1997

University of St. Francis
GEN 809.933 A456
Alpers, Paul J.
What is pastoral? /

3 0301 00086304 9

S0-AHN-016

What Is Pastoral?

THE UNIVERSITY OF CHICAGO PRESS
Chicago & London

WHAT IS PASTORAL?

Paul Alpers

Paul Alpers is the Class of 1942 Professor of English
at the University of California, Berkeley.

The University of Chicago Press, Chicago 60637
The University of Chicago Press, Ltd., London
© 1996 by The University of Chicago
All rights reserved. Published 1996
Printed in the United States of America
05 04 03 02 01 00 99 98 97 96   1 2 3 4 5

ISBN: 0-226-01516-5 (cloth)

This book has been published with the generous assistance of the
Ingram Merrill Foundation.

Library of Congress Cataloging-in-Publication Data

Alpers, Paul J.
  What is pastoral? / Paul Alpers.
     p.   cm.
  Includes bibliographical references and index.
     1. Pastoral literature—History and criticism.   I. Title.
PN56.P3A43   1996
809'.93321734—dc20   95-35356

⊗The paper used in this publication meets the minimum require-
ments of the American National Standard for Information Sciences—
Permanence of Paper for Printed Library Materials, ANSI Z39.48-1984.

809.933
A456

This book is for
BEN and NICK

$35.62

4.3-97

158,337

Contents

Preface

This book seeks to explain the sense in which various literary works and genres count as pastoral, or can be considered versions of pastoral. It seeks to account for the main features of pastoral writings and for their historical variety and relation to each other. Two main irritants have led to my writing it (I grant that it is up to me to produce the pearl). The first is the view that pastoral is motivated by naive idyllicism; the second is the way modern studies tend to use "pastoral" with ungoverned inclusiveness.[1] A literary definition is revealing and useful, it seems to me, not when it plants its banner everywhere, but when it is clear about what does and does not count as an example of the phenomenon in question. Hence when a colleague asked me what would be the book's surprising examples, I answered, "None." My endeavor is rather to treat evident examples, of which I seek to give convincing critical accounts that are also accurately suggestive in their implications and extensions.

The answer to the question posed in the title is that pastoral is a literary *mode* based on what Kenneth Burke calls a *representative anecdote*. Part I (chapters 1–3) concerns these two concepts and the idea of pastoral convention—both what convention means in pastoral and why pastoral is so "conventional" a form. These chapters can be thought of as synchronic, while those in Part II are diachronic. They trace two large developments of pastoral writing: poetry (chapters 4–7) and prose narrative (chapters 8–9), from ancient writers

---

1. More than one example will occur to those who cultivate this field. For a self-aware statement of the principle, see Lawrence Buell, "American Pastoral Ideology Reappraised," *American Literary History* 1 (1989): 23:

> "Pastoral" is used in an extended sense, familiar to Americanists, to refer not to the specific set of obsolescent conventions of the eclogue tradition, but to all literature—poetry or prose, fiction or nonfiction—that celebrates the ethos of nature/rurality over against the ethos of the town or city. This domain includes for present purposes all degrees of rusticity from farm to wilderness.

through works of the nineteenth and twentieth centuries. If there is anything surprising in what the book offers, I think it is that its account of pastoral extends beyond the Renaissance. (My desire to make this emphasis led to what some may feel is a culpable omission—a separate treatment of pastoral drama as a form.)

Most of the post-classical works I discuss are English. This reflects limitations on my part, of course, and also of what I could expect readers to bring to the book. Tasso's *Aminta* and Garcilaso de la Vega's eclogues are generally known, I fear, only to specialists in their respective national literatures, and their literary distinction (unlike that of *Don Quixote*) does not survive translation. But there is a further, more interesting justification for emphasizing works in English. Pastoral, at least in the Renaissance, has always seemed a literary form that crossed national boundaries easily, so that if one had the knowledge, one could treat English, Italian, French, Spanish, Portuguese, German, Dutch, and neo-Latin examples interchangeably, as parts of a single account. In working on this book, I discovered that the differences among the cultures and vernacular literatures of Europe make for decisive differences even in this classicizing and genre-conscious form. We are used to recognizing the importance of understanding literary and cultural phenomena diachronically. I would call the analogous understanding, as it applies to historically contemporary phenomena, *diachoric* (from Greek *chōra*, place, country).

This is a formalist account of pastoral and its literary history. It argues that the central fiction of pastoral—in Burke's terminology, its representative anecdote—is not the Golden Age or idyllic landscapes, but herdsmen and their lives. My first purpose in advancing this argument and pursuing its implications is to clarify the formal motives of pastoral and thus convey the life and intelligence of pastoral writings. Clarifying formal motives should also enable students of literature to see that pastoral does not include all poems about nature or landscape, nor does it include all poetry, drama, and fiction about rural life. What it does include is a large number of literary works, from Hellenistic times to our own, whose writers have found pastoral usages to be an "enabling resource," as the poet Seamus Heaney called them in reviewing an anthology of pastoral verse.[2]

To interpret literature and write its history on these terms runs counter, I am well aware, to what many today regard as the proper work of understanding and historicizing the writings of the past. The anthology reviewed by Seamus Heaney devotes itself to demystifying, not to say trashing, the poetry it collects. The general point at issue is whether one should take these writings on their own terms—criticism, in my sense, as interpretation—or rather view

2. Seamus Heaney, *Preoccupations: Selected Prose, 1968–1978* (New York: Farrar, Straus, and Giroux, 1980), 180.

them critically, in another sense, by questioning their grounds and exposing what they repress or occlude. The differences of principle here concern the regard one has for individual works and for the whole enterprise of literature. A book of this sort is not the occasion for debating these central principles. It does not even provide the opportunity for addressing some questions of literary history for which a just view of pastoral is essential. I have not incorporated a previously published article which argues that new historicist interpretations of *The Shepheardes Calender* give an inadequate account of its place in literary history, because what is at stake in that argument is the situation of poetry in Elizabethan culture, not the character of pastoral in and by itself.[3] Nor can my account of certain poems by Wordsworth stand by themselves as an alternative to recent attempts to question the course of his literary career and demystify his poetry. If my account of pastoral and my individual analyses are convincing, their effect should be to discourage reading specific works as mere instances or allegories of (what the interpreter conceives to be) their ideologies or historical situations. I note my resistances or disagreements as they occur, but as an example, consider Marjorie Levinson's complaint, in discussing "The Solitary Reaper," that "no one is exercised by the fact that Wordsworth's narrator represents himself as the 'profound' and redemptive composer."[4] The reason no one is exercised by this fact is that it is not a fact at all. Whatever may be true of the way Wordsworth represented himself in life or in other poems, the speaker of "The Solitary Reaper" does not represent himself and his relation to the reaper as Levinson says he does. That relation, as I hope my account of the poem makes clear, is a pastoral one, and one main purpose of this book is to argue that when pastoral writing is properly understood, it can be seen to be far more aware of itself and its conditions than it has usually been thought to be, or even capable of being.

I do not, however, want to suggest that Levinson's inaccuracy means, ipso facto, that the questions she raises are not significant—that we should simply let the writing of the past be what it is. "What it is" is what we make it out to be, and it is precisely this that is so variously and profoundly in question at present. I hope this book contributes to our consideration of literature and its claim on us: pastoral is a form that arose from and has continuously meditated this question. But it will do so by reevaluating an important literary mode and exemplifying a way of reading, rather than by directly engaging in our current debates.

3. Paul Alpers, "Pastoral and the Domain of Lyric in Spenser's *Shepheardes Calender*," *Representations* 12 (1985): 83–100.
4. Marjorie Levinson, *Keats's Life of Allegory* (Oxford: Blackwell, 1988), 79.

Acknowledgments

Parts of the following chapters, often in somewhat different form, appeared in the journals indicated: "Prologue" (*The Threepenny Review*), chapter 1 (*Critical Inquiry*), chapter 3 (*ELH, New Literary History*), chapter 4 (*Arethusa*), chapter 5 (*ELH*), chapter 8 (*Compar(a)ison*). I thank all these journals and their editors for permission to reprint this material. I also thank Scholars Press for permission to reprint, in chapter 1, a revised version of my contribution to *Cabinet of the Muses: Essays in Honor of Thomas G. Rosenmeyer*, ed. M. Griffith and D. J. Mastronarde.

My work on this book has been supported by fellowships from the National Endowment for the Humanities and the John Simon Guggenheim Foundation. I am very grateful to both these organizations for their generosity, and I am equally grateful to my own institution, the University of California at Berkeley, for a Humanities Research Fellowship and for annual grants from the Committee on Research. A semester of teaching at Princeton University, as Visiting Senior Fellow of the Council of the Humanities, was of great help in getting this study under way.

I have been working on this project for many years, and many friends and colleagues have commented on drafts of chapters and contributed to my thinking about it. I particularly wish to thank Janet Adelman, Svetlana Alpers, Charles Altieri, Jonas Barish, Will Batstone, Harry Berger, Carol Christ, Jennifer Clarvoe, Louise George Clubb, Andrew Escobedo, Stephen Greenblatt, David Halperin, Leslie Katz, Jeffrey Knapp, Steven Knapp, Nita Krevans, D. A. Miller, Louis Montrose, Michael Putnam, Elizabeth Rhodes, Catherine Robson, Thomas Rosenmeyer, Roger Sale, Charles Segal, Katherine Snyder, and Dorothy Stephens. My colleagues on *Representations* have continually enlivened my intellectual life and broadened my perspectives.

Frequently Cited Works

References to the following will be made parenthetically in the text.

William Empson, *Some Versions of Pastoral* (Norfolk, Conn.: New Directions paperback, 1960) (Cited in text as *SVP*)

Andrew Marvell, *The Complete Poems*, ed. Elizabeth Story Donno (Harmondsworth: Penguin, 1972)

John Milton, *Poems*, ed. John Carey and Alastair Fowler (London: Longmans, 1968)

The Riverside Shakespeare, ed. G. Blakemore Evans et al. (Boston: Houghton Mifflin, 1974)

Edmund Spenser, *Poetical Works*, ed. J. C. Smith and E. de Selincourt (Oxford: Oxford University Press, 1912)

Theocritus, ed. A. S. F. Gow, 2 vols. (Cambridge: Cambridge University Press, 1952)

Theocritus, *Idylls*, trans. R. C. Trevelyan (New York: Albert and Charles Boni, 1925)

Virgil, *Eclogues*, Latin text and translation from Paul Alpers, *The Singer of the Eclogues* (Berkeley and Los Angeles: University of California Press, 1979)

PART ONE

Prologue

The reader of this book may ask, as I have often asked myself, why pastoral poetry deserves the kind of attention I have given and ask the reader to give it. Some of the reasons are brought out, unwittingly, by a powerful moment in Irving Howe's introduction to a translation of Primo Levi's novel, *If Not Now, When?* Howe recalls an episode in Levi's earlier book, *If This Is a Man,*[1] an account of his imprisonment in Auschwitz:

> Levi recalls a day when he and a few other prisoners were put to work scraping an underground gasoline tank. They worked in almost total darkness, and the work was very hard. Then, from some inner fold of memory, Levi began telling young French prisoners about Dante's great poem, reciting the lines
>
> > Think of your breed; for brutish ignorance
> > Your mettle was not made; you were made men
> > To follow after knowledge and excellence.

1. The book is published in England under this title, which correctly translates the Italian title, *Se questo è un uomo.* In the United States it is called *Survival in Auschwitz.* I quote from *Survival in Auschwitz and The Reawakening: Two Memoirs,* trans. Stuart Woolf (New York: Summit Books, 1986). Irving Howe's essay is in *If Not Now, When?* trans. William Weaver (New York: Summit Books, 1985).

Coming "like the blast of a trumpet, like the voice of God," these lines flood the hearts of the prisoners, so that "for a moment I forget who I am and where I am" and the wretched might suppose they are still human beings.

This incident, stirring enough as Howe recounts it, is made even more poignant by the clarity, energy, and confidence which its main terms have in Dante's Italian:

> Considerate la vostra semenza:
> fatti non foste a viver come bruti,
> ma per seguir virtute e canoscenza.
> (*Inf.* 26.118–20)

These noble lines had themselves outlived Dante's apparent condemnation of their human presumption. Levi's quoting them in the midst of a modern hell makes literature confront the human situation with an almost shocking directness. The incident thus evokes the heroic and tragic modes in whose terms we have learned to speak of the power of literature to move us and illuminate our lives. But in recounting this extraordinary episode, Irving Howe's memory has played him false. Primo Levi did quote these lines to a fellow prisoner, and his recalling them affected him as powerfully as the quoted phrases suggest. But the circumstances were different and have their own unheroic poignancy.

There were six of us [Levi's chapter begins], scraping and cleaning the inside of an underground petrol tank; the daylight only reached us through a small manhole. It was a luxury job because no one supervised us; but it was cold and damp. The powder of the rust burnt under our eyelids and coated our throats and mouths with a taste almost like blood.

Because they were unsupervised, the men were able to loaf, so they sprung to work when the swaying of their rope ladder showed that someone was coming. It proved to be Jean, the "Pikolo" of the working group and the most humane and trusted of the "Prominents"—prisoners placed in minor supervisory positions, who acquired not only enviable privileges, but also a certain amount of power (if, like Jean, they chose to use it) to ease the plight of their fellows. The prisoners were perpetually hungry, and since Levi and the others were working underground, neither perceptions of light and temperature nor the state of their bellies would have assured them in advance that Jean was coming on his daily mission of getting someone to help him fetch the vat of soup for the group's midday meal. On this day he chose Levi, and the story continues as follows:

He climbed out and I followed him, blinking in the brightness of the day. It was warmish outside, the sun drew a faint smell of paint and tar from the greasy earth, which made me think of a holiday beach of my infancy.

Pikolo gave me one of the two wooden poles, and we walked along under a clear June sky.

I began to thank him, but he stopped me: it was not necessary. One could see the Carpathians covered in snow. I breathed in the fresh air, I felt unusually light-hearted.

"*Tu es fou de marcher si vite. On a le temps, tu sais.*" The ration was collected half a mile away; one had to return with the pot weighing over a hundred pounds supported on the two poles. It was quite a tiring task, but it meant a pleasant walk there without a load, and the ever-welcome chance of going near the kitchens.

We slowed down. Pikolo was expert. He had chosen the path cleverly so that we would have to make a long detour, walking at least for an hour, without arousing suspicion. We spoke of our houses, of Strasbourg and Turin [their native towns], of the books we had read, of what we had studied, of our mothers: how all mothers resemble each other! His mother too had scolded him for never knowing how much money he had in his pocket; his mother too would have been amazed if she had known that he had found his feet, that day by day he was finding his feet.

At this point an SS man passes on a bicycle, and when he has gone, Jean says, "*Sale brute, celui-là. Ein ganz gemeiner Hund.*" Levi is intrigued by and comments on the Alsatian's bilingualism, and Jean replies that he had once spent a month in Liguria and would like to learn Italian. "I would be pleased to teach him Italian: why not try? We can do it. Why not immediately, one thing is as good as another, the important thing is not to lose time, not to waste this hour." And so the lesson begins—at first a few simple nouns until, for no apparent reason, Dante's canto of Ulysses comes into Levi's head. He begins to recite the episode, translating it into French and explaining it as he goes along.

The reader will recognize that Levi's and Jean's sense of physical and conversational ease at noontime replicates, under painfully unlikely circumstances, a situation conventionally found in pastoral poems. In the pastorals of Theocritus, Virgil, and their Renaissance imitators, shepherds gather at noon in what is both fictionally and metaphorically a space for exchanging conversation and song. Levi's episode is particularly close to Virgil's ninth Eclogue, in which two shepherds, obliged to walk to a neighboring town, first discuss the social upheavals that have put one of them on the road and then recite fragments of songs to each other. The poem even shares with its real-life counterpart one speaker's inability to remember all the verses he wishes to recite. Whether or not this is more than a superficial similarity, the theme Virgil engages by this motif has deep connections with the significance Dante's verses acquire for Levi. The Ninth Eclogue imitates one of Theocritus's greatest poems and quotes some of his verses, but it qualifies its imitation by the initiating political circumstances (completely absent from Theocritus) and by the motif of imperfect memory. Thus in the very act of re-singing their predecessors, Virgil's shepherds and the poet himself question the extent to which such revoicing is possible. When the shepherds puzzle over the obscure fate of Menalcas—who was unable with his music to prevent the devastation of the countryside, but whose songs they still sing and whose return they still hope for—they both question and hold out the possibility that is felt so strongly in Levi's episode, that the song of an absent master can have power in our present circumstances. When Levi remembers, blessedly without faltering, the tercet that sounds in his ear like the voice of God,

> Pikolo begs me to repeat it. How good Pikolo is, he is aware that it is doing me good. Or perhaps it is something more: perhaps, despite the wan translation and the pedestrian, rushed commentary, he has received the message, he has felt that it has to do with him, that it has to do with all men who toil, and with us in particular; and that it has to do with us two, who dare to reason of these things with the poles for the soup on our shoulders.

I certainly do not mean to say that Levi's episode is in itself pastoral. It has a pastoral feeling at the beginning, with the warmth of the sun, the fresh air, and the free perambulation, with purpose temporarily suspended; Jean the Pikolo has a pastoral feeling throughout, in his human ease and continuing solicitude for his less fortunate companion (in this he resembles the young Lycidas of Virgil's poem). But as Irving Howe suggests, the episode acquires a thoroughly unpastoral urgency: time grows short, the feelings and recognitions prompted by Dante become almost insupportable, and Levi increasingly feels distress, even anguish, at his inability to remember all the verses. But however unpastoral it becomes, the episode forcibly suggests the importance of the kind of poetry whose conventions it enacts. Irving Howe's false recollection of the episode was perfectly natural, the way any of us would be likely to remember this overwhelming moment in Levi's narrative. Howe, in effect, made the episode a "representative anecdote": he gave it a form in his mind that conveys his sense of the human value of literature. What the true form of the episode tells us is that conventions of pastoral that sometimes seem callow and in bad faith—the pretense that poor, humble, and deprived people are simply free to sing and woo—these fictions convey the sobering truth that literature can give us our sense of human worth only if we have the kind of space Levi and Jean the Pikolo found on that midday in June and that is represented by the pleasures of the *locus amoenus*. This is, at least in the present context, a sobering awareness, because if anything is clear from Primo Levi's book about Auschwitz, it is that the episode as Howe recounts it could not have happened. Under ordinary conditions of life in the camp, one did not remember lines of poetry. The desperate weariness, the unappeasable hunger, the brutal hardships of the work, the soreness and chills, impossible to be rid of, and the way life was ordered so as to create a pervasive distrust of one's fellows and a wretched but absolutely necessary selfishness—all these, so one feels, made impossible as simple an act of the inner life as remembering lines of verse. What is most deeply disturbing about *If This Is a Man* is that the creators of Auschwitz very nearly succeeded in their project of denying fellow creatures their humanity. The serious case against pastoral is precisely that, for all its acceptance of limitation, it does not envisage deprivation of this extent and severity. But the pastoral lineaments of Levi's Ulysses episode show why this mode of poetry has been and should remain part of the way we value and understand our lives and our writings.

One

REPRESENTATIVE ANECDOTES AND
IDEAS OF PASTORAL

I

Pastoral is a familiar topic in the academic study of literature. It seems an accessible concept, and most critics and readers have a fairly clear idea of what they mean by it. Yet there is no principled account of it on which most people agree, and it sometimes seems as if there are as many versions of pastoral as there are critics and scholars who write about it. Apart from the happy confusion of definitions, it is clear to no one, experts or novices, what works count as pastoral or—perhaps a form of the same question—whether pastoral is a historically delimited or permanent literary type. It does seem that we should know what we are talking about, the more so as "pastoral" can still be a word to conjure with—whether the conjuror is practicing white magic (using "pastoral" as a critical cult-word, to impress) or black (using it to mean "naively idyllic" and thus to put a curse on the work or author so named).

Literary pastoral first appeared in classical antiquity, and it had an enormous vogue in the Renaissance. A modern theorist of pastoral might therefore want to begin with ancient and Renaissance criticism and literary theory. Unfortunately and surprisingly, there is not much help in this quarter. Pastoral is not mentioned in the two ancient treatises that shaped and influenced Renaissance criticism. Bucolic poetry could not have been treated by Aristotle since it was not a classical Greek form; Horace, who must have read Theocritus and who refers to Virgil's Eclogues elsewhere, says nothing about it in the *Ars Poetica*. In the Renaissance, the Horatian tradition of surveying all known or approved kinds of poetry produced passages in various *artes poeticae* from Vida to Boileau, and in prose treatises chapters and paragraphs of differing worth: the finest examples in English are a paragraph in Sidney's *Apology for Poetry* and a short chapter in Puttenham's *The Arte of English Poesie*. The most common schematic placing of pastoral was by means of the *genera dicendi*—the high, middle, and low styles to which, by a coincidence which had a great deal of weight for critics since late antiquity, Virgil's three major works seemed to correspond. Thinking of pastoral as the humble member of this stylistic triad clearly affected writers' sense of it, perhaps mainly through giving pastoral poems a place in Renaissance schooling. But nothing very sustained came out of all this—nothing that can serve us as a critical starting point, much less a model. This is true even for those rare cases in which pastoral has a significant role in a systematic poetics. It is the first type of poetry discussed in Julius Caesar Scaliger's *Poetices libri septem* (1561), and Scaliger tries to deduce its forms and themes from general considerations. But he never discusses how pastoral fulfills the end of poetry, to please and instruct, and his chapter soon turns to anthropology—an account of the origins of pastoral and a sort of ethnography of pastoral objects. Some twenty years later, Antonio Viperano published *De Poetica Libri Tres* (Antwerp, 1579). The treatment of genre in the first book is genuinely theoretical: Viperano tries to generate all genres from the fundamental stances of praise and blame, and he explicitly asks why pastoral has been neglected in treatises such as his. But when he turns to pastoral in Book III (devoted to the minor genres of satire, mime, bucolic, and lyric), he too lapses into an account of origins and concludes with a miscellany of practical rules and observations. From such writings one can gather various opinions that may illuminate an issue or a poem, but nothing that has critical power or coherence.[1]

1. For the historical details of many of the matters mentioned in this paragraph, see the informative article by Fred J. Nichols, "The Development of Neo-Latin Theory of the Pastoral in the Sixteenth Century," *Humanistica Lovanensia* 18(1969): 95–114. Nichols begins by pointing out how skimpy is the body of material he surveys, and his analyses and conclusions suggest the degree to which sixteenth-century "theory of pastoral" fell short of indicating the interest and achievement of the pastoral poetry prior to and contemporary with it. The first two chapters of J. E. Congleton, *Theories of Pastoral Poetry in England, 1684–1798* (Gainesville: University of Florida Press, 1952) contain as much information about pastoral criticism and theory in the Continental and English Renaissance as most readers will want. Congleton seems not to have known Viperano's treatise, but his conclusion that "the pastoral criticism of the Italian Renaissance except for that in Scaliger's *Ars Poetica* and in Trissino's *Poetica* is fragmentary" (22) is not modified by the exhaustive summaries and analyses of Bernard Weinberg, *A History of Literary Criticism in the Italian Renaissance*, 2 vols. (Chicago: University of Chicago Press, 1961). Even in the famous controversy over Guarini's *Il Pastor Fido* (Weinberg, 2: 1074–1105), the main issues concern not pastoral but tragicomedy as a dramatic

Renaissance poetics fails to tell us much about pastoral, because any scheme or survey of the whole of poetry inevitably emphasizes what it considers the major forms. Given this bias, it is not surprising that much Renaissance criticism of pastoral occurs in prologues or prefaces to pastoral works—where, in effect, the reader is introduced to a "simple" work and is asked to take its humility seriously. Some major works of Renaissance pastoral have critically significant or suggestive prologues: Sannazaro's *Arcadia*, Cervantes' *Galatea*, Spenser's *The Shepheardes Calender*, d'Urfé's *Astrée*. Sidney's fullest discussion of the poetics of pastoral is not the paragraph in the *Apology for Poetry*, but the narrator's introduction of the "First Eclogues" in the *Old Arcadia*.[2] Serious criticism of pastoral begins with one of these prefaces, René Rapin's introduction to his *Eclogae Sacrae* (1659). Unlike the brief prologues of Sannazaro, Cervantes, and d'Urfé, this preface is a lengthy "Dissertatio de Carmine Pastorali." It soon became detached from the poems it introduced and appeared as an independent essay on pastoral, taking and expounding it on its own terms. A generation later, Fontenelle wrote an influential "Discours sur la nature de l'eglogue," which, like Rapin's "Dissertatio," appeared as a commentary on his own pastorals, but was detached and became influential as a separate essay.[3]

Like Rapin's and Fontenelle's essays, most modern studies define pastoral simply by saying what it is. It turns out to be a number of things. We are told that pastoral "is a double longing after innocence and happiness"; that it is based on the philosophical antithesis of Art and Nature; that its universal idea is the Golden Age; that its fundamental motive is hostility to urban life; that its "central tenet" is "the pathetic fallacy"; that it expresses the ideal of *otium*; that it is founded on Epicureanism; that in the Renaissance it is "the poetic expression *par excellence* of the cult of aesthetic Platonism" or, alternatively, of the philo-

genre. In Guarini's final theoretical statement, *Il Compendio Della Poesia Tragicomica* (1601, a synthesis of two earlier treatises), only ten of the seventy pages concern pastoral, and it is never central to the argument about tragicomedy. See Giambattista Guarini, *Il Pastor Fido e Il Compendio della Poesia Tragicomica*, ed. Gioachino Brognoligo (Bari: G. Laterza, 1914), 219–88.

2. Sir Philip Sidney, *An Apology for Poetry*, ed. Geoffrey Shepherd (London: Nelson, 1965), 116; *The Countess of Pembroke's Arcadia (The Old Arcadia)*, ed. Jean Robertson (Oxford: Clarendon Press, 1973), 56.

3. René Rapin, *Eclogae cum Dissertatione de Carmine Pastorali* (Leyden, 1672); Bernard le Bovier de Fontenelle, *Poesies Pastorales, avec un Traité sur la Nature de l'Eglogue, & une Digression sur les Anciens & les Modernes* (Paris: Michel Guerout, 1688). Rapin's and Fontenelle's essays were translated into English before the end of the seventeenth century—Rapin's by Thomas Creech (1684, see below, n. 14) and Fontenelle's by Peter Motteux, in Le Bossu, *Treatise of the Epick Poem* (London, 1695), 277–95. As Congleton points out (above, n. 1), these two essays were the foundation of neoclassical criticism of pastoral in England. Pope's youthful *Discourse on Pastoral Poetry* amalgamates the two. See the editorial comments in Alexander Pope, *Pastoral Poetry and An Essay on Criticism*, ed. E. Audra and Aubrey Williams (London: Methuen, 1961), 15–16.

sophical *vita contemplativa*.[4] Such definitions are heterogeneous in the literal sense. After a painstaking survey, one scholar says:

> Critics are justifiably unsure whether to locate the identity of pastoral in certain enduring literary norms and conventions, or in a specific (if perennial) subject, or in some continuity of feeling, attitude, "philosophical conception," or mode of consciousness which informs the literary imagination but originates outside it.[5]

It is no surprise, then, that the most important recent book on the subject is altogether impatient with definition:

> Nor will this book launch another attempt to define the nature of pastoral—a cause lost as early as the sixteenth century, when the genre began to manifest the tendency of most strong literary forms to propagate by miscegenation, and a cause reduced to total confusion by modern criticism's search for "versions of pastoral" in the most unlikely places. . . . Perhaps now is the time for the central question to be restated. It is not what pastoral *is* that should matter to us.[6]

4. The allusions are to the following books and essays: (1) "double longing": Renato Poggioli, *The Oaten Flute: Essays on Pastoral Poetry and the Pastoral Ideal*, (Cambridge: Harvard University Press, 1975), 1; (2) art and nature: Frank Kermode, *English Pastoral Poetry: From the Beginnings to Marvell* (London, 1952; repr., New York: Norton, 1972), 37; Leo Marx, *The Machine in the Garden: Technology and the Pastoral Ideal in America* (New York: Oxford University Press, 1964), 35; (3) Golden Age: Walter W. Greg, *Pastoral Poetry & Pastoral Drama: A Literary Inquiry, with Special Reference to the Pre-Restoration Stage in England* (London: A. H. Bullen, 1906; repr., New York: Russell and Russell, 1959), 5; (4) hostility to urban life: K. W. Gransden, "The Pastoral Alternative," *Arethusa* 3 (1970): 103–21; cf. Raymond Williams, *The Country and the City* (London: Chatto & Windus, 1973); (5) pathetic fallacy: Edward William Tayler, *Nature and Art in Renaissance Literature* (New York: Columbia University Press, 1964), 154; (6) otium: Hallett Smith, *Elizabethan Poetry: A Study in Conventions, Meaning, and Expression* (Cambridge: Harvard University Press, 1952), 2; (7) Epicureanism: Thomas G. Rosenmeyer, *The Green Cabinet: Theocritus and the European Pastoral Lyric* (Berkeley & Los Angeles: University of California Press, 1969), 42–44; (8) aesthetic Platonism: Richard Cody, *The Landscape of the Mind: Pastoralism and Platonic Theory in Tasso's "Aminta" and Shakespeare's Early Comedies* (Oxford: Clarendon Press, 1969), 6; (9) *vita contemplativa*: John D. Bernard, *Ceremonies of Innocence: Pastoralism in the Poetry of Edmund Spenser* (Cambridge: Cambridge University Press, 1989), 10.

5. David M. Halperin, *Before Pastoral: Theocritus and the Ancient Tradition of Bucolic Poetry* (New Haven: Yale University Press, 1983), 76.

6. Annabel Patterson, *Pastoral and Ideology: Virgil to Valéry* (Berkeley & Los Angeles: University of California Press, 1987), 7. Quotations in the next sentence are also on this page.

Cf. Andrew V. Ettin, *Literature and the Pastoral* (New Haven: Yale University Press, 1984): "Writing about a literary kind always means mediating between the description too inclusive to be a definition and the definition too exclusive to be a description" (2). The relaxed good sense of this observation unfortunately leads Ettin, in my view, to a far too inclusive and impressionistic account of pastoral.

Since Patterson's project involves the cultural and ideological afterlife of a single work, Virgil's Eclogues, she can circumvent the question of definition. But if we accept more broadly her recommendation that we think about what pastoral "can do"—that is, "how writers, artists, and intellectuals . . . have *used* pastoral for a range of functions and intentions that the *Eclogues* first articulated"—then we will need to have some idea of what counts as pastoral and what does not.

As Patterson suggests, definition, in the literal sense of determining boundaries, involves dealing with the range and variety of pastoral writings as they present themselves historically. From the perspective of a formalist literary history, the central question is the relation of literary works to their predecessors. In an essay on generic theory, Fredric Jameson offers a choice between two historical models—one "based on the identity between its various stages" and the other "based on difference and discontinuity, thereby projecting a very different view of history itself as a series of irrevocable qualitative breaks." This absolute division between identity and discontinuity seems to me belied by the history of at least some literary forms. Jameson says, of his first historical model, that "its ideological function lies in its apparent reinforcement of the notion of a tradition, of some deep and unbroken continuity between the mythic imagination of primitive man and the sophisticated products of the modern societies."[7] But one is not necessarily seeking to aggrandize or revere literature if one argues that certain literary forms or conventions or modes enable new expression, which can be seen both to derive and be different from its models or preceding instances. "Continuity," unmodified by a phrase like "deep and unbroken," seems to me the word for this phenomenon, because it less prejudges questions than "tradition," which does have ideological weight, or "development," which cannot avoid implications of progress, natural growth, or inevitability. To assume the continuity of literary forms and expression is, in a sense, to say simply that language and literature are social phenomena and that any verbal activity occurs not de novo but in some institutional context, what Wittgenstein called a "language game." Literary expression, in this view, is a particularly formalized or institutionalized activity, and continuity between present and past poems therefore would seem to be simply in the nature of poetry.

Nevertheless, there is still something to be said against this view of poetry, to wit, whatever the institutional *facts* of language and literature, literary *value* consists precisely in breaking old molds, doing some kind of violence to received conventions and forms of expression. I think we all assume that good poems either extend the possibilities of expression or in some way revitalize the capacities of literary forms and language. The question is whether we re-

---

7. Fredric Jameson, "Magical Narratives: Romance as Genre," *New Literary History* 7 (1975–76): 156.

gard these effects as enabled by existing forms and modes—so that new works realize or develop or extend something implicit in them—or whether they come about through resisting and undermining them. To speak of continuity between literary works, then, is to take a particular view of their individuality and newness. To the extent that this view is rejected, pastoral poems—which not only exemplify continuity but mythologize it as an account of poetry— will be felt to be slight and uninteresting. To the extent that continuity is thought to be at least an important half-truth about poetry, pastoral, with its unusual self-consciousness about these issues, can be thought of as an exemplary literary form.

II

A definition of pastoral must first give a coherent account of its various features—formal, expressive, and thematic—and second, provide for its historical continuity, the change and variety within the form. The basis of such a definition is provided by what Kenneth Burke calls a "representative anecdote." Burke comes up with this term in *A Grammar of Motives*, at the beginning of the chapter on "Scope and Reduction":

> Men seek for vocabularies that will be faithful *reflections* of reality. To this end, they must develop vocabularies that are *selections* of reality. And any selection of reality must, in certain circumstances, function as a *deflection* of reality. Insofar as the vocabulary meets the needs of reflection, we can say that it has the necessary scope. In its selectivity, it is a reduction. Its scope and reduction become a deflection when the given terminology, or calculus, is not suited to the subject matter which it is designed to calculate. Dramatism suggests a procedure to be followed in the development of a given calculus, or terminology. It involves the search for a "representative anecdote," to be used as a form in conformity with which the vocabulary is constructed.[8]

Burke's use of "anecdote," instead of a more philosophically respectable term (like "paradigm"), brings out the contingencies inherent in all such intellectual choices. "Anecdote" implies that they are inseparable from the stuff of reality with which they deal, and that their selection does not escape the conditions of ordinary summary accounts of our lives. (On the other hand, the term does not carry its normal implications of a story, as the examples cited in the next paragraph show.) "Representative," as Burke uses it here, has a double meaning. An anecdote is representative in that (1) it is a typical instance of an aspect of

8. Kenneth Burke, *A Grammar of Motives* (Berkeley & Los Angeles: University of California Press, 1969), 59. Parenthetical page references in the text are to this edition.

reality and (2) by being typical, it serves to generate specific depictions, or representations, of that reality.

Burke's own representative anecdote is the drama, from which he derives the "pentad" of terms (act, scene, agent, agency, purpose) which provide a grammar of human motives. But he also considers some other anecdotes as a way of analyzing human relations: tribal rituals and the communion service, which are both rejected as unrepresentative of modern society; war, which is rejected as being "more of a *confusion* than a *form*"; the Constitution of the United States, which becomes the representative anecdote of the last third of the book; and a railway terminal, which provides a wonderful inventive page, but which is finally rejected because it is so physical that the human realities and connections it represents "could not be located in the idiom of [the] chosen anecdote."[9] One can see that all these examples are genuinely "anecdotal"— they briefly and tellingly summarize some specific phenomenon in the world or form of human life—and that they are representative: they stand for whole fields of study or types of discourse, which we can generate by pursuing the details of these anecdotes, spelling them out, as it were. Burke claims that a representative anecdote is the foundation of *every* theoretical discourse, but whether or not this is so—and it is at least a striking way of suggesting that no theory is free of the conditions of discourse—it is an especially appropriate way to analyze literary criticism and theory. By grounding the informing structure of a discourse in the reality it concerns, the idea of the representative anecdote acknowledges both the inseparability of form and content in literary works and the fact that this field of human knowledge, at least, is constituted only by following its specific historical manifestations and development. The representative anecdote is compatible with historical realities, because it is conceived not as a paradigm or authoritative example, against which other examples are checked or measured, but as a "summation" which has generative powers. In Burke's words, it "contains *in nuce* the terminological structure that is evolved in conformity with it" (60). Critical discourse so conceived seems eminently suited to following the course of a literary type, especially one like pastoral, which begins with a single historical example and which evolves by transforming the structures and the stock of conventions provided by its previous instances.

Before appropriating Burke's idea for my own purposes, I should say something about the way he uses it. His conception of it is global. He seeks something on a par with the social contract or the state of nature—not *a* but *the* anecdote which will be representative of all human motives. It may well be asked whether the representative anecdote so conceived can legitimately be

---

9. These examples of representative anecdotes are found in the opening pages of Part Three ("On Dialectic"), 323–30.

scaled down to the task of defining a literary type or mode. I think that it can; for one thing, Burke of all our general thinkers has most encouraged us to look to literary processes and structures for insight into the workings of society and the human mind. And I think that this scaling down retrieves from Burke's own treatment a central truth of the idea of a representative anecdote. One of the great insights of the notion and of the term (the suggestions of the particular and the casual in "anecdote," clashing fruitfully with the general and "centrist" claims of "representative") is the recognition that any concept or representation, by its very formulation, generates its own limitations: scope and reduction, to invoke the title of the chapter in which the idea appears, are mutually implicated in human myths and concepts. It would seem, then, that a search for *the* representative anecdote is a contradiction in terms. If representative anecdotes, justly conceived, are at the heart of our conceptions, it is in the nature of the case that there will be a number of such conceptions, since no one of them can exhaust all of reality. The generous, pluralistic, democratic, and playful side of Burke knows this perfectly well. Early in *A Grammar of Motives* he says that "the Edenic paradigm" would be "applicable if we were capable of total acts that produce total transformations. In reality, we are capable of but partial acts, acts that but partially represent us and that produce but partial transformations" (19). But Burke's dramatistic recognitions are never wholly separate from a totalizing vein which seeks what he calls God-terms. This side of his intellectual character leads him to turn the chapter on "Scope and Reduction" into an account of divine Creation as the act of acts; in his later work it has caused him to replace dramatism by the transformed theology he calls "Logology."[10]

These elisions and shifts may be regarded with irritation, as signs of Burke's carelessness and confusion; with aesthetic pleasure, as characteristic American modes of oratory and tinkering; or with committed interest, as polarities and tendencies in Burke's thought. For our purposes, we need only concern ourselves with what is valid and useful in the idea of the representative anecdote. I take that to be the form in which it acknowledges that the scope of representation cannot avoid the reductions of language. Representative anecdotes, like proverbs and titles (those other brief compendia around which Burke's thought has often revolved) contain *multum in parvo* but not *omnia in parvo*. By the same token, Burke's favorite trope, synecdoche, which he equates with representa-

10. For an account of a similar tension in Burke, between his accepting historical change and seeking to transcend it, see Frank Lentricchia, "Reading History with Kenneth Burke," in Hayden White and Margaret Brose, eds., *Representing Kenneth Burke* (Baltimore: Johns Hopkins University Press, 1982), 119–49. In a later essay, "Terministic Screens," Burke resumes some of the interests contained in the idea of a representative anecdote and even repeats the changes rung on re-, se-, and de-flection of reality. But he no longer uses the term "representative anecdote," because, in my view, it is not wholly consonant with his "logological" interests. See *Language as Symbolic Action* (Berkeley & Los Angeles: University of California Press, 1966), 44–62, esp. 44–47.

tion, is valuable as a tool of analysis precisely when and to the extent that one recognizes the partiality and selectivity inherent in it. Burke's own tendency to conceive his terms as absolutes does not rule out our using them in, so to speak, their lowercase forms.[11] Indeed, it may help explain why the concept of representative anecdote is particularly useful in analyzing pastoral. For pastoral makes explicit a certain disproportion between its fictions, conspicuously modest and selective, and the meanings they bear or imply: there is always a suggestion that "more is meant than meets the ear." "In pastoral," Empson says, "you take a limited life and pretend it is the full and normal one."[12] If so, then the fictions of pastoral may be the representative instance of the representative anecdote.

From its beginnings, modern criticism of pastoral has been founded on representative anecdotes. The first part of Rapin's treatise, on the antiquity and origins of pastoral poetry, bears a superficial resemblance to Scaliger's chapter on pastoral and to the opening sections of Guillaume Colletet's *Discours du Poème Bucolique* (1657), published two years before Rapin's essay and the first critical work devoted entirely to pastoral.[13] But Rapin's treatment of his materials is quite new. Instead of simply recording, as his predecessors do, various ancient tales and notions about the origins of pastoral, he expresses dissatisfaction with them as foolish fables. "Things and solid truth," he says, "is that we seek after."[14] What is striking is the form this solid knowledge takes. After surveying the ancient sources and concluding that no reliable knowledge is available from them, he says:

> Yet what beginning this kind of Poetry had, I think I can pretty well conjecture: for tis likely that first Shepherds us'd Songs to recreate themselves in their leisure hours whilst they fed their Sheep; and that each man, as his wit served, accommodated his Songs to his present Circumstances: to this Solitude invited, and the extream leisure that attends that employment absolutely requir'd it: For as their retirement gave them lei-

11. For Burke's urge to capitalize his terms (a pun he would approve), cf. his "Dialectician's Hymn," in which he hails the Logos as a "Vast Almighty Title" and calls "Thy name a Great Synecdoche/ Thy works a Grand Tautology." In *Language as Symbolic Action,* 55–57; also in *The Philosophy of Literary Form: Studies in Symbolic Action,* 3d ed. (Berkeley & Los Angeles: University of California Press, 1973), 448–50.

12. William Empson, *Some Versions of Pastoral* (Norfolk: New Directions, paperback, 1960), 110. Throughout the rest of this book, references to *SVP* will be parenthetical, in the text.

13. Congleton, *Theories of Pastoral,* 31. Nichols (113, above n. 1) is mistaken to give this dubious honor to Gerrit Vossius, "De bucolico carmine" (1647). This is simply a chapter (Book 3, chap. 8) in a long, general work: Gerardi Joannis Vossii, *Poeticarum institutionum libri tres* (Amsterdam: L. Elzevir, 1647).

14. Thomas Creech, *The Idylliums of Theocritus with Rapin's Discourse of Pastoral Done into English* (Oxford, 1684), 11. Subsequent page references are in the text.

sure, and Solitude a fit place for Meditation, Meditation and Invention produc'd a Verse. (pp. 13–14)

This brief narration is, in the strictest sense, a *representative* anecdote. To follow Foucault's account of "classical" representation, it seeks to signify a reality that is separate from it (and thus has the effect of bypassing the question of actual historical origin) but of which it permits a clear and compendious understanding. Rapin goes on to give his representative anecdote its final form, its title, as Burke would say:

> Pastorals were the invention of the simplicity and innocence of [the] Golden age, if there was ever any such, or certainly of that time which succeeded the beginning of the World: For tho the Golden Age must be acknowledged to be only in the fabulous times, yet 'tis certain that the Manners of the first Men were so plain and simple, that we may easily derive both the innocent imployment of Shepherds, and Pastorals from them. (14–15)

By taking representation to be the mode of knowledge, Rapin transforms Guillaume Colletet's pointless surveying and opining into what we can recognize as critical discourse.[15] The anecdote of the Golden Age enables him to resolve some traditional problems about pastoral. On the appropriate subject matter, he says: "All things must appear delightful and easy, nothing vitious and rough. . . . Every part must be full of the simplicity of the *Golden Age,* and of that Candor which was then eminent" (25). This is a critical remark, because it is applicable to literary phenomena and it is coherent enough to be discussable: making good the implications of "every part must be full," Rapin later extends its principles and terminology to other aspects of pastoral. The image of life in the Golden Age—"free and modest, honest and ingenuous" (35)—enables him to deal with the problems uncovered when he turns his Aristotelian analysis to other categories. In depicting the "manners" of shepherds, one must avoid the

---

15. The difference between Colletet's *Discours* (a 47-page duodecimo) and Rapin's *Dissertatio* is the more striking because their materials are often similar. Rapin's anecdote of the shepherd singing alone resembles Colletet's portrait of the shepherd (12–13), which itself derives from Scaliger (1.4, in Frederick M. Padelford, ed. and trans., *Select Translations from Scaliger's Poetics* [New York: Henry Holt, 1905], 21). But Colletet's discourse is genuinely pointless. It was written, he tells us, as one of a series of discourses on types of poetry, and was prompted by discussions in the French Academy about the idyll, which, he felt, was not sufficiently well defined. After twenty pages of rehashing Scaliger, surveying French eclogues, and the like, he finally comes to the idyll—about which he then says nothing except that the word, unlike "eclogue," indicates that the poem is short and is therefore truer to the scope of a pastoral (22). When he surveys modern French "idylls" (31ff.), the only criterion of the genre seems to be imitation of Theocritus, Bion, Moschus, and their Italian imitators. As for the stipulation that a pastoral be short, it collapses when Colletet defends as a pastoral St-Amant's 6,000-line long *Moÿse sauvé* ("*idylle heroique*").

extremes of coarse rusticity (some of Theocritus, all of Mantuan) and of undue courtliness (*Il Pastor Fido*). The "mean may be easily observed if the manners of our Shepherds be represented according to the *Genius* of the *golden Age*" (33). The word "genius" shows that Rapin's concern is not mere imitation of an external reality (which he knows never existed) but an informing notion that produces the phenomena and details that make poems poems. Hence when he goes on to the category of "thought," he can once more appeal to the Golden Age (35, quoted above) to recommend a mean between extremes—this time of "too scrupulous a Curiosity in Ornament" (34) on the one hand, and an insipid plainness on the other.

None of this will satisfy anyone today *as* criticism, but one can see that it *is* criticism. And it is criticism largely because its central idea takes the form of a representative anecdote. Even when Rapin does not explicitly appeal to the Golden Age, one feels its presence as an informing idea. The most important single word in the essay, "simplicity," gets its specific meanings and its reliability as a forceful word from the critic's accounts of the Golden Age: we have here a direct instance of an anecdote generating a terminology. Similarly, Rapin supports stylistic recommendations—brevity, delicacy, sweetness, "neatness"— with images that derive their critical point and force from the central image of life in the Golden Age. These images include attractive maidens (42, 44, 46), Adonis gardens (43), country fare (43), and the fruits of the land (56).

The history of pastoral criticism can be described as a series of representative anecdotes: Rapin's Golden Age and Fontenelle's innocent love; childhood and maturity in Schiller's *On Naive and Sentimental Poetry;* and, in our own time, Poggioli's pastorals of innocence and happiness and Empson's social encounter of courtier and rustic. Perhaps the most remarkable example occurs in Book VIII of *The Prelude,* in which Wordsworth surveys and, in some sense, dismisses traditional pastoral. The lines follow the statement, "And shepherds were the men that pleased me first," and go as follows in the 1805 version:

> Not such as, in Arcadian fastnesses
> Sequestered, handed down among themselves,
> So ancient poets sing, the golden age;
> Nor such—a second race, allied to these—
> As Shakespeare in the wood of Arden placed,
> Where Phoebe sighed for the false Ganymede,
> Or there where Florizel and Perdita
> Together danced, Queen of the feast and King;
> Nor such as Spenser fabled. True it is
> That I had heard, what he perhaps had seen,
> Of maids at sunrise bringing in from far
> Their May-bush, and along the streets in flocks

Parading, with a song of taunting rhymes
Aimed at the laggards slumbering within doors—
Had also heard, from those who yet remembered,
Tales of the maypole dance, and flowers that decked
The posts and the kirk-pillars, and of youths,
That each one with his maid at break of day,
By annual custom, issued forth in troops
To drink the waters of some favorite well,
And hang it round with garlands. This, alas,
Was but a dream: the times had scattered all
These lighter graces, and the rural ways
And manners which it was my chance to see
In childhood were severe and unadorned,
The unluxuriant produce of a life
Intent on little but substantial needs.[16]

The longest and most interesting section is on Spenser. Rather than character-izing one of Spenser's poems, Wordsworth rewrites a passage from the May eclogue of *The Shepheardes Calender* and presents it as a literal anecdote which was told to him when young—perhaps for its representative force, as if to say what things were like in the old days. In doing this, Wordsworth suggests how ap-posite Burke's term is, and nowhere more so than in the May eclogue itself. That poem is a debate between two old shepherds, in whom, the commentator E.K. says, "be represented two formes of pastoures or Ministers."[17] Their debate concerns the spiritual shepherd's attitude towards his flock, and it centers pre-cisely on two competing representative anecdotes. The easy-going shepherd defines himself by the account of the May Day ceremonies that Wordsworth rewrites. His antagonist not only criticizes the "lustihede and wanton mery-ment" (40) of this scene, but opposes to it a different pastoral anecdote—an account of shepherds' lives in biblical times, which serves as an allegory of the primitive church. In telling how May Day rites disappeared in the severities of the life he knew as a child, Wordsworth suggests that he well understood the pastoral contention represented by Spenser.[18]

16. William Wordsworth, *The Prelude: 1799, 1805, 1850*, ed. Jonathan Wordsworth et al. (New York: Norton, 1979) 8.183–209. All further references to this work will be included in the text.

17. Edmund Spenser, *Minor Poems*, ed. Ernest de Selincourt (Oxford: Clarendon Press, 1910), 46 ("Maye," Argument).

18. Wordsworth also, I feel I must add, shows himself a better critic than his descendant and editor, who says, in his note to these lines, that in the May eclogue we see "Spenser's idealization of pastoral life." My discussion below of the lines about *As You Like It* will suggest that there is a similar diminishing and trivializing of Wordsworth's sense of his predecessors, in the editorial as-sertion that "Wordsworth stresses the unreality of Shakespeare's pastoral world."

In the 1805 *Prelude* the point of the whole passage is that traditional pastoral falsely represents the life of shepherds as Wordsworth knew it. In Burke's terms, the anecdotes do not provide an adequate descriptive terminology. But in revising the poem, Wordsworth brought out the continuity between past versions of pastoral and present lives; the 1850 version thus suggests that such representations have representative force. The passage on Spenser remains essentially as it was, but the opening lines are much expanded and revised:

> Not such as Saturn ruled 'mid Latian wilds,
> With arts and laws so tempered, that their lives
> Left, even to us toiling in this late day,
> A bright tradition of the golden age;
> Not such as, 'mid Arcadian fastnesses
> Sequestered, handed down among themselves
> Felicity, in Grecian song renowned;
> Nor such as, when an adverse fate had driven,
> From house and home, the courtly band whose fortunes
> Entered, with Shakespeare's genius, the wild woods
> Of Arden, amid sunshine or in shade,
> Culled the best fruits of Time's uncounted hours,
> Ere Phoebe sighed for the false Ganymede.
>
> (1850: 8.129–41)

The additions and changes engage us more fully in these past representations. A number of the details recall aspects of the modern country festival in a "secluded glen" at the foot of Mount Helvellyn, which Wordsworth celebrates in the opening passage of Book VIII—the account of Saturn's shepherds, who were temperate in the wilds; the "felicity" of the Arcadians, sequestered in their fastnesses; the respite from time in the Forest of Arden. In this way, the clean separation of past and present in the 1805 version is revised to a tradition left "even to us toiling in this late day."

Like every good critic of pastoral, Wordsworth is attentive to the representing consciousness as well as to the lives represented. This comes out most strikingly in the new account of *As You Like It*, which connects it to the double implication of "even to us toiling in this late day." "Us" is poised between the poet and the lives he represents. *As You Like It* is made to anticipate this suspended meaning by the account of how the characters of the play become inhabitants of Arden. In 1805 Wordsworth merely says that Shakespeare placed them there. Now he describes them, accurately, as driven from home by an adverse fate, and the phrase, "entered, with Shakespeare's genius," brilliantly suggests the double relation of the poet and his human community—a doubleness certainly felt by the egotist who called the poet a man speaking to men, and one mythologized in traditional pastoral, with its singing contests that sometimes have winners and sometimes end in ties, and with its double notion of all Arcadians being singers and yet of there being master singers who are preeminent among them.

The passage concludes with two lines that are genuinely pastoral in mode. Wordsworth's mind seems to have dwelt on Phoebe sighing for the false Ganymede, but the reasons do not become clear until the 1850 version gives the line a context which releases its meanings. "Time's uncounted hours" is a beautiful bit of pastoral, because it is full of idyllic feeling and at the same time true to reality. It thus exemplifies Empson's account of pastoral by fusing, in a single phrase, a simple and a sophisticated awareness of an experience. A similar double perspective accounts for the power of the final line. The first thing we notice is that by changing "Where" in 1805 to "Ere," Wordsworth makes Phoebe's love dissipate the suspension of time in Arden. But the effect is so keen, because the line does not simply describe the plot of the play, as an observer, the sophisticated consciousness, knows it. It also renders Phoebe's sighing and disappointment from her point of view: "false" is felt to mean not simply "not actual," but "untrue," "false to me," as so often in love poetry. We can open up the sense of "representative" in pastorals by saying that in representing (i.e., depicting) Phoebe, the poet represents (i.e., speaks for) her, and she thus becomes representative (i.e., characteristic) of the way desire dissipates a sense of the idyllic. In representing Shakespeare's shepherdess, Wordsworth's genius takes us *out* of the woods of Arden and into the world of the modern shepherd and, perhaps, of a modern pastoral.

III

Our idea of pastoral will be determined by what we take to be its representative anecdote. To see the issues and choices involved, let us turn to the beginning of pastoral poetry as we know it—the opening lines of Theocritus's first idyll:

> *Thyrsis.* Sweet is the whispering music of yonder pine that sings
>   Over the water-brooks, and sweet the melody of your pipe,
>   Dear goatherd. After Pan, the second prize you'll bear away.
>   If he should take the hornèd goat, the she-goat shall you win:
>   But if he choose the she-goat for his meed, to you shall fall
>   The kid; and dainty is kid's flesh, till you begin to milk them.
> *Goatherd.* Sweeter, O shepherd, is your song than the melodious fall
>   Of yonder stream that from on high gushes down the rock.
>   If it chance that the Muses take the young ewe for their gift,

> Then your reward will be the stall-fed lamb; but should they
>   choose
> To take the lamb, then yours shall be the sheep for second
>   prize.[19]

This passage presents several features that are regarded as pastoral's defining characteristics: idyllic landscape, landscape as a setting for song, an atmosphere of *otium*, a conscious attention to art and nature, herdsmen as singers, and, in the account of the gifts, herdsmen as herdsmen. This multiplicity of features itself suggests that we should treat these lines as an anecdote—that is, as a brief and compendious rendering of a certain situation or type of life. Viewing the passage this way, we would not try to pick out one or two features as definitive. Rather, we can see that all its features belong to a central fiction and that different features can be emphasized and developed in various ways as this central fiction itself is developed and transformed in this and other poems.

But if this passage provides the informing anecdote of pastoral, what does it represent? There have been, in general, two ways of answering this question, and they lead to different accounts of pastoral. For many critics, these lines represent a landscape, while for others they represent two herdsmen in a characteristic situation. In either case, we must keep in mind the double meaning of "representative." It means both that the informing anecdote is a means of depiction, and also that what is depicted stands as a representative, a summary or characteristic example, or that it is in a synecdochic relation to something else, for which it stands or of which it is part. Hence there can be a double answer to the question: what do these representations represent? For those nineteenth-century critics who regarded Theocritus as a realist, the passage depicts herdsmen in the countryside (Sicilian, it was thought). We ourselves, though acknowledging the realistic aspect of the proposed gifts, might draw attention to the emphasis on singing and say that these herdsmen represent poets. The question of what is represented is more elusive if we take the landscape to be the heart of the passage. In that case, most critics and readers seem to regard it as representative of some state of mind—an ethical attitude or a psychological yearning or a realm of the imagination. Earlier critics might have thought that it represents the Golden Age, but that fiction itself would now be taken to represent a state of mind.

This book will argue that we will have a far truer idea of pastoral if we take its representative anecdote to be herdsmen and their lives, rather than landscape or idealized nature. The difference between these two anecdotes can be seen in the way they represent the opening lines of Virgil's first eclogue:

19. Theocritus, *Idylls*, trans. R. C. Trevelyan (New York: Albert and Charles Boni, 1925), Idyll 1, 1–11. See chap. 4, n. 1, for comment on this and other translations.

Meliboeus. *Tityre, tu patulae recubans sub tegmine fagi*
    silvestrem tenui musam meditaris avena;
    nos patriae finis et dulcia linquimus arva.
    nos patriam fugimus; tu, Tityre, lentus in umbra
    formosam resonare doces Amaryllida silvas.
Tityrus. *O Meliboee, deus nobis haec otia fecit.*
    namque erit ille mihi semper deus, illius aram
    saepe tener nostris ab ovilibus imbuet agnus.
    ille meas errare boves, ut cernis, et ipsum
    ludere quae vellem calamo permisit agresti.

M. You, Tityrus, under the spreading, sheltering beech,
    Tune woodland musings on a delicate reed;
    We flee our country's borders, our sweet fields,
    Abandon home; you, lazing in the shade,
    Make woods resound with lovely Amaryllis.
T. O Melibee, a god grants us this peace—
    Ever a god to me, upon whose altar
    A young lamb from our folds will often bleed.
    He has allowed, you see, my herds to wander
    And me to play as I will on a rustic pipe.[20]

We can regard these lines, which set an exchange about pastoral song at the head of a collection of bucolics, as a version of Theocritus's opening lines.[21] Our understanding of the character of the two passages and the relation between them both determines and is determined by our idea of pastoral.

Theocritus's passage is full of lovely symmetries. Each speech begins with two lines comparing the other herdsman's music to nature's and concludes with three lines (each set structured in the same way) promising a gift to honor a song. These formal symmetries perfectly convey the atmosphere of this meeting and the attitude of the herdsmen. They do not mirror each other (we later learn that they have individual circumstances and histories), but they do understand each other and their situations and can therefore exchange speeches, just as they propose to exchange songs and gifts. By the same token, the herdsmen are in a harmonious relation to the natural setting which they share. The

20. Eclogue 1, 1–10. Text and translation (slightly revised) from Paul Alpers, *The Singer of the "Eclogues": A Study of Virgilian Pastoral* (Berkeley & Los Angeles: University of California Press, 1979). The Latin text is based on that of R. A. B. Mynors, *P. Vergili Maronis Opera*, Oxford Classical Texts (Oxford, 1969). In discussing details from Theocritus and Virgil, I sometimes give more literal renderings than in my verse translation.

21. For the relation between Theocritus and Virgil, see chapter 4, where I argue that Virgil's transformation of Theocritean bucolic established pastoral as a literary form.

first sentence suggests the harmony between human and natural music by its unusual grammar, which can roughly be described as supplying a double "both-and" construction.[22] Human and natural music are thus coordinated but remain separate. The landscape is discretely and lucidly sketched in the phrase "by the brooks" (1. 2). It neither dominates the herdsmen nor is unduly responsive to them, but, in its parallel activity, is an appropriate setting for human song.

When we turn to Virgil we find two herdsmen who have shared a way of life but who are now in opposite situations. Tityrus is secure in the way of life he has known, while Meliboeus has been dispossessed of his farm and is going into exile. If we take landscape as the representative anecdote, these lines appear to criticize and undermine the very notion of pastoral: its idyllic landscape represents a fantasy that is dissipated by the recognition of political and social realities. The rest of the eclogue seems to confirm this assumption. It has no pastoral singing, explicitly refers to contemporary Rome, and concerns a countryside disrupted by the aftermath of civil war. But if we take herdsmen's lives as the representative anecdote of pastoral, we can see that Virgil is reinterpreting Theocritus. The situation he presents does not flatly deny but rather questions and makes explicit the conditions under which, in the Roman world, the beginning of Idyll 1 can be representative of human singing and a way of life. After all, there is nothing surprising about a pastoral representation of the situation in Eclogue 1. In their simplicity and vulnerability, shepherds fittingly represent those whose lives are determined by the actions of powerful men or by events and circumstances over which they have no control. Even though they are among the least powerful members of society, they are far from alone in experiencing the dependency and victimization presented in this eclogue. In this sense, the situation of Meliboeus and Tityrus, though not perhaps the universal condition of mankind, is common enough to show why this eclogue exemplifies Empson's dictum that "you can say everything about complex people by a complete consideration of simple people" (*SVP*, 131).

Virgil's new representation of shepherds brings about a modification of pastoral song. The homogeneity of Theocritus's opening exchange divides here into two versions of pastoral. Tityrus's speech separates out the realistic aspect of Theocritus's lines and presents *otium* in circumstantial terms. Tityrus is a real herdsman; the god he praises turns out to be a powerful young man in Rome, presumably Octavian; and the sacrifices he promises were common in Roman rural and domestic life. The indication of real circumstances carries with it a sense of real time: Tityrus promises future acts and remembrances in gratitude for a condition that is due to a past action. Meliboeus's speech, on the other hand, brings out and intensifies what is idyllic, in the modern sense, in Theoc-

---

22. As pointed out in K. J. Dover, ed., Theocritus, *Select Poems*, (London: Macmillan, 1971), 77: "*kai* . . . *kai* [both . . . and] is superimposed on *hadu* . . . *hadu de* [sweet . . . and sweet]."

ritus. Tityrus is represented as living in a "timeless" present, his *otium* an expanded, blissful moment rather than a complete way of life. His song is represented not as the piping in the fields that he himself describes but rather as, in Marvell's phase, an "echoing song" that fills the space around him. Similarly, we find in each speech a characteristic account of the relation between human song and nature. The natural scene, with its wandering herd, is the setting for Tityrus's freedom, but is not central to his representation of it. The focus is rather on the human conditions of his *otium*. "He has allowed me to play as I will on a rustic pipe" both indicates his dependence on his patron and brings out, in balancing "quae vellem" (what I want) and "permisit" (has allowed), the problematic relations of freedom and dependency. The word "ludere" has all the meanings of the English word "play," so that the half-line "ludere quae vellem" has larger suggestions of freedom, which I have tried to convey by translating, "play as I will." But the line concludes by scaling down these intimations to the music played *calamo agresti*, on a rustic pipe.

The final line of Meliboeus's speech, on the other hand, gives a quite different version of pastoral song: *formosam resonare doces Amaryllida silvas* (you teach the woods to resound lovely Amaryllis). Here man and landscape are intimately responsive to each other, in what the French call a *cadre sonore*. The singer teaches the woods to sound his beloved's name; on the other hand, the actual sounding is attributed to the woods alone, so that the song is not what he utters but what he hears: hence the echoing effect in *Amaryllida silvas*, where the "-il" syllables receive the metrical emphasis, and the general sense of intimate responsiveness. The singer's love, which prompts his song, has a similar double aspect, active and receptive. Is his song dependent on his mistress who inspires him, or is it he who, in proclaiming her, in a sense makes her *formosam*, lovely?

Virgil has changed Theocritus's responsive exchange into something that looks like drama. Hence some scholars call Eclogue 1 a rustic mime, and critics who imagine a confrontation of "pastoral myth" and "contemporary reality" will seek out elements of the dramatic in it. But the "dramatic" effect comes less from depicted conflict or confrontation, of which there is hardly any, than from the separateness of the two speakers in a responsive exchange. Where the opening of Idyll 1 is close to the formal responsiveness of singing contests, Virgil's exchange produces two versions of pastoral—Meliboeus's, idyllic because colored by his sense of separation, and Tityrus's, pragmatic and concretely rural, however protected. The passage itself supplies tags (or what Burke would call "titles") for these versions of pastoral. We have already noted Tityrus's *calamo . . . agresti* (rustic pipe), where the adjective *agrestis* comes from *ager* (field). This phrase answers to *silvestrem . . . musam* (woodland muse) in the second line of Meliboeus's speech.

Eclogue 1 shows us how pastoral historically transforms and diversifies itself. As we shall see in chapter 4, Virgil could not have written this poem (or

158,337

the others in his Eclogue book) had he not taken Theocritus as a model; but at the same time he reinterprets Theocritean bucolic. His representing pastoral song and its conditions—as he understood them in the literary, social, and political world of Rome—leads him to develop, in this eclogue, two versions of pastoral. From a poem like this, one can trace much of the subsequent course of pastoral poetry. An important descendant, for example, is the pastoral episode in Book 6 of *The Faerie Queene*, in which we find two distinct versions of pastoral, corresponding to the *calamus agrestis* and the *musa silvestris* of Virgil's poem. In canto 9, which is set in "open fields" (st. 4) and in "a cottage clad with lome" (st. 16), Sir Calidore meets the old shepherd Melibee (a *fortunatus senex*, like Tityrus) and learns to accommodate his courtly desires, notions, and manners to the "mean" condition of the country. The word "mean," an important one in the canto, suggests both modest, even poor, conditions and the ethical ideal of moderation, which these conditions nurture. In canto 10, the knight finds himself in quite another pastoral world—Mount Acidale, a woodland which is Venus's pastoral retreat and is explicitly off bounds to "the ruder clowne" (st. 7). Here Calidore meets a different kind of shepherd—Colin Clout, the poet's pastoral self-representation—and his pastoral experience is to see the Graces dance and to hear Colin Clout describe them and praise his beloved. When the vision of the Graces disappears because of Calidore's naive desire to apprehend it, the shepherd-poet makes the woods resound with lovely Rosalind.

We can trace the continuity between Virgil's eclogues and Book 6 of *The Faerie Queene* by asking how these and various intermediate works deal with the representative anecdote of pastoral. These dealings can involve a given literary culture, so that Sannazaro's *Arcadia*, a fountainhead of Renaissance pastoral, grafts Petrarchan love poetry onto Virgilian pastoral; or the social existence of literary works, so that one pays attention to the pleasures sought and demands made by various royal and princely courts; or larger historical situations, such as the strains in English society in the first half of the seventeenth century, when civil war was in the making and pastoral poetry flourished. But what connects pastoral works to each other, what makes them a literary "kind," is the way each deals, in its circumstances and for its reasons, with the representative anecdote of herdsmen and their lives.

To say that this is the representative anecdote of pastoral means that pastoral works are representations of shepherds (and, in post-classical literature, shepherdesses) who are felt to be representative of some other or of all other men and/or women. But since all the terms in this definition are subject to modification or reinterpretation, pastoral is historically diversified and transformed. Various writers at various times modify the way shepherds are depicted, on the grounds that it either does not truly represent them or that it deprives them of their representative force. In Shakespeare and Wordsworth we find shepherds portrayed in accordance with what is claimed to be the truth of their lives, but most modifications in the depiction of shepherds involve the ways in which it is claimed that they are representative. The biblical metaphor of the good shepherd enters pastoral for this reason, and—to take a quite different branch of Renaissance pastoral—literary shepherds are often lovers because their lives are felt to represent some (not all) fundamental aspects of love as a human experience. Similarly, old shepherds, who rarely appear in Theocritus and Virgil, become a recognizable character type in the Renaissance, because they utter various kinds of moral counsel which are felt to be implicit in accepting that shepherds' lives represent human lives. The old shepherds of *The Shepheardes Calender,* for example, speak for various forms of the reality principle—accepting old age or warning more easygoing pastors to heed the deceptions of the Roman Catholic church. Similarly, the dramatis personae of pastoral can be extended to include other rustics or socially inferior persons on the grounds that they are the equivalent, in a given society or world, of shepherds, or that they more truly have the representative status that traditional pastoral ascribes to its herdsmen. It is the latter consideration that enables us to answer the old question about whether Marvell's mower is an innovation. Mowers do appear in earlier pastorals, but Marvell's figure is new because, for reasons that clearly have to do with his view of the realities of love and the imagination, Marvell was the first poet to make the mower the representative pastoral lover.

A similar account, similarly based on Burke's ideas, allows us to understand the place of landscape in pastoral. However much we argue (as I shall in a moment) that Romantic poetics has caused us to exaggerate the importance of idealized nature, it is still the case that certain representations of landscape have always been characteristic of pastoral. The question is whether we can account for pastoral landscapes in the terms of our representative anecdote. I think that we can: in both life and poetry, after all, certain kinds of landscape are the setting in which herdsmen lead their lives. Our guiding principle here should be what Burke calls the scene-agent ratio, "the synecdochic relation . . . between person and place."[23] The presence, emergence, and history of pastoral landscape is not a matter of nature poetry or of visionary or psychological projection but rather an interpretation, a selective emphasis determined by individual or cultural motives, of the central fiction that shepherds' lives represent human lives. To conceive pastoral landscape this way enables us to understand what is clear from the history of pastoral—that it is susceptible to presenting different accounts of nature as the "scene" of shepherds' lives (as in the various landscapes

23. *A Grammar of Motives,* 7.

of *The Shepheardes Calender*) or to varying the importance attributed to natural setting (as the setting of *A Midsummer Night's Dream* is more important than that of *As You Like It*).

But whatever the specific features and emphases, it is the representative anecdote of shepherds' lives that makes certain landscapes pastoral. Burke exemplifies the scene-agent ratio by citing a passage in *Heroes and Hero-Worship*, in which Carlyle speaks of Arabia as the "fit habitation" of the people among whom Mohammed was born. This notion is a thematic concern of pastoral poetry: we may say that landscapes are pastoral when they are conceived as fit habitations for herdsmen or their equivalents, like the child around whom emerges the magical landscape of Virgil's fourth Eclogue. We remind ourselves again that the interpretation of "herdsmen or their equivalents" changes historically. In Virgil's works, pastoral and georgic are distinct: in the latter, nature's uncertainties and harshness are more prominent, because it is conceived as the habitation of farmers. In the Renaissance the two types merge in various ways, largely because in Christian thought ideas of humility are connected with the curse of labor. But the principle remains: poetic representations of nature or of landscape are not all of a piece; they answer to and express various human needs and concerns; *pastoral* landscapes are those of which the human centers are herdsmen or their equivalents.

IV

Nature and idyllic landscape figure prominently in most scholarly and critical accounts of pastoral and are regularly associated with the Golden Age, innocence, and nostalgia. It is not self-evident that these are the defining features of pastoral. The idea that they are derives from a specific poetics, which, so far as it concerns pastoral, has its profoundest statement in Friedrich Schiller's *On Naive and Sentimental Poetry* (1795–6). Schiller understands what is at stake in attributing value to certain representations and modes of simplicity. His essay thus provides an anatomy of modern thinking about pastoral and enables us to see connections and implications in a way no later criticism does.

Schiller's account of pastoral is embedded in a general theory of poetry, and particularly of the nature of modern poetry. The intellectual imperatives and cultural urgencies of this theory derive from an analogy between the growth of the individual and the progress of human history. "Th[e] path taken by the modern poets," he says at one point, is "that along which man in general, the individual as well as the race, must pass."[24] Schiller represents man's original

24. "On Naive and Sentimental Poetry," in H. B. Nisbet, ed., *German Aesthetic and Literary Criticism: Winckelmann, Lessing, Hamann, Herder, Schiller, Goethe* (Cambridge: Cambridge University Press, 1985), 194. Nisbet reprints in full and slightly modified the translation by Julius A. Elias (New York:

condition—in the childhood of the individual and historically in ancient Greece—as one of unity within himself and with the world around him: "sense and reason, passive and active faculties, are not separated in their activities, still less do they stand in conflict with one another" (193). But as man develops and civilization and art lay their hands upon him, "that *sensuous* harmony in him is withdrawn, and he can now express himself only as a *moral* unity, i.e. as striving after unity. The correspondence between his feeling and thought which in his first condition *actually* took place, exists now only *ideally*" (194). Nature, which once was simply the world in which man found himself and acted, is now seen to be separate from him, and presents itself as the ideal of harmonious existence which he seeks to achieve.

To these types of man, which are also stages of development, correspond two types of poetry, the naive and the sentimental:

> In the earlier state of natural simplicity [poetry] is the completest pos- sible *imitation of actuality*—at that stage man still functions with all his powers simultaneously as a harmonious unity and hence the whole of his nature is expressed completely in actuality; whereas now, in the state of civilisation where that harmonious cooperation of his whole nature is only an idea, it is . . . the *representation of the ideal*, that makes for the poet. (194)

What might appear a slippage between types of poetry and types of poet con- veys one of Schiller's deepest insights and contributions to theory. His atten- tion to structures of temperament and their relation to historical and cultural situations enables him to reject traditional generic categories of poetry and instead to classify all poetry by modes of feeling or perception (*Empfindungs- weise*). Naive poetry is always characterized by simplicity, whatever its subject or emotional level: "since the naive poet only follows simple nature and feeling, and limits himself solely to imitation of actuality, he can have only a single relationship to his subject" (195). From this single relationship arises our own singleness of feeling as we read Homer and other naive poets. Sentimental po- etry, on the other hand, arouses complex feelings, because the sentimental poet does not realize himself in his relation to actuality:

> He *reflects* upon the impression that objects make upon him, and only in that reflection is the emotion grounded which he himself experiences and which he excites in us. . . . The sentimental poet is thus always in- volved with two conflicting representations [*Vorstellungen*] and perceptions [*Empfindungen*]—with actuality as a limit and with his idea as infinitude;

Frederick Ungar, 1966). Parenthetical page references in the text to "Naive and Sentimental Poetry" will be to Nisbet's volume.

and the mixed feelings that he excites will always testify to this dual source. (196)

From the sentimental poet's relation to the ideal on the one hand and actuality on the other, Schiller derives all modes of modern poetry:

> Since in this case there is a plurality of principles it depends which of the two will *predominate* in the perception of the poet and in his representation [*Darstellung*], and hence a variation in the treatment is possible [as it is not in naive poetry]. For now the question arises whether he will tend more toward actuality or toward the ideal—whether he will realize the former as an object of antipathy or the latter as an object of sympathy. His presentation will, therefore, be either *satirical* or it will be . . . *elegiac;* every sentimental poet will adhere to one of these two modes of perception. (196)

Schiller here speaks of elegiac poetry in a broad sense—as the kind of poetry in which pleasure in [*Wohlgefallen*] and representation of the ideal predominate over the sense of actuality. This broadly elegiac poetry can take one of two forms:

> Either nature and the ideal are an object of sadness if the first is treated as lost and the second as unattained. Or both are an object of joy represented as actual. The first yields the *elegy* in the narrower sense, and the second the idyll. (200)

On Naive and Sentimental Poetry has been said to "constitute the intellectual foundation for all modern approaches to pastoral," on the grounds that it established modal (as opposed to traditional generic) definitions of the various kinds of poetry.[25] But the essay is more specifically a "mirror for modern critics," as the Elizabethans might have said, because Schiller's categories of sentimental poetry correspond remarkably to what many critics still describe as the uses of pastoral. Like Schiller, these critics consider a longing for the ideal, prompted by a reaction against the ways of civilization, to be at the heart of (pastoral) poetry. Hence when not indulging in pure representations of the ideal (Schiller's idyll), the pastoral sensibility will either turn to criticism of corrupt or sophisticated ways of life (Schiller's satire) or will look back nostalgically to a simpler, vanished past (Schiller's elegy). The satiric potentialities of pastoral are a commonplace—to the extent that in some accounts, satire is not simply an aspect or potential use of pastoral but its main motive. And the extraordinary emphasis on the Golden Age in modern accounts of pastoral—far beyond what is justified by ancient or even Renaissance writers—is due to critics' accepting

25. Halperin, *Before Pastoral* (above, n. 5), 43.

a structure of relationships which makes the elegy, in Schiller's sense, a definitive manifestation of the impulse at the heart of this kind of poetry.

However suggestive Schiller's theory of modern poetry, it is unlikely that
we would accept the specific terms in which he frames it. But pastoral still seems
to us to be defined by the problem of man's relation to nature and the phenomena and issues which Schiller derives from it. Hence we find modern critics
channeling the general issues of *On Naive and Sentimental Poetry* into the specific
problematic of pastoral. Adam Parry's well known essay, "Landscape in Greek
Poetry," develops a framework almost identical to Schiller's:

> Man in the youth of a culture possesses a kind of confidence which does
> not allow him to feel alien from the world about him. . . . As long as man,
> though different from the rest of nature, (using the word in a wider sense)
> is not of another world from it, he will not choose nature as a whole, or
> nature in a multiple aspect, to figure something of himself. For this would
> involve his conceiving nature as something *other*.[26]

Having outlined this version of the naive, Parry goes on to define the later stage
of culture and poetry:

> Interest in landscape, or nature, *for its own sake* could be best understood
> as applying to that literary art wherein man looks to nature for something
> which he has not within himself or which exists in an imperfect and adul-
> terated manner in his daily life. . . . Nature no longer tells us what we are:
> it tells us what we are not but yearn to be. Pastoral poetry—and romantic
> poetry, where it deals with nature—fits into this category.[27]

The main difference between this and the original scheme of "naive and sentimental poetry" is that Schiller's model of nature is the child and its maturing,
whereas Parry, like most modern critics of pastoral, makes landscape representative of nature and the issue it raises. The foregrounding of landscape is evident in the title of his essay (which as much concerns metaphors drawn from
nature and the representation of heroes) and in such other titles as "Arcadia:
The Discovery of a Spiritual Landscape," *Vergil's "Eclogues": Landscapes of Experience*, and "*Lycidas*: The Poet in a Landscape." The modern emphasis on landscapes and settings as the definitive features of pastoral presumably reflects a
diminished belief in the value of childhood and a continuing commitment to
imaginative worlds. Whatever its cause, the shift from childhood to landscape
has an important theoretical and interpretive consequence. It removes time and
its necessities from the model of nature and poetry, and thus conceals from us

26. Adam Parry, "Landscape in Greek Poetry," *Yale Classical Studies* 15 (1957): 4, 6.

27. Ibid., 7–8. Parry does not mention Schiller, but he is well aware of his debt to writers in the
romantic tradition, notably Wordsworth, Hölderlin, and Ruskin.

the reasons, which (as we shall see) were clear to Schiller, why pastoral often seems jejune or callow.

The point of tracing these modern emphases back to Schiller is to show that what have seemed obvious ways of understanding pastoral carry with them a certain poetics and certain attendant emphases. It is not enough to point to the presence in pastoral of *loci amoeni* and echoing woods. They are certainly there, but they have as much to do with establishing a space for song as with man's relation to nature. We need a stronger explanation for the fact that idyllic landscape—or its associated phenomenon, the Golden Age—is often singled out as the definitive feature of pastoral. Only in Schiller's terms can we understand the links assumed when Parry says that pastoral appears in Plato's *Phaedrus* "in the form of both indulgence in natural beauty and criticism of society,"[28] or when Frank Kermode explains "the nature of pastoral poetry" by moving, in the space of two pages, from "contrasts between the natural and the cultivated" to the opposition of country and city to the Golden Age to Juvenalian satire.[29] Again, it is not that Schiller's poetics are espoused as such, but rather that they in effect predetermine what seem the evident features, interests, and uses of pastoral. Once you decide innocence or the Golden Age or landscape are of the essence of pastoral, you are likely to be drawn into the field of force represented by *On Naive and Sentimental Poetry*.

Of course it may be that Schiller's poetics are appropriate to pastoral. But if this is so, we must face Schiller's own argument that pastoral is an inherently compromised form. After developing the distinction between satire and elegy as the two main branches of sentimental poetry, he turns to the third type, the idyll, in which the real and the ideal come together:

> The poetic representation of innocent and contented mankind is the universal concept of this type of poetic composition. Since this innocence and this contentedness appear incompatible with the artificial conditions of society at large and with a certain degree of education and refinement, the poets have removed the location of idyll from the tumult of everyday life into the simple pastoral state and assigned its period before the *beginnings of civilisation* in the childlike age of man. (210)

Schiller has a strong, even a noble sense of the way idyllic poetry expresses dissatisfaction with modern society and the individual's desire for harmony within himself and with his environment. He therefore does not regard idyllic imaginings as merely reactive or wishful. In a memorable passage, he says:

28. Ibid., 16.
29. Kermode, *English Pastoral Poetry* (above, n. 4), 13–15.

All peoples who possess a history have a paradise, a state of innocence, a golden age; indeed, every man has his paradise, his golden age, which he recalls, according as he has more or less of the poetic in his nature, with more or less inspiration. Experience itself therefore supplies features enough for the depiction [*Gemälde*] of which the pastoral idyll treats. For this reason it remains always a beautiful, an elevating fiction, and the poetic power in representing it [*Darstellung*] has truly worked on behalf of the ideal. (211)

But although the idyll has its source in human nature and the natural history of culture, there is a "shortcoming grounded in the essence of the pastoral idyll [*Hirtenidylle;* Schiller also uses the word *Schäferidylle*]" (211). It can be stated in more than one way, in accordance with the various dualisms which inform Schiller's thought. He states it first as a conflict between past and future. If, as he claims, the idyll is not a chimera and holds out a real human possibility, then its effect should be to make us look to the future in hope: the condition of harmony which it depicts is the one which civilization "aims at as its ultimate purpose" (210). Unfortunately, by presenting a state of innocence in the past, the idyll, precisely by affecting us, leads us backwards and "imbues us only with a sad feeling of loss" (211). The aesthetic weakness is inherent and necessary, because idyllic poems do not accept the necessities of time. "The childlike age of man," which the idyll depicts, can no more be recovered than the actual childhood of individual men.

Schiller goes on to develop the contradictions of the modern, "sentimental" idyll—he explicitly says that he is not concerned with the "naive" idyll of the Greeks [30]—in broader historical and cultural terms:

Set *before the beginnings of civilisation,* [such poems] exclude together with its disadvantages all its advantages, and by their very nature they find themselves necessarily in conflict with it. . . . Since they can only attain their purpose by the denial of all art, and only by the simplification of human nature, they possess together with the utmost value for the *heart,* all too little for the *spirit,* and their narrow range is too soon exhausted. (211)

Hence the value of these poems is at the same time their limitation: "We can love them and seek them out only when we stand in need of peace, but not

---

30. Schiller does not discuss Theocritus, but he is presumably thinking of him when, in his critique of the modern idyll (of which German poetry in the eighteenth century provided abundant examples), he says: "What I am here criticising in the bucolic idyll applies of course only to the sentimental; for the naive can never be lacking content since here it is already contained in the form itself" (211). It is to Schillerian poetics, in the main, that we owe the view of Theocritus as a realist that dominated nineteenth-century criticism.

when our forces are striving for motion and activity. Only for the sick in spirit can they provide *healing*, but no *nourishment* for the healthy; they cannot vivify, only assuage" (211).

Schiller's analysis has a clarity and authority unmatched by any later critic in his tradition. He gives a persuasive account of the appeal of pastoral, to which he in no way suggests he is immune, while at the same time his sense of its spiritual debility is as urgent, broadly based, and decisive as Samuel Johnson's. It is also less easily discounted than Johnson's. Schiller's argument brings out and helps us understand the fact that many modern critics of pastoral find it difficult to take their subject seriously. Bruno Snell represents Virgil's pastorals as "the discovery of a spiritual landscape," prompted by the loss of the connection, which existed in the Greek city-state, between poetry and the world of experience and action. This analysis derives, whether consciously or not, from *On Naive and Sentimental Poetry*. (The second half of Snell's essay is devoted to Horace, whom Schiller called "the founder of this sentimental mode of poetry" [190]). It is Schiller's critique of the idyll which explains why Snell does not treat the Eclogues simply as a form of modern poetry, but makes them sound peculiarly feeble and self-indulgent:

> Virgil needed a new home for his herdsmen, a land far distant from the sordid realities of the present. . . . He needed a far-away land overlaid with the golden haze of unreality. . . . [Theocritus] still shows some interest in realistic detail. Virgil has ceased to see anything but what is important to him: tenderness and warmth and delicacy of feeling.[31]

Renato Poggioli, who expended so much wit and intelligence on analyzing the pastoral ideal, had no qualms about saying that it "shifts on the quicksands of wishful thought":

> The psychological root of the pastoral is a double longing after innocence and happiness, to be recovered not through conversion or regeneration but merely through a retreat. . . . The pastoral longing is but the wishful dream of a happiness to be gained without effort, of an erotic bliss made absolute by its own irresponsibility.[32]

Rosalie Colie praises Marvell's Mower poems in the same vein:

31. Bruno Snell, *The Discovery of the Mind: The Greek Origins of European Thought*, trans. T. G. Rosenmeyer (Cambridge: Harvard University Press, 1953), 282, 288.

32. Renato Poggioli, *The Oaten Flute* (above, n. 4), 1, 14. The phrase about the quicksands of wishful thought is on page 2. The easy and sophisticated Poggioli sometimes sounds simply like a latter-day Fontenelle. But his involvement with Schiller's problematic (he was, after all, most importantly a critic of modern literature) is evident in his hostility to Rousseau and his championing of Goethe. Schiller (188–89) has a striking and brilliant expostulation with the cultured person who feels the longings Poggioli describes here.

The pastoral cannot provide a satisfactory working-model for lives as men and women must live them, complicated beyond help from the pastoral paradigm. Just because the pastoral is so "useless" in interpreting human life, it is important for its recreative, dreaming beauty all the same.[33]

These uneasy and condescending accounts can be referred to and explained by Schiller not only because they still discern in pastoral the features of the sentimental idyll, but also because they measure them by similar criteria. They share with Schiller ideas of psychological integrity and fullness of experience that make pastoral appear callow or self-indulgent, and they share a sense of the necessities of history that make it appear escapist.

Modern critics are of course aware that pastoral writing is urban and sophisticated. But by accepting a Schillerian account of the essential ingenuousness and debility of "pure" pastoral, they can speak of its sophistication not as one of its properties, but only as a conflict with itself. One reason for emphasizing the satiric potentialities of pastoral is to associate it with a stronger form of poetry, one that is explicitly ironic and schooled by experience. But the characteristic way of making pastoral interesting is to claim that it undermines or criticizes or transcends itself. Thus Harry Berger speaks of Spenser's *Shepheardes Calender* as a critique of "the paradise principle." In terms that again remind us of Schiller, he argues that Spenser represents "the longing for paradise as the psychological basis of the pastoral retreat from life. This longing may be inflected toward wish-fulfilling fantasy or toward bitter rejection of the world that falls short of such fantasy."[34] What makes *The Shepheardes Calender* worth our attention, in Berger's view, is that it takes as jaundiced a view of the paradise principle as we do and proves to be "an ironic portrait of the tradition it claims for itself."[35] Irony is not the only way in which pastoral can be interpreted as something other than it seems. Allegory too has been much favored by modern critics, who often invoke the tradition that Virgil's fourth Eclogue prophesied the birth of Christ in order to justify their own abstruse or high-minded interpretations.

33. Rosalie L. Colie, *"My Ecchoing Song": Andrew Marvell's Poetry of Criticism* (Princeton: Princeton University Press, 1970), 41.

34. Harry Berger, Jr., "Orpheus, Pan, and the Poetics of Misogyny: Spenser's Critique of Pastoral Love and Art," *ELH* 50 (1983): 27. This article has been incorporated into a monograph on *The Shepheardes Calender* that forms the second part of Berger's *Revisionary Play: Studies in the Spenserian Dynamics* (Berkeley & Los Angeles: University of California Press, 1988). The sentences quoted above appear at the head of this monograph (277–78).

35. *ELH* 50 (1983): 53. Berger has to some extent modified this view (though for our purposes its representative force still holds). In *Revisionary Play* he says, "I think pastoral that criticizes itself rather than (or as well as) the great world is an enduring element of the mode" (282). But since he wants to call this *meta*pastoral, the Schillerian "paradise principle" is still at the heart of the mode.

Such attempts to transcend the felt limitations of pastoral are once again anticipated and prospectively analyzed in *On Naive and Sentimental Poetry*. The contradiction in sentimental idylls, Schiller says, is that they "implement an ideal, and yet retain the narrower indigent pastoral world" (212). In traditional pastoral, the poetic value of this world derives solely from the naive mode of representation. The writer of modern idylls therefore "should absolutely have chosen . . . another world for the ideal (212)," which he should represent in wholly other terms:

> Let him not lead us backwards into our childhood in order to secure to us with the most precious acquisitions of the understanding a peace which cannot last longer than the slumber of our spiritual faculties, but rather lead us forward into our maturity in order to permit us to perceive that higher harmony which rewards the combatant and gratifies the conqueror. Let him undertake the task of idyll so as to display that pastoral innocence even in creatures of civilisation and under all the conditions of the most active and vigorous life, of expansive thought, of the subtlest art, the highest social refinement, which, in a word, leads man who cannot now go back to Arcady forward to Elysium. (213)

This is a call for what our leading witness of Romantic prophecy calls "strong" poetry. Schiller's terms are less ironized and embattled than Harold Bloom's, but his words bring to mind such Bloomian heroes as Blake, Wordsworth, Shelley, and Whitman, and he looks back to the same historical antecedent: "A loftier satisfaction is aroused by Milton's superb representation of the first human couple and the state of innocence in paradise: the most beautiful idyll known to me of the sentimental type" (212). When modern critics of pastoral emphasize allegorical interpretation, the theme of art and nature, Edenic motifs, and the higher flights of irony and self-reflexiveness, they assume the authority of Romantic poetry in its heroic aspect and seek to make pastoral interesting in its terms. Not all continue the Romantic tradition as frankly and grandly as Northrop Frye, who assimilates pastoral to the mode of romance,[36] and not all are as self-aware as Berger, who explicitly seeks a "strong" version of pastoral to recuperate the "weak";[37] others, like Poggioli and Kermode, have their own interesting quarrels with Romanticism. But just as accepting a Schillerian account of pastoral leads to dissatisfaction with it, so embracing Schiller-

---

36. For Frye's elevation of pastoral, see *Anatomy of Criticism* (Princeton: Princeton University Press, 1957), 141–44, 152, 296–97.

37. *ELH* (1983): 37; *Revisionary Play*, 349. Berger's championing of *"strong pastoral or metapastoral,"* as opposed to "the great quantity of pastoral that . . . may be classified as *weak pastoral*" motivates his excellent essay, "The Origins of Bucolic Representation: Disenchantment and Revision in Theocritus' Seventh *Idyll*," *Classical Antiquity* 3 (1984): 1–39. The words quoted are on p. 2.

ian solutions leads to implausible claims. If "strong" poetry is our criterion, there is no avoiding the conclusion that pastoral is "weak."

V

The alternative to calling pastoral "weak" is to say, with Empson, that "the pastoral process" consists of "putting the complex into the simple" (*SVP,* 23). Though *Some Versions of Pastoral* is widely recognized as the one really profound treatment of the subject, its coruscating brilliance and idiosyncracies of manner have made it as difficult to use as it is easy to admire. Empson's view of pastoral has been regarded as either unmanageably inclusive or narrowly social and political. It in fact lies between these extremes, wide-ranging indeed but consistent. Empson develops an account of the central and defining simplicity of pastoral not from the natural model of childhood and maturity, but from a basic social situation—the encounter of "high" and "low" persons, the sophisticated and socially privileged confronting (as courtiers and rustics meet in Renaissance pastorals) the socially and economically humble. Empson's view that poetry is rhetorical and social—its permanent forces unavoidably mediated by the realities of given societies and historical moments—offers an alternative to Schiller's view of poetry as psychological and universal.

One finds ethical, social, and rhetorical emphases in some of the most valuable interpretations of pastoral written since Empson—notably Thomas G. Rosenmeyer's *The Green Cabinet* (1969) and Richard Cody's *The Landscape of the Mind* (1969). (Note the concession to Schillerian poetics in these titles, both of which, as Rosenmeyer in his case frankly admits, are irrelevant to the arguments of the books). By grounding their accounts of pastoral in intellectual history—Epicureanism, in Rosenmeyer's case, and Renaissance Neo-Platonism, in Cody's—both these studies imply a pre-Romantic poetics of pastoral, to which not nature but certain kinds of human beings and human experience are central. Neither of these studies considers itself "Empsonian." But it is Empson who provides a modern poetics that explains why attending to the human figures of pastoral leads one to find its identifying features in elements of voice, style, and representation, and why interpreters like Rosenmeyer and Cody emphasize ethical stability in one's present world, rather than a yearning for one's past.

The way Empson's account of the poetic mind is different from Schiller's is implicit in remarks that begin the chapter on "They that have power to hurt":

> There is no reason why the subtlety of the irony in so complex a material must be capable of being pegged out into verbal explanations. The vague and generalised language of the descriptions, which might be talking about so many sorts of people as well as feeling so many things about

them, somehow makes a unity like a cross-roads, which analysis does not deal with by exploring down the roads; makes a solid flute on which you can play a multitude of tunes, whose solidity no list of all possible tunes would go far to explain. (86)

This "solidity" might at first call to mind the unity of (complex) effect that most of our critical forebears attribute to poetry. One of Empson's contemporaries at Cambridge tells us that Coleridge's definition of the poet's activity—"the balance or reconciliation of opposite or discordant qualities, of sameness with difference; of the general with the concrete, the idea with the image . . . a more than usual state of emotion with more than usual order"—"could have been recited by any pupil of Richards as surely as a Presbyterian could recite the Shorter Catechism."[38] This view of the poet implies, for the critic, that completeness of understanding is of the essence of imaginative apprehension: the mind that grasps the literary work holds within it all that can be relevantly said about it. But though he was Richards's greatest pupil, Empson does not share this view of either the poet or the critic.[39] The unity of a crossroads (such as it is) is a fact of social existence, with no grounding in nature or analogy to the human individual; the solid flute suggests the limits of the minds that write and interpret, for of course no tune can be played upon it.

Most of the chapters of *Some Versions of Pastoral* begin by remarking that the poetic forces in question lie beyond individual calculation or control. Of Marvell's "The Garden": "The chief point of the poem is to contrast and reconcile conscious and unconscious states, intuitive and intellectual modes of apprehension; and yet that distinction is never made, perhaps could not have been made; his thought is implied by his metaphors" (113). Of *The Beggar's Opera*: "Some queer forces often at work in literature can be seen there unusually clearly; its casualness and inclusiveness allow it to collect into it things that had been floating in tradition" (185). "Double Plots" begins: "The mode of action of a double plot is the sort of thing critics are liable to neglect; it does not depend on being noticed for its operation, so is neither an easy nor an obviously useful thing to notice" (25). Any individual—the writer as well as the reader—has an essentially pastoral relation to an artwork, in that he or she cannot, in the strong and literal sense, comprehend it all. The point with which Empson begins the book, and which leads him to argue that all good "proletarian" literature is "pastoral," is that "good writing is not done unless there are serious forces at work; and it is not permanent unless it works for readers with opinions different from the author's" (3). Hence "two people may get very different experiences from the

38. M. C. Bradbrook, "The Ambiguity of William Empson," in Roma Gill, ed., *William Empson: The Man and His Work* (London: Routledge & Kegan Paul, 1974), 4.

39. For a fuller account of this aspect of Empson's thought, see Paul Alpers, "Empson on Pastoral," *New Literary History* 10 (1978–79): 101–23.

same work of art without either being definitely wrong" (5). His reflections on the double plot lead him to say: "Once you break into the godlike unity of the appreciator you find a microcosm of which the theatre is the macrocosm; the mind is complex and ill-connected like an audience, and it is as surprising in the one case as the other that a sort of unity can be produced by a play" (66). Under these conditions, every figure in a work and every writer and reader is in the situation represented by literary herdsmen. The imagined unity of god-like comprehension dissolves into a social coherence of which each person is only a part.

The "versions of pastoral" Empson puts on display are everywhere determined by the ideas encoded in the phrase, "putting the complex into the simple." For all the variety and unorthodoxy of his examples, he is consistently concerned with the range of suggestion and implication in apparently simple effects, whether these are due to humble characters, or to certain literary devices or qualities of style, or to certain words and images (like the "green thought in a green shade" that absorbs so much of his attention in the chapter on "The Garden"). The Elizabethan double plot counts as pastoral because it is "an easy-going device" that "has an obvious effect . . . of making you feel the play deals with life as a whole" (25). The point of discussing *Paradise Lost* under the rubric of "Milton and Bentley" is to show that Milton's style prompts full feeling and reflection because of qualities of suggestiveness, even vagueness, that elude the grasp of critics who insist—like Bentley in his notorious rewriting of the poem—that poetry be accountable to the analytic intelligence alone. Remarks (quoted above) introducing "The Garden" and *The Beggar's Opera* emphasize poetic devices and effects that are both accessible and inclusive. What makes "the process of putting the complex into the simple" in these works a *pastoral* process is shown by a characteristic they all share. Each contains characters or images traditionally considered "simple," sometimes straightforwardly pastoral, to whom or which Empson's analysis continually returns: the comic or "low" characters in Elizabethan plays, the "summer's flower" in Shakespeare's sonnet 94 ("They that have power to hurt"), Marvell's "green thought in a green shade;" Adam and Eve before the Fall, the thieves and Polly Peachum in *The Beggar's Opera*, and "the child as swain" in *Alice in Wonderland*. The account given of these figures is continually associated with the effect and presence of the work as a whole and with the qualities of the mind that produced and the mind that apprehends it.

Most important, each of these simple figures, and the scores of others discussed in the book, is presented as itself containing contradictions or multiple judgments or complexities of experience. In other words, each in itself has the power attributed to the literary work. This power of the simple is most immediately evident in "ambiguous" words and in a phrase like "a green thought in a green shade," which has a fullness of implication we expect to find in poetic

images. A more striking example—both because it is outside our usual literary
expectations and because it involves manifestly simple characters—is the trait
that Empson calls "comic primness." This is a form of irony which works by
having a character say something in (apparently) perfect innocence which at
the same time is felt to open up a range of critical attitudes and ironic perspectives. It is not surprising to be told of Polly Peachum that "the fascination of the
character is that one has no means of telling whether she is simple or ironical"
(232). The Empsonian twist is that this puzzle and the power it implies are
attributed to all speakers, even the most sophisticated, including the author of
the work in which Polly appears. This view emerges in Empson's range of illus-
trations (of which the most astonishing is Aristotle on judicial torture [203]),
in the general remark that "the force of irony is its claim to innocence" (221),
and in the definition of "full Comic Primness," which applies equally to a prim
character or to the author himself: "It is a play of judgment which implies not
so much doubt as a full understanding of issues between which the enjoyer,
with the humility of impertinence, does not propose to decide" (201).

As the idea of "comic primness" suggests, the difference between Empson
and Schiller comes out most pertinently in the ways they construe simplicity.
Schiller speaks of the simplicity (*Einfalt*) of naive poetry, but the element of the
paradoxical or problematic in Empson's formula—its consciousness that "in pastoral you take a limited life and pretend it is the full and normal one" (110)—
does not come into play, since by definition the naive as a mode of representation is expressive of full human experience. The tension between the complex
and the simple emerges when Schiller considers simplicity in real life, in a discussion of what he calls "childish" (*kindisch*) and "childlike" (*kindlich*) tempera-
ments and behavior (182ff.). "Childish" behavior and character cannot compel
our unreserved assent, he says, for they are at the expense of a mature and
cultured sense of reality. Certain individuals, however, have an inner strength
and innocence that enable them to transcend considerations of the world and
its ways; in their presence, our "mockery of ingenuousness [*Einfältigkeit*] yields
to admiration of simplicity [*Einfachheit*]" (182). In a rather tortuous discussion,
Schiller tries to reserve the honorific term "naive" for those persons who are
genuinely child*like*, and at one point he represents them as pastoral figures: in
their ignoring of "the artificial circumstances of fashionable society," he says,
they "comport themselves even at the courts of kings with the same ingenuousness and innocence that one would find only in a pastoral society [*Schäferwelt*]"
(184). But his main emphasis is on heroically naive individuals—poets, artists,
even statesmen and generals; the childlike then becomes a characteristic of
genius, whose expressions are "the utterances of a god in the mouth of a child"
(187). This is as paradoxical as Empson's "complex in simple," but the terms are
too extreme to have the humbler pole modulate the style of life or art that

expresses it. Schiller's attitude towards human simplicity is divided exactly as is his attitude towards the literary idyll—between uneasiness at the limitations of the childish and admiration of the genuinely childlike, which proves to be heroic and godlike.

Empson's idea of simplicity in social presence and behavior has some superficial similarities to Schiller's. A defense of the courtly pastoralist's pretence of humility—that "in its full form" it is not "merely snobbish"—sounds some Schillerian notes:

> The simple man becomes a clumsy fool who yet has better "sense" than his betters and can say things more fundamentally true; he is "in contact with nature," which the complex man needs to be, so that Bottom is not afraid of the fairies; he is in contact with the mysterious forces of our own nature, so that the clown has the wit of the Unconscious; he can speak the truth because he has nothing to lose. (14)

This could be squared with Schiller's statement that "we ascribe a naive temperament to a person if he, in his judgement of things, overlooks their artificial and contrived aspects and heeds only their simple nature" (184). But the differences of substance are revealed in the two styles—Schiller's philosophical mode of ontological characterization and universal responses, versus Empson's flexible play between the complex man and the simple, jumping from one to the other in the space between "clumsy fool" and "better 'sense'," and ending by both facing and assuming as his own the clown's forthright speech. Not subscribing to an ideology of Nature and childhood, Empson can regard the simple person appreciatively, taking on some of his stances without expecting him to resolve the divisions and dilemmas of ordinary human experience. On the contrary, "both versions, straight and comic, are based on a double attitude of the artist to the worker, of the complex man to the simple one ('I am in one way better, in another not so good'), and this may well recognise a permanent truth about the aesthetic situation" (15). This double attitude responds, and the aesthetic situation corresponds, to what Empson regards as permanent conditions of life in human societies. Hence, the pastoral process is not called into question by reality as we know it, nor is it to be expected to transcend or transform it. Empsonian pastoral lives in the present, because that is all it has. It can "give strength to see life clearly and so to adopt a fuller attitude to it" (19), because it includes the self-conscious and critical, as Schiller's idyll (unlike other forms of sentimental poetry) does not.

The idea of "putting the complex into the simple" has clear affinities with Burke's pairing of "scope and reduction," and like Burke, Empson has a strong sense of the representative. From the monarchs represented in history plays and court entertainments to "the child as swain," *Some Versions of Pastoral* presents a historical sequence of representative figures.[40] Though they are of diminishing social authority, Empson regards their literary presence as fundamentally the same from the start. He says of the "hypostatised hero" of Elizabethan works that "his machinery is already like that of pastoral" (29). After mentioning Christ as the ultimate representative figure, "the Logos who was an individual man," Empson quotes Donne's "Air and Angels" (Love assuming the beloved's body), and then says:

> This at once leads to the dependence of the world upon the person or thing treated as a personification: "This member of the class is the whole class, or its defining property: this man has a magical importance to all men." If you choose an important member the result is heroic; if you choose an unimportant one it is pastoral. (79).

The fundamental likeness between heroic and pastoral figures is "inherent in the double plot convention": "this power of suggestion is the strength of the double plot; once you take the two parts to correspond, any character may take on *mana* because he seems to cause what he corresponds to or be Logos of what he symbolises" (32). At either end of the scale, Empson sees characters as both limited and "inclusive" (his term for the White Queen in *Alice* [280]). What limits them is their being placed in a larger world (real or literary), whose complexities they nevertheless are felt to stand for: they are thus both pastoral and representative. However idiosyncratic Empson's examples, his account of them prepares us to see the interests and claims of the shepherds in traditional pastoral, just as he points us to the historical foundations of literary pastoral when he reflects on the interconnections of heroic and pastoral conventions.

Given the ironic and somewhat marginal character of his two final examples (*The Beggar's Opera* and *Alice in Wonderland*), one might argue that Empson conceives the modern writer as ineluctably "belated," in Harold Bloom's terms, or "sentimental," in Schiller's. *Some Versions of Pastoral* would thus offer less an alternative to Schiller than a latter-day development of one aspect of the critical system and problematic that derive from him and his contemporaries. This is probably true, if one looks to Empson for theory and a general poetics as such. But insofar as what matters in literature is represented by acts of reading and practical criticism, *Some Versions of Pastoral* is a major alternative to Schiller's account of the idyll and its disabilities. The book's strength and suggestiveness come from the way it relinquishes visionary heroism and identifies writing and its human significance with a fundamentally ironized mode. The formula, "putting the complex into the simple," is as important as it has seemed, because it means what it says. Not only does the simple have a claim on us, both in life

---

40. On the historical vision of *Some Versions of Pastoral*, see Roger Sale, *Modern Heroism* (Berkeley & Los Angeles: University of California Press, 1973), 107–92.

and in literature; literature, in Empson's view, invites the complex person to see himself and his condition in the simple. One of the most decisive definitions of pastoral in the book is that "you can say everything about complex people by a complete consideration of simple people" (131). At the same time, Empson is aware that "complete consideration" is a matter of literary representation and self-representation: "in pastoral you take a limited life and pretend it is the full and normal one" (110). This is both a "trick" and a fundamental truth "which must at last be taken alone." "The business of interpretation is obviously very complicated," he goes on to say in the paragraph from which these phrases are taken, and his own truthfulness, independence, and the "ironic pliancy" which Burke praised in a review ensure a sufficiently complex view of pastoral simplicities.[41] But not *too* complex—that is an important point of all that we have been saying. Empson enables us to view pastorals without condescension and yet without exaggerating our claims for them. On his terms, we can acknowledge that they are limited and have a specific character, and that they need not lay claim to the whole of literary power in order to be of genuine interest to us.

41. *The Philosophy of Literary Form* (above, no. 10), 424.

Two

MODE AND GENRE

Pastoral is commonly said to be a mode, not a genre. Like most truisms, this one is true, but in one important respect it is misleading. Its truth lies in the suggestion that pastoral is a broad and flexible category that includes, but is not confined to, a number of identifiable genres. What is mistaken in the formula is the assumption that genre is opposed to mode. Once we understand what we mean by "mode"—it is a surprisingly unexamined concept—we will be able to see its continuity with "genre" as we presently understand it. We shall also see why pastoral in particular is identified as a mode. Among literary kinds, it self-consciously attends to the fundamental idea of mode—that literary usages encode or imply views (in Angus Fletcher's phrase) of human "strength relative to world."

Though the theory of literary genres can often seem a whirligig of reifying and hairsplitting, there is something of a shared sense, in work of the past few decades, of what is meant by a genre. In the first place, most theorists and critics agree that the term should not be used for the ultimate categories—the most familiar of which are narrative, drama, and lyric—which include all that we mean by literature.[1] Goethe called these categories *Naturformen;* some mod-

---

1. See Karl Viëtor's classic essay, "Die Geschichte Literarischer Gattungen," in *Geist und Form* (Bern: A. Francke, 1952), 292.

ern theorists still treat them or similar categories as "universals" and seek to ground them in extraliterary realities, whether linguistic, anthropological, phenomenological, or existential. But genres are now generally agreed to be historical phenomena, and there is a tendency to think of them as well demarcated, both historically and aesthetically. Definitions of genre as a principle of matching matter and form,[2] or a way of connecting topic and treatment,[3] convey a sense of the term which is most usefully formulated by Wellek and Warren:

> Genre should be conceived, we think, as a grouping of literary works based, theoretically, upon both outer form (specific metre or structure) and also upon inner form (attitude, tone, purpose—more crudely, subject and audience). The ostensible basis may be one or the other (e.g., "pastoral" and "satire" for the inner form; dipodic verse and Pindaric ode for outer); but the critical problem will then be to find the *other* dimension, to complete the diagram.[4]

Similarly, Alastair Fowler, in the most substantial recent treatment of these matters, says a literary "kind" (the term he prefers to "genre") is "marked by a complex of substantive and formal features that always include a distinctive (though not usually unique) external structure."[5] Fowler calls these identifying features "the generic repertoire," and they range from meter, size, and style to values and attitude.

Identifying genre by both "outer" and "inner" features corresponds to our intuitive sense of the term and reduces the confusion caused by the fact that generic characteristics tend to be of many different sorts. It does, however, make for an emphasis on literary kinds that are particularly well defined. Wellek and Warren single out the Gothic novel as "a genre by all the criteria one can invoke": "there is not only a limited and continuous subject matter or thematics, but there is a stock of devices . . . [and] there is, still further, a *Kunstwollen*, an aesthetic intent."[6] The genres which one now encounters in criticism and theory tend to be, like the Gothic novel, specific, definable, and readily identified. A genre is conceived as a literary form that has clear superficial features or marks of identification and that is sufficiently conventional or rule-governed

---

2. Claudio Guillen, *Literature as System* (Princeton: Princeton University Press, 1971), 111.

3. Rosalie L. Colie, *The Resources of Kind: Genre-Theory in the Renaissance*, ed. Barbara K. Lewalski (Berkeley & Los Angeles: University of California Press, 1973), 29.

4. René Wellek and Austin Warren, *Theory of Literature*, 2d ed. (New York: Harcourt, Brace, 1956), 221.

5. Alastair Fowler, *Kinds of Literature: An Introduction to the Theory of Genres and Modes* (Cambridge: Harvard University Press, 1982), 74.

6. Wellek and Warren, 223.

to enable us to say, for example, that a given work is a pastoral elegy or a Petrarchan love poem or a verse satire or a Plautine comedy or an encomium and not another thing. Literary pastoral includes many genres so conceived. It includes not only the whole range of formal eclogues—pastoral elegies, love complaints, singing-contests, and the like—but also pastoral romances, pastoral lyrics, pastoral comedies, and pastoral novels. If all these are pastoral, then we are certainly right to say that pastoral is not a genre. Rather, it seems to be one of the types of literature—like tragedy, comedy, novel, romance, satire, and elegy—which have generic-sounding names but which are more inclusive and general than genres proper. We seek to recognize that pastoral is one of these literary types, when we say that it is not a genre, but a mode.

But what precisely do we mean by calling pastoral (or any other literary type) a mode? Our answers to this question are very vague, and at times seem to be so on principle. Take, for example, Paul H. Fry's discussion of "ode" as the name of a poetic type:

> The reason why the words "elegy" and "satire" seem more usefully to rope off poetic kinds than "ode" does is that "elegy" and "satire" are *modal* terms that allow enormous flexibility of reference. They describe orientations but tend not to prescribe a set style, form, or occasion—or even, necessarily, a set theme. It is in the loose spirit of such terms that I propose the "ode of presentation" as a mode.[7]

It is, if anything, an understatement to speak of the "loose spirit" of modal terms. There is positively a tradition of not defining the concept. You will not find a definition of "mode" in Angus Fletcher's *Allegory: The Theory of a Symbolic Mode* or in Earl Miner's books on seventeenth-century poetry, *The Metaphysical Mode* and *The Cavalier Mode,* or in the introduction and selections of a recent anthology of criticism called *The Pastoral Mode.*[8] Ralph Cohen, whom no one will accuse of theoretical naiveté, concludes an essay on "The Augustan Mode" by saying, "By this term 'mode' I mean no more than a range of special poetic uses of conventionalized figures, images, ideas and syntactical, metrical, or organizational structures in the poetry of 1660–1750."[9] The definitional plight of this term is summed up by yet another critic, who says, "A work's mode, then, let us say, is whatever it seems to be in its most general aspect."[10]

When critics do define "mode," they tend to equate it with "attitude." The critic last quoted goes on to say: "In general . . . the mode of a work will be

7. *The Poet's Calling in the English Ode* (New Haven: Yale University Press, 1980), 5.

8. Bryan Loughrey, ed., *The Pastoral Mode: A Casebook* (London: Macmillan, 1984).

9. "The Augustan Mode in English Poetry," *Eighteenth-Century Studies* 1 (1967): 32.

10. Allan Rodway, "Generic Criticism," in M. Bradbury and D. Palmer, ed., *Contemporary Criticism* (London: Edward Arnold, 1970), 94.

largely a matter of attitude or tone rather than style or form of writing."[11] Robert Scholes proposes that the "primary modes of fiction" derive from the way fictional worlds "imply attitudes." He emphasizes that "in this modal consideration," terms like "tragedy" and "comedy" "refer to the quality of the fictional world and not to any form of story customarily associated with the term."[12] Mode, then, refers to feelings and attitudes as such, as distinguished from their realization or manifestation in specific devices, conventions, structures. This tendency to associate "mode" with "attitude" is very clear in David Halperin's survey of pastoral criticism. Halperin notes that modern critics "refer to pastoral quite matter-of-factly as a 'mode.'" This, he says, is consistent with "the recent trend in criticism . . . to substitute the literary *mode* for the literary *genre*." He associates this substitution with Wellek and Warren's distinction between "outer form" and "inner form,"[13] and he attributes the shift of emphasis above all to Empson. *Some Versions of Pastoral*, he says, represents "the triumph of inner form over outer form in critical definitions and the predominance of pastoral as theme over pastoral as convention." He cites a well-known study of pastoral to justify this remark, and concludes:

> Many readers will feel that Empson has succeeded in adumbrating what Greg called the "philosophical conception" underlying most versions of pastoral. Empson established that pastoral is a literary mode for expressing a view of life equal in scope to that conveyed by tragedy, comedy, and other primary modes.[14]

If mode really is an "inner" matter of attitude or philosophical conception, then it is hard to see how it can be continuous with the concept of genre, in which "outer form" is of the essence. Some such objection, as well as sheer impatience with broad uses of "mode" (he calls it "the easiest of all terminological recourses"), prompts Fowler to rein in the term and make it "structurally

---

11. Ibid., 95.

12. *Structuralism in Literature* (New Haven: Yale University Press, 1974), 133.

13. David M. Halperin, *Before Pastoral: Theocritus and the Ancient Tradition of Bucolic Poetry* (New Haven: Yale University Press, 1983), 33–5.

14. Halperin, 53, 55. The first remark about Empson follows a quotation from Harold Toliver, *Pastoral Forms and Attitudes* (Berkeley & Los Angeles: University of California Press, 1971), p. vii: "Most critics who have dealt with pastoral theoretically since Empson . . . have extended the principles of the old shepherd poem freely to literature that abandons many of its conventions while illustrating its themes and attitudes." See also Leo Marx, "Pastoralism in America," in Sacvan Bercovitch and Myra Jehlen, eds., *Ideology and Classic American Literature* (Cambridge: Harvard University Press, 1986), 46: "Pastoral is not a genre but a mode—the broadest, most inclusive category of composition. It derives its identity not from any formal convention but from a particular perspective on human experience." Marx too attributes the emergence of this view of pastoral to Empson.

dependent" on genre. Historically, he claims that there is no mode without a "parent kind" or an "antecedent kind"; as he put it in an earlier article, "genre tends to mode" and historically precedes it.[15] Analytically, he defines mode as "a selection or abstraction from kind," but he seems to conceive this as simply a selection from the complete generic repertoire. He explicitly opposes the idea that modes are "distillations, from these relatively evanescent forms [the genres], of the permanently valuable features."[16] He means to tie modes closely to the generic indicators and repertoires; troubled by "the vague intimations of 'mood,'" he insists that "a mode announces itself by distinct signals."[17] One can sympathize with Fowler's resistance to the idea that modes are "timeless," but his insistence that they, as much as genres, are historical phenomena leads to his undue emphasis on the details of "outer form," at the expense of the feelings and attitudes that motivate them.

It is ironic that these recent accounts of mode oscillate between inner attitudes and external traits, because the term is preeminently one that connects, indeed treats as inseparable, "inner form" and "outer form." We can see this not by gleaning statements from theoretical discussions, but by examining the way the word is used in practice. Helen Vendler invokes it to qualify her summary of the argument of a section of Stevens's "The Man with the Blue Guitar."

> Such a paraphrase of the poem does not reveal its mode, which is the depressed opposite to the persiflage of ai-yi-yi [referring to another section of the poem]. The poem is not tragic, but drawn and wry, spoken not by the struggling guitarist, but by a preceptor well versed in ennui, with his frenchified "Regard." Rhythm is practically abrogated; rhyme is prohibited; syntax seems reduced to the simple declarative sentence; rhetoric is cramped to simple indication. . . . "And" is dropped from the language. The sentences stand like epitaphs, in strict autonomy.[18]

There are psychological interests in these sentences, but Vendler is concerned mainly with qualities of diction, syntax, and rhythm. Moreover, she does not view these usages as *expressing* an attitude, but rather as somehow encoding it, as having an attitude implicit in them. It is precisely this sense of literary lan-

15. Fowler, *Kinds of Literature*, 106, 108, 111. "The Life and Death of Literary Forms," in *New Directions in Literary History*, ed. Ralph Cohen (London: Routledge & Kegan Paul, 1974), 92. Cf. *Kinds of Literature*, 167: "Mode is not only a looser genre collateral with the fixed kind, but also its successor. . . . The two are in diachronic relation: kind tends to mode."

16. Fowler, *Kinds of Literature*, 56, 111.

17. Ibid., 107.

18. Helen Hennessy Vendler, *On Extended Wings: Wallace Stevens' Longer Poems* (Cambridge: Harvard University Press, 1969), 130.

guage—that there is a reciprocal relation between usages and attitude—that makes us invoke the term "mode" to give a summary sense of a work or passage. It is the term we use when we want to suggest that the ethos of a work informs its technique and that techniques imply an ethos.

"Mode" is thus the term that suggests the connection of "inner" and "outer" form; it conveys the familiar view that form and content entail each other and cannot, finally, be separated. This is the sense that is registered when Josephine Miles says, "We should look for a new mode where a new complex of idea, material, and structure clearly began," or when Richard Cody observes of Tasso's *Aminta* that it went "far enough to establish the pastoral as a whole literary mode, with an ethos and style of its own."[19] "Mode" is a suitable term for the literary category that includes a number of individual genres, because it is continuous with the idea that a genre is identified by both outer and inner form.

Miles's and Cody's remarks show an awareness of what a mode is, but they hardly constitute definitions of the term. For that we must turn to the most important treatment of the concept, the chapter of Northrop Frye's *Anatomy of Criticism* entitled "Historical Criticism: Theory of Modes." Frye says:

> In literary fictions the plot consists of somebody doing something. The somebody, if an individual, is the hero, and the something he does or fails to do is what he can do, or could have done, on the level of the postulates made about him by the author and the consequent expectations of the audience. Fictions, therefore, may be classified, not morally, but by the hero's power of action, which may be greater than ours, less, or roughly the same.[20]

Frye then goes on to specify five modes—myth, romance, high mimetic (epic and tragedy), low mimetic (comedy and the novel), and ironic—according to the hero's stature in relation to other human beings and to the environment in which they live. After surveying these fictional modes, as he calls them, Frye turns from "the internal fiction of the hero and his society" to the relation between writer and audience or writer and reader. "There can hardly be a work of literature," he rightly observes, "without some kind of relation, implied or expressed, between its creator and its auditors."[21] He then goes on to outline a scheme of five "thematic modes," which have the same rationale as the "fictional modes."

19. Josephine Miles, *Eras and Modes in English Poetry* (Berkeley & Los Angeles: University of California Press, 1957), 115. Richard Cody, *The Landscape of the Mind* (Oxford: Clarendon Press, 1969), 78.
20. *Anatomy of Criticism* (Princeton: Princeton University Press, 1957), 33.
21. Ibid., 53.

Frye himself never tells us why he calls these categories "modes." But we find an explanation in Angus Fletcher's wonderfully illuminating comment on the idea that fictions may be classified according to the hero's power of action. "The term 'mode' is appropriate," Fletcher says, "because in each of the five the hero is a protagonist with a given strength relative to his world, and as such each hero—whether mythic, romantic, high mimetic, low mimetic, or ironic—is a *modulor* for verbal architectonics; man is the measure, the *modus* of myth."[22] On the basis of this formulation, we can say that mode is the literary manifestation, in a given work, not of its attitudes in a loose sense, but of its assumptions about man's nature and situation. This definition in turn provides a critical question we implicitly put to any work we interpret: what notions of human strength, possibilities, pleasures, dilemmas, etc. are manifested in the represented realities and in the emphases, devices, organization, effects, etc. of this work? As we shall see, the key to all these questions—and this is the brilliance of Fletcher's remark—is the implicit view of the hero's or speaker's or reader's strength relative to his or her world. I specify all three of these figures, because we need not maintain Frye's separation of fictional and thematic. He distinguishes the two for theoretical reasons, but as he himself says, "every work of literature has both a fictional and a thematic aspect."[23]

II

It is clear that pastoral has consciously modal interests. The figure of the shepherd is felt to be representative precisely in figuring every or any man's strength relative to the world. A great many citizens of late Republican Rome could read their situation in that of the two herdsmen of Virgil's first Eclogue—one victimized by the aftermath of civil war, the other dependent on the protector he has been fortunate to find. Such representative vulnerability goes naturally with the figure of the literary shepherd. At other times, the herdsman's simplicity is a source of moral authority, and one feels in him a strength in humility. In both secular and ecclesiastical contexts, he can speak out against corruption and excessive refinement and for values that range from stoic acceptance to the loving care of the good shepherd of the Gospels. Modal considerations are particularly explicit in pastoral, because from its beginnings the poet has represented himself as a herdsman. In a passage that suggested a turning point in *Lycidas*, Virgil, representing himself as Tityrus, is called to a sense of himself—which means a sense of his present powers—by the god of poetry:

22. "Utopian History and the *Anatomy of Criticism*," in Murray Krieger, ed., *Northrop Frye in Modern Criticism* (New York, 1966), 34–35.
23. Frye, 53.

Prima Syracosio dignata est ludere versu
nostra neque erubuit silvas habitare Thalea.
cum canerem reges et proelia, Cynthius aurem
vellit et admonuit: "pastorem, Tityre, pinguis
pascere oportet ovis, deductum dicere carmen."

(Ecl. 6.1–5)

My playful muse first chose Sicilian verse:
She did not blush to dwell among the woods.
When I tried a song of kings and battles, Phoebus
Plucked my ear and warned, "A shepherd,
    Tityrus,
Should feed fat sheep, recite a fine-spun song."

These lines allude to a programmatic rejection of epic by the Alexandrian poet Callimachus, and they recall that Theocritus's bucolics (the Sicilian verse of the first line) were a conscious reduction of Homeric verse to the felt range and possibilities of poetry in a post-heroic, cosmopolitan world.[24] Gestures like these are not merely modest or plaintive. The self-awareness and wit with which pastoral poets scale down their verse is a way of reclaiming a degree of strength relative to their world: "tomorrow to fresh woods and pastures new."

However, it is not enough to observe that pastoral is interested in the issue of strength relative to world. Sidney defended pastoral by recalling Eclogue 1:

Is it then the Pastoral poem which is misliked? . . . Is the poor pipe disdained, which sometime out of Meliboeus' mouth can show the misery of people under hard lords or ravening soldiers? And again, by Tityrus, what blessedness is derived to them that lie lowest from the goodness of them that sit highest.[25]

This observation could be considered purely thematic, whereas the idea of mode involves an inherent connection between manner and matter, so that when these themes are sounded on the "poor pipe" of pastoral, they have a distinctive range and significance. Similarly, the paradox of poetic strength in modesty can take a nonpastoral form, as in Donne's "The Canonization":

We can die by it, if not live by love,
    And if unfit for tombs and hearse

---

24. On Theocritus and Homer, see chapter 4. The passage from Callimachus is quoted in that chapter.

25. Sir Philip Sidney, *An Apology for Poetry*, ed. Geoffrey Shepherd (London: Nelson, 1965), 116.

Our legend be, it will be fit for verse;
And if no piece of chronicle we prove,
We'll build in sonnets pretty rooms;
As well a well wrought urn becomes
The greatest ashes, as half-acre tombs.

One sees the similarity in sentiment, including a sense of dialectical relation to
the heroic, but this poem, though it concerns withdrawal from the world, is
not a pastoral. From his opening gestures of contempt for the claims of society,
to the resolution of "We can die by it," to the grandeur with which he represents
"us canonized for love," the speaker has a capacity to stand free from the world
and triumph over it in a way that is unknown to the literary shepherd.

A comparison of two seventeenth-century poems on the same subject will
show what is at issue in considerations of mode—the way motifs and attitudes
are affected by and implicit in poetic realization. One is Marvell's "The Mower
to the Glowworms," usually regarded as the slightest of the "Mower poems":

Ye living lamps, by whose dear light
The nightingale does sit so late,
And studying all the summer night,
Her matchless songs does meditate;

Ye country comets, that portend
No war, nor prince's funeral,
Shining unto no higher end
Than to presage the grass's fall;

Ye glowworms, whose officious flame
To wandering mowers shows the way,
That in the night have lost their aim,
And after foolish fires do stray;

Your courteous lights in vain you waste,
Since Juliana here is come,
For she my mind hath so displaced
That I shall never find my home.

The other poem, probably written in the same decade, is Thomas Stanley's
"The Glowworm":

Stay, fairest Chariessa, stay and mark
This animated gem, whose fainter spark
Of fading light its birth had from the dark.

A star thought by the erring passenger,
Which falling from its native orb dropped here,
And makes the earth, its center, now its sphere.

Should many of these sparks together be,
He that the unknown light far off should see
Would think it a terrestrial galaxy.

Take't up, fair saint; see how it mocks thy fright;
The paler flame doth not yield heat, though light,
Which thus deceives thy reason through thy
    sight.

But see how quickly it, ta'en up, doth fade,
To shine in darkness only being made,
By th'brightness of thy light turned to a shade;

And burnt to ashes by thy flaming eyes,
On the chaste altar of thy hand it dies,
As to thy greater light a sacrifice.[26]

No one, presumably, would have any difficulty saying which of these two poems is a pastoral. Yet locutions like "living lamps" and "country comets," to go no further, seem as witty as anything in Stanley's poem. The question is how we can spell out the differences between the poems and the impression they make. We can appeal to the fact that Marvell's speaker is a mower, but he has not been given the touches of rusticity that identify the speakers of other pastoral lyrics. In "The Mower to the Glowworms," we might even imagine that the first two stanzas are spoken by a courtier. Yet it seems clear that the "wholly Marvellian ambience" to which Frank Kermode attributes the "witty delicacy" of the poem has a great deal to do with its pastoralism.[27]

    The first thing to notice in discriminating the speakers of these two poems is that Stanley's addresses his mistress and asks her to observe, to "stay and mark," an amusing insect. Hence the first phrase he uses about it—"this animated gem"—is a way of fixing and identifying it, capturing in a phrase its oddness and interest. The first phrase of Marvell's poem—"Ye living lamps"—is a less pointed and brittle paradox, not only because the phrase could refer to eyes or heavenly bodies, but because of the speaker's relation to the creatures he names. He addresses not another human observer, with whom he shares his amused interest and capacity for coining phrases, but the glowworms themselves, who are therefore treated, if not exactly as his equals, then at least as belonging to the same world, occupying the same space, more than an idle curiosity. When he speaks of their "dear light," it is impossible not to feel, as the poem will confirm, that the meaning is "dear to me" as well as "dear to the

---

26. From Stanley's *Poems* (1651). The standard edition is *The Poems and Translations of Thomas Stanley*, ed. G. M. Crump (Oxford: Clarendon Press, 1962). I quote the modernized version in Hugh Maclean, ed., *Ben Jonson and the Cavalier Poets* (New York: Norton, 1974), 358.

27. Andrew Marvell, *Selected Poetry*, ed. Frank Kermode (New York: Signet, 1967), xx.

nightingale." By the same token, the phrase "living lamps" is not used to fix the glowworms for observation, but is the starting point of a sentence that fills the first stanza and that creates a whole situation, even a little world.

The difference between the poems is even more striking in the way they treat the idea that glowworms appear like stars fallen to earth. This is not sheer poetic fancy, as the idea comes from a passage of agricultural lore in Pliny.[28] But for Stanley's speaker, the idea is clearly a false perception, though an interesting and amusing one, and his awareness that these are illusions underlies his ability to be witty. He is witty in respect to scientific knowledge, when the paradox about the fallen star—that it "makes the earth, [formerly] its center, now its sphere"—is balanced by a consciousness of its false premise. In the next stanza, he is witty on the side of gallantry. The illusion that the cluster of glowworms is a "terrestrial galaxy" (another cosmological paradox, though less focused and interesting than the one that precedes it) lays the foundation for complimenting his mistress, with her "greater light," as an earthly sun. The speaker's security of knowledge and of social relation is nowhere clearer than at the end, in the tribute to his mistress's powers. The familiar conceit has a different effect here than in other modes of love poetry—which are other modes precisely because the lover has a different "strength relative to the beloved," and because he and the poems attribute to her a different strength relative to the world. The acknowledgment of the mistress's powers here is rather cool, because the speaker attributes the power to darken the glowworm, in the first instance, to the light of day and the light of reason (Stanley was a founding member of the Royal Society). The glowworm would have faded had it been taken up into the light by anyone's hand. Hence the final conceits are confined to the powers, which are real ones, of social compliment and devotion. The lover's sacrifice to the mistress's chastity, a fictive reality in other modes, is here only a gallant hint.

As we compare the poems, we might take Marvell's speaker, who characterizes himself as a "wandering mower," to be in the position of Stanley's "erring passenger," who mistakes the glowworm for a star. The mower does have the capacity to be misled, but on the other hand the point of that stanza is that a mower can tell the life-saving difference between the glowworm's light and the delusive will-o'-the-wisp. So the issues of strength relative to world are intricate ones, as we can see in the second stanza:

> Ye country comets, that portend
> No war, nor prince's funeral,
> Shining unto no higher end
> Than to presage the grass's fall.

28. See J. B. Leishman, *The Art of Marvell's Poetry* (New York: Minerva Press, 1968), 152.

In the mouth of a courtly speaker, "country comets" might seem a piece of tender condescension, as the country is clearly out of bounds for serious portents. (We do not know exactly when Marvell wrote this poem, but at any of the conceivable dates, wars and a prince's funeral were serious matters for England.) On the other hand, commentators have often noticed the closing allusion to the biblical "all flesh is grass." In the light of this motif, "country comets" turn out to be portents, and some of Marvell's commentators have been quite portentous themselves about their symbolic force. As so often with Marvell, we want to resist undue solemnity without denying intimated meanings: to recall Kermode's praise, we want to stay in touch with all aspects of the poem's wit and delicacy. Marvell's poise here derives directly from his pastoralism. "The grass's fall" can be seen as nothing more than the natural result of the mower's normal activity. This way of taking the line is supported by the fact that glowworms, according to Pliny, literally presage the mowing of the grass: they "neuer appeare before hay is ripe vpon the ground, ne yet after it is cut downe."[29] The line is a perfect instance of "putting the complex into the simple." It represents a natural phenomenon and a human activity that are not only normal and benign, but complete unto themselves. The suggestive phrase thus retains, as Empson puts it, its "claim to innocence" (*SVP*, 221). Hence its implications are not grasped by extending its significance into the world of wars and princes—this is what makes for portentous interpretations—but by assimilating to itself all forms of death and suggesting that they are fundamentally the same.

Marvell's phrase opens up two views of death, without (to recall another of Empson's formulations) proposing to decide between them. On the one hand, death in any shape can be seen to be as natural as the seasonal round of mowing; on the other hand, the inclusion of normal death in the completeness of the country world suggests that the world of violent death, of wars and princes, is unnatural. The poised presence of these alternatives reveals the depth of wit that Eliot praised and that is signalled, in this stanza, by the opening phrase. "Country comets" feels witty in the ordinary sense, because it is rather paradoxical, but unlike Stanley's "terrestrial galaxy," it cannot be grasped without giving it some credence. Though we might at first take its basis to be visual (the glowworms look like comets), the meanings the phrase acquires require us to take on the role of someone who inhabits a world in which glowworms are normal and humans have "no higher end" than a mower's. The wit is pastoral, because unless you know what the glowworms presage (that it is time to mow), you cannot know what they portend.

If it seems right to say that the wit of Marvell's stanza is pastoral, we must still justify comparing the poems as if their speakers retain their identities

29. Ibid.

throughout. Stanley's speaker clearly does: his security is the source of his wit and charm. It *feels* as if Marvell's speaker does, but that is the effect we have to explain. He does not at first have even as much pastoral identity as Marlowe's lover, who—though cunningly poised between being a sophisticated courtier and an inhabitant of the country—begins with a gesture, "Come live with me," that recalls the *huc ades* of Virgil's Corydon and many another passionate shepherd. The mower's identity (first hinted by "the grass's fall") only emerges in the third stanza, when he addresses the glowworms by their proper name, associates himself with "wandering mowers," and suggests his own susceptibility to "foolish fires." But oddly enough, the speaker's vulnerability, which seems to establish his pastoral identity, leads to the separation from the pastoral world of which he speaks in the last stanza. Given this movement, how can we take either poem or speaker to retain a pastoral character?

Our answer to this question depends on what we take to be the pastoralism of the opening stanzas. To a critic like Rosalie Colie—for whom "the pastoral setting, invented by a wish-fulfilling poetic imagination . . . , assumes without question a *pathétique* conjunction of mind with landscape"—the mower at the end "is left alienated by the power of his love from his otherwise cherishing environment, driven out of his natural context by the violence of love's force."[30] But this natural context, this "home" from which the mower is "displaced," is not idyllic in Schiller's sense, and is not represented by landscape or a fully depicted pastoral world. The sense of secure completeness, which the mower has lost and which underlies the wit of stanza 2, is due to a particularly Marvellian kind of pastoral representation:

> Ye living lamps, by whose dear light
> The nightingale does sit so late,
> And studying all the summer night,
> Her matchless songs does meditate.

Nightingales are of course not confined to pastoral poetry, but they are very much at home in it. By the time Marvell wrote, the bird had long since been associated with shepherds whose frustrated love has isolated them and whose pains are expressed in beautiful laments.[31] The scene the mower sketches in this stanza is thus not a "cherishing environment" but a self-representation, a version of his own situation: he too is a suffering lover, singing alone, in the company of glowworms. The sense of benign companionship ("by whose *dear* light") and

30. Rosalie Colie, *"My Ecchoing Song": Andrew Marvell's Poetry of Criticism* (Princeton: Princeton University Press, 1970), 15, 31.

31. Virgil, *Georgics* 4.511–15; Petrarch, *Rime* 311; Spenser, *The Shepheardes Calender*, "August," 183, "November," 25, 141 (following Clement Marot, "Eglogue sur le Trespas de Loyse de Savoye," 29, 125); Garcilaso de la Vega, *Egloga* 1.324–40.

fullness of expression ("her matchless songs") makes this self-representation pastoral—that is, what a divided or suffering mind might be if it were *not* displaced.

On the Schillerian model, we would view the mower's self-consciousness itself and his capacity for wit as due to his separation from nature. But this stanza is an odd, though perfectly pertinent, reminder that pastoral poetry has always been "sentimental." The final word of the stanza strikingly confirms that the poem's emphasis on the mind is not inherently at odds with its pastoral character. "Meditate" is something of a technical term in pastoral poetry. In a line which Milton anglicized, the fortunate Tityrus of Virgil's first Eclogue is said to "meditate his woodland muse on a slender oaten stalk or pipe" (*silvestrem tenui musam meditaris avena*). Latin *meditari* is cognate with our "meditate," but in using it of piping, Virgil calls up its other meaning, "practice" or "rehearse." Marvell's phrases, "sit so late" and "studying all the summer night," would seem to tip the balance to "meditate" as an act of the mind. But the last line of the stanza maintains suggestions of actual utterance—not only because of the meaning authorized by Virgil,[32] but also because "matchless," with its sense of wonder and immediacy, suggests that we are hearing the song as if sung. The line as a whole conveys the sense that the isolated mind can exist in a mode of simplicity, because alliteration makes "meditate" answer to and seem the equivalent of "matchless song." The artfulness of the line assimilates human song, which may be studied and meditated before it is uttered, to the natural song of a bird.

In the first stanza of this poem, unlike those of "Damon the Mower" and "The Mower's Song," the generic "markers"—the figure of the nightingale and the word "meditate"—do not add up to much by themselves. It takes considerations of mode to draw out their implications and perhaps even establish them as pastoral: it is not the use of "meditate" as a code word but its force in the final line that confirms the nightingale's poignant strength relative to its world. When we turn to the final stanza, attention to mode again enables us to fill out its generic hints and enables us to see why, despite its gesture of separation, the poem as a whole is pastoral.

The mower's simultaneous likeness to and difference from the nightingale anticipates his relation to the mowers of stanza 3. These ordinary mowers live in the world represented by the double meaning of the grass's fall—a world of normal labor, bounded by natural death. They may stray after foolish fires, but the glowworms save them, show their way home, simply by making light in the dark. Our mower, who calls the glowworms "officious" and "courteous," is

---

32. Cf. *Comus* 545–46, where the word must mean "play" as well as "contemplate": the Attendant Spirit, in the guise of a shepherd, says that "wrapt in a pleasing fit of melancholy," he began "to meditate my rural minstrelsy."

no longer at home in this world, but he remains sufficiently of it to have become its poet. Like other literary shepherds—including Virgil's Corydon, the model for "Damon the Mower"—love has prompted him to utter his emotional distress and sense of displacement. Like his predecessors, he can only do so by pastoral representations. The first three stanzas give one measure of the relation between what the mower is and what he has been. Each completes an initial vocative phrase, as if filling out in its representations the implications of the selected name for the glowworms. Each stanza is a sort of miniature pastoral, and one aspect of the poem's mode is the way we can dwell on and within each of them, poised and suspended, before moving on.

The grammar of these stanzas perfectly conveys their status. We must move on, because the sentence and the mower's utterance are not complete. When the vocatives end, it is with a statement that the relation which underlay them, the mutual solicitude between mowers and glowworms, has come to an end: "Your courteous lights in vain you waste." This is pastoral precisely because the gesture ends the poem. Once the relation is broken, once "I" (first used here)[33] is separated from the grammar of vocatives and the representation of "wandering mowers," the mower has only one power of song left—to name his distress. The distance between "courteous" and "waste" suggests that his loss is disastrous. But his capacity to give that loss measured expression is sustained through the sentence precisely by his naming what he has lost and thus bringing it to consciousness. The negative "displaced" produces the positive awareness of "home," and no stroke in the poem is more brilliant than its ending with this word. In the represented world of ordinary mowers, there was no need to use it: it was simply implicit in the details and relationships of the first three stanzas, even the third. With Marvellian fineness, the word "home" measures what the degree of awareness it registers has cost the mower. But the formal effect of the word is equally fine and more powerful. The last line, produced as the result clause in a "so . . . that" construction, suggests utter displacement, giving a slight shock (that surprise which Eliot prized in metaphysical wit) as we realize that the mower is driven not elsewhere but nowhere. Some such feeling must lie behind Colie's speaking of "the violence of love's force" in this stanza. But most readers do not take the poem this way, and for good reason. For while "home" registers the mower's sense of his extremity, it also completes his song. It not only completes the sentence of which the poem consists, but also supplies its central motif.

The sense of satisfying closure is available not only to the reader but, implicitly, to the mower. For when we say he has nowhere to go, we must remember that "here," where he has been, is a representation of his condition, and that

---

33. As pointed out by Judith Haber, *Pastoral and the Poetics of Self-Contradiction: Theocritus to Marvell* (Cambridge: Cambridge University Press, 1994), 100.

the severer self-representation of the last stanza remains a place for the mind to dwell. A final modal consideration, it seems to me, confirms this point. Marvell's speaker dwells within his poem, because, unlike Stanley's, he cannot initiate a new sentence. This is directly a matter of strength relative to world. The closure on "home" reveals, on the one hand, his vulnerability and weakness, his incapacity to proceed farther, and, on the other, his self-awareness and his firm hold on values of affectionate relation (it is in this stanza that he calls the glowworms "courteous") and spiritual security. He is a pastoral poet not only in his initial self-representation as the nightingale, but also in the self-representation implicit in his sense of kinship with the glowworms. Once their light is, in his eyes, wasted, so too, in a sense, is his breath.

The pastoral vignettes of the first three stanzas involve love-suffering, death, and the possibilities of moral error. Neither this poem nor any good pastoral denies such realities of life, but it does make them seem natural and acceptable by turning them into pleasing aesthetic form. Seen this way, the poem itself can be thought of as like the glowworm—small, amusing, interesting, doing us good by going about its natural business. But at the same time the poem acknowledges its source in the human complexities and interests represented by the displaced mower, who can address these glowworms and associate them with emblems of mental poise and acceptance which he himself can savor and appreciate, because he once knew them, but which he has now lost. Indeed, the poem makes us ask whether the mower can be said to have known this pastoral peace and stability before he lost it. Questions like this show the mower's likeness both to earlier literary shepherds[34] and to the sophisticated poets who invented this form of poetry. His sense of mental displacement, his loss of his "home," is itself a reduction or simple representation of the situation of any poet who looks for ways of representing or speaking of his situation and world in such a way as to make himself feel at home in it. The poem, then, is something of a double pastoral: the glowworms are pastoral creatures to the mower, but the mower himself is a pastoral creature to us.

III

Modal analysis helps us understand the pastoralism of "The Mower to the Glowworms," but it is not necessary for the simple purpose of identifying it as a pastoral. With more syncretic or idiosyncratic works, an appeal to mode is

---

34. For example, Spenser's Colin Clout, who represents himself as a displaced lover and expresses a sense of paradise lost at the beginning of the June eclogue. *SC* "June" puts on full display several motifs that are exquisitely tuned in "The Mower to the Glowworms"—the wandering mind, birds as pastoral singers, the pastoral lover's sense of diminishment, and his withdrawal to his song and what it can express of himself.

necessary in order to say whether or not they are pastoral. Taxonomic anxiety is the last thing one wants to promote, but the purpose of making modal and generic distinctions is interpretation, not classification as such. Our stake in defining pastoral is coextensive with our stake in understanding poems. When a critic as important as Raymond Williams can use "pastoral" to undermine Jonson's "To Penshurst," we have some interest in saying why the term is wrongly used of the poem.[35] And when critics load Marvell's "Upon Appleton House" with grandiose meanings, we may be pleased to find a way of understanding how this most brilliantly inventive of poems can delight as well as instruct. Moreover, in saying one of these poems is pastoral in mode and one not, we can hardly be accused of comparing apples and oranges, since both are what are called "country house poems."[36]

"To Penshurst" depicts a fertile, idealized landscape; it portrays benign relations between the owner of the estate and his tenants; and it praises simple, traditional virtues which are set off against modern acquisitiveness and extravagance. It is therefore not surprising that talk of pastoral is found in many critical discussions of the poem, and that it appears in a recent anthology of pastoral poetry. And yet "To Penshurst" is clearly not a pastoral in the generic sense, and it is not in the modal sense either. A very intelligent essay by Harris Friedberg enables us to examine this question with some clarity. Friedberg makes the following argument about the beginning of the poem:

> In [the] first section, borrowing a domesticated version of pastoral from Martial, Jonson superimposes natural and literary landscapes to confirm Penshurst's claims to ideality. But this mythopoeic mode is essentially a foreign one to Jonson. . . . Penshurst itself is capable of announcing its own value without relying on the poet's importation of a fictive landscape. Thus pastoral gives way to a more georgic mode.[37]

Friedberg is speaking of the following lines:

> Thou hast thy walks for health as well as sport:
>   Thy Mount, to which the dryads do resort,
> Where Pan and Bacchus their high feasts have made,
>   Beneath the broad beech and the chestnut shade;
> That taller tree, which of a nut was set
>   At his great birth, where all the muses met.

35. Raymond Williams, *The Country and the City* (London: Chatto & Windus, 1973), 26–34.

36. The reader may ask whether poems in different modes can belong to the same "kind." Defining the country house poem has become a veritable cottage industry of criticism, but my sense is that these poems, which are few in number, are so different as to defy attempts to define them as a genre.

37. "Ben Jonson's Poetry: Pastoral, Georgic, Epigram," *ELR* 4 (1974), 130.

> There, in the writhèd bark, are cut the names
>   Of many a sylvan taken with his flames;
> And thence the ruddy satyrs oft provoke
>   The lighter fauns to reach thy lady's oak.[38]

Friedberg calls this "pastoral" because it represents a landscape inhabited by the mythological figures of Pan, Bacchus, and the dryads. "Through these pastoral allusions," he says, "Jonson is able to show the harmony [of the human world] with the natural world." Furthermore, the Latin deities, reminding us as they do of a passage in one of Martial's epigrams (9.61), "serve as metaphor both for a relationship with the landscape and with a cultural tradition; they are no mere ornaments, but part of the primary experience of the poem, mediating between natural and literary landscapes and stressing their essential oneness at Penshurst." "At Penshurst," he says, "the realms of poetry and history miraculously intersect."[39] It is clear that Friedberg is not innocent of the literary sophistication of pastoral. Yet his emphasis on landscape and harmony with nature betray the Schillerian assumptions that underlie his observations about the "essential oneness" of the natural and the literary and the "miraculous" intersection of poetry and history. These terms suggest an underlying idyllicism in the way the mind apprehends the elements of the situation and the overall force of the passage. Hence Friedberg is eager to have the poem move on to the georgic and epigrammatic modes with which, he claims, it continues and concludes.

Modal terms are appropriate here, but these seem to me the wrong ones. Consider the speaker's presence in the opening lines:

> Thou are not, Penshurst, built to envious show
>   Of touch or marble, nor canst boast a row
> Of polished pillars, or a roof of gold;
>   Thou hast no lantern whereof tales are told,
> Or stair, or courts; but stand'st an ancient pile,
>   And these grudged at, art reverenced the while.
>
> (1–6)

The list of negatives might suggest "satiric" as a modal term, but most critics reject that idea, because the main intent of these lines is not to expose abuses. Their rhetorical shaping subordinates critical points scored to the praise registered in the clinching phrases, "stand'st an ancient pile" and "art reverenced the while." The intent to praise is so clear that we might turn to "encomiastic" as the appropriate modal term. But that word seems inconsistent with the speaker's

---

38. Lines 9–18, in *Ben Jonson*, ed. Ian Donaldson (Oxford: Oxford University Press, 1985), 282–85.

39. Friedberg, 129. The other sentences quoted are on p. 130.

critical energy in enumerating details and with the sense of discriminating judgment he displays. There may not, indeed, be any single adjective that conveys the mode of these lines. But it is clear that we are in the presence of a speaker whose judgments give authority to the praise in the next couplet:

> Thou joy'st in better marks, of soil, of air,
> Of wood, of water; therein thou art fair.
>
> (7–8)

Later in the poem, the speaker's praises are explicitly based on his strength relative to the world of Penshurst. The lines "whose liberal board doth flow/ With all that hospitality doth know!" (59–60) could, in isolation, be called encomiastic hyperbole. But the next lines make clear that this speaker knows what he is talking about—both in the sense that he knows in general what makes for true hospitality, for what makes guests welcome, and in the sense that he has experienced this at firsthand:

> Where comes no guest but is allowed to eat
> Without his fear, and of thy lord's own meat;
> Where the same beer and bread and self-same wine
> That is his lordship's shall be also mine.
>
> (61–64)

A few lines later, the speaker directly invokes his strength relative to the world of Penshurst:

> Nor, when I take my lodging, need I pray
> For fire or lights or livery: all is there,
> As if thou then wert mine, or I reigned here.
>
> (72–74)

What does all this tell us about the pastoralism Friedberg attributes to the opening landscape? Primarily, that a speaker so discriminating and so firmly judging is not going to regard the associations of the literary and the real as miraculous or naively harmonious. He is in a knowing, not a wondering relation to the worlds of men, nature, and books. This becomes explicit in a telling usage at the climax of the lines that invoke the pastoral deities:

> Thou hast thy walks for health as well as sport:
> Thy Mount, to which the dryads do resort,
> Where Pan and Bacchus their high feasts have made,
> Beneath the broad beech and the chestnut shade;
> That taller tree, which of a nut was set
> At his great birth, where all the muses met.
>
> (9–14)

The last line refers to Sir Philip Sidney. The muses—who at first seem mythological beings on a par with Pan, Bacchus, and the dryads just mentioned—can also be taken simply as a metaphor for Sidney's extraordinary gifts and versatility. The sense of mythological presence is not denied by this rational underpinning—for Sidney cut a heroic figure, as both man and poet—but it is put on a certain footing. Someone who speaks with this kind of wit knows why mythological figures are invoked in speaking of human affairs, just as he knows his way around the estate and knows the passage in Martial that suggests his own praise.

Now let us turn to a country-house poem in a different mode. Here is the opening stanza of "Upon Appleton House":

> Within this sober frame expect
> Work of no foreign architect,
> That unto caves the quarries drew,
> And forests did to pastures hew,
> Who of his great design in pain
> Did for a model vault his brain,
> Whose columns should so high be raised
> To arch the brows that on them gazed.
>
> (st. 1)

Like "To Penshurst," "Upon Appleton House" begins with a negative representation. But where Jonson's speaker defines himself by ethical criticism of showy extravagance, Marvell's speaker fancifully imagines the foreign architect's mental effort, and in this way makes us feel its extravagance is absurd: the "great design" is manifestly no more than the product of a single mind unable to go outside itself. "Of his great design in pain" coolly deflates by revealing a contradiction, which then produces the wit of the closing couplet. Read one way, the final lines play out the absurdity of the architect vaulting his brain, as they present the creator's brows elevated to extravagant heights in wonder at his own conception. At the same time, the lines leave room to imagine that the raised eyebrows belong to a sensible English spectator looking at the ridiculously lofty columns of a foreigner's building.

Marvell's wit always has a hint of pastoral about it—most apparent in this stanza in the line "And forests did to pastures hew," which has the accent of "The Mower Against Gardens." But it is in the next stanza that we see why the mode of this poem is pastoral:

> Why should of all things man unruled
> Such unproportioned dwellings build?
> The beasts are by their dens expressed:
> And birds contrive an equal nest;

> The low-roofed tortoises do dwell
> In cases fit of tortoise shell:
> No creature loves an empty space;
> Their bodies measure out their place.
>
> (st. 2)

This stanza is pastoral because the question asked in the first couplet is answered by the example of simple creatures. We can see the modal effect by comparing the way the idea of proportion is invoked in "To Penshurst." Jonson's poem concludes:

> Now, Penshurst, they that will proportion thee
>   With other edifices, when they see
> Those proud, ambitious heaps, and nothing else,
>   May say, their lords have built, but thy lord dwells.
>
> (99–102)

We note again the knowing firmness, the capacity to have the whole poem close on and reside in the word "dwells." When this speaker uses the word "proportion," he invokes an idea of conscious measurement, and this appeal to aesthetic and moral judgment concludes a poem which itself has in mind the traditional analogy between a poem and a building.[40] When Marvell calls human dwellings unproportioned, his mode conveys a different sense of the way we inhabit our buildings and our poems. The example of the birds and beasts, who are said to proportion their dwellings naturally, has modal consequences that are first seen in the wittiest lines in the stanza. "The low-roofed tortoises do dwell/In cases fit of tortoise shell." The wit lies in the play on "cases," which in seventeenth-century English can directly mean the tortoises' shells, but which also, of course, refers to boxes made of tortoise shell. The wit is pastoral because the reference to these luxurious objects is absorbed into the charming tautology of the couplet. Of course tortoises "do dwell/In cases fit of tortoise shell": where else should they dwell? It is a splendid Empsonian moment. The refined and the exquisite are perfectly contained by the natural fact, as when Damon the Mower says the evening bathes his feet in cowslip water—something he would splash through in his meadows, but also a decoction used by gentleladies ("Damon the Mower," 47–48). Here the charming turn on tortoise shell leads to the aesthetic adumbrated in the next couplet: "No creature loves an empty space;/Their bodies measure out their place." Where the authority of Ben Jonson's clinching lines comes from the active, individuated, sometimes muscular workings of syntax, word choice, meter, and lineation, Marvell's dic-

---

40. Alastair Fowler, "The 'Better Marks' of Jonson's *To Penshurst*," *RES* 24 (1973): 266–82.

tum gets its firmness from being preferred as obvious and from the closeness of the speaker's verbal performance to the model of proportion held up by this stanza. As the words too "measure out their place," the final line seems itself to exemplify or enact the beasts' natural mode of being.

The rub, of course, is that human nature consists of both mind and body. The elements that clash in the foreign architect's "great design in pain" must somehow be brought into harmony, and so the project of measuring out a place produces the most wide-ranging, fantastical, and brilliantly performative of all the country-house poems. But it is all in the service of finding the human equivalent, in both the represented dwelling and the poem about it, of the birds contriving their equal nest: one could indeed view the whole poem as concerned with the naturalness of "contriving." This is not the place for a complete tour of "Upon Appleton House," but let us recall how full of pastoral concerns and topoi it is. The stanza we have just examined brings into play the question that underlies *The Shepheardes Calender*—the proportion that exists between human beings and nature.[41] Two stanzas after this, Marvell is praising "that more sober age and mind" when men stooped to enter a dwelling, and he goes on to imagine—and again think how differently "To Penshurst" deals with the same phenomenon, the simple house—that later ages will smile at this house, as they do at "Romulus his bee-like cell" (st. 5). The heart of the poem is the question of withdrawal from the world, first seen in the undue rigidity of the nunnery, then in Fairfax's transformation of his heroic career into the modesty of a garden drawn up in military fashion, and finally in the poet's excursion in the meadows and withdrawal to the woods. The last stanza of the poem is a familiar pastoral topos, the return home as evening falls, and it invokes the pastoral figures of the salmon-fishers. But it is perhaps misleading to survey the poem in this way. Though it uses a number of pastoral conventions, they are not deployed in a way that tells us that this is a particular kind of poem. Nor is it the case that all poems about withdrawal from the world or man's place in nature are pastoral. "Upon Appleton House" is pastoral because of the mode in which it develops its main theme, which is the human imagination and the home it finds and makes for itself in this world.[42] The figure of the poet, his various gestures and usages, the very stanzas themselves—with their even pace, their separateness, and mutual equality—all these manifest the strength relative to world that in more conventional pastoral is represented by the simplicity of the shepherd-singer, whose capacity to dwell in his natural home

41. The commentator E. K. uses the word in the argument to "December": "He [Colin Clout] proportioneth his life to the foure seasons of the yeare."

42. For a full discussion of the pastoralism of "Upon Appleton House," see Haber (above n. 33), 124–52.

and voice his relation to it is bound up with the fact that he must accommodate to its realities and that he cannot control it.

IV

Marvell's unusual self-consciousness about pastoral fictions and conventions makes him not just a poet to study, but a collaborator in critical analysis and definition. (This is not unusual in Renaissance poetry, and particularly not in pastoral, which has always been a self-conscious form.) But we should correct two possibly misleading suggestions that might arise from using his poems to exemplify the ideas of mode itself and of pastoral as a mode. The first is Fowler's argument that modes historically arise later than genres, in which type-specific traits are abundant and coherent. In Fowler's terms, only a poet as late as Marvell could play so loosely with the generic repertoire and permit the kind of analysis we have given. But the history of pastoral disproves this argument. Pastoral is itself a late form, the product of a sophisticated literary culture (Alexandria, in the third century B.C.) that was conscious of its distance from Homeric poetry and from the culture of classical Greece. Modal interests underlie Theocritus's invention of bucolic poetry. It was his consciousness of his relation to the older world of Greek literature—evident in Idylls we shall examine in a later chapter—that prompted him to write poetry about herdsmen and ordinary folk, and to make the herdsman-singer the characteristic figure of the poet. However, Theocritus did not give ancient pastoral its definitive *generic* form. As we shall see, there are no clear boundaries between his "pastoral" and "nonpastoral" Idylls and no coherently developed set of conventions that mark certain "bucolics" as what we would call "pastoral." That was the work of later Greek pastoralists and was brought to completion by Virgil, whose Eclogues give ancient pastoral its generic identity. In the case of pastoral, at least, one is tempted to reverse Fowler's dictum and say that mode tends to genre. The real point, of course, is that the two are always mutually implicated.

A second impression that might arise from our use of Marvell is that modal analyses involve working on a small scale. But when we turn to pastoral drama and the forms of pastoral narrative, both romance and novel, we see that important conventions of structure and organization have a modal rationale. The disposition of scenes in *As You Like It* is consistent with (and perhaps reflects) the handling of episodes in its source, Thomas Lodge's *Rosalynde*, which in its turn reflects the organization of eclogue-sequences. However, this is not a matter of external rules but of the way the fictions of pastoral determine its literary usages.

The sixteenth-century pastoral romance, the form that Shakespeare knew and that Cervantes practiced, begins with an imitation of Virgil, Jacopo Sannazaro's *Arcadia* (1504). Sannazaro saw that the Eclogues were conceived as a single book, and he decided to go his model one better by providing his own series of eclogues with prose links. These prose passages are usually no longer than the poems they introduce, and several are themselves based on classical eclogues. Sannazaro's *Arcadia*, then, is a sort of double eclogue-book, half prose and half verse. The pastoral romance did not take the form in which we know it until Jorge de Montemayor's *Diana* (1559), which derives from Sannazaro, but in which the prose narration dominates and the poems appear embedded in it. The origins of pastoral romances explain an important aspect of their structure: they are not only episodic, like most romances, but the episodes tend to be set-pieces, of a similar character, often centering on or issuing in a song, a poetic performance, or a recited tale.[43] They are, in other words, transformed eclogues, and the romance as a whole tends to respect their separate character. *Rosalynde* is a good example. It represents three love situations: Rosalynde and Rosader (Shakespeare's Orlando); Alinda and Saladyne (Shakespeare's Celia and Oliver); and Phebe and Montanus (Shakespeare's Phebe and Silvius). In contrast to *As You Like It*, where Orlando and Rosalind dominate, Lodge's three wooings have equal weight and occur seriatim. The Rosalind-Rosader wooing occurs first, and even though Rosalind is disguised as a boy and the lovers are merely playing, it is effectively resolved in the one scene devoted to it. Moreover, its climax occurs not in prose but in what Lodge calls a "wooing eclogue" in verse. Lodge then moves on to Alinda and Saladyne, who also come to an understanding in one scene, and then to Phebe and Montanus who—and this is the greatest difference between *Rosalynde* and *As You Like It*—provide the most complex of the three love situations, both in its poetry and its action.

Why should a prose romance like *Rosalynde* respect the eclogue-like character of the episodes of which it is composed? If one is thinking along generic lines, the answer to this question would emphasize conventions and rules of procedure: one does the thing this way, in effect, because this is the way such things are done. Only by paying attention to the modal aspects of these structural practices can we understand why they remained in force—that is, why writers and readers continued to find life and interest in them. To understand the episodic structure of pastoral romance, we must return to Virgil's Eclogues and the question of their mode. In a memorable passage, Erwin Panofsky says:

> In Virgil's ideal Arcady human suffering and superhumanly perfect surroundings create a dissonance. This dissonance, once felt, had to be resolved, and it was resolved in that vespertinal mixture of sadness and

---

43. This is not true of some later romances, which identify themselves as pastoral but in their scope, ambition, and attitudes depart from the pastoralism of the original form in *La Diana*. Sidney's *Arcadia* is the most important English example. For a fuller discussion of the *Diana*, see chapter 8.

tranquillity which is perhaps Virgil's most personal contribution to poetry. With only slight exaggeration one might say that he "discovered"
the evening.[44]

This is clearly an observation about mode: sadness reflects the shepherd's vulnerability to loss and tranquillity his ability to accept his life and the simple
good things in it. At the same time, the passage is steeped in Schillerian assumptions, which prompt Panofsky to note a dissonance between "human suffering" and "superhumanly perfect surroundings" in Virgil's "ideal Arcady." But
there is no such dissonance in Eclogue 1. The landscape of this eclogue is the
real country of flocks and farms described by Tityrus;[45] these surroundings appear superhumanly perfect only when and because one is denied or deprived of
them. The sense the poem gives of idyllic surroundings comes solely from the
speeches of the exiled Meliboeus, who lavishes on Tityrus's good fortune his
own intense longing for the actual cottage and fields (67–72) which have been
taken from him. If anything, Virgil perceives a consonance between suffering
and ideal landscape. Rather than expressing nostalgia, the poem anatomizes it.

   Hence we should turn to a different account of the way literary mode
determines pastoral mood. Speaking (as Panofsky apparently was) of the end
of Eclogue 1, Charles Segal says:

> Despite the temporary effort toward calm and rest the tensions between
> sadness and peace, settledness and dispossession are unresolved. Rest is
> promised, it is true, but exile is no less pressing. The morrow still awaits.
> This atmosphere of suspension amid contraries, of rest amid disturbance,
> sets the tone for the *Eclogues*.[46]

"Suspension" is the word that best conveys how the oppositions and disparities
of Virgilian pastoral are related to each other and held in the mind. As opposed
to words like "resolve," "reconcile," or "transcend," "suspend" implies no permanently achieved new relation, while at the same time it conveys absorption in
the moment. It thus suggests a poised, even secure contemplation of things
disparate or ironically related, and yet at the same time does not imply that
disparities or conflicts are fully resolved. "Suspension" is a modal term, in that
it directly reflects the protagonist's strength relative to his world. The herdsman
of pastoral poetry is conceived as the opposite of the hero: he is able to live

---

44. Erwin Panofsky, "*Et in Arcadia Ego*: Poussin and the Elegiac Tradition," in *Meaning in the Visual
Arts* (New York: Anchor Books, 1955), 300.

45. The settings are more fully indicated in other speeches of Tityrus's than what has been quoted
in chapter 1 (see lines 19–25, 27–35).

46. "*Tamen Cantabitis, Arcades*: Exile and Arcadia in *Eclogues One* and *Nine*," *Arion* 4 (1965): 243–44.
Reprinted in *Poetry and Myth in Ancient Pastoral* (Princeton: Princeton University Press, 1981),
277–78.

with and sing out his dilemmas and pain, but he is unable to act so as to resolve or overcome them, or see them through to their end.

The effect of suspension is found at crucial moments of the Eclogues, particularly their endings; it is also characteristic of the organization of the whole sequence. The ten eclogues in the book can be regarded as being organized in three different ways: as a sequence culminating in the two final poems, which seem to bid farewell to pastoral poetry; as two halves, of which the second recapitulates the first in a more self-consciously poetic way; and in a more static, less sequential fashion, in which love laments and song contests surround a central group of three eclogues composed in what Milton called "a higher mood." The individual eclogues and the way they are organized enable us to entertain all these possibilities, so that we cannot insist on one at the expense of the others: that is, the possible relations between the individual eclogues are suspended, not decisively ordered or resolved.[47] Again, this is a matter of poetic mode. Just as the shepherds in these poems are viewed as equals and just as their characteristic way of being with each other is responsive song, so the ten eclogues are of equal weight and are variously paired off so as to seem responsive to each other.

Unlike Sannazaro, Lodge was not directly imitating Virgil, but the example of Virgil's eclogue book helps us understand why *Rosalynde* is organized as it is. On the one hand, its court characters have been driven into exile; on the other hand, they find in Arden a landscape of love, where all shepherds, native or immigrant, are equals. Either consideration of strength relative to world—the loss of dominion in the courtly world or the equality of those who are subject to love—indicates why this romance underplays the role of its apparent hero and is not structured by a plot. Rosalind and Rosader are nominally the most important of the lovers, but, like Virgil, Lodge finds ways to distribute the weight of emphasis among his episodes. Thus it is in Saladyne's wooing of Alinda that the "debate" between court and country is most fully played out, while the most poetical lover in Lodge's Arden, and the one most threatened with genuine love suffering, is not Rosader but the shepherd Montanus. It is the native shepherd, reduced by Shakespeare to the dimensions of Silvius, whose love story provides the concluding episode—less, however, as a climax than as the completion of a frame, for his love woes are what the reader and the courtiers first encounter in Arden.

Like the pastoral romance, pastoral drama developed in the sixteenth century from Virgil's Eclogues. Our own sense of poetry leads us to associate eclogues with lyrics, and we therefore assume that they are characteristically

47. For a full account, see Paul Alpers, *The Singer of the Eclogues: A Study of Virgilian Pastoral* (Berkeley & Los Angeles: University of California Press, 1979), 103–13; also below, chapter 4. For a very different view, emphasizing intricate structure and the dynamic effect of sequence, see John Van Sickle, *The Design of Virgil's Bucolics* (Rome: Edizioni dell'Ateneo e Bizzarri, 1978).

monodies. But the majority of Virgil's Eclogues have more than one speaker—sometimes participants in a singing contest, sometimes interlocutors in a dialogue—and it was therefore perfectly natural to perform them, or imitations of them, as little theatrical pieces at court. From these *egloghe rappresentative*, as they were called, the pastoral drama developed in mid-sixteenth-century Italy.[48] There was nothing like the Italian vogue for these plays in England, but some Elizabethan examples show their genealogy. John Lyly's *Gallathea* begins as if it were a prose eclogue:

> *Tityrus.* The sun doth beat upon the plain fields, wherefore let us sit down, Gallathea, under this fair oak, by whose broad leaves being defended from the warm beams we may enjoy the fresh air which softly breathes from Humber floods.
> *Gallathea.* Father, you have devised well, and whilst our flock doth roam up and down this pleasant green you shall recount to me, if it please you, for what cause this tree was dedicated unto Neptune, and why you have thus disguised me.[49]

George Peele's court entertainment *The Araygnement of Paris* (subtitled "A Pastorall" when published in 1584) is a succession of eclogue-like scenes, some of them deriving from *The Shepheardes Calender*, which had recently given English literature its first Virgilian eclogue book.[50]

Like pastoral romances, pastoral dramas are episodic, characterized by set pieces, relatively unmarked by the shapings and energies of plot. The pastoral source and the pastoral character of *As You Like It* explain its unusual dramaturgy, which has been noted by many critics:

> It is in the defectiveness of its action that *As You Like It* differs from the rest of the major comedies—in its dearth not only of big theatrical scenes but of events linked together by the logical intricacies of cause and effect.[51]

48. For the history of pastoral drama in Italy, see Marzia Pieri, *La scena boschereccia nel Rinascimento italiano* (Padova: Liviana Editrice, 1983). The most important recent treatment of Italian pastoral drama in English is Louise George Clubb, *Italian Drama in Shakespeare's Time* (New Haven: Yale University Press, 1989). Clubb's emphasis, however, is not on the filiations between eclogues and pastoral plays, but rather on their differences—the way these plays, absorbing the usages of other genres, became full-fledged dramas.

49. John Lyly, *Gallathea and Midas*, ed. Anne Begor Lancashire (Lincoln: University of Nebraska Press, 1969).

50. For details about the date and circumstances of *The Araygnement of Paris*, see the edition of R. Mark Benbow in *The Dramatic Works of George Peele* (New Haven: Yale University Press, 1970).

51. Harold Jenkins, "*As You Like It*," in *Pastoral and Romance: Modern Essays in Criticism*, ed. Eleanor Terry Lincoln (Englewood Cliffs: Prentice-Hall, 1969), 103. This essay first appeared in *Shakespeare Survey VIII*, ed. Harold Jenkins (Cambridge: Cambridge University Press, 1955), 40–51.

As You Like It comes nearer in form to a discussion play or a symposium than any other of Shakespeare's comedies. Not only is the action punctuated by songs; there is much reporting of meetings and conversations, and the comparatively uneventful plot marks time while the actors talk.[52]

What seems puzzling and idiosyncratic, when we view the play as a comedy, appears explicable, even "normal," when we view it as a pastoral. Some of the scenes in Arden have a clear relation to the eclogues that are the foundation of pastoral romance and drama: the dialogue between Silvius and Corin about the pains of love (2.4, derived from a formal eclogue in Lodge); the exchange between Touchstone and Corin on the virtues of life in the court and the country (3.2); the scene between Silvius and Phebe (3.5), which Corin calls "a pageant truly play'd" between true love and scorn (3.4.52); and above all the songs, which, with one exception, are the occasion and centerpiece of separate scenes (2.5, 3.2, 5.3). Other scenes have a looser, but nonetheless real, relation to eclogues. When Rosalind persistently interrupts Celia's description of Orlando lying under a tree, in order to elaborate her own conceits on the descriptive details, Celia's impatient outburst—"I would sing my song without a burthen" (3.2.247)—reveals the scene's descent from amoebean eclogues. A common eclogue-type, in which an older shepherd reproves a younger for the follies of love, lies behind Rosalind/Ganymede's first scene with Orlando, in which she attributes her antidote for love to "an old religious uncle of mine" (3.2.344). More broadly, the pastoral dramaturgy is seen in the fact that though there is a large cast of characters, one encounters them, as Harold Jenkins notes, "most often two at a time."[53]

A modal view of the dramaturgy of *As You Like It* implies not only that its scenes have a pastoral genealogy, but also that they retain a pastoral character. Many critics vindicate the play's pastoralism by connecting its variety of wit and its brilliant ease with the "golden world" imagined by the wrestler Charles and the atmosphere of the Forest of Arden. These critics usually acknowledge a certain tension between the play's critical energies and awarenesses and the idyllicism that is assumed to be of the essence of pastoral. Rosalie Colie, who was keenly aware of the generic presences in the play, says:

> *As You Like It*'s beautiful finish seems the greater achievement precisely because of the playwright's uncompromising insistence upon the problematical within pastoral thematics. . . . We are forced to attend to the tensions underlying even this most idealized of literary modes.[54]

52. Leo Salingar, *Shakespeare and the Traditions of Comedy* (Cambridge: Cambridge University Press, 1974), 293.

53. Jenkins, 117.

54. Rosalie L. Colie, *Shakespeare's Living Art* (Princeton: Princeton University Press, 1974), 261.

There will always seem to be a conflict between Shakespearean tough-mindedness and pure pastoralism if we think that "the literary pastoral cele-brates the glorious unrealities of the imagination," that "pastoral myths" offer "wish-fulfilling satisfactions," and that "the forest, then, shelters a counter-society, idyllic and playful, offering a model of possibility to the real world."[55] When the pastoral world is conceived this way, it is hard to regard it as the locale of critical wit and realistic perceptions, and hence difficult to connect the play's pastoralism with its self-consciousness and what Colie well calls its "perspectivism."

The play itself helps us understand the critical problem by offering us a choice of mottos. Critics most frequently take up the one first offered:

> They say he is already in the Forest of Arden, and a many merry men with him; and there they live like the old Robin Hood of England. They say many young gentlemen flock to him every day, and fleet the time carelessly, as they did in the golden world. (1.1.114–19)

After what we have seen of Oliver's treatment of Orlando, this speech indeed suggests "a countersociety, idyllic and playful." But it is a view from the court world, and there is something searching and impressive in Shakespeare's putting it in the mouth of the wrestler Charles. The paradox of the brutish character intuiting ease and freedom anticipates Caliban, and Charles's words have a cer-tain pastoral authority. It is as if his own occupation at court—"low" and physi-cal, utterly dependent yet providing an admired spectacle—gives him the ca-pacity to see what his social superiors cannot. (We should remember that he arrives on the scene not to do Oliver's bidding but to warn him not to let Orlando wrestle that day.)

The play never denies the force of Charles's speech, but it adjusts our un-derstanding of what it means to be "careless," i.e. without care:

> Now, my co-mates and brothers in exile,
> Hath not old custom made this life more sweet
> Than that of painted pomp? Are not these woods
> More free from peril than the envious court?
> Here feel we not the penalty of Adam,
> The seasons' difference, as the icy fang
> And churlish chiding of the winter's wind,
> Which when it bites and blows upon my body
> Even till I shrink with cold, I smile and say,
> "This is no flattery: these are counsellors

55. Ibid., 249, 250, 261.

That feelingly persuade me what I am."
Sweet are the uses of adversity,
Which like the toad, ugly and venomous,
Wears yet a precious jewel in his head;
And this our life, exempt from public haunt,
Finds tongues in trees, books in the running brooks,
Sermons in stones, and good in every thing.

(2.1.1–17)

These are the first words we hear in the Forest. What marks the place out is not idyllic nature but a way of life, for which the Duke can speak because he appears in the guise of—in our terminology, represents himself as—a forester, an inhabitant of the woods.[56] Hence he establishes his claims by rhetorical questions that are addressed to his "co-mates and brothers in exile" and that register a felt obviousness in values and a shared sense of life. This is a style very different from the pronouncements of a Prospero, who remains a monarch even in exile. The distinctiveness of the Duke's mode is even more striking in the sentence that follows his opening questions. The imagery of the winter's wind reminds us of *King Lear,* and the clinching line—"That feelingly persuade me what I am"—could well be imagined to come from that play, as if it incorporated into Lear's recognitions on the heath Gloucester's anguished "I see it feelingly" (4.4.149). What can make such a line so different in this context? Though it is said in the Duke's own person it is put at one remove from the present utterance, by being attributed to a characteristic scene. That scene is a pastoral encounter, between a nobleman, suspicious of flattery and used to being addressed by counsellors, and a natural force that is represented, in the phrase "churlish chiding," as a rustic interlocutor. The Duke has in effect imagined and internalized a pastoral of the type we know best from the Sixth Book of *The Faerie Queene,* where the knight Sir Calidore finds his blandishments and his gold resisted and reproved by the old shepherd Melibee. By the same token, the Duke's statement of self-knowledge is not, like Gloucester's, an utterance wrenched from experience, but is, in true pastoral fashion, made out to be the responsive iteration of something impressed upon him. Hence almost identical words can be pastoral rather than tragic in mode: they bear witness not to the individual's attempt to make sense of his own and others' suffering, but to a common condition acknowledged as obvious. In his response to the Duke's rhetorical poise, Amiens provides an alternative motto to the wrestler Charles's:

56. Cf. the stage direction of 2.1: "Enter Duke Senior, Amiens, and two or three Lords, like foresters."

> I would not change it. Happy is your Grace,
> That can translate the stubbornness of fortune
> Into so quiet and so sweet a style.
>
> (2.1.18–20)

The claim, initiated by the double meaning of "translate," is that a style of speech is a style of life. The Duke has given an epigrammatic example in his final lines, where the translation of nature's lessons into apparently simple verbal patterns is seasoned by the wit that switches "tongues" and "books" from the natural objects to which they might be thought to belong and thus makes clear that, in pastoral, nature's meanings are uttered by man.

Amiens's praise of the Duke can be applied very widely in *As You Like It:* all the characters can be seen as dealing in a recognizable style of speech with what their lives and fortunes have imposed upon them. As so often, Touchstone gives his own formulation when he arrives in the Forest: "Ay, now am I in Arden, the more fool I. When I was at home, I was in a better place, but travellers must be content" (2.4.16–18). Commentators usually say that this disputes the "conventional" preference of country to court, but it is a thoroughly pastoral remark—less because it speaks of content (for it does so wryly, as if discontentedly) than because of the comic primness of "the more fool I," where Touchstone's self-mockery also contains the main claim for the Forest, that it enables its inhabitants to be themselves. Touchstone, of all the characters, shows us that a style of speech is a style of life, and it is this that explains why the dominance of wit and talk over action in *As You Like It* can be so satisfying. It is a pastoral phenomenon, for its ultimate model is the literary shepherd's translation of experience into song and the stylish exchanges we find in singing contests and other dialogic eclogues. But if most of the characters are from the court world and if the two characters Shakespeare added to *Rosalynde,* Touchstone and Jaques, seem resistant to Arden and critical of life in it, we need to explain how the modes of self-presentation in the play can be viewed as and assimilated to pastoral.

All the court figures in *As You Like It* can be seen as playing out Spenser's metaphor for himself as a pastoral poet: "Lo I the man, whose Muse whilome did maske,/As time her taught, in lowly Shepheards weeds" (*FQ* 1.Proem.1). It is by willingly stepping into the forester's garb that the Duke and his men accept their exile; Orlando, thus appareled, manages to stay in his suit (the pun is Rosalind's, 4.1.87); Rosalind's guise, first adopted out of necessity, allows her the freedom to play out her courtship with Orlando, and Celia's tests the integrity of Oliver's love. Surrounding these courtly pastoralists are characters in whom we see the extremes of naive and masked self-presentation. Though the natives of Arden are conspicuously stylized and associated with literary roles— as if to insure in the audience's pastoralism as much critical awareness as in the

Duke's or Rosalind's—each is what he or she seems to be, in dress and in rhetoric. Touchstone and Jaques, the two characters who have not changed costume, are at the other extreme. Both are caught up in, and indeed strikingly exemplify, the problematic of pastoral masking: they self-consciously play out and test for us the relation between one's dress, one's style of speech, and one's adopted role. Their mockery and realism thus have no privileged or even separate grounds. They are as much part of life in Arden as anyone else, willy-nilly involved in the play of styles of speech.[57]

The vitality and sufficiency of roles and gestures gives *As You Like It* its characteristic tone. Not surprisingly it is Touchstone who defines this element of the play, when he teases us into looking for a statable attitude towards the pastoral world:

> Truly, shepherd, in respect of itself, it is a good life; but in respect that it is a shepherd's life, it is naught. In respect that it is solitary, I like it very well; but in respect that it is private, it is a very vild life. Now in respect it is in the fields, it pleaseth me well; but in respect it is not in the court, it is tedious. (3.2.13–19)

"Through the apparent nonsense of his witty clown," Poggioli says,

> Shakespeare seems to reply to three important questions. The first is whether he values or scorns the pastoral ideal. The second is whether this comedy is a pastoral play. The third is whether it reaffirms or denies the traditional poetics of the pastoral. The equivocal answer that the clown gives to all three on behalf of the poet amounts to an echo of the comedy's title: as you like it.[58]

This is well said, but whether truly or not, let the forest judge. Poggioli calls the play's pastoralism equivocal, because for him true pastoral is irredeemably committed to idyllic impulses and innocent needs. But the self-pleasuring performance he relishes is itself pastoral in character, the more so as Touchstone's speech, with its sophisticated redundancies, prompts the plain rustic redundancies—e.g. "the property of rain is to wet and fire to burn"—with which Corin stands up to him. Colie, for all her Schillerian assumptions, understands better the literary genealogy of *As You Like It* and therefore its modal character:

> Perspectivism is built into this play; it is the play's method, but it relies on traditional implications within the mode, by developing an inherent

---

57 Edwin Greenlaw long ago argued that Jaques derives from the melancholy solitaries of pastoral romance, like Sannazaro's Sincero, Sidney's Philisides, and Spenser's Colin Clout. "Shakespeare's Pastorals," *Studies in Philology* 13 (1916): 122–54; reprinted in *Pastoral and Romance*, ed. Lincoln; see esp. 88–92.

58. Renato Poggioli, *The Oaten Flute* (Cambridge, MA: Harvard University Press, 1975), 39.

dialectical tendency in pastoral eclogues to an astonishing degree. Many contests question the traditions which ultimately they endorse.[59]

The role playing, the welcoming of one's situation, the satisfactions of wit and playfulness, and thus the play's pastoralism all come together in the figure of Rosalind. No one doubts her centrality to the play. It is not simply that her impulsiveness, wit, and strength of feeling can be seen to associate her with characters as different as Silvius (for romantic love), Phebe (for coyness and literalizing wit), and Touchstone (for mocking realism and willingness to perform). Her character seems so to dominate the play that one critic compares her in this respect to Hamlet.[60] The finest of the older essays argues that the play's "two polar attitudes" towards love, "romantic participation" and "humorous detachment," "meet and are reconciled in Rosalind's personality": "she possesses as an attribute of character the power of combining wholehearted feeling and undistorted judgment which gives the play its value."[61] One understands the reasons for such statements, but critics in this vein tend to confuse the authority of Rosalind's presence with dramatic and moral autonomy. As she herself recognizes—"Alas the day! What shall I do with my doublet and hose?" (3.2.219–20)—the disguise which gives her freedom is also her dilemma. She is thus in the situation of all the other pastoralists: constrained to adopt a costume, she learns to play a role that expresses her needs and nature more truly than would have been possible in the "workaday world."

Taking Rosalind at her word, critics say she administers physic to the sentimentally romantic Orlando, but the scene in which she undertakes his cure does not put them in the relation suggested by this metaphor. It is the last of the brilliant encounters in Act 3, scene 2 (Corin-Touchstone, Touchstone-Rosalind with the former's mocking verses, Celia-Rosalind, Jaques-Orlando), all of which display responsive wit and give the audience a sense of a pleasurable standoff. Rosalind prepares to meet Orlando by saying, "I will speak to him like a saucy lackey, and under that habit play the knave with him."[62] Their encounter is no less marked than the earlier ones by conscious performance and appreciative response. Orlando is not mooning about but is clearly charmed by this youth, willing to give rein to his saucy wit. Rosalind, whose vulnerability has been evident in the preceding dialogues, exercises this wit not to cure Orlando but to elicit declarations of his love and find ways of safely expressing her own: in her own way, to adapt the Duke's words of Touchstone (5.4.106), she uses her wit like a stalking horse. The structure of Rosalind's performance

59. Colie, 256.

60. Anne Barton, Introduction to *As You Like It* in *The Riverside Shakespeare*, 366.

61. C. L. Barber, *Shakespeare's Festive Comedy* (Princeton: Princeton University Press, 1959), 233.

62. 3.2.295–7. The role Rosalind proposes to play is a standard one in Lyly's pastoral comedies.

comes out in the exchange that follows her telling Orlando he does not look like a lover:

> *Orlando.* Fair youth, I would I could make thee believe I love.
> *Rosalind.* Me believe it? You may as soon make her that you love believe it, which I warrant she is apter to do than to confess she does.

> (3.2.385–89)

This is absolutely transparent to us—it states exactly what is true of Rosalind at the moment she utters it—but quite opaque to Orlando, not simply because Rosalind is in disguise but because the statement is rhetorically disguised by the role she has adopted of mocking women.

At such moments, when acting in disguise enables her to express her love, Rosalind plays out the double meaning of Touchstone's motto for a poetics of pastoral: "The truest poetry is the most feigning" (3.3.19). But all her turns, gestures, and performances are versions of pastoral. The great set piece on dying for love (4.1.94–108)—perhaps too often regarded as the ultimate wisdom on its subject—is pastoral not only by virtue of being a performance under a mask (a motif charmingly doubled in its opening phrase, "No, faith, die by attorney"), but also because, in its youthful breeziness, it yields to the pleasures of affection and performance. It is followed by an equally splendid pastoral gesture:

> *Rosalind.* Men have died from time to time, and worms have eaten them, but not for love.
> *Orlando.* I would not have my right Rosalind of this mind, for I protest her frown might kill me.
> *Rosalind.* By this hand, it will not kill a fly.

> (4.1.106–11)

This both mocks Orlando's hyperbole and makes a pledge from an equally extravagant love. Its pastoralism comes from the apparent wholeheartedness and simplicity of its rhetorical form, whether we take it to be oath, promise, or asseveration. At such a moment, one can imagine that nothing more need be said, and we can understand why this scene of mock-wooing feels, to audiences and readers, like the thing itself.

But even though Rosalind can express her desires by her pretense, the play cannot leave her or us satisfied with the pastoral presence we have described. "Wedlock would be nibbling," Touchstone says (3.3.81), and Orlando will soon announce, "I can live no longer by thinking" (5.2.50). Precisely to the extent that the play of these middle acts is self-sufficient and satisfying, there will be an awkwardness felt about bringing the comedy to a close. In the concluding scenes, Barber says, "the treatment becomes more and more frankly artificial," and he speaks of it apologetically: "The lack of realism in presentation does not matter, because a much more important realism in our attitude towards the substance of romance has been achieved already by the action of the comedy."[63] There is unquestionably a problem here, as G. K. Hunter points out:

> The central episodes . . . show a series of contrasting attitudes to love and to the country; these are developed through the meaningful *play* of Rosalind . . . and Orlando. This *play* is a uniquely powerful way of presenting the richness and complexity of a relationship; but it requires a suspension of place, time and intrigue, and this becalming of the play makes it difficult to steer it to a satisfactory conclusion.[64]

Everything we have seen about pastoral as a mode suggests that it minimizes the energies of plot, and it is therefore not surprising that the pastoralism of *As You Like It* gives rise to this dilemma. What our account has not yet provided for—and what we defer until the next chapter—is the pastoral solution Shakespeare found.

63. Barber, 236.
64. G. K. Hunter, *William Shakespeare: The Late Comedies* (London: Longmans Green, 1962), 39.

Three

PASTORAL CONVENTION

Pastoral writings are notoriously conventional, and no statement of what that means is more familiar than Samuel Johnson's animadversions on *Lycidas*. Johnson complained that the poem

> is not to be considered as the effusion of real passion; for passion runs not after remote allusions and obscure opinions. Passion plucks no berries from the myrtle and ivy, nor calls upon Arethuse and Mincius, nor tells of rough *satyrs* and *fauns with cloven heel.* Where there is leisure for fiction there is little grief.[1]

"Remote allusions" and "obscure opinions" serve to suggest a gap between the machinery of the poem and the feelings it purports to express. But Johnson's real complaint is that this machinery is not obscure but commonplace: "Among the flocks, and copses, and flowers, appear the heathen deities—Jove and Phoebus, Neptune and Aeolus, with a long train of mythological imagery, such as a college easily supplies." Hence there is a double indictment, which sums up what it means to say that a poem is "conventional" or "merely conventional": "In

---

1. Samuel Johnson, "Life of Milton," in *Milton's "Lycidas": The Tradition and the Poem,* ed. C. A. Patrides, rev. ed. (Columbia: University of Missouri Press, 1983), 60. Cited hereafter as Patrides.

this poem there is no nature, for there is no truth; there is no art, for there is nothing new."[2]

Johnson's criticisms derive from an assumption that often governs much friendlier accounts of pastoral—that there is an inherent contradiction between what is conventional and what is individual, whether in expression or poetic handling. Critics have been much readier to see poems as undermining or criticizing pastoral conventions than to see those conventions as themselves permitting the self-consciousness, individuation, and wit that maintain the life of conventional "kinds." Pastoral may be particularly resistant to the recognition, by now widespread, that all literary forms are in some sense conventional. One can imagine intelligent readers and critics acknowledging this general truth and still thinking that some conventions are more conventional than others. Moreover, certain favorable views of convention serve to reinforce the ideas of strictness and impersonality—playing the game according to the rules—that cause readers to dismiss pastorals or praise them inappropriately. Even if we acknowledge the importance of recognizing generic intentions and therefore of recognizing the conventions that identify and differentiate genres, we may still construe conventions too exclusively in terms of "outer form" at the expense of underlying rationale or implicit attitude. Pastoral conventions need not be as artificial and repetitious as they appeared to Johnson, because they have modal motivations that are always ready to be freshly engaged or acknowledged.

One source of our difficulty with the idea of convention is that its root meaning, "coming together" (from Latin *convenire*) has dropped out of sight when the word is used in literary contexts. Here are the definitions from a desk dictionary (*OED*'s treatment of the word is quite unhelpful): (1) A formal meeting of delegates or members; (2) The persons attending such a meeting; (3) An agreement or contract; (4) General consent or approval; accepted custom, rule, opinion, etc.; (5) A rule or approved technique in conduct or art; a custom or usage. The last two definitions are the ones most germane to literary convention. They seem obvious and unexceptionable, but they have a bias that is characteristic and misleading: they minimize the element of convening that is evident in the other definitions, such as an agreement or a meeting. These other usages keep in view individuals coming together either literally or in their attitudes and commitments. This element is evaded or buried in the definitions that concern us: "a rule or approved technique," "general consent" (the least evasive), "accepted custom or rule." Such definitions represent literary conventions as prior, impersonal realities. Thus the relevant definition in *OED* runs, "A rule or practice based upon general consent, or accepted and upheld by society at large; an arbitrary rule or practice recognized as valid in any particular art or

2. Patrides, 61, 60.

study." This definition reflects a felt opposition between the individual and the social that is a heritage of European thought and politics at the turn of the nineteenth century, when "convention" first became a term in literary discourse and took on other meanings germane to its literary use.[3] *OED*'s definition may speak of "general consent," but it leaves no room for ideas of agreement and assembly—involved in all earlier meanings of "convention" and "conventional"—that engage the root meaning.

Pastoral poems make explicit the dependence of their conventions on the idea of coming together. Pastoral convenings are characteristically occasions for songs and colloquies that express and thereby seek to redress separation, absence, or loss. The inaugural poem of Western pastoral, Theocritus's first Idyll, brings herdsmen together for the pleasure of hearing a lament for Daphnis. It is therefore no accident that in this chapter we will be discovering the self-conscious conventionality of pastoral in pastoral laments—Virgil's fifth Eclogue, Milton's *Lycidas,* and the double sestina, "Ye goatherd gods," from Sidney's *Arcadia.* Literary herdsmen need each other to hear their complaints and share the sentiments and pleasures that sustain them: singing for someone, we shall see, is fundamental to these poems. By the same token, the pastoral poet depends on prior usages and texts, either accommodating their grander modes to bucolic modesty, or imitating, echoing, and adapting, as if the responsive singing represented in eclogues were a model of the poet's own activity. Literary shepherds often recall and sing for each other the songs of their masters and predecessors; so too the intertextuality of pastoral brings poet and reader(s) together in a literary space whose modulor (to recall Angus Fletcher's definition of mode) is the representative herdsman.[4] Virgil's Eclogues, the source of most of the details Johnson stigmatizes, show that pastoral writing involves a consciousness of the reasons that underlie its conventions. Eclogue 7 begins as follows:

> *Forte sub arguta consederat ilice Daphnis,*
> *compulerantque greges Corydon et Thyrsis in unum,*
> *Thyrsis ovis, Corydon distentas lacte capellas,*
> *ambo florentes aetatibus, Arcades ambo,*
> *et cantare pares et respondere parati.*
>
> (7.1–5)

3. For the emergence of the term, see Harry Levin, "Notes on Convention," in *Perspectives of Criticism,* ed. Harry Levin (Cambridge: Harvard University Press, 1950), 55–83.

4. See above, chap. 2. Jane O. Newman, *Pastoral Conventions: Poetry, Language, and Thought in Seventeenth-Century Nuremberg* (Baltimore: Johns Hopkins University Press, 1990), describes a historical project (the "Order of Flowers on the Pegnitz") which consciously and literally acted out the idea of pastoral convening and convention.

Under a whispering holm-oak, Daphnis sat,
Corin and Thyrsis drove their flocks together,
Thyrsis his sheep, Corin goats swollen with milk,
Both in the flower of youth, Arcadians both,
Equal in song and eager to respond.

These lines turn from a literal coming together to the social cohesion that underlies poetic practices. The process is seen in miniature in the second line, in which the concluding *in unum* fully establishes the force of the prefix in *compulerant* (drove together)—itself anticipated in *consederat*, a verb which elsewhere (in the plural) describes shepherds sitting together to sing (3.55, 5.3). The rest of the passage presents Corydon and Thyrsis as, so to speak, identical twins, differentiated only by their flocks, and they are given what was to become the title of many literary shepherds, *Arcades ambo*. It is not surprising that these lines introduce a singing contest so artfully conducted and closely matched that the main critical question about this Eclogue has always been why one of the shepherds is declared the winner.

If these lines and the singing contest were all we had, Eclogue 7 might exemplify the kind of pastoral Johnson scorned. But the introduction of Eclogue 7 continues for fifteen more lines, making it far longer than its Theocritean prototypes, the opening passages of Idylls 8 and 9. It tells of the arrival of the narrator, Meliboeus, whose relation to the group is more problematic than that of the other herdsmen: he is seeking a stray goat, and when he accepts the invitation to rest in the shade, he feels a conflict between the play of the song contest and the work that awaits him at home. These fictional complications—which concern "strength relative to occasion" and "strength relative to world"—give a rationale for setting the singing contest in a separate space and serve to represent it as a formal ritual in the shepherds' world. Because of this self-conscious staging, the poem, though indubitably artificial, wards off the Johnsonian charge of presuming on its machinery.

Other eclogues develop more broadly the way in which acts of convening, the shepherds' coming together, give rise to convention, poetic and social practice. Eclogue 5 begins by drawing attention to the act of coming together:

Cur non, Mopse, boni quoniam convenimus *ambo,*
tu calamos inflare levis, ego dicere versus,
hic corylis mixtas inter consedimus *ulmos?*

(5.1–3)

Mopsus, as we have met, both of us skilled—
You piping on light reeds and I at verse—
Why not sit here, where elms and hazels mingle?

The pastoral lament Mopsus agrees to sing begins and ends with scenes of mourners gathered around the dead shepherd-hero Daphnis:

> Exstinctum Nymphae crudeli funere Daphnin
> flebant (vos coryli testes et flumina Nymphis),
> cum complexa sui corpus miserabile nati
> atque deos atque astra vocat crudelia mater.
>
> (5.20–3)

> Snuffed out by cruel death, Daphnis was mourned
> By nymphs—you streams and hazels told their grief—
> While clasping her son's pitiable corpse,
> His mother reproached both gods and cruel stars.

By the end of the song, this immediate mourning at the actual scene of death has become a commemorative gathering at Daphnis's tomb:

> *spargite humum foliis, inducite fontibus umbras,*
> *pastores (mandat fieri sibi talia Daphnis),*
> *et tumulum facite, et tumulo superaddite carmen:*
> *"Daphnis ego in silvis, hinc usque ad sidera notus,*
> *formosi pecoris custos, formosior ipse."*
>
> (40–44)

> Strew foliage on the ground and shade the springs,
> You shepherds—Daphnis calls for rites like these.
> Build him a mound and add this epitaph:
> "I woodland Daphnis, blazoned among stars,
> Guarded a lovely flock, still lovelier I."

The idea of convening is implicit in these scenes and is confirmed by verbs of motion elsewhere in the song. The first effect of Daphnis's death is that no one drove herds to water at the streams (24–25). One of the deeds for which Daphnis is praised is teaching the shepherds to lead Bacchic dances (30). Most important, his death is described in terms of departures:

> *postquam te fata tulerunt,*
> *ipsa Pales agros atque ipse reliquit Apollo.*
>
> (5.34–35)

> After the fates took you,
> Pales herself and our own Apollo left the fields.

Though Mopsus's final vignette does not directly represent shepherds coming together, the idea of convening appears in the first line of his address to the other shepherds: *Spargite humum foliis, inducite fontibus umbras* (40). The second phrase literally means "draw shade over the fountains." Commentators have dealt with this rather difficult expression by interpreting the active verb as a static image. But the sense of purposeful motion towards a spot, or a gathering at or over it, is crucial to the phrase. It makes the celebration of Daphnis an act on and for an occasion, not an instance of a ritual that is predetermined or otherwise guaranteed by a stable context or setting. The special character of the ceremonial action is seen in the verb *inducite*, which is repeated from the account of Daphnis's deeds, ten lines earlier:

> *Daphnis et Armenias curru subiungere tigris*
> *instituit, Daphnis thiasos* inducere *Bacchi*
> *et foliis lentas intexere mollibus hastas.*
>
> (5.29–31)

> Daphnis instructed us to harness tigers
> On chariots, to *lead on* Bacchus' revels
> And intertwine stout spears and delicate leaves.

When the hero was alive, the verb *inducere* represented real ceremonial action; now, in the absence of the hero, it opaquely refers to an action and draws attention to itself as a locution.

The displacement of action to utterance is coextensive with the fact that Mopsus speaks for Daphnis. Just as the hero's actions no longer directly establish (*instituit*) the activities of the pastoral world, so the authority attributed to him in this commemoration depends on the shepherd's calling his fellows together (one sense of English "convene," though not of Latin *convenio*):

> *spargite humum foliis, inducite fontibus umbras,*
> *pastores (mandat fieri sibi talia Daphnis).*
>
> (5.40–41)

> Strew foliage on the ground and shade the springs,
> You shepherds—Daphnis calls for rites like these.

With *mandat* coming on the heels of Mopsus's own imperatives, these lines make it seem that Mopsus has taken on some of Daphnis's powers. We accept the hero's commands because of the shepherd's. At the same time, these are pastoral commands; they depend on the presence and sometimes the consent of other persons than the speaker himself. This is not simply a matter of what is inherent in imperatives, which depend, for their completion, on the compliance of one or more auditors. Dependence on another's presence is also conveyed in the phrasing *mandat fieri sibi talia Daphnis* ("Daphnis commands that such things be done for him"). Mopsus's claim to speak directly for Daphnis is held in suspension with the sense that he is simply one more shepherd who heeds the hero's injunction. The urgency with which he speaks thus depends on the implied presence of Daphnis. In convoking his fellow shepherds, the singer brings into their presence the dead companion they commemorate.

In uttering words attributed to Daphnis, Mopsus takes on a role fundamental to the Virgilian shepherd—that of singing a song *for* someone. This idea appears most fully at the beginning of the tenth and last Eclogue:

> *Extremum hunc, Arethusa, mihi concede laborem:*
> *pauca meo Gallo, sed quae legat ipsa Lycoris,*
> *carmina sunt dicenda: neget quis carmina Gallo?*
>
> (10.1–3)

> Grant this, my final effort, Arethusa:
> A song for Gallus—but may Lycoris read it—
> Is to be sung: who would not sing for Gallus?

Pauca meo Gallo . . . carmina sunt dicenda can mean either "A few songs must be sung *for* my Gallus" or "*to* my Gallus" or "*by* my Gallus." The final phrase has the same range of meanings. *Carmina Gallo* can mean songs for his benefit (with Lycoris) or sung to him as a listener or, construing more loosely, sung on his behalf or instead of him. The tenth Eclogue (of which the central passage is a love complaint put in Gallus's mouth) proceeds to play out all possible meanings of the English phrase, "a song for Gallus." Seen in the light of this motto, a conventional song is a song sung for you ("conventional" in Johnson's negative sense) and that you in turn sing or sing back: this is the particular emphasis or inflection of Virgilian pastoral, with its emphasis on convening for song. The line *mandat fieri sibi talia Daphnis* exemplifies this structure exactly, as Daphnis's injunction is both heard and restated by Mopsus.

Everything that makes these lines conventional appears in the last three lines of Mopsus's song:

> *et tumulum facite, et tumulo superaddite carmen:*
> *"Daphnis ego in silvis, hinc usque ad sidera notus,*
> *formosi pecoris custos, formosior ipse."*
>
> (42–44)

> Build him a mound and add this epitaph:
> "I woodland Daphnis, blazoned among stars,
> Guarded a lovely flock, still lovelier I."

Again the rhetorical basis is the shepherd calling upon his fellows, and the concluding inscription depends on convening all the persons hitherto involved:

the shepherds, who are to hear and inscribe the epitaph; Daphnis, in whose person the words are spoken; and Mopsus, on whose voice everything depends. The epitaph has the same doubleness as the earlier line about Daphnis's commands: we can feel Mopsus's identification with the hero for whom he speaks, while at the same time we can imagine a certain distance between Mopsus and these words, which may be simply an epitaph he tells others to inscribe. These two aspects of the epitaph involve two different meanings of singing a song "for" Daphnis—singing in his stead and on his behalf. But a conventional song, we have said, is not simply one you sing for someone, but one that is in the first place sung for you. These lines fulfill this condition precisely—not simply because, as with Daphnis's first command, we can *imagine* a prior utterance of the dead shepherd, but because there is in fact a prior utterance which produces Virgil's and Mopsus's and Daphnis's words here. These lines imitate the moment in Theocritus's first Idyll when the shepherd Thyrsis represents, that is, both depicts and takes on the character of, the heroic shepherd as he dies:

> I am that Daphnis, he who drove the kine to pasture here,
> Daphnis who led the bulls and calves to water at these springs.
>   (1.120–21)[5]

To the presences essential to Virgil's lines—the shepherds, Daphnis, Mopsus—we must add that of Theocritus. In doing so, we bring our account of these lines around to the ordinary sense in which one would call them conventional—that is, in accordance with a previously established model or practice.

In pastoral poetry, the model for close imitation is the singing contest, in which the challenge for the second singer is to accept the terms set by the first and at the same time establish his own images or voice or claims. Virgil takes up Theocritus as one shepherd answers another, by giving his own version of the song in his predecessor's poem. But in literary imitation the prior poet is not fictively present in the poem. Hence taking up a predecessor's words, re-singing what was sung, implies calling him into the presence of the shepherds said to be gathered together in the poem. The analogy with Mopsus, who seeks to restore the absent Daphnis to his world, brings out the modal assumptions of pastoral conventions. Though he represents Daphnis in more than one sense, Mopsus no longer has the power of autonomous act or utterance. Effective act, speech, and song depend, in the world of this poem, on the presence of one's fellows. Hence monodies are less common in ancient pastoral than dialogues. Song and heightened utterance characteristically emerge from speeches exchanged in small dramatic situations or in the formalities of the singing contest. The impassioned speech of pastoral lovers, whose separation from their love

---

5. Information about texts and translations of Theocritus is given in chap. 4, n. 1.

objects produces emotions that separate them from their fellows, is sometimes put in the mouths of shepherds who impersonate and sing for them. The ultimate separation of death is represented in Eclogue 5 not in direct lament, but in performed songs which Mopsus and Menalcas sing to each other on the normal occasion of coming together to escape the heat of noon. What in the represented world is a limited power of action—the lover's helplessness, the mutual solicitudes and dependencies of ordinary shepherds, the vulnerability to death and the acts and impositions of Rome and its rulers—manifests itself, in poetic practice, in the way expressive clarity, loveliness, and coherence are achieved at the cost of autonomous utterance, full expression, and direct dramatic representation.

These modal considerations underlie usages now dulled to us by familiarity, but fresh and finely modulated in their Virgilian forms. Mopsus laments the dead Daphnis in the following terms:

> *vitis ut arboribus decori est, ut vitibus uvae,*
> *ut gregibus tauri, segetes ut pinguibus arvis,*
> *tu decus omne tuis.*

> (5.32–34)

> As vines adorn the trees and grapes the vine,
> Great bulls the herds and harvests the rich fields,
> So you adorned us all.

This is what Rosenmeyer calls a priamel, "a series of brief statements or propositions which are felt to be based on an underlying pattern, and which usually lead up to a terminal proposition of somewhat greater weight."[6] Mopsus's lines respond to Theocritean prototypes, of which the closest is in Idyll 8:

> As acorns are a glory [*kosmos* = Lat. *decus*] to the oak, to the apple-tree
>   its apples,
> So to the heifer is her calf, to the cowherd his kine.

> (79–80)

Virgil adapts these items to provide a compendium of rural well-being. By emphasizing plural numbers and by linking the first two items by the common element of the vine, he suggests a complete pastoral world. But this world lies under the shadow of an absence, which is adumbrated in the final item. The force of *tu decus omne tuis* (you the entire honor or adornment of your fellows) is brought out by Dryden's expansion:

---

6. Thomas G. Rosenmeyer, *The Green Cabinet: Theocritus and the European Pastoral Lyric* (Berkeley & Los Angeles: University of California Press, 1969), 338 n. 22.

> As Vines the Trees, as Grapes the Vines adorn,
> As Bulls the Herds, and Fields the Yellow Corn;
> So bright a Splendor, so divine a Grace,
> The glorious *Daphnis* cast on his illustrious Race.[7]

In the phenomena to which Daphnis is compared, the adornments (grapes, bulls, rich crops) are the product of what they in turn adorn. By contrast, *tu decus omne tuis* represents Daphnis as wholly the source of the splendor cast on his people. The hero's priority suggests his separateness, which is also intimated by placing the phrase at the end of the list and the beginning of a new line. Separateness, in turn, is an augury of the separations represented in the lines the phrase initiates:

> *postquam te fata tulerunt,*
> *ipsa Pales agros atque ipse reliquit Apollo.*
>
> (5.34–35)

> After the fates took you,
> Pales herself and our own Apollo left the fields.

These separations and departures reveal the true force of the priamel which lists rural goods: its authority comes not from fullness of representation but from the verbal formalities which are precisely what is left to ordinary shepherds when separated from the hero. Another English Augustan provides a valuable piece of creative interpretation. John Martyn, in his edition of 1734, says of the departure of Pales and Apollo:

> This desertion of the fields by the goddess of shepherds and the god of music and poetry is a figurative expression of the grief of the shepherds for the loss of Daphnis. They were so afflicted, that they neglected the care of their sheep, and had not spirits to sing, in which their chief diversion consisted.[8]

The priamel can be seen as the form song takes when the shepherds recover their voices. The idea of convention, then, is crucial to it: not only the idea of gathering for song on a specific occasion and the gathering of items in a list, but also the idea of a usage that implicitly convenes an absent predecessor— the poet who instituted the practice of these priamels as Daphnis, in the immediately preceding lines, is said to have instituted ceremonial practices.

---

7. *The Works of John Dryden*, vol. 5 ("The Works of Virgil in English, 1697") ed. William Frost and Vinton A. Dearing (Berkeley & Los Angeles: University of California Press, 1987), 101.

8. John Martyn, *The Bucolicks of Virgil, with an English Translation and Notes*, 4th ed. (Oxford, 1820), re 5.35. As Servius pointed out, Apollo is also the god of pastures (Apollon Nomios).

Eclogue 5 suggests that a pastoral convention is a poetic practice that makes up for a loss, a separation, or an absence. Even Menalcas's song, with its full representation of the pastoral world and its evident intent to restore Daphnis to it, sings for Daphnis under conditions determined by his absence. The relative grandeur of the song and the tradition of identifying Daphnis with Julius Caesar lead one critic to say, "Virgil's fictional Daphnis is not . . . a hero of pastoral withdrawal, but an inspirational leader who brings peace and harmony to the agricultural world."[9] This sounds as if Menalcas represents the dead Daphnis as doing, in his new form, what he did when alive—harnessing wild beasts, instituting Bacchic dances, and the like. But what is striking is that Daphnis does not appear as an active agent or even influence:

> *Candidus insuetum miratur limen Olympi*
> *sub pedibusque videt nubes et sidera Daphnis.*
> *ergo alacris silvas et cetera rura voluptas*
> *Panaque pastoresque tenet Dryadasque puellas.*
> *nec lupus insidias pecori, nec retia cervis*
> *ulla dolum meditantur: amat bonus otia Daphnis.*
> (5.56–61)

Radiant at heaven's unfamiliar gate,
Daphnis marvels at clouds and stars below.
At this, keen pleasure quickens woods and fields,
Pan and the shepherds and the Dryad maidens.
Wolves lay no ambush for the flocks, no nets
Wait to betray the deer: Daphnis loves peace.

From the initial scene of his wondering at the unaccustomed threshold of Olympus, rather like a shepherd awed by a new place, Daphnis is rather passive. The crucial phrase about him—which makes Brooks Otis say that "Daphnis, become immortal . . . *reverses* nature"[10]—is *amat bonus otia Daphnis,* good Daphnis loves peace. The suggestion, reinforced by the preceding *meditantur* (the verb Meliboeus used of Tityrus's music-making), is that *otia,* the benign peacefulness of the countryside, is not what Daphnis creates or empowers, but what he loves to contemplate, what he enjoys. The active energy in this scene of peace is the keen desire that seizes the shepherds and the woodland demigods. The active verbs in the following scene represent utterance and song:

9. Eleanor Winsor Leach, *Vergil's "Eclogues": Landscapes of Experience,* (Ithaca: Cornell University Press, 1974), 182.
10. *Virgil: A Study in Civilized Poetry* (Oxford: Clarendon Press, 1964), 140; emphasis mine.

> *ipsi laetitia voces ad sidera iactant*
> *intonsi montes; ipsae iam carmina rupes,*
> *ipsa sonant arbusta: "deus, deus ille, Menalca!"*
>
> (5.62–64)

> The shaggy mountains hurl their joyous cries
> Up to the stars; now rocky cliffs and trees
> Sing out, "A god! he is a god, Menalcas!"

As if empowered by this cry of joy, Menalcas represents the ceremonies and convivialities that will honor the new god. He promises annual commemorations, in which the presence the hero had when alive is reduced and displaced onto communal, seasonal rites. The Bacchic dances Daphnis established (30–31) recur as pastoral song and dance:

> *cantabunt mihi Damoetas et Lyctius Aegon;*
> *saltantis Satyros imitabitur Alphesiboeus.*
>
> (5.72–73)

> Damoetas and Cretan Aegon will sing to me,
> Alphesiboeus mimic the leaping fauns.

The afterlife Menalcas envisages for these celebrations is made good in responsive imitations like Milton's:

> Rough satyrs danced, and fauns with cloven heel,
> From the glad sound would not be absent long,
> And old Damaetas loved to hear our song.

The concluding pledge to Daphnis reflects the emphasis on ceremony and song:

> *dum iuga montis aper, fluvios dum piscis amabit,*
> *dumque thymo pascentur apes, dum rore cicadae,*
> *semper honos nomenque tuum laudesque manebunt.*
>
> (5.76–8)

> While boars love mountain ridges, fish the streams,
> Bees feed on thyme and grasshoppers on dew,
> Your honor, name, and praises will endure.

The difference between these lines and Mopsus's priamel reflects the difference between the two songs. Daphnis is not separate, as he was in the phrase *tu decus omne tuis:* his honor and praises are absorbed into the natural preferences and habitats which represent their continuance. Similarly, the speaker is absorbed into the representation of external processes: what looks like a pledge, for which the appropriate verb would be in the first person, is here conveyed by the third person future, *manebunt*. Finally, this list has no specific Theocritean antecedent. It presents itself as conventional simply in the sense of being the accepted practice of a given world. In its freedom from the self-consciousness of Mopsus's song, it bears witness to Menalcas's sense of the stability of the shepherds' world. Nevertheless, the priamel cannot be thought to be free of the conditions of conventional song in the sense we have defined it. However much it elides the fictional and textual separations relevant to it, it is emphatically a rhetorical performance, an instance of poetic practice. Even when it suggests heroic dimensions, what remains of Daphnis is not represented action or presence, but precisely what is due to human utterance—honor and praise.

Menalcas's song continues the work of Mopsus's and exemplifies the form the pastoral community takes in the absence of the hero. Just as it begins as a response to Mopsus's song, so its conclusion shows how thoroughly it is grounded in pastoral convening. Menalcas's last words—*damnabis tu quoque votis*, referring to the obligation to give in return when one is favored by a god[11]— are transformed by Mopsus's response into a similar obligation between singers. Mopsus responds to Menalcas's song by saying *Quae tibi, quae tali reddam pro carmine dona?* (81, "What can I give to you in return for such a song?")—where *reddo*, "give in return," is the word used earlier for offering vows to the nymphs (75). We might say that Mopsus is obliquely returning Menalcas's praise of him (45–49), in effect calling him *divine poeta* and a surrogate for Daphnis. But any such implications are colored by, indeed subject to, the conditions of pastoral convention. Mopsus's question returns us to the world of pastoral rivalry and exchange, and of occasion and variety in song and nature. The gifts exchanged at the end of the poem are attractively problematic symbols: the frail reed, which represents the power of song, and the artfully decorated crook, which represents pastoral work (85–90). In diminishing representational fullness and foregrounding poetic performance and practice, the poem shifts its emphasis from the hero himself to his commemoration by ordinary humans. It is in this that the poem is a *pastoral* elegy. The ending of Eclogue 5, with its recollections of Theocritean language and practice, shows that continuity is conceived in terms of the conventions that ensure repetition and that constitute the world of pastoral song.

Though the pastoral elegy is a special kind, we can use it to define pastoral convention, because death is the ultimate form of the separations and losses that pervade pastoral poetry. The most common repository of these motifs is the love complaint, which in the Renaissance was often modelled on Virgil's

---

11. In his edition of the *Eclogues* (Cambridge: Cambridge University Press, 1977), Robert Coleman translates the phrase, "you too will hold them to their vows," and explains: "the petitioner made his vow to the god; if the petition was granted, then the god obliged him to keep the vow."

tenth Eclogue—itself an imitation of Theocritus's pastoral elegy for Daphnis, but with a metaphoric dying of love substituted for the putatively real death in its model. Separation and loss are also central in pastoral representations of social injustice, like the dispossessed homesteaders of Virgil's first and ninth Eclogues; in ecclesiastical satire, in which there is a direct or implicit appeal to the Gospels and the primitive church; and in gestures like Marvell's invoking Eden and the Fall at crucial moments in "The Garden" and "Upon Appleton House." The usual ideas of nostalgia and idyllic retreat wrongly construe the way pastoral deals with such themes, but there is no doubt that from its beginning, the form has been concerned with various human separations and their implications. Theocritus, like all his Alexandrian contemporaries, was aware of a cultural distance from the Greek city-state and its major literary forms, epic and tragedy. His first Idyll, the inaugural poem of Western pastoral, registers this awareness in both its main parts—the description of a decorated cup, a conscious reduction of Homer's description of the Shield of Achilles, and the song which bids farewell to the heroic herdsman Daphnis.

It is no mistake that Idyll 1 is a pastoral elegy. But the poem's character shows how differently pastoral deals with its human situations than the Schillerian model suggests. The cup and its description are diminished versions of their Homeric forebears, but the description is a virtuoso performance on Theocritus's part, and the cup itself is represented as prized and admired, "a wonder fit for goatherd's eyes." The song of Daphnis is represented as a famous set piece, the finest thing in the repertory of Thyrsis its singer; the pleasure it gives is represented by the cup for which it is exchanged. Pastoral songs and representations are conceived as dealing with, not avoiding or retreating from, present situations and occasions. Like the left-wing Protestants he represents, Spenser's "Puritan" shepherd gives an account of the primitive church in order to criticize present practices; he begins not nostalgically but with "The time was once, and may againe retorne" (*SC* "May," 103). With pastoral poise, Marvell leaves open the sense in which Appleton House is "Paradise's only map" (st. 96). The song of Frost's ovenbird does not cease in midsummer, because, like its creator's verse, it "knows in singing not to sing," and it sustains us precisely by asking "what to make of a diminished thing." Pastoral elegy plays out the motives of the whole mode by directly engaging the question of how a world continues after a loss or separation. And pastoral elegy is characteristic also in representing song and its associated practices as the means by which the world of shepherds—whatever or whomever, in any given case, they represent—sustains itself. Hence pastoral elegies, from Theocritus's lament for Daphnis to Virgil's fifth Eclogue to the November eclogue of *The Shepheardes Calender* are performed songs. They include expressions of grief, but they are not represented as spontaneous or dramatic utterances at the moment or the scene of death, or even (as opposed to other funeral poems) at the moment of burial. *Lycidas*, which explores and sums up the whole genre, can be seen as turning the direct experience of loss—"Bitter constraint and sad occasion dear"—into the performance of a pastoral elegy. Its general intent, to speak for its fellow mourners, and its calling up of pastoral usages and voices test and fulfill the idea of pastoral convention.

A convention is a usage that brings human beings together; a pastoral convention brings them together under the figure of shepherds. When shepherds and their lives are taken to be representative, literary conventions take on a certain character, which historically is due to Virgil's transformation of Theocritean bucolic and which can be specified theoretically in modal terms. The literary conception of the shepherd's strength relative to his world explains why pastoral is so "conventional" a form: as opposed to epic and tragedy, with their ideas of heroic autonomy and isolation, it takes human life to be inherently a matter of common plights and common pleasures. Pastoral poetry represents these plights and these pleasures as shared and accepted, but it avoids naiveté and sentimentality because its usages retain an awareness of their conditions— the limitations that are seen to define, in the literal sense, any life, and their intensification in situations of separation and loss that can and must be dealt with, but are not to be denied or overcome.

II

Lycidas is the last great example of the traditional pastoral elegy, and ever since Johnson's assault it has occasioned anxieties and misconceptions about pastoral convention.[12] To say, as critics frequently do, that the poem exposes the inadequacies of pastoral conventions assumes that Johnson was right about the conventions, even if wrong about the poem. *Lycidas* does indeed subject the conventions of pastoral elegy to a searching critique, but it is in the interest of sustaining their uses and intent—bringing shepherds together for commemorative song that will sustain the community or world which has felt the grievous loss of one of its members. But in one respect, crucial it would seem to our whole account, the poem differs from its predecessors: there is no represented gathering of shepherds to lament their dead fellow. This makes the poem less predictable and rule-governed than earlier pastoral elegies, but the effect is to enhance the depth and energy with which it reveals the significance of their conventions. The convening that underlies them is implicit in the fact that it

---

12. The account of *Lycidas* that follows adapts the interpretation presented in my article, "*Lycidas* and Modern Criticism," *ELH* 49 (1982): 468–96. This article has a more polemical edge and a somewhat different conceptual frame. It treats some details of the poem more fully and the issues of interpreting it more broadly than I do here; in particular, it confronts the challenging reading of Stanley Fish, "*Lycidas*: A Poem Finally Anonymous," *Glyph* 8 (1981): 1–18; reprinted in Patrides (above, n. 1), 319–40.

was first published in a volume of memorial poems written by Edward King's contemporaries at Cambridge.[13] The force of *Lycidas*, which is the concluding poem of this volume and its only pastoral elegy, is that the poets and readers of such a collection are metaphorically brought together as shepherds. In this way it "makes new," in Pound's phrase, the poetical kind whose history it sums up. Like Marvell's pastoral lyrics (roughly contemporary with it), it stands at the end of a generic practice which it is in a position to understand deeply and, in some ways, to exhaust.[14]

The ordinary reader's sense of *Lycidas* is well stated by Isabel MacCaffrey:

> Many readers have observed . . . that *Lycidas* is only intermittently "pastoral"; the bucolic tone and rural setting are repeatedly left behind as new ranges of awareness open in the speaker's memory and imagination. This alternation of tones and landscapes reflects the two worlds of the poem: of innocence and of experience. The second invades the first, with effects of violation and distress, both emotional and aesthetic, that have caused commentators to speak of "digressions." . . . The speeches of Phoebus and St. Peter . . . [are followed by] returns in space to the pastoral landscape where fountains, rivers, and Muses mourn the dead shepherd, offering consolation which becomes more poignant but less satisfying as the poem develops.[15]

This sense of shifts in the poem and strong, even disruptive, interventions is of course right. What is mistaken is to identify as pastoral only what is innocent and cannot stand up to experience. For MacCaffrey, pastoral is the landscape of the Schillerian idyll, whereas for Milton it consisted of a much wider repertory of poetic representations, including two which provide the interventions thought to violate the pastoralism of the poem. The source of Phoebus's intervention is a moment at the beginning of Virgil's sixth Eclogue, when Phoebus checks the rising ambition of the shepherd-poet by plucking his ear (6.3–5). St. Peter's speech is based on the parable of the good shepherd and is in a vein of satiric harshness that was domesticated in English pastoral by Spenser's imi-

---

13. *Justa Edovardo King* (Cambridge, 1638) contains 36 elegies, 20 in Latin, 3 in Greek, and 13 in English; the latter have a separate title page, *Obsequies to the memorie of Mr. Edward King.* A revised and corrected version was published in *Poems of Mr. John Milton* (London, 1645), in which was added the headnote that now routinely appears with the poem. 1645 is the basis of John Carey's text, in the Longman *Poems of John Milton.* There is also a manuscript of *Lycidas* (dated November 1637) in Trinity College, Cambridge.

14. See my article "Convening and Convention in Pastoral Poetry," *New Literary History* 14 (1982– 83): 277–78, 287–97, for an account of the way Marvell's "Damon the Mower" engages poet and reader in the convening implicit in pastoral conventions.

15. "*Lycidas:* The Poet in a Landscape," in *The Lyric and Dramatic Milton: Selected Papers from the English Institute,* ed. Joseph H. Summers (New York: Columbia University Press, 1965), 71–72; in Patrides, 250–51.

tations of Mantuan in *The Shepheardes Calender*. It will be less surprising to think of these passages as pastoral, if we think of pastoral in terms of voice, dialogue, and representative roles. Nevertheless, no mere shift of paradigm can deny the effect of these speeches. Any account of their place in the poem must stay in touch with the fact that they do not feel conventional in the sense established by Virgil's fifth Eclogue.

If accepting established roles is one thing that makes poems conventional, then one reason *Lycidas* seems to challenge its conventions is that the speaker does not appear at first in the character of a shepherd.[16] The title leads us to expect an eclogue, but the opening words seem to be spoken by the poet himself. Even though they use pastoral imagery and two Virgilian locutions, "yet once more" seems meaningless unless we take them this way, and the suggestion is confirmed by the headnote added in 1645: "In this monody, the author bewails a learned friend." When the speaker says, of the dead youth,

> He must not float upon his watery bier
> Unwept, and welter to the parching wind,
> Without the meed of some melodious tear,
>
> (12–14)

he sounds like the other poets in the memorial volume to Edward King. Like them, he dwells on the manner of King's death and the way it frustrates proper burial and mourning. The phrase "melodious tear" is a characteristic conceit, playing on the fact that funeral elegies were often called *Lachrymae* or "Tears." It takes twenty lines for the pastoralism of the poem fully to emerge:

> For we were nursed upon the self-same hill,
> Fed the same flock; by fountain, shade, and rill.
>   Together both, ere the high lawns appeared
> Under the opening eye-lids of the morn,
> We drove a-field, and both together heard
> What time the grey-fly winds her sultry horn,
> Battening our flocks with the fresh dews of night,
> Oft till the star that rose, at evening, bright,
> Toward heaven's descent had sloped his westering wheel.
> Meanwhile the rural ditties were not mute,
> Tempered to the oaten flute,
> Rough satyrs danced, and fauns with cloven heel,
> From the glad sound would not be absent long,
> And old Damaetas loved to hear our song.
>
> (23–36)

16. This point has been made by MacCaffrey (Patrides, 248) and by Robert Martin Adams, "Bounding 'Lycidas,'" *Hudson Review* 23 (1970): 299.

This remembered scene satisfies both Johnsonian and Schillerian accounts of pastoral. It is a tissue of Virgilian phrases; at the same time it has an air of idyllic innocence, because individual identity is submerged in the plural pronouns and in the sights, atmosphere, and sounds of nature. But in the midst of all the pastoral details, we still miss the single thing we most expect to find in an eclogue, a shepherd-singer. The passage is full of sounds, but the human figures are represented as listening to them: "both together heard" the grey-fly; "old Damaetas loved to hear our song"; "Meanwhile the rural ditties were not mute"—no doubt sung by shepherds, but the locution suggests that they simply occur, like the sounds of nature.

The shepherd who is the singer of this poem finally emerges as a new verse paragraph begins:

> But O the heavy change, now thou art gone,
> Now thou art gone, and never must return!

The pronoun "we" has been divided into "thou" and the "I" implicit in this strongly vocalized utterance. Separation and loss give the speaker his voice and establish the conventional role the title of the poem leads us to expect. It is in this passage that we first encounter some of the familiar topoi of the pastoral elegy—the landscape and its echoes mourning the dead shepherd, the landscape devastated by his loss, and the serial listing conveying the dead shepherd's worth by analogies from nature. It is by this long and oblique process (a matter of some fifty lines) that *Lycidas* arrives at the question which usually occurs at or near the beginning of a pastoral lament: "Where were ye nymphs when the remorseless deep/Closed o'er the head of your loved Lycidas?" [17]

Pastoral conventions in Virgil's elegy for Daphnis manifest the loss of the hero to the shepherds' world, but they remain the represented social and poetic practices of that world. In *Lycidas* the speaker's role and the conventions of pastoral elegy emerge at the moment when the death of Lycidas casts in the past the world in which shepherds sang together. This decisive turn would seem to confirm the usual accounts of the poem, for what place is left for pastoral conventions—or rather, how can they remain "conventional"—when no fictional shepherds come together for song? Whether or not "old Damaetas," as once was thought, represents a college tutor, the benign and protected world in which he "loved to hear our song" fittingly represents a time of youth, when Milton and Edward King were students at Cambridge. Once the poem undergoes its "heavy change," its putative world becomes contemporary and dangerous. Yet there is a sense in which its practices maintain its pastoralism. The

17. Lines 50–51. For the usual placement of the invocation to the nymphs, see Theocritus, Idyll 1.66–69 (the lament for Daphnis is the second half of the poem), and Virgil's imitation, Eclogue 10.9–12.

topoi which register the loss of the pastoral world envisage readers who are connected by their knowledge of poems and traditions which, in the case of this poem, they once studied in each other's company. They have now metaphorically come together again, by collecting in a volume the poems in which they lament their fellow student. In substituting shared literary usage for the represented pastoral world, *Lycidas* seals the endeavor of the book which it concludes.

This is not at all to deny the questionings and instabilities of the poem. The situation of a memorial volume in a world of hostile natural and social forces suggests precisely the problems on which the poem dwells:

> Alas! What boots it with uncessant care
> To tend the homely slighted shepherd's trade,
> And strictly meditate the thankless muse?
>
> (64–66)

In one sense, these are obviously pastoral questions, because they concern the power of song and the roles represented by the figure of the shepherd. But what has usually not been recognized is that the poem's acts of questioning are themselves pastoral. They do not occur because a merely naive and innocent consciousness is invaded by sterner realities to which it is inherently inadequate. Rather, they arise from the internal workings of usages and conventions whose "strength relative to world" is indeed at issue in the poem but is finally confirmed by it.

Thus the first "shock of recognition" is produced by a close imitation of a classical prototype:

> Where were ye nymphs when the remorseless deep
> Closed o'er the head of your loved Lycidas?
> For neither were ye playing on the steep,
> Where your old bards, the famous Druids, lie,
> Nor on the shaggy top of Mona high,
> Nor yet where Deva spreads her wizard stream:
> Ay me, I fondly dream!
> Had ye been there—for what could that have done?
>
> (50–57)

By way of imitating the geographical questions addressed to the nymphs by Theocritus's and Virgil's speakers, Milton's swain depicts the Welsh landscape near which Edward King drowned in terms which make it eligible to be the scene of a native and post-classical pastoral. His representation of a rugged landscape ("the shaggy top of Mona high"), which also engages the powers of ancient poet-priests ("your old bards, the famous Druids"), reaches a climax and an impasse in the line on the River Dee, where the adjective "wizard" recalls the powers of divination attributed to the river, personifies them (so as to suggest the powers of a bard in touch with nature), and makes them suspect by associations with superstition and witchcraft.[18] "Ay me, I fondly dream," then, is a self-correction, due to the speaker's grasping where his imaginings have led him.

It is surely significant that such self-correcting turns occur in Virgil's Eclogues.[19] But where the Virgilian turns occur in the impassioned speeches of lovers separated from their fellows, Milton adapts the device to a topos that is more stable and "public." He thus indicates the particular pressures which *Lycidas* puts on pastoral convention. Because the literary usages of the poem are not attributed to a fictional world and its roles, there is an unusual emphasis on the speaker's vocal and imaginative energies. The first topos distinctly belonging to pastoral elegy shows the shift from represented world to voice:

> Thee shepherd, thee the woods, and desert caves,
> With wild thyme and the gadding vine o'ergrown,
> And all their echoes mourn.
>
> (39–41)

In most pastoral elegies, there is a rather full detailing of the way birds and beasts, fountains and streams, trees and mountains lament the dead shepherd, often with natural sounds. Milton reduces the scene and makes the only source of sound the human voice. Though the woods and desert caves are subjects of the verb "mourn," the intervening line about the thyme and gadding vine makes them a perceived scene and throws all the emphasis onto the echoes as the agent in the sentence. Since the scene contains no apparent sources of sound, we refer these echoes to the sound we are actually hearing—the speaker's voice addressing the dead shepherd and producing its own echoes in doing so: "O the heavy change, now thou art gone,/Now thou art gone," the internal half-rhyme of "thyme" and "vine," and "Thee shepherd, thee."

The shift from the lost world, where all sounds are heard, to the landscape filled with the sound of the speaker's voice establishes a tension in *Lycidas* between individual utterance and voices heard. In earlier pastorals, the relation between what is uttered and what is heard is stable and in all senses conventional. It is most secure and reliable in singing contests, but even when free from the set rules of these exchanges, the speeches in pastoral dialogues often

18. On the River Dee's powers of divination, see *A Variorum Commentary on the Poems of John Milton*, vol. 2: *The Minor English Poems*, ed. A. S. P. Woodhouse and Douglas Bush (New York: Columbia University Press, 1972), ad loc., citing Camden's *Britain* and Drayton, *Polyolbion* (10.186–218). Information not otherwise accounted for is to be found in this commentary.

19. One of them appears on the title page of the first edition (1637) of *Comus: Eheu quid volui misero mihi! floribus austrum/Perditus* (Alas, what have I wished on my wretched self! Desperate, [I have unleashed] the southwind on my flowers, Ecl. 2.58–59).

have the character of responsive set pieces. In Virgil, pastoral impersonation and responsiveness lead to harmony and interplay between voices in dialogue and the multiplication and re-hearing of voices in ostensible monodies. In *Lycidas*, where pastoral voices are detached from fictional speakers said to be gathered at a specified scene, the interconnections of monody and dialogue, utterance and listening, are less stable than in Virgil. The first notorious moment of instability occurs after the self-correction of "Ay me, I fondly dream!" and the imaginings it prompts of Orpheus and his fate:

> Alas! What boots it with uncessant care
> To tend the homely slighted shepherd's trade,
> And strictly meditate the thankless muse,
> Were it not better done as others use,
> To sport with Amaryllis in the shade,
> Or with the tangles of Neaera's hair?
> Fame is the spur that the clear spirit doth raise
> (That last infirmity of noble mind)
> To scorn delights, and live laborious days;
> But the fair guerdon when we hope to find,
> And think to burst out into sudden blaze,
> Comes the blind Fury with th' abhorred shears,
> And slits the thin-spun life. But not the praise,
> Phoebus replied, and touched my trembling ears.
> (64–77)

As in the earlier passage, it is the speaker's imagination that prompts the correcting awareness. Early in the passage, the meditation on the "homely slighted shepherd's trade" produces an answering voice, when the question about sporting with Amaryllis prompts the counter-assertion, "Fame is the spur that the clear spirit doth raise." These internal voices emerge from powerful identifications and engagements. The blind Fury's act completes a sentence which, in its building up, corresponds to the striving represented. The actions of voice and mind, culminating in the intensity of "And slits the thin-spun life," make "But not the praise" seem to come from within, from the speaker's internal contention with himself.[20]

As opposed to the self-correction of "Ay me, I fondly dream!" the speaker's yearnings, imaginings, and conflicts of attitude here produce a voice he can attribute to another speaker. It is that fact, not simply the Virgilian source, that shows the compatibility of Phoebus's intervention with the pastoral endeavors

---

20. Modern editors who enclose Phoebus's speech in quotation marks (unknown in Renaissance texts) destroy this effect. This passage shows the importance of the Longman editors' decision to reproduce the original punctuation of Milton's texts.

of the poem. The speaker's voicing of distress at the loss of Lycidas has led him to the first successful act of convening in the poem. It is true that Phoebus's speech is said to be of a "higher mood," but its main result, as of the god's intervention in Virgil, is to set the poem back on its pastoral course:

> O fountain Arethuse, and thou honoured flood,
> Smooth-sliding Mincius, crowned with vocal reeds,
> That strain I heard was of a higher mood:
> But now my oat proceeds,
> And listens to the herald of the sea.
>
> (85–89)

So completely has the speaker's voice, at this point, gone over into what he hears that we accept as a flat claim the statement that an oaten pipe listens. Rather than establishing a "higher mood' for the poem, Phoebus's voice motivates a convention of pastoral elegy that directly involves convening fictive speakers—the procession of mourners who come to speak to the dying shepherd or to sing at his tomb.

This is the opposite effect from that envisaged by views of the poem as a dramatic process in which pastoral innocence gives way to a fuller sense of reality. In the most intelligent of these accounts, appropriately entitled "The Swain's Paideia," Donald M. Friedman recognizes the difficulty here. Phoebus's speech, he says, "does not disturb the flow of pastoral conventions in the swain's repertory. . . . It is as if the swain [when he goes on to the procession of mourners] has forgotten that both the inquiry into causes and the notion of the protective muses have been discovered to be fond dreams"[21] But if the purpose of the poem is not psychological progress and ontological inquiry, but to "bewail a learned friend" (as the headnote says) and to "sing for Lycidas," then the procession of mourners does further its endeavor by bringing into it fictional speakers who can properly lament the dead youth and represent the significance of his death. This significance largely lies in the questions it raises. Nothing more strikingly shows that the conventions of pastoral enable their own questioning than the fact that the last of the speakers convened by this convention is "the pilot of the Galilean lake" (109). His accents are harsh, but they do not, as some critics say, break the frame of the poem, because one of the things the poem has done is reestablish the frame in which such a voice can be heard.

This argument may be accepted for the way St. Peter enters the poem, but it can hardly be thought to meet the usual account of his effect *on* it.[22] After his speech, the speaker recoils with the words, "Return Alpheus, the dread voice is past" (132), and proceeds to a lengthy catalogue of flowers that is usually

21. "*Lycidas*: The Swain's Paideia," *Milton Studies* 3 (1971): 13 (in Patrides, 289).
22. On St. Peter's speech itself, see chapter 4.

taken to represent the fragility and fallaciousness, however poignant, of pastoral and its conventions. This view seems abundantly confirmed by the lines that conclude the passage: "For so to interpose a little ease,/Let our frail thoughts dally with false surmise" (152–53). Once more, it seems, the pastoral speaker has caught himself up in imagining a vain thing.

Evident as it seems, this interpretation fails to account for the positive presence implied by the length of the flower passage and the fact, which we know from the Trinity manuscript, that Milton labored over and expanded it. Why should he as a writer or we as readers give so much attention to these lines if they are, as Friedman puts it, "a demonstration of the pastoral's commitment to a life of ease, disengagement, even immaturity and a denial of responsibility"?[23] Some of the reasons begin to appear if we read the passage for its rhetoric and not simply its imagery:

> Return Alpheus, the dread voice is past,
> That shrunk thy streams; return Sicilian muse,
> And call the vales, and bid them hither cast
> Their bells, and flowrets of a thousand hues.
> (132–35)

Though the opening lines register the felt vehemence of St. Peter's speech—as if all humans, good as well as bad, were threatened by the prophetic finality of "stands ready to smite once, and smite no more"—the speaker's responsiveness is greater, more capable of an answering utterance, than the vulnerable recoiling he attributes to Alpheus. Earlier, after Phoebus's speech, the address to Arethusa and Mincius led to a declarative mode, in which he spoke of his oat proceeding to listen. Here he recovers pastoral convening by his own vocatives. He addresses Alpheus in a tone poised between urgent request and friendly encouragement. There is a confidence, even a companionship, here which is confirmed and clarified in the next lines, when the speaker's request to the Sicilian muse turns, as he utters it ("bid them"), into his own command. He himself then addresses the vales, and the imperative in the next sentence is unequivocally his own:

> Ye valleys low where the mild whispers use,
> Of shades and wanton winds, and gushing brooks,
> On whose fresh lap the swart star sparely looks,
> Throw hither all your quaint enamelled eyes.
> (136–39)

This is the first command in the speaker's own voice since he addressed the Muses at the beginning of the poem ("Begin, and somewhat loudly sweep the

23. Friedman, 16 (in Patrides, 291).

string," 17). In itself it does not strike a newly authoritative note, but the next imperative shows what is emerging here:

> Throw hither all your quaint enamelled eyes,
> That on the green turf suck the honied showers,
> And purple all the ground with vernal flowers.
> Bring the rathe primrose that forsaken dies.
>
> (139–42)

The last imperative is sharply registered, particularly if we take "purple" in the preceding line as an indicative. The line is distinctive too for being the first in the passage to name a specific flower, and it inaugurates a list of six such lines which lead to the end of the passage. But what is most importantly new here is more oblique. Who is urged or commanded to bring the primrose and the other flowers? It is not a likely verb to address to the valleys, who were explicitly addressed and urged to "Throw hither all your quaint enamelled eyes." The command "Bring the rathe primrose" sounds as if it were spoken to human companions, as in Spenser's "April" eclogue: "Bring hether the Pincke and purple Cullambine,/With Gelliflowres," and so on (136ff.). The speaker's imperatives, which explicitly take the form of convenings ("Return," bid them hither cast," "throw hither," "bring") finally establish him in a role played by various of his predecessors in pastoral elegies—calling on companions to bring flowers to the tomb of the dead shepherd.

As at earlier moments in the poem, the speaker's openness and flexibility have led him not away from but rather to roles and conventions of pastoral elegies and other kinds of eclogue. His very ability to initiate new speech after St. Peter's "dread voice" can be referred to the dialogue form of ordinary eclogues, in which speeches of different character are assigned to different shepherds. On this model, the speaker's response to St. Peter can be imagined as somewhere between ordinary responsive song and the direct debates (e.g. about the value of love, characteristically between a harshly critical old shepherd and a vulnerable young one) that are an important Renaissance development of the Virgilian eclogue. But as we have been saying all along, *Lycidas* is an eclogue with a difference, and that difference is that its roles and conventions are not tied directly to a represented fictional world. In an ordinary eclogue, the catalogue of flowers would conclude in something like the following way:

> Bring the rathe primrose that forsaken dies,
> The tufted crow-toe, and pale jessamine,
> The white pink, and the pansy freaked with jet,
> The glowing violet,
> The musk-rose, and the well-attired woodbine,
> To strew the laureate hearse where Lycid lies.

In this form, in which four lines have been left out, the passage would resemble the lists of flowers that we find in Marot's pastoral elegy for the queen mother, Louise de Savoie, and Castiglione's for his young friend Matteo Falcone.[24] With the omitted lines restored, the passage goes:

> The musk-rose, and the well-attired woodbine,
> With cowslips wan that hang the pensive head,
> And every flower that sad embroidery wears:
> Bid amaranthus all his beauty shed,
> And daffadillies fill their cups with tears,
> To strew the laureate hearse where Lycid lies.
>   (146–51)

The first thing we notice is that the list of brief, descriptive phrases has given way to personifications. Each fills a line, and they provide the context of the final imperative: "Bid amaranthus all his beauty shed." This can scarcely be a literal command, on the order of "throw hither" or "bring." But it is made to seem quite natural, because the personifications prepare us to transfer the sense of urgency from the literal bringing of flowers to the significance of these flowers and the way they represent our mourning. This new mode of exhortation is powerful enough to make the real flower amaranthus—also known as "love-lies-ableeding" and mentioned in relevant contexts by Sannazaro, Castiglione, and Spenser—take on a suggestion of the imaginary flower which was long thought, because the name means "unfading," to adorn the blessed in heaven.[25]

By concluding the passage this way, Milton draws on a traditional equation of flowers and poems. This metaphor is old and widespread, but it has a particular place in the tradition of pastoral elegy. In *Astrophel*, Spenser introduces the series of elegies he and others wrote for Sidney, as

> dolefull layes vnto the time addrest.
> The which I here in order will rehearse,
> As fittest flowres to deck his mournfull hearse.[26]

In other pastoral elegies, the metaphor appears in the commemorative song itself, but what is striking is that it does not take the form of an actual list of flowers. The lament for Androgeo, in Sannazaro's *Arcadia*, simply mentions

24. Clement Marot, "Eglogue sur le Trespas de ma Dame Loyse de Savoye," 225–40; Baldassare Castiglione, "Alcon," 142–50. These poems and the elegies by Ronsard and Sannazaro discussed below are collected in T. P. Harrison, Jr., and H. J. Leon, eds., *The Pastoral Elegy* (Austin: University of Texas Press, 1939).

25. The *Variorum Commentary* discusses the two flowers and the claims of each to be recognized here. The earthly amaranthus is mentioned in Sannazaro, *Arcadia*, 11.38 (cf. *Pisc. Ecl.* 1.95); Castiglione, "Alcon," 149; Spenser, *Virgils Gnat*, 677 and *FQ* 3.6.45.

26. "The Lay of Clorinda," 106–8, in *Minor Poems*.

fresh garlands in a stanza that promises immortalization in verse.[27] Ronsard's elegy for Henri II ends with a resonant use of the image, but the flowers are metaphoric, not literally present:

> *nous ferons aux forests*
> *Apprendre tes honneurs, afin que ta louange,*
> *Redite tous les ans, par les ans ne se change,*
> *Plus forte que la mort, fleurissante en tout temps,*
> *Par ces grandes forests, comme fleurs au Printemps.*[28]

> We will make the woods know your honors, so that your
> praise, repeated every year, will not be changed by the
> years—more powerful than death, flowering at all times,
> in these great woods, like flowers in springtime.

On the other hand, in the pastoral elegies we have mentioned, in which lists like Milton's occur, the floral tributes are not associated with poetry and the powers claimed for it. Milton combines these two traditions. Only detailed listing could have the effect described by Rosemond Tuve: "[The flowers] are the precisest possible counterpart of the offered-up verses which men strew upon a laureate hearse; all alike mourn for the death of a part (as poet, an Orphean part) of that fabric to which all belong, and all alike, reaffirming life, make an answer to death's power."[29] But Tuve resists recognizing that these claims on behalf of nature entail the separateness and the powers of the poet. Only speakers can mourn, reaffirm, and "make an answer." Nature is present in this passage because of the voice that bids the muse, and that then assumes a ceremonial role established in earlier poems. The concluding personifications and the symbolizing force of "Bid amaranthus all his beauty shed" emphasize the powers of human poetizing, which are confirmed by calling Lycidas's a "laureate hearse." But as Sannazaro's and Ronsard's brief and metaphoric uses recognize, actual flowers can hardly sustain or represent the human powers that seem to be claimed—and precisely because of the natural loveliness and fragility that make them appropriate tributes and expressions of grief. This too *Lycidas* recognizes, particularly in the image of the "daffadillies," and sums up in the phrase "frail thoughts." And in this recognition, the poem follows yet another of its models, the November eclogue of *The Shepheardes Calender*, in which flowers are consistently images of mortality and human weakness.

---

27. "Ergasto sovra la Sepultura," *Arcadia* 5.53–65, in Iacopo Sannazaro, *Opere*, ed. Enrico Carrara (Turin: UTET, 1952).

28. *Oeuvres Complètes*, ed. Gustave Cohen (Paris: Pléiade edition, 1950), 1:930.

29. *Images and Themes in Five Poems by Milton* (Cambridge: Harvard University Press, 1957), 103; in Patrides, 197.

As with the invocation of the nymphs and the procession of mourners, so with the floral tributes: the conduct of the poem both establishes (or reestablishes) a convention and uses it in so full a way that it reaches its limits of expression and representation. Most of St. Peter's speech would not shrink any streams, in that it is evidently a version of pastoral. It is no shock to hear a faithless shepherd called a bad singer, and the most strident line, "Grate on their scrannel pipes of wretched straw," imitates a line in Virgil's consciously Theocritean Eclogue 3 (line 27). Moreover, the final prophetic outburst comes from full responsiveness to the "hungry sheep," to the imagery of "foul contagion," and to the depradations of "the grim wolf"—all well within the compass of pastoral representation. Similarly, Milton tests the adequacy of the flower catalogue by concentrating into it all that previous poets had brought to the convention—the listed floral tributes of Marot and Castiglione, the metaphors for poetry of Sannazaro and Ronsard, Spenser's sense of mortal loveliness. For this reason, the phrase "false surmise" has not only the weight of the genuinely problematic but implies a positive value, which we can appreciate when we go on to the passage that is usually thought to confirm its dismissal of ordinary pastoral:

> Ay me! Whilst thee the shores, and sounding seas
> Wash far away, where'er thy bones are hurled,
> Whether beyond the stormy Hebrides
> Where thou perhaps under the whelming tide
> Visit'st the bottom of the monstrous world;
> Or whether thou to our moist vows denied,
> Sleep'st by the fable of Bellerus old.
>
> (154–60)

For most critics, these lines represent brute actuality. MacCaffrey says the speaker "merely records the facts of Lycidas's condition as they assault the anguished imagination."[30] For M. H. Abrams, the passage renders "the horror of the actual condition of the lost and weltering corpse."[31] Friedman speaks of "the flow of intractable experience" and of the "unillusioned contemplation" of "the facts of King's death."[32] One understands the intent of such rhetoric, but what is actually said seems to me wholly wrong. The entire mode of this passage is one of imagination and surmise. Even its grammar is suspended—the uncertain scope and connection of "whilst" initiating what is the real "flow" of the passage, its speculative identifications. The intricate syntax and the delicate solicitude of a word like "perhaps" do not represent a mind assaulted or horror-

---

30. MacCaffrey, 85; in Patrides, 260.
31. "Five Types of *Lycidas*," in Patrides, 233.
32. Friedman, 17; in Patrides, 292–93.

stricken, and if being "unillusioned" is at issue, the most poignant detail in the passage—imagining that Lycidas *visits* the bottom of the monstrous world—is as deeply illusioned as anything in the poem. These lines prove what the flower passage seemed to disprove, the adequacy of poetic imagination. The answer to "false surmise" is not the truth *tout court*, but what poets have always claimed, "true surmise."

The true imaginings of this passage do not contradict or undermine the pastoralism of the poem. It is true that there is a certain demythologizing. Instead of attributing human feelings and powers to the mythical figures of nymphs, Druids, and the personified River Dee—and denying them to the impersonal "remorseless deep"—Milton locates them directly in the speaker and his alter ego, the dead Lycidas. But the imaginative endeavor of the earlier passage is not rejected but sustained—the solicitude for "thy loved Lycidas," the seeking of a companion in an alien landscape, the endowing of nature with human and particularly poetic associations and qualities. For this speaker— whose words imitate Sannazaro's lamenting fisherman, wondering in what region he should seek his drowned mistress[33]—this speaker has not lost his pas-

---

33. *Piscatory Eclogues* 1.69–76. G. W. Pigman denies that this passage is Milton's source, claiming that it is merely an instance of a widespread "whether . . . or" convention of cletic hymns, in which the speaker addresses a god wherever he dwells. Pigman relevantly cites *Paradise Lost* 1.10–13 and *Paradise Regained* 4.596–602. The fact that this is the passage that speaks of "moist vows" and that ends with "Look homeward angel" suggests that there is something to this point, though I think it overstates the case to say that "it is the very use of the convention which alerts the reader to Lycidas' apotheosis." Pigman goes on to say that not St. Michael but "the spirit of Lycidas is the angel." G. W. Pigman III, *Grief and English Renaissance Elegy* (Cambridge: Cambridge University Press, 1985), 118–19, 162–63.

Still, I have invoked Sannazaro to indicate the pastoral character of the speaker, and I leave it to the reader to decide whether the cited passage, which Milton certainly knew, has not contributed specifically to these lines in *Lycidas*:

> *Me miserum, qua te tandem regione requiram?*
> *Quave sequar? per te quondam mihi terra placebat,*
> *Et populi, laetaeque suis cum moenibus urbes:*
> *Nunc juvat immensi fines lustrare profundi,*
> *Perque procellosas errare licentius undas*
> *Tritonum immistum turbis, scopulosaque cete*
> *Inter, et informes horrenti corpore phocas,*
> *Quo numquam terras videam.*
>
> (*Pisc. Ecl.* 1.69–76)

Alas for me, in what region shall I now seek you out? Or where shall I follow you? Because of you the land once pleased me, and its peoples, and happy cities with their walls. Now my pleasure is to pace the boundaries of the vast deep, and to wander uncontrollably through stormy waves, mingling with crowds of Titans, among rock-like sea-monsters and hideous seals with shaggy bodies, where I shall never see land.

Jacopo Sannazaro, *Egloghe, elegie, odi, epigrammi*, ed. Giorgio Castello (Milan: Carlo Signorelli, 1928).

toral character. The phrases which most powerfully render the physical realities of Lycidas's death, "where'er thy bones are hurled" and "under the whelming tide," both derive their force from the speaker's sense of his own vulnerability. And Lycidas himself—like Virgil's Daphnis, wondering at the unaccustomed threshold of Olympus (Ecl. 5.56)—is imagined as a shepherd in an alien world: he *visits* the bottom of the monstrous world and *sleeps* by the fable of Bellerus old. Pastoral representations are at the heart of the poignancy, the awe, and the mysteriousness of this passage.

Moreover, the locution, "our moist vows," continues the work of convening fellow shepherds that was begun in the flower passage. The accepted gloss, "tearful prayers,"[34] is not adequate to this extraordinary phrase. A vow is different from a prayer: it is not a supplication, but a solemn engagement, with an implication, sometimes strong, of earnest desire. A prayer in this context could only be directed to the true deity. But vows can be directed to mortals—rulers, lovers, or friends—and the object of these "moist vows" is Lycidas himself. The importance of an utterance devoted to him is stated at the beginning of the poem:

> He must not float upon his watery bier
> Unwept, and welter to the parching wind,
> Without the meed of some melodious tear.
> (12–14)

The double meaning of "tear" ("tear" and "funeral poem") anticipates "moist vows," and the speaker goes on to wish

> So may some gentle muse
> With lucky words favour my destined urn
> (19–20),

where "lucky," with its sense of "well-omened," continues the atmosphere of weighty intentions. The mutual obligations of companions and fellow singers are the motivation of this poem, both internally and externally in the volume in which it appeared. "Moist vows" are therefore tearful utterances owed or dedicated to Lycidas, like the vows, *vota*, promised to Virgil's Daphnis and Sannazaro's Androgeo.[35] Furthermore, these are "*our* moist vows." This is only the third use of this pronoun since the passage about the shepherds' youth together, where the first-person pronominals were all "we" and "our." Between that passage and this phrase, there is first

---

34. This is the gloss given in the *Variorum Commentary* and in the editions of Carey and Merritt Y. Hughes.
35. Ecl. 5.79–80; *Arcadia* 5.55.

> But the fair guerdon when we hope to find,
> And think to burst out into sudden blaze
>
> (73–74)

where the "we" is gnomic, referring to all humans. Next is "Let *our* frail thoughts dally with false surmise," where there is a general sense—as if to say, all human thoughts are frail—but where one can imagine a more specific reference to the companions whom the speaker seems to have called upon to "bring the rathe primrose." Now there is no uncertainty in the reference. "Our moist vows" can only be those of Lycidas's companions, those who have made vows to him, who are singing for him, and whose vows are "moist" not only because they "weep for Lycidas," but also because they are imaginatively seeking him in the bosom of the deep.

This coming together in imaginative endeavor, in a situation of loss and separation, once more returns us to pastoral convention. We have been tracing two movements in the poem: the first is the use and, in a sense, exhaustion of certain conventions of pastoral elegy; the second is the calling up and hearing of certain pastoral voices. The poem comes to its conclusion by bringing these voices into the speaker's, in effect absorbing dialogue into monody, and by settling on a conventional ending, the apotheosis of the dead shepherd. The transition to this passage is the most condensed instance in the poem of the way imaginings lead to utterance—the interpenetration of pastoral representations and voices:

> Or whether thou to our moist vows denied,
> Sleep'st by the fable of Bellerus old,
> Where the great vision of the guarded mount
> Looks toward Namancos and Bayona's hold;
> Look homeward angel now, and melt with ruth.
> And, O ye dolphins, waft the hapless youth.
>   Weep no more, woeful shepherds weep no more,
> For Lycidas your sorrow is not dead.
>
> (159–66)

Though the body of Lycidas is "to our moist vows denied," it is imaginatively given a resting place in two locutions for places on the Cornish coast—Land's End ("the fable of Bellerus old," a phrase to which we shall return) and St. Michael's Mount, not named as such, but called "the great vision of the guarded mount." This phrase presumably refers to a vision of St. Michael which occurred on the promontory and which led to its being dedicated to him. But when the speaker says "Looks toward Namancos and Bayona's hold," "vision" becomes an action and the guarded mount becomes an agent. These grammatical and rhetorical shifts show how active the speaker is in these representations—how much, at this point, his locutions generate and direct the poem. "Looks," in turn, prompts the first word, as if he were responsive now to his own utterance, of his address to a newly constituted pastoral world—of protective deity, benign natural forces, and fellow shepherds:

> Look homeward angel now, and melt with ruth.
> And, O ye dolphins, waft the hapless youth.
> Weep no more, woeful shepherds weep no more.

The fusion here of beseeching, exhortation, and command makes grander and more intense the earlier blending of command, request, and encouragement in the address to Alpheus and the Sicilian muse. Without denying its human needs and identifications, the poet's voice assumes the strength hitherto associated with the voices of Phoebus and St. Peter. In the more tender urging of the dolphins, the speaker takes on the character of the sea deities who had earlier mourned Lycidas. All the voices of the poem are here drawn into the speaker's: dialogue has returned to monody. Now the poet can speak to his imagined companions as fellow shepherds and reveal to them the kind of knowledge earlier attributed to separate and not wholly human figures.

It has long been recognized that the passage which assures the shepherds that "Lycidas your sorrow is not dead" is conventional, but this has been taken in an invidious and mistaken sense. For it is not the fact, as is commonly thought, that the apotheosis of the dead shepherd is the usual or traditional ending of pastoral elegies.[36] In Virgil's fifth Eclogue, the apotheosis of Daphnis occurs in the middle, and Menalcas's song, which responds to Mopsus's lament, concerns the way the pastoral world will commemorate and honor the hero who has left it. This is the pattern that is followed in the pastoral elegies of Marot, Sannazaro, Castiglione, and Ronsard.[37] In all these poems, what is at issue is not the dead person's salvation, which is assumed, but the way he will continue to be a presence on earth and the way human life will sustain itself in his absence. The various rites of pastoral worship and commemoration are concerned with these issues. Strewing flowers on the grave is one of these rites, and one meaning of "false surmise" is that the catalogue of flowers is the wrong

---

36. The *Variorum Commentary* says that lines 165–85 "form the conclusion of the third movement, and of the monody proper, in a pattern set by Virgil, *E.* 5.56–80, and widely adopted by Christian elegists, namely, the apotheosis of the departed" (725). For reiterations of this misconception, see Clay Hunt, *"Lycidas" and the Italian Critics* (New Haven: Yale University Press, 1979), 144, and Renato Poggioli, *The Oaten Flute* (Cambridge: Harvard University Press, 1975), 21.

37. Spenser's ending SC "November" with the apotheosis is exceptional, and it is significant that this poem has a much looser relationship to Virgil's fifth Eclogue than *Lycidas* and the Continental elegies we have cited. Spenser may have meant the poem to be a revisionist version of the pastoral elegy, but he does not engage its conventions and their implications to anything like the degree Milton does.

way to conclude a pastoral elegy. By placing the apotheosis at the end of his pastoral elegy, Milton implicitly claims that its poetic representation is the true act of commemoration, the true way in which our knowledge of what we have lost can sustain our lives on earth. Milton "corrects" the pastoral elegy from within—not by going beyond its conventions or criticizing them *as* conventional, but by giving them what he conceived to be their true form.

The flowers are inadequate to proper commemoration because of what their earthly fragility suggests of the poetry they represent, but *not* because they represent human poetizing as such. Poetry, fictive making, is the grounds of this poem's vision of truth, and nowhere more strikingly than in the line that initiates the movement to the apotheosis: "Sleep'st by the fable of Bellerus old." Rather than frustrating or rebuking "our moist vows" (as we might expect from the earlier corrections and interventions), the line makes good all that the phrase conveys of the striving and solicitude at the heart of the making of the poem. "Sleep'st," like earlier details, imagines the vulnerability, the mere humanity of the shepherd. But the telling phrase is "the fable of Bellerus old." It is intensely textual, as we can see by asking either how one can sleep by a fable or how "the fable of Bellerus old" can refer, as it does, to Land's End, a real place. Moreover, the phrase is pure fiction: not even the fable is real, for Milton invented the name Bellerus from the Roman name for Land's End. Why should we believe or accept such a locution? What authority does it have? We can only say that it is authorized, in all senses, by what the poem has brought to its production here—the human obligations and imaginings registered in "our moist vows," the sense of traditional fictions conveyed by "old," and through these all that seemed earlier to be rejected, the nymphs and Druids, those "old bards," and other humanizers of nature. Most remarkable, in a way, is "fable." Coming from the same root as "fame," it retrieves some of its valuing of what humans say of each other, perhaps even gives a benign cast to "broad rumour." In this bizarre locution, the poem manifests and sustains its central purpose—to "sing for Lycidas," that is to find the proper commemorative song for a human world.

Hence human imaginings and representations are fulfilled, not superseded, by the turn to revealed truth in the apotheosis of the dead shepherd. Most critics simply treat this passage as the promised land, but Friedman rightly recognizes that it is not a redaction of the Book of Revelation: "It is important to notice that, as a part of the elegy, the description of heaven's 'other groves,' the 'blest Kingdoms meek of joy and love,' is no less an imaginative fiction than the fields that first appeared 'under the opening eyelids of the morn.'"[38] This observation is confirmed by the fact that when the speaker says, "Weep no more," he takes on an identifiable role in the pastoral elegy; by the gaudy diction of the sun simile (168–71), which draws attention to its own rhetoricity

38. Friedman, 22; in Patrides, 297–98.

as it elevates Lycidas to heaven; by the genuinely conventional phrase, "other groves and other streams";[39] and by the way "hears the unexpressive nuptial song" (vs. the prophet's "I heard" in Revelation) merges, in the climactic representation of heard song, the experience of the speaker and the companion whose singing was lost to him.

The grounding of the apotheosis in poetic convention and usage explains why the poem returns to the human world not simply in the coda about the "uncouth swain," but at the end of the song for Lycidas:

> There entertain him all the saints above,
> In solemn troops, and sweet societies
> That sing, and singing in their glory move,
> And wipe the tears for ever from his eyes.
> Now Lycidas the shepherds weep no more.
> (178–82)

The speaker's exhortation to his fellow shepherds to weep no more is fulfilled when he translates what Revelation promises—"God shall wipe away all tears from their eyes" (21.4)—into an action of Lycidas's fellows in heaven and then, remarkably, by his bringing it down to earth. What he apprehended imaginatively becomes not simply a counsel but a speech-act of comfort: "Now Lycidas the shepherds weep no more" in effect wipes the tears from the eyes of his companions on earth. Such power to comfort and assuage does not come solely from revealed truth, as the final lines make clear:

> Now Lycidas the shepherds weep no more;
> Henceforth thou art the genius of the shore,
> In thy large recompense, and shalt be good
> To all that wander in that perilous flood.
> (182–85)

The older commentators were troubled by the phrase, "genius of the shore." One objected that "the *Genius loci* can have no counterpart in modern religious

---

39. The *Variorum Commentary* cites several examples of the "other . . . other" figure, including instances in the pastoral elegies by Sannazaro and Ronsard, which we have discussed, and in William Drummond of Hawthornden's pastoral elegy for Prince Henry, "Tears on the Death of Moeliades" (1613). Wherever used, the "other . . . other" frame can emphasize likeness to or difference from earthly settings. For a double-edged Marvellian instance, in which registering difference leads to establishing pastoral presence, see "Upon the Hill and Grove at Bilbrough," 65–66.

David Quint argues that in Sannazaro the figure represents heaven as simply another pastoral bower and that the immortality of which his and Virgil's elegies speak is primarily that conferred by commemorative poetry itself: *Origin and Originality in Renaissance Literature* (New Haven: Yale University Press, 1983), 53–59. The representation of Lycidas's new home is not contained by the "other . . . other" frame, but Quint's account nevertheless suggests how much the afterlife of the shepherds mourned in pastoral elegies depends on human poetizing.

belief, being a product of that localizing tendency of Pagan theology which it was one special aim of Christianity to abolish."[40] Insofar as the concept can be squared with Christian belief, it is with the form most inimical to Milton. "It is pleasant to see," said an eighteenth-century editor, "how the most anti-papistical poets are inclined to canonize and then to invoke their friends as saints."[41] These are real objections, and the poem takes care of them only by the appeal to usage and the rhetorical shaping we have been tracing in it. There could be a full stop after "shore," but instead the speaker continues with the phrase, "in thy large recompense." The meaning now seems to be metaphorical: "Because of or in respect to your heavenly reward, you can be thought of as 'the genius of the shore.'" But the pagan term survives in a very precise way. "Thy large recompense" has a double meaning which beautifully encapsulates the point of these lines: it is Lycidas's reward in heaven, which, at the same time, is the compensation for his loss which he bestows on us. "Thy" is both the object and the agent of "large recompense." The second meaning, in which Lycidas compensates the shepherds, maintains the literal meaning of the pagan genius, the protective local deity. In using the term and keeping its meaning alive this way, Milton confirms his allegiance to Virgil and to the conventions of the pastoral elegy. In Eclogue 5, Daphnis becomes a local deity who will protect his former companions. Milton's phrase, "and shalt be good," directly renders Menalcas's cry to the newly deified Daphnis—*sis bonus o felixque tuis* (65)—and it can be understood only with reference to the suggestions of deity in "the genius of the shore." In this way, the poem fulfills the offices of poetry and of the pastoral elegy in particular. By giving assurance to "all that wander in that perilous flood," it sustains the human world, enabling it to continue both despite and in the light of what it has lost.

III

A literary convention, by definition, invites repeated use, though the repetitions can range from the routine ("conventional" in the invidious sense) to the individualized turns and reinventions of poems like *Lycidas* and *Upon Appleton House*. Any performance is inherently repeatable—Theocritus's goatherd, in Idyll 1, asks Thyrsis for his song of Daphnis, because it is already famous—and

---

40. C. S. Jerram, ed., *The Lycdas and Epitaphium Damonis of Milton* (London, 1874). This is the most important Victorian commentary.

41. Thomas Newton, in his edition of *Paradise Regained* and other poems (London, 1752). This and Jerram's comment, just cited, are quoted in Scott Elledge's edition of *Lycidas* (New York: Harper and Row, 1966), but not in the *Variorum Commentary*, which simply mentions them disapprovingly.

pastoral draws out this fact by associating performances with various ritual occasions for song. Nowhere are the motives of pastoral convention more strikingly evident than in the most remarkably ritualistic poem in English, the
double sestina, "Ye goatherd gods, that love the grassy mountains," in Sir Philip
Sidney's *Arcadia*. This poem is a lament by two shepherds for the departure from
Arcadia of their goddess-like beloved; it was originally conceived as the first of
a series of laments ("The Fourth Eclogues" of the *Old Arcadia*), which were
prompted, in part, by the apparent death of the Arcadian king. Despite this
staging, the poem has an ironic and critical relation to pastoral conventions,
just as *Astrophil and Stella* has to Petrarchan conventions. Its austerity, its crescendo of despair, its transformation of the setting recorded in its end words
into emblems of psychological distress, and its separation to the point of turning against the pastoral world make it clear why David Kalstone, its most patient and sensitive analyst, calls it "un-Arcadian" and concludes that it "must be
taken . . . as a criticism of the easy resolutions of Sannazaro's *Arcadia*."[42] Yet the
power that prompts Kalstone to his analysis and that was first recognized in a
famous passage in *Seven Types of Ambiguity* is due to a pastoral conception of the
poem's regularities of rhetoric and verse form.

We may begin by asking, why a *double* sestina? The obvious answer is that
it makes for a doubled expression of love woe or despair. This is what is suggested by Empson's account: "The poem beats, however rich its orchestration,
with a wailing and immovable monotony, for ever upon the same doors in
vain. . . . A whole succession of feelings about the local scenery, the whole way
in which it is taken for granted, has been enlisted into sorrow and beats as a
single passion of the mind."[43] Similarly, Kalstone says that Sannazaro, on whose
poem Sidney modelled his, "realized that the very form of the double sestina
could signify the unavoidable pains of love in the pastoral world";[44] like Empson he draws attention to the effect of the end-words and their continual recurrence. In this view, the double sestina is simply an augmentation of the normal
sestina—remarkable as a technical feat, but perfectly predictable, since repetition is of the essence of the basic form. Petrarch seems to have understood the
form this way. The one double sestina in the *Rime* concerns the absoluteness of
Laura's death, which has made impossible both the poet's ordinary experience
of love suffering and his capacity to nurture and record it in his verses. The
seventh stanza, which is crucial, because it initiates the second sestina, makes
explicit the relation between theme and form:

42. David Kalstone, *Sidney's Poetry: Contexts and Interpretations* (Cambridge: Harvard University Press,
1965), 83.
43. *Seven Types of Ambiguity*, 3d ed. (London: Chatto & Windus, 1963), 36, 38.
44. Kalstone, 76.

Nesun visse giamai più di me lieto,
nesun vive più tristo et giorni et notti,
et doppiando 'l dolor, doppia lo stile
che trae del cor sì lacrimose rime.
Vissi di speme, or vivo pur di pianto,
né contra Morte spero altro che morte.

(My emphasis)

No one ever lived more glad than I,
no one lives more sorrowful both day and night
or, sorrow doubling, redoubles his style
that draws from his heart such tearful rhymes.
I lived on hope, now I live only on weeping,
nor against Death do I hope for anything but death.[45]

But Sidney's poem is not just an augmented sestina. Unlike Petrarch's it has two speakers, and it is this which shows its pastoral ancestry and nature. The formal innovation is due to Sannazaro. The double sestina in his *Arcadia* is a conspicuous imitation of Petrarch's—not only in the form itself, but also in its representation of love experience, in its imagery, and in some shared end-words. At the same time, Sannazaro gives it a full pastoral staging. Each section of the *Arcadia* consists of a prose narration or set piece which introduces or motivates a poem. These introductions are essentially prose pastiches of classical verse, including, of course, passages from eclogues. In this case, the gathered shepherds wish to hear Logisto and Elpino compete in song, and the two shepherds are described in words taken directly from the opening passage of Virgil's Eclogue 7.[46] This imitation and the call for competitive singing set these two lovers apart from the solo singer of the preceding poem, a Petrarchan canzone adapted to Arcadian modes.

Sannazaro's double sestina does not initially fulfill the expectations aroused by its staging, for it proves not to be a singing contest. Though the singers alternate verses, the effect at first is a cumulative detailing of the Petrarchan lover's experience. But in the middle of the poem, where the second sestina begins, the speakers begin to respond to each other, with two views of love, one hopeful, one despairing. Kalstone, thinking of the poem as a doubled ex-

---

45. *Rime* 332.37–42. Text and translation from Robert M. Durling, trans. and ed., *Petrarch's Lyric Poems* (Cambridge: Harvard University Press, 1976).

46. "Pastori belli de la persona, e di età giovenissimi: Elpino di capre, Logisto di lanate pecore guardatore; ambiduo coi capelli biondi più che le mature spiche, ambiduo di Arcadia, et egualmente a cantare et a rispondere apparecchiati" (Prosa 4, ed. Carrara, 80). (Shepherds lovely of body and in age at the height of youth: Elpino a keeper of goats, Logisto of woolly sheep, both with hair more yellow than ripe ears of grain, both Arcadians, and equally ready to sing and to respond.) Cf. Virgil, Ecl. 7.1–5, quoted above.

pression of the isolated lover's inner experience, rightly finds this development unmotivated psychologically. It is, however, formally and modally motivated. Where the doubleness represents two figures, *Arcades ambo*, who have come together to sing, the poem as a whole can balance alternative perspectives on the world and the experience they share. The poem thus sums up one main endeavor of Sannazaro's *Arcadia*—to mitigate the isolation and extremity of the Petrarchan love experience by various rituals, most of them rituals of song, that make love and its sufferings appear a shared experience, less singular than the sufferer feels, and susceptible of alleviation by narration to a fellow or by song and measured utterance.

If these are the motives and effects of Sannazaro's poem, then it seems all the more appropriate to view Sidney's double sestina, with its crescendo of isolating despair, as un-Arcadian. Though the two speakers are different in character, Strephon being the more vulnerably innocent and Klaius loftier in intellect and temperament, these differences are not strongly registered in the poem itself.[47] The fact that Strephon sings first and Klaius overgoes him is consistent with their characters, but as the poem moves to its climax Strephon increasingly takes his cue from the point reached by Klaius, so that the effect is more of steady building than of alternation. Our attention is so unremittingly on the distress of the isolated lover, the pronominals "I" and "my" so dominate the poem, that one readily imagines it as a solo utterance, whatever the official designation of speakers.

Yet the climactic effect of the poem is a pastoral one, and it is due to the fact that there are two speakers.[48] The first four pairs of stanzas proceed according to the rules which we see exemplified in the last of them:

47. Sidney made the differences between the two explicit when he revised the *Arcadia*. See "A shepherd's tale no height of style requires" (33–38), an unfinished narrative poem that tells how they fell in love with Urania, in *The Poems of Sir Philip Sidney*, ed. William A. Ringler, Jr. (Oxford: Clarendon Press, 1962), 243. Hereafter cited as *Poems*. Similarly, in the revised *Arcadia*, Kalander speaks of the two, but "especially Claius," as learned shepherds. See *The Countess of Pembroke's Arcadia (The New Arcadia)*, ed. Victor Skretkowicz (Oxford: Clarendon Press, 1987), 24. Hereafter cited as *NA*.

48. In the sentence which introduces the poem in the *Old Arcadia*, they are said to utter their complaint "eclogue-wise." *The Countess of Pembroke's Arcadia (The Old Arcadia)*, ed. Jean Robertson (Oxford: Clarendon Press, 1973), 328. Hereafter cited as *OA*. I cite Robertson's text of the poem, which is a modernized version of that found in *Poems*, ed. Ringler.

The later textual history of the poem shows the possibility of imagining its two speakers as one. In the first edition of the revised *Arcadia*, published posthumously in 1590, it appears in the First Eclogues and, in the absence of Strephon and Klaius themselves, is performed by one singer. See *NA*, 486. In the enlarged edition of 1593, which the Countess of Pembroke put together, it appears in the Second Eclogues and is performed by two other shepherds. 1593, which is fuller but has less authority than 1590, is the basis of the most available modern edition, *The Countess of Pembroke's Arcadia*, ed. Maurice Evans (Harmondsworth: Penguin, 1977). "Ye goat-herd gods" is on pp. 413–15; it can also be found in various anthologies.

> Strephon. Meseems I see the high and stately mountains
>   Transform themselves to low dejected valleys.
>   Meseems I hear in these ill-changed forests
>   The nightingales do learn of owls their music.
>   Meseems I feel the comfort of the morning
>   Turned to the mortal serene of an evening.
>   Klaius. Meseems I see a filthy cloudy evening
>   As soon as sun begins to climb the mountains.
>   Meseems I feel a noisome scent the morning
>   When I do smell the flowers of these valleys.
>   Meseems I hear (when I do hear sweet music)
>   The dreadful cries of murdered men in forests.

Not only does Klaius repeat Strephon's opening words; the rest of his stanza responds closely to his fellow's locutions and images. This responsiveness is characteristic of the poem to this point, as is the augmentation felt in Klaius's more energetic syntax and his more active representation of his perceptions: where Strephon perceives a world already distorted, Klaius seems actively to distort his. These stanzas, the last thoroughly regular ones in the poem, are the first two of the second sestina. Sidney displaces the turning point of the poem from the formal center to the next, and penultimate, pair of stanzas:

> Strephon. I wish to fire the trees of all these forests;
>   I give the sun a last farewell each evening;
>   I curse the fiddling finders-out of music;
>   With envy I do hate the lofty mountains,
>   And with despite despise the humble valleys;
>   I do detest night, evening, day, and morning.
>   Klaius. Curse to myself my prayer is, the morning;
>   My fire is more than can be made with forests;
>   My state more base than are the basest valleys;
>   I wish no evenings more to see, each evening;
>   Shamed, I hate myself in sight of mountains,
>   And stop mine ears lest I grow mad with music.

There is a vehement rupture here: the rhythm and sentiment of Klaius's "Curse to myself" mark the first time he does not begin his stanza with the same words as Strephon. The responsive details ("fire," the delayed "I wish," "hate") are not enough to recover the earlier regularities of utterance. This effect is thematized in the two most powerful lines, which make harmonious sound distinctly more distressing than in the preceding stanzas: "I curse the fiddling finders-out of music" and "And stop mine ears lest I grow mad with music." Even when Klaius had claimed to hear "the dreadful cries of murdered men in forests," he knew the actual sounds were "sweet music." Now at the point where music itself di-

rectly conveys the extremities of anguish and distress, the responsive procedures of the poem start to disintegrate, and the poem itself seems to come to
an end. Strephon's final line—"I do detest night, evening, day, and morning"—
has the character of a final line, both in its summary effect (very different from
the last lines of his preceding stanzas) and in its suggestion of the listing of
terminal words that ends a sestina.[49] Hence Klaius, speaking from his own isolation and distress, begins his stanza by a dramatic inversion of Strephon's "I
curse, etc." and not by a formal repetition of Strephon's initial words. The ag-
gressions that Strephon turns outward, he directs against himself, until his final
line seems to take the poem to its limit—to burst the bounds of identity and
feeling, and hence of utterance.

And yet the poem does not end and does not burst its bounds. Instead it
makes an astonishing turn:

> Shamed, I hate myself in sight of mountains,
> And stop mine ears lest I grow mad with music.
> *Strephon.* For she, whose parts maintained a perfect music,
> Whose beauties shined more than the blushing morning,
> Who much did pass in state the stately mountains,
> In straightness passed the cedars of the forests,
> Hath cast me, wretch, into eternal evening,
> By taking her two suns from these dark valleys.

At just the point at which music seems utterly discomposed, the line "For she
whose parts maintained a perfect music" enacts its image and maintains the
formalized and harmonious utterance that seemed to be destroyed. It makes
good the formal requirement that the poem continue, for its completion,
through two more stanzas, and it shows why two speakers are necessary to
make such programmatic formalities adequate to the love experience represented. No single lyric speaker (not even the Donne of "A Nocturnal Upon
St. Lucy's Day") could move directly from the liminal distractedness of "And
stop mine ears lest I grow mad with music" to the grand affirmation of this line.
The very first word, "For," conveys a sense of consequence and coherence that
is breathtaking in context. Its promise is fulfilled as the first line initiates a sentence that, for the first time in the poem, is sustained for the length of the entire
stanza. The sustaining of formal order brings with it a restoration of the pastoral landscape: the mountains, valleys, and forests, the morning and evening
that bound the shepherds' world are no longer, in Empson's phrase, doors upon
which the singers beat in vain, but become, in this final exchange, measures of
value. Klaius's response maintains the music of the poem by once more beginning, as it should, with Strephon's initiating words:

49. This line internally contains one of the terminal words, "evening," so it could in fact be used
in the required three-line ending.

> For she, with whom compared the Alps are valleys,
> She, whose least word brings from the spheres their music,
> At whose approach the sun rase in the evening,
> Who, where she went, bare in her forehead morning,
> Is gone, is gone from these our spoiled forests,
> Turning to deserts our best pastured mountains.

The sentence that sustains this stanza exactly corresponds to the one that prompts it—subject in the first line, followed by two subordinate clauses, with the main verb in the fifth line, followed by a participial phrase in the last. The image of the lady as the sun is more central and affirmative than in Strephon's stanza, where it still expresses personal loss. Even the final images keep their attention on Urania's worth. It is her departure, like that of Astraea in older pastoral myth, that spoils (both ruins and robs) the forests, whereas earlier in the poem it was the lovers' projected anguish. The different tone of these lines is due not simply to this explicit claim—most firmly conveyed by the "best pastured mountains," which remain in place as a liminal image, measuring her worth—but also to the emergence, for the first time, of the first-person plural pronoun. By speaking of "our spoiled forests" and "our best pastured mountains," Klaius represents his situation as a shared plight: the phrase suggests not only his fellowship in love with Strephon, but what belongs to the shepherds' world. This simple pronominal affirms what is implicit in the responsive form of the double sestina and enables the poem to conclude by representing song as the means by which loss is sustained and the shepherds' world defined:

> These mountains witness shall, so shall these valleys,
> These forests eke, made wretched by our music,
> Our morning hymn this is, and song at evening.

These lines, spoken together,[50] stabilize the shepherds' loss by representing its utterance as ritual expression. The one detail that registers the distress at the heart of the poem—"made wretched by our music"—recapitulates the ambiguities of the pastoral love lament. On the one hand, it is not inconsistent with earlier assertions that the lover's music is itself wretched: "fill the vales with cries instead of music," "my deadly swannish music," "my strange exclaiming music," "the nightingales do learn of owls their music" (a detail from Theocritus's dying Daphnis, *Id.* 1.136). At the same time, the line can equally mean that the harmony and power of their song, an expression of the loss of Urania such as we find in the last two stanzas, will leave the forests wretched. In this case, though

---

50. Skretkowicz (*NA*, 488) is the only editor to understand that when the manuscripts and the printed editions show the two shepherds' names together, one beneath the other, it means that they speak all three lines together. Other editors mistakenly attribute the first line to Strephon and the last two to Klaius.

there is no recovering Strephon's "I that was once esteemed for pleasant music," there is a sense in which the two together, sharing their loss, have restored Klaius's wonderful response to that line: "I that was once the music of these valleys." It is this sense of love lament with which the poem closes, as "hymn" and "song" dominate the obligatory end-words "morning" and "evening" and make music and its regularities weigh as much in the close as the three aspects of pastoral landscape that witness it.

The Double Sestina is a surprising but powerful illustration of Empson's remark that "the way [the] sense of isolation has been avoided in the past is by the conventions of pastoral" (*SVP*, 18). For all the extremity of their love, it is clear that Sidney conceived Strephon and Klaius in this way. In the Third Eclogues of the *Old Arcadia* they are briefly identified as "stranger shepherds," as opposed to "Arcadian-born shepherds."[51] In the Fourth Eclogues, when they sing their double sestina, we learn that they are gentlemen who have "taken this trade of life" because of love of Urania, thought to be a shepherd's daughter but "indeed of far greater birth."[52] Sidney kept returning to Strephon and Klaius and reconceiving their story. He wrote a long narrative poem, "A shepherd's tale no height of style requires," never completed, which represents them as Arcadian shepherds who fall in love with Urania, the country lass, while playing the rustic game of barley-break.[53] The fact that Strephon and Klaius appear in this poem as ordinary shepherds presumably explains Sidney's decision to use this version of their story in the revised *New Arcadia*. There they appear as the central figures in the opening episode, where they lament, in more Platonic terms than the Double Sestina's, the departure of Urania, now unequivocally a figure like Astraea. They are grander than in "A shepherd's tale," but the crucial change remains, that they have become natives of Arcadia. Because they are no longer said to be gentlemen, their experience of spiritual growth in the noble impossibility of their love is set apart from the more entangling and morally ambiguous love experiences of Pyrocles and Musidorus.

The revised conception of Strephon and Klaius as Arcadians not only serves to discriminate different modes of heroic love suffering; it also draws out the pastoral assumptions of the Double Sestina, which itself remained unchanged. First, the poem can be seen to exemplify the striking phrases that conclude the set-piece describing the land of Arcadia:

---

51. *OA*, 245.

52. *OA*, 328.

53. "A shepherd's tale" does not appear in *OA* and, according to Ringler (*Poems*, 494), must have been written after Sidney had finished it. It is not in the 1590 edition of *NA*, but was included by the Countess of Pembroke, who "apparently found the uncompleted poem among her brother's papers," in the First Eclogues of the 1593 edition. It can be found in the Penguin *NA*, ed. Evans, 197–212.

. . . here, a shepherd's boy piping, as though he should never be old;
there, a young shepherdess knitting and withal singing, and it seemed
that her voice comforted her hands to work, and her hands kept time to
her voice's music. As for the houses of the country (for many houses came
under their eye), they were all scattered, no two being one by th'other,
and yet not so far off as that it barred mutual succour—a show as it were
of an accompanable solitariness, and of a civil wildness.[54]

Given the violence paced out by the double sestina and its using "forests" and
"mountains" as end-words, it is not unreasonable to apply the phrase "civil wildness" to it. "Accompanable solitariness" applies directly: the companionship
Strephon and Klaius find in their love distress, marked by the form of the poem
and by its concluding shift from "I" and "my" to "our," is in sharp contrast to the
genuine solitariness experienced by the figure of Philisides, the courtier-lover
who haunts the world of the Arcadian eclogues, looking in as a stranger like a
latter-day version of Virgil's Gallus. In the romance itself, the narrator and his
spokesmen express considerable anxiety about solitude, whether it is due to
Basilius's foolish withdrawal from the court or the passionate love of the heroes
Pyrocles and Musidorus. Though less manifestly benign than it appears in the
description of Arcadia, the "accompanable solitariness" of Strephon and Klaius
is equally pastoral, because it represents an achieved and steady condition.
Where the tension between society and solitude generates actions and conflict
for all the noble figures in the romance, Strephon and Klaius, as Sidney came
finally to conceive them, are as fixed in their situation as Colin Clout piping to
the Graces on Mount Acidale in Book 6 of *The Faerie Queene*.

From the standpoint of its "music," the double sestina is a grand and austere
example of the harmonies exemplified by the responsive song to which the
shepherds dance, while introducing the first set of Eclogues:

> A. We love, and have our loves rewarded.
> B. We love, and are no whit regarded.
> A. We find most sweet affection's snare.
> B. That sweet, but sour despairful care.
> A. Who can despair whom hope doth bear?
> B. And who can hope who feels despair?
> AB. As without breath no pipe doth move,
>   No music kindly without love.[55]

---

54. *NA*, 11.

55. *OA*, 57–58. Here, as elsewhere, I use *OA*'s modernized text, but present the poem in the form
in which it appears in *Poems*, 14. In *OA* the utterance of the poem is directly narrated, with each
line being introduced as responsive verse (e.g. "the others would answer").

In its ease and lightness, gliding past "And who can hope who feels despair?" to the final joint affirmation, this poem is at a great distance from the Double Sestina. Yet they are the extremes of the same scale: in each case, rule-governed responses bring together lovers apparently separated in their plights, and it is as true of the massive lament as of the graceful dance that love finds its natural expression in music and music its natural motive in love.

We can appreciate the pastoral interdependency of love and music in the Double Sestina by considering, once more, how it differentiates its singers from the princely heroes of the romance. When Musidorus falls in love with Pamela, he disguises himself as a shepherd. The first poem he utters—when, like the other noble figures, he goes off by himself to unburden his feelings—concludes:

> Then pour out plaint, and in one word say this:
> Helpless his plaint who spoils himself of bliss.[56]

Whatever his disguise, Musidorus remains in character with this aphoristic conclusion, which is characteristic of courtly lyric. But a speaker who encapsulates his woes "in one word" is doing something very different from what is indicated by the phrase "then pour out plaint," and Sidney, if not his characters, was quite aware of this. Two pages after this poem, when Musidorus is discovered by his friend the disguised Amazon, the narrator says:

> But Musidorus, looking dolefully upon her, wringing his hands, and pouring out abundance of tears, began to recount unto her all this I have already told you, but with such passionate dilating of it that, for my part, I have not a feeling insight enough into the matter to be able lively to express it. Sufficeth it that whatsoever a possessed heart with a good tongue, to a dear friend, could utter was at that time largely set forth.[57]

Precisely what cannot be represented on the part of the noble figures—passionate dilating and large setting forth to a dear friend—is preeminently what we find in the lament Sidney put in the mouths of his shepherd-lovers.[58]

The Double Sestina, with its austere fixity, seems a distinctly Sidneian representation of love. But one other aspect of its pastoralism, again brought out in Sidney's revisions, shows its connection with other pastoral love laments. In

---

56. *OA*, 40.

57. *OA*, 42.

58. Cf. the sentence which follows the responsive song ("We love, and have our loves rewarded") and introduces the first of the eclogues: "Having thus varied both their songs and dances into diverse sorts of inventions, their last sport was one of them to provoke another to a more large expressing of his passions" (*OA*, 58).

the *Old Arcadia* Strephon and Klaius uttered their woe only because of its fitness to Arcadia's general grief for the apparently dead Basilius. In the *New Arcadia,* their double sestina is not only sung in the course of the eclogues regularly staged for Basilius, but is performed by other shepherds. Its effect suggests what it means to have a love plight so stabilized in song: "So well were these wailful complaints accorded to the passions of all the princely hearers, while every one made what he heard of another the balance of his own fortune, that they stood a long while stricken in sad and silent consideration of them."[59] This again is a Sidneian effect: he is so attentive to dramatic situation, to the princely identities of those assembled, and therefore to the problematic nature of their love, that he represents them as struck with silence. But in other romances, whose authors and lovers more willingly accept their representation as shepherds, there is a different effect when "wailful complaints accord to the passions of the hearers." In these romances, love complaints not only strike a responsive chord in each bosom, but call forth responsive utterance, usually in the form of a love narration with its own built-in poems. When love is viewed more benignly than it is by Sidney, the fixity of the love complaint becomes a sign of fidelity, and it is eligible for the reward of faithful love.

The monument to this view of love is Jorge de Montemayor's *Diana* (1559), which established the form of the Renaissance pastoral romance. The "action" of the *Diana* consists largely in shepherds and shepherdesses (some putatively real and some courtiers and townspeople in disguise) uttering love complaints, which when heard by others prompt expressions of sympathy and accounts of shared and analogous experience. The great issues in the romance are fidelity, memory, and hope, and the whole work is designed to resolve unhappiness and reward truth in love. The *Diana* too has its double sestina, and its use confirms the implications we have drawn out of Sidney's. By itself it is a solo utterance of unrelieved woe, reviving the memory of what the singer thinks is a hopeless love. So described, its ritual repetition would seem more Petrarchan than pastoral, were it not that it is performed at the request of and to give pleasure to a fair shepherdess, the shepherd's companion in his grief. In this static form—"forever piping songs forever new"—the reiterated double sestina sounds like its analogues in Sannazaro's *Arcadia* and the Eclogues of Sidney's. But what

59. This revises a sentence in the Second Eclogues of *OA* describing the company's reaction to the love complaint of Plangus (performed by another shepherd): "So well did Histor's voice express the passion of Plangus that all the princely beholders were stricken into a silent consideration of it; indeed everyone making that he heard of another the balance of his own troubles" (*OA,* 152). This same sentence, with the beginning rewritten ("So well did Lamon's voice express the passions of those shepherds") follows the Double Sestina (performed by Lamon solo) in the Second Eclogues of 1590 (*NA,* 520). The version I have quoted in the text appears in 1593, after the second of Strephon and Klaius's double complaints (Penguin *NA,* 418–19). Though of less certain authority, I cite it for the sake of the phrase about complaints according to the passions of the hearers.

makes the *Diana* a romance is that it treats love's fixities and dilemmas as susceptible to change and resolution. It does so by the simple, but in this work tireless, device of having complaints and dialogues overheard by additional shepherds, whose sympathies and stories in various ways work to complicate or resolve the situation to which they have been introduced. In the case of the double sestina, it is overheard by a character who can inform the woeful singer that his beloved, who thought him dead, is longing for him; he leaves posthaste to achieve a happiness that corresponds to and rewards his persistence in woe.

IV

One can hardly believe that such nonsense carries conviction, and there is no way to become a believer short of reading the *Diana.* We shall examine its pastoral machinery in a later chapter; meanwhile, let us return to *As You Like It,* which we left as a play in need of a conclusion. From the wrestler Charles's evocation of the young gentlemen who flock to the exiled Duke, to Jaques's discordant nonsense word "ducdame"—"a Greek invocation, to call fools into a circle" (2.5.59)—to the Duke's feast, the various pastoral encounters, and Rosalind's appointments with Orlando, until Hymen makes "earthly things . . . atone [=at one] together" (5.4.109–10), the thematics of convening bear the burden of the play. But is it thereby a "conventional" pastoral? There are a number of reasons one might think it is not; one is the transformation of Montanus, in *Rosalynde,* into Silvius. Montanus is the poet of Lodge's Arden: his complaints greet Rosalind and Alinda when they come to the forest and it is he who performs for the exiled King Gerismond before the weddings that conclude the romance. One might say from Silvius's mode of speech that the gods have made him poetical, but he never performs a song or writes a poem, and therefore no special status is granted to his expression of his passion. Quite the contrary, the cool breeze of Rosalind's wit blows over him and Phebe and is one of the ways the tone of the play is established. C. L. Barber's comment suggests the way it seems to treat this pair of lovers and, with them, pastoral convention:

> Rosalind is not committed to the conventional language and attitudes of love, loaded as these inevitably are with sentimentality. Silvius and Phebe are her foils in this: they take their conventional language and their conventional feelings perfectly seriously, with nothing in reserve. As a result they seem naïve and rather trivial.[60]

This may be enough to say about Silvius and Phebe as characters, but they play rather important roles in the play's patterns and dynamics. In Act II, in which all the characters except Oliver are assembled in the Forest of Arden, it

---

60. *Shakespeare's Festive Comedy* (Princeton: Princeton University Press, 1959), 233–34.

is Silvius, and Silvius alone, who lets us know that this is a locale in which love can flourish. When Rosalind and Celia arrive in the forest, weary in body and spirits, they come upon Silvius protesting the extremity of his love to Corin. In Lodge, this exchange is a formal eclogue, with Corydon reproving love in the usual manner of old shepherds. Shakespeare's Corin is quite sympathetic to Silvius's plight, but his age leaves him insufficiently attuned to his young friend's present state. Silvius therefore improvises a set speech—not a song and not a composition but half-way to being a poem and with a pseudo-refrain ("Thou hast not lov'd")—and exits calling "O Phebe, Phebe, Phebe!" Rosalind reacts precisely in the "conventional" way:

> Alas, poor shepherd, searching of thy wound,
> I have by hard adventure found mine own.
>
> (2.4.44–45)

Touchstone steps forward with a burlesque version of what Silvius calls the follies that love does "make thee run into," and he concludes with an aphorism that critics often treat as a motto of the play: "We that are true lovers run into strange capers; but as all is mortal in nature, so is all nature in love mortal in folly" (2.4.54–56). Rosalind endorses the sentiment—"Thou speak'st wiser than thou art ware of"—but not the tone, as she proves by a final gesture in Silvius's vein:

> Jove, Jove! this shepherd's passion
> Is much upon my fashion.
>
> (2.4.60–61)

The kinship Rosalind first feels with Silvius does not cease to be an element in the drama, even in the scene in which she mocks him and Phebe. Barber gives an account of the scene as we tend to remember it:

All-suffering Silvius and his tyrannical little Phebe are a bit of Lodge's version taken over, outwardly intact, and set in a wholly new perspective. A "courting eglogue" between them, in the mode of Lodge, is exhibited almost as a formal spectacle, with Corin for presenter and Rosalind and Celia for audience. It is announced as

> a pageant truly play'd
> Between the pale complexion of true love
> And the red glow of scorn and proud disdain.
>
> (3.4.53–5)

What we then watch is played "truly"—according to the best current convention. . . . Shakespeare lets us feel the charm of the form; but then he has Rosalind break up their pretty pageant.[61]

---

61. Ibid., 230.

What Barber omits is that Rosalind has an investment in this scene even before she comes to it. Corin comes upon her when she is impatient at Orlando's failure to keep his appointed hour and Celia is teasing her for her impulsive shifts of mood. When Corin proposes to show the "pageant truly played," Rosalind replies with alacrity, in the final speech of the scene:

> O, come, let us remove,
> The sight of lovers feedeth those in love.
> Bring us to this sight, and you shall say
> I'll prove a busy actor in their play.
>
> (3.4.56–59)

In effect, she would rather watch Silvius and Phebe than be subjected to Celia's teasing. The last line is prophetic, but she cannot, at this point, know or intend what it proves to mean. Her meaning here must be that she will somehow enter into the love sports of Arden: the shepherd's passion is still much upon her fashion.

Rosalind is thus not a mere spectator of the scene between Silvius and Phebe, and the issue is therefore not whether she responds conventionally, on the one hand, or with independent wit on the other. Shakespeare has brought her to the scene by dramatizing the conventional response to the lover—the sense of sharing his plight—and her response to what she sees and hears is an equally dramatic response to the scornful mistress.

> Why, what means this? why do you look on me?
> I see no more in you than in the ordinary
> Of nature's sale-work. 'Od's my little life,
> I think she means to tangle my eyes too!
> No, faith, proud mistress, hope not after it.
> 'Tis not your inky brows, your black silk hair,
> Your bugle eyeballs, nor your cheek of cream
> That can entame my spirits to your worship.
> You foolish shepherd, wherefore do you follow her,
> Like foggy south, puffing with wind and rain?
> You are a thousand times a properer man
> Than she a woman. 'Tis such fools as you
> That makes the world full of ill-favor'd children.
>
> (3.5.41–53)

Rosalind's vehemence and impatience reveal something other than an impartial supervising intelligence.[62] Her mockery responds dramatically to Phebe's scorn of Silvius, in the most prominent speech in their pageant of love:

62. Cf. Barber's remark that "she reminds them that they are nature's creatures, and that love's purposes are contradicted by too absolute a cultivation of romantic liking or loathing" (230). Simi-

'Tis pretty, sure, and very probable
That eyes, that are the frail'st and softest things,
Who shut their coward gates on atomies,
Should be called tyrants, butchers, murtherers!
Now I do frown on thee with all my heart,
And if mine eyes can wound, now let them kill thee.
Now counterfeit to swound; why, now fall down,
Or if thou canst not, O, for shame, for shame,
Lie not, to say mine eyes are murtherers!

(3.5.11–19)

Phebe mocks the lover's extravagance by pretending to take his claims literally. This makes her rather less dignified and attractive than her prototype in Lodge, but it also makes her a good deal more like Rosalind herself, who will deal with Orlando in a similar vein in the next scene. Phebe's refusal to credit hyperboles is exactly the weapon that Rosalind will turn on her. Phebe thus appears to be a pastoral simplification of one side of Rosalind, just as Silvius is of another. If he represents her capacity for romantic extravagance, she represents her capacity for mocking her lover and the need she seems to feel, at this point in the play, for controlling him and protecting herself from fully acknowledging her feelings.[63] Once smitten, Phebe fills out another aspect of Rosalind's pastoralism, her sense of love's imperatives. Phebe's first utterance, after Ganymede/Rosalind leaves, is:

Dead shepherd, now I find thy saw of might,
"Who ever lov'd that lov'd not at first sight?"

(3.5.81–82)

This is pure pastoral convention. The words of the departed shepherd "accord to the passions of the hearer," and they are true of all the lovers in Arden—Rosalind and Orlando, Silvius and Phebe, Celia and Oliver, and, for all we know, Touchstone and Audrey.

Rosalind's association with Silvius and Phebe is only the most explicit sign that she plays a pastoral role in the middle acts of *As You Like It*. Her vitality, wit, and sense of freedom are such that critics understandably treat her as the controlling intelligence in the play. But her freedom and control are bound up with her disguise and its constraints. She discovers the depths of her own love

---

larly, Thomas McFarland views her scoffing wit as proper medicine for the unhealthy emotions of not only Silvius and Phebe but Orlando. *Shakespeare's Pastoral Comedy* (Chapel Hill: University of North Carolina Press, 1972), 114–17.

63. Cf. Rosalie L. Colie, *Shakespeare's Living Art* (Princeton: Princeton University Press, 1974), 255: "Ganymede assumes with his disguise . . . one proper pastoral love-attitude, that conventionally assigned the shepherdess, of coolness to the lover."

and Orlando's open-eyed persistence in his, because she can mock, tease, and openly show her hand to everyone except the person to whom she will eventually have to. The question, for her and for the play, is how the revelation of herself will come about. The problem is neatly presented by an implication Helen Gardner draws from her fine observation that "the center of *As You Like It*" is the "discovery of truth by feigning and of what is wisdom and what folly by debate." Thinking along these lines, Gardner says, "By playing with [Orlando] in the disguise of a boy, [Rosalind] discovers when she can play no more."[64] This represents Rosalind as the play's controlling intelligence, able to act on what the scenes in the Forest of Arden make known.[65] But Rosalind's playing with Orlando does not lead her to discover the limits of play. On the contrary, at the end of the mock-wooing scene (4.1), it is not at all clear that she is not ready to play through several more such scenes; this is presumably what she has in mind when she sends Orlando off with a fine display of teasing and fooling and makes him promise to return in two hours. Rosalind recognizes that she can play no more only because of events that are beyond her control.

The resolution of the play is precipitated by Oliver's arrival in the forest and Orlando's being wounded by the lioness from whom he rescues his brother. Rosalind—who has once more been impatient with her lover and who has been working off some of her energy by teasing Silvius about Phebe's love poem to her—swoons when she sees the bloody handkerchief that explains why Orlando failed to come (4.3.156). At the level of plot, there is really nothing in this episode that should force Rosalind to remove her disguise, but there is a great change in her strength relative to world. However she is costumed, she has revealed herself by swooning, and the first indication of this turning point is a motif that associates her with Silvius and Phebe. "Now counterfeit to swound," Phebe had challenged Silvius, and Rosalind attempts to disguise her fainting by claiming, again and again, that it was "counterfeit" (4.3.167–82). In the scenes with Orlando, Rosalind had been able to express her own love by seeming to mock his: the play's truest poetry was indeed the most feigning. But when she swoons, she can no longer pretend that she and her prose are in control: she cannot successfully feign that her body's expression of faining was mere feigning.

It looks as if the poise of pastoral masking is to be disrupted and caught up in the larger forces of romance and dramatic comedy. But from this point on,

64. Helen Gardner, "*As You Like It*," in *As You Like It*, ed. Albert Gilman (New York: Signet, 1963), 225; originally in *More Talking of Shakespeare*, ed. John Garrett (London: Longmans, 1959).

65. For a more up-to-date account of Rosalind as in control of herself and the play, see Barbara J. Bono, "Mixed Gender, Mixed Genre in Shakespeare's *As You Like It*," in Barbara Kiefer Lewalski, ed., *Renaissance Genres* (Harvard English Studies 14) (Cambridge: Harvard University Press, 1986), 203–4.

the workings of the play, whatever their sources in literary tradition, can be described as making good the claims of pastoral convention. The consequences of Rosalind's swoon are revealed when she next meets Orlando, and they play with another of Silvius and Phebe's motifs:

> *Ros.* O my dear Orlando, how it grieves me to see thee wear thy
> heart in a scarf!
> *Orl.* It is my arm.
> *Ros.* I thought thy heart had been wounded with the claws of a lion.
> *Orl.* Wounded it is, but with the eyes of a lady.
>
> (5.2.19–24)

It is as if Rosalind intended him to produce this sentiment. Certainly she is no longer in a position to mock such an expression of devotion but can only return to her feeble pretence: "Did your brother tell you how I counterfeited to sound when he show'd me your handkercher?" (5.2.25–26) "Ay, and greater wonders than that," says Orlando, whereupon Rosalind, taking his meaning and at last having something on which to exercise her wit and energy, gives a playfully rhetorical account of the sudden love of Oliver and Celia. This little performance prompts a decisive action. Orlando is moved by the impending wedding to express impatience for his ("I can live no longer by thinking"), and Rosalind, as if to acknowledge that her hand is forced, concocts her story of the magician uncle as the guise under which she can reveal herself. This conjuncture of feigning and faining is one way in which the play works the magic it thematizes here. All it really takes to bring everything round is for Rosalind to reveal herself, but the various modes of "holiday humor"—wit, fancy, imaginative staging—make us half believe that their charm is an exercise of charms.

So far as plot goes, the scene could end with Ganymede's promise to bring Rosalind to Orlando, but its poetry is still to be played out. Silvius and Phebe enter, and when Rosalind tries to turn away the importunate shepherdess by telling her to love her "faithful shepherd," the two native lovers set in motion a little eclogue:

> *Phebe.* Good shepherd, tell this youth what 'tis to love.
> *Silvius.* It is to be all made of sighs and tears,
> And so am I for Phebe.
> *Phebe.* And I for Ganymed.
> *Orl.* And I for Rosalind.
> *Ros.* And I for no woman.
>
> (5.2.83–88)

The claims of pastoral convention are not to be resisted. Rosalind's "And I for no woman" may protect her "cover"—it ostensibly denies that she is caught up in this round of love, while leaving open the meaning that she loves a man—

but she cannot avoid the effect given here, that she too is chiming in. Her prose wit has one more gesture left to it. Phebe initiates the fourth and last round of the quartet:

> *Phebe.* If this be so, why blame you me to love you?
> *Silvius.* If this be so, why blame you me to love you?
> *Orl.* If this be so, why blame you me to love you?
> *Ros.* Why do you speak too, "Why blame you me to love you?"
> *Orl.* To her that is not here, nor doth not hear.
>   (5.2.103–7)

This is a pretty enough answer by Orlando and could keep the music going, but it is too much for Rosalind, who cuts it all off with her "Pray you, no more of this, 'tis like the howling of Irish wolves against the moon." This is usually taken to be simply a healthy expression of good sense. But this comparison was proverbial for a vain desire,[66] so it suggests Rosalind's impatience not only with her fellow lovers but with her own disguise. As if feeling its force, she concludes the scene by prosing the conventionality of the quartet in which she has just participated:

> To-morrow meet me all together. I will marry you [Phebe], if ever I marry woman, and I'll be married to-morrow. I will satisfy you [Orlando], if ever I satisfied man, and you shall be married to-morrow. I will content you [Silvius], if what pleases you contents you, and you shall be married to-morrow. As you love Rosalind, meet. As you love Phebe, meet. And as I love no woman, I'll meet. (5.2.112–20)

The parallel phrases and the motif of meeting lay the ground for the final scene, in which Rosalind, promising "to make all this matter even" (5.4.18), brings in Hymen, who unites the couples and leads them in a wedding dance.

Ending with marriages is hardly specific to pastoral and may have nothing to do with it. But in this play, as the characters come together in the guise of shepherds and foresters, pastoral conventions carry the comic dramaturgy and concerns. After the lovers' quartet there is a brief scene (5.3), a kind of prologue to the long finale, in which two pages—stock figures from Lyly's pastoral comedies but coming from nowhere in this play—sit down with Touchstone and Audrey to sing "It was a lover and his lass." The scene consists almost entirely of the song, whose dramaturgic effect is registered at its conclusion. Touch-

---

66. In *Rosalynde*, Rosalind/Ganymede uses the comparison to dissuade Montanus from loving Phebe. See *Narrative and Dramatic Sources of Shakespeare*, ed. Geoffrey Bullough, vol. 2 (New York: Columbia University Press, 1963): 242. In her Arden edition of *As You Like It* (London: Methuen, 1975), Agnes Latham notes that "dogs or wolves howling at full moon were a proverbial image of ineffective clamour." In addition to her references, cf. Robert Greene's pastoral romance *Menaphon*, ed. G. B. Harrison (Oxford, 1927), 61, and Michael Drayton, *The Shepheards Garland* 7.29–30.

stone, predictably trying to trip up his companions, says: "Truly, young gentlemen, though there was no great matter in the ditty, yet the note was very
untuneable." To which one page replies, truly and with perfect sufficiency: "You
are deceiv'd, sir. We kept time, we lost not our time" (5.3.34–38). They did
keep time in their singing, and it was not a waste of time. The song—the most
innocent and idyllic in the play, the one springtime song in a play which usually
sings of "winter and rough weather"—thus assimilates to its self-sufficient pleasures and to its pastoral moral ("And therefore take the present time") the various paces of Time about which Rosalind/Ganymede first displayed her witty
wares to her charmed lover (3.2.302–33).

The final scene confirms the confluence of pastoral and comedy by remaining in the Forest of Arden to celebrate the coming together of its various inhabitants. Commentators, aware that most of the characters are courtiers, associate *As You Like It* with other plays in which a sojourn in a "green world"
enables a return to court.[67] But where *Love's Labour's Lost, A Midsummer Night's
Dream, The Winter's Tale,* and *The Tempest* bring the characters back to court or
show them on the point of departure, *As You Like It* is content to finish its business in the woods. The Duke, no longer exiled, nevertheless says:

> First, in this forest let us do those ends
> That here were well begun and well begot;
> And after, every of this happy number,
> That have endur'd shrewd days and nights with us,
> Shall share the good of our returnèd fortune,
> According to the measure of their states.
> Mean time, forget this new-fall'n dignity,
> And fall into our rustic revelry.
> Play, music, and you brides and bridegrooms all,
> With measure heap'd in joy, to th' measures fall.
>
> (5.4.170–79)

"The measure of their states" indicates the differentiated and hierarchical social
order that awaits them all. But for the moment society's measure is turned into
the "dancing measures" in which only Duke Frederick and Jaques will not take
part. The pastoral idea of space set apart for song meets and is adequate to what
the comic theater provides.

As You Like It can end both conventionally and satisfactorily, because the
play throughout is attentive to the motives and powers of pastoral convention.
Just as *Lycidas* presses certain traditional usages to their limits, so *As You Like It*

---

67. See the comments of Mary Lascelles and John Wain quoted in The New Variorum edition of
As You Like It, ed. Richard Knowles (New York: The Modern Language Association, 1977), 524,
526.

tests by dramatizing and validates in its dramaturgy two practices that are at the heart of pastoral—responsive rivalry in performance of set pieces and the translation of experience into song and other forms of verbal finish and display. Amiens's praise of the Duke—

> happy is your Grace,
> That can translate the stubbornness of fortune
> Into so quiet and so sweet a style—
>
> (2.1.18–20)

could be said of a hermit and perhaps of a stoic. One can also imagine the virtuous spirit controlling its fortunes in other styles than the sweet and quiet. The Duke's style is pastoral, because it is shared, held in common on the basis of a recognized strength relative to his world. This understanding of pastoral is made explicit at the end of Act 2, when Orlando breaks into the Duke's company and demands food. His wonder that "in this desert inaccessible" there is gentleness where he expected savagery makes him put up his sword and turn his demand into a plea—"If ever you have look'd on better days,/If ever been where bells have knoll'd to church," etc.— to which the Duke, enacting the idea of welcome and a common style, answers as responsively as if this were a formal eclogue (2.7.113–26). Then while Orlando goes to get Adam, the Duke says:

> Thou seest we are not all alone unhappy:
> This wide and universal theater
> Presents more woeful pageants than the scene
> Wherein we play in.
>
> (2.7.136–39)

This sense of a shared plight counts as pastoral because its speaker stands by his experience and awareness but does not presume on its centrality. He can imagine that his exile is a pageant merely played, like the scene between Silvius and Phebe. Hence he can display the quiet and sweet style of his life by having Amiens conclude this act with a musical version of the speech with which he himself began it—the song, "Blow, blow, thou winter wind."

But between the Duke's appeal to his fellows and Amiens's song comes Jaques's "All the world's a stage," which defiantly picks up the Duke's metaphor. The speech challenges and, so far as Jaques himself is concerned, denies the idea that rivaling performances bring foresters together. More broadly, it raises the question—played out by Touchstone and Rosalind, as well as by Jaques—of whether pastoral conventions can stand up to critical wit. In a sense, we have been arguing all along that they can, but we can conclude with a representative moment of pastoral convention and its testing. The first song we hear in Arden also engages an element of the Duke's speech, but attunes an experience less stubborn than the human ingratitude at the center of "Blow, blow thou winter wind":

> Under the greenwood tree
>   Who loves to lie with me,
> And turn his merry note
>   Unto the sweet bird's throat,
> Come hither, come hither, come hither!
>   Here shall he see
>   No enemy
> But winter and rough weather.
>
> (2.5.1–8)

The exclusive *huc ades* of the lover's pastoral appeal—"Come live with me and be my love"—here becomes a general invitation. The song beautifully plays out the idea of pastoral convention by making it impossible to tell whether the represented dweller in the greenwood is the singer or the companion invited to join him. But his present companion—and here again we see Shakespeare giving a more sharply dramatic form to something potential in pastoral practices—is Jaques, whose responsive song is a parody of this invitation:

> If it do come to pass
> That any man turn ass,
> Leaving his wealth and ease
> A stubborn will to please,
> Ducdame, ducdame, ducdame!
>   Here shall he see
>   Gross fools as he,
> And if he will come to me.
>
> (2.5.50–57)

This mockery ignores that what has brought the courtiers to Arden is not willfulness but a pastoral choice—free but within imposed limits or necessities. (This may be true of all "free" choices, hence the representativeness of pastoral; but pastoral choosers are aware of the constraints on them, hence the distinctness of the mode.) Jaques then acts out his defiance of pastoral convention by explaining "ducdame" as "a Greek invocation, to call fools into a circle."

So be it, as you like it. What is splendid about the play is that its lovers, its actors, its audience can accept this motto for themselves. *As You Like It* continually moves to attune what is discordant or dissonant, thus taking up a pastoral endeavor we have already observed in Sidney's double sestina and in *Lycidas*, with its hearing and absorbing of sterner pastoral voices. The attuning of discord is most direct in the woodland songs, in the last of which, the song of the deer, the foresters willingly "bear the burden," in the musical and physical sense, both of the horns which they bring home as a trophy and of their symbolic import, about which Rosalind has just been teasing Orlando (4.1.160–76).[68] Dissonant utterance occurs throughout the play, and not only in the speeches of Touchstone and Jaques. It is at the heart of the pastoral kinship between Rosalind and Phebe. Phebe falls in love with Ganymede not, as in Lodge, because of his/her pretty face, but because of her mocking, irritated voice:

> Sweet youth, I pray you chide a year together,
> I had rather hear you chide than this man woo.
>   (3.5.64–65)

The word Phebe settles on here is more frequent in this play than in any other of Shakespeare's. It engages a motif first sounded when the Duke praises "the churlish chiding of the winter's wind" and that later focuses his and Orlando's distancing themselves from Jaques. The Duke's sense that harsh sounds can be sweet is matched by the way various lovers, from Rosalind to Touchstone, mingle mockery and affection. But it is Phebe the chider who brings this word into the love plot, and it is Rosalind who puts it on full pastoral display. When Silvius brings Phebe's letter to her, Rosalind rags him by pretending that Phebe's conventional little love poem is "railing." Phebe's word sounds both within her poem—"Whiles you chid me, I did love"—and in Silvius's response when Rosalind has read it: "Call you this chiding?" "Alas, poor shepherd!" Celia says, as well she might (4.3.40–65). This playful juggling of harsh and sweet can be seen as fooling that liberates, as a salutary abrasiveness (best displayed here in Rosalind's wonderful remark, "She Phebes me" [4.3.39]), and as a working off of social and erotic energies: Rosalind's abuse has something to do with Silvius's arriving just when she was impatiently expecting Orlando. All these elements are again apparent in the pastoralism of the final scene. Touchstone's set piece on dueling and the virtues of "if"—Shakespeare's substitution for the love complaints with which Lodge's Montanus entertains King Gerismond— shows how verbal performance can disarm rivalry. As even Touchstone "press[es] in here . . . amongst the country copulatives," Hymen draws the fools of love into a circle. Even Jaques, who mockingly hails "the couples coming to the ark" at the beginning of the scene, makes his exit by a ritual farewell that, with its final rhyme on "dancing measures," is as close as he can come to pastoral song.[69]

This account of the pastoralism of *As You Like It* should, like the play itself,

---

68. Cf. J. C. Scaliger, *Poetices* 1.4: "The contestants [in the original pastoral singing contests] were also crowned, and we even read of their wearing the horns of deer" (Padelford [chap. 1, n. 15], 26).

69. Anne Barton comments on Jaques's new character in the ending, in the context of a discussion of the way *As You Like It* attunes its discords. "*As You Like It* and *Twelfth Night*: Shakespeare's Sense of an Ending," in *Shakespearian Comedy* (Stratford-Upon-Avon Studies 14), ed. Malcolm Bradbury and David Palmer (London: Edward Arnold, 1972), 166.

have an epilogue. We have continually spoken of pastoral expression as due to and reflecting felt limitations, and we have spoken of pastoral conventions as practices that bring "shepherds" together after a separation or loss. What happens in the Forest of Arden is certainly initiated by the courtiers' loss of the world in which they belong, but the play is so assured and liberating that by its end we may simply take the world of Arden to be the world itself. *As You Like It* is usually thought to be one of the supreme achievements of Shakespearean comedy. On the other hand, even its most fervent admirers, its truest believers, have often felt the need to defend or explain away elements of the play, like the supposed unreality of the pastoral world, the "fairy-tale" nature of its plot devices, and the artificial character of its ending.[70] However strongly such reservations were felt in older criticism, they have been replaced by reservations grounded in sociohistorical observations. Recent studies emphasize that the world of the play is hierarchical and that it is in the final analysis dominated by men. The finest of these essays—which by no means intends to debunk the play, only to understand the conditions of its accomplishment—observes that "if *As You Like It* is a vehicle for Rosalind's exuberance, it is also a structure for her containment," and adds: "Several generations of critics—most of them men, and quite infatuated with Rosalind themselves—have stressed the exuberance and ignored the containment."[71] It is certainly the case that Celia says not a word once she is engaged to Oliver,[72] and that Rosalind's taking off her disguise, which we have treated as the "purpose" of the play, means that she is handed over to the Duke as a daughter and to Orlando as a wife. It is altogether an odd play—robust and liberating, and at the same time requiring a certain delicacy in treatment. Too great an insistence on social hierarchy or "patriarchal structures" seems to ignore the character of the play, while avoiding these matters would seem to miss some of the play's own lessons of critical self-awareness. What the title's wry permissiveness suggests is Shakespeare's own pastoral self-awareness, the sense of the play's limits he displayed by keeping his foresters in Arden and not following the ending of *Rosalynde,* in which there is a decisive return to the world of wars and kingdoms. Critics have often felt the connections of this play with *Hamlet,* through Jaques, and through various motifs and locutions, with *King Lear.* Presumably, the Duke and his company return to court better individually and as a society. But had Shakespeare actually brought them home, he might have set them on the road to the tragedies.

70. Barton (171) gives a full account, along traditional lines, of the reservations that attend and are dealt with by the ending.

71. Louis Adrian Montrose, "'The Place of a Brother' in *As You Like It:* Social Process and Comic Form," *Shakespeare Quarterly* 32 (1981): 52.

72. As pointed out by Peter Erickson, *Patriarchal Structures in Shakespeare's Drama* (Berkeley & Los Angeles: University of California Press, 1985), 36.

PART TWO

Four

REPRESENTATIVE SHEPHERDS

I

Critical ideas of pastoral have taken the form of representative anecdotes, because pastoral poetry has been concerned with issues of representation from its beginnings as a literary form. The beginnings, so far as we know, were in certain poems (called "idylls" since Roman times) by Theocritus, one of a remarkable group of poets and scholars patronized by the Ptolemaic dynasty in Alexandria, in the third century B.C.[1] I shall argue in this chapter that pastoral

---

1. In writing about Theocritus, I have had to assume that my reader is unacquainted with his poetry and does not read ancient Greek. I have therefore erred on the side of generosity in quoting passages and giving information about various Idylls, and I have used a translation which, though rather stiff and old-fashioned, follows the Greek text closely in language and lineation: R. C. Trevelyan, trans., *The Idylls of Theocritus* (New York: Albert and Charles Boni, 1925). For those readers who want to read Theocritus— and I hope there are many, he is as great a poet as Keats—I would recommend Theocritus, *Idylls and Epigrams*, trans. Daryl Hine (New York: Atheneum, 1982), a tour-de-force of English dactyls. Two other translations, which have been well received and are in different poetic manners, are those of Anna Rist, *The Poems of Theocritus: Translated with Introductions* (Chapel Hill: University of North Carolina Press, 1978), with useful introductions to each poem, and Barriss Mills, *The Idylls of Theokritos: A Verse Translation* (West Lafayette: Purdue University Studies, 1963).

It seems unnecessary to give full scholarly documentation and support to every point made

was, as the horsebreeders say, by Virgil out of Theocritus. Historically it was the work of both poets, with Virgil coordinating and making more explicit what was implicit in Theocritus's bucolic representations. For example, the various senses in which a pastoral singer sings *for* someone are all present in the Idylls, but it is Virgil who made them thematically explicit and connected them with each other. His transformation of Theocritean bucolic is as much a matter of form as of theme and symbol: where Theocritus's pastorals are part of a larger collection of poems, from which they are not easily differentiated, the Eclogues are a coherent book. The older view of the relation between the two poets was that, in Schiller's terms, Theocritus played "naive" to Virgil's "sentimental." It is now well understood, and will become clear in our account, that the Greek poet—self-consciously post-heroic and (to use Harold Bloom's term) belated— is as "sentimental" as his Roman imitator. Still, some poets are more sentimental than others. It is from Virgil's self-conscious handling of Theocritean representations and usages that the figure of the herdsman emerged as representative, both of the poet and of all humans. Without doing violence to the texture and energy of the poetry, one can derive from the Eclogues the formula which established pastoral as a poetic kind and which at the same time made possible its historical variety. The Virgilian formula is: the poet represents (himself as) a shepherd or shepherds.

We shall begin with Theocritus's Idyll 1, both for its intrinsic importance and because it addresses matters of bucolic representation with unusual full-

---

and detail discussed. For a student of the modern literatures, it is daunting to realize how much uncertainty surrounds many aspects and details of Theocritus's poems. My assertions about lexical matters and other details are based on Liddell and Scott's Greek Lexicon and the two standard commentaries in English: A. S. F. Gow, ed., *Theocritus*, 2 vols. (Cambridge: at the University Press, 1950; 2d ed. 1952), and K. J. Dover, ed., *Theocritus: Select Poems* (London: Macmillan, 1971). I have used and cite Gow's Greek text. Gow provides a facing prose translation and a full scholarly commentary. Dover is a very useful school edition, critically more up-to-date than Gow, with no translation but with a glossary. My ad hoc translations of lines and phrases, which sometimes differ from Trevelyan, are based on Gow, with occasional modifications from Dover.

It will be seen that much of what I say draws on the large amount of scholarly and critical interpretation of the *Idylls*, but here again I think continual detailed references would be merely burdensome. These can be found in the three books to which I am most indebted and which I think readers of this book will find most profitable, if they wish to pursue matters Theocritean: Thomas G. Rosenmeyer, *The Green Cabinet: Theocritus and the European Pastoral Lyric* (Berkeley & Los Angeles: University of California Press, 1969); Charles Segal, *Poetry and Myth in Ancient Pastoral: Essays on Theocritus and Virgil* (Princeton: Princeton University Press, 1981); and David M. Halperin, *Before Pastoral: Theocritus and the Ancient Tradition of Bucolic Poetry* (New Haven: Yale University Press, 1983). Steven F. Walker, *Theocritus* (Boston: Twayne Publishers, 1980) is a useful introduction. Kathryn J. Gutzwiller, *Theocritus' Pastoral Analogies: The Formation of a Genre* (Madison: University of Wisconsin Press, 1991), which appeared after this chapter was written, is the most up-to-date in its scholarly references and has considerable interest for the nonspecialist reader.

ness.[2] Idyll 1 is best known as a pastoral elegy, for its centerpiece is a song about the death of the heroic herdsman Daphnis. But there are extensive preliminaries to this song. The poem begins, as we have already seen,[3] with the shepherd Thyrsis and an anonymous goatherd complimenting each other's music-making. Thyrsis requests that the goatherd play his pipe, but the goatherd refuses, for fear of arousing Pan's wrath at noontime. He in his turn requests Thyrsis to sing the song about Daphnis for which he is well known, and he promises to reward him with three milkings of a goat and a beautiful cup. This promise is made good, in anticipation, by the goatherd's long description of the exquisite workmanship of the cup and the three scenes depicted on it:

> Within, a woman is designed, such as the Gods might fashion,
> Clad in a robe, with snooded hair; and upon either side
> Two men with fair long locks contending in alternate speech
> One with the other; but her heart is touched by naught they say:
> For now at one she glances with a smile, and now again
> Flings to the other a light thought; while they, with heavy eyes
> Long wearied out for love of her, are wasting toil in vain.
> Beyond these there is carved an ancient fisherman, who stands
> On a jagged rock, and busily the old man gathers in
> His great net for a cast, like one who toils with might and main.
> You'd say that he was fishing with the whole strength of his limbs
> Such swelling sinews everywhere stand out around his neck;
> For grey-haired though he be, his strength is worthy of youth still
>
> (32–44)

In the third scene, which we shall examine later, a boy who is supposed to be guarding a vineyard has become absorbed in making a cricket cage and ignores two foxes who are raiding the vineyard and pilfering the food he has brought for himself.

The cup has representational interests that go beyond its mimetic felicity. In its literary relations, it literally re-presents two august predecessors—Homer's description of Achilles' shield (*Iliad* 18.478–607) and the pseudo-

---

2. The term "idyll" (Gr. *eidullion*), is ancient but later than Theocritus, and its meaning is uncertain. It has nothing to do with "idyllic" in our sense. The order in which the Idylls are printed is that of the first Renaissance edition; ancient evidence varies, but it seems likely that Idyll 1 was meant to stand first in the collection. Several of the Idylls are now thought not to be by Theocritus. For students of pastoral, Idylls 8 and 9 are the most important of these. As Dover points out, these "were regarded as Theokritean in ancient times" (and were imitated by Virgil), "and suspicion of their authenticity . . . is modern; they give the impression of rather ill-judged parodies of Theokritos, and are probably the work of Hellenistic imitators" (xviii–xix).

3. Above, chap. 1

Hesiodic fragment known as the *Shield of Heracles*. Theocritus's verse form, dactylic hexameter, itself establishes a connection with heroic poetry, and the description of the cup imitates scenes from both its epic forebears. The scene of the lovers contending recalls the judicial dispute on Achilles' shield (*Iliad* 18.497–509); the description of the old man fishing imitates a scene from the *Shield of Heracles* (211–15); both shields contain scenes of vineyards.[4] The language too alludes to these epic models. Starting with *daidalma*, a Theocritean congener of the noun (*daidalon*) and adjective (*daidalos*) used of Achilles' shield and other Homeric artifacts, the description of the cup is shot through with Homeric and Hesiodic diction and allusions. The goatherd's cup is thus the bucolic representative of Homer's and Hesiod's shields. In emulating their craft and reducing their heroic dimensions, it means to take their place, to stand in for them in the hexameter verse of a post-heroic age.

As a Hellenistic representation of Achilles' shield, the goatherd's cup reveals further interests of the sort for which we use the word "representative." By their very scope and the number of their scenes, Homer's and Hesiod's descriptions lay claim to being, as Lessing said of Homer's, an "Inbegriff von allem, was in der Welt vorgeht."[5] In spite of the fact that he reduces their surveys to three scenes, Theocritus maintains the suggestion that what he presents sums up human life. This effect is partly a matter, as Burke puts it, of selection: the cup presents three ages of man (boyhood, youth, old age) and three characteristic activities (love, work, play). The effect is also due to Theocritus's mode of representation. By comparison with Homer's scenes, some of which have a great deal of action, Theocritus's are static—fixed in single places, even if there are small or suggested actions within them. Furthermore, the situations depicted do not seem to involve individual stories or plots, such as would require completion by further scenes or actions. The sufficiency of what we are shown supports the suggestion that these situations are "typical of a class, conveying an adequate idea of others of its kind" (OED, s.v. "representative").

The goatherd's cup has one further representational function. The goatherd offers it to Thyrsis by way of declining to sing himself. But his description is so long and conspicuous a set piece that it acts as a substitute for the song he refuses to sing. This substitution is important for the ethos of the poem, because it maintains the equality between the two speakers that was expressed in the balance and reciprocity of their opening exchange. But it also serves to augment the large issue of the representer's relation to what he represents. The verbal self-consciousness of the *ekphrasis* and its appeals to the viewer could be attributed to the poet himself, but the passage also brings out the goatherd's

---

4. For detailed discussion, see Halperin, 176–81.

5. Quoted by Halperin, 177. Hesiod's shield is largely devoted to personifications and mythological figures, but it includes a survey of human life (270–313).

stake in the cup. His concluding words speak both of the good things he exchanged for it and of his sensory and aesthetic prizing of it:

> And all around the cup is spreading soft acanthus leaf,
> A wondrous thing to goatherds, that will amaze your soul.
> I bought it of a merchant who came from Calydon,
> And the price I paid him was a goat and a great white cream-cheese.
> Never yet has it touched my lip, but still unstained by wine
> It lies. This bowl with all my heart would I bestow on you,
> If you'll be kind and sing that song I yearn so much to hear.[6]

As opposed to the more impersonal description of the scenes on the cup, these
lines dramatize the speaker's relation to what he represents. The cup's function
as the goatherd's "song" also engages this issue, and it is directly and self-
consciously taken up in Thyrsis's song itself.

Thyrsis's song begins by setting a scene: we are shown the dying Daphnis
surrounded by animals and then visited and challenged by various rural characters and deities. So summarized, this may seem close to the mode of representation on the goatherd's cup. But this passage has almost no descriptive
detail. As soon as the visitants appear, they begin to expostulate, either in sympathy or mockery, with the dying hero. Theocritus's passage lacks the purely
descriptive detail found in Virgil's imitation of it—for example, the description
of Menalcas as "wet from the winter acorns" or Silvanus as "tossing flowery
fennel stalks and lilies" on his head.[7] In such a context, the narrator can become
an impersonator, like the actor who is said to represent a character on the stage.

Daphnis takes Thyrsis to the limits of bucolic impersonation. At first,
the dying hero's speeches are like those of the other characters: we might as
easily say that the singer reports them as that he enacts them. But Daphnis
becomes something of an impersonator himself when, in his parting shot at
Venus, he tells her what to say when she goes off to her Diomedes (112–13).
After that his utterances change in character: they are not engaged in the
scene represented by Thyrsis, but address the whole natural world. His words
parallel those with which Thyrsis began—identifying himself ("I am that
Daphnis," 120; cf. "This is Thyrsis of Etna," 65) and then asking Pan to come
from whatever mountain he roams, as Thyrsis sought the nymphs in their
various haunts. At first, the voices of Thyrsis the singer and Daphnis the hero
remain distinct:

6. Lines 55–61. I have changed Trevelyan's translation of the first half of line 56 to accommodate
Gow's and Dover's reading *aipolikon*.

7. *Ecl.* 10.20, 25. Later, Daphnis describes a pastoral setting (106–7, = Idyll 5.45–46), but the
lines have always puzzled commentators precisely because their argumentative force is hard to
make out.

> I am that Daphnis, he who drove the kine to pasture here,
> Daphnis who led the bulls and calves to water at these springs.
> Lead yet awhile, ye Muses, lead you the pastoral song.
>   (120–22)

Throughout the song, this refrain has served to keep Thyrsis's voice separate from those of the represented characters. But at this point the refrain changes:

> O Pan, Pan, whether thou art on the high hills of Lykaios,
> Or whether o'er great Mainalos thou roamest, hither come
> To the Sicilian isle, and leave the tomb of Helike,
> And Lykaonides' lofty cairn, which even the Gods revere.
>   Break off, I pray, ye Muses, break off the pastoral song.
> Come, lord, and take this shapely pipe, fragrant with honeyed breath
> From the sweet wax that joins it, curved to fit the lip so well.
> As for me—down to Hades Love is haling me already.
>   Break off, I pray, ye Muses, break off the pastoral song.
>   (123–31)

Who utters this new refrain?[8] We can attribute it to Thyrsis, bringing his song to a close, but it can also be put in the mouth of Daphnis, conscious of speaking his last words and handing over the instrument on which he made pastoral music. At this most heightened moment of the song, the singer's refrain comes close to being the hero's dramatic utterance.

Just as the goatherd's cup stands in for its heroic models, so Thyrsis comes to represent the bucolic hero whom he laments and celebrates. Thyrsis stands in for Daphnis in a double sense: the climax of his *impersonation* occurs when we are most aware of Daphnis as a master of pastoral song, a role in which Thyrsis can be thought to *replace* him. We can also see a resemblance between Daphnis's self-dramatization and the gestures with which Thyrsis begins and ends his song—the expostulation, "Where were ye, nymphs?" and his farewell to the Muses. Yet just as the cup reduces the shield of Achilles to an aesthetically pleasing object whose scenes we contemplate with interest but also detachment, so Thyrsis remains at a certain distance from the heroic herdsman whom he represents. The distinction between the hero who dies and the narrator/ impersonator who is still on the scene at the end of the song might be thought to go without saying. But this poem makes a point of saying it, of bringing out the distinction. The poem continues from the point in Daphnis's farewell at which our last quotation broke it off:

---

8. Dover (83) asks whether this new refrain might begin at 114, before Daphnis begins his farewells. But the evidence Gow presents (vol. 2: 16) seems decisive—that the scholiasts "comment on [this refrain] at 127, and the mss agree in introducing it at that point and using it from there on."

Bear violets henceforth, ye brambles, and ye thistles too,
And upon boughs of juniper let fair narcissus bloom,
Let all things be confounded; let the pine-tree put forth figs,
Since Daphnis lies dying! Let the stag tear the hounds,
And screech-owls from the hills contend in song with nightingales.
 Break off, I pray, ye Muses, break off the pastoral song.
These words he spoke, then said no more: and him would Aphrodite
Fain have raised back to life; but no more thread for the Fates to spin
Was left him: down to the stream went Daphnis: eddying waves
 closed o'er
The man loved by the Muses, whom every Nymph held dear.
 Break off, I pray, ye Muses, break off the pastoral song.
And now give me the she-goat and the bowl, that I may milk her
And pour forth to the Muses. O Muses, fare you well,
And again farewell. Another day a sweeter song I'll sing you.
(132–45)

The first of the refrains could be uttered by either Daphnis or Thyrsis. It could certainly be the parting shot of the hero, whose vision of nature upside down concludes with a dissonant chorus of owls and nightingales (the meaning of the verb in the line is unsure and much disputed). Even if attributed to Thyrsis, the refrain intervenes in and terminates the hero's utterance, and thus could take on some of his urgency. Where the separation of hero and singer becomes decisive, even startling, is after the last refrain, where the illusion of impersonation completely ceases, and the song, as Rosenmeyer says, is frankly "characterized as a performance."[9] Thyrsis's farewell to the Muses does not have heroic finality: it is simply *au revoir*.

 The quotidian sense of reality is at the heart of the poem's pastoralism. The mysterious line in which the eddying waves close over Daphnis, where identification with the hero's fatality is strongly felt, is balanced by the goatherd's words immediately preceding Thyrsis's song:

This bowl with all my heart would I bestow on you,
If you'll be kind and sing that song I yearn so much to hear.
I am in earnest. Come, friend; surely you will not hoard your song
Until you come to Hades where all things are forgot?
(60–63)

From the perspective of these lines, the poem sharply distinguishes Daphnis from Thyrsis. Whatever lies behind Daphnis's fate—and here the poem is

---

9. Rosenmeyer, 121.

opaque and mysterious, some argue purposely so—it is certain that he goes down to Hades resolutely preserving some self-defining notion or secret. The goatherd and Thyrsis, more ordinary herdsmen, are willing to identify themselves by concrete and disparate pleasures and recognitions. It is the goatherd, not the master singer, who has the last word in the poem:

> Thyrsis, may your fair mouth for this be filled and filled again
> With honey and the honey-comb; and may you eat dried figs
> From Aigilos; for more lovely than the cricket's is your song.
> See, here's the bowl; and mark, my friend, how savourly it smells.
> In the well-spring of the Hours you might think it had been dipped.
> Come here, Kissaitha!—She is yours to milk.—Beware, you kids;
> Skip not about so, or you'll have the he-goat after you.
>   (146–52)

The last line should not lead us to exaggerate the "down-to-earth" outlook here. The speech is remarkable for the range of its modes of praise and its intimated sensory and imaginative experiences—a range made possible by the capacity of the ordinary herdsman, as he is represented in this poem, to value experiences and awarenesses disparately and as they come. Even the last line, which could be thought to deflate by its appeal to coarser realities, exemplifies the poise of the whole poem, for it brings back to the stabilities of ordinary life the rather brutal common sense with which Priapus mocked Daphnis (81–92).

To repeat: just as the cup reduces Homer's shield to an aesthetically pleasing object that can be valued and exchanged in the regular course of our lives, so Thyrsis and the goatherd live, as we say, in a different world from Daphnis, much less Achilles and Heracles. And yet Thyrsis can sing not only about Daphnis but in his stead, and the goatherd's acceptance of the here and now is not in ignorance of larger forces and disturbing mysteries. His initial refusal to pipe, for fear of Pan's wrath, is answered, at the end of his speech, by his recognizing the powers against which humans define themselves:

> Come, friend, surely you will not hoard your song
> Until you come to Hades where all things are forgot?

The last line comes to a focus on a single grand epithet for Hades—*eklelathonta*, "making utterly forgetful," a word with Homeric resonances and filling almost two hexameter feet. The line thus suggests an awareness not only of death as a limit, but also of its power to blot out all by which we know ourselves. The goatherd and Thyrsis do not embrace the powers of Hades, as Daphnis does, but they recognize the penumbra surrounding our lives.

By the same token, the goatherd's cup does not merely miniaturize human life. Its scenes register problematic realities (physical need and difficulty, aggressiveness, emotional uncertainty and distress) that pastoral, on some views of it, seeks to ignore. The craftsman's attention to border devices and the cup's general effect of framing its scenes suggest that the bucolic artisan's aim is both to acknowledge what lies outside his boundaries and to include and set off as much as can be taken in without loss of moral and aesthetic poise. Viewed this way, the cup is not only, as David Halperin has suggested, a programmatic presentation of bucolic themes.[10] It also is representative of the art of bucolic poetry, and suggests its strength relative to world. The cup both substitutes for the song the goatherd refuses and is a fitting token of exchange for Thyrsis's song. In framing what is humanly problematic, it not only matches Thyrsis's aesthetic distance from Daphnis's defiant fatality, but also brings out one of the main devices for achieving it—the refrain which, recurring every three or four lines, has the effect of framing the represented scenes and utterances and containing and distancing their energies.

II

Virgil's clarifying and unifying interpretation of Theocritus's bucolics turned their representational interests and practices into a "representative anecdote" in Burke's sense. But if this is how pastoral developed, there remains a prior question: if the beginnings of pastoral are in Theocritus's poems, why can we not develop the idea of a representative anecdote and the specific representative anecdote of pastoral from them?

This question has been given a rather surprising answer in David M. Halperin's *Before Pastoral*. Halperin argues that the literary idea of pastoral arises later than Theocritus; that we therefore should not seek in his poems generic purposes or boundaries which he did not have in mind; and that "bucolic," the term Theocritus coined for his poems, is a different type of poetry from what we mean by pastoral. Halperin surveys the way "bucolic" is used in Theocritus and in post-Theocritean commentary, and shows that ancient commentators did not limit the application of the term to poems about herdsmen. After thus clearing the ground, Halperin takes as his starting point the generic centrality of meter:

> At the time Theocritus was composing the Idylls, the principle of classifying poetic genres according to meter and the doctrine of the fixity and separateness of the poetic genres had been long and powerfully established.... The most reasonable way to discover the form, and hence the "generic" concept, underlying the bucolic poetry of Theocritus is to regard his use of the dactylic hexameter as programmatic and to investi-

10. Halperin, chap. 9, esp. 177–89.

gate the relation between bucolic poetry and the other kinds of poetry traditionally composed in that meter.[11]

On this view, any one of Theocritus's hexameter poems (i.e., all his poems except epigrams and a few idylls) can be regarded as belonging to the bucolic genre—or strictly speaking, the bucolic subgenre of *epos*, the class of all poems written in epic meter. Since the *Idylls* include mythological poems, urban love complaints, and short comic street dramas ("mimes"), this claim may seem implausible. But Halperin would say that is because we take "bucolic" to mean "pastoral," and he would go on to point out how much Theocritus's "pastoral" and "non-pastoral" bucolics have in common. In subject and theme, they concern the lives of ordinary people, the ups and downs of love, and minor or marginal episodes from myth and heroic poetry; in poetic handling, they are short, sophisticated, and playful or comic in tone. Many of these characteristics are what Halperin calls "inversions" and "subversions" of heroic *epos*. Indeed, he argues that bucolic poetry "does not possess an autonomous identity or definition," but is "defined by opposition" to "the characteristics of the traditional *epos* in response to which it arose."[12]

Even if, as is likely, Halperin has overplayed his hand, his argument is helpful and liberating. There is clearly something to his point that Theocritus has an interest not just in herdsmen but in ordinary people in general. He helps us recognize the continuity in poetic project between the idylls about herdsmen and other distinctively Theocritean poems: Idyll 15, a mime in which two Syracusan housewives attend an Adonis festival; Idyll 13, which concerns Heracles' infatuation with the boy Hylas; and Idyll 2, in which an urban adolescent recounts her unhappy love affair and attempts to cast a spell on the man who has jilted her. (The fact that Virgil turned Idyll 2 into a pastoral love complaint, in Eclogue 8, suggests that he regarded it as "bucolic," or at least eligible to be considered bucolic.) By the same token, it seems to be misplaced critical anxiety to ask whether Idyll 10, a contention about love between two reapers, or Idyll 11, Polyphemus's complaint for the nymph Galatea, are or are not "pastoral": in Halperin's terms, they are clearly bucolic.[13]

The question of whether most or all of the *Idylls* belong to the same poetic

---

11. Halperin, 211.

12. Ibid., 249. On "inversion" and "subversion," see 219–37.

13. Idyll 11 has usually been regarded as pastoral, but Rosenmeyer's comments on it (87, 102, 129, 254) show the uneasiness that thoughtfully applied criteria can induce. In comparing Idyll 6, which also concerns Polyphemus, Rosenmeyer sketches the kind of argument that might be made against Halperin: "From the whole range of the legendary tale, a particular moment is chosen; it is a moment of inaction, of relaxation, but also of suspense. The procedure is similar to what happens in many epyllia; but the moment is chosen for its stillness, its balanced simplicity, and not, as in the typical epyllion, for the refracted light it sheds on the old legend" (88).

kind must be left to students of Hellenistic poetry. From our standpoint, the most important weakness in Halperin's argument is his failure to explain why Theocritus called his poems "bucolic." The term comes from *boukolos* (cowherd) and appears prominently in poems that appear "pastoral" to us. The goatherd praises Thyrsis's mastery of bucolic singing (*boukolikas moisas*, 1.20), and the refrain of the song for Daphnis the *boukolos* (1.92, 116) uniformly speaks of it as bucolic song (*boukolikas aoidas*). In Idyll 7, which is explicitly concerned with poetic principles, the verb *boukoliasdesthai* ("bucolicize," apparently a word coined by Theocritus) refers to the exchange of songs between a goatherd who is a master singer and an urban poet who is on his way to a harvest festival. Late in his study, Halperin acknowledges Theocritus's use of the herdsman as "a vehicle for poetic self-expression" and "a figure which could serve as the type of the Alexandrian poet."[14] For him, this observation has little force or centrality. But its pertinence both to a number of idylls and to the terms used in them makes one think that the "bucolics" may be a distinct group within the Idylls.

It is therefore not surprising that one study identifies seven Idylls (1, 3, 4, 5, 6, 7, 11) as pastoral and excludes others because "the figure of the Herdsman-Poet, the hallmark of the genre, does not appear in them."[15] What is surprising is that this criterion does not work out very well. Idyll 4 has always been included among the pastoral idylls, because it is a dialogue between two herdsmen. But neither of them sings or offers to sing a song, and only one even mentions his abilities as a singer. It therefore seems legalistic to count this poem as pastoral and exclude Idyll 10, in which the interlocutors, though they are reapers, not herdsmen, both sing songs, one of which closely resembles the love complaint of the goatherd in Idyll 3. Even the programmatic Idyll 7 presents difficulties if we take the representation of herdsmen-poets as "the hallmark of the genre." Most scholars think Idyll 7 in some way concerns a poetic initiation, a latter-day analogue of a famous scene in which Hesiod says the Muses came to him while he was herding his lambs on Helicon, gave him a staff of laurel, and breathed into him a divine voice (*Theogony* 22–32). Theocritus's goatherd Lycidas is not only a master singer but may in some way represent a divinity of song; he offers his "bucolic song" as an example of well-crafted poetry, more modest than Homer's; and when the two poets have performed for each other, he gives his herdsman's staff to Simichidas. All this would be quite straightforward if Simichidas—who narrates the poem and is usually thought

14. Halperin, 243.

15. Walker, 34. These seven idylls are the ones Gutzwiller singles out. But she views pastoral not as generically fixed in and by Theocritus, but as emerging from his focusing, in a way that was new to Greek literature, on the figure of the herdsman. She agrees with other scholars that what Theocritus began was completed by Virgil (ix). At least from our standpoint, her views are thus not inconsistent with Halperin's, though she keeps a certain distance from him.

in some way to represent Theocritus—showed any signs of having undergone a pastoral initiation. But he remains to the end a visitor to the country, and most important, the song in which he displays his prowess is emphatically urban—a witty exhortation on behalf of an absent friend who is foolishly in love with a boy. Even Lycidas's song, which certainly should be a representative "bucolic" poem, begins as a recognized type of urban love poetry—a *propemptikon*, or amatory farewell to a traveler—before it turns, as we shall see, to a recognizably "pastoral" conclusion.

If "bucolic" is a generic term, it must in some sense be attributed to the poet himself and not simply to various characters in some of his poems. If neither the herdsmen of the *Idylls* nor the singers and poets nor the represented songs sufficiently illuminate the term, Virgil's example prompts us to ask how the poet of the *Idylls* represents himself. The figure of Simichidas in Idyll 7, whom scholars at one time simply identified with Theocritus, is too urban and elusive to be taken as a pastoral self-representation.[16] However, there are two other passages in the *Idylls* in which we can see pastoral self-representation of a fullness which anticipates Virgil. The first is the last scene on the goatherd's cup:

> Then, but a little space beyond that sea-hardened old man,
> Is a vineyard, richly laden with clusters fiery-red,
> And guarding it a little lad upon a rough wall sits,
> Two she-foxes on either side; one ranging up and down
> The vine-rows, pilfering the ripe grapes; the other against the wall
> Is marshalling all her cunning, and vows she will not leave
> That boy, till she has set him down to breakfast on dry crumbs.
> But he with stalks of asphodel is plaiting a pretty cage

---

16. It is true that Simichidas utters the neologism *boukoliasdōmestha*, "let us bucolicize." But even if this means "let us sing country songs," it can only be with reference to the occasion, not to Simichidas's social character, for the goatherd's teasing has just made it clear that his new companion is a man of the city. By the same token, scholars now agree that if Simichidas is a pseudonym for Theocritus, it is not a rustic name in which the poet disguises himself, but a known urban nickname, like the name Sicelidas by which the poet Asclepiades was known and which is used to refer to him in Idyll 7 (40). Simichidas may seem to represent himself as a herdsman when he responds to Lycidas' song (91–3):

> Dear Lycidas, many things else the Nymphs
> Have taught me too, while I was pasturing kine among the hills,
> Good songs, that fame perchance has brought even to the throne of Zeus.

But the self-conscious allusion to Hesiod's encounter with the Muses and the way the last line hints at the patronage of Ptolemy Philadelphus show that the speaker's acts of herding are fleeting and metaphoric. Rosenmeyer (63) speaks of Theocritus as playing cat and mouse with the identification of himself as Simichidas, and the same can be said of his representing the narrator and poet of Idyll 7 as a herdsman.

For locusts, binding it with a reed; nor cares he for his wallet,
Nor for the vines so much as in his plaiting he finds joy.

(45–54)

Like the first two scenes on the cup, this one includes suggestions of painful experience. But the threat to the boy and the vineyard are treated lightly, and unlike the first two scenes, what is (potentially) distressing is no part of the experience of the central human figure. The scenes have progressed from the presumably urban setting of the love triangle; to a rather stern natural world (cf. the rough rock and the old fisherman as "sea-worn") in which the appropriate human activity is toil; to a rural setting, in which the central figure is a boy occupied with something that amuses him. This progression in the scenes of the cup thus suggests the situation of Thyrsis and the goatherd, sharing the pleasures of rural art in a *locus amoenus* which is set off from the surrounding world but which still contains elements, like Pan's choler at noon or the foxes in the vineyard, whose danger must be acknowledged. The representative force of this third scene—the way it suggests the processes and pleasures of bucolic art—is confirmed by the likenesses between the boy's plaiting and the art of the cup itself. His fitting of rushes and stalks to each other suggests the skillful working of the cup (especially in the words *kalan*, lovely, *plekei*, plaits, and *epharmosdōn*, binding, all of which can be used of less miniature objects or of other arts).[17] The making of a cage or trap recalls the way the cup is surrounded by trails of ivy and acanthus and "captures" human situations in discreet scenes.[18] The boy's absorption in his craftsmanship matches the responses the poet elicits from us: two lines after speaking of the boy's joy in his plaiting, the goatherd calls the cup "a spectacle indeed for goatherds, a wonder that will strike your heart with amazement" (56).

If the boy's situation and activity represent those of the shepherds within the poem, and if the plaiting in which he is absorbed represents the art of the cup itself, then it may not seem far-fetched to take the boy's pleasure and activity as representative of the pastoral art of Theocritus himself. There is representative force even in the miniaturization of the boy and his cricket cage, for they are connected in two ways with the self-conscious diminutions of

17. Cf. Segal, 27: "The concentrated weaving of the 'beautiful' cage for the grasshopper is a palpable symbol of poetry." Elsewhere, Segal associates this figure with "the making of poetry, for the association of 'weaving' and poetry goes back to archaic times" (182).

18. There is probably no way to determine whether the boy is making a cage or a trap. The manuscripts have both readings, as do the manuscripts of the analogous passage in *Daphnis and Chloe*, 1.10. The charms of the *Wissenschaft* involved in these matters can be seen in Dover's note, justifying his reading "grasshopper-cage": "The variant 'grasshopper-trap' is unattractive; the easiest way to catch grasshoppers is simply to walk into the grass and pounce on them (catching cicadas is a different matter)."

Alexandrian poetry. First, the scene plays on and brings out our awareness that the goatherd's cup is itself a diminished, handcrafted version of epic predecessors. Second, the *akris* for which the cage is being made is a generic name for the class of insects which includes the cicada (*tettix*)—Callimachus's symbol of his own poetic skill and the standard by which the goatherd praises Thyrsis's song at the end of this poem.[19]

If the boy on the cup represents the poet by conspicuous diminution, Lycidas's song in Idyll 7 exemplifies the possibilities of expansive self-representation. The first half of the song has nothing pastoral about it. Lycidas wishes a safe voyage for Ageanax, the youth for whom he burns in love. At the point where he imagines Ageanax's ship safely in port, he imagines himself rejoicing— garlanded, lying on a soft couch, and drinking excellent wine "luxuriously"[20] while calling to mind his beloved. The song now takes a pastoral turn:

> Two shepherds, from Acharnae one, the other from Lykope,
> Shall be my flute-players; and beside me Tityrus shall sing
> How once Daphnis the herdsman loved Xenia the nymph,
> And how the mountain grieved for him, and the oak-trees sang his dirge
> (The oaks that grow along the banks of the river Himeras),
> When he lay wasting like a streak of snow beneath tall Haimos,
> Or Rhodope, or Athos, or far-off Caucasus.
>
> (7.71–77)

There is a double reflexiveness in this passage. On the one hand, Lycidas, having sung himself into an imagined state of pleasure, now represents as an element of that pleasure hearing a song sung to him. Second, the subject of that song is an image of himself—a herdsman deprived of his love and accompanied, instead, by song. The Daphnis of these lines (evidently the same figure as the dying hero of Idyll 1) differs from Lycidas in the grand setting of his love grief, in nature's solicitude for him, and in the tragic cast of his love. But these differences too have a self-referential aspect, for they recall Lycidas's distinguishing himself from poets who seek to rival Homer and build as high as a mountain.

As Lycidas continues singing the song he imagines hearing, he produces a second self-representation, fuller and more striking:

19. "Your singing outdoes the cicada" (148). For Callimachus, see the next section and n. 35. Without mentioning this passage, Rosenmeyer (55) speaks of the interest of Hellenistic poets and painters in children, by way of discussing "Theocritus's reduction of complex experiences by means of a concentration upon youthful inexperience" (56). Halperin observes, in discussing the boy on the cup, "The playful child came to be a fitting figure for the Alexandrian poet dedicated to upholding standards of artistic modesty" (181).

20. This is Trevelyan's rendering of *malakōs* (69), and is repeated by Gow in his note (though not in his translation).

And he shall sing how once the goatherd was enclosed alive
In a great coffer by his lord's outrage and cruel spite;
And how the blunt-faced bees, as from the meadows they flew home
To the fragrant chest of cedar-wood, fed him with tender flowers,
Because with sweet nectar the Muse had steeped his lips.
O fortunate Komatas, such joys indeed were thine;
Yea, prisoned in the coffer, by the bees thou wast fed
With honey-comb, and didst endure thy bondage a whole year.

(78–85)

Komatas is an image of Lycidas not only because he is a goatherd whose lips have been favored by the Muse, but also because his confinement—strict and distressing and yet characterized by sweetness—replicates Lycidas's condition of self-pleasuring separation, perhaps even deprivation, in his love. The Komatas of this episode appears nowhere else in Greek poetry. His living in a past time, his unusual fate, the miracle which preserved him, and the frequent Homeric diction of the passage all suggest that he is intended, as if displacing the fated Daphnis, as the mythical founder of herdsmen's song. This is what emerges in the address to him that concludes Lycidas's song:

Would that thou hadst been numbered with the living in my days,
That so I might have grazed thy pretty she-goats on the hills,
Listening to thy voice, whilst thou under the oaks or pines
Hadst lain, divine Komatas, singing sweet melodies.

(86–89)

In the immediately preceding lines, Lycidas has addressed "divine Komatas" in a manner "reminiscent of the way in which gods and heroes are sometimes praised."[21] The energy of the speaker's invocation and the return to the kind of mountain scene where Lycidas says he worked out his song make the counterfactual imagining of this passage feel like a present reality. Lycidas represents himself still as the listener here, but it is precisely by singing of himself in this role that he has come to establish the presence of his mythical forebear. The poetic handling makes good the claim implicit in producing an ad hoc myth of origin: it suggests the latter-day poet's capacity to mythologize the origins even of a mode of poetry that is self-consciously derivative and at a distance from august predecessors.

   Though Komatas, like Lycidas, was a goatherd (*aipolos*), the sophistication and breadth of this inset make one wonder why it does not define what makes Theocritus bucolic. The mainstream of Theocritean criticism would give an

---

21. Dover on 7.83ff., referring to the use of *tu thēn* immediately after a vocative in 83 and followed by *kai tu* twice.

ethical answer to this question. Rosenmeyer might argue that the mythological fullness and the highly conscious self-mirroring are precisely what make the passage unrepresentative of Theocritean pastoral, with its Epicurean emphasis on accessible goods and lightness of touch.[22] He might point to the fact that Lycidas is answered by Simichidas's witty and not very high-minded song, which among other things mocks a friend's passionate love. Theocritean bucolic, he might say, lies in the play between these two songs, the balance and poise they give the whole poem, and the kind of friendship they establish between the two singers. Halperin would certainly endorse this "dialogic" view of bucolic, and other interpreters of Idyll 7 would give various accounts of the way Simichidas is necessary to the balance and economy of the poem.[23] Our own inquiry leads to an analogous conclusion. Theocritus's appearance as Simichidas and the two passages we have analyzed as representing "the poet of the bucolics" are all very different from each other. The boy on the cup and Komatas do share important attributes: they are bounded, surrounded by danger, self-sufficient, possessed by pleasure and sweetness. On the other hand, they are literally worlds apart—the boy with his innocent self-absorption, doing what any boy would do, and the adult goatherd exposed to the dangers of the heroic world[24] and made pastoral only by a miracle. And just as Lycidas and Komatas are balanced by Simichidas, so in Idyll 1 the boy is balanced by Thyrsis, whose very different artistic powers, vocal and performative, enable him to reach out to Daphnis's experience, represent him, and sing his song. In short, there is a wide range of figures who can be thought to represent "the poet of the bucolics." Even among the herdsmen-singers, we would include not only the skillful youths who sing Polyphemus's love in Idyll 6, but also the Polyphemus of Idyll 11—whose complaint, the poet says, shows how song can cure

22. Cf. his remarks (112) on the slightly unsettling effects of Komatas's presence as a heroic herdsman.

23. See Segal, 135, 155 and N. Krevans, "Geography and the Literary Tradition in Theocritus 7," *Transactions of the American Philological Association* 113 (1983): 201–20, and George B. Walsh, "Seeing and Feeling: Representation in Two Poems of Theocritus," *Classical Philology* 80 (1985): 1–19. As with just about everything concerning Idyll 7—Dover rightly says that "no other poem of Theokritos poses problems of interpretation so numerous and interesting as this" (145)—there is no unanimity about this matter. Harry Berger, Jr., mentions "the growing critical abuse to which poor Simichidas must submit": "The Origins of Bucolic Representation: Disenchantment and Revision in Theocritus' Seventh *Idyll*," *Classical Antiquity* 3 (1984): 1–39 (cf. 15, n. 28). In this extremely interesting and suggestive article, Berger does some of his own dumping on Simichidas, but he avoids giving Lycidas a privileged position in the poem's poetics by making him subject to the irony inherent in the fact that a poem which is written to be read displaces the putative presence of speech and song.

24. In saying Komatas was enclosed in a chest "by the impious presumption of a king," Theocritus uses a Homeric phrase (*kakaisin atasthaliaisin*, 79; cf. *Odyssey* 12.300, 24.458) of great ethical severity.

love—and the lovesick goatherd of Idyll 3, whose pretentious serenade is a parody of the way a sophisticated bucolic poet uses epic locutions. The gallery of Theocritean singers and "makers"—whose extremes are defined by Komatas and the boy on the cup—are sufficiently like each other to show why Theocritus's poems are called "bucolics." They are sufficiently individual and differentiated to show why no one or selected group of them can be taken as representing the poet himself or a hypothetical poet who is responsible for a clearly distinguished group of poems. The representative personages and the representational interests of pastoral are to be found in Theocritus, but only, so to speak, in solution. It was Virgil who crystallized them out.[25]

III

Some of Virgil's codification of Theocritus is anticipated in post-Theocritean Greek bucolic. The straightforward representation of herdsmen as poets and poets as herdsmen begins to emerge with clarity in the pseudo-Theocritean Idylls 8 and 9, and takes the form in which we know it in the *Lament for Bion*, where for the first time a real urban poet is called a herdsman.[26] We can see similar developments leading to Virgil's conceiving his Eclogues as a book. If Theocritus intended a specific ordering of his hexameter poems, the evidence for it is extremely sparse and elusive. The manuscript tradition of the Eclogues, on the other hand, consistently observes the order of the poems as we know them, and various formal relations among the poems make it clear, as a recent editor says, "that Vergil himself intended [the order] to have some significance."[27] It is thought that the example for a book of bucolics was set by a collection made in the first half of the first century B.C. by the grammarian Artemidorus of Tarsus. We do not know the precise contents of this collection, but we have an epigram that stood at its head:

25. See Frances Muecke, "Virgil and the Genre of Pastoral," *AUMLA: Journal of the Australasian Universities Language and Literature Association* 44 (1975): 169–70.

26. See John Van Sickle, "Theocritus and the Development of the Conception of Bucolic Genre," *Ramus* 5 (1976): 18–44, esp. p. 27: "the [post-Theocritean] mannerists seize on a generic tendency which was inchoate in Theocritus and make it more coherent, but cut-and-dried." On Idyll 8, cf. Kathryn Gutzwiller, "Character and Legend in *Idyll* 8," *Transactions of the American Philological Association* 113 (1983): 171–82.

27. Vergil, *Eclogues*, ed. Robert Coleman (Cambridge: Cambridge University Press, 1977), 18. Virgil's book of pastorals is known by two titles, each with ancient authority, *Bucolica* and *Ecloga* (literally, "selections"). It is possible that some of the Eclogues were published individually, but at some point Virgil clearly conceived them as a book. The precise significance of the order of the Eclogues and the degree of significance to give it are, not surprisingly, much disputed. See Brooks Otis, *Virgil: A Study in Civilized Poetry*, (Oxford: Clarendon Press, 1964): 128–43, and above, chapter 2, n. 47.

> Bucolic Muses, scattered once, but now together all
> within a single fold, within a single flock.[28]

A few decades before Virgil gave pastoral its definitive form, we find the figure of the shepherd representing not only the writers of bucolic poems, but also the critical intelligence that recognizes their distinctness.

Nevertheless, it would be a mistake to think of the history of ancient pastoral in purely linear terms, as if Virgil simply picked up post-Theocritean developments and moved forward on his own.[29] The Eclogues return to, realize, and transform Theocritean interests and practices. Virgil established pastoral as a genre by turning the Idylls into a book coherently conceived in both formal and representational senses—that is, in respect to both the arrangement of the poems and the consistency of the world depicted in them. By comparison with the rural characters in Theocritus, Virgil's herdsmen are more like each other and more evidently share the same way of life. This comparative uniformity is often due to Virgil's modifying a Theocritean model. Eclogue 2 closely imitates the love complaint of Polyphemus the Cyclops, but it is put in the mouth of the shepherd Corydon. In Eclogue 9, an imitation of Idyll 7, two herdsmen who know each other, not a townsman and a goatherd, meet on the road; as in Idyll 7, there is an offstage herdsman who embodies the power of song, but far from being a mythical figure like Komatas, he belongs to the world of the two interlocutors. In other respects too, Virgil reduces the differences between Theocritus's herdsmen. When he imitates the coarse banter of Idylls 4 and 5 in Eclogue 3, he not only smooths the rough edges of Theocritus's herdsmen, but literally composes their differences by turning their quarrel into a singing contest. Unlike its model in Idyll 5, this contest does not break down into renewed quarreling, and whereas Theocritus's poem ends with the victor mocking his defeated rival, Virgil's concludes with praise all around and a suspended judgment.

Taking a hint from Latin *condo*, which has a similar double meaning, we can use the word "composing" to describe the way Virgil interprets and harmonizes Theocritean conventions and poems. With what one scholar calls his "penchant for the significant,"[30] he regularly makes them more susceptible to interpretation and more internally consistent. The one case in which Virgil does not bring a Theocritean figure into the world of ordinary herdsmen confirms the consistency of that world. In imitating Idyll 1, Virgil preserves Daphnis's special

28. *A.P.* 9.205. Gow includes this epigram in his edition, but I quote the neat translation by Van Sickle, 27.

29. Cf. Halperin, 17: "In the light of these developments within the post-Theocritean Greek tradition, Virgil's subsequent 'pastoralization' of bucolic poetry may be seen not as a rupture but rather as the continuation (highly original, to be sure) of a previously established interpretative tendency."

30. Friedrich Klingner, *Virgil* (Zürich, 1967), 94.

status. In Eclogue 5, he is a dead shepherd praised for his acts as a leader, represented as raised to the heavens, and finally installed as a local deity. (Some scholars still accept his identification, widely accepted in the Renaissance, with the recently assassinated Julius Caesar.) In Eclogue 10, he appears as the poet's friend Gallus, a love poet and military leader, who is metaphorically dying of love. Virgil's Daphnis is more distinctively set apart from his fellows, both by certain depicted acts of leadership and by his clear separation from the present scene. The dying asseveration of Theocritus's Daphnis—"I am that Daphnis," etc.—reappears in Virgil as the dead hero's epitaph. Insofar as Virgil imagines song restoring the hero's presence, it is by memorial honors and not by fictional re-presentation of the living figure, as in Thyrsis's song. Similarly Gallus, like his prototype, is visited and addressed by herdsmen and rural deities, but Virgil makes explicit his separation from them: he is not a herdsman, and his love-suffering drives him from Arcadia, whose peace he longs vainly to share. Thus even though Virgil in this case does not assimilate his Theocritean model to the world of ordinary herdsmen, his consciousness of boundaries and differences preserves the consistency and coherence of that world.

By reducing Theocritus's figures and usages to a more homogeneously rendered world of shepherds, Virgil established the conventions of pastoral. This may seem the opposite of what we want from a great poet, and there is certainly an invidious sense in which Virgil's shepherds are conventional: by comparison with the figures in Theocritus's poems, they can seem artificial and somewhat interchangeable. But the reduction of mimetic variety and substance brings different and compensating powers. A convention, precisely because it is that, enables us to grasp and make something of the likenesses between motifs and practices that seem disparate or at best loosely connected in a more mimetic poet. In reducing Theocritus's bucolic representations, Virgil's pastoral conventions develop some of their implications.

This is not a matter of greater poetic self-consciousness as such. There is plenty of that in Thyrsis's song of Daphnis and in Idyll 6, where Damoetas and Daphnis sing a double song of Polyphemus. In both these poems, we see the double sense in which the singer represents (depicts and takes the role of) someone else; in both we see Theocritus's awareness that a performer both becomes someone else and remains himself; in both there is a certain pastoral inflection of this doubleness, in the singers' poise and the ease of their separation from the figures they represent. But if we try to take this sense of the pastoral singer elsewhere in the Idylls, we find ourselves blocked. When Theocritus presents the love song of Polyphemus to his friend Nicias, in Idyll 11, do we think of him taking on a role, in the sense his herdsmen do? Is Idyll 3, a monologue spoken entirely by a lovesick goatherd, on the same or a different footing from Idyll 11, in which the poet, in his own voice, introduces Polyphemus's song and comments briefly at its end? In Virgil, we can pursue the implications of the Theocritean relation between singer and what is sung—not because Virgil dwells exclusively on this great puzzle, but because he grasps its relation to other aspects of Theocritus's world of song. When Simichidas proposes to Lycidas that they "bucolicize" while walking together, he says:

> But come, since we are sharers alike of road and morn,
> Let us sing pastoral lays: perchance each will delight the other.
>
> (7.35–36)

> *all' age dē, xuna gar hodos xuna de kai aōs,*
> *boukoliasdōmestha: tach' hōteros allon onasei.*

The word *onasei*, which Dover defines as "bring good to," includes the meanings of both Trevelyan's "delight" and Gow's "profit"; Hines's "advantage" (the verb) may be the best one-word equivalent. The idea that songs bring mutual benefits is clear in the exchange between Thyrsis and the goatherd in Idyll 1, and in the singing contest in Idyll 6, which ends with Daphnis and Damoetas embracing and exchanging gifts. But the idea of song for someone else's benefit—which is of clear relevance to the songs of Idyll 7 (Lycidas's for Ageanax's voyage and Simichidas's for his friend in love)—does not seem to apply to Thyrsis's relation to Daphnis or the singers of Idyll 6 to Polyphemus. Conversely, the paradoxes of performance seem marginal to the songs of Idyll 7, even in Lycidas's imagining of the songs that will be sung to him.

When Virgil begins Eclogue 10 by opening up the meanings of "a song for Gallus,"[31] he brings out the connections between these two ways of construing song. He represents the poem as an act of friendship, to benefit Gallus, and it begins with a scene in which various Arcadians, concerned about his woes, speak solicitously to him. But the heart of the poet's "song for Gallus" is a love lament put in the mouth of Gallus himself. The ambiguities of representation in this monologue, which is the central passage in the poem (10.29–69), are brought out by the line which follows it:

> *Haec sat erit, divae, vestrum cecinisse poetam.*

> Your poet, goddesses, has sung enough.
>
> (10.70)

"Your poet," the singer of the song we have just heard, can refer to either Virgil or Gallus, who was well known as a poet and who is addressed earlier as *divine poeta* (17). Though the succeeding lines dispel the ambiguity, it is firmly enough

31. Cf. chapter 3, p. 85.

registered to raise the question of who speaks the utterance of a represented character.

The point is not simply that Virgil replicates Theocritus's merging of singer and represented speaker but that he associates it directly with what was, in Theocritus, a quite separate aspect of bucolic singing, the idea of mutual benefit. We can see the same connection at the end of Mopsus's song for Daphnis, in Eclogue 5:

> Strew foliage on the ground and shade the springs,
> You shepherds—Daphnis calls for rites like these.
> Build him a mound and add this epitaph:
> "I woodland Daphnis, blazoned among stars,
> Guarded a lovely flock, still lovelier I." [32]

Mopsus, the singer, calls on his fellows to do something in honor of Daphnis or for his benefit. But his commanding them to do what Daphnis commands (*mandat*) suggests at the same time a sense of identification with the dead hero. Similarly, the epitaph may be seen as words he tells others to inscribe, or it may suggest that he speaks for Daphnis in the strong sense. In the latter case, Mopsus represents Daphnis, both in his momentary impersonation, at the climax of his song, and as the successor who orders rites on his behalf and who is later said to take his place as a master singer.

Just as Eclogue 10 plays out the full meaning of "a song for Gallus," so in Eclogue 5, all shepherds are imagined to be singing for one other. As in its Theocritean model, the occasion of the funeral song is the ordinary meeting of two herdsmen at noontime and the proposal to sing for each other's pleasure. But instead of the asymmetry between the goatherd's description of the cup and Thyrsis's song of Daphnis, Virgil's shepherds sing reciprocal songs of equal length—one lamenting Daphnis's death, the other envisaging his deification and future honors. Menalcas's response to Mopsus's song shows that he sings not only for his companion but also for Daphnis:

> Tale tuum carmen nobis, divine poeta,
> quale sopor fessis in gramine, quale per aestum
> dulcis aquae saliente sitim restinguere rivo.
> nec calamis solum aequiperas, sed voce magistrum:
> fortunate puer, tu nunc eris alter ab illo.
> nos tamen haec quocumque modo tibi nostra vicissim
> dicemus, Daphinque tuum tollemus ad astra;
> Daphnin ad astra feremus: amavit nos quoque Daphnis.
> (5.45–52)

---

32. 5.40–44. This passage is discussed in chap. 3, where the Latin is also quoted.

> Your song, inspired poet, is like slumber
> On soft grass to the weary, or a brook
> Of sparkling water, quenching noontime thirst.
> Piping and singing both, you are his equal,
> Fortunate lad, his one and true successor.
> But in response to you, as best I can,
> I'll sing and raise your Daphnis to the stars:
> Yes, to the stars—for Daphnis loved me too.

The closest Menalcas comes to impersonating Daphnis is in his opening lines, which represent the newly elevated hero wondering at the unfamiliar threshold of Olympus. Nevertheless, his is very much a song for Daphnis. It imagines unusual harmony filling the countryside because "Daphnis loves peace" (61); it voices a cry of joy (*"Deus, deus ille, Menalca!"*) which the singer imagines hearing nature express at Daphnis's deification; finally, the second half of the song is addressed to Daphnis himself, as a new local deity. In all this, the shepherds' intention to give each other pleasure (a purpose represented by the gifts they exchange at the end) extends to and becomes the broader purpose of restoring and representing the dead hero to the world from which death separated him. They depict him to that world and provide substitutes for him, both in their own persons and in the rites they call for. Singing for each other, Mopsus and Menalcas sing for Daphnis, and in singing for Daphnis, they come to sing for the world they represent and therefore for each other in a fuller sense.

Just as Virgil integrates the Idylls' treatment of impersonation and the benefits of song, so he brings the bucolic poet's representation of himself into the world and conventions of his Eclogues. The poet's self-representation in Eclogue 10 is implicit in his invoking Arethusa, who as a Sicilian nymph had become an unofficial bucolic muse.[33] Later the poet describes the arrival of Pan, "Arcadia's god, whom we ourselves/Saw stained with crimson dye and blood-red berries."[34] In the closing passage, Virgil speaks of himself as having sung for Gallus while weaving a basket—we may think of the boy and his cricket cage, though the image of poetry as weaving is widespread—and he speaks the last line of the poem, and of the whole Eclogue book, in the character of a shepherd: *ite domum saturae, venit Hesperus, ite capellae* ("Go home well fed, my goats: go: Vesper comes"). As even these few examples suggest, the poet represents himself as a shepherd with various degrees of explicitness. He is most direct and programmatic at the beginning of Eclogue 6:

---

33. See the *Lament for Bion*, 77, and Halperin, 129–30, 251–53.

34. 10.26–27: *Pan deus Arcadiae venit, quem vidimus ipsi/sanguineis ebuli bacis minioque rubentem.* The first-person plural can be used as the equivalent of the first-person singular, so the words here can mean either "whom I myself saw" or "whom we [Arcadians] ourselves saw."

Prima Syracosio dignata est ludere versu
nostra neque erubuit silvas habitare Thalea.
cum canerem reges et proelia, Cynthius aurem
vellit et admonuit: "pastorem, Tityre, pinguis
pascere oportet ovis, deductum dicere carmen."
nunc ego (namque super tibi erunt qui dicere laudes,
Vare, tuas cupiant et tristia condere bella)
agrestem tenui meditabor harundine Musam.

(6.1–8)

My playful muse first chose Sicilian verse:
She did not blush to dwell among the woods.
When I tried a song of kings and battles, Phoebus
Plucked my ear and warned, "A shepherd, Tityrus,
Should feed fat sheep, recite a fine-spun song."
Now I—for poets enough will long to speak
Your praises, Varus, and compose sad wars—
Tune rustic musings on a delicate reed.

The poet not only depicts himself as a shepherd and adopts a pastoral name; he also makes this self-representation central to bucolic poetics. The opening lines are modelled on a famous passage in Callimachus:

> Do not look to me for a song loudly resounding. It is not mine to thunder; that belongs to Zeus. For, when I first placed a tablet on my knees, Lycian Apollo said to me: " . . . poet, feed the victim to be as fat as possible, but, my friend, keep the Muse slender. . . . For we sing among those who love the shrill voice of the cicala and not the noise of the . . . asses." Let others bray just like the long-eared brute, but let me be the dainty, the winged one.[35]

These lines are strongly reminiscent of Lycidas's attack, in Idyll 7, on those who would emulate Homer, and both Callimachus and Theocritus are close to pastoral self-representation—Callimachus in the image of the cicada and Theocritus in Lycidas and the other figures, Simichidas and Komatas, who are associated with his statement. Virgil's calling himself Tityrus thus completes the development of a pastoral convention already implicit in his Alexandrian predecessors.

Virgil does not confine his self-representation to a passage like this, but builds it into his pastoral world. For self-reflexive richness, the Komatas inset in Idyll 7 matches any single passage of the Eclogues, but its elements suffuse

---

35. Callimachus, *Aetia, Iambi, Lyric Poems, Hecale, and Other Fragments*, ed. and trans. C. A. Trypanis (Cambridge: Harvard University Press, Loeb Classical Library, 1975), frag. 1.17–33.

Virgil's world. Some of the energies of Lycida's song appear in the utterances of other figures than the poet himself—for example, Gallus's praise of the Arcadians as singers:

> tristis at ille "tamen cantabitis, Arcades" inquit
> "montibus haec vestris, soli cantare periti
> Arcades. o mihi tum quam molliter ossa quiescant,
> vestra meos olim si fistula dicat amores!"
>
> (10.31–34)

> He, full of sorrow, said, "Still you will sing
> All this, here in your hills, Arcadians, masters
> Alone of song. What soft rest for my bones
> If your pipes sometime will rehearse my love."

As in Lycidas's song, blocked erotic feelings are transferred to other imagined pleasures—most notably in *molliter*, which occurs here uniquely in Virgil and in its range of meanings (softly, tenderly, luxuriously) is the equivalent of Theocritus's *malakōs*, used of Lycidas's drinking to Ageanax's safe arrival.[36] Perhaps Gallus is imagining himself as Lycidas imagined his prototype Daphnis—dying while the love-laments, sung either in or to the mountains (the Latin will bear both meanings) sound around him. There is implied self-representation, again wishfully inflected, when Gallus, famous as a poet, calls the Arcadians the *only* skilled singers (*soli cantare periti*); later he explicitly imagines himself tuning his witty verses on a pastoral pipe. Gallus does not represent Virgil in any simple sense, but he is also not as dramatic a figure as Theocritus's Lycidas. In addressing the Arcadians—in whose number the poet has just included himself, in the lines about Pan—Gallus gives back an image of the poet's undertaking to sing a pastoral song for him. Indeed, in these and the following lines, Gallus takes on an imaginative "project" very close to Virgil's: to represent himself as a shepherd.

Gallus may seem too like the poet—and Eclogue 10 too unusual a poem—to establish much in general about the Eclogues. But even the representation of ordinary shepherds contributes elements to the poet's self-representation. A striking example derives from Meliboeus's invocation of Tityrus's well-being at the beginning of the first Eclogue.[37] Like Gallus's account of the Arcadians' life, Melboeus's account of Tityrus's is heightened by his sense of separation from it. In giving a particular representation of Tityrus, in speaking for as well as to him, Meliboeus can be seen to resemble the poet himself. But this likeness arises

36. Cf. Coleman ad loc, who points out the uniqueness of the adverb and supplies the meanings cited.

37. Quoted and discussed, in chap. 1.

from the dramatic circumstances of the eclogue, and it is made good not by any on-the-spot reflexiveness, but five eclogues later, when Meliboeus's speech supplies part of Virgil's own self-representation. In adopting the name Tityrus, the poet describes himself in words taken from Meliboeus's depiction of his namesake: *nunc ego . . . agrestem tenui meditabor harundine Musam* ("Now I will tune rural musings on a delicate reed," 6.8).[38]

The conventions of Virgilian pastoral can be encapsulated in the formula, "the poet represents (himself as) a shepherd or shepherds." The fictional representations and the self-representation are implicit in each other, and together they constitute the representative anecdote of pastoral. To return to Burke's terms, it will certainly be agreed that Virgil's composing of Theocritus is a feat of reduction. The question remains whether the reductions of Virgilian pastoral have or are capable of human scope. If "the representative anecdote of pastoral" simply means the set of fictions and conventions that will generate further pastorals, we might imagine looking down a historical hall of mirrors and seeing example after example of what has been a notoriously artificial and self-replicating form. To take this literary kind seriously, we must be able to say that the representational conventions of pastoral constitute a representative anecdote in the larger sense—that its reductions produce accounts of life and art in which one can take a serious interest and from which one can derive serious pleasure.

IV

It would seem obvious that Virgilian pastoral is serious, for it is well known that Virgil introduced strains of what Milton called a "higher mood" and that he extended pastoral to engage social and political realities that were excluded by Theocritus. The difficulty is that such matters are usually taken to go beyond the representational possibilities of pastoral. The poem Virgil put first in his book of Eclogues seems to confirm this assumption. Eclogue 1 has no pastoral singing, explicitly refers to contemporary Rome, and concerns a countryside disrupted by the aftermath of civil war. It is not surprising to find a recent editor summarizing it in the following terms: "There is little of Theocritus in the poem; it is a boldly original and highly wrought piece presenting in dramatic form the confrontation between pastoral myth and contemporary Italian reality."[39]

Eclogue 1 is a dialogue between two herdsmen who have shared a way of

---

38. Cf. 1.2: *silvestrem tenui musam meditaris avena* ("You tune woodland musings on a delicate oaten reed").

39. Coleman, 90–91. This is the view taken by Michael C. J. Putnam's influential book, *Virgil's Pastoral Art* (Princeton: Princeton University Press, 1970), chap. 1.

life but are now driven apart by events over which they have no control. In the opening speech, which we have already looked at for other reasons, Meliboeus draws the contrast with which the poem is concerned—between Tityrus's well-being and his own unwilling departure from his home. Later passages reveal that Meliboeus's land has fallen victim to the expropriations of land (40–39 B.C.) with which Octavian and Antony rewarded their veterans after the battle of Philippi. Tityrus is not exempt from the circumstances that have determined Meliboeus's fate: he has simply been more fortunate and enjoys the protection of a powerful young man in Rome, whom he calls a god and who is presumably Octavian. However unanticipated by Theocritus, a pastoral representation of this situation is not surprising. Shepherds, as we have said earlier, fittingly represent those whose lives are determined by the actions of powerful men or by events and circumstances over which they have no control.

But a piece of writing is not pastoral simply because it makes herdsmen examples of a more general plight. We can readily imagine a poem or other writing in which shepherds are used as examples, but in which the literary form or the mode of representation is not determined by the fiction of shepherds' lives. In calling Eclogue 1 a pastoral, we must have in mind not simply the character and situation of its interlocutors, but the way they are realized in the poem. Against the view that contemporary realities disrupt the pastoral myth, our claim is that Virgilian pastoral is capable of representing these realities without losing its character as pastoral. The central critical questions, then, are how these realities enter the poem and make their presence felt and how the poem makes us feel the representative character of its two speakers.

In addressing these questions, the issue is not the number of Theocritean imitations and allusions in Eclogue 1—about that there is considerable scholarly disagreement—or whether the poem is "Theocritean" in the sense one can use that term of more narrowly imitative Eclogues like 3 and 7. What matters is whether Eclogue 1 is of a piece with the development of Virgilian pastoral from Theocritean bucolic. If that is the question, we can properly compare the opening passages of Idyll 1 and Eclogue 1 without worrying about precise questions of imitation. The most important point from a formal standpoint—and pastoral's capacity to represent political realities is a formal question—is that Virgil has turned Theocritus's responsive exchange into something that looks like drama. Hence some scholars call Eclogue 1 a rustic mime, and critics who imagine a confrontation of "pastoral myth" and "contemporary reality" will seek out elements of the dramatic in it. But the "dramatic" effect comes less from depicted conflict or confrontation, of which there is hardly any, than from the separateness of the two speakers in a responsive exchange. Where the opening of Idyll 1 is close to the formal responsiveness of singing contests, Virgil's exchange produces two versions of pastoral, for which the passage provides tags in *calamo . . . agresti* (rustic pipe), and *silvestrem . . . musam* (woodland muse).⁴⁰

   If it is Virgilian to turn differences between speakers into versions of pastoral, differentiations and separations as such are perfectly Theocritean. The exchanges that follow the opening of Idyll 1 bring out clear distinctions between the goatherd and Thyrsis, and these underlie the various asymmetries of the Idyll—between, for example, the goatherd's anonymity and the attention paid Thyrsis's name and, on the largest scale, between the goatherd's cup and Thyrsis's song of Daphnis. Even the opening passage reveals certain slight differences and asymmetries, of which Virgil's exchange can be regarded as a charged or enhanced version. The "prizes" offered by Thyrsis and the goatherd—different, to be sure, but of the same kind and perfectly exchangeable— become, on the one hand, a symbolic instrument of pastoral (the *avena*, Milton's "oaten flute"),⁴¹ and, on the other, the real lamb sacrificed to Tityrus's god. Instead of speaking from and of a shared situation, Meliboeus and Tityrus each speaks, with considerable urgency, from his own situation. The felt difference gives a dramatic effect, but the means are pastoral. Meliboeus's speech is strongly felt as his version of Tityrus's life, because Virgil infuses into it the lover's experience of being separated from what he desires. It is not only that Meliboeus represents the *silvestrem musam* as a song of love, but that he imagines something close to erotic pleasure in the auditory plenum of the echoing woods.

   Just as the drama, such as it is, of Eclogue 1 is within the capacities of bucolic and pastoral, so the poem limits its representation of social forces, both disruptive and protective, to what can be accommodated to pastoral utterance. Rome, the young Octavian, and the expropriations are seen only as they impinge on the lives of the shepherds. The passages about them are modulated by uncertainty, wonder, gratitude, or dismay—all of which reflect the herdsman's vulnerability and limited comprehension—and are shaped by rhetorical devices, like serial listing, that are associated with bucolic. The pastoral character of the speakers is particularly apparent in their consciousness of boundaries. Tityrus's awareness of Rome revolves around its difference and distance from the world he knows (19–25). His most fervent praise of his benefactor

---

40. Above, chap. 1.

41. Peter Smith argues that in the unusual use of *avena* (oatstraw) as a musical instrument, "Virgil intended the literal meaning to yield to the symbolic." *Tenui*, as Servius observed, not only has the physical meaning "slender" but also "slight" or "humble" with reference to literary style. Virgil's purpose, Smith argues, was "to invent . . . a personal and literary musical instrument, an instrument that may symbolize the creative process of pastoral composition without violating musical commonsense." "Vergil's *Avena* and the Pipes of Pastoral Poetry," *Transactions of the American Philological Society* 101 (1970): 507.

pledges his feelings of gratitude against a vision of violated boundaries, both natural and human:

> *Ante leves ergo pascentur in aethere cervi*
> *et freta destituent nudos in litore piscis,*
> *ante pererratis amborum finibus exsul*
> *aut Ararim Parthus bibet aut Germania Tigrim,*
> *quam nostro illius labatur pectore vultus.*
>
> (1.59–63)

> Sooner light-footed stags will graze in air,
> The waves will strand their fish bare on the shore;
> Sooner in exile, their borders having been crossed,
> Will Gauls and Persians drink each other's streams,
> Than shall *his* features slip out of our hearts.

Meliboeus, whose first expression of his distress is *nos patriae finis . . . fugimus* (we flee our country's borders), responds to Tityrus's vision by applying it to his own case:

> *At nos hinc alii sitientis ibimus Afros,*
> *pars Scythiam et rapidum cretae veniemus Oaxen*
> *et penitus toto divisos orbe Britannos.*
>
> (1.64–6)

> Ah, but we others leave for thirsty lands—
> Africa, Scythia, or Oxus' chalky waves,
> Or Britain, wholly cut off from the world.

The last line makes imagined exile the inversion of dwelling securely within one's native borders. Meliboeus then imagines the sight that might greet him on returning to his *patrios finis:*

> *en umquam patrios longo post tempore finis*
> *pauperis et tuguri congestum caespite culmen,*
> *post aliquot, mea regna, videns mirabor aristas?*
> *impius haec tam culta novalia miles habebit,*
> *barbarus has segetes. en quo discordia civis*
> *produxit miseros: his nos consevimus agros!*
>
> (1.67–72)

> Shall I ever again, within my country's borders,
> With wonder see a turf-heaped cottage roof,
> My realm, at last, some modest ears of grain?
> Think of these fields in a soldier's cruel hands!

These crops for foreigners! See how discord leaves
Countrymen wretched: for *them* we've tilled and
sown!

It is these lines that tell us that the turmoil in the countryside, earlier mentioned in general terms (11–12), is due to the expropriations. How can we say that these realities disrupt pastoral as a literary mode, when our knowledge of them in the poem is inseparable from their pastoral representation?

The poetry of boundaries is most intimate and powerful in the speech which prompts and sets the level of Tityrus's outburst—Meliboeus's evocation of his friend's good fortune:

> *Fortunate senex, ergo tua rura manebunt*
> *et tibi magna satis, quamvis lapis omnia nudus*
> *limosoque palus obducat pascua iunco.*
> *non insueta gravis temptabunt pabula fetas,*
> *nec mala vicini pecoris contagia laedent.*
> *fortunate senex, hic inter flumina nota*
> *et fontis sacros frigus captabis opacum;*
> *hinc tibi, quae semper, vicino ab limite saepes*
> *Hyblaeis apibus florem depasta salicti*
> *saepe levi somnum suadebit inire susurro;*
> *hinc alta sub rupe canet frondator ad auras,*
> *nec tamen interea raucae, tua cura, palumbes*
> *nec gemere aëria cessabit turtur ab ulmo.*
>
> (1.46–58)

Lucky old man! your lands will then remain
Yours and enough for you, although bare rock
And slimy marsh reeds overspread the fields.
Strange forage won't invade your heavy ewes,
Nor foul diseases from a neighbor's flock.
Lucky old man! here by familiar streams
And hallowed springs you'll seek out cooling shade.
Here as always, the neighboring hedge, whose bees
Feed on its flowering willow, will induce
Your gentle slumber with sweet murmurings.
The hillside pruner will serenade the air;
Nor will the throaty pigeons, your dear care,
Nor turtledoves cease moaning in the elms.

At the heart of Meliboeus's nostalgia is a desire for protective boundaries and a fear of their violation. His sense of blight is expressed by muddy reeds covering the pastures[42] and by diseases spreading from a neighboring flock. He places his fortunate friend *hic inter flumina nota*, where the emphasis on *known* streams is augmented by the preposition *inter*, which suggests not simply location but surroundings. Most remarkably, the grammatical subject of the following sentence is not the bees whose murmurings will induce slumber, but *vicino ab limite saepes*, the hedge on the neighboring boundary. Details like these show the particular way in which Virgil accommodated pastoral song to historical realities. The shepherd's sense that known boundaries assure the security and pleasure he values enables him to register the pain and measure the significance of the violation of boundaries.

Eclogue 1 remains true to its bucolic heritage not simply in the character of its two speakers, but in its whole poetic enterprise. We have already noted that in his first speech Meliboeus resembles the poet in speaking for Tityrus, and the opening exchange brings out a larger sense in which Virgil's shepherds and the poet himself mutually reflect each other. Both Meliboeus and Tityrus represent the shepherd's situation as it manifests itself in song. Meliboeus's *formosam resonare doces Amaryllida silvas* is answered by Tityrus's *calamo agresti*, which gathers together the rural details of *ovilibus*, *agnus*, and *errare boves* (the sheepfolds, the lamb for sacrifice, and the wandering cattle). Throughout Eclogue 1, each shepherd speaks out of the heart of his experience, the shepherd's situation as he understands it. Each in a sense thinks his version of pastoral is *the* version of pastoral. Hence the discontinuities that have concerned commentators. None of the speeches respond directly, in the manner of drama, to what prompts them: rather, in this eclogue without performed songs, they are set pieces with something of the character of songs. (The conventions of opera may be the most helpful analogy to those new to the poem.) The lack of dramatic interaction proves to be a Virgilian extension of the bucolic responsiveness on which the first speeches were based. At the center of the poem, each shepherd has an emotional speech which conveys his sense of his own situation, but which has the effect of representing his companion's. Tityrus's *adynata*, quoted above, praise his benefactor, but their terms project, with painful accuracy, the fate that lies in store for the exiled Meliboeus.[43] Meliboeus's speech about Tityrus's good fortune is often quoted as if it gave Tityrus's own sense of his situation: it well might, since it prompts his expression of gratitude, but it is far more idyllic than anything Tityrus says of himself. What happens,

---

42. *Pascua*, from *pasco*, feed. The phrase *obducto limo* occurs at *Georgics* 1.116 to show the consequences of an overflowing river.

43. This fact is often used to criticize Tityrus for his insensitivity and contributes to the antagonism to Tityrus that now dominates criticism of Eclogue 1. In my judgment, this view rests partly on a mistaken view of pastoral and partly on taking Eclogue 1 to be more dramatic than it is. I discuss these issues in *The Singer of the Eclogues*, 65–95.

then, is that each shepherd comes to speak for the other, as if singing the other's song. The mutual responsiveness of Theocritean bucolic—exemplified in the opening of Idyll 1 and formalized in singing contests—becomes mutual representation. The likeness of *each* shepherd's speech to the poet's own activity suggests why dialogue, not monody, is the dominant form of Virgilian pastoral, and shows why it is possible to say that the pastoral poet represents himself not only as *a* shepherd but sometimes as shepherds. Even when he directly calls himself Tityrus and is thus necessarily represented as a single shepherd, Virgil brings together the first Eclogue's two versions of pastoral. He speaks of his muse inhabiting the woods (*silvas habitare*), but then changes *silvestrem*, in Meliboeus's line about Tityrus, to *agrestem tenui meditabor harundine Musam*.

True to the poet's own mode of self-representation, the doubleness of Eclogue 1's pastoralism is exemplified in speeches by each of the shepherds. When Meliboeus evokes Tityrus's good fortune, he expands the *cadre sonore* depicted in his first speech and represents Tityrus as enveloped in rural music (53–58, quoted above). This speech is of course in character for Meliboeus, but it is also a characteristic piece of Virgilian pastoral. We can imagine Theocritus contributing to it the music of Thyrsis's first speech in Idyll 1 (*psithurisma . . . melisdetai . . . surisdes*) and the sounds that Lycidas imagines surrounding Daphnis and that he wishes he could have heard as Komatas's companion. Seen in this light, Virgil's lines enhance the *locus amoenus* by the desire bred of separation; its final detail is a bird whose natural song makes pleasurable the sound of mourning.[44] At the same time, this landscape is far from imaginary. The sounds Meliboeus imagines Tityrus hearing occur in the normal course of country life. Bees are present because they make honey as well as a pleasant sound; the *frondator* trims leaves, a task performed for various purposes (e.g. providing fodder for cattle); doves were kept on some Roman farms, so they are a *cura* not only as objects of affection but also as animals to be tended.[45] In representing Tityrus, Meliboeus has incorporated something of his friend's "agrarian" version of pastoral into his own. This is one reason why the speech is not only "Meliboean" (i.e., in dramatic character) but "Virgilian."

The final speech—when Tityrus invites Meliboeus to delay his departure

---

44. *Gemere* characteristically includes the idea of mourning, lamenting; presumably for this reason Servius remarks that here it means "sing: properly of the dove" (*canere: proprie de turture*). Tennyson's "moan of doves" gives the force in this context and the desired overtones.

45. For practical details, see K. D. White, *Roman Farming*, (Ithaca: Cornell University Press, 1970). Coleman says that *limite*, in the phrase about the hedge on the neighboring boundary, "was originally used of the path that marked the boundary. . . . The very notion of land-ownership entailed by the word belongs to the realities of country life, not to the pastoral myth." This and similar comments on the realism of Eclogue 1 (e.g. re *peculi*, 32) are useful and illuminating, even if one rejects Coleman's assumption that anything "realistic" cannot be "pastoral."

for one night—is notoriously Virgilian, and it too shows that the poet's presence in the poem is established by the two shepherds he represents:

> *Hic tamen hanc mecum poteras requiescere noctem*
> *fronde super viridi: sunt nobis mitia poma,*
> *castaneae molles et pressi copia lactis;*
> *et iam summa procul villarum culmina fumant,*
> *maioresque cadunt altis de montibus umbrae.*
>
> (1.79–82)

> Still, you could take your rest with me tonight,
> Couched on green leaves: there will be apples ripe,
> Soft roasted chestnuts, plenty of pressed cheese.
> Already, in the distance, rooftops smoke,
> And lofty hills let fall their lengthening shade.

These lines engage both Tityrus's and Meliboeus's versions of pastoral and bring to its fullest expression the eclogue's poetry of boundaries. The sense of well-being comes from the rustic fare and the green couch that Tityrus offers. Even in the final lines, rural detail is essential to the achieved poise and suggestiveness. The penultimate line begins by seeming to lead out from Tityrus's rustic meal to the larger world and its uncertainties, to which Meliboeus must go: *et iam summa procul.* Both *summa* (highest) and *procul* (far off) suggest the limits of our awareness, and both are indefinite words. But in the second half of the line, *villarum culmina fumant,* these suggestions of the unknown are fixed in a rural sight that defines the shepherds' world. On the one hand, it marks a time of day and prompts the herdsmen to their meal; on the other, it adumbrates the social powers that determine their lives.[46] Similarly, the landscape of the last two lines includes both the world of human habitations and uninhabited nature. The range of representation gives the final word of the poem, *umbrae* (shadows), the ambiguity that all commentators have noticed. These are the foreboding shadows of night but also, as the pleasurable sound of the line suggests, a remembrance of the *umbra* in which Tityrus, in Meliboeus's first description of him, fills the woods with song—as these lines, with their lovely and haunting music, more elusively and ambiguously fill out the landscape of evening and its intimations for the human beings at its center.

---

46. I owe this point to Stephen V. Tracy, in a comment on an earlier version of this chapter, in *Arethusa* 23 (1990): 49–57. Tracy corrected my rather too upbeat account by pointing out that *villarum* "carries the image of a large farming estate or grand residence." Hence "the end of the line points outward to the powerful figures of the external world who are impinging on the pastoral pleasance" (50–51).

Tityrus's speech is so suggestive because it heeds the limit of Virgilian pastoral—that human experience is represented only to the extent that it can be turned into or accommodated to song. The pastoral poet's claim on our attention is not due to representational scope in its obvious sense, but to the self-understanding and the awareness of the conditions of song implicit in imagining himself in the role of a shepherd. Poetic self-consciousness thus becomes a way of acknowledging what cannot be controlled, what lies outside our limits, and therefore what it is possible to represent. Tityrus's final speech has often been felt to be the quintessential expression of Virgilian pastoral. But its poise and measure are due to its remaining in touch with the separateness normal to bucolic speakers, and not to any grander mode of lyrical summation. The speech responds to the conclusion of Meliboeus's last speech, in which he says farewell to his flock:

> *ite meae, felix quondam pecus, ite capellae.*
> *non ego vos posthac viridi proiectus in antro*
> *dumosa pendere procul de rupe videbo;*
> *carmina nulla canam; non me pascente, capellae,*
> *florentem cytisum et salices carpetis amaras.*
>
> (1:74–8)

> Go now, my goats; once happy flock, move on.
> No more shall I, stretched out in a cavern green,
> Watch you, far off, on brambly hillsides hang.
> I'll sing no songs, nor shepherd you when you
> Browse on the flowering shrubs and bitter willows.

Tityrus's speech responds to these lines not simply by being an invitation but by answering to several of the details with which Meliboeus represents pastoral well-being: lying in a green spot; seeing a far off (*procul*) sight which both bounds one's world and gives play to the imagination; and, finally, the details and pleasures of innocent feeding. Just as Tityrus takes on some of Meliboeus's mode of pastoral song—as if to modify the finality of "I'll sing no songs"—so these lines of Meliboeus's have some of Tityrus's vein of detailing rural circumstances. This is a remarkable and touching conclusion to a poem that concerns the divergence of its characters' lives. By making these final speeches answer each other and by making Meliboeus's and Tityrus's modes of pastoral interpenetrate, Virgil restores to the harsher and more ambiguous world of his poem the humane responsiveness exemplified in the opening speeches of Idyll 1. The pastoralism of the poem measures well-being and the experience of loss, and finally suspends the difference between the two speakers in the harmonies of verse.

V

Eclogue 1 shows the scope of pastoral usages and their implicit strength relative to world: its suspension of issues is reflected in the historical division of opinion about whether Tityrus's gratitude to Octavian or Meliboeus's bitterness at being dispossessed represents the poet's view of Rome in the aftermath of civil war. When Virgil returns to the expropriations at the end of the Eclogue book, it is to question explicitly the power of pastoral song. Like Eclogue 5 (to which it more than once alludes), Eclogue 9 begins with a meeting of shepherds whose discourse dwells on loss—the absent mastersinger Menalcas, the diminished countryside, and the threatened homestead and community. But this poem, like Eclogue 1, takes place in a Roman countryside disrupted by the expropriations, and it makes problematic aspects of pastoral convention that are central to the poetics of Eclogue 5. The speakers of Eclogue 9 do not settle down to perform-ing songs, and there is a diminished confidence that poetic practice can recall presences or reestablish connections. Rather, poetry and its powers are explic-itly at issue: the pressing questions are whether songs can be remembered and repeated and whether Menalcas, who (like the absent Daphnis in 5) is directly addressed, will return to his companions and enable them to resume normal pastoral singing. When the poem is described this way, one can see why many critics regard it as ironic, even antipastoral. At the same time, there are reasons for the more positive readings of other critics. These find their justification in the marked increase in poetic richness and political confidence of the songs the shepherds quote to each other in the course of the poem. We can augment and support this account in the terms provided by Virgilian convention. The quoted songs are successful repetitions or imitations (two are direct reworkings of Theocritus), and each begins with and is informed by direct address to an-other person. In the action of the poem, addressing Menalcas may not assure that he will rejoin his companions; in the quoted songs, on the other hand, absent persons are adequately addressed and even celebrated, and thus in some sense made present.

This last observation confirms what we have said about Virgilian pas-toral—that in the face of loss, heroic acts and fully represented worlds give way to poetic practice. Eclogue 9 displays the shift explicitly. In the first half of the poem, the speakers discuss scenes of disruption and disturbance in the world of the poem. These give way to the quoted songs, the last of which foretells a period of fruitful Caesarean peace; it engages some of the Roman themes of Eclogue 5, and its last line rewrites, in positive terms, one of the bitterest utterances of the displaced Meliboeus.[47] Our awareness of pastoral

---

47. 9.50: *insere, Daphni, piros: carpent tua poma nepotes* (graft pear trees, Daphnis; your sons will pluck the fruits). Cf. Meliboeus's ironic address to himself at 1.73: *insere nunc, Meliboee, piros, pone ordine vitis* (go graft your pear trees, Melibee, plant your vines).

convention should enable us both to understand the poetic self-consciousness of this shift in the poem, and to acknowledge the force of all its modes of representation. Critical disagreement about Eclogue 9 comes from treating one or another of its aspects as dominant, whereas what is remarkable is that its critical, ironic, and affirmative elements are held in suspension. This poise is largely due to Virgil's sense of the shepherds' world—the relations between shepherds within the poem and the analogous relation between the poet himself and Theocritus. This pastoral world is neither as fragile as it has seemed to some critics nor as adequate to the realities of the Roman world as it has seemed to others. Virgil's shepherds regularly come together for song, and song is what unites them. But they and their creator understand that separation and loss are the conditions of their utterance, and that poetic conventions are determined by the character of the convenings that underlie them.

Eclogue 9 begins with the same external situation as Eclogue 1, the expropriation of the farm belonging to one of the speakers. But its dramaturgy and rhetoric, brief colloquial speeches of men who meet on the road, have a more accidental character. Hence the songs are fragments, not the performed pieces of Eclogue 5, and none of the speeches has the quotable fullness of those in Eclogue 1. The ending has the same quality of suspending differences as that of Eclogue 1, but in a distinctly more astringent mode. The old shepherd Moeris, urged to "sing as we walk, it makes the trip less painful" (64), replies:

> *Desine plura, puer, et quod nunc instat agamus;*
> *carmina tum melius, cum venerit ipse, canemus.*
>
> (9.66–67)

> No more, my boy, let's do what must be done;
> We shall sing all the better when he [Menalcas] comes.

Superficially this seems to reject song because of present necessities. But the very phrase, *desine plura, puer,* recalls contexts of exchanging song,[48] and the final line not only holds out the promise of future song, but, framing its promise with *carmina . . . canemus,* sings a bit in doing so. This interdependency of occasion and mode of singing is matched in a self-reflexive gesture by the poet. He represents his first imitation of Theocritus as a song remembered by Lycidas,[49] wondering who will sing pastoral songs in Menalcas's absence. This is the kind of pastoral self-representation with which we are familiar. But beyond that, these lines quote as song the kind of Theocritean utterance that is the model

---

48. In Eclogue 5.19, *desine plura, puer* is the phrase Menalcas uses to urge Mopsus to cease speaking and begin his song; in Eclogue 8, *desine* is twice used of ending song (8.11, 61), the second time as part of a concluding refrain.

49. Ecl. 9.23–5, which closely follow Idyll 3.3–5.

for the "realistic" opening lines of this Eclogue. Of all Virgil's pastorals, Eclogue 9 is the one that most knows (like Frost's oven-bird) "in singing not to sing."

Whether realistic, as in Eclogue 9, or formalized, as in Eclogue 7, Virgil's pastoral world is represented in a way determined by the modes of speech and song to which it gives rise. Its usages always carry with them an awareness of their own conditions, both in the represented world and in the order of literature. Eclogue 1 appears critical of pastoral only if we take Meliboeus's account of Tityrus's life as the pastoral norm and fail to recognize that in representing idyllic perfection it expresses Meliboeus's sense of loss. Accepting, confronting, and seeking to restore loss are normal situations for Virgil's shepherds. When it is not "public" loss in the shepherds' world—Meliboeus's dispossession, Daphnis's death, or the arbitrary removal of Menalcas—it is the private love loss which is central to Eclogues 2, 6, 8, and 10. It may well be that before the dispossessions, Tityrus and Meliboeus, *Arcades ambo*, spoke to each other like the shepherds in Eclogues 5 and 7. But those shepherds, too, understand the conditions of their utterances: that is the point of the long prologue to the singing contest in Eclogue 7. When the shepherds of Eclogue 9 discuss the power, uses, pleasures and availability of song—a continual topic of their conversation, replacing the more impersonally programmatic statements of Idyll 7—they are not questioning the foundations of Virgilian pastoral but displaying its capacities.

In Eclogues 1 and 9 particularly, speakers extend pastoral utterance to represent the situation in which they find themselves. But there are limits to the capacities of pastoral representation, and they are most readily apparent in the poems about love. With the exception of Eclogue 2, where Corydon is a somewhat comic figure, all the love complaints in the Eclogues are uttered by someone other than the lover, the one who directly experiences loss or deprivation. In Eclogue 8, a singing match, the singers are pure performers, even less distinguishable than the pastoral twins of Eclogue 7; they are thus strikingly set apart from the distressed victims of love whose songs they sing. The extraordinary narration of Pasiphae's mad longing in Eclogue 6—in which Brooks Otis rightly sees the first outlines of Dido[50]—is part of a cosmological and mythological poem sung by Silenus in consequence of some silvan horseplay. Gallus's love complaint, in Eclogue 10, can be thought to be sung in his own person, but only the possibility that Virgil sings it for him makes it eligible for inclusion in a pastoral. What this pattern in the Eclogues makes apparent is that situations and experiences of distress tend to be represented only insofar as they can be sung: the "realistic" attempt to recover song in Eclogue 9, the ambiguity about who utters Gallus's complaint, and the aria-like speeches of Eclogue 1 set the limits of this mode of representation.

The poetic limits of Eclogue 1 are determined by the very pastoral convening, the meeting and responsive speech of shepherds, that makes possible its expression of uneasiness and distress in the world of the civil wars. Critics who want the poem to be other or more than pastoral invariably treat Tityrus's last speech as a dramatic manifestation of his inadequacy to Meliboeus's situation—his insincerity, his lack of sufficient sympathy, even his failure to issue his invitation until Meliboeus has already wandered out of earshot.[51] Such readings are an attempt to deny the pleasures and force of the final verses, whose blandishments are felt to be spiritually limited. So they may be, but such as they are, they are to be acknowledged and accepted. The poem ends with differences and distress suspended and with human fellowship sustained, in the face of loss, by pastoral representations and poetic practice. These practices are not themselves formalized within the fictive world: the concluding speeches are a putatively real exchange. But they are certainly formalized in their composition, and their bucolic responsiveness must be seen as the pastoral poet's way of concluding his poem. The note of suspension, so memorable at the end of Eclogue 1, is characteristic of all the endings of the Eclogues.[52] It is a way of bringing matters to a close without resolving issues—very much a pastoral way of ending, since it suggests the necessity of limits but an inability to impose or determine them. The formal satisfactions of the poem are similarly unimposed, oblique. The final five lines of Meliboeus's last speech are seen as separable when Tityrus responds to their motifs in a speech of equal length; *umbrae*, closing the poem, picks up the *umbra* in which Meliboeus represented Tityrus singing of Amaryllis, but responsively, as a pastoral echo, not by authorial fiat. The quality of suspension, anticipating the elusive gravity of the *Aeneid*, sets one kind of example or standard for later pastoral writings. If at the same time it indicates the limits of these poems—so conscious of boundaries, so poised in their formal orderings and in relation to each other—it at the same time bears witness to the integrity of Virgil's pastoral self-representation.

VI

Virgil established herdsmens' lives as the representative anecdote of pastoral, but the phrase should not be taken in its novelistic or sociological sense. Virgil's

---

51. This possibility arises because the imperfect *poteras*, which is usually taken as a polite form of invitation (hence my translation, "You could take your rest"), can also convey a contrary to fact meaning—"you could have taken your rest." Critics who take a strong view of the divisions in Eclogue 1 and a severe view of Tityrus prefer this latter meaning, and imagine Meliboeus walking down the road, out of earshot, leaving Tityrus looking foolish. It is hard to see how both meanings of *poteras* can come into play, but see the acute comments by William Batstone on the ambiguities of the whole ending: "On How Virgil's Pastoral Makes a Difference," *Arethusa* 23 (1990): 11–12.

52. See Alpers, 96–105.

practice, with its basis in Theocritean bucolic, makes it clear that the shepherds of pastoral are figures devised to engage certain issues of poetry and poetics, to express certain ethical attitudes, and to locate poets and readers in cultural and political history. In both Theocritus and Virgil, there is considerable variation, from poem to poem, in the degree to which the physical and social realities of herdsmen's lives are acknowledged, engaged, and involved in literary effects. Later pastoral works are variously "artificial," "fictional," and "realistic," depending on their authors' cultures, poetics, and views of reality. From the Burkean point of view we have adopted, the historical variety of pastoral has two general or theoretical explanations. The first is the complexity of representation, which at once derives from, is distinct from, and is responsible to the realities of human life. Second, the representative anecdote is conceived not as a fixed formula but as a generative fiction, which can be elaborated or transformed in accordance with the needs of representation or the claims of representativeness. Our argument is not simply that pastoral *has* changed in certain ways, but that its founding conception makes it susceptible of such change.

Much of the history of Renaissance pastoral could be written in terms of various versions of the representative shepherd. The first important book of pastorals in English, Spenser's *The Shepheardes Calender*, is consciously various and inclusive. The idea that an eclogue book should have variety goes back to the fourth-century grammarian Servius, who said (in his commentary on Virgil, which appeared in most sixteenth-century editions): "He who writes bucolics ought to take care, above all, that the eclogues not be alike."[53] Spenser built in the recommended variety by framing his book as a calendar and assigning an eclogue to each month. Seasonal decorum was not his only principle of differentiation. According to the commentator known as E. K., the eclogues are "deuided into three formes or ranckes," which he calls "plaintive," "recreative," and "moral."[54] The several versions of pastoral in *The Shepheardes Calender*, which are reflected in its variety of verse forms and poetic styles, entail and can be seen to derive from several kinds of representative shepherd.

The most obvious difference between Spenser's eclogues and those of his ancient models—his concern with Christian life and institutions—is usually associated with the Gospel parable of the Good Shepherd (John 10:1–18). But Spenser's good shepherds do not represent the clergy alone—the simple but forthright Thomalin of "July," who reproaches ambitious prelates, seems to be a layperson—and their style of speech derives from a literary source which imitates Virgil, but revises the terms on which his herdsmen are conceived as

---

53. "Qui enim bucolica scribit, curare debet ante omnia, ne similes sibi sint eclogae" (note on 3.1, observing with approval how much this eclogue differs from 1 and 2).

54. E. K. introduces these categories in "The generall argument of the whole booke" (*Minor Poems*, 11).

representative. The Latin eclogues of Baptista Spagnuoli, a Carmelite monk known from his birthplace as Baptista Mantuanus and in England as Mantuan, were a standard textbook in sixteenth-century schools. Here is what Spenser as a schoolboy would have found at the beginning of Mantuan's eclogues:

> *Fauste, precor, gelida quando pecus omne sub umbra*
> *ruminat, antiquos paulum recitemus amores,*
> *ne, si forte sopor nos occupet, ulla ferarum*
> *quae modo per segetes tacite insidiantur adultas*
> *saeviat in pecudes; melior vigilantia somno.*
>
> (1.1–5)
>
> Friend Faustus, pray thee, once our flock
>   in shade and pleasaunt bale
> Doth chew the cudde: of auncient love
>   let us begin to tale.
> Least if by hap unhappy sleepe
>   our senses should begyle,
> Some savage beast in sprouted corne
>   our cattell catch the while:
> For many such about the fields
>   do lurking lye in wayte
> Wherfore to watch is better far
>   than sleepe in my conceyte.[55]

The opening words imitate, and were once as famous as, *Tityre, tu patulae recubans* (cf. *Love's Labour's Lost* 4.2.93). But once past the cool shade in which the herd ruminates, we find ourselves in a different world from Virgil's. Wild beasts were a threat to flocks in ancient Italy, as Virgil makes clear in the *Georgics* (e.g. 3.407). In the *Eclogues*, the poet, like a good shepherd, keeps the threat on the borders of his world. It is acknowledged, in a way reminiscent of the framing effect of Theocritus's cup, only in formal listings (2.63, 3.80, 7.52, 8.52) and in visions of more than natural peace (4.22, 5.60). In the lives of Mantuan's shepherds, predatory beasts are a normal reality. Their presence in the opening speech of his first Eclogue may remind us of the parable of the Good Shepherd, but his world is Christian in a broader and more common sense: it is the world and nature after the Fall, when human beings are subject to the curse of labor. Eclogue 2, which concerns the madness of love, begins with the kind of scene—the flooding of the River Po and the repairing of its banks—that Virgil reserves for the *Georgics*. Eclogue 5, the model for Spenser's "October," speaks

---

55. Baptista Mantuanus, *Eclogues*, ed. W. P. Mustard (Baltimore: Johns Hopkins University Press, 1911). The translation is from *The Eclogues of Mantuan, Translated by George Turbervile* (1567), ed. Douglas Bush (New York: Scholars' Facsimiles and Reprints, 1937).

of a sharp conflict between the physical demands of tending sheep and the *otium* that song requires (5.13–19).

By insisting that certain realities and experiences are representative of shepherds' lives, Mantuan produces a distinct version of pastoral. His shepherds are not in the least Arcadian, but their style of speech is nonetheless pastoral. Its characteristic modes of expression—proverbs, moral judgments, homely comparisons, georgic imagery, hard-bitten invectives—have a directness and vigor that claim to derive from simple experiences and needs. Literary shepherds very frequently seek to avoid the heat of the sun, but the Mantuanesque shepherd sounds like this:

> And now the Sonne hath reared vp
>   his fyriefooted teme,
> Making his way betweene the Cuppe,
>   and golden Diademe:
> The rampant Lyon hunts he fast,
>   with Dogge of noysome breath,
> Whose balefull barking bringes in hast
>   pyne, plagues, and dreery death.
> Agaynst his cruell scortching heate
>   where hast thou couerture?
> The wastefull hylls vnto his threate
>   is a playne ouerture.
>
> ("July," 17–28)

This is Spenser's Thomalin, who goes on to call himself a "seely shepherds swayne" (30). But his challenging manner already suggests the moral authority with which he will speak against the symbolism of the hills and on behalf of the safe and humble valleys. Even his modest self-characterization has an element of moral challenge, since it responds to the goatherd's calling him "thou iollye shepheards swayne" (5) when he invites him to join him on the hill.

Mantuan's shepherds are much given to moral invective, and true to their literary provenance, Spenser puts long satiric speeches in the mouths of Thomalin ("July," 169–204) and Diggon Davie ("September," 104–35). The greatest of such speeches is the invective against false pastors in *Lycidas*. In using Virgil's miming of Theocritean coarseness to register a central moral criticism, it recapitulates the history we have sketched:

> What recks it them? What need they? They are sped;
> And when they list, their lean and flashy songs
> Grate on their scrannel pipes of wretched straw.[56]

---

56. Lines 122–24. The source is Virgil, Ecl. 3.26–27: *non tu in triviis, indocte, solebas/stridenti miserum stipula disperdere carmen?* (Wasn't it you, you dolt, who at the crossroads used to murder a wretched song on a squeaking straw?)

The Virgilian source is given stylistic authority by Mantuan and Spenser's moral vein, but these lines are pastoral for stronger reasons than their literary descent. They engage central questions of *Lycidas*: what "shepherd" most importantly represents (poet or pastor?), what kind of poet one should be, and the value of poetry if the figure of the shepherd represents human capacities. What sense, after all, does it make to attack bad ministers for their "lean and flashy songs"? On the model of *The Shepheardes Calender*, it would be as plausible to imagine that those who neglect their flocks are piping merrily in the shade (cf. "May," 19–44). Milton's lines suggest not only that a good poet must be a good man, but that the whole character of one's life has the quality of a poem, good or bad. St. Peter is no doubt a privileged speaker (though we should note he is identified by a rather pastoral kenning, "the pilot of the Galilean lake"), but his words remain true to their pastoral origins by their vigor and felt obviousness—as if all these large issues come down to saying that only a good shepherd can judge of good singing.

To say that St. Peter's speech is a version of pastoral does not deal with the question of how the rest of the poem accommodates it. In *Lycidas* this is a pressing question, but something like it has been present from the beginnings of pastoral. It is as if claiming that shepherds are representative immediately raises the question of what they represent. Servius's recommendation of variety can be seen to recognize an important capacity of the genre, rather than being simply a warning against boring your reader. The brilliance of Spenser's calendar device is that it not only accommodates different versions of pastoral, but suggests that they all belong to and emerge from one fundamental fiction. Nor does Spenser merely assign each kind of pastoral to its season. In the most interesting of the ecclesiastical eclogues, "May," the season is the occasion for a debate between two ways of construing shepherds' lives. The easy-going Palinode sets a scene of rural festivities, from which he feels unnaturally cut off. Piers, his companion, reproves him for desires unbecoming "men of elder witt," but as their debate develops, it concerns not youth and age (the subject of the nonecclesiastical "February") but appropriate behavior for both clergy and laypersons. Though the severe Piers speaks with more authority and has the central speech of the poem (73–131, with its account of the primitive church), it is not clear that the eclogue promotes a single ecclesiastical agenda.[57]

Spenser clearly had sympathies with the Protestant left. In both "May" and "July" he appeals to the authority of the shepherd "Algrind," i.e. Edmund Grindal, the Archbishop of Canterbury, who supported a reformed church and in doing so had incurred the Queen's displeasure. On the other hand, he gives a

---

57. For a review of the various positions on this matter and of the pertinent historical circumstances, see John N. King, "Was Spenser a Puritan?" *Spenser Studies* 6 (1986): 1–31. King argues that Spenser's position was that of a "progressive Protestant" within the Elizabethan church settlement.

good deal of play to those who speak against a severe view of the shepherd's life.[58] We will not attempt to settle the matter here; perhaps, given the design and strategies of *The Shepheardes Calender* and the anxieties Spenser must have felt about speaking too plainly on public matters, they cannot be settled. What is important for us is that the representational practices of pastoral—the forms of responsive dialogue, the way literary shepherds tend to present themselves as representative—lead to a sense of both sides being heard. Moreover, the tendency we have seen in Virgil, to conclude eclogues on a note of suspended differences, is implicit in the pastoral idea of human lives as mutually dependent and lived on common terms. It is certainly the case that the question of composing differences interests Spenser. In "September," he directly averts a confrontation of principle, after Hobbinoll protests that flesh is too weak for Diggon Davie's call to endless vigilance. "Puritan" controversialists would have supplied Spenser with plenty of arguments on this point;[59] instead, he concludes the poem on a note of fellowship in need and with an invitation to rest and shelter based on Virgil's first Eclogue. "May" raises the question, which reflects current controversies, of whether shepherds should or should not seek concord with each other (Palinode for, with considerable dignity, 152–63; Piers against, with appeal to Scripture, 164–71). The concluding fable, of the fox and the kid, allows Spenser to suspend the disagreement in a shared moral entertainment. Finally, the capacity of "shepherds' lives" to generate more than one version of pastoral is born out by the literary afterlife of the May eclogue. Not surprisingly, Piers's account of the primitive church was quoted by Milton as a "presage" of his own "reforming times."[60] But Palinode's festive descriptions became the basis of Wordsworth's representation, in surveying pastoral poetry and pastoral life, of the tales he had heard about celebrating the May.[61]

VII

The shepherds of *The Shepheardes Calender* play a number of other roles than those connected with church affairs and the Christian life. The most important of these roles, the lover and the poet, are familiar from Virgil, but in them too

---

58. This is not only a matter of explicit argumentation. Elements of Palinode's representation of the May celebrations recall the pastoral tributes in "April" (cf. "May," 9–14, with "April," 136–44. The nymphs and fairies of "May," 30–33, appear unambiguously in "June," 25–27, and "April," 118–22 (cf. E. K.'s note on "Ladies of the lake" as nymphs).

59. Cf. the note on "September," 228–35, in *The Shepherd's Calendar*, ed. W. L. Renwick (London: Scholartis Press, 1930), 213; Anthea Hume, *Edmund Spenser: Protestant Poet* (Cambridge: Cambridge University Press, 1984), 38.

60. *Animadversions upon the Remonstrants Defence, Against Smectymnuus* (1641), in *Complete Prose Works*, ed. Don M. Wolfe, 8 vols. (New Haven: Yale University Press, 1953–82), 1:722–23.

61. *Prelude* (1805), 8.191–203; see above, chap. 1.

we see how the representative character of the shepherd changed historically. One kind of change can be seen in the "June" eclogue, a dialogue between Colin Clout, who is suffering from unrequited love, and the shepherd Hobbinoll, a friend who is solicitous of his condition. The situation appears to replicate that of Virgil's tenth Eclogue, but with one crucial difference. Gallus, Virgil's suffering lover, does not belong to the shepherds' world, indeed is explicitly unable to enter and become part of it; Colin Clout, on the other hand, once shared the life of the shepherd who addresses him, and even though his distress has cost him his innocence, he is still represented as a shepherd.

Colin Clout is comparable to Gallus, because he is a master-poet and because his love-suffering, redefining his world, retains some of the heroic scale that derives from Theocritus's Daphnis. Hence we can reasonably ask how the "Gallus-figure" in European pastoral changed from an outsider to a shepherd—or, to take it back to its historical original, how Daphnis became a shepherd again. In terms of literary history, the answer is Petrarch and Sannazaro. The opening setting of Sannazaro's *Arcadia* is an elaborately described *locus amoenus*, where the Arcadian shepherds gather for games and musical contests, but the scene "discovers" the shepherd Ergasto, alone and wretched under a tree. In the *poesia*, the eclogue proper, a sympathetic companion inquires into Ergasto's condition and is told of a cataclysmic love which in every respect—the narrative of its inception, its obsessiveness, and the language used of it—is a pastoralized version of Petrarchan devotion. With the exception of the old shepherds, who are beyond such things and critical of them, all the participants in the eclogues of the *Arcadia* are lovers. Their characteristic verse forms, the canzone and the sestina, are Petrarchan, and they are spared the fate of the Petrarchan lover, *vergogna* and isolation, only because their condition is common and hence eligible, in its shared humbleness and vulnerability, for pastoral representation. Such plot as the *Arcadia* has is provided by the tension between the sense of love as a shared plight and the isolations of desire; the narrator Sincero, a figure of the author (like Sidney's Philisides), is a Gallus who is able to sojourn, if not finally to remain, in Arcadia. The Petrarchan conception of love in Sannazaro makes its energies and deprivations central to poetic power and makes the literary shepherd almost by definition a lover.

This change in the literary shepherd is ultimately due to changing ideas of love and the beloved that are almost as profound as the advent of Christianity. The continuity of Virgilian pastoral comes from the way its resources and conventions can adapt to and develop such new experiences and interests. Thus, Spenser's "June" combines two Virgilian prototypes. Its basic situation is that of Eclogue 10, but its form, the way its dialogue represents issues of innocence and suffering, derives from Eclogue 1. Colin Clout is depicted as exiled by love from the world which he once shared with his fellows and to which Hobbinoll urges him to return. Two changes in the tactics of Eclogue 1 show the flexibility of pastoral usages. In "June," the depiction of the secure, idyllic setting is not given to the shepherd separated from and yearning for it, but to the shepherd who has remained there, the equivalent of Tityrus. The effect is to make the poem more emphatically a confrontation of two versions of pastoral. At the same time, the Tityrus-figure is not himself represented as a singer. His two main speeches show his capacity for describing musical occasions, but both passages are set pieces about the music-making of the young Colin Clout. Hence the two versions of pastoral are not simply identified with the two speakers but come to represent "Colin before" and "Colin after," two stages in the experience and modes of expression of the master-singer. Placed in the middle month of *The Shepheardes Calender*, the eclogue thus engages the symbolism of the year and enables Spenser, though more ambivalent about love than Sannazaro, to open up the relation of song, full and harmonious utterance, to love in particular and distress in general. If the echo of Colin's former music "taught the byrds . . . frame to thy songe their cherefull cheriping" (53–5), the Colin who now says "Enough is me to paint out my vnrest" (79) can imagine a more powerful complaint that would "learne these woods, to wayle my woe,/ And teache the trees, their trickling teares to shedde" (95–96). To put it in Virgilian terms, it is not Tityrus but Meliboeus, both before and after his exile, who teaches the woods to resound in this poem.

Many critics argue, as one puts it, that Colin's "failure as a lover . . . is intimately related to his failure as a poet."[62] But what do "success" and "failure" mean in the world of *The Shepheardes Calender?* Far from suggesting that others succeed where Colin fails, the poem is filled with shepherds who share with him the experience of frustrated love and thwarted ambitions. "October" is particularly revealing, because it most directly concerns the powers and offices of poetry to which Colin Clout is purportedly inadequate. Like "June," the poem is a dialogue between a naive shepherd, who offers various encouraging and "official" views of poetry, and his more experienced companion, who both understands the powers of poetry more deeply and at the same time is skeptical about the possibility of realizing them in the present time. Specific allusions to the Queen and the Earl of Leicester show that the author himself has a stake in what these shepherds say, and the second speaker's rhetorical and emotional range, from intuiting the sacred rage of poetry to bitterness at the present state of letters, is similar to that of Colin Clout, Spenser's persona. Nevertheless, Spenser does not give this role in the poem to Colin, but to a shepherd named Cuddie. The reason, presumably, is that he does not want to identify Colin's plight as a poet with him as a single character, but means to suggest that it is a general condition among Elizabethan "shepherds." Similarly, in "September,"

---

62. Richard Mallette, "Spenser's Portrait of the Artist in *The Shepheardes Calender* and *Colin Clouts Come Home Againe*," *SEL: Studies in English Literature* 19 (1979): 22.

the expression of sobering experience and frustration of youthful hopes is put in the mouth of a shepherd named Diggon Davie—Spenser's adaptation of a figure from ecclesiastical satire[63]—who explains to the naive Hobbinoll the facts about ecclesiastical greed and careerism and the threats Rome poses to the English church, and at the same time expresses his own sense of weariness and defeat. Colin Clout can only be judged a failure by standards of "strength relative to world" that *The Shepheardes Calender* seems explicitly designed to deny. Because Colin's experience is representative of that of other shepherds—as their experience is of his—the figure of the shepherd comes to represent the situation of the Elizabethan poet, courtier, and churchman.

It is of course possible, and not uncommon, to say that the poet views Colin Clout ironically. There is every reason to accept E. K.'s word that Colin Clout represents the poet. The tradition that Virgil used a pastoral pseudonym is directly invoked in *The Shepheardes Calender*;[64] Spenser's contemporaries referred to him as "Colin"; later in his career, Spenser unambiguously used the name of himself in Book VI of *The Faerie Queene* and in his last pastoral poem, *Colin Clouts Come Home Againe*. Nor is there reason to doubt that other shepherds in the poem in some sense speak for the poet. The "Argument" to "October" firmly associates Spenser with Cuddie, who is called "the perfecte paterne of a Poete," and who espouses a doctrine of "celestiall inspiration" that Spenser himself is said to have set forth in a treatise (otherwise unknown to us) called "The English Poete." The praise of Archbishop Grindal, then in disgrace with the Queen, has to be taken as a view endorsed by the poet (otherwise, why risk offending the monarch?) and is consistent with other passages espousing the church reform supported by Spenser's patrons. Yet the praise of Grindal (made quite outspoken by the transparent pseudonym "Algrind") is modulated by being put in the mouth of the shepherd who speaks, in "July," for the humble life of the valleys. Thomalin's final words on this matter—"But I am taught by *Algrins* ill,/to loue the lowe degree" ("July," 219–20)—show that Spenser felt the force of George Puttenham's remark that poets use "the homely persons" and "rude speeches" of pastoral "to insinuate and glaunce at greater matters, and such as perchance had not bene safe to haue been disclosed in any other sort."[65] This is not a matter of simply retreating from temerity. Both forthrightness and diffidence are inherent in pastoral representation. The moral authority of a speaker like Thomalin derives from the simplicity of his perceptions and state-

63. Hallett Smith, *Elizabethan Poetry* (Cambridge: Harvard University Press, 1952), 210.

64. E. K. in the first gloss in the poem, on the name Colin Clout ("January," Arg.): "Vnder which name this Poete secretly shadoweth himself [*SC* was first published anonymously], as sometime did Virgil vnder the name of Tityrus." See also "October" 55 and gloss.

65. George Puttenham, *The Arte of English Poesie*, ed. Gladys Doidge Willcock and Alice Walker (Cambridge: Cambridge University Press, 1936), I.18 (p. 38).

ments and is thus coextensive with his powerlessness and vulnerability. Irony may be inherent in speaking through such a figure, because the conscious humility and simplicity suggest that the poet holds something in reserve. But in eclogue books like Spenser's and Virgil's, this reserve strength is not attributed to a poet-figure implicitly located outside the shepherds' world, but is distributed among other pastoral figures and representations. Critics who claim that the poet keeps himself separate from Colin Clout require a stronger than bucolic irony—a Schillerian, not an Empsonian irony—and they assume that the question is whether Spenser identifies himself with Colin Clout alone. But as in Virgil's Eclogues, pastoral representation and self-representation interpenetrate in *The Shepheardes Calender*, and involve not simply a single shepherd but all the shepherds of the poem.

The limitations and dilemmas of various social roles—on which the most interesting recent studies of *The Shepheardes Calender* have placed their emphasis[66]—are not the only reason the figure of the shepherd was important to Spenser. The book was famous in its time and held its place in literary history as a display piece, showing (in a spirit not foreign to pastoral emulation) that English poetry could match that of the Continental vernaculars. The whole book has to be seen in this light—for its emulation of Virgil's Eclogues, for the conspicuous variety of its metres and poetic types, and for the calendar device, whose claims of substance and coherence are made explicit in the Envoi: "Loe I haue made a Calender for euery yeare,/That steele in strength, and time in durance shall outweare." But three poems, metrically the most elaborate in *The Shepheardes Calender*, stand out as staking an English claim in the poetry of the European Renaissance: the "lay" in "April," which celebrates Elizabeth I as "*Eliza*, Queene of shepheardes all"; the sestina in "August," along with Sidney's the first example of the form in English; and the elegy for Dido in "November." Each of these derives from a recognized type of pastoral poem. "April," the fourth poem in the book, is a version of Virgil's fourth Eclogue; it emulates its model not only in its imperial and mythological aspects but also by keeping open the possibility that the "queen of shepherds" is herself to be seen as a shepherdess. The "August" sestina replicates Sannazaro's pastoral adaptation of the Petrarchan form by emphasizing the power of vocalizing distress and by resolving, at the end, to "take part" with the nightingale, "in songs and plaintiue pleas." "November," a pastoral elegy, imitates Clément Marot's "Eglogue sur le Trespas de ma Dame Loyse de Savoye, Mere du Roy Françoys," which itself brought into

---

66. See especially the remarkable articles by Louis Adrian Montrose: "'The perfecte paterne of a Poete': The Poetics of Courtship in *The Shepheardes Calender*," *Texas Studies in Literature and Language* 21 (1979): 34–67; "'Eliza, Queene of shepheardes' and the Pastoral of Power," *English Literary Renaissance* 10 (1980): 153–82; "Of Gentlemen and Shepherds: The Politics of Elizabethan Pastoral Form," *ELH* 50 (1983): 415–59.

French poetry the pastoral elegies of Virgil and the Greek bucolic poets. The importance of Marot, as Annabel Patterson has recently shown, goes beyond his providing the model for "November" and for Colin Clout's retrospective account of his life in "December." Marot's use of the Virgilian shepherd to represent himself as courtier, as humanist poet, and as Protestant exile gives him a pervasive presence in *The Shepheardes Calender* and must have provided Spenser with an important example of the multiplicity and flexibility of the poet's pastoral roles. "Marot's response to the Virgilian dialectic," she argues, "was sufficiently alert to its cultural transferability to produce a new story, in which the lots of the fortunate and unfortunate shepherd might alternate in a single life (or the life of a nation, perhaps)."[67]

Patterson's emphasis, which she can justly claim is corrective, is on the Virgilian shepherd as an instrument of political criticism and as a conscious recorder (as opposed to an epiphenomenal manifestation) of social dilemma and conflict. But in placing this emphasis, she loses sight, in *The Shepheardes Calender*, of an aspect of Marot's pastoralism that she herself identifies—its engagement with ideals "of intellectual privacy and of artistic liberty" and of "vernacular Neoclassicism."[68] The brilliance of Spenser's calendar device is that it made room for this, along with other kinds of pastoral. Moreover, the pastoralisms of the major showpieces—the "April," "August," and "November" songs—are coordinated by the fact that each is attributed to Colin Clout and by the way they represent, as a group, his career as a pastoral singer. The "April" lay of Eliza is said to have been composed in his youth, before he experienced the pains of love to which he gives vent in the "August" sestina. Lying on either side of "June," in the middle of the year, the two poems thus play out its two versions of pastoral. Hobbinoll's evocation of the muses and fairies flocking to hear the young Colin ("June," 25–32, 57–64) directly recalls some of the scenes in "April," while the elaborated distress of the "August" sestina can be thought to fulfill Colin's present desire to "learne these woods, to wayle my woe." The two poems are connected not simply by the fiction of Colin's life, but by the idea of poetry it embodies. The erotic energies of each—the innocent poem as well as the experienced, "April" as well as "August"—show the centrality of love, both as desire and fidelity, to the Renaissance figure of the shepherd-poet. The fact that both poems are performed by other shepherds, not sung by Colin himself, brings out what it means to be a master-singer: utterances of such elaboration and finish survive the experience or stage of life

---

67. Annabel Patterson, *Pastoral and Ideology* (Berkeley & Los Angeles: University of California Press, 1987), 115.

68. Patterson, 114, 118. I spell out my disagreements with Montrose and (prospectively) Patterson in "Pastoral and the Domain of Lyric in Spenser's *Shepheardes Calender*," *Representations* 12 (Fall 1985): 83–100.

that prompted them and remain to be sung by others. At the same time, there is more than the ready transference of these songs to other singers to show the pastoralism of the mastery they represent. The way these performed songs are set off against other kinds of expression and experience—within the "April" and "August" eclogues themselves, as well as in the context of the whole book— shows that no one utterance can sum up Colin Clout's career, much less the life of man represented by the calendar device itself.

Five

PASTORAL SPEAKERS

I

The Virgilian figure of the representative shepherd is inherently capable of fresh interpretation and application. Its possibilities provide one way of accounting for both the importance and the variety of pastoral poetry in the sixteenth century. Even when conventional pastoral genres seem to lose their vitality (roughly, around the turn of the seventeenth century) pastoral retains its capacity for fresh realization and for extending its range. The effect of Shakespearean pastoral—historically in England and "typologically" in our account—was to unsettle and diversify the Virgilian formula, "The poet represents (himself as) a shepherd or shepherds." When pastoral values and usages are located in a variety of figures and are no longer closely identified with the literary shepherd—and this, in effect, is the shift from Spenser to Shakespeare—the poet need not represent himself as a shepherd in order to sustain the pastoral mode. The characteristic figure then becomes what we will call a pastoral speaker. A pastoral speaker is one whose mode of utterance and strength relative to world derive from the literary shepherd, but who is not represented as a herdsman or similar humble figure. In the same way, Shakespearean drama produces what we will call shepherd-equivalents—socially humble figures who may not be identified with the country and its occupations, but whose function and presence are like those of the herdsmen of traditional pastoral.

The emergence of the pastoral speaker from representative shepherds is played out in the pastoral episode (cantos 9 and 10) of Book 6 of *The Faerie Queene*. Sir Calidore, pursuing the Blatant Beast of slander, comes upon a world of shepherds, falls in love with the fairest shepherdess, and as a sort of reward or confirmation of his decision to cast his lot with them, happens upon Mount Acidale, said to be Venus's earthly retreat, where he sees the Graces dancing to the music of a shepherd. In the context of *The Faerie Queene*, the leading question about this long episode has been the hero's so-called truancy: whether or not he is to be blamed for choosing a pastoral life and forsaking the quest imposed upon him. However, coming to the cantos as we do, what is most notable is that each is centered on the figure of a representative shepherd. In canto 9, the old shepherd Melibee speaks for the values of the "lowly, quiet life" of shepherds which Calidore desires to share; in canto 10, the shepherd who pipes to the Graces and then instructs Calidore about them is Colin Clout, a figure of the poet himself.

Melibee and Colin Clout play out the two versions of pastoral, *agrestis* and *silvestris*, in Virgil's first Eclogue. Melibee inhabits and speaks for the ordinary life of the fields, which are repeatedly identified as his local (9.4,14,20); Colin Clout is placed in a mythical landscape, a wooded hill inhabited by the deities of love, that is explicitly off bounds to "wylde beastes" and "the ruder clowne" (10.7). Melibee speaks with the forthrightness, the cultivated simplicity that we have seen as the hallmark of one kind of literary shepherd. Colin Clout not only makes the woods resound with his beloved (10.10), but his music has the power to prompt her appearance (whether as apparition or real presence) and that of the local nymphs and the Graces themselves. Most important, the confrontation of these figures with a hero from the court world brings out the pastoral character of their modes of representation. When Calidore sees the Graces dancing and steps forward, resolved to know what they are, the vision disappears, leaving only the shepherd, who "for fell despight of that displeasure" (10.18) breaks his bagpipe. This might seem to "break off the pastoral song," but it is in fact its occasion and beginning. However bitterly Colin Clout reacts to Calidore's interruption of the vision, the Knight of Courtesy's expression of regret prompts the shepherd not to "learne these woods, to wayle my woe," as would an isolated lover, but to explain to this new shepherd (for so he takes Calidore to be) the nature of what he has just seen. The ensuing speech is as long as the poet's own representation of the vision; in recapitulating myths and motifs and expanding the moral explication initiated by the poet, it is clearly meant to be a substitute for it. As the two shepherds come together, Colin Clout turns from piping to speech, and we are given a definitive instance of the way pastoral utterance can be thought to restore the loss that occasioned it. In the final stanzas of Colin's speech, the fervent listing of the beloved's moral attributes seems to restore her to his presence—what else can be suggested by "She made me often pipe *and now to pipe apace*"?—and in the concluding address to Gloriana, the voice of the poet merges with that of his persona in the plea to "pardon thy shepheard" for exalting a "poore handmayd" (10.27–28).

The encounter with Melibee also concerns the motives and scope of pastoral utterance. After supper in the old shepherd's cottage, Sir Calidore thanks his host and self-consciously initiates a pastoral discourse:

> And drawing thence his speach another way,
> Gan highly to commend the *happie* life,
> Which Shepheards lead, without debate or bitter strife.
>
> How much (sayd he) more *happie* is the state,
> In which ye father here doe dwell at ease,
> Leading a life so free and *fortunate,*
> From all the tempests of these worldly seas,
> Which tosse the rest in daungerous disease;
> Where warres, and wreckes, and wicked enmitie
> Doe them afflict, which no man can appease,
> That certes I your *happinesse* enuie,
> And wish my lot were plast in such *felicitie.*
>
> (9.18–19, my emphasis)

Calidore, like many modern readers, takes the point of the pastoral life to be escape from worldliness and its discontents. His speech encapsulates these motives in the key word, "happie," which, as the courtier may well know, has plenty of pastoral authority. Both its meanings are registered in this speech. Like Virgil's Meliboeus, Calidore calls the shepherd he addresses "fortunate," while "felicity" looks to its root, *felix,* the word which initiates Virgil's praise of country life in a famous passage in the *Georgics* (2.490ff.). "Happy" is the epithet Shakespeare's Amiens bestows on the Duke in his pastoral guise. But Melibee denies both the suggestion of unalloyed pleasure and the implication (explicitly reproved in their next exchange) that it depends on luck:

> Surely my sonne (then answer'd he againe)
> If happie, then it is in this intent,
> That hauing small, yet doe I not complaine
> Of want, ne wish for more it to augment,
> But doe my self, with that I haue, content.
>
> (9.20)

Pastoral contentment may sometimes be due to innocence, but for Melibee it is a knowing virtue. He speaks with more self-awareness and nuance than other moralizing old shepherds, because he corrects his younger antagonist by revising his implied account of desire and choice. His speech ends with the story of the false choice he himself made "when pride of youth forth pricked my desire" and, disdaining "shepheards base attire" he sought his fortune at court (9.24). Dismayed by the "vainnesse" and "idle hopes" he found there,

> After I had ten yeares my selfe excluded
> From natiue home, and spent my youth in vaine,
> I gan my follies to my selfe to plaine,
> And this sweet peace, whose lacke did then appeare.
> (9.25)

The last line exactly replicates Calidore's ostensible motive for praising Melibee's life, and shows the connection between the knight and the shepherd. At the same time, Calidore's eager desire is checked by the double force of Melibee's verb "plaine" (i.e. complain): because, with "follies" as its object, it first registers self-reproach, it expresses a just appreciation, not mere regretful longing, for its second object, the "sweet peace" of his "natiue home." The final words of this stanza and of the whole speech speak of desire not only chastened by but transformed into moral choice:

> Tho [then] backe returning to my sheepe againe,
> I from thenceforth haue learn'd to loue more deare
> This lowly quiet life, which I inherite here.
> (9.25)

Melibee's espousal of contentment is neither austerely stoical nor hard-bitten and defiant, in the manner of Mantuan's shepherds. On the contrary, his speech has a rather idyllic character—which is what prompts his critical antagonists to speak of his "laziness," his "dream world," and the "soft pastoralism" of the canto.[1] Remarks like these replicate Calidore's misunderstanding, for the idyllic touches in Melibee's speech are grounded in chosen tasks and satisfactions. He defines pastoral content by topoi of golden age poems—the land's self-sufficiency and freedom from foreign trade—but scales them down to a life of conscious simplicity:

---

1. "Laziness": Harry Berger, Jr., "A Secret Discipline: *The Faerie Queene*, Book VI," in *Form and Convention in the Poetry of Edmund Spenser*, ed. William Nelson (New York: Columbia University Press, 1961), 61; reprinted in Berger's *Revisionary Play: Studies in the Spenserian Dynamics* (Berkeley & Los Angeles: University of California Press, 1988), 233. "Dream world": Humphrey Tonkin, *Spenser's Courteous Pastoral* (Oxford: Clarendon Press, 1972), 292. "Soft pastoralism": Isabel G. MacCaffrey, *Spenser's Allegory: The Anatomy of Imagination* (Princeton: Princeton University Press, 1976), 364. In her discussion of Melibee (365–70), MacCaffrey rightly resists the implications of this phrase, but the result is that she has difficulty making his moral authority consistent with the nature of his life.

So taught of nature, which doth litle need
Of forreine helpes to lifes due nourishment:
The fields my food, my flocke my rayment bred;
No better doe I weare, no better doe I feed.

(9.20)

His statement that "all the night in siluer sleepe I spend" is not advanced as a
leading claim (though it is a familiar point in poems praising the country), but
appears on the heels, as if the result and reward, of his criticism of ambition
and his consequent confidence in "my minds vnmoued quiet" (9.22). Melibee's
pastoral rhetoric similarly modifies another golden age topos, the spontaneous
growth of crops:

They that haue much, feare much to loose thereby,
And store of cares doth follow riches store.
The little that I haue, growes dayly more
Without my care, but onely to attend it.

(9.21)

Until the final half-line, this distinction between worldly care and pastoral carelessness, may seem conventionally innocent. But the last phrase denies the
absolute meaning of "without my care" and thus revises our sense of what is at
issue in pastoral security (*se-curus* = without care). The suggestion of freedom
is maintained, but scaled down to the claim that one is without care if one
knows what truly to care about—in this case the flocks mentioned in the next
lines or the rural tasks detailed two stanzas later.

As if recapitulating the way pastoral was historically inscribed within the
heroic, the romance context brings Melibee and Colin Clout face to face with
a courtier who is responsive to their discourses. Their encounters therefore
make unusually clear what is involved in the representative status of the literary
shepherd. Melibee represents a way of life that Calidore values and desires; he
can even be said to represent the knight himself, in that his rejection of the
court and return to the country offer a challenging version of the choice Calidore claims to want to make. Colin Clout has a similar relation to the knight,
in that his life is devoted to celebrating a "countrey lasse" (10.25) who seems a
"miracle of heauenly hew," as Pastorella did when Calidore first saw her "enui-
ron'd with a girland, goodly graced,/Of louely lasses" and piping shepherds
(9.8). Moreover, the vision of the Graces is first mentioned by way of explaining why Calidore would be justified in remaining in the country (10.4), and the
effect of Colin Clout's "discourses," as of Melibee's, is that the knight "wisht,
that with that shepheard he mote dwelling share" (10.30). Both Melibee and
Colin Clout hold out, to the hero and implicitly to the reader, alternatives of
attitude and role.

But how, in fact, can the courtier-hero take these alternatives seriously? It is one thing for the poet to present considerations for and against renouncing the "shadowes vaine/Of courtly fauour" and seeking "the happy peace" and "perfect pleasures" which one finds "amongst poore hyndes, in hils, in woods, in dales" (10.1–4). It is another to translate the awareness of pastoral values into the choice of a life so completely defined by a single place and a single round of activities as Melibee's and Colin Clout's. Pastoral envisages this possibility, and many fine poems—from "His golden locks time hath to silver turned" to *Upon Appleton House*—examine and praise it. But the value of pastoral is not confined to such situations. Rather, it is equally represented by the Shakespearean pattern, in which time spent in a pastoral locale restores courtiers to their homes and to themselves. Since the country is not Calidore's "native home," the question is what in his case can be the equivalent of Melibee's choice.

Spenser's handling of the episode shows his awareness of the problem. Calidore reacts to Melibee's praise of the shepherds' life with what the poet calls "double rauishment" (9.26): he is enraptured with the speech itself and with the country maiden with whom he has fallen in love. These pastoral erotics underlie the sentimental vehemence of his response. After a stanza in which he tries to "insinuate his harts desire" by aping his host's praises of the country,[2] he says:

> That euen I which daily doe behold
> The glorie of the great, mongst whom I won,
> And now haue prou'd, what happinesse ye hold
> In this small plot of your dominion,
> Now loath great Lordship and ambition.
>   (9.28)

The insistence still on "happinesse," the grand word "dominion" (which represents "small plot" precisely as a form of "Lordship"), and the use of "loath" to express moral recognition show that the knight has not yet taken in what he has heard. The very structure of the sentence, a sustained period quite unusual in *The Faerie Queene*, suggests that he has still not adopted the style he professes to admire. What Melibee reproves, however, is not this rhetoric itself, but the wish it prompts:

> And wish the heauens so much had graced mee,
> As graunt me liue in like condition;

2. 9.27. Calidore's first words are a Meliboean pastiche. His opening phrase, "this worlds gay showes," is picked up from Melibee (9.22), while key words in the next two lines, "vaine" and "lowlinesse," echo the alexandrines of the last two stanzas of Melibee's speech (9.24, 25).

> Or that my fortunes might transposed bee
> From pitch of higher place, vnto this low degree.
>   (9.28)

Melibee replies that it is vain to accuse the heavens of "fortunes fault" and says: "fittest is, that all contented rest/With that they hold: each hath his fortune in his brest" (9.29). This is a pastoral moral, but so generalized as to be detached from particularities of place or social role. Melibee then goes on to state a moral—"It is the mynd, that maketh good or ill" (9.30)—that is certainly not confined to pastoral. But its corrective point is what enables Calidore to find a mode adequate to his situation:

> Since then in each mans self (said *Calidore*)
> It is, to fashion his owne lyfes estate,
> Giue leaue awhyle, good father, in this shore
> To rest my barcke, which hath bene beaten late
> With stormes of fortune and tempestuous fate,
> In seas of troubles and of toylesome paine,
> That whether quite from them for to retrate
> I shall resolue, or backe to turne againe,
> I may here with your selfe some small repose obtaine.
>   (9.31)

In Melibee's speech, the truth that each man fashions his life takes the form of apothegms, a rhetorical form conventional with the old shepherds of pastoral and expressive of the notion that all humans have the same simple needs. Calidore's courtly metaphor (and his deployment of it in what would have been called an "allegory") might thus seem once more to miss the point. In fact it shows, unlike his previous mimicry and literalism, that he now understands Melibee's pastoral moral—that knowledge of self is inseparable from knowing and accepting one's circumstances. The image of the ship in the port suggests genuine rest, but does not deny that the courtier spends his life on the high seas. Its justness is confirmed by the moral poise of the final lines. As he suspends the choice he knows he will have to make, the knight's understanding takes the form of the "small repose" of this stanza itself. Calidore here has achieved his own version of pastoral. Like the poets of "The Garden" and "L'Allegro," he does not represent himself as a shepherd, but the mode in which he speaks has been determined by the literary shepherd(s) whom he has encountered.

Calidore eventually does become a shepherd. When the erotics that underlie his rhetoric take the form of wooing, Pastorella will have nothing to do with his knightly manner. In a passage that repeats the pattern of having his courtliness corrected, he learns to accommodate himself to what Melibee calls "our rudenesse" (9.33) and dons "shepheards weed" (9.36) in order to be with his beloved. This leads to a stanza (9.37) in which we see him guarding and folding Pastorella's sheep and humbling himself to learn to milk ("loue so much could"), but after this it is difficult to keep his pastoral guise in view or mind. Though nominally a shepherd, he is repeatedly referred to as "the knight," for it is his behavior in that role that concerns the poet—e.g., "Thus did the gentle knight himselfe abeare/Amongst that rusticke rout in all his deeds" (9.45). Hence his most memorable appearance as a shepherd is not in the putative reality of the story, but in a simile that represents his accommodation to Pastorella:

> Which *Calidore* perceiuing, thought it best
> To chaunge the manner of his loftie looke;
> And doffing his bright armes, himselfe addrest
> In shepheards weed, and in his hand he tooke,
> In stead of steelehead speare, a shepheards hooke,
> That who had seene him then, would haue bethought
> On *Phrygian Paris* by *Plexippus* brooke,
> When he the loue of fayre *Oenone* sought,
> What time the golden apple was vnto him brought.
>
> (9.36)

We are made to imagine Paris in a state of innocence, merely loving his fair shepherdess, even though the stanza closes by reminding us of the fierce war that will result from his forsaking her. These fatal intimations, which might be thought to disrupt the idyll, are balanced by fixing the moment just before Paris's choice and by the golden apple itself, with its physical appeal and its evocation of a glamorous scene that is not unlike what we will see on Mount Acidale—the appearance of three goddesses to a shepherd in love.[3] As in Calidore's speech about the "small repose" he may obtain in the shepherds' world, the effect here is to suspend events and issues that will take the protagonist into the world of heroic action. The simile thus creates for the reader a pastoral encounter of his own. We have to recognize both the appeal of idyllic simplicities and the dilemmas that attend the courtly figure in pastoral guise. This is genuinely pastoral writing, but it is discontinuous with the narration that is unfolding in this canto.[4] Unlike the world of Lodge's *Rosalynde*, where Paris and

---

3. The convention, in Elizabethan poems and pageants, of presenting the golden apple to the Queen may even be thought to give a benign cast to its introduction here, where Paris is compared to a knight of Gloriana. Examples of this device in Tudor court entertainments are cited in R. Mark Benbow's introduction to his edition of Peele's *Araygnement of Paris*, in *The Life and Works of George Peele* (New Haven: Yale University Press), vol. 3 (*The Dramatic Works of George Peele*, 1970), 20.

4. For fuller discussion of this point and of what this episode implies for *The Faerie Queene*, see Paul Alpers, "Spenser's Late Pastorals," *ELH* 56 (1989): 797–817.

many of his mythological brothers and sisters are very much at home,[5] neither the world of Melibee nor of Colin Clout can accommodate the Phrygian shepherd. He can only appear to us in a simile, one part of the poet's rather piecemeal representation of his hero in these cantos. But the stanza is one of the great moments in the episode. Brief though it is, it shows that the resources of pastoral representation and the claims of representativeness are not confined to the shepherds of the eclogue tradition.

Finally, this episode reveals not only the nature and resources of pastoral representation, but a limitation of some of its forms. One of the striking things about Calidore's sojourn among the shepherds is that none of them, besides Melibee, utters a word. Their speech (though not very much of it) is reported indirectly; we are told of their pipings and carolings; we are shown Coridon, Calidore's rival in love, bringing Pastorella gifts and biting his lip for jealousy; but Melibee is the only shepherd whose speech is directly quoted.[6] The canto as a whole thus brings out the fact that Melibee represents a way of life in the specific sense that he can speak for it. The presence of the knight and the context of heroic romance make explicit what in eclogues is assumed but unstated: that what makes a shepherd representative is his ability to represent. To put the matter most pointedly, the shepherd Melibee is able to be a pastoral figure because he has been at court. This detail in the story comes from its source in *Gerusalemme Liberata* (7.12–13), but it is impossible to ignore its connection with Melibee's powers and privilege of speech. The poem itself is clear about this connection, insofar as it concerns pastoral thematics and poetics. Melibee's having crossed the boundary within which he now dwells makes him conscious of it and the choice it represents. He is even a figure of the poet, in that his ability to represent himself (which is necessarily to represent himself as a shepherd) enables him to represent the lives of shepherds. He

---

5. For example, when Rosalynd and Aliena first come to Arden, they come upon Montanus and Coridon singing "a pleasant eglog" in the following setting:

> The ground where they sat was diapred with *Floras* riches, as if she ment to wrap *Tellus* in the glorie of her vestments: round about in the forme of an Amphitheater were most curiouslie planted Pine trees, interseamed with Limons and Citrons, which with the thicknesse of their boughes so shadowed the place, that *Phoebus* could not prie into the secret of that Arbour; so united were the tops with so thicke a closure, that *Venus* might there in her jollitie have dallied unseene with her deerest paramour. Fast by (to make the place more gorgeous), was there a Fount so Christalline and cleere, that it seemed *Diana* with her *Driades* and *Hemadriades* had that spring, as the secret of all their bathings.

Thomas Lodge, *Rosalynde* (1590), in *Narrative and Dramatic Sources of Shakespeare*, ed. Geoffrey Bullough, vol. 2 (1963), 183. The amorous shepherd Paris is a point of reference throughout *Rosalynde* (cf. 206, 247, 248, 252, 253).

6. Coridon finally speaks in 11.30–32. But this is after the brigands have wiped out the shepherds' world. It is as if this devastation gives him a voice: what he recounts is the brigands' slaughter of the shepherds, including Melibee and, he thinks, Pastorella.

thus suggests that pastoral is essentially a mode of courtly and humanist self-representation.

One need not view this with indignation: it is no secret that pastoral is of the country, but by and for the city. But its insufficiencies become clear in Spenser's treatment of Coridon. Unlike his confrontation with Melibee and his learning to woo Pastorella, Calidore's dealings with Coridon do not count as a pastoral encounter, because they do not make him imagine himself as a shepherd and hence reconsider what he is and what he values. On the contrary, in this context Spenser praises his hero as if he had arrived fresh from court and had never put on shepherd's weeds:

> Thus did the gentle knight himselfe abeare
> Amongst that rusticke rout in all his deeds.
>
> . . . .
>
> For courtesie amongst the rudest breeds
> Good will and fauour.
>
> (9.45)

In his own person, the Knight of Courtesy can only condescend to the rustic. He pats Coridon on the head for his country gifts to Pastorella (9.40)—gifts which can have real charm and erotic expressiveness when represented by the passionate shepherds of eclogue and lyric—and commends his prowess in wrestling when he has in fact just humiliated him (9.43–44). When we go on to canto 10, we find that the poet's own treatment of the rustic is worse than the knight's condescension. After staging a scene in which Calidore rescues Pastorella from a tiger, while Coridon runs away in fear, the narrator says:

> From that day forth she gan him [Calidore] to affect,
> And daily more her fauour to augment;
> But *Coridon* for cowherdize reiect,
> Fit to keepe sheepe, vnfit for loues content.
>
> (10.37)

These lines reject not only cowardice but the herdsman's condition punningly linked to it. The last line in effect renounces pastoral, whose claim on us is precisely the acknowledgment that our condition in love, as in other fundamental human situations, can be represented by keepers of sheep. Coridon fails to be a pastoral figure (and Spenserian pastoral fails the rustic), because the courtly poet is unable or unwilling to represent him in the full sense: in depicting him, he does not speak in his stead or on his behalf. Hence Coridon cannot be imagined to speak for himself and therefore cannot be met in a pastoral encounter.

II

Not surprisingly, it is in the drama that rustic figures speak for themselves in ways that extend the repertory of the representative shepherd and enlarge the possibilities of pastoral. Shakespeare's interest in representative rustics is made evident early in his career, in the first scene of *Love's Labor's Lost*. After the King and his fellows reaffirm their vows to study for three years and make their court "a little academe," Berowne, already restive under the disavowal of love, asks whether they shall have no "quick recreation." The King replies that Don Armado, the fanciful, rhetoric-mongering Spaniard, will serve "for my minstrelsy," and Longaville concludes:

> Costard the swain and he shall be our sport;
> And so to study three years is but short.
>
> (1.1.179–80)

This sounds as if country entertainment will be as neatly separated and contained as the eclogues which the natives of Sidney's Arcadia stage for King Basileus in his rural retreat. At this very moment entertainment arrives, but not in the anticipated form. Costard is brought in by Dull, the constable:

> *Constable.* Which is the Duke's own person?
> *Berowne.* This, fellow. What wouldst?
> *Constable.* I myself reprehend his own person, for I am his Grace's farborough [petty constable]; but I would see his own person in flesh and blood.
>
> (1.1.181–85)

Any malapropism suggests the capacity of language to go haywire, and a malapropism on "represent" calls attention (in modern lingo) to the arbitrariness of signs and hence the inherent capacity of words to be substituted for one another. But the potentially dizzying effect is balanced here by the obviousness of the meaning: "reprehend" not only can be mistaken for but can adequately represent "represent." By transforming our own verbal consciousness into simplicity of apprehension and the release of laughter, the rustic's malapropism becomes a piece of pastoral representation.

The pastoralism of this moment initiates a more far-reaching pastoral encounter in the scene. Costard has been "taken with a wench," thus violating an edict that represents, in the ordinary world of constables and actionable offenses, the King's high-minded vow to avoid all commerce with women. The letter from Don Armado, which Dull bears to the King and which makes known Costard's offense, puts on display the substitutability of words to which Dull's malapropism called attention. The scene then concludes with a pastoral encounter on this theme:

> *King.* Did you hear the proclamation?
> *Costard.* I do confess much of the hearing it, but little of the marking of it.
> *King.* It was proclaim'd a year's imprisonment to be taken with a wench.
> *Costard.* I was taken with none, sir, I was taken with a damsel.
> *King.* Well, it was proclaim'd damsel.
> *Costard.* This was no damsel neither, sir, she was a virgin.
> *King.* It is so varied too, for it was proclaim'd virgin.
> *Costard.* If it were, I deny her virginity; I was taken with a maid.
> *King.* This maid will not serve your turn, sir.
> *Costard.* This maid will serve my turn, sir.
>
> (1.1.284–99)

This joke has some of the decisiveness of farce, but it translates physical need into verbal force, and its mode is pastoral. Not only does "Costard the swain" represent what he himself ruefully calls "the simplicity of man to hearken after the flesh" (217); he takes on this role by speaking up for, i.e., representing himself to the King. Whether his devastating reply is naive or consciously witty—and it is pastoral precisely in that one cannot tell—its effect, true to the word of his rustic companion, is to "reprehend the Duke's own person." The swain's behavior and self-representation enact both the literal meaning and the pun in "reprehend": by representing human needs and nature, he criticizes the King's outlawing of love. In hearkening after the flesh—a locution set off against much talk of hearing verbal displays—Costard has already enacted the protest Berowne couches in sophistry: "Com' on then, I will swear to study so,/ To know the thing I am forbid to know" (1.1.59–60).

In terms of literary genealogy Costard is not a pastoral figure like Spenser's Melibee, who derives from the moralizing old shepherds of Renaissance eclogues. Costard comes from the world of festive comedy, and as a literary type is a clown or fool (the two other epithets, besides "swain," used of him in the play). Empson might argue, as he certainly suggests, that all these figures in Shakespeare are "versions of pastoral." Leo Salingar's description of Shakespeare's fools could similarly have had Empson in mind: "They may be simpletons or jesters, or a mixture of both, so that it becomes difficult to distinguish their unconscious humour from their wry wit; but in general, they stand for instinctive human nature as contrasted with culture, for the naïve man or the physical man as against the man of sentiment."[7] But in Costard, Shakespeare assimilates the clown to a pastoral context—an aristocratic retreat to the country to pursue a life of contemplation—and a pastoral problematic, the transformation of erotic energies into play and utterance. In this context, it might ap-

---

7. Leo Salingar, *Shakespeare and the Traditions of Comedy* (Cambridge: Cambridge University Press, 1974), 16.

pear that Costard's pastoral representativeness is subject to the same limiting observation we made about Spenser's Melibee—that the pastoral figure is ultimately a piece of courtly self-representation. But the conditions of drama, and particularly the drama of the Shakespearean theater, give the country figures a certain independence. Melibee speaks Calidore's language, for there is no other in *The Faerie Queene*. Costard speaks his own language, which turns out, at times, to have a representative authority of its own.

One sometimes feels that Costard's verbal bumbling and naive attitudes are simply stock representations of the comic rustic. To the extent that this is true, he is speaking the courtier's language, in the sense that his verbal powers are limited to the way courtly writing (as in the Miso, Mopsa, and Dametas of Sidney's *Arcadia*) mocks country folk. The difficulty of saying when this is true of Costard and when not is a sign of the limitations of *Love's Labor's Lost*. But *As You Like It* makes clear what is already at work in the earlier play. The difference between the figure of Corin and his prototype in *Rosalynde* shows how Shakespeare, as many critics have recognized, strikes a new note in pastoral writing. Lodge's Alinda and Rosalynde first see the old shepherd Corydon in his "pleasant eclogue" with Montanus, just as Celia and Rosalind first see Corin discussing Silvius's love with him. When the eclogue is finished, Alinda steps forward, identifies herself as "a distressed Gentlewoman" wandering in the forest, and requests "some place of rest":

> . . . May you appoint us anie place of quiet harbour, (be it never so meane) I shall be thankfull to you, contented in my selfe, and gratefull to whosoever shall bee mine hoste.
>
> Coridon hearing the Gentlewoman speak so courteously returned her mildly and reverentlie this aunswere:
>
> Fair Mistres, we returne you as heartie a welcome, as you gave us a courteous salute.[8]

This little exchange perfectly exemplifies what Empson calls "the essential trick of the old pastoral, which was felt to imply a beautiful relation between rich and poor" (*SVP*, 11). Here the "trick" takes the form of Alinda making her request in exactly the terms that are to be attributed to the shepherd: quiet harbor, acceptance of meanness, thankfulness, content. Hence there cannot fail to be a perfect harmony between courtier and rustic. The conventionality, in all senses, of the passage makes one appreciate the way Spenser tests the courtier's representation of pastoral ideals, the way he uses the shepherd to hold the courtier to his terms. On the other hand, Lodge's far simpler version of the

---

8. In Geoffrey Bullough, ed., *Narrative and Dramatic Sources of Shakespeare*, 8 vols. (New York: Columbia University Press, 1961–75), 2:187–88. Subsequent references will be parenthetical in the text.

encounter is not without its charms. Here is the end of the speech in which Corydon represents "the shepherd's life":

> Envie stirres not us, wee covet not to climbe, our desires mount not above our degrees, nor our thoughts above our fortunes. Care cannot harbour in our cottages, nor doo our homely couches know broken slumbers: as we exceede not in diet, so we have inough to satisfie; and Mistres I have so much Latin, *Satis est quod sufficit.* (189)

This is a quite entrancing bit of self-reflexiveness. Corydon's motto reiterates "we have enough to satisfy" and thus enacts its own sufficiency: "the Latin I have tells me I need no more." The shepherd is thus saved from the pretentiousness of Holofernes the schoolmaster, who misquotes this apothegm in *Love's Labor's Lost* (5.1.1). But in addition, the gesture acknowledges the self-reflexiveness of this pastoral—the fact that the shepherd represents the gentleman's values because he speaks the gentleman's tongue. The writer's pleasure in the piece of wit is also a willingness to stand by this motto, and he thus makes good the ritual diffidence of his prefatory address "to the Gentlemen Readers":

> Gentlemen, look not here to find anie sprigs of Pallas bay tree, nor to heare the humour of any amorous Lawreate, nor the pleasing veine of anie eloquent Orator: *Nolo altum sapere,* they be matters above my capacitie. (159)

Shakespeare's characters do not take for granted "the beautiful relation between rich and poor," and therefore, as Judy Z. Kronenfeld points out in an excellent article,[9] Shakespeare's pastoralism does not presume upon it. Far from presenting herself as having already made pastoral virtues of her necessities, the exhausted Celia urges her companions to ask Corin "if he for gold will give us any food" (2.4.65). It is in such terms that Rosalind makes their request:

> I prithee, shepherd, if that love or gold
> Can in this desert place buy entertainment,
> Bring us where we may rest ourselves and feed.
> Here's a young maid with travel much oppressed,
> And faints for succor.
>
> (2.4.71–75)

If Melibee refused Calidore's gold, it would certainly be possible for the figure addressed here to reject the idea of payment for the help he gives. Instead, economic necessities are brought to the fore:

9. Judy Z. Kronenfeld, "Social Rank and the Pastoral Ideals of *As You Like It,* " *Shakespeare Quarterly* 29 (1978): 333–48.

Fair sir, I pity her
And wish, for her sake more than for mine own,
My fortunes were more able to relieve her;
But I am shepherd to another man,
And do not shear the fleeces that I graze.
My master is of churlish disposition,
And little reaks to find the way to heaven
By doing deeds of hospitality.
Besides, his cote, his flocks, and bounds of feed
Are now on sale, and at our sheep-cote now
By reason of his absence there is nothing
That you will feed on; but what is, come see,
And in my voice most welcome shall you be.[10]

(2.4.75–87)

One's first thought is that this speech undermines pastoral values. It first suggests that charity and succor are dependent on one's means and then that the citizen of Arden who has the means is charitable neither to his servants nor to strangers. But as a number of critics have observed and as Kronenfeld says most precisely, "Shakespeare first defines the situation as unconventional, then finds within it the conventional virtues, thus revitalizing the idea of pastoral charity."[11]

The question is how Shakespeare manages to restore pastoral values here; or rather, how he manages to do it without falling back on the fact (as much a trick of the old pastoral as any) that "good owners" come along just when their money and decency are needed. The answer is in Corin's rhetoric and presence, which are very much those—or better, Shakespearean developments of those—of other representative shepherds. The astringent precision of "And do not shear the fleeces that I graze" is pastoral not only because it states the simple fact, as Empson puts it (*SVP*, 11) in "learned and fashionable language." Though more self-conscious than apothegms (mainly because it doubles the literal and metonymic use of "fleeces") it is in touch with their mode. Furthermore, the way in which it represents the shepherd's economic status itself expresses pastoral values, for the meanings and associations of "graze" (feeding, protective supervision, ease of pasture) suggest that not being able to shear the fleeces of one's flock is to have a natural sequence blocked and even a natural right denied. The assertion of pastoral values is direct and explicit in the por-

---

10. The only detail Shakespeare adds is the master's churlish disposition, for Lodge's shepherd also serves a "landlord" who means to sell his farm and flock. But this information appears *after* Alinda has declared her intention "to buy some farme, and a flocke of sheepe, and so become a shepheardesse, meaning to live low, and content me with a countrey life" (188).

11. Kronenfeld, "Social Rank," 344.

trait of the "churlish" master, and it enacts, both in this epithet and its criticism, the traditional pastoral paradox that the humble person reproves his social superior by representing the virtues he should exemplify. Finally, the speech ends with a remarkable pastoral gesture. "In my voice most welcome shall you be" says in Corin's dignified plain style what the younger Shakespeare conveyed by rustic malapropism. For it is tantamount to saying "I myself reprehend my master's own person": that is, I give the welcome in his stead (represent him) and implicitly rebuke him for being unwilling to give it himself. Moreover, the line is a self-fulfilling moment: coming at the end of Corin's speech, it does not project its welcome into the future but enacts it on the spot. The somewhat odd locution, "in my voice," draws attention to the self-reflexiveness, and it completes the revitalization of pastoral values by representing human solicitude as responsive speech.[12]

Indeed, so clear is the pastoralism of Corin's speech that one may well ask what was the point of the realistic "swerve" with which he began. For it cannot be claimed that Corin makes us cognizant of a permanent element in the world he represents. In the speech most often quoted as an example of his homespun dignity, he says:

> Sir, I am a true laborer: I earn that I eat, get that I wear, owe no man hate, envy no man's happiness, glad of other men's good, content with my harm, and the greatest of my pride is to see my ewes graze and my lambs suck. (3.2.73–77)

The first phrases may indicate the status of a hired hand, but the speech as a whole suggests the independent proprietor—especially the final detail, which is reminiscent of the way Spenser's Melibee and Lodge's Corydon speak of their flocks as their only care. (What is critically searching in this line is that what makes "pride" pastoral—its conversion into pure satisfaction—is its representation in terms of maternal feeding.)[13] One understands why commentators

---

12. All editors gloss "voice" as "vote," following Dr. Johnson's explanation: "As far as I have voice or vote, as far as I have power to bid you welcome." But surely "vote" is not a possible meaning here. Rather we should look to two extended meanings of "voice" (7c, 10c), under which OED gives only quotations from Shakespeare. None of these examples is difficult to understand, but they apparently strike a lexicographer as unusual. What they have in common is the literal idea of "voice," speaking up for something. E.g. *Measure for Measure* 1.2.179–81: "Acquaint her with the danger of my state;/Implore her, in my voice, that she make friends/To the strict deputy." Also *Merry Wives* 1.4.156; *Cymbeline* 3.5.115. In two examples, the phrase "father's voice" is used for parental authority over a daughter's marriage (*MSND* 1.1.54, *All's Well*, 2.3.54). Corin's "in my voice" includes both ideas contained in these other examples—social authority and speaking on behalf of someone or for some purpose. Johnson's gloss indicates both these ideas, but they are not usefully codified in the gloss "voice = vote."

13. Touchstone immediately seizes this point and rags the old shepherd for getting his living by "the copulation of cattle" and betraying "a she-lamb of a twelve-month to a crookèd-pated

with politics more radical than Kronenfeld's feel irritated at the way the play lapses into conventional pastoralism. Without endorsing the dismissiveness of some of these critics,[14] we can take the questions they raise seriously and ask what purpose is served by Corin's moment of social realism. Is the speech any more than an on-the-spot display by Shakespeare that, as always, he is too smart to be taken in by a convention? After all, the very title of this play can call to mind the opportunism or cynicism of its leading wits, Touchstone and Jaques.

The questions the speech raises about pastoral values and relationships serve to ground them in situations and relationships more dramatic than in earlier pastorals, including pastoral dramas. Instead of the pretty speechifying of Lodge's Alinda, we have Rosalind asking for help in circumstances of distress. Even if Rosalind's courtesy to Corin suggests a conventional sense of noblesse oblige, Corin's reply reveals that gentle values depend on the individual gentleperson. But beyond the relation between the characters, Corin's words about his master introduce a broader idea—that the kind of thing we have seen happening at court can happen anywhere, even in Arden. Arden may prove to be the "better world" in which the courtier LeBeau, bidding farewell to Orlando, imagines he would "desire more love and knowledge" of the disgraced man whom he cannot befriend (1.2.285). It may even prove to be the golden world of carelessness imagined by the wrestler Charles. But if so, it is because it allows room for decency as knowing as LeBeau's. There is no presumption of any virtue inherent in the place (commentators have often noted the absence of magic in these woods), just as Corin's speech makes it clear that there are no virtues inherent in the social ranks that, ideally, express them. The economic and social realism specific to Corin's speech is simply one manifestation of the broader and more conservative human realism of the play.

---

old cuckoldly ram." The clown's coarseness here irritates some critics and certainly seems "antipastoral," but in fact his responsive wit restores to this topos the male presence it has with Spenser's Melibee:

> The litle that I haue, growes dayly more
> Without my care, but onely to attend it;
> My lambes doe euery yeare increase their score,
> And my flockes father daily doth amend it.
>
> (6.9.21)

It is hardly "realism" to say this: Lodge's Corydon knows as much when, saying that shepherds only experience "meane misfortunes, as the losse of a few sheepe" he says, "The next yeare may mend al with a fresh increase" (188–89). Touchstone simply steps in and performs his version of this knowledge. To the extent that Shakespeare makes pastoral new by dramatizing its situations, attitudes, conventions, and characters, its truths and values will emerge dramatically—here, mainly by sharpening the characterization of responsive speakers. To adapt the cryptic remark of Holofernes the schoolmaster, the pastoral allusion holds in the exchange (*LLL* 4.2.45).

14. E.g. John Barrell and John Bull, eds., *The Penguin Book of English Pastoral Verse* (London: Allen Lane, 1974), 108.

But if this is so, if virtues are not inherent in locale, then there is no reason why so-called pastoral values should be represented by shepherds. This is precisely what is conveyed by the scene preceding the courtiers' entrance into Arden and their encounter with Corin. When Orlando returns home from the wrestling match, he is met by the old family servant Adam, who warns him that his brother intends to kill him; when Orlando says he will take his chances at home, rather than beg or rob, Adam offers him his life's savings,

> Which I did store to be my foster-nurse,
> When service should in my old limbs lie lame,
> And unregarded age in corners thrown.
> Take that, and He that doth the ravens feed,
> Yea, providently caters for the sparrow,
> Be comfort to my age!   (2.3.40–45)

The pathos that makes these lines celebrated is mitigated by the play. Adam is spared the fate of being "unregarded"—not by acts of providence or the magic that does duty for them on the stage, but because his generosity insures an answering care and generosity in his young master. Similarly, when Orlando, seeking food for Adam, breaks violently in upon the Duke and his men, his act of desperate loyalty is met with civil generosity. If the play makes us feel that such responsiveness and solicitude are not conventional in the invidious sense, it is because we are persuaded that either of these episodes could have developed differently. A young master like the Bertram of *All's Well* (not to mention the Oliver of this play) might have accepted Adam's gold in a different spirit; Jaques would have dealt differently, as he is at pains to show, with the desperate Orlando. If the virtues and values are pastoral, it is because of the characters (in all senses) of the individuals who espouse and exemplify them. When Adam offers his gold and his service, Orlando exclaims:

> O good old man, how well in thee appears
> The constant service of the antique world,
> When service sweat for duty, not for meed!
>   (2.3.56–58)

These words present Adam as, in Kronenfeld's phrase, "a model of pastoral virtue."[15] Precisely because they call to mind pastoral ideas, they detach Adam and the virtues he represents from pastoral representation in the narrow, literal sense. By dividing the figure of the virtuous old shepherd between Corin and Adam, Shakespeare reveals the possibility of "shepherd-equivalents"—humble figures who are not shepherds but who have their literary characteristics and representative presence.

---

15. Kronenfeld, 339.

The equivalence between Adam and Corin may seem so conscious, even programmatic (making a deliberate point about conventional pastoral) as to be of merely local interest in *As You Like It*. But Shakespeare's dramaturgy can produce shepherd-equivalents in unexpected contexts. The grave-digger in *Hamlet* is simply a "clown," as the stage direction calls him, when he expounds the law and quizzes his fellow at the beginning of the scene. But he becomes a pastoral figure in the presence of courtiers. When Hamlet and Horatio enter, they find him singing in the grave and tossing skulls about him as he does his job. The hero's presence makes us aware of the pastoral value of his earlier "clownish" speeches. His talk about Adam as the first gentleman is simple not only in its manner but in its secure knowledge of what we must all come to. The self-reflexiveness of his clinching point, that Adam "bore arms" because he was a digger, reveals the confidence in his own representativeness, already suggested when he says, "There is no ancient gentlemen but gard'ners, ditchers, and grave-makers; they hold up Adam's profession" (5.1.29–30). This claim anticipates all the elements of Hamlet's meditations as he watches him—on the jawbone of Cain, the social inversions of death and their suggestion of "fine revolution," and the lawyer's attempt to contract out of death—and it also reveals the hero's painful, performative self-consciousness.

When Hamlet finally addresses him, the grave-digger is as good as his word: "Whose grave's this, sirrah?" "Mine, sir" (5.1.119). He, if no other man, could be associated with the birds and the low-roofed tortoises who reveal, to the pastoralizing speaker of *Upon Appleton House*, the folly of man who, "superfluously spread/Demands more room alive than dead" (st. 3). (Marvell's poem can be regarded as a reprise of this scene, Theocritus to its Homer. The narrator coolly encompasses both the prince whose "imagination trace[s] the noble dust of Alexander" [5.1.202–3] and the grave-digger, whose riddle to his companion, to which he himself is the answer, is "What is he that builds stronger than either the mason, the shipwright, or the carpenter?" [5.1.41–2]) There is no sentimentality here, perhaps not even any pathos in the ordinary sense. The grave-digger's sense of the whole tragedy comes down to clownish tautologies:

> *Hamlet.* How came he mad?
> *Grave-digger.* Very strangely, they say.
> *Hamlet.* How strangely?
> *Grave-digger.* Faith, e'en with losing his wits.
> *Hamlet.* Upon what ground?
> *Grave-digger.* Why, here in Denmark.
>
> (5.1.156–61)

Tired jests, we have heard them before, but the grave-digger knows the grounds on which he stands. His pragmatic answers to Hamlet's morbid question about ground—"How long will a man lie i'th'earth ere he rot?"—take on their full human value in the subsequent exchange about Yorick's skull. Hamlet's improvisation on it shows, *in parvo*, the intellectual and existential range of the first modern hero. It has all his performative energy, charm, and finesse, and at the same time reveals his mordant wit, his revulsion at the flesh, his self-disgust and despair. For the grave-digger, exclaiming "A pestilence on him for a mad rogue!" Yorick is the same fellow, "alive as dead." Unlike the melancholy prince, he is at home with death.

III

The final Shakespearean transformation of the representative shepherd occurs in Act 4 of *The Winter's Tale*. It is no secret that the pastoralism of this act turns the tragic beginnings of the play to its comic end. But when we look for the figures we expect to find, the representative shepherds of eclogues and of pastoral drama and romance, they seem to be reduced and marginal. Hence Greg's astonishing statement that "the shepherd scenes of [the] play . . . owe nothing of their treatment to pastoral tradition, nothing to convention, nothing to aught save life as it mirrored itself in the magic glass of the poet's imagination."[16] Critics tend to poach these scenes for what can be absorbed into accounts of the whole play: the exchange on art and nature; the Old Shepherd's statement, "thou met'st with things dying, I with things new-born" (3.3.113–14); and Perdita's phrase, "great creating Nature" (4.4.88), which is assumed to state the quintessence of pastoral. The motivic and symbolic weight of these moments is consonant with the solemnities of the rest of the play, but is often felt to be at odds with the conditions of their utterance. The Arden editor wants to cut the Old Shepherd's statement down to size, as a piece of rustic wit, and critics regularly find it awkward that Polixenes, who is up to no good, takes the "right" side in the debate about art and nature. Autolycus presents similar difficulties—is he a life-enhancing figure or a corrupt scoundrel?—and even Perdita goes in and out of focus as we try to understand the relation between her innocence and her authority. All these figures count as pastoral speakers. Their variety—less obvious, because less programmatic, than in *As You Like It*—has obscured what they have in common. Those who are not inhabitants of the countryside are court figures who represent themselves as country folk, and the sheep-shearing festival convenes them all.

The most obvious courtly pastoralist is Florizel, who when we meet him has already undergone the change of guise that Spenser's Calidore learns to accept for the sake of love. The test of his "swain's wearing" (4.9) is the character of his speech:

16. Walter W. Greg, *Pastoral Poetry and Pastoral Drama* (London: A. H. Bullen, 1906), 411.

> Apprehend
> Nothing but jollity. The gods themselves
> (Humbling their deities to love) have taken
> The shapes of beasts upon them. Jupiter
> Became a bull and bellow'd; the green Neptune
> A ram and bleated; and the fire-rob'd god,
> Golden Apollo, a poor humble swain,
> As I seem now. Their transformations
> Were never for a piece of beauty rarer,
> Nor in a way so chaste, since my desires
> Run not before mine honor, nor my lusts
> Burn hotter than my faith.
>
> $\qquad\qquad\qquad\qquad\qquad\qquad$ (4.4.24–35)

In other contexts, like the tapestries of Spenser's House of Busyrane, Ovidian transformations involve humiliation, the god within laid low by his need. Florizel's is a pastoral transformation. His initial locution—"The gods themselves . . . have taken/The shapes of beasts upon them"—conveys the swain's humility, for it represents what one suffers as a willing choice. The loving prince seems as good as his word, which is to say as good as his costume. But the purity of avowal here—the "way so chaste" Florizel claims for himself—involves an additional element of pastoral costuming, the festivity which has Perdita "most goddess-like prank'd up" (10) and which allows the lover to say, "Apprehend nothing but jollity." Because of the occasion, there is an element of sheer play in the young prince's self-representation, and he therefore, like other pastoral lovers but without their frustration, can distill his desire into lovely utterance. Indeed the playwright himself can be said, like his young hero, to be playing with pastoral in this long scene.[17] Not in the sense (which it is a main purpose of this book to discourage) that something must be done to pastoral to make it interesting, but in the strong and specific sense that he brings out the possibilities in pastoral of playing and of making a play.

After the anguish of Leontes' Sicily, where fantasies of bestial sex and the wearing of horns poison the imagination, this speech has the liberating effect promised by its opening line. If "Leontes' state of mind is a parody of the imagination of lover and poet," as Northrop Frye says,[18] Florizel gives new and saving qualities to the lover's avowals. He provides an alternative to the courtly habit of hyperbole that is implicated in the tragedy of the first three acts. We first see it in the convoluted courtesies of the opening scene, then in the playful ex-

17. I owe this suggestion to Janet Adelman, who made many helpful comments about this chapter.
18. "Recognition in *The Winter's Tale*," in *Fables of Identity* (New York: Harcourt, Brace, & World, 1963), 115.

travagancies (e.g. "Your queen and I are devils," 1.2.82) that help fire Leontes' imagination, and finally in the state of desperation that embraces Paulina's indignation and Antigonus's willingness to stake his wife's and daughters' virtue on Hermione's (2.1.133–57). Florizel's pastoralism acts as a protection against courtly hyperbole. The delicate absurdities of Jupiter's bellowing and Neptune's bleating treat erotic utterance with affectionate irony and thus register a saving difference from the courtly representation of innocence, which sex invades like a catastrophe: "We were as twinn'd lambs that did frisk i' th' sun,/And bleat the one at th' other" (1.2.67–68). The speech guarantees the claims implicit in its central lines:

> the fire-rob'd god,
> Golden Apollo, a poor humble swain,
> As I seem now.

"The fire-robed god," his epithet suggestive of erotic urgency, is renamed first as the god of poetry and then as the pastoral speaker who is his equal in love and who wields, as these very lines suggest, equivalent powers of rhetorical transformation. Well may Florizel assure Perdita that youthful lovers can escape the rages of their fathers.

Yet one may wonder whether Florizel's purity of avowal is not subject to all the limitations of fragile innocence usually attributed to pastoral. Is this young sir, breathing forth his chaste desires, any more than the male equivalent of those floral virgins Perdita imagines dying "ere they can behold/Bright Phoebus in his strength" (4.4.123–24)? Is this the son whose erotic insistence ("Or I'll be thine, my fair,/Or not my father's," 4.4.42–43) can redeem the devastation wrought by the adult male imagination? Why do this speech and this scene not seem to us, in the context of this play, as the madness of Ophelia—Perdita's predecessor in bestowing flowers on her elders—seems to Laertes: "Thought and afflictions, passion, hell itself/She turns to favor and to prettiness" (*Hamlet*, 4.5.188–89)?

The answer lies in the way Shakespeare makes pastoral usages answerable to a dramatic situation and dramatic relations productive of pastoral values. Though his source, Robert Greene's *Pandosto*, provided scenes in the country, it was Shakespeare who made these scenes a pastoral occasion. He developed the sheep-shearing festival from a single sentence in *Pandosto*[19] and did more than make it a site of convening—though that motif is itself made prominent by scenes which show Polixenes and Camillo setting off for the country (4.2) and then Autolycus and the Clown (Perdita's "brother") heading for the festival (4.3). By turning Greene's country episodes into a single gathering, Shakespeare brings together what Greene keeps separate—ordinary country life and

19. In the Arden Edition of *The Winter's Tale*, ed. J. H. P. Pafford (London: Methuen, 1963), 204.

the prince's pastoral wooing—and to them adds the disguised Polixenes and Camillo, whose analogues in *Pandosto* do not cross the border that separates court and country. These changes are both pastoral—in that the festive convening makes all the characters "shepherds," rural celebrants, for the nonce— and dramatic, in that the various elements of the situation are brought into contact (and therefore potential conflict) with each other.

The full dramatic potential, as one might expect of a pastoral, is suspended. True conflict does not occur until Polixenes throws off his disguise; the fact that he thus breaks off a mock marriage—which, like those of *Rosalynde* and *As You Like It*, seems as good as the real thing—makes it explicit that this is a disruption of pastoral.[20] At the same time, the festive pastoral is, from its opening lines, deeply attentive to dramatic realities:

> These your unusual weeds to each part of you
> Does give a life; no shepherdess, but Flora
> Peering in April's front.
>
> (4.4.1–3)

This is a double pastoral: the princess who is represented as a shepherdess (knowingly within the play, though not by herself) is here recostumed as a rural goddess. At the same time, these lines are made dramatic by the way the circumstances of their utterance engage their most striking detail. "Peering in April's front" is usually taken to mean "peeping out in early April." This takes the subject to be flowers, not their goddess,[21] but Florizel's loving praise and Perdita's presence make it impossible not to think of the goddess herself. Imagining Flora "in person" brings out the personification in "April's front" (i.e. brow or face, a much more likely meaning, in any case, than "first days").[22] These personifications make the phrase mean either "Flora looking out through or appearing in the face of April" or "Flora looking in(to) April's face." In a direct authorial description of the costumed Perdita, the first reading might come into play, but the words are spoken by her lover, who is presumably looking at her as he speaks and she at him. Though not literally "proud-pied," like the April

---

20. Cf. Florizel's words to Perdita at 4.4.49–51, which directly associate pastoral feasting with effective mock-marriage: "Lift up your countenance, as it were the day/Of celebration of that nuptial, which/We two have sworn shall come."

21. Hence the note in Frank Kermode, ed., *The Winter's Tale* (New York: New American Library, 1963): "i.e. Flora in April, when the flowers peep out rather than boldly appear." The gloss quoted above is the Riverside Shakespeare's.

22. Cf. OED: "front" in the meaning required by Riverside and Kermode is largely a military term, which is wholly inappropriate, nor does "front of an object" (e.g. table or building) really do here. Other Shakespearean uses of "front" support "front = brow or face" (*Ham* 3.4.56, *Lear* 2.2.108, *A&C* 1.1.6, *Mac* 4.3.232, 5.9.13), though the one valid counterexample in OED is Shakespearean: "As Philomel in summer's front doth sing" (Sonnet 102).

of Sonnet 98,[23] both his youth and the spirit of the occasion allow us to imagine him as the month who "dressed in all his trim/Hath put a spirit of youth in everything." When Perdita replies to his playful aggrandizing, she draws out the motif implicit in the lovers' mutual gaze:

> But that our feasts
> In every mess have folly, and the feeders
> Digest 't with a custom, I should blush
> To see you so attir'd—swoon, I think
> To show myself a glass.
>
> (4.4.10–14)[24]

To look at him is both to see someone disconcertingly different and at the same time to see herself reflected (as, indeed, the flower-prince Florizel can be thought to reflect Flora).

The pastoral development of lovers' mutual reflection is immensely liberating for the play. For the tragedy that seems to have befallen Sicily is generated by a powerful misconstruction of erotic mirroring. Leontes imagines Hermione and Polixenes "paddling palms and pinching fingers" and then "making practic'd smiles/As in a looking-glass" (1.2.115–17). As this fantasy leads him to the verge of distraction, he turns for relief to Mamillius and initiates a more painful and grotesque fantasy of mirroring. "Art thou my boy?" he asks his son. He tries out on himself the cuckold's familiar torment, and resists (but in fact reinstates) it by gazing on the boy's face and seeing himself there. "What? hast smutch'd thy nose?/They say it is a copy out of mine" (1.2.121–22) Whether the lad's nose is running or dirty, Leontes' thought leads to a contorted play on "neat," with its double sense of "cleanly" and of cattle, horned beasts. This prompts a metaphorical statement of the first question: "How now, you wanton calf,/Art thou my calf?" "Yes, if you will, my lord," comes the reply, and indeed he will:

> Thou want'st a rough pash and the shoots that I have,
> To be full like me; yet they say we are
> Almost as like as eggs.
>
> (1.2.128–30)

These lines, in which Leontes simply equates his adult sexuality with wearing the cuckold's horns, begin the speech which will explode in the distracted so-

23. It is probable, however, that he is quite dressed up for a swain. At the end of scene 4, he exchanges his garb with Autolycus, who is then able to pass himself off, admittedly to the rustics, as a courtier.

24. Like J. H. P. Pafford, the Arden editor, and Stephen Orgel, in his forthcoming edition in the Oxford Shakespeare series, I accept Theobald's emendation "swoon" for the Folio reading "sworn," which Riverside adopts.

liloquy, "Affection, thy intention stabs the center!" The lines that bring him to that point are an insistent claiming that Mamillius is his likeness. We see here the habit of desperate asseveration that both reflects and helps create Sicily's frame of mind:

> Women say so [that we are like as eggs]
> That will say anything. But were they false
> As o'er-dy'd blacks, as wind, as waters, false
> As dice are to be wish'd by one that fixes
> No bourn 'twixt his and mine, yet were it true
> To say this boy were like me.
>
> (I.ii.130–35)

Leontes imagines the dicer in terms that cannot help but bring Polixenes to his mind, but they also bring out, for us, the terrible burden he imposes on his son by not recognizing a "bourn 'twixt his and mine." It is this psychological imposition, Leontes' use of Mamillius as a narcissistic reflector,[25] that makes credible the strong suggestion, in the romance plot, that he kills him.

Leontes' self-mirroring gradually extends to the whole world around him, until the only retreat from his diseased mind—the only place "Sicily" the country can be different from "Sicily" the monarch—is the prison, that other locale of doomed enclosure, to which the women of the play withdraw or are confined. The pastoralism of Bohemia frees the play and, eventually, Sicily from these segregations and self-enclosures. Dramatized in Florizel's and Perdita's wooing, pastoral masking makes erotic mirroring at once delighted and self-conscious. The underlying notion might be put as follows: "If I, dressed up for festivity and loving, am not myself, then you in whom I see myself, are also not myself." Perdita's imagined swooning at her own image is itself differentially reflected, a dozen lines later, when Florizel's phrase—"Golden Apollo, a poor humble swain,/As I seem now"—raises the question of how he mirrors the god.

Perdita registers the sense of others' otherness when she speaks of the disparity in rank between herself and her prince: "To me the difference forges dread" (4.4.17). Her fear derives from differences seen dramatically—that is, as fixed and ineluctable, leading to conflict and consequences. But so long as Polixenes remains in pastoral guise, dread is suspended and difference emerges in the checks and balances of the dialogue—always dramatically plausible, but conceived in and sustaining a pastoral mode. Many of the speeches are set pieces, manifestly related to what we might find in eclogues. When the Old Shepherd enters on the festival scene with his rustic companions, he speaks, like many of his literary ancestors, as *laudator temporis acti.* (His first appearance,

---

25. The phrase is that of Peter Erickson, "Patriarchal Structures in *The Winter's Tale,*" *PMLA* 97 (1982): 821.

in 3.3, was in a familiar role in eclogues and romances—the herdsman searching for his lost sheep.) He reproaches Perdita for shirking her duties as a hostess
by portraying the behavior of his "old wife" on such days. This is a pastoral
register different from the play of Florizel and Perdita, but related to it by innocent utterance and the motifs of festivity and country bearing. It has a similar
effect in and on the play. The old man's wholehearted insistence that his virgin daughter "quench [her] blushes" (4.4.67) and put herself forth to entertain
her guests has the effect of undoing the confusions of insistent entertainment
and sexual boldness with which Leontes' tragedy began. The Old Shepherd's
speech is immediately followed by the most famous set piece in the play, the
exchange on art and nature between Perdita and Polixenes. In the pleasure
given by its rivaling responsiveness, it is related to exchanges in eclogues, and
it is the dramatic device of the festival, to which all come in the character of
shepherds, that enables it to occur. Polixenes' speech gives critics pause because
it seems out of character: there is a disparity between his defense of mingling
base and gentle and his actual purpose in coming to the countryside. But it is
precisely that he *is* out of character here. The liberating quality of the feast,
suspending for a while the dramatic realities that will reassert themselves, allows him to speak as if he belonged to Perdita's world and to register his differences in the role of sympathetic elder.

The benign registration of differences between genders and generations sustains a major development in the play. In a brief but important essay, C. L. Barber
drew attention to the centrality of what seems to be Leontes' homosexual attrac-
tion to Polixenes. He points to the "twinn'd lambs" speech, of course, but also to
the way Leontes' paranoid jealousy conforms to the Freudian account and to "the
remarkable insistence on identification of the two kings with their sons."[26] He
then makes the following structural argument about the whole play:

> The primary motive that must be transformed before Hermione can be
> recovered in *The Winter's Tale*, as the father-daughter motive is trans-

---

26. "'Thou that Beget'st Him That Did Thee Beget': Transformation in *Pericles* and *The Winter's Tale*,"
Shakespeare Survey 22 (1969): 59–67. In revised form, this essay has been incorporated into C. L.
Barber and Richard P. Wheeler, *The Whole Journey: Shakespeare's Power of Development* (Berkeley & Los
Angeles: University of California Press, 1986). Both the phrase just quoted and the next quotation
are on p. 330.

In using Barber for the purposes of practical criticism, I do not mean to prefer his interpretation
to the more deeply elaborated psychoanalytic accounts of Murray Schwartz, "Leontes' Jealousy in
The Winter's Tale," *American Imago* 30 (1973): 250–73, and "*The Winter's Tale*: Loss and Transformation,"
American Imago 32 (1975): 145–99, and of Janet Adelman, *Suffocating Mothers* (New York: Routledge,
1992), 220–38. Perhaps this is the place to say that my thinking about issues of identity and
difference in Shakespeare owes much to the work of Stanley Cavell, though my account of *The
Winter's Tale* is along quite different lines from his, in *Disowning Knowledge* (Cambridge: Cambridge
University Press, 1987), 193–221.

formed in *Pericles*, is the affection of Leontes for Polixenes, whatever name one gives it. The resolution becomes possible because the affection is consummated, as it could not otherwise be, through Perdita and Florizel.

I think our analysis enables us to state more clearly what Barber somewhat elides here. He draws attention, in the opening acts, to a homoerotic hall of mirrors: Leontes sees himself in Polixenes, and the power of this bond is manifested by the way the two monarchs mirror each other in seeing themselves in their sons. For the children to fulfill the fathers' love for each other, one son must be killed off and a daughter substituted for him. The pastoral scene turns this stern necessity into a far stronger version of "favor and prettiness" than could be represented by Ophelia and the Oedipal drama that claims her as victim. Nor is the movement from homoerotic bonds to heterosexual love in itself uncommon in Shakespearean comedy.[27] What is distinctive in *The Winter's Tale* is that the children's love frees both them and their elders, who return at the end of the play not simply as authority figures but as lovers. This realignment of eros requires that the fathers as well as the children take part in the pastoral transformations of Act 4. We may feel that Polixenes's behavior after unmasking deprives him of any personal right, so to speak, to the cultivated dignity of his speech on art and nature. But his masking has caught him up in the play's work of freeing erotic devotion; his words to Perdita, as pastoral *raisonneur*, can therefore serve as a motto for the great final scene, in which he is one of the wondering observers as Hermione's statue takes flesh.

The ancillary characters of Bohemia extend the way pastoral disguising plays out erotic and social differentiation. After the "eclogue" which begins the feasting—with Perdita's flower speech, the last set piece, as its apogee—the celebration gives way to "a dance of Shepherds and Shepherdesses." This introduces a scene of rural merriment, at the heart of which is Autolycus, selling his knacks and singing his ballads. The question for critics—and for those staging the play as well—is whether this adds anything of importance to what Derek Traversi calls the "rarified idealism" of the verse pastoral that has preceded. Traversi is typical in his uneasiness about Autolycus: he likes the "note of wayward humanity" and the "direct evocation of the flesh" but he does not want to attribute too much importance, in the central conceptions of the play, to the rogue's "vivacious spontaneity."[28] This interpretive uncertainty comes, in the first instance, from failing to see Autolycus's connection with other aspects of the play's pastoralism. He is one more Shakespearean variation on the literary shepherd: a fugitive from the court who has attired himself in country garb, he

27. Cf. Janet Adelman, "Male Bonding in Shakespeare's Comedies," in *Shakespeare's Rough Magic: Renaissance Essays in Honor of C. L. Barber*, ed. Peter Erickson and Coppélia Kahn (Newark, Del.: University of Delaware Press, 1985), 73–103.

28. *Shakespeare: The Last Phase*, 155, 138.

achieves his ends by means of entrancing songs. The scene over which he pre-
sides makes its pastoral conception evident when it concludes with a dance of
"three carters, three shepherds, three neatherds, [and] three swineherds," who
are costumed as satyrs. One expects to find herdsmen and satyrs in pastoral
drama and romance, and there is no pointed disparity with Autolycus, as there
is between Silvius and Touchstone in *As You Like It*. For the satyr dance, turning
sexual energy into musical pleasure, stages the significance of Autolycus's ballads, which occasion innocent bawdry and which themselves are sold as love-
gifts.

The importance of Autolycus's pleasures becomes apparent when Polixenes
decides to make his move. He asks Florizel why he purchased no love-gifts
from the pedlar:

> How now, fair shepherd?
> Your heart is full of something that does take
> Your mind from feasting. Sooth, when I was young,
> And handed love as you do, I was wont
> To load my she with knacks.
>
> (4.4.345–49)

These lines beautifully illustrate the doubleness of pastoral masking. Polixenes
challenged Perdita in this same tone of elderly solicitude, which we can take as
honest (to use one of the play's key words) insofar as the speaker accepts his
country guise. An old shepherd speaking these lines would suggest a tolerant
awareness of the folly he once played out himself: this is the tone Corin takes,
in the first words Rosalind hears in the Forest of Arden, as he counsels the
enamored Silvius (2.4.22ff.). But Polixenes, preparing to throw off his disguise,
is "angling" here, in the manner of his brother-king (1.2.180). His dramatic
purpose gives a disparaging inflection to "handed" and "load my she with
knacks": it brings into the countryside a whiff of Leontes' physical loathing
("paddling palms and pinching fingers") and contemptuous locutions ("My
wife's a hobby-horse, deserves a name/As rank as any flax-wench" 1.2.275–76).
Florizel replies that his gifts are those of the heart, and he shows what he means
by redeeming his beloved's hand:

> I take thy hand, this hand,
> As soft as dove's down and as white as it,
> Or Ethiopian's tooth, or the fann'd snow that's bolted
> By th' northern blasts twice o'er.
>
> (4.4.362–65)

Polixenes professes to admire this protestation, but his admiration is compromised by an undertone of mockery ("How prettily th' young swain seems to
wash/The hand was fair before!") We must be able to resist such mockery our-

selves, if these extravagant speeches are to redeem the hyperboles of love that Leontes corrupted and that underlie the wonders of the statue scene.

Our admiration of Florizel can be more wholehearted, it can admit wonder, because of the comic erotics of the preceding scene. There Autolycus and his companions play out the words with which the Old Shepherd's servant announces his arrival:

> He hath songs for man or woman, of all sizes; no milliner can so fit his customers with gloves. He has the prettiest love-songs for maids, so without bawdry, which is strange; with such delicate burthens of dildos and fadings, "jump her and thump her." (4.4.191–95)

Here, as in the rest of the scene, gloves and ballads are interchangeable love-gifts, each felt to express the lover's desires and to pay suitable tribute to the mistress's powers. Florizel's verbal decking of his beloved's hand does not feel excessively rarefied, because it is seen to be of a piece with these more common exchanges. It is Polixenes's spirit, not his son's, that will scorn such commerce and the erotic extravagance it too expresses. The young lover deifying the mistress he has "most goddess-like prank'd up" is reinscribed in the balladeer who is said to "sing over" ribbons, smocks, and cuffs "as they were gods and goddesses" (207–8). When Autolycus enters singing "Lawn as white as driven snow" he is as good as his herald's word. Even the innocent obscenity of "dildos" is not left as a mere joke against the rustics, as Polixenes might view it. The malapropism, taking the name of the phallus as a ballad refrain, is one more instance of pastoral transformation—a "delicate burthen" indeed.

To redeem the play from Leontes, Sicily, the world of the fathers, there was needed—so the dramaturgy of Act 4 argues—both the innocent extravagance of the princely lover and a figure who has a more ironic and earthbound sense not only of human desires but of poetizing as a form of pleasure, self-expression, and advantage-seeking. This diversifying of pastoral roles engages a promise of innocence first stated in Act 1, as the Sicilian tragedy unfolds. When Hermione and Polixenes, having seen his exchange with Mamillius, ask Leontes what troubles him, he dismisses their concern by saying he was carried away by seeing himself in "the lines of my boy's face" (1.2.153–54). What he sees there—himself as a boy "unbreech'd," with his "dagger muzzled"—shows how he reads his own sexual disturbance into Mamillius. As if to turn everyone's attention, including his own, from these suggestions, he asks: "Are you so fond of your young prince as we /Do seem to be of ours?" Polixenes replies:

> If at home, sir,
> He's all my exercise, my mirth, my matter;
> Now my sworn friend, and then mine enemy;
> My parasite, my soldier, statesman, all.

> He makes a July's day short as December,
> And with his varying childness cures in me
> Thoughts that would thick my blood.
>
> (1.2.165–71)

This representation of innocence is as important to the play as the more frequently cited lines about the boyhood of the two kings. Both terms in the
phrase "varying childness" bring out the difference from Polixenes's earlier por-
trayal of "twinn'd lambs," who "bleat the one at th' other" as if absolutely identical. Here innocence is not only seen in human form but is manifested by the
human capacity to play a variety of roles.

It is precisely this power of our nature that Leontes corrupts the moment
Polixenes and Hermione leave:

> Gone already!
> Inch-thick, knee-deep, o'er head and ears a fork'd one!
> Go play, boy, play. Thy mother plays, and I
> Play too, but so disgrac'd a part, whose issue
> Will hiss me to my grave: contempt and clamor
> Will be my knell. Go play, boy, play.
>
> (I.ii.185–90)

What first strikes us, of course, is the ugly twist Leontes gives to the innocent
word. But this moment initiates a more fearsome corruption of playing. Leontes'
paranoid fantasy—imagining himself onstage in his own part, the object of all
eyes—is augmented by an additional need to play out the parts of those who
betray and mock him. It is this that provides the finishing touch, the sting at
the end, of the scene of loathing with which his speech continues:

> There have been
> (Or I am much deceived) cuckolds ere now,
> And many a man there is (even at this present,
> Now, while I speak this) holds his wife by th' arm,
> That little thinks she has been sluic'd in 's absence,
> And his pond fish'd by his next neighbor—by
> Sir Smile, his neighbor.
>
> (1.2.190–96)

Leontes' capacity to take on all the parts in his drama appears in his vehement
imaginings of the love-play of Hermione and Polixenes—a vein he regularly
draws on, as if playing Iago to his own Othello. Nowhere is this playing of
parts more evident than in his carryings on after he invades the scene in the
nursery (2.1), where Mamillius, in his "varying childness," is about to tell his
winter's tale. As he pulls the boy from his mother, she asks, "What is this?
Sport?" and soon sees the games her husband plays:

> You, my lords,
> Look on her, mark her well; be but about
> To say she is a goodly lady, and
> The justice of your hearts will thereto add
> 'Tis pity she's not honest—honorable.
> Praise her but for this her without-door form
> (Which on my faith deserves high speech) and straight
> The shrug, the hum or ha (these petty brands
> That calumny doth use. . . .)
>
> (II.i.64–72)

The solipsism of Leontes' Sicily is evident. Everywhere he turns he sees his suspicions confirmed—in Camillo's dismay (cf. 1.2.384–87), in Polixenes' flight, and in Mamillius's pining away. But bound up with self-mirroring and its misinterpretations is the active self-projection by which the monarch populates his realm with fantasy figures of his own enactment.

Perhaps it is this ludic twist that enables *The Winter's Tale* to be a tragicomedy. In any case, one of the most important functions of the pastoralism of Act 4 is to redeem the capacity to play—to restore "varying childness" to the world, under the aspect of festivity. Autolycus's centrality is clear here. Not only does he diversify, in respect to Florizel, the role of pastoral singer, he is himself a notorious player of parts. This is the way he represents himself to the Clown as he pretends, as if in parody of Leontes, to be his own victim:

> I know this man well [says Autolycus]; he hath been since an ape-bearer, then a process-server, a bailiff, then he compass'd a motion of the Prodigal Son, and married a tinker's wife within a mile where my land and living lies; and, having flown over many knavish professions, he settled only in rogue. Some call him Autolycus. (4.3.94–100)

The rogue's role-playing is assimilated to pastoral in the sheep-shearing scene. Of all Autolycus's songs, the one that most achieves his ends is neither "Lawn as white as driven snow" nor "Will you buy any tape," both of which hawk his wares, nor one of the fantastical ballads he summarizes, which themselves parody the tragic events in Sicily (4.4.262–81). Rather it is the trio ballad, in which he joins the country folk, of "Two maids wooing a man." He has scarcely begun his pitch to sell this song, when Mopsa and Dorcas inform him they have known it a month since and invite him to join them in singing it. "I can bear my part," says Autolycus; "you must know 'tis my occupation" (4.4.295–96). It is this song which entrances the Clown: "He would not stir his pettitoes [Autolycus tells us later] till he had both tune and words, which so drew the rest of the herd to me that all their other senses stuck in ears" (4.4.606–9). It is this moment that makes Northrop Frye speak of Autolycus as "a kind of rascally

Orpheus"[29]—with perfect truth to pastoral tradition, since it recalls the beginning of Virgil's eighth Eclogue, when the herds leave off grazing, in wonder at
the songs of two shepherds. Shakespeare seems to have remembered this
passage (whether or not through intermediaries) when Camillo praises Perdita:
"I should leaving grazing, were I of your flock,/And only live by gazing"
(4.4.109–10). The fullness of pastoral conception here perhaps justifies a fussy
correction of Frye's remark: it is the Clown, the rustic, whose singing of this
song has such Orphic effect, while Autolycus, the original singer, goes about
picking pockets.

In Perdita's flower speech, pastoral playing lies at the heart of pastoral
speaking. Perdita is a pastoral speaker here, because in her dramatic character
she takes on the function of the literary shepherd. In a double act of convening,
she welcomes her lover and her companions by imaginatively gathering the
flowers of springtime:

> Now, my fair'st friend,
> I would I had some flow'rs o' th' spring that might
> Become your time of day—and yours, and yours,
> That wear upon your virgin branches yet
> Your maidenheads growing. O Proserpina,
> For the flow'rs now, that, frighted, thou let'st fall
> From Dis's wagon!
>
> (4.4.112–18)

The invocation of Proserpina brings out the conventional function of pastoral
song—to bring the singer and her fellows together in the face of separation or
loss. But if the speech has the underpinnings of pastoral elegy, it does not have
the tone: Perdita does not feel Proserpina's fate as a loss to herself, nor does she,
like the ordinary literary shepherd, feel in a diminished situation. On the contrary, her poetizing, like her character, seems to restore the maiden-goddess
and the season that is associated with her. Hence the grandeur critics attribute
to her innocence in this speech. She is "more truly representative of the age of
innocence than Milton's Eve." "Like Hermione's, unlike Autolycus's, [hers] is an
achieved innocence."[30] She is said to be like "great creating Nature" herself:
"She so excels nature—or, at least, nature's norm—that her imagination can
dispense with the objects [i.e. the flowers] themselves."[31] If the pastoral singer's
invoking of an absent companion or predecessor has the effect of convening

29. *Fables of Identity*, 117.

30. S. L. Bethel and A. D. Nuttall, as quoted by Michael Taylor, "Innocence in *The Winter's Tale*,"
Shakespeare Studies 15 (1982): 236.

31. Rosalie L. Colie, *Shakespeare's Living Art* (Princeton: Princeton University Press, 1974), 278.

him, Perdita has been so successful that some critics mistakenly think that this scene takes place in springtime.[32]

Nevertheless, however understandable the critics' rhetoric and however much this speech thematizes natural recovery and the finding of that which is lost, Perdita cannot bring about the resolution which depends on that recovery. It is of the essence of the play's mode that no single character has that power—even Leontes, to Sicily's great good fortune, does not have the tragic hero's strength relative to his world—and Perdita most assuredly does not. She can lay claim to being Flora in this scene, but not Astraea.[33] But the playing that enables her to "be" Flora explains both the character of her innocence in this speech and the compatibility of its power with its pastoralism. The speech begins in play—Perdita's merry rebuke of Camillo's extravagant praise (quoted above)—and it leads to the self-conscious avowal, "Methinks I play as I have seen them do/In Whitsun pastorals." However we imagine her accompanying gestures or behavior, variable role-playing is implicit in the rhetoric of her catalogue of flowers. We can see this most readily by comparing Ovid's account of Perdita's prototype:

> *Haud procul Hennaeis lacus est a moenibus altae,*
> *nomine Pergus, aquae: non illo plura Caystros*
> *carmina cycnorum labentibus audit in undis.*
> *silva coronat aquas cingens latus omne suisque*
> *frondibus ut velo Phoebeos submovet ictus;*
> *frigora dant rami, Tyrios humus umida flores:*
> *perpetuum ver est. quo dum Proserpina luco*
> *ludit et aut violas aut candida lilia carpit,*
> *dumque puellari studio calathosque sinumque*
> *inplet et aequales certat superare legendo,*
> *paene simul visa est dilectaque raptaque Diti:*
> *usque adeo est properatus amor. dea territa maesto*
> *et matrem et comites, sed matrem saepius, ore*
> *clamat, et ut summa vestem laniarat ab ora,*
> *collecti flores tunicis cecidere remissis,*
> *tantaque simplicitas puerilibus adfuit annis,*
> *haec quoque virgineum movit iactura dolorem.*
>
> (5.385–401)

---

32. E.g. F. C. Tinkler, "*The Winter's Tale,*" *Scrutiny* 5 (1936–37): 358. Students who use the *Riverside Shakespeare* are told that the Bohemian scenes "celebrate . . . the awakening of spring" (p. 1565), but are not informed that sheep-shearing takes place in late June or that 4.4.79–81 indicates that the feast in this play is later (see Arden note at 4.3.37).

33. She has a clear relation to the Flora of Peele's *The Arraignment of Paris.*

Not far from Henna's walls there is a deep pool of water, Pergus by name.
Not Caÿster on its gliding waters hears more songs of swans than does
this pool. A wood crowns the heights around its waters on every side,
and with its foliage as with an awning keeps off Phoebus's rays. The
branches afford a pleasing coolness, and the well-watered ground bears
bright-coloured flowers. There spring is everlasting. Within this grove
Proserpina was playing, and gathering violets or white lilies. And while
with girlish eagerness she was filling her basket and her bosom, and striving to surpass her mates in gathering, almost in one act did Pluto see and
love and carry her away: so precipitate was his love. The terrified girl
called plaintively on her mother and her companions, but more often
upon her mother. And since she had torn her garment at its upper edge,
the flowers which she had gathered fell out of her loosened tunic; and
such was the innocence of her girlish years, the loss of her flowers even
at such a time aroused new grief.[34]

I quote the whole passage to bring out the many thematic connections—
playing itself, protection from Phoebus's strength, the profusion of flowers and
some specific flowers (lilies and violets), the motif of spring outlasting its time.
Moreover, Ovid's passage, though not a pastoral, is conscious of song at its
beginning—where it enhances and identifies the special character of this
spot—and of its distortion in the virgin's cries of distress at the end. But what
is particularly revealing for us is the way Ovid characterizes Proserpina: his
whole emphasis is on her *simplicitas*.[35] This passage, like the entire narration,
sharply differentiates innocence and experience, children and parents. Innocence has its pathos, but it is seen from the outside and as itself a simple thing.
The experience of pathos belongs to Ceres, who has moments of rage that
come close to those of the rapist Dis. The cooler complexity of the poet's supervising intelligence, registered here by *usque adeo est properatus amor* (396), is
matched in the story by Jove, who takes on the poet's tone when Ceres tells
him of their daughter's fate:

> *commune est pignus onusque*
> *nata mihi tecum; sed si modo nomina rebus*
> *addere vera placet, non hoc iniuria factum,*
> *verum amor est.*
>
> (5.523–26)

34. Text and translation (slightly modified) from Ovid, *Metamorphoses*, ed. Frank Justus Miller, 3d
ed. (rev. G. P. Goold), 2 vols. (Cambridge: Harvard University Press, Loeb Classical Library).

35. This emphasis recurs in the brief scene of her eating the pomegranate in the underworld, *cultis
dum simplex errat in hortis* (5.535).

She is, indeed, our daughter, yours and mine, our common pledge and
care. But if only we are willing to give right names to things, this is no
harm that has been done, but only love.

Ovid tells the story of Proserpina as it would be seen by Polixenes. What
is astonishing about Perdita, as critics in various ways have tried to say, is her
knowingness in innocence. In the flower speech, this characteristic—which
elsewhere manifests itself in frank playfulness—appears in a fluent assumption
of identities and roles. What shall we say is the character of the speaker who
evokes "daffodils,/That come before the swallow dares, and take/The winds of
March with beauty" (4.4.118–20)? Does the idea of coming before the swallow
dares reveal the maiden's fearfulness? Or does the virgin feel an identity with
the spring flower, the daffodil, and its imputed boldness? This would be consistent with her imagined gathering of the flowers her frightened prototype let
fall—the frankness of the country maid coming in to surpass the goddess in
virginal presence. The range of her identifications is extended in the next detail,
which evokes the erotic appeal of the flower's bold fragility and puts the
speaker, momentarily, in the role of the forceful lover. "Take," which here
means "charm" or "seize the affections" (OED), retains a suggestion of vehemence; the word is not a pun, but it has a range that could include everything
in Ovid's one-line narration of the rape of Proserpina. *Paene simul visa est dilectaque
raptaque Diti* is the way a self-conscious poet rolls up items into a single moment;
Perdita's "take" is pastoral in its simplicity, its resistance to being discomposed.
At the same time, one would not say of this speaker, *tantaque simplicitas puerilibus
adfuit annis.* Rather her speech displays "the pastoral process of putting the complex into the simple," and it here depends on a flexibility of identification that
sublimates, makes grand and exquisite, the power of "varying childness"—a
phrase, we recall, used of the very Florizel who now stands before us in his
youth.
There is a similar effect in

> pale primroses,
> That die unmarried, ere they can behold
> Bright Phoebus in his strength (a malady
> Most incident to maids).
>
> (4.4.122–25)

Traversi, an ideologue of maturity, says, "The beauty of these lines is devoid of
strength, even clings pathetically to its own lack of vigor."[36] This is the accent
of Polixenes. But how can we dispute the assumption that the maiden speaker

36. Traversi, 149.

is identical with the maidens represented? She surely feels some sense of identification with them—not only because of her virginity, but because she herself justly fears she may die unmarried. Her locution for sexual experience recalls, by its similar structure, the social fears she expressed earlier: "Or how/Should I, in these my borrowed flaunts, behold/The sternness of his [Polixenes's] presence?" (4.4.22–24) Nevertheless, the suggestions of maidenly pathos do not determine Perdita's character as speaker here. For one thing, she could not speak as she does without some implicit experience, denied to the primroses, of "bright Phoebus in his strength." That her grasp of the virgins' situation goes beyond the *simplicitas* belonging to girlish years is confirmed by the element of wit in her final phrase. The Arden editor explains that the reference is to chlorosis, "the green sickness," and refers us to Herrick's "How Primroses came green," which records the legend that virgins, "troubled with Green-sicknesses," were transformed into the flower which retains their hue. There is no doubt about the actuality of chlorosis, but neither grammar nor rhetoric allows us to refer "a malady most incident to maids" to the adjective "pale." It can only refer to the preceding line and a half, which concerns the condition of being unmarried. Perdita wittily distances herself from maidenhood and suggests that to live beyond it—as she very much wants to—is a condition of health. (This suggestion is also consistent with the seasonal doubling—recuperating the values of spring for life in the summer, when the sun is in his strength.) Moreover, the phrase, rightly understood, borders on tautology: being unmarried is, of course, "most incident to maids," for it defines them. The virgin speaker thus absorbs her desires and self-awareness into a phrase that, on the one hand, looks like a piece of comic primness, and on the other like its sophisticated partner, Marvellian wit.

One final consideration shows how this speech turns the workings of ordinary pastoral to the uses of drama. For whom do we imagine Perdita to be "singing" here? She speaks *to* her companions and her shepherd-lover, as she would in an eclogue. But when we ask in whose stead or on whose behalf she speaks, we are aware of another figure than those present. When she calls on Proserpina to bring the flowers of spring, Perdita—conscious of presenting "flow'rs of middle summer" to "men of middle age" (4.4.106–8)—intuits the role of the maiden's mother, the absent Ceres. Perdita thus speaks not only for herself but for Hermione, and it is in this way—deeply consistent with the pastoralism of both situation and character—that her presence in this scene, as many critics have felt, adumbrates the play's resolution. The final flowers of her catalogue, "bold oxlips" and "the crown imperial," and the wonder of her presence, which has Florizel saying "all your acts are queens" (4.4.146) and Camillo calling her "the queen of curds and cream" (161), prepare us to be believers of the greater wonder when her royal mother comes to life and is told that "our Perdita is found."

The main figures in Shakespeare's Bohemia are all conceived in terms provided by traditional pastoral. Florizel, Perdita, Autolycus, and Polixenes map out the possible ways in which court personages assume pastoral guise, and each speaks importantly in the character of a shepherd. But in their range and presence they quite dwarf the "real" shepherds who are their hosts, those whom one would expect—thinking of works like Sannazaro's *Arcadia*, *Il Pastor Fido*, *Diana*, and *Rosalynde*—to populate and determine the character of the pastoral world. We can locate the diminishment of the representative shepherd by the way *The Winter's Tale* deals with pastoral encounters. Immediately after Polixenes storms off, uttering his dire threats, Perdita says:

> Even here undone!
> I was not much afeard; for once or twice
> I was about to speak, and tell him plainly
> The self-same sun that shines upon his court
> Hides not his visage from our cottage, but
> Looks on alike.
>
> (4.4.441–46)

The plain talk she imagines here is precisely what courtly interlocutors have heard from Spenser's Melibee and Shakespeare's Corin. Why does this pastoral encounter not occur face-to-face? Surely because the dramatic tensions are too strong for pastoral exchange. Perdita, in fact, did stand up to Polixenes in the art-nature "debate," but the conditions there are explicitly those of eclogue, where the courtier accepts his role as shepherd. Shakespeare's dramaturgy, in other words, is conscious of the fact which Spenser's could not fully acknowledge—that the shepherd encountered by the sophisticated speaker is really a self-representation. Hence the pastoral encounters of *The Winter's Tale* occur between like characters, or, to put it another way, pastoral encounters are seen to be versions of pastoral exchange.

The dramaturgy of Act 4 is thus expressive and cognizant of the limitations of pastoral. Nevertheless, the power of the act as a whole is not in spite of but due to its commitment to pastoral usages. The possibility of exchange—which is to say, the possibility of action and utterance that establish connections between separate persons, the recognition of likeness in apparent difference (Perdita's imagined rebuke to Polixenes), the possibility represented by the grafting Polixenes defends when it is understood in the spirit of Perdita (i.e. when we understand the art-nature dialogue as responsive song, not debate)—these pastoral usages and thematics are the means by which the play transforms the disasters with which it began. Moreover, the fact that the tragic beginnings are identified with the *court* of Sicily means that the play as a whole engages the way in which pastoral figures are self-representations: we come to see the courtly pastoralists of Act 4, in themselves and in their relations, as alternatives to the courtiers of Acts 1 – 3. The pastoralism of Act 4 thus recovers the uses of pastoral encounter; but the encounter takes place not so much between the characters as within the mind of the audience.[37] This is clearest in the episodes between Autolycus and the rustics, the last of which, concluding Act 4, parodies pastoral encounters, as Autolycus acts the role of the courtier to intimidate the Old Shepherd and his son. Our interest in these episodes is expressed less by what is going on between the characters on stage than by what goes on between us and the scenes as comic and pastoral wholes. What is crucial is that we not view any of the figures, either the rustics or Autolycus, in the spirit of Polixenes. It is because we feel the generosity and freedom Autolycus brings into the play—in the liberating sexual playfulness of his first song ("When daffodils begin to peer") and then in the scene about love gifts—that we feel the alternatives, eventually to be realized in Hermione and the repentant Leontes, to Polixenes' disparaging of erotic devotion. We thus feel a pastoral alternative for ourselves, but it is no longer represented by a putatively real shepherd like Spenser's Melibee.

37. One way Shakespeare achieves this effect is by juxtaposing scenes: Antigonus's soliloquy, recounting his vision of the sorrowing Hermione, and his exit pursued by a bear are followed by the appearance of the Old Shepherd and his son (3.3); the scene in which Polixenes and Camillo set off for the country (4.2) is followed by the entrance of Autolycus and his encounter with the Clown (4.3).

Six

PASTORAL LYRICS AND
THEIR SPEAKERS

I

In the account we have so far given, the figure of the pastoral speaker emerges when formal pastoral, based on Virgilian eclogues, is amalgamated with epic and drama. These forms bring with them the direct representation of courtly and heroic personages. "The pastoral process of putting the complex in the simple" is therefore played out explicitly, as these persons encounter humble figures and take on their accents and (sometimes) habiliments. But the pastoral speaker can also be seen to emerge from eclogues themselves, as if a refinement or natural outgrowth of their modes of representation and utterance. Lyrics with pastoral speakers are among the definitive poems of the English Renaissance—from "Come live with me and be my love," with its pellucid sophistication, to Marvell's "The Garden," a quintessential instance both of "putting the complex in the simple" and of the contemplative ideal that one is "never less alone than when alone."

"Come live with me and be my love" is in a direct line of descent from Theocritus's Idyll 11 and Virgil's imitation of it in Eclogue 2. Like his predecessors, Marlowe's speaker offers his beloved a subtly eroticized account of the country pleasures they will share; his opening gesture, which was to be repeatedly imitated in English poetry, itself imitates striking moments in Theocritus

223

and Virgil. Nevertheless, this speaker is different from Theocritus's Polyphemus and Virgil's Corydon. Not only is he more refined; despite the title by which we know the poem, "The Passionate Shepherd to His Love," it is not even clear that he is represented as a shepherd:

> Come live with me, and be my love,
> And we will all the pleasures prove
> That valleys, groves, hills and fields,
> Woods, or steepy mountain yields.[1]

Polyphemus says, "Come to me," and Corydon, a truly passionate shepherd, urges the lovely boy he desires *huc ades*—a charged phrase which literally means "be hither."[2] "Come live with me" beautifully elides indications of place, just as it reduces the distance between lover and beloved. The words could as well be spoken by a courtier setting out for the country with his lady as by a fictional shepherd inviting his love to join him where he already is. The poem never entirely decides between these possibilities. The second stanza would seem to be spoken by an outsider:

> And we will sit upon the rocks,
> Seeing the shepherds feed their flocks.

Two stanzas later, the lover seems to be a country swain:

> A gown made of the finest wool
> Which from our pretty lambs we pull.

Yet even if these are "our" lambs, the love gift is exquisite (*"finest* wool"), and the stanza ends with the most unambiguously courtly items in the poem: "Fair linèd slippers for the cold, / With buckles of the purest gold." The balancing of refined and rustic, in the pleasures and gifts offered, is of a piece with the way the poem suspends the difference between, in our terms, a represented shepherd and a pastoral speaker.

As opposed to an eclogue, which is committed to the fiction that its speakers are shepherds, a lyric allows its speaker to slip in and out of pastoral guise and reveal directly the sophistication which had prompted him to assume it in the first place. But even if the guise of a "passionate shepherd" is not continuously maintained—indeed the most evident pastoral guise is not the speaker's, but the costume offered the beloved—"Come live with me" remains a pastoral

1. Christopher Marlowe, *The Complete Poems and Translations*, ed. Stephen Orgel (Harmondsworth: Penguin, 1971), 211.

2. As Coleman points out, ad loc., it conflates *hic ades* (be here) and *huc adveni* (come hither). Virgil also uses this phrase when he directly quotes the parallel Theocritean passage in Eclogue 9 (39). The Greek phrase itself, *all' aphikeuso poth' hame* (Idyll 11.42), has strong directional markers.

lyric. Beyond the putatively rustic details, which are sporadic, its workings sustain the pastoral character of the speaker. Its secure balancing of courtly and rural is made clear by some contemporary imitations and alternative versions. In *England's Helicon* (1600), the pastoral anthology in which the definitive form of the poem appears and which bestowed its pastoral title, it is followed by "The Nymph's Reply" (usually attributed to Raleigh) and then by "Another of the Same Nature," which begins:

> Come live with me and be my dear,
> And we will revel all the year.

"Revel" already tips the hand of the courtier speaker, and his identity is made explicit by the deictic of place that begins the next stanza:

> There shall you have the beauteous pine,
> The cedar and the spreading vine.[3]

Virgil's *huc ades* is reversed. The country is no longer the place from which the lover speaks but the place whither he sets out, and the poem remains true to its beginnings by representing not Marlowe's refined simplicities but an erotic *locus amoenus* that is finally called "love's paradise." The balance of Marlowe's poem is similarly upset by a stanza inserted when it was published as a broadside ballad:

> Thy silver dishes for thy meat,
> As precious as the gods do eat,
> Shall on an ivory table be
> Prepared each day for thee and me.[4]

At first this seems similar in character to much of Marlowe's poem. But the hyperbolic "as precious as the gods do eat" is quite foreign to the passionate shepherd, who only allows himself the refined superlatives, "finest wool," and "purest gold." Moreover, the way the syntax of this stanza builds up a single scene is quite inconsistent with the discreteness of detail and gesture in the poem in which it has been inserted.

    This last comparison indicates why the poem is pastoral in mode. The poetic presentation, the fictional offering, of these pleasures never exceeds the character attributed to them. Though the poem is the summation of its offered gifts, it can at the same time appear to be simply one among them. When the

---

3. Reprinted in Marlowe, *Poems*, ed. Orgel, 213.

4. As quoted in J. William Hebel and Hoyt H. Hudson, *Poetry of the English Renaissance, 1509–1660* (New York: Appleton-Century-Crofts, 1929), 946. This is the stanza as it appears in the second edition of Izaak Walton's *Complete Angler* (1655). For the fullest textual history, see Hyder Edward Rollins, ed., *Englands Helicon, 1600, 1614*, 2 vols. (Cambridge: Harvard University Press, 1935), 2: 187. Rollins cites the slightly different broadside version, beginning, "Thy silver dishes, filled with meat."

lover says, "And I will make thee beds of roses, / And a thousand fragrant posies," "posies" and "poesies" seem almost to be (what they actually were in Elizabethan English) the same word. The double sense does not feel like a pun, because there is as little distance between the two meanings as there is between the lovers themselves. Urgency of desire, so marked in the shepherd's Virgilian prototype, has evaporated; instead of being prompted by the lover's frustration, the transformation of eros into song becomes the characterizing mark of eros itself. The gifts, the physical appurtenances of love, maintain this sense of being transparent to desire, its wholly sufficient expression. The clogs of physical nature—whether the lover's (we recall that the Cyclops is the original passionate shepherd) or that of the rustic gifts that are usual in these poems—are here distilled and purged.[5] By so reducing desire, the poem achieves its exquisite fulfillment. It thus makes good the promise, which other poems express with greater coarseness of all sorts, that love is best fulfilled in country simplicities.

The ending of the poem confirms its pastoral security, the way it turns its sophistication to felt simplicities. In its first published version (in *The Passionate Pilgrim*, 1599, a miscellany attributed to Shakespeare), the poem ended with what we know as its penultimate stanza:

> A belt of straw and ivy buds,
> With coral clasps and amber studs:
> And if these pleasures may thee move,
> Then live with me, and be my love.[6]

This is of a piece with the poem we have described. The balancing of country and court in the details of the belt and the heightening of their physical presence in the second line put the emphasis on "pleasures" and not—as in poems in which fictional shepherds proffer their robins' eggs and squirrels' nests—on moving the obdurate mistress. And yet the jump from the physical specificity of the first couplet to the general formulas of the next make this too abrupt an ending for the poem. Satisfying closure is achieved by the last stanza as it appears in *England's Helicon*:

> The shepherd swains shall dance and sing
> For thy delight each May morning.
> If these delights thy mind may move,
> Then live with me, and be my love.

---

5. The next step in the representation of rustic gifts is taken in Marvell's "Damon the Mower," where they are made emblematic and newly problematic.

6. Quoted from Riverside Shakespeare, p. 1793. The last line begins with "Then," versus "Come" in *England's Helicon*; that this word signals closure is shown by the fact that the version in *England's Helicon* uses it to begin *its* last line. The presentation of the poem in *The Passionate Pilgrim* continues with the first stanza of "The Nymph's Reply," under the title, "Love's Answer."

The frank repetition in line 4, turning the poem's opening gesture into a refrain, makes into rhetoric the celebratory simplicity represented by "dance and sing." What were earlier called "pleasures" are now "delights," acknowledged to be aesthetic. The foregrounding of "dance and sing" is self-reflexive without being unduly self-conscious. It is simply that these activities, more directly than the previous gifts, resemble the offering poem itself: even the short distance between "posies" and "poesies" is no longer to be traversed. Hence the sophistication of "thy *mind* may move" can be apprehended as simplicity, as the alliteration of this phrase chimes in with the refrain-like repetition of the final couplet. The speaker still does not unambiguously represent himself as a shepherd. But the "shepherd swains" of this stanza are more decidedly his companions and counterparts than the shepherds he earlier imagined observing as they fed their flocks. In the course of the poem, though we are scarcely aware of it, the speaker has been drawn into the world whose "pleasures" he sets out to "prove," and the delights of his song become those of its inhabitants.

The elements which compose the speaker of a pastoral lyric are those that underlie the main fiction of eclogues—that the sophisticated poet and his peers are simple herdsmen—and that are dramatized in pastoral encounters. The pastoral lyric can be described as reducing the larger forms from which it derives—either distilling the monody of a Virgilian shepherd or condensing into one speaker and style the courtier and countryman who meet in pastoral dramas and romances. Sometimes a lyric will maintain this separation of roles. In Sidney's "Dispraise of a Courtly Life,"[7] the courtier-speaker overhears the complaint of a former shepherd, now a courtier; the body of the poem is his lament for his prior life. It is as if Sir Calidore had overheard Melibee as a young man, before he returned to the country. Because it represents an encounter, the poem is more a mini-eclogue than a pastoral lyric of the sort we are discussing. Indeed, given the insistent complexity of all Sidney's pastoral writing, it is hard to imagine that this poem could have been such a lyric. It is unlikely that Sidney could have found a way to utter such a dispraise of the courtly life, which bases itself on known and intuited simplicity, in a courtly or urbane speaker's voice, like the one we hear in "The Garden." Sidney needed the figure of the shepherd to voice this complaint, and the form of lyric he adopted is one found in earlier Tudor poetry (e.g. Surrey, "In winter's just return")—the neutral listener hearing the lament of a lover or someone bereaved.

Many Elizabethan pastoral poems are the result of lyricizing eclogue speakers and situations. Sometimes the derivation from eclogues is manifest, as in the lyrics of Lodge's *Rosalynde* or the rivaling songs of Spring and Winter

---

7. This poem is one of "Two Pastoralls, made by Sir *Philip Sidney*, never yet published" that appeared in Francis Davison's miscellany *A Poetical Rhapsody* (1602). See *The Poems of Sir Philip Sidney*, ed. William A. Ringler, Jr. (Oxford: Clarendon Press, 1962), 262–64, 498.

that conclude *Love's Labour's Lost.* In other cases, certain lyrics of love, praise, or complaint display a vague pastoralism which can be firmed up by adding titles and modifying details. This tactic enabled the editor of *England's Helicon* to fill the page of his anthology (it is he who gave "Come live with me" its unambiguously pastoral title). For example, the only poem by Shakespeare in the volume—the "sonnet" which reveals Dumaine's betrayal of his vow in *Love's Labour's Lost* (4.3.99–118)—is claimed for pastoral by being titled "The passionate Sheepheards Song" and by changing the word "lover" to "Sheepheard" in the line, "That the lover, sick to death."[8] The diffusion of eclogue in and by lyric is nicely represented by Thomas Lodge's volume *Phillis* (1593). The title page announces that this is a collection of "Pastorall Sonnets, Elegies, and amorous delights"; its eponymous mistress has a pastoral name; and the volume includes two eclogues. For all that, the sonnets which make up the bulk of the collection look to be simply Petrarchan love poems touched up with pastoral details. But in certain poems, as the editor of *England's Helicon* saw, there is a fuller conception of pastoral situation:

> Ah trees, why fall your leaves so fast?
> Ah Rocks, where are your roabes of mosse?
> Ah Flocks, why stand you all agast?
>   Trees, Rocks, and Flocks, what, are ye pensive for my losse?
>
> The birds me thinks tune naught but moane,
> The winds breath naught but bitter plaint:
> The beasts forsake their dennes to groane,
>   Birds, winds and beasts what, dooth my losse your powers attaint?
>
> Floods weepe their springs above their bounds,
> And Eccho wailes to see my woe:
> The roabe of ruthe dooth cloath the grounds,
>   Floods, Eccho, grounds, why doo ye all these teares bestow?
>
> The trees, the Rocks and Flocks replie,
> The birds, the winds, the beasts report:
> Floods, Eccho, grounds for sorrow crie,
>   We greeve since *Phillis* nill kinde *Damons*
>   love consort.[9]

We could regard this poem either as reducing a love eclogue and sounding one of its notes, or as pastoralizing an ordinary love poem by the proper names chosen and the inclusion of flocks as a detail of nature. In either perspective its

---

8. The poem is eligible for this conversion because of its Maytime imagery. The poem also appears, as one of several "Sonnets to Sundry Notes of Music," in *The Passionate Pilgrim.*

9. *Englands Helicon,* ed. Hugh Macdonald (Cambridge: Harvard University Press, 1950), 91.

rhetoric is interesting and secure, because it grasps the nature and situation of the pastoral speaker. The questioning mode of the refrain, the indications that the season is winter and some of the details therefore natural, rhetorical gestures like "The birds *me thinks* tune naught but moane"—all show that the speaker is conscious of being separate from the world which he claims represents his feelings. These claims therefore do not exemplify the pathetic fallacy in Ruskin's sense; instead, the poem makes clear that their use, as in the grander instances of pastoral elegy, is to mitigate a loss by poetic practice. This is the motive of pastoral convention, which in an eclogue would be located in a shepherd represented as singing his loss. In this poem, where the speaker is even more thinly represented than in "Come live with me and be my love," one attributes conventional motives and practices to the poem itself. Nevertheless, it is the awareness of a pastoral speaker that explains why the poem succeeds in adhering to its rules without becoming mechanical. It progresses from the questioning of the first stanza, to the emphasis on sound in the second, to the fuller voicing of "And Eccho wailes to see my woe"—as why should it not, since it is echoing his woeful wailing?—and then completes this progression by the pastoral convening of the final stanza, in which nature and the speaker come together in the absence of the beloved. In this stanza, nature's sounds seem fully absorbed into the speaker's. The verbs are more thoroughly humanized than the beasts' groaning and the winter wind's "bitter plaint"; the human maker's presence is underscored by multiplying the listing that is the poem's main rule of procedure. Still the speaker and his situation retain their pastoral character. The end words—"replie," "report," and "for sorrow crie"—form a progression from passive to active echoing, and the final line makes good the implicit idea that human voicing fulfills itself in company. With wonderful deftness the speaker joins his song to nature's: "we" is officially the pronoun used by assembled nature, but its force is due to the implicit presence of the human "I." This delicate calling together is completed by the speaker's final word, which tells the whole story of the poem. Its ostensible meaning is that his beloved will not associate with him, but "consort," in its very utterance, confirms the responsive song to which this loss has prompted him and for which it in some sense compensates.[10]

II

To speak of these pastoral lyrics as "exquisite," "poised," or "delicate" raises the question, most famously voiced by Raleigh in "The Nymph's Reply," whether such posies can endure the rude winds of winter or even behold bright Phoebus

10. According to OED, the verb *consort* appears at the end of the sixteenth century, and from the beginning displays the overlapping of social and musical meanings that Lodge exploits here.

in his strength. One cannot seek the answer in *England's Helicon*, a rather mo-
notonous and old-fashioned collection. It is Herrick who shows what the pastoral lyric could be after Shakespeare had opened up the workings of pastoral
and after Donne and Jonson had transformed the English lyric. Herrick can be
over-delicate himself. But he wrote a number of pastoral lyrics that are as self-
aware and witty as they had to be after Donne and Shakespeare, and at the
same time achieve a mode of simplicity. His main formula was to shift the
sophisticate's pastoral encounter, which in sixteenth-century verse is with a
herdsman or rustic, to other simple beings of the countryside—nymphs, maidens, and above all, flowers. There is a hint of this development in "Come live
with me and be my love":

> And we will sit upon the rocks,
> Seeing the shepherds feed their flocks
> By shallow rivers, to whose falls
> Melodious birds sing madrigals.

These lines imitate a moment in *The Shepheardes Calender* which became known
as a kind of signature of Spenserian verse:

> Contented I: then will I singe his laye
> Of fayre *Eliza*, Queene of shepheardes all:
> Which once he made, as by a spring he laye,
> And tuned it vnto the Waters fall.
> ("April," 33–36)[11]

Apart from the wonderfully knowing "*shallow* rivers," Marlowe records the shift
that will be a foundation of Herrick's pastoral lyricism. The simple creature
whose voice is attuned to the water is no longer a shepherd but a part of the
natural setting in which a Virgilian or Spenserian shepherd would sing.[12]

---

11. These words, which are spoken of the absent Colin, become a memorial to Spenser himself,
three years after his death:

> Attentiue was full many a dainty eare,
> Nay, hearers hong vpon his melting tong,
> While sweetly of his Faiery Queene he song,
> While to the waters fall he tun'd her fame,
> And in each barke engrau'd Elizaes name.

The Second Part of the Return From Parnassus (1602), lines 209–13, in *The Three Parnassus Plays*, ed. J. B.
Leishman (London, 1949), 236–37.

12. There is precedent for this in *The Shepheardes Calender* itself. The opening stanza of "June," in
which Hobbinoll speaks of pastoral delights, concludes: "Byrds of euery kynde/To the waters fall
their tunes attemper right" (7–8). But when Hobbinoll describes Colin Clout's youthful "rymes and
roundelayes" (49), it is clear that the shepherd remains the representative singer:

> [Their] Echo made the neyghbour groues to ring,
> And taught the byrds, which in the lower spring

Where Marlowe's speaker imagines birds singing to the water's fall, Herrick's lyricized encounters are with creatures wanting voice, as Milton called them at a critical moment of pastoral convening in Eden (*PL* 9.199). This can be regarded as one more consequence of the Shakespearean self-awareness:

> And this our life, exempt from public haunt,
> Finds tongues in trees, books in the running brooks,
> Sermons in stones, and good in everything.

These lines wittily deny humanizing sounds in the "running brooks" (where our books have most led us to expect them), but retrieve them and retain their pastoral feeling by alliteration and internal rhyme. Compared to this, "melodious birds sing madrigals" has the innocence of Spenser's Hobbinoll. As a lyric poet, Herrick has no pastoral character—exiled duke or naive rustic—to whom to attribute such expressions. His sophistication discovers a relation to simple creatures through lyrical virtuosity:

> Faire Daffadills, we weep to see
> You haste away so soone:
> As yet the early-rising Sun
> Has not attain'd his Noone.
> Stay, stay,
> Untill the hasting day
> Has run
> But to the Even-song;
> And, having pray'd together, we
> Will goe with you along.[13]

The first line could initiate a wittily conceited poem. But the emergent details suggest that "we" are country companions of the flowers addressed, and the short lines and the fluency of the stanza suggest an identification with the flowers' vulnerability. One would be tempted to say that the stanza of "To Daffadils"

Did shroude in shady leaues from sonny rayes,
Frame to thy songe their cherefull cheriping.
(52–55)

Unlike Marlowe's lyric, in which eros and innocence are conflated, the June eclogue as a whole is a negotiation and debate between the songs of youth and the utterances of experience and loss. Hence Virgil's representation of Tityrus making the woods resound with the name of his beloved (Ecl. 1.5) is divided into the lines just quoted, attributed to Colin before he fell in love, and the later Colin's desire to "learne these woods, to wayle my woe" (95).

13. "To Daffadils," in *The Poems of Robert Herrick*, ed. L. C. Martin (London: Oxford University Press, 1965), 125. Not all poems addressed to flowers establish a pastoral relation to them and are thus pastoral in mode. "To Primroses fill'd with morning-dew" (104) begins with a sense of identification with the flowers, but moves to the human separateness of wit and epigram.

imitates the brief *cursus vitae* of its objects, were it not that the voicing of its shortest line—"Stay, stay"—establishes a separate human presence, which is evident again at the end of the stanza. The specificity of "the Even-song" prompts one to take the "we" who pray together to be the humans envisaged from the beginning of the poem: there is no fiction of praying with the flowers before joining them, in the last line, in our final journey. The speaker is related to the flowers not by the full identification of pathetic fallacy, but by a pastoral convening, where the parties are associated in all that matters, but are known to be separate. The speaker thus has a double character, suspended between complex and simple, of the sort we found in "Come live with me and be my love." This doubleness has yet another dimension. If we imagine the "we" who speak the poem to be country persons, it is not clear what their gender is. On the one hand, grieving over the flowers suggests the maidens evoked by Perdita. On the other hand, the urgency of "Stay, stay" suggests a (male) pastoral lover—perhaps even a reduction of Apollo or Pan, proleptically pursuing a plant. ("And Pan did after Syrinx speed, / Not as a nymph, but for a reed," to quote the greatest statement, in the line of wit, of the pastoral transformation of eros into song.) Androgyny is elsewhere part of Herrick's repertoire, but in this case, where genders are not strongly marked and where the details just noticed have simplicity in common, the doubleness of the pastoral speaker resembles that of Perdita, who, when she addresses the "daffodils that take the winds of March with beauty," identifies partly with the virgins she represents and partly with the male lovers who adore and yet seem to threaten them.

Because of the first stanza, the second and last draws its moral in a pastoral mode:

> We have short time to stay, as you,
>   We have as short a Spring;
> As quick a growth to meet Decay,
>   As you, or any thing.
>   We die,
>   As your hours doe, and drie
>   Away,
>   Like to the Summers raine;
> Or as the pearles of Mornings dew
>   Ne'r to be found againe.

The fullness and formal satisfaction of the first stanza, counteracting without contradicting the haste it thematizes, make plausible the notion, in the first four lines here, of a brief but genuine space of time. The somewhat paradoxical locution "short time to stay" is magnified into "as short a Spring," where despite the adjective the season is longer than any unit of time previously envisaged. The next line again allows a *spatium*, as well as a *cursus*, *vitae*: it represents decay not as a process but as something met (like even-song and the flowers) by the erotic eagerness first expressed in "Stay, stay" and here by "quick." The separateness of associated creatures registered in the first stanza makes possible the fineness of "As you, or any thing," which makes the daffodils representative precisely by not making them out to be other than they are. The pastoral character of these lines is confirmed by the images that close the poem. The summer's rain adds another season to the conceived duration of our life while representing its evanescence, and its association with the moisture of tears and the delicate pathos of the four lines it concludes lead to the final image, "the pearles of Mornings dew." These precious objects relocate us at the beginning of the poem, weeping at daybreak. But our tears are now transferred to the natural scene, whose beauty, as here represented, is due precisely to the sense of transience that prompts both our tears and their memorializing in a poem.

Identification with a flower's *cursus vitae* is the "invention," as Renaissance critics would have called it, of other pastoral lyrics in *Hesperides* and is one element in Herrick's greatest pastoral, "Corinna's going a Maying." But it is not the only form taken by poems that address flowers:

> To Marygolds
> Give way, and be ye ravisht by the Sun,
> (And hang the head when as the Act is done)
> Spread as He spreads; wax lesse as He do's wane;
> And as He shuts, close up to Maids again.
>   (196)

This is a male version, if such can be imagined, of Perdita's address to the "pale primroses, / That die unmarried, ere they can behold / Bright Phoebus in his strength." The difference in the flowers addressed already indicates the difference in the speaker's gender. Herrick replaces the permanently virginal flowers with the one which, because it follows the sun, was mythologized as a maiden in love with Phoebus. Yet Herrick's speaker does not directly identify with the masculine sun, as Carew does when he commends "Boldnesse in love":

> Marke how the bashfull morne, in vaine
> Courts the amorous Marigold,
> With sighing blasts, and weeping raine;
> Yet she refuses to unfold.
> But when the Planet of the day,
> Approacheth with his powerfull ray,
> Then she spreads, then she receives
> His warmer beames into her virgin leaves.
> So shalt thou thrive in love, fond Boy, etc.[14]

14. *The Poems of Thomas Carew*, ed. Rhodes Dunlap (Oxford: Clarendon Press, 1949), 42.

Herrick speaks in imperatives, but they are those of a spokesman and intermediary. His initial command, "Give way," suggests a servant preceding his lord's
progress, while the next two commands may suggest an intermediary of a different sort. What saves these lines from prurience—a malady most incident to
Herrick in other poems—is the way the speaker's identifications are suspended
between the two parties in this erotic transaction. An Empsonian analysis might
say that the servant extends fellow feeling to someone else who is subject to
his master, as if he were a pastoral alternative to Leporello. But such underpinnings are only hinted at here: the sense of shared humility emerges only in the
extraordinary locution, "be ye ravisht," which brings together active and passive imaginings, and the impersonality of "hang *the* head." These are enough to
prepare for the next couplet, which recapitulates, this time with pastoral identifications, the action imagined in the first two lines.

In fully representing "the act" of the sun, the final couplet imagines that
the marigolds are its agent. "Spread as He spreads" defines the sexual encounter
by the flowers' role: the sun in its progress can be said to spread, but the word
transforms its expected erotic role, which is (as in Carew's poem) to penetrate.
Similarly, in the second half of the line, the sun follows the flowers, not only in
the order of the verbs, but because it is the flowers who "wax" (even if paradoxically waxing less) while the sun wanes. Finally, as the last line names the
sun's action ("shuts") by the flowers' ("close up"), it both completes the reduction
of the sun's progress to the cycle of the flowers, and more remarkably, envisages
the re-virgining of the flowers. This is odd stuff—hardly what one would expect, as Carew's poem shows, from a male wit of the seventeenth century. But
in this poem Herrick's fluid and variegated erotic identifications lead the verse
to locate eros in innocence itself. This is not necessarily a function of pastoral—the most remarkable fancy of re-virgining in Herrick is in the poem in
which he woos "His Winding-sheet"—but in "To Marygolds" it is the effect of
pastoral encounter and address. The poem's closure joins with that of the flowers and its brief compass is identified with theirs, because the speaker's urgings
take on the dimensions of the simple creatures another poet might lord it over.

Herrick is the laureate of floral innocence, and *Hesperides,* in one of its aspects, is an anthology of the flowers Perdita let fall in her great speech. In one
poem, "The Apron of Flowers," those flowers are directly and in every sense
recollected:

> To gather Flowers *Sappha* went,
>   And homeward she did bring
> Within her Lawnie Continent,
>   The treasure of the Spring.
>
> She smiling blusht, and blushing smil'd,
>   And sweetly blushing thus,

She lookt as she'd been got with child
By young *Favonius*.

Her Apron gave (as she did passe)
An Odor more divine,
More pleasing too, then ever was
The lap of *Proserpine*.

The most interesting thing about this poem is not its fancy of virgin pregnancy but the suggestion, due to the double sense of "Lawnie Continent" in stanza 1, that "the lap of *Proserpine*" is the earth itself—in which case, Sappha with her apron of flowers becomes a local deity of the place she sums up. The poem exemplifies the principle Empson states about "all those conceits," like personification, "where the general is given a sort of sacred local habitation in a particular":

This at once leads to the dependence of the world upon the person or thing treated as a personification: "This member of the class is the whole class, or its defining property: this man has a magical importance to all men." If you choose an important member the result is heroic; if you choose an unimportant one it is pastoral. (*SVP*, 79)

The fields in which Corinna is invited to go a-Maying are celebrated in several poems. In the most remarkable of these lyrics, the locale of innocent eros becomes the scene of love loss:

To Meddowes

1. Ye have been fresh and green,
       Ye have been fill'd with flowers:
   And ye the Walks have been
       Where Maids have spent their houres.

2. You have beheld, how they
       With *Wicker Arks* did come
   To kisse, and beare away
       The richer Couslips home.

3. Y'ave heard them sweetly sing,
       And seen them in a Round:
   Each Virgin, like a Spring,
       With Hony-succles crown'd.

4. But now, we see, none here,
       Whose silv'rie feet did tread,
   And with dishevell'd Haire,
       Adorn'd this smoother Mead.

> 5. Like Unthrifts, having spent,
>   Your stock, and needy grown,
>   Y'are left here to lament
>   Your poore estates, alone.

This has a clear before-after structure: three stanzas beginning "You have" represent the plenum of innocent eros; "But now" then introduces the diminished present. But the poem does not traffic in the harsh oppositions of Raleigh's reply to "Come live with me and be my love" or the scenes of winter that begin and end *The Shepheardes Calender*. What is poignant is precisely the continuity between then and now: the initial representation of the maids and the meadows, who seem so to belong together, makes inevitable their final separation. This is most immediately evident in the second stanza, where the observing meadows can feel richer as their flowers are kissed and deprived as they are borne home by the maidens. But apart from this premonitory action, separateness inheres in the maidens' very presence. What "The Apron of Flowers" mythologizes as a "Lawnie Continent"—both the piece of earth (lawn) itself and the apron of linen (lawn) in which flowers are contained—is here divided between the pristine moment of the opening lines—"Ye have been fresh and green, / Ye have been fill'd with flowers"—and the wicker arks which the maidens bring to the fields. Even the third stanza—in which the maidens' "round" forestalls linear movement from the meadows—represents presence by the miniaturized deification of "*each* Virgin," summing up the season in herself and crowned with flowers that are as surely taken from the meadows they once filled as the cowslips of the preceding stanza. Fully playing out the fantasy encoded in "the lap of *Proserpine*" entails a separation of scene and human agent; the present deprivation is simply this separation made decisive. "But now" seems to indicate precisely this decisive turn, but the fourth stanza represents one more scene of past festivity—only now loveliness is a memory, recounted as past action and no longer experienced as pleasure. "Whose silv'rie feet did tread" recalls "And ye the Walks have been." But where the earlier line suggests the sufficiency of the scene for the acts it contains—the amplitude of the meadows providing paths ("walks" in one sense) where the maidens can pass their time (by "walks" in another sense)—"silv'rie feet" is touchingly metonymic. The effect of representing the maidens by a bodily part, however beautiful,[15] is doubled by the reduction of the earlier scenes of celebration to the physical contact between foot and ground. "Adorn'd this smoother Mead" similarly casts the shadow of separation over loveliness. For what makes the meadow "smoother"—a term which in itself can register present attractiveness—is the loss of the springtime flowers which the maidens have gathered and with which they are garlanded.

---

15. In another meadow poem "silver feet" is used in a scene like that of stanza 3: "The meddow verse or Aniversary to Mistris Bridget Lowman," 7.

In adorning themselves they have adorned the meadows, as if truly their tutelary deities, but this very act of fulfillment has made the pleasures of the meadow a thing of the past.

The sense of separation and loss are made pastoral in "To Meddowes" by the character of the speaker. On the one hand, he addresses the meadows as one past his prime and touched by experience—like the figure who speaks "To the Virgins, to make much of Time." On the other hand, the speaker of this poem about memory can be thought to be confronting his own youth, as if saying, in the words of that other great lyric addressed to meadows:

> My mind was once the true survey
> Of all these meadows fresh and gay,
> And in the greenness of the grass
> Did see its hopes as in a glass.
>
> ("The Mower's Song")

One can allow the hint of personification in speaking, as we did, of the pleasures of the meadows, because the speaker's pastoral identification goes out not only to the maidens but even more to the scene that contains and is imagined to enjoy them. The poem bypasses the eroticism of "men of middle age," to use Perdita's phrase: there is nothing here of sun and wind or their mythological embodiments. The eroticism is passive—viewing, hearing, containing, being kissed, even being walked upon. As if reducing those pastorals where youth and age meet to speak of love, it brings early or preadolescent fantasies together with those of the many poems in which Herrick imagines himself tended by virgins in old age or death.

The poem opens up these imaginings with such clarity—wit in the sense of awareness—because it is cast as a pastoral encounter. The turning point, "But now, we see, none here," associates speaker and scene with all the poise of a pastoral convening. The first person pronoun (the first in the poem) can be thought to include either the speaker and the meadows—in which case, it acknowledges the meadows as a personification of himself—or the speaker and fellow observers, whose implicit presence is called up by the deictic in "*this* smoother Mead" and the way remembered scenes are presented more as externalized sights than previously. The complexities of identification and association can be seen by considering alternative kinds of pronouns in the last stanza:

> Like Unthrifts, having spent,
>   Your stock, and needy grown,
> Y'are left here to lament
>   Your poore estates, alone.

If the pronouns were in the first person ("my [or 'our'] stock," etc.), this stanza would tip the balance to the side of complaint; the poem would then resemble

Spenser's June eclogue, moving from the innocent pleasures of Hobbinoll to Colin Clout bewailing the frustrations of love. If the pronouns were in the third person ("their stock," etc.), the stanza would be a frigid personification—egregiously using the figure while cutting off the human association that justifies it. From the standpoint of grammar and address, either of these developments would have been possible after the fourth stanza. The return to the second person sustains all the pastoral relations of the poem. It permits a reckoning, at once rueful and unblinking, of the economy of eros. The poem makes a clear connection between the maidens who "spent their houres" and those who invested desire in them and find their "stock" now "spent." But one cannot determine which party is the agent of this joint spending or locate the line that is crossed when the freedom suggested in the final erotic memory, "with dishevell'd Haire," is reproved as unthriftiness. Even the maids could be thought to be included in this sober awakening—a similar moral is addressed to them in "Gather ye rosebuds while ye may"—but the sense of loss and solitude here is that of a male lover. All that mitigates it is the sense that loss is shared by the scene that bears witness to it. But this is enough—as Lodge's Corin says, *satis est quod sufficit*—because of the companionship of pastoral encounter. The reduction of echoing woods to smooth meadows enfolds and dissipates the isolation that threatens the passionate shepherds of eclogues.

III

In Herrick's poems, the range potential in eclogues—strikingly manifested by Spenser when he returns to Colin Clout in *Faerie Queene* VI and *Colin Clouts Come Home Againe*—is reduced to the felt coherence of a single speaker. If Elizabeth's reign is the heyday, for English literature, of representative shepherds and the genres associated with them (eclogue, drama, romance), the seventeenth century is the age of the pastoral speaker and the pastoral lyric. Marvell is the representative figure here. He is a great pastoral poet not simply because of the Mower poems and "The Nymph Complaining for the Death of Her Fawn," but because of a mode of wit that pervades many of his lyrics and that is realized most fully in the pastoral speakers of "The Garden" and "Upon Appleton House." The character of the Marvellian speaker is made particularly clear by "The Mower Against Gardens." Though nominally spoken by a conventional figure,[16] the poem sounds as much spoken in the poet's voice as "On a Drop of Dew," "The Coronet," and "The Picture of Little T.C." For most of the poem,

---

16. What counts for us here is the generic likeness of Marvell's mower to literary shepherds—particularly clear in "Damon the Mower"—and not the fact that mowers are unusual figures in traditional pastoral. On the relation of "Damon the Mower" to Theocritus, Idyll 11, and Virgil, Eclogue 2, see Paul Alpers, "Convening and Convention in Pastoral Poetry," *New Literary History* 14 (1982–83): 287–97.

the only indication that this speaker has a special identity is the cool partiality of his argument. But in this the poem is not easily distinguished from "The Garden," which begins in a similar vein—a wittily reductive but serious view of what human nature leads to—and which has analogous singularities of gesture and argument. Only at the end of "The Mower Against Gardens" does the speaker's identity emerge or—if we take the title to involve an official commitment—make itself felt. The poem thus enacts a general truth about Marvell's pastoralism: conventional figures, literary shepherds or their equivalents, are no longer the sine qua non of pastoral expression but are special cases, precipitates as it were, of the pastoral speaker. When the speaker of "The Coronet" refers to the flowers that "once adorned my shepherdess's head," he might be taken to refer to a past poetic role, now discarded. Yet his representing his poem as a floral gathering, his discovery of "the serpent old" interwoven in his garland (giving Edenic suggestions to the Virgilian [Ecl 3.93] snake in the grass), and his gestures of humility at the end—these suggest that this is still a pastoral speaker, turning the shepherd's erotic project to devotional purposes, just as do Thyrsis and Dorinda, Clorinda and Damon in the poems that bear their names.

Milton would seem to be the seventeenth-century counterexample, but a similar argument can be made about his pastoralism. Even *Lycidas*, which consciously sums up the eclogue tradition, does not explicitly represent its speaker as a shepherd until the end. His identity is implicit from early on in the poem (though *not* from the beginning),[17] but readers usually feel a slight jolt at "Thus sang the uncouth swain to the oaks and rills." In *Lycidas* this feels like a fixing and distancing of the speaker, whereas in an ordinary eclogue he would have been represented this way from the beginning.[18] There is a similar tension— between the pastoral speaker, flexibly conceived, and the figure of the shepherd—in "On the Morning of Christ's Nativity." This poem is a version of Virgil's Fourth Eclogue, and like its prototype, its speaker retains his pastoral character by locating himself in a historical moment and deflecting his song from a full representation of the new world for which he speaks.[19] The conclud-

---

17. See above, chap. 3, pp. 95–96.

18. Compare Spenser's "Astrophell," an elegy for Sidney. Though not strictly speaking an eclogue, it from the beginning represents speaker, audience, and subject as shepherds.

19. Twice in the middle of the poem, the speaker turns from his vision of last things to the occasion and needs of the present (itself a conflation of the poem's present time, Christmas Day 1629, with the historical event it commemorates: this anniversary song to commemorate a heroic shepherd is exactly what is envisaged in Virgil's fifth Eclogue and the tradition of pastoral elegy it inaugurates). The two stanzas that begin "For if such holy song/Enwrap our fancy long,/Time will run back, and fetch the age of gold" (133–35) are checked by "But wisest fate says no,/This must not yet be so,/The babe lies yet in smiling infancy" (149–51). This sequence is repeated in the next two stanzas, when a movement towards representing the Last Judgment is held in by "And then at last our bliss/Full and perfect is/But now begins" (165–67). These gestures themselves

ing dismissal of the pagan gods, which centers on the sounds of distress and of worship now made vain, ironizes but does not transcend the pastoral practice of convening one's predecessors, constituting one's voice by hearing theirs. The speaker of the poem does not cross the threshold implicitly established by this exercise in negation. He does not break into the realm of "unexpressive notes" (116); instead, he concludes the poem with the image of the sun going to rest (a gesture out of *Midsummer Night's Dream*) and the brief scene in the "courtly stable." The body of the poem thus sustains the speaker's pastoral characterization in the introductory stanzas:

> See how from far upon the eastern road
> The star-led wizards haste with odours sweet,
> O run, prevent them with thy humble ode,
> And lay it lowly at his blessed feet.
>
> (22–25)

This directly associates the muse, who is here addressed and who represents the poet, with the shepherds of the Nativity. Yet when this pastoral speaker comes to represent the shepherds of the biblical narrative, there is a feeling of diminution more jolting than in *Lycidas:*

> The shepherds on the lawn,
> Or ere the point of dawn,
>   Sat simply chatting in a rustic row;
> Full little thought they then,
> That the mighty Pan
>   Was kindly come to live with them below;
> Perhaps their loves, or else their sheep,
> Was all that did their silly thoughts so busy keep.
>
> (85–92)

The Nativity Ode has a pastoral speaker, but one cannot conceive that these shepherds, "chatting in a rustic row," are his self-representation.

In a more normal vein—more normal, because the Fourth Eclogue and its descendants consciously press the limits of pastoral expression—the speaker of "L'Allegro" is pastoral by virtue of his receptivity, the fluidity of his identifications (his ego scarcely defined, much less seeking to establish itself and dominate), and his constant turning of heard sounds into the "linked sweetness" of his own utterance. His is the poem of the figure Milton represented, decades later, as the pastoral alternative to the heroic ego of Satan:

---

imitate the way the fourth Eclogue turns from its brief foretelling of the reign of peace and the hero's reception in heaven with *at tibi prima, puer* (18), which begins the main body of the poem.

As one who long in populous city pent,
Where houses thick and sewers annoy the air,
Forth issuing on a summer's morn to breathe
Among the pleasant villages and farms
Adjoined, from each thing met conceives delight,
The smell of grain, or tedded grass, or kine,
Or dairy, each rural sight, each rural sound.

(PL 9: 445–51)

L'Allegro catches (cf. line 69) several rural sights and sounds, increasingly moving among them until at one point his voice becomes that—or rather those—of rustic storytellers (100–114). Like Sir Calidore in his pastoral sojourn, he speaks in a mode which has been determined by the literary shepherds whom he has encountered, but the shepherds his poem represents are only one part, and somewhat specialized at that, of his pastoral repertoire.[20]

Inclusiveness is the hallmark of the major first-person pastorals and, it would seem, their conscious motive: poetic excursiveness is explicit in "L'Allegro" and "Upon Appleton House," "Lycidas" condenses into one poem the range of an eclogue book, and each stanza of "The Garden" strikingly adds to the worlds and roles it imagines. Among other earlier pastorals, *Colin Clouts Come Home Againe* anticipates these poems in its individuality and range; but it is narrated in the third person, even though it has first-person force for Spenser, and it adheres to the convention of representing the poet and his peers as shepherds. The first-person speaker of seventeenth-century pastorals himself plays out or calls up the various roles and characters—shepherds, nymphs and satyrs, rural and Olympian deities, lovers, poets, celebrants, lamenters—that are separately represented in eclogues, pastoral dramas, and pastoral romances. Just as the plotting and dramaturgy of these larger forms make them pastoral in mode, so the first-person speakers do not exceed their pastoral characters. The "green thought in a green shade" to which "The Garden" is willing to reduce its imagined selves and worlds is an emblem of the simplicity these speakers cultivate, the diffidence which enables their flexibility and inclusiveness, the humility which, in the words of "Upon Appleton House," "alone designs / Those short but admirable lines" (st. 6).

Nowhere is the speaker's pastoral character more brilliantly maintained than in the mowing passage (st. 47–55) of "Upon Appleton House." From Lord Fairfax's neatly emblematic garden the poet passes to the meadows, with their "unfathomable grass." A whole stanza is devoted to playing out this epithet:

20. For the role shepherd figures play in the poem, see below, pp. 249–51.

To see men through this meadow dive,
We wonder how they rise alive,
As, under water, none does know
Whether he fall through it or go.
But, as the mariners that sound,
And show upon their lead the ground,
They bring up flowers so to be seen,
And prove they've at the bottom been.

(st. 48)

The double sense of "unfathomable," physical and mental, represents the doubleness of wit itself in this stanza. The aphoristic formulation of lines 3 and 4 acknowledges the speaker's susceptibility to immersion and its disorienting effects, while at the same time it assumes wit's capacity to stand apart from a represented experience—just as, in the metaphor that follows, one plumbs the depths from shipboard. The wit here is distinctly Marvellian, not only in the poised ambiguity of whether one is within or without (a main motif of the poem), but also because this effect is doubled and infolded by representing immersion as itself prompting one to examine its character.[21] Marvellian poise can always shade into pastoral suspension, and in this case the wit is given a direct pastoral representation. For the point of the sounding metaphor is not simply that one gauges the depths by staying above them, but the fact that the human agents of this measurement are mariners doing a job of work. By the same token, penetrating water to "show the ground" smacks of paradox—like those put on display when the meadows are flooded (st. 59–60)—but is here no more than a practical reality. The simplicity of the mariners and their activity absorbs the speaker's self-consciousness, and the stanza can therefore conclude on a note of play, the pleasurable mastery that is repeatedly the sign of this poem's wit. The vague referent of "they" (perhaps the mowers, certainly not the mariners), need not be more precise. For it is the poet's job to come up with flowers, and in doing so he shows that he has sounded the depths of this image.

This stanza enacts the process by which a pastoral speaker precipitates shepherds and their equivalents as ad hoc self-representations. The mariners doing their work lead to the mowers, in the next stanza, doing theirs:

For when the sun the grass hath vexed,
The tawny mowers enter next;

---

21. On "meanings for 'within' and 'without,'" see Rosalie L. Colie, *"My Ecchoing Song": Andrew Marvell's Poetry of Criticism* (Princeton: Princeton University Press, 1970), 219–38. See also Christopher Ricks, "'Its own resemblance,'" in C. A. Patrides, ed., *Approaches to Marvell: The York Tercentenary Lectures* (London, 1978), 108–35.

Who seem like Israelites to be,
Walking on foot through a green sea.

(st. 49)

"With whistling scythe, and elbow strong," the mowers "massacre the grass along." One of them literalizes this metaphor by killing a rail (a small land-bird), and he thus becomes a surrogate of the poet:

The edge all bloody from its breast
He draws, and does his stroke detest,
Fearing the flesh untimely mowed
To him a fate as black forebode.

(st. 50)

Scarcely have we taken in this emblematic pun—the mower here enacts the fact that his work is a metaphor for the death we will all suffer—when a star-tling intervention occurs:

But bloody Thestylis, that waits
To bring the mowing camp their cates,
Greedy as kites, has trussed it up,
And forthwith means on it to sup:
When on another quick she lights,
And cries, "He called us Israelites;
But now, to make his saying true,
Rails rain for quails, for manna, dew."

(st. 51)

Bloody or not, Thestylis can be taken to be another surrogate of the poet. She confirms his power of turning up metaphors wherever he looks in the country scene, and as a figure from Virgil's Eclogues, where she is also in charge of feeding the mowers, she would seem to confirm our notion that conventional pastoral figures are, in Marvell, precipitates of the pastoral speaker.[22]

But this stanza has the effect of a pastoral encounter. The moral astrin-gency of Spenser's Melibee, rebuking the sentimental courtier, is here trans-formed into rustic rudeness. Thestylis does not even address the wit who has brought her on the scene: by displaying him in the third person, whether in mockery or hearty amazement, she cuts him down to size. This does not re-pudiate the play of wit—for Thestylis's job of work, like the mower's, has led her to be something of a poet—but rather represents it in a way that is deci-sively pastoral. How would the poet claim to be different from Thestylis, ea-

---

22. *Thestylis et rapido fessis messoribus aestu/alia serpyllumque herbas contundit olentis* ("Thestylis pounds thyme, garlic, and pungent herbs/For reapers weary in the consuming heat," Ecl. 2.10–11).

gerly pouncing on supper? Both he and she are in the game of finding grist for
their mills, and the rustics have the advantage of sweating and laboring, of
being more directly in touch with their work. Hence one of the triumphant
pieces of wit, a few stanzas later:

> And now the careless victors play,
> Dancing the triumphs of the hay;
> Where every mower's wholesome heat
> Smells like an Alexander's sweat.
>
> (st. 54)

Commentators refer the last line to the myth that Alexander's sweat smelled as
sweet as perfume. But as Hamlet could have told them, the comparison works
the other way too, and in this context, which has already provided the easy
release of the pun on "hay" (the mown grass and a country dance), the comparison, as Dogberry says, is not odorous.

"I am in one way better, in another not so good," as Empson (*SVP,* 15) puts
the relation of poet and rustic. The speaker of "Upon Appleton House" will
never cease to be a stager of scenes, a manipulator of perspective; he will freely
range, as Sidney says of the poet, within the zodiac of his own wit. But Marvell
plays Theocritus to the heroic mind Sidney imagined. From this point in the
poem, the natural scene repeatedly answers the poet's wit, diverting and upend-
ing his inventions even as it confirms them. Even in Fairfax's emblematic garden,
so much the product of the hero's choice and the artist's conscious control, wit
discovers what Eros learned in the Anacreontic fable of Cupid and the bee: [23]

> But when the vigilant patrol
> Of stars walks round about the Pole,
> Their leaves, that to the stalks are curled,
> Seem to their staves the ensigns furled.
> Then in some flower's belovèd hut
> Each bee as sentinel is shut,
> And sleeps so too: but, if once stirred,
> She runs you through, nor asks the word.
>
> (st. 40)

It is of course the poet who imagines and represents the bee, just as he calls up
Thestylis, a Virgilian avatar who quotes Scripture. But the play of his wit leads

---

23. This little poem is one of the late Greek *Anacreontea,* which were published in Latin versions by
Henri Estienne (Stephanus) in 1554. There are translations by Ronsard (*Odes* 4.16), Herrick ("The
wounded Cupid. Song" and also "Upon Cupid"), and Thomas Stanley ("The Bee"). *England's Helicon*
includes an expanded version by Thomas Lodge ("The Barginet of Antimachus"), which has links
with the March eclogue of *The Shepheardes Calender.* Herrick's "The showre of Blossomes" is a variant
in which, as in Marvell, it is the poet who is wounded by the bee.

to moments like these, where the pastoral interpenetration of monody and dialogue reveals itself with the sharpness of pastoral encounter. Using a pastoral epithet, Marvell's speaker can call himself an "easy philosopher," because he submits to the transformations of what he himself summons and imagines.

IV

Herrick and Marvell, to say nothing of Milton, had a stake in traditional pastoral, and it is therefore plausible to claim that their pastoral speakers are developments of the shepherd-singers of the Virgilian tradition. But what of later writers, whose literary culture was not that of the European Renaissance? In what terms can we call the following poem a version of pastoral?

> Behold her, single in the field,
> Yon solitary Highland Lass!
> Reaping and singing by herself;
> Stop here, or gently pass!
> Alone she cuts and binds the grain,
> And sings a melancholy strain;
> O listen! for the Vale profound
> Is overflowing with the sound.
>
> No Nightingale did ever chaunt
> More welcome notes to weary bands
> Of travellers in some shady haunt,
> Among Arabian sands:
> A voice so thrilling ne'er was heard
> In spring-time from the Cuckoo-bird,
> Breaking the silence of the seas
> Among the farthest Hebrides.
>
> Will no one tell me what she sings?—
> Perhaps the plaintive numbers flow
> For old, unhappy, far-off things,
> And battles long ago:
> Or is it some more humble lay,
> Familiar matter of to-day?
> Some natural sorrow, loss, or pain,
> That has been, and may be again?
>
> Whate'er the theme, the Maiden sang
> As if her song could have no ending;
> I saw her singing at her work,
> And o'er the sickle bending:—
> I listened, motionless and still;

> And, as I mounted up the hill,
> The music in my heart I bore,
> Long after it was heard no more.[24]

"The Solitary Reaper" represents an encounter with a rustic singer. But it has none of the superficial usages of traditional pastoral, nor, more importantly, the address to a fellow creature and the fictional coming together that had sustained their vitality. At the same time, the poem has important pastoral interests and motifs. Responsiveness to song is at the heart of the images in the second stanza, and the imaginings themselves respond to the song of the reaper. The sense that human bonds are established by song prompts the question that begins the third stanza and informs its intuitions about the reaper's plaintive theme. As Geoffrey Hartman says, what the poet hears "spreads sociably from one person to another over great spaces of fantasy and solitude."[25] The final lines not only make the claim of human connection but, in the coalescing of the poem itself with the experience it records, exemplify the recovery of song after separation from an original fullness.

Hartman, whose book on Wordsworth takes its bearings from this poem, raises the question of its mode:

> It might be useful to consider the Romantic lyric as a development of the surmise. We have no proper definition, formal or historical, of this kind of lyric, which disconcertingly turns all terms descriptive of mode into terms descriptive of mood. When we say, for example, that "The Solitary Reaper" is a blend of idyll and elegy we refer more to states of mind expressed by it than to formal genres. (11)

We shall see later why Schiller's terms, idyll and elegy, enter here, but for the moment let us stay with the question as Hartman defines it. What he later calls "the relation of mood to mode" is his formulation of the problem that troubled Wordsworth's earliest critics—the relation between the modest or even trivial occasions of his poems and the powerful feelings the poet elicits from them.[26]

---

24. E. de Selincourt and Helen Darbishire, eds., *The Poetical Works of William Wordsworth*, 5 vols. (Oxford: Clarendon Press, 1940–49), 3: 77. This is the final version of the poem written in 1805 and first published in 1807. Unlike other poems by Wordsworth, "The Solitary Reaper" does not benefit from the recent trend to prefer the poet's first versions. Stephen Gill's excellent volume, *William Wordsworth* (Oxford: Oxford University Press, 1984) in the "Oxford Authors" series prints the 1807 text and does not inform the reader of Wordsworth's revisions, which I discuss and try to justify below.

25. Geoffrey H. Hartman, *Wordsworth's Poetry: 1787–184* (New Haven: Yale University Press, 1964), 15. Further references will be in the text.

26. Unlike many of Wordsworth's poems, this one was not motivated by an actual encounter, felt to be memorable. Dorothy Wordsworth introduces it in her *Recollections of a Tour Made in Scotland* by saying: "It was harvest time, and the fields were quietly (might I be allowed to say pensively?)

Whether or not we agree with Hartman that the figure of the reaper acts as a literal *memento mori*, it is certain that it motivates both the psychology and the rhetoric of the poem. The emphasis on her being "single," "solitary," and "alone" already registers the speaker's anxieties of isolation, which emerge when her "melancholy strain" prompts imaginings of desolate situations. At the same time, the reaper's singing at her work sets the agenda of the poem, which is to dispel solitude by utterance.

When the speaker imagines the content of the reaper's song, his alternatives bring out the importance, to him, of this lone figure's being in touch with the world of the past and the human world around her. As with the country singers of earlier pastoral, her simplicity measures the poet's condition. But the relation between them is one specific to Romantic poetry. When the second stanza shifts to remote and enchanting scenes, one feels the separation between rustic utterance and the poetic imagination. For Arnold, this stanza illustrated the "magical power of poetry," and Bradley cited it to show that Wordsworth was not "deficient in romance" and that "the 'Arabian sands' had the same glamour for him as for others."[27] The reaper's song, on the other hand, is imagined (in the third stanza) to be a ballad, the form of poetry that most caught the Romantic imagination by its local and historical rootedness and its being a communal expression. In Schiller's terms, this is a sentimental poem about a naive song.

But though the second stanza is set apart, it is responsive to the reaper's song, and the first version of the poem makes clear that there is a pastoral conception in its imaginings.

> No Nightingale did ever chaunt
> *So sweetly to reposing bands*
> Of Travellers in some shady haunt,
> Among Arabian Sands:
> *No sweeter voice was ever heard*
> In spring-time from the Cuckoo-bird,
> Breaking the silence of the seas
> Among the farthest Hebrides.[28]

---

enlivened by small companies of reapers. It is not uncommon in the more lonely parts of the Highlands to see a *single* person so employed." *Journals of Dorothy Wordsworth*, ed. E. de Selincourt (London: Macmillan, 1959), 1: 380. This comment, with its pensive parenthesis, indicates both the usualness of the scene in itself and the way it might strike an outsider with peculiar force. On the poem's actual, literary occasion, see the end of this chapter and n. 42.

27. Arnold quotes the lines about the cuckoo (along with, *inter alia*, Perdita's lines about the daffodils) to illustrate the "magical power of poetry." "Maurice de Guérin," in *Lectures and Essays in Criticism*, ed. R. H. Super (Ann Arbor: University of Michigan Press, 1962), 13–14. A. C. Bradley, *Oxford Lectures on Poetry* (Bloomington: Indiana University Press, 1961), 114.

28. I quote this stanza from Gill (above, n. 24), 319. I have italicized the lines Wordsworth revised.

Both the reiterated "sweet" and the image of "reposing bands" show that the poet conceived his accommodation of the reaper's song in pastoral terms. Wordsworth's revisions do not eliminate this pastoralism, but rather, by changing the neoclassical coding and its suggestion of too easy an absorption of native song, make it a modern pastoral. The new adjective for the cuckoo's song, "thrilling,"[29] makes the character of the heard sound consonant with the extremity of the situation it relieves. To have the nightingale sing "more welcome notes to weary bands" not only carries out the original pastoral conception, but shows a deepened awareness of its significance. Song is now said to have sustaining powers, not because it gives merely benign pleasure but because it makes for human connection and scale in a situation of deprivation and reduced strength.

The third stanza more directly accommodates naive song to the observer's language and consciousness. Its modern, Schillerian poetics are connected to older pastoral by the way the speaker's utterance is modified by the song he hears. In its first lines, the speaker's poetical character is felt in the anxiety of his opening gesture, in the sense of identification with the flowing of "plaintive numbers," and in the characterization of traditional ballads, where we have not left the exotic wholly behind. But the second half of the stanza assimilates these imaginings to present utterance, and it brings together both the alternatives posed and the two speakers in question. Consider the alternatives that are presented. Would the reaper consider the second kind of song "more humble" than an old ballad? Would she even recognize the difference between the two kinds of song? Presumably not: these are the poet's distinctions and hierarchies. But although he cannot avoid them, the stanza mitigates their force and approaches the naive singer's indifference to them. For if one is still singing the old ballads, it is because their "old, unhappy, far-off things" express "some natural sorrow, loss, or pain / That has been, and may be again." And if these songs are being sung as one works, they are, in an important sense, "familiar matter of to-day." The second surmise, far from being a sharply felt alternative to the first, states the value for present utterance of the old ballads. Thus the poet becomes a pastoral speaker: he represents the reaper's song and his attentiveness to it so as to take on its sense of widespread human connection, "whate'er the theme."

The speaker's utterance and the reaper's song do not merge—a possibility glimpsed in "Perhaps the plaintive numbers flow"—nor do the alternatives posed become indistinguishable. The verse form, respecting boundaries of line and stanza, does not allow for strong movements of assimilation; it sustains the poem's pastoralism by sharing the powers of song between singer and speaker.

---

29. In *Poetical Works* (1827), Wordsworth revised line 13 to "Such thrilling voice was never heard"; he gave it its final form in 1836. See Jared Curtis, ed., *Poems, in Two Volumes* (Ithaca: Cornell University Press, 1983), 184.

The division of the stanzas in half, ensured by the rhyme scheme and the short fourth line, gives rise to the kind of responsiveness one finds in pastoral singing contests. Just as the representation of a "humble lay" confirms the significance of the traditional ballads, so in the second stanza the imagining of the cuckoo's song is a re-representation of the nightingale's. If, as Hartman suggests, this is radically a lyric of surmise, its verse form and representations make for a sense of stability and equality among its imaginative alternatives. With its frequency of end-stopping, the verse turns the song's "overflowing sound" into a well-modulated flow.[30] It is in this way that "the influx of an unusual state of consciousness," as Hartman puts it, "is quickly normalized" (16).

But there is still an obvious difference from older pastorals. No words are given to the reaper herself, and the responsiveness between the imaginings in the second and third stanzas is not between singers or speakers but within the poet's mind. The difference this makes to pastoral lyric can be seen by comparing a passage from "L'Allegro":

> Towers, and battlements it [the eye] sees
> Bosomed high in tufted trees,
> Where perhaps some beauty lies,
> The cynosure of neighbouring eyes.
> Hard by, a cottage chimney smokes,
> From betwixt two aged oaks,
> Where Corydon and Thyrsis met,
> Are at their savoury dinner set
> Of herbs, and other country messes,
> Which the neat-handed Phillis dresses;
> And then in haste her bower she leaves,
> With Thestylis to bind the sheaves.
> (77–88)

Explicit gestures—"Where perhaps some beauty lies" and "if the earlier season lead"—indicate that in this poem too imaginings are regularly matters of surmise. Our question concerns the speaker's relation to the scenes and figures thus called up. In the second couplet, "The cynosure of neighbouring eyes" associates the speaker's act of seeing—here, more than anywhere in the poem, attributed to the detached eye—with that of those whom he was presumably observing. Hence "neighboring," though it strictly refers to others' imagined proximity to the inhabited tower, has the effect of drawing the speaker within the rural circle. One might even suggest that these eyes are "neighboring" to the speaker's; certainly it is true that because of this couplet, one cannot tell

---

30. In both the second and third stanzas, it is possible to stop—not the stanza, of course, but the particular sentence—after almost every line.

whether the next scene is "hard by" the towers and battlements seen from a distance or "hard by" the observer himself.

In viewing the country scene, the speaker of "L'Allegro" associates himself with its inhabitants, and this leads to something close to self-representation as a shepherd. Phyllis's leaving her bower becomes, as the passage continues, the initiating surmise for another of the speaker's excursions:

> Or if the earlier season lead
> To the tanned haycock in the mead,
> Sometimes with secure delight
> The upland hamlets will invite,
> When the merry bells ring round,
> And the jocund rebecks sound
> To many a youth, and many a maid,
> Dancing in the chequered shade;
> And young and old come forth to play
> On a sunshine holiday.
>
> (89–98)

Here again the speaker's imagining leads him to associate himself with the country figures in the represented scene. The generalizing "sometimes" and the couplet about the bells and rebecks seem to make it clear that the invitation of the upland hamlets is felt by the speaker as well as (if at all) by Phillis, the country girl. Yet no sooner is this indicated than the verse, unfolding, specifies that the country music sounds "to many a youth, and many a maid, / Dancing in the chequered shade." These fluid identifications, the picking up and dropping and reassuming of roles, are what make us say that this poem has a pastoral speaker—one who takes on the character(s) of the country figures he encounters—and is not a formal pastoral, in which speakers are represented as shepherds. But as this speaker's surmises take him into the festive upland scene, his accents become those of his rural companions:

> And young and old come forth to play
> On a sunshine holiday,
> Till the livelong daylight fail,
> Then to the spicy nut-brown ale,
> With stories told of many a feat,
> How Faëry Mab the junkets eat,
> She was pinched, and pulled she said,
> And he by friar's lantern led
> Tells how the drudging goblin sweat,
> To earn his cream-bowl duly set,
> When in one night, ere glimpse of morn,

His shadowy flail hath threshed the corn,
That ten day-labourers could not end;
Then lies him down the lubber fiend,
And stretched out all the chimney's length,
Basks at the fire his hairy strength.

(97–112)[31]

The sense of taking one's ease by the fire comes from complex identifications. The rustic locution "the lubber fiend"[32] introduces a feeling of direct quotation into the reported speech and thus allows us to imagine that the pleasures of the last couplet are shared between the urban poet and the country speaker he represents. The rural storyteller's delight in an impressive account leads to and informs the last line, whose sophisticated formulation, on the other hand, can hardly be imagined as country utterance (compare "She was pinched, and pulled she said"). Similarly, the vignette of comfortable pleasure both suggests the storyteller's own situation (since the nighttime ale-drinking and tale-swapping presumably take place around the fire) and at the same time anticipates the poet's final self-representations. The vision of city and court entertainments which follows this passage is called (showing that it too is surmise) "such sights as youthful poets dream / On summer eves by haunted stream" (129–30). The concluding appeal to Mirth transforms its initial gesture, "Lap me in soft Lydian airs," into a final self-representation as Orpheus waking "from golden slumber on a bed / Of heaped Elysian flowers" (146–47). In the windings of this poem, where details and scenes are both firmly registered and easily give way to others, the lubber fiend basking his strength becomes a version of a familiar posture of the pastoral poet.

The imagined scenes of "The Solitary Reaper," by contrast, are set apart from the situation that prompts them, taking us, in the second stanza, to remote settings, realms of poesy. This is not to say that scene and situation in poems like "L'Allegro" and "The Garden" are not imaginative: on the contrary, these poems assume less tension between the work of the imagination and a plausible here and now, and therefore can dwell more securely within their projected worlds. Even Marvell's great stanza about the oceanic mind begins by firmly locating the turn inward—"Meanwhile the mind, from pleasure less, / Withdraws into its happiness"—and closes when the mind's powers at their most awesome produce an emblem of the poet in his garden of retirement: "Annihilating all that's made / To a green thought in a green shade." Hence as the poem

---

31. At 104 I have restored the reading of 1645 (*Poems of Mr. John Milton*), where Carey follows *Poems* (1673): "And by the friar's lantern led."

32. OED points out the association of "lubber" ("a clumsy fellow") with "lob" ("a country bumpkin"). Shakespeare's Puck is addressed by a fairy as "thou lob of spirits" (*MSND* 2.1.16).

continues, it knows exactly where it is, even when offering alternatives: "Here at the fountain's sliding foot, / Or at some fruit-tree's mossy root," etc. Wordsworth, by contrast, returns to the here and now with a gesture tinged by anxiety: "Will no one tell me what she sings?" And as this sense of a gap to be overcome suggests, the imaginings from which he turns have a different character from Marvell's and Milton's. Compared to the lark who greets l'Allegro as he rises in the morning, the nightingale and cuckoo are marked as symbolic, summing up the significance of the reaper's song. As the hyperbolical framing ("no X was ever") and the scenes of existential extremity suggest, each imagining attempts a total transformation of this experience, as if seeking to be, by itself, its poem. The two surmises—scaled down by their responsive iteration of each other, by the stanza and their disposition in it, and by the way each starts with secure perceptions and unfolds intimations of extremity—are the pastoralisms of a poet whose grandeurs are those of mountain apocalypse and the abysses of the mind.

The poet of such imaginings takes on a simple character, becomes a pastoral speaker, in a distinctive way. "Perhaps the plaintive numbers flow" is more than an observer's assessment. The troubled character of the question that has reconnected him to the human scene suggests, if not his own plaintiveness, then receptivity to the song's. Hence his representation of the song takes on some of its felt character. Its entering his voice—as, the previous stanza implied, it had entered his consciousness—is foregrounded by the end-word "flow." We have said that the "overflowing" sound of the song as first heard is modulated by the "flow" of verse: in this sense the poem enacts the transformation of music into language, song into speech, and naive into sentimental utterance. But at the same time, the potentialities of "flowing" are not simply channeled or contained. The modulation of this verse is very different from that of Denham's famous couplets on the Thames, a model for Augustan poetry:

> O could I flow like thee, and make thy stream
> My great example, as it is my theme!
> Though deep, yet clear, though gentle, yet not dull,
> Strong without rage, without ore-flowing full.[33]

For all its end-stopping, the verse of "The Solitary Reaper" has an easier, fuller, more innocent projection, and nowhere more evidently than in the lines we are considering:

33. *Coopers Hill* (1655 ed.), 189–92, in Brendan OHehir, *Expans'd Hieroglyphicks: A Critical Edition of Sir John Denham's "Coopers Hill"* (Berkeley & Los Angeles: University of California Press, 1969), 150–1.

> Perhaps the plaintive numbers flow
> For old, unhappy, far-off things,
> And battles long ago.

The first line seems not to be a complete sentence, yet the effect of its continuation is not a strong enjambment, rather a kind of spilling over.[34] Thinking of the words of Theocritus's goatherd in Idyll 1—"Pleasanter, shepherd, this musical cadence of yours than the water / Yonder that falls splashing down from the rocks up above"—we can call this a pastoral fluency. It is sustained in these lines by the way the iteration first of adjectives and then of a second noun phrase, all in diction of marked simplicity, carry the verse forward. In the same spirit, Hartman speaks of "the many 'fluidifying' doublings of this poem" (9).

This fluency is that of a different pastoral speaker from the poet of "L'Allegro," miming rustic vocabulary in "lubber fiend" and bringing complex and simple speech together in the couplet that follows. Where the Renaissance poet takes on roles, the Romantic poet seeks wholeness of utterance. Consider the most remarkably simple line in the poem, the last of the third stanza:

> Or is it some more humble lay,
> Familiar matter of to-day?
> Some natural sorrow, loss, or pain,
> That has been, and may be again?

Nothing could be plainer, yet it would be wrong to say that the poet is miming country utterance or even reducing his normal discourse to accord with its simplicity. This is indeed the "language really used by men," as the Preface to *Lyrical Ballads* calls it, but for Wordsworth it is the language of poetry itself. The Renaissance poet imagines a populated world which offers a variety of parts to play; this poet absorbs the conceived utterance of the only other figure in his landscape. (Another poem written after the 1803 tour of Scotland, "Stepping Westward," begins by quoting a phrase spoken to the poet in a country encounter, and then proceeds to absorb it into the poet's consciousness so readily and thoroughly that it prompts intimations of his spiritual destiny.)

Consider the plainness of another seventeenth-century pastoral speaker:

---

34. The effect is due to a rhetorical complication of the grammar. The main clause, "The plaintive numbers flow," is complete, but "perhaps" leaves the sentence unfinished, since the meaning which would make it complete—"the numbers may be flowing or they may not"—seems impossible to entertain here.

And now in age I bud again,
After so many deaths I live and write;
I once more smell the dew and rain,
And relish versing.[35]

This is pastoral because, in its imagery and its sense of human powers—its vulnerability, its treasuring of the senses and its giving over the earlier fantasies of conquering heaven—the speaker accepts the likeness between himself and the flower that gives the poem its title. It is a famous and striking passage, but that is just the point: it is a specific rhetoric for a decisive spiritual moment. Its poignant directness gives way, in the final stanza, to simplicity of a different sort—a gnomic plainness that suggests a different pastoral role, that of the older shepherd, with his sense of distance from youthful rashness.[36] In "The Solitary Reaper," simple utterance is a pervasive stylistic ideal, expressing the whole character of a poet. Hence the coalescence of utterance between speaker and reaper can only be a matter of intuition, not explicit representation. In the absence of mimetic sounding, in the fact that responsiveness, for this pastoral speaker, manifests itself as consciousness and not answering utterance, the only music of which we are capable is that which is felt in the silence of the heart. For at the same time as the poem makes the real language of men its own, it reflects Schiller's sense that the naive, for the modern poet, is unrepresentable. The reaper's song cannot be quoted or mimed; it must remain simply the ideal of solitary utterance, integrated with work, human experience, historical time, and natural setting. Hartman was exactly right to invoke the Schillerian categories of idyll and elegy for this poem and to suggest that the two combine here. The poem is a modern pastoral lyric in that the achieved simplicity of imagining and utterance (which suggests the idyllic) does not ignore the separateness and distance that in other poems might lead to the openly elegiac.

The pastoral character of the poem and its speaker are made clear in the final stanza:

35. George Herbert, "The Flower," 36–39, in *George Herbert and Henry Vaughan*, ed. Louis L. Martz (Oxford: Oxford University Press, 1986), 151.

36. I think the failure to understand the capacity of a lyricist like Herbert to take on different (pastoral) roles accounts for the widespread disappointment, not to say irritation, with this stanza. See, for example, Helen Vendler, *The Poetry of George Herbert* (Cambridge: Harvard University Press, 1975), who speaks of the final lines as "grim" and says their "homiletic neatness is probably a flaw in the poem" (53). A response of this sort is grounded in Romantic poetics, according to which the previous wholeness of utterance is denied in the intellectual imposition of a moral. Whether or not this happens elsewhere in Herbert, pastoral roles in "The Flower" are motivated by the speaker's humility and by the way the poem addresses the question, equally central to *The Shepheardes Calender* and "Upon Appleton House," of the proportion between man and nature.

> Whate'er the theme, the Maiden sang
> As if her song could have no ending;
> I saw her singing at her work,
> And o'er the sickle bending:—
> I listened, motionless and still;
> And, as I mounted up the hill,
> The music in my heart I bore,
> Long after it was heard no more.

The crucial line is the fifth, which is the crossing point from reaper to poet, linking them and initiating their separation. In the first version of the poem, Wordsworth wrote, "I listened till I had my fill." What are we to make of this astonishing line? John Danby says:

> Wordsworth at the end of the poem is curiously *comfortable*. . . . Originally, as the poet turned away from the girl to continue his own solitary journey, he was filled with a sense of satisfaction amounting to repletion. The comfortableness is a strange yet typically Wordsworthian thing to emerge from the experience we are led through by the poem.

Danby thinks the revision of this line "was a mistake. We need the deep sense of satisfaction that the song has brought with it—the sense of repletion which sets Wordsworth free to turn away, on his own axis, and continue in his own vast orbit."[37] I want to argue that the revision, like those in stanza 2, realizes the essential workings of the poem—in our terms, brings out its pastoralism. Danby's remark about the poet's "own vast orbit" indicates what is wrong with the metaphor of ingestion here. As John Jones points out, this metaphor is "a typical statement of the fact of mutual fitting" between "the [Wordsworthian] child and the visible scene."[38] Jones cites lines written of the Pedlar (later the Wanderer of *The Excursion*), when he was a boy living in the mountains:

> Sound needed none
> Nor any voice of joy: his spirit drank
> The spectacle.[39]

The 1850 *Prelude* adds the metaphor to say that the infant babe "Drinks in the feelings of his Mother's eye" (vs. 1805, "Doth gather passion," 2.237), and both versions have it in

37. John F. Danby, *The Simple Wordsworth* (London: Routledge & Kegan Paul, 1960), 123, 126.

38. John Jones, *The Egotistical Sublime* (London: Chatto and Windus, 1964), 84.

39. *Poetical Works* 5.382; = *Excursion* 1.205–7. These lines first appear in one of *The Pedlar* manuscripts (Ms. E, 196–98; date probably 1803–4). See William Wordsworth, *"The Ruined Cottage" and "The Pedlar,"* ed. James Butler (Ithaca: Cornell University Press), 398.

> Thence did I drink the visionary power
> (2.330 [1805], 2.311 [1850])

and in

> Even then,
> A child, I held unconscious intercourse
> With the eternal beauty, drinking in
> A pure organic pleasure from the lines
> Of curling mist, etc.
> (1.588–92 [1805], 1.561–5 [1850])[40]

All these passages concern the child, to whom the sensuous and naively self-centered metaphor is appropriate; moreover, the relation represented by the metaphor (except in the case of the nursing child, where it has literal force), is between the child and the natural scene. In "The Solitary Reaper," on the other hand, the observer is an adult and is "taking in" another human being. It is true that the metaphor can be powerfully used of adult experience—as when the Snowden vision becomes "the emblem of a mind / That feeds upon infinity" (1850, 14. 70–71). But this again is the solitary mind, and all the instances we have cited are in blank verse—representations, verging on loftiness, of the essential relation between man and nature. In the situation and mode of "The Solitary Reaper," the metaphor of ingestion could do none of its work, because it could not represent an action, it could not be used as a verb.

The line Wordsworth substituted, "I listened, motionless and still," is deeply true to the character of the poem. Just when the reaper is represented most externally (hinting the impending separation, as past tenses enter the poem), the speaker's situation is most literally and directly narrated. He registers the song's effect not by the poetizing of stanza 2, but by the fact that he was held attentive, as we ourselves are by the line's workings—the strong pause after "listened," the suggestive length of "motionless," and the way the meaning of "still" brings out the effect of the adjectival doublet it completes. This moment of suspended attention is pastoral, because its effect is grounded in the speaker's strength relative to his situation: his natural condition is the movement that follows in the next line and that expresses the existence in time which the poem seeks to resist, to hold still. Where "I listened till I had my fill" claimed a complete incorporation of the reaper's endless song, the new line brings singer and listener together in and for the moment of the poem: the reaper, moving at her work and continually singing, but in the preceding lines represented with a certain aesthetic fixity; the speaker, who can only take in her freedom and the flowing of her song by his own stillness.

40. William Wordsworth, *The Prelude: 1799, 1805, 1850,* ed. Jonathan Wordsworth et al. (New York: W. W. Norton, 1979).

This stillness must give way to the movement of traveller and verse. But the moment of pastoral suspension is sustained for the stanza and the poem. The main "action" of the stanza is to turn the imputed power of the reaper's song—"the Maiden sang / As if her song could have no ending"—into the claim with which the poem ends. In the first version, this claim, as Danby's justification suggests, is too bald and grand. The phrase, "till I had my fill," skips over the moment of absorption and represents the poet's power of enduring song as equivalent to the reaper's and as purely a matter of consciousness. The revision rhetorically enacts the moment of absorption, and thus brings out the way in which the putative inner experience is coincident with the workings of the poem. This more decisively distinguishes naive song from sentimental poem, but its truth to the conditions of its utterance counteracts, in pastoral manner, the pastness of the experience. The final lines become a claim not simply about the poet's (past) inner experience, but about its realization in the poem—and therefore its capacity for re-realization, as the reader repeats, in relation to the poem, the poet's represented experience in relation to the reaper.[41]

In this implicit chain of responsive listening, "The Solitary Reaper" is true to its character as a modern pastoral. As is well known—and as William and Dorothy Wordsworth always stated in presenting it—the poem was prompted by "a beautiful sentence," as they called it, in Thomas Wilkinson's

---

41. Some critics would take Wordsworth's revision as an attempt—all the more irritating because successful—to cover his tracks, to conceal his appropriation of the reaper and her song. Marjorie Levinson says that "Wordsworth ravishes his reaper." *Keats's Life of Allegory: The Origins of A Style* (Oxford: Basil Blackwell, 1988), 80. The implications of this remark are spelled out in Nancy A. Jones, "The Rape of the Rural Muse: Wordsworth's 'The Solitary Reaper' as a Version of Pastourelle," in Lynn A. Higgins and Brenda R. Silver, eds., *Rape and Representation* (New York: Columbia University Press, 1991), 263–77. This essay is full of melodramatic claims (e.g., "He has made off with her music to ascend to literary fame, much as the knight [in pastourelles] makes off with the shepherdess's virginity," 272). But the crucial charge is that the modern poet, like the medieval knight, is intent on conquest (267) and mastery (270).

Far from denying that Wordsworth could be guilty of such a thing, I would argue that misplaced eroticism and objectionable appropriation are distinctly evident in "To a Highland Girl," another of the "Poems Written During a Tour of Scotland" (in *Poems, in Two Volumes,* 1807) and one with which "The Solitary Reaper" is regularly associated, e.g. by Marlon Ross, "Naturalizing Gender: Woman's Place in Wordsworth's Ideological Landscape," *ELH* 53 (1986): 404–5. The question of critical principle here is whether we are to distinguish one poem from another. What is impressive about "The Solitary Reaper" is that it recognizes (no more clearly, in my view, than in its revisions) the conditions of its own production, and hence the extent to which the modern poet can appropriate, in a neutral and legitimate sense, not the reaper and her life but her unlettered song. "To a Highland Girl" involves no such recognition of separateness and distance. It begins by confronting the girl in her habitat, and by directly addressing her throughout the poem represents her simply by telling her what she is. This is overcoming the language barrier (40–41) with a vengeance.

Tours to the British Mountains: "Passed a female who was reaping alone: she sung in Erse as she bended over her sickle; the sweetest human voice I ever heard: her strains were tenderly melancholy, and felt delicious, long after they were heard no more."[42] Like the bucolics of Theocritus and Virgil, "The Solitary Reaper" is motivated by a prior text. But the nature of this text brings out the literary and cultural situation in which Wordsworth made pastoral new. It does not belong to a separate literary system which the innovating poem both heeds and claims to revise or extend. Nor was it a published text, but like Dorothy Wordsworth's *Recollections of a Tour in Scotland,* a manuscript that circulated among friends. Its lack of privilege as a piece of writing gives it a claim to be—what, despite eighteenth-century misconceptions, Theocritus's Doric never was—the language really used by men.[43] Both its charac-

42. I quote the sentence from the published version of Wilkinson's *Tour* (London, 1824), as it appears in Curtis, ed., *Poems, in Two Volumes,* 415. In a note to the poem (printed with it, 1807– 1820), Wordsworth says: "This Poem was suggested by a beautiful sentence in a MS. Tour in Scotland written by a Friend, the last line being taken from it *verbatim.*" Dorothy Wordsworth referred in similar terms to this sentence in two letters, the earliest of which (November 7, 1805) allows us to date the poem. See *Letters of William and Dorothy Wordsworth: The Early Years, 1787–1805,* ed. Ernest de Selincourt (2d ed., rev. Chester L. Shaver; Oxford: Clarendon Press, 1967), 639, 652–55. For other mentions, see Mark L. Reed, *Wordsworth: The Chronology of the Middle Years, 1800– 1815* (Cambridge: Harvard University Press, 1975), 315, 707. Because neither Dorothy nor William seem ever to have actually quoted the sentence while acknowledging its relation to the poem, it seems particularly inappropriate for critics to refer to the fact that the reaper was singing in Erse, as a way of explaining why the speaker of the poem does not know "what she sings." Surely it is possible to hear the melody of a song, heard from a certain distance, without being able to make out the words, even in one's own language.

43. Or rather, Peter J. Manning would remind us, men of a certain class and political outlook. In his study of the poem—in *Reading Romantics* (Oxford: Oxford University Press, 1990), 241–72— Manning shows that Wordsworth's enthusiasm for Wilkinson himself (a man of great probity, living in retreat on his family estate) and for the Scottish Highlanders and their traditions is of a piece with his increasingly conservative politics—his associating himself with the landed aristocracy and gentry, as opposed to the commercial classes. Manning's essay impressively contextualizes "The Solitary Reaper," both in Wordsworth's life and thought and specifically in *Poems, in Two Volumes.* But if he succeeds in questioning the aesthetic status of "The Solitary Reaper"—and in particular, Hartman's representation of it as solely a product of memory and poetic imagination—he fails to provide a revisionist reading that accounts for its distinctive character. Indeed, in saying that the poem's "nostalgia [the wrong word, I think] is polemical" (268) and that its apparent "timelessness" manages still to have designs upon us (264), he almost denies that it is a lyric. The question is whether the method of his essay can meet the challenge it presents—to give an account of later Wordsworthian lyrics (i.e. those written after *Lyrical Ballads*) that leaves them standing as individual poems.

In *The Romantic Ideology* (Chicago: University of Chicago Press, 1983), the book that inaugu- rated much revisionist interpretation of the Romantics, Jerome J. McGann argues that "between 1793 and 1798 Wordsworth lost the world merely to gain his own immortal soul" (88). McGann can honestly admire *The Ruined Cottage* and "Tintern Abbey," because, in his terms, they enact the spiritual displacement he criticizes. But it is hard to see how his critique leaves room to feel the

ter and the poem it prompted bring out the modernity of Wordsworthian pastoral.

---

power and distinction of the 1807 lyrics that were once among Wordsworth's most admired poems—"The Solitary Reaper," "To the Cuckoo," "Composed upon Westminster Bridge," "It is a beauteous evening," "I wandered lonely as a cloud," "My heart leaps up." McGann includes these poems in his *New Oxford Book of Romantic Period Verse,* but the question remains how historicizing critics can value them.

Some of these questions are raised by Manning himself, in the final essay of his volume, "Placing Poor Susan: Wordsworth and the New Historicism."

Seven

MODERN PASTORAL
LYRICISM

Wordsworth's use of classical and Renaissance pastoral is evident in a number of his poems. *The Ruined Cottage* is modelled on the traditional eclogue; "The Brothers" "was intended to be the concluding poem of a series of pastorals," and Coleridge called it "that model of English pastoral";[1] two of the three "Matthew" poems in *Lyrical Ballads*, "The Fountain" and "The Two April Mornings," are lyric versions of eclogue, in their settings, motifs, and dialogue form; in the second part of "Hart-Leap Well," which begins as a narrative ballad, the poet assumes a pastoral character ("'Tis my delight, alone in summer shade, / To pipe a simple song to thinking hearts"), and much of the burden of the poem is given to an old shepherd who tells him the story of the fountain and interprets its meaning to him. We can apply to all these poems what Wordsworth's friend John Stoddart said of "The Brothers"—that it is "a local eclogue, of a new, and original species."[2] That is, each poem shows clear affiliations with older pastorals, while at the same time the older conventions and usages take on a distinct

---

1. These statements about "The Brothers" are in a note to the poem, in *Lyrical Ballads*, and in Samuel Taylor Coleridge, *Biographia Literaria*, ed. James Engell and W. Jackson Bate (Princeton: Princeton University Press, 1983), 2:80.

2. Quoted in R. S. Woof, "John Stoddart, 'Michael' and Lyrical Ballads," *Ariel* 1, no. 2 (1970): 21.

and (so far as is possible in literary innovation) unprecedented form. These poems in which Wordsworth transforms older pastoral usages provide the readiest way of seeing how he made a modern pastoral possible for writers in English.

In respect to his establishing a mode of modern pastoral, as in so many other ways, *The Ruined Cottage* is the crucial poem in his development. It consciously revises and "makes new" the traditional eclogue, and it shows an eclogue-like range in its interlocutors' speeches, which are variously narrative, dramatic, lyric, and argumentative. It thus led to both the pastoral narrations and the pastoral lyrics that Wordsworth wrote in the months and years after he completed its first version.[3] Its opening passage makes clear its generic filiation:

3. For 150 years *The Ruined Cottage* was known as part of Book 1 of *The Excursion* (1814). But an integral version of the poem, now known as MS. B, was completed by March 1798 and was offered to Wordsworth's publisher, Joseph Cottle. About a year later, Dorothy Wordsworth transcribed in a notebook a revised version, now known as MS. D, which is the centerpiece of Jonathan Wordsworth, *The Music of Humanity* (New York: Harper & Row, 1969). Mainly because of this book, MS. D is widely regarded as the best version of the poem (it is the one printed, for example, in *The Norton Anthology of English Literature*). My discussion of the way it revised MS. B will show why I agree with this assessment. All my quotations of *Ruined Cottage* material are from the "Cornell Wordsworth" edition: James Butler, ed., *"The Ruined Cottage" and "The Pedlar"* (Ithaca: Cornell University Press, 1979), hereafter cited as "Cornell." All information in this note and elsewhere about the stages of composition of *The Ruined Cottage* is from this indispensable edition.

MS. D differs considerably from the form in which it was first published, Book 1 of *The Excursion*, in which the story of Margaret and her cottage is preceded by an equally long account of its narrator, the Wanderer, whose emerging spiritual portrait (originally as "The Pedlar") is part of the complicated history of this poem. The problematic relation between the Pedlar/Wanderer half of *Excursion* 1 and the "Ruined Cottage" half is evident in the various stages of the poem's composition. The two important features of MS. D are (1) that it bypasses the problem (because it provides no separate account of the Pedlar) and (2) it most fully realizes the pastoral usages that underlie and enable all the versions of Margaret's story. Because my emphasis is on the way *The Ruined Cottage* "made new" these usages, I have found it awkward to refer to and engage other interpretations from which I have learned a great deal. I think in particular of Geoffrey H. Hartman, *Wordsworth's Poetry: 1787–1814* (New Haven: Yale University Press, 1964), esp. 302–6; Reeve Parker, "'Finer Distance': The Narrative Art of Wordsworth's 'The Wanderer,'" *ELH* 39 (1972): 87–111; Peter J. Manning, "Wordsworth, Margaret, and The Pedlar," *Studies in Romanticism* 15 (1976): 195–220, repr. in *Reading Romantics* (Oxford: Oxford University Press, 1990), 9–34. These interpretations all make the Pedlar (later, the Wanderer) the center of attention in the poem—an emphasis which leads both Parker and Manning to prefer the *Excursion* (1814) version (Hartman's book predated Jonathan Wordsworth's publication of MS. D). I think my account most significantly resists or adjusts theirs by distributing our attention more evenly to the Pedlar and the narrator. This more pastoral emphasis—or rather, the more fully realized pastoralism of MS. D (as detailed below, in my account of its additions and revisions)—allows us to see not only the two interlocutors, but also Margaret and Robert, as figures of the poet.

Of more recent interpretations, the most important is Alan Liu's "new historicist" critique, in *Wordsworth: The Sense of History* (Stanford: Stanford University Press, 1989), 311–58. See below,

'Twas summer and the sun was mounted high.
Along the south the uplands feebly glared
Through a pale steam, and all the northern downs
In clearer air ascending shewed far off
Their surfaces with shadows dappled o'er
Of deep embattled clouds: far as the sight
Could reach those many shadows lay in spots
Determined and unmoved, with steady beams
Of clear and pleasant sunshine interposed;
Pleasant to him who on the soft cool moss
Extends his careless limbs beside the root
Of some huge oak whose aged branches make
A twilight of their own, a dewy shade
Where the wren warbles while the dreaming man,
Half-conscious of that soothing melody,
With side-long eye looks out upon the scene,
By those impending branches made more soft,
More soft and distant.

(1–18)

In all its versions, the poem begins with these lines; somewhat revised, they are the first words one reads in *The Excursion*. The range of critical views of "the dreaming man" suggests the complexity of this figure. On one hand, some view it as the narrator's wishful fantasy—one strikingly at odds with his true condition, as revealed in the next lines ("Other lot was mine. / Across a bare wide Common I had toiled"), and suggestive of his need for the spiritual instruction bestowed by the Pedlar/Wanderer. Others associate the dreaming man with the Pedlar himself, who is first seen stretched out beneath the trees of the cottage (27–34), and interpret him in accordance with the view they advance of the Pedlar.[4] There is a similar difference in accounts of the literary genealogy of the dreamer. Taking their cue from the fact that the opening landscape description adapts lines from Wordsworth's youthful poem, *An Evening Walk*, some critics view this figure as a version and critique of the poet as he appears in works

---

n. 19, for the point on which my account most pertinently disputes his. But we may note here that he too gives almost exclusive attention to the Pedlar, an emphasis reflected in his taking MS. B as the poem's truest version.

My thinking about the relation between *The Ruined Cottage* and pastoral elegy was first stimulated by Thomas Joseph Wolf, "Wordsworth and the Pastoral Tradition" (Ph.D. dissertation, University of California, Berkeley, 1975).

4. J. Wordsworth, *The Music of Humanity*, 100. Geoffrey Hartman makes the opening passage authoritative for the poem in the development of "finer distance." See *Wordsworth's Poetry: 1787–1814*, 303–4.

by Thomson, Collins, and Cowper.[5] This may well be, but the figure himself goes back much further. Annabel Patterson rightly views these lines as a re-writing of Virgil's first Eclogue. "It would have been impossible," she says, "for Wordsworth to write these lines *without* conceiving of his 'dreaming man' as Tityrus, whose late-eighteenth-century version of *otium* renders everything as 'soft and distant.'" This figure is rudely displaced by the narrator's heat-oppressed toil across the common, because for Wordsworth "pastoral medita-tion . . . had to be redeemed from its negative associations with Tityrus": "the soft pastoral [of antiquity and the eighteenth century] is displaced by the hard pastoral of the mind at serious work."[6] But Patterson's eagerness to stigmatize Tityrus and champion Meliboeus's version of pastoral causes her to ignore the way Wordsworth conflates the two Virgilian shepherds. His dreaming figure derives from both the opening description of Tityrus, *recubans sub tegmine fagi*, and Meliboeus's final words, bidding farewell to his "once happy flock":

> *non ego vos posthac viridi proiectus in antro*
> *dumosa pendere procul de rupe videbo.*
> > (*Ecl.* 1.75–6)

> No more shall I, stretched out in a cavern green,
> Watch you, far off, on brambly hillsides hang.

Wordsworth quoted these lines, in the Preface to his 1815 *Poems*, to exemplify the powers of the imagination, and they provide the heart of the passage in *The Ruined Cottage*—the relation between the man, comfortably stretched out, and the distant scene that gives him pleasure. Perhaps in conscious acknowledg-ment, a later revision placed the dreamer not "beside the root / Of some huge oak," but "along the front / Of some huge cave."[7]

The fact that Wordsworth's figure combines the ease of Tityrus with Meli-boeus's remembered posture of pleased contemplation suggests that it is mis-taken to identify him with one or the other of the interlocutors of *The Ruined Cottage.* Rather, the dreaming man presents an image of the poetic imagination that is put in play and worked out—just as one would expect in an eclogue—by both narrator and pedlar, country figures who come together at a scene of loss. The problematic at the heart of this image is indicated by Wordsworth's

5. Parker, "'Finer Distance,'" 90ff.; Liu, *Wordsworth: The Sense of History*, 314.

6. Annabel Patterson, *Pastoral and Ideology* (Berkeley & Los Angeles: University of California Press, 1987), 277–78.

7. *Excursion* 1.10–11. To my knowledge, the only one of Wordsworth's critics to have noticed this connection is Susan J. Wolfson, *The Questioning Presence* (Ithaca: Cornell University Press, 1986), 112.

own comment on Virgil's lines, which he uses to illustrate the imagination as "employed upon images in a conjunction by which they modify each other": "the apparently perilous situation of the goat, hanging upon the shaggy precipice, is contrasted with that of the shepherd contemplating it from the seclusion of the cavern in which he lies stretched at ease and in security."[8] The question this brief comment raises is the relation between the feeling, intuiting, and observing mind and the surrounding life which it takes in and seeks to integrate. Depending on which way one tilts the passage, one could emphasize either the unifying power of the imagination (the mind absorbing and integrating the surrounding world) or the importance, for true imaginative grasp, of sensing a "perilous situation," the difference and disparity between the mind and the world. This is, of course, a pervasive question in Wordsworth's poetry, but the 1815 Preface shows its pertinence to his use of Virgil's image at the beginning of *The Ruined Cottage*. The languor of the dreaming man suggests a jejune and inadequate imagination. What is external to him, the warbling of the wren, is already within the shade where he reposes, and the coloring of the bird's song ("Half-conscious of that soothing melody") is then extended to the whole external scene, "made . . . more soft and distant." The succeeding lines are starkly opposed:

> Other lot was mine.
> Across a bare wide Common I had toiled
> With languid feet which by the slipp'ry ground
> Were baffled still, and when I stretched myself
> On the brown earth my limbs from very heat
> Could find no rest nor my weak arm disperse
> The insect host which gathered round my face
> And joined their murmurs to the tedious noise
> Of seeds of bursting gorse that crackled round.
> (18–26)

By itself, this seems an obvious antipastoral, not only because of the toil, the lack of shade, and the impossibility of repose, but also because "the insect host" and the "bursting gorse," which in Theocritus would have made an agreeable noontime music, here produce only a "tedious noise." Nevertheless, this negation of the *locus amoenus* does not rule out the Virgilian shepherd as a figure of the imagination for this poem. The final lines of part 1 recuperate the image by restoring the melody of the once oppressive insects and by making the shade of immense trees a locale that promises spiritual calm:

8. "Preface to *Poems* (1815)," in *William Wordsworth*, ed. Stephen Gill (Oxford: Oxford University Press, 1984), 632–33. This is a volume in the "Oxford Authors" series, and will henceforth be cited as Gill.

> At this the old Man paus'd
> And looking up to those enormous elms
> He said, "'Tis now the hour of deepest noon.
> At this still season of repose and peace,
> This hour when all things which are not at rest
> Are chearful, while this multitude of flies
> Fills all the air with happy melody,
> Why should a tear be in an old man's eye?
> Why should we thus with an untoward mind
> And in the weakness of humanity
> From natural wisdom turn our hearts away,
> To natural comfort shut our eyes and ears,
> And feeding on disquiet thus disturb
> The calm of Nature with our restless thoughts?"
>   (185–98)

These lines end part 1 of "The Ruined Cottage." The fullness of the speech and the centrality of its image give a sense of closure, which, however, is premature. The "disquiet" and the "restless thoughts" at the heart of the scene prompt the narrator's request, at the beginning of part 2, that the Pedlar complete his narration of Margaret's story. Its conclusion leads to the conclusion of the poem:

> By this the sun declining shot
> A slant and mellow radiance which began
> To fall upon us where beneath the trees
> We sate on that low bench, and now we felt,
> Admonished thus, the sweet hour coming on.
> A linnet warbled from those lofty elms,
> A thrush sang loud, and other melodies,
> At distance heard, peopled the milder air.
> The old man rose and hoisted up his load.
> Together casting then a farewell look
> Upon those silent walls, we left the shade
> And ere the stars were visible attained
> A rustic inn, our evening resting-place.
>   (526–38)

Whereas in the opening lines the wren warbled within the dreamer's bower, several melodies—no single one charged with symbolic weight—now "peopled the milder air." Similarly, the oblique glance and the soft pastoralism of the opening passage become the "slant and mellow radiance" of the sun. The inner calm of the two humans who sit in the shade is now manifested by the multiplicity and sweetness of the surrounding world, and the single word "peopled" registers, with a delicacy consonant with the air and the light, the humanizing of the imagination that, as Geoffrey Hartman says, is a main endeavor of this poem.

The image of the Virgilian shepherd thus marks the beginning, the middle, and the end of *The Ruined Cottage*, and we can account for this device in quite conventional terms. The movement from the Pedlar's speech at the end of part 1 to the end of the poem is from noontime, the usual beginning of eclogues, to evening, the typical moment of closure from Virgil's first Eclogue to *Lycidas*, both of which are surely remembered here. The scene at evening, in another movement provided by older eclogues, brings the two country figures together in the same place of repose, after their earlier separateness from each other. But if all this means that Wordsworth modelled *The Ruined Cottage* on the classical and Renaissance eclogue, it is equally certain that he meant to make the eclogue new, to reconceive it as a modern poem. As Patterson suggests, it is this purpose, rather than ordinary antipastoralism, that explains the account of the narrator toiling across the "bare wide Common." These lines are in a vein that is prominent in Wordsworth's poetry of the mid-1790s—in the "Salisbury Plain" poems notably, and in the "Incipient Madness" fragment that is one of the earliest pieces of the *Ruined Cottage* project.[9] In these poems, the narrator crosses a vast and barren plain or moor, the reverse, as "Salisbury Plain" makes explicit, of a pastoral landscape: "No shade was there, no meads of pleasant green, / No brook to wet his lips or soothe his ear" (46–47).[10] The traveller seeks shelter, but in such terrain he will not find even "a shepherd's lowly thorn / Or hovel" (59–60); instead he comes upon a Gothic ruin, in which the main psychological and moral encounter of the poem takes place. This pattern seems to be sustained when the narrator of *The Ruined Cottage* discerns "a group of trees / Which midway in that level stood alone" (27–28) and finds "beneath [their] shade" "a ruined house, four naked walls / That stared upon each other" (31–32). It is such a sight that produces "incipient madness" in the narrator of that fragment—the obsession with a single spot that is, as Hartman says, a chief danger of the Wordsworthian imagination. The narrator of *The Ruined Cottage*, as evidently a figure of the poet as his predecessors, is spared this fate. Instead of locking his stare within the ruined walls, which represent and invite just such self-reflexive regard, he "looked round." What he sees is "an aged Man"— in no such posture as the leech-gatherer, whom another Wordsworthian poet-narrator will encounter, but "alone and stretched upon the cottage bench" and

9. The "Incipient Madness" fragment is reprinted in Cornell, pp. 468–69. It is discussed by Jonathan Wordsworth (*The Music of Humanity*, 7–8) and is the starting point of Hartman's discussion of *The Ruined Cottage* (*Wordsworth's Poetry*, 136–37). See also Manning, *Reading Romantics*, 11ff.

10. Quoted from Gill's text, which is that of the first version (1793–94). Like *The Ruined Cottage*, this poem went through several revisions.

(again unlike the leech-gatherer) a friend whom the narrator recognizes. The description that follows makes it clear that this is a pastoral meeting:

> Two days before
> We had been fellow-travellers. I knew
> That he was in this neighbourhood and now
> Delighted found him here in the cool shade.
> He lay, his pack of rustic merchandize
> Pillowing his head—I guess he had no thought
> Of his way-wandering life. His eyes were shut;
> The shadows of the breezy elms above
> Dappled his face. With thirsty heat oppress'd
> At length I hailed him, glad to see his hat
> Bedewed with water-drops, as if the brim
> Had newly scoop'd a running stream.
>
> (40–51)

This pastoral convening of narrator and pedlar could have been the beginning of an eclogue on the older model. By arriving at it in the way he does, Wordsworth provides new grounds and motives for pastoral and its usages. For Wordsworth, poetry in general and pastoral as one of its modes directly and essentially involve our relation to external nature and the related question of whether and how the earth is a fit habitation for human beings. The bareness of the common may be simply that—"bare, bare," as Stevens says of the earth—not barrenness made intelligible as the negation of fertility, much less an openness to imaginative play, such as is offered by the village common ("this naked equal flat") and its cattle in "Upon Appleton House":

> They seem within the polished grass
> A landskip drawn in looking-glass,
> And shrunk in the huge pasture show
> As spots, so shaped, on faces do—
> Such fleas, ere they approach the eye,
> In multiplying glasses lie.
> They feed so wide, so slowly move,
> As constellations do above.
>
> (st. 58)

Over every conceivable change of distance, there is a relation between observer and thing seen on which one can rely. This relation is not constituted by the imagination in Wordsworth's sense, but by the wit of a mind that can imagine itself as an ocean and contract itself to a green thought in a green shade. Its secure mobility comes from thinking of the world as analogous to man and everywhere amenable to human habitation and construction. Such a sense of the world underlies the variety of Renaissance pastoral and its ability to range widely. The scenes near the end of "L'Allegro"—though they are called (in another reminiscence of the Virgilian shepherd in repose) "such sights as youthful poets dream / On summer eves by haunted stream" (129–30)—are urban, courtly, and social. Hence one fulfillment of the Virgilian pastoralist is Pope's brilliant evocation of "Miss Blount, on her leaving the Town, after the Coronation," bored and offended by country life and country manners:

> In some fair evening, on your elbow laid,
> You dream of triumphs in the rural shade;
> In pensive thought recall the fancy'd scene,
> See Coronations rise on ev'ry green;
> Before you pass th' imaginary sights
> Of Lords, and Earls, and Dukes, and garter'd Knights;
> While the spread Fan o'ershades your closing eyes;
> Then give one flirt, and all the vision flies.
> Thus vanish sceptres, coronets, and balls,
> And leave you in lone woods, or empty walls.[11]

Nothing could be further from Wordsworth's dreaming man, whose imagination does not summon scenes of any sort, but registers and then seems to bestow a tone and atmosphere on the world. The lone woods and empty walls—which for Pope are within the power of a flick of the fan or the turn of wit in a couplet—become, in Wordsworth, the foundation of a new kind of poetry and a corresponding revision of pastoral.

This revision begins, so far as *The Ruined Cottage* is concerned, the moment the narrator and pedlar come together in the shade. The narrator assumes, as if an habitué of the older pastoral, that the Pedlar has slaked his thirst at a "running stream." Instead the Pedlar directs him to a well, half overgrown, in "a plot / Of garden-ground, now wild" (54–55). When he returns, the old man says:

> "I see around me [   ]
> Things which you cannot see. We die, my Friend,
> Nor we alone, but that which each man loved
> And prized in his peculiar nook of earth
> Dies with him or is changed, and very soon
> Even of the good is no memorial left.
> The waters of that spring if they could feel
> Might mourn. They are not as they were; the bond
> Of brotherhood is broken.
>   (MS. B., 129–37)

11. *The Poems of Alexander Pope*, ed. John Butt (London: Methuen, 1963), 243–44.

These are the lines as Wordsworth first wrote them. He soon expanded the line about the waters mourning in a way that makes clear why relief from the oppressive heat came not from a natural source but from something made by humans, a well in a garden:

> and very soon
> Even of the good is no memorial left.
> The Poets in their elegies and songs
> Lamenting the departed call the groves,
> They call upon the hills and streams to mourn,
> And senseless rocks, nor idly; for they speak
> In these their invocations with a voice
> Obedient to the strong creative power
> Of human passion.
>
> (MS. D, 71–79)

The poet plays out the intuition that the waters might mourn by justifying the older pastoral convention that nature laments the dead. But for Wordsworth and his spokesman this is clearly a thing of the past—nowhere more evidently than in the strong vocalizing that comes to the Pedlar as he is speaking on behalf of these older poems. The modern outlook is most tellingly revealed in "They call upon the hills and streams to mourn, / And senseless rocks." The Renaissance convention depends on thinking of nature as animate, so that one can attribute an answering intention to the echoes that human utterance arouses.[12] Virgil's formula is *teaching* the woods to resound the name of the beloved. But Wordsworth's term, "call upon," reveals an underlying skepticism "in these their invocations"—the awareness, perhaps even the fear, that physical nature, as represented by "senseless rocks," is neutral and inanimate. Hence we are thrown back on what, in the modern view, the older poems most truly bear witness to, "the strong creative power / Of human passion."

The question then is how, in the absence of direct analogy, the mourner's passion is related to the scene he laments. One expects the point of the Pedlar's first words—"We die, my Friend, / Nor we alone"—to be the human fellowship of death. To ask "Who would not weep for Lycidas?" assumes that the common physical course of our lives guarantees common feelings and desires. Instead, the Pedlar says:

> Nor we alone, but that which each man loved
> And prized in his peculiar nook of earth

12. This is Lucretius' skeptical etiology of pastoral (*De Rer. Nat.*, 4.572–92); animating this idea produced the remarkable poem, "To Joanna," one of the two in the second volume of *Lyrical Ballads* that Wordsworth thought showed "the greatest genius." See Mary Moorman, *William Wordsworth, a Biography: The Early Years* (Oxford: Oxford University Press, 1957), 506.

> Dies with him or is changed, and very soon
> Even of the good is no memorial left.
>
> (69–72)

The key word "peculiar" (i.e., "particular to an individual") calls up precisely the spectre of isolation that the Pedlar claims to dispel and that was nakedly presented in the image of the lone traveller toiling across the common—the more so as it seems that the imagined objects of love are surroundings and artifacts, rather than other humans. Along with the loss of the bond between human beings and external nature, we almost seem to have lost the bond of human nature itself. What then can constitute a memorial? How can a modern poem fulfill the office of pastoral elegy, of speaking for the dead to the fellow humans who survive her? (No wonder the writer of these lines was to produce intensely interesting "Essays upon Epitaphs," whose underlying question is how words on a stone can address us.) The mode of memorializing implicit in the Pedlar's words here proved to be the way of Wordsworthian pastoral narrative—of *The Ruined Cottage* itself and of "Michael," "The Brothers," and "Hart-Leap Well." In each of these poems, the remnants of what was peculiarly prized and loved are made to yield the story of the "strong creative power of human passion" with which they were endowed.

But we cannot know directly the humanizing love that was originally bestowed on natural objects and on human habitations and structures. As the opening passage of "Michael" makes explicit, the poetry of these ruins and remnants stands in a belated relation, to use Harold Bloom's term, to the experiences that ultimately prompt it. Hence the poet must establish a link between present and past, and in each of these poems it is said to lie in personal acquaintance or local tradition—that is, in his own or someone else's "peculiar" attachments. This idea of what makes for human connection explains why pastoral elegy here takes the form of narrative: it is the Pedlar's story of Margaret and her cottage that makes her known, so as to be mourned and commemorated. But modern narration does not recover the imagined voice of the older pastoral. It leads to a form of commemoration that emerges in the rest of MS. D's expansion of the Pedlar's original fancy that the waters of the well "might mourn":

> a voice
> Obedient to the strong creative power
> Of human passion. Sympathies there are
> More tranquil, yet perhaps of kindred birth,
> That steal upon the meditative mind
> And grow with thought. Beside yon spring I stood
> And eyed its waters till we seemed to feel

One sadness, they and I. For them a bond
Of brotherhood is broken.

                              (77–85)[13]

Though he feels the power of the older pastoral, the Pedlar, eyeing the waters, does not represent his feeling of shared sadness by the fiction of mutual utterance. Instead, these lines register a shift from direct vocalizing to the more inward ways of meditation. This shifting of the vocal to the meditative, of which "The Solitary Reaper" is the lyrical epitome, is necessitated by the ideas of poetry and reality that continue to make themselves felt in these lines. Despite the suggestions of the verse—attuned, we may feel, to "the still, sad music of humanity"—the "bond of brotherhood" which the Pedlar attributes to the waters is not identical with the "sympathies" and the "one sadness" he feels in their presence. It refers specifically to Margaret's relation to the well—to the fact that "every day the touch of human hand / Disturbed their stillness, and they ministered [through Margaret's mediation] / To human comfort" (86–88). What is left to the Pedlar is the sight of "a spider's web" on the margin of the well and "the useless fragment of a wooden bowl" (unnoticed by the narrator when he drank). "It moved my very heart," the Pedlar testifies, but his task as poet is to fill in the story of Margaret and her cottage so as to yield, in the "sentimental" mode that remains to us now, the human bonding that was once physically manifested when Margaret offered to travellers the "cool refreshment" of the waters with which the narrator has slaked his thirst.

The poem as a whole carries out both the narrative and lyric endeavors that are indicated by the Pedlar's words. The most distinctively lyrical moment, perhaps the most famous detail in the poem, occurs in his last speech, after he has told Margaret's story:

"My Friend, enough to sorrow have you given,
The purposes of wisdom ask no more;
Be wise and chearful, and no longer read
The forms of things with an unworthy eye.
She sleeps in the calm earth, and peace is here.
I well remember that those very plumes,
Those weeds, and the high spear-grass on that wall,
By mist and silent rain-drops silver'd o'er,
As once I passed did to my heart convey
So still an image of tranquillity,
So calm and still, and looked so beautiful

---

13. It is perhaps worth noting that through all the revisions by which *The Ruined Cottage* became Book I of *The Excursion,* Wordsworth never altered these lines or the dozen that preceded them.

> Amid the uneasy thoughts which filled my mind,
> That what we feel of sorrow and despair
> From ruin and from change, and all the grief
> The passing shews of being leave behind,
> Appeared an idle dream that could not live
> Where meditation was. I turned away
> And walked along my road in happiness."
>
> (508–25)

These lines, with their central image of the spear-grass, appear at the end of the poem in MS D. But Wordsworth first drafted them to be inserted after the following passage:

> O Sir! the good die first,
> And they whose hearts are dry as summer dust
> Burn to the socket . . . .
> . . . . She is dead,
> The worm is on her cheek, and this poor hut,
> Stripp'd of its outward garb of houshold flowers,
> Of rose and sweet-briar, offers to the wind
> A cold bare wall whose earthy top is tricked
> With weeds and the rank spear-grass. She is dead,
> And nettles rot and adders sun themselves
> Where we have sate together while she nurs'd
> Her infant at her breast.
>
> (96–111)

Both the vocalizing ("O Sir! the good die first" and the repetition of "She is dead") and the topos of inverted nature show that this is the Pedlar's version of the laments sung by the older pastoral poets. The lines about the beautified spear-grass were originally intended as his own self-correction.[14] This single speech would thus have encapsulated the revision of pastoral from the old, falsely humanized form—in which "weeds and the rank spear-grass" were thought to be *infelix*, like the *lolium* of Virgil's fifth Eclogue, because inimical to ordinary human life—to the poetry of meditation, in which they become emblems of the tranquillity of nature and our sense of it.

When Wordsworth moved the spear-grass speech to the end of the poem, he had the Pedlar address it not to himself, but to the narrator. The speech thus appears, especially to readers of *The Excursion* (where it was augmented by Christianizing additions), simply to manifest the old man's spiritual strength

---

14. The passage originally began: "But I have spoken thus/With an ungrateful temper and have read/The forms of things with an unworthy eye" (Cornell, p. 203). The lines were originally inserted after a further vignette of the natural relations inverted (111–16, quoted and discussed below).

and to sustain his role as moral authority. But in the revisions which turned MS. B into MS. D, Wordsworth not only wrote and then moved this speech, he also reduced the Pedlar's moral separateness and added passages that show him sharing the human susceptibilities of his young companion.[15] MS. D, as opposed to the later revisions, thus permits the spear-grass speech to appear as the second half of a pastoral exchange, of which the first half is the narrator's response to the end of Margaret's story:

> ".   .   .   here she died,
> Last human tenant of these ruined walls."
> [These were the last lines of the poem in MS. B.]
>   The old Man ceased: he saw that I was mov'd;
> From that low Bench, rising instinctively,
> I turned aside in weakness, nor had power
> To thank him for the tale which he had told.
> I stood, and leaning o'er the garden-gate
> Reviewed that Woman's suff'rings, and it seemed
> To comfort me while with a brother's love
> I blessed her in the impotence of grief.
> At length [towards] the [Cottage I return'd]
> Fondly, and traced with milder interest
> That secret spirit of humanity
> Which, 'mid the calm oblivious "tendencies
> Of nature, 'mid her plants, her weeds, and flowers,
> And silent overgrowings, still survived.
> The old man, seeing this, resumed and said,
> "My Friend, enough to sorrow have you given,"
>   etc.
>
> (491–508)[16]

---

15. The biographical portrait of the Pedlar in MS. B (40–105) is omitted. The added passages are MS. D, 116–19 and 362–75. Conversely, Wordsworth omitted from *Excursion* 1 all of the Pedlar's lament for Margaret, beginning "She is dead" (MS. D, 105–19), and substituted these few lines of chastened verse:

> She is dead,
> The light extinguished of her lonely hut,
> The hut itself abandoned to decay,
> And she forgotten in the quiet grave.
>
> (*Exc.* 1.507–10)

Following these lines, which may be thought to exemplify the excellence of the verse of *The Excursion*, Wordsworth introduced a ponderously moral double portrait of Margaret and Robert (*Exc.* 1.511–23), which exemplifies it at its worst.

16. The lacunae in line 501 are erasures in MS. D. The words I have supplied, following Cornell (p. 73), are from MS. E (1803–4).

The narrator's account of his thoughts is marked at the beginning (495–96) as replacing the speech of praise or thanks with which one shepherd, in traditional eclogues, acknowledges another's impressive performance.[17] The ensuing meditation, the substitute for direct utterance, is pastoral in mode, in that its effects depend on the narrator's vulnerability to Margaret's story and his sense of the weakness he shares with her. The structure of their relationship is given when he says "with a brother's love [making fraternal equality an alternative to the love of Robert the husband and the paternal Pedlar] / I blessed her in the impotence of grief." The double force of this last phrase, which refers equally to Margaret's sufferings and to the narrator's sense of them, is a pastoral suspension in the new mode. While it thematizes a lack of resolving power, its doubleness provides the grounds for the following lines, in which Margaret, the narrator, and nature come together in a pastoral convening that is "sentimental" in precisely Schiller's sense. Just as Margaret, when alive, had the character of a local nymph,[18] because of the restorative effects travellers felt in the waters of her well, so here her care of the cottage underlies the suggestion that nature now tends this spot: it is not simply that nature is personified in "her plants, her weeds, and flowers," but that the personifying pronouns half seem to refer to Margaret. The narrator's share of this convening appears not only in quotable locutions, like "the secret spirit of humanity," but in the intimacies and process of the verse. In the older pastoral elegy stable recognitions are achieved by vocalizing in a world of known relations—invocations of nature, addresses to one's fellow mourners, apostrophes to the deceased. Wordsworth's meditative pastoral absorbs vocalizing into its own inner movement and music. Because of the way the large formulations absorb feeling (as when the key consonantal sounds of "traced with . . . interest" provide the alliteration and thus exemplify the operation of "secret spirit") and because of the vocal effects (both repetition and projection) in "'mid the calm oblivious tendencies" and "'mid her plants, her weeds, and flowers," the "tendencies" that are felt in these lines are of the verse, rather than of nature, whose agency is made marginal in a prepositional phrase. Because the verse participates in and bears witness to both elements in the final line—"silent overgrowings" and "still survived"—their ostensible opposition is overcome, and the effect is that nature and humanity are reconciled.

This is what Wordsworth would always claim to be the power of the poetic imagination. In this poem, it is exercised by modern equivalents of the literary shepherd—two rural speakers who come together to share the work of mourn-

17. This convention is widespread not only in eclogues generally, but in pastoral elegies in particular—e.g. Theocritus 1, Virgil 5, *The Shepheardes Calender* "November."

18. I owe this suggestion to Virginia Ireys, "Pastoral Heroines in Eighteenth-Century English Poetry" (Ph.D. dissertation, University of California, Berkeley, 1988).

ing and commemoration. The Pedlar's words, responding to the narrator's inner speech, are similarly pastoral in character. They recount a moment of his own vulnerability and appear here as a kind of recursion of the narrator's experience of calm emerging from troubled contemplation. The Pedlar's gnomic assurance, which is almost an epitaph—"She sleeps in the calm earth, and peace is here"— derives its beauty from the way its inner music, "peace" rhyming with and almost a palindrome of "sleeps," sustains the central spondee of "calm earth." But its deeper force comes from the fact that it caps, as if recalling the responsive song of older eclogues, the way the narrator had personified nature. Just as he imagined Margaret's "secret spirit" absorbed into the spot she tended, so the Pedlar can call the earth "calm" because she sleeps in it; for all the generality of the phrase, it still refers to a "peculiar nook of earth." The line was of course the same when Wordsworth originally drafted it as the Pedlar's self-correction. Restaging it in a pastoral exchange, he made clear that its force depends not on resisting grief, but on transforming it imaginatively.

Imaginative transformation is preeminently felt when the "weeds and the rank spear-grass" (108) of the cottage's ruin become "an image of tranquillity." Though this is "hat every reader knows" about the poem, its underlying poetics have not been well understood. Most critics treat the spear-grass as what Alan Liu, in his recent adversarial account, calls an "icon."[19] Thus M. H. Abrams

19. Liu (above, n. 3), 312. The animus of Liu's chapter on *The Ruined Cottage*, titled "The Economy of Lyric," is directed at the "image," both for being "a separate principle of form not only fundamental but exclusive in generating Wordsworth's meaning" (311) and for being the poetic device most favored by the humanism of the New Criticism. The poem's most famous image arouses his especial disgust: "the humanity of spear-grass, as it were, sticks in the craw" (320).

At one level, one can dispute Liu's account by saying that he misreads the poem and therefore misconstrues its poetics. His analysis of *The Ruined Cottage* depends on his fetishizing the image (as his favored term "icon" reveals), and his historicist critique everywhere depends on his representing the poem in these terms. "What economy," he asks, "underwrote the 'iconomy' of lyric?" (325). Liu needs to hypostatize the image in order to claim that the poem engages in suspect forms of exchange (his main image of its "iconomy" is the black market). It is therefore essential to his account that he ignore the forms of vocalizing that pervade *The Ruined Cottage*—the direct utterance of speeches, the modes of narrative representation, and the meditative verse whose movements transform the vocalizing of older pastorals. For a historicizing account that understands how central are the "motions" of Wordsworth's verse, see Celeste Langan, *Romantic Vagrancy: Literature and the Simulation of Freedom* (Cambridge University Press, forthcoming).

I recognize that a different reading of the poem, even if thought to be truer, does not fully meet Liu's critique, since he means to call in question the very practice of close reading which is the basis of my disagreement with him. Moreover, I think that his is one of the most challenging and fully considered of recent arguments against the idea that taking poems on their own terms is the truest way to read them. So even though I think that his reading of *The Ruined Cottage* is sufficiently skewed to cast doubt on his larger account, I do not think this settles the general issues he raises. Furthermore (he would surely point out), to take MS. D as the "true" form of *The Ruined Cottage* ignores the figure of the Pedlar, which Wordsworth certainly kept wanting to attach to the story of Margaret and which is central to Liu's account of the "economy" of MS. B. But here again

says that the two evocations of it bring about a "visual peripety," an "alteration of the eye" with which we regard human suffering.[20] The poem certainly permits this kind of account. It is the Pedlar, after all, who speaks of viewing things with an unworthy eye. Yet the silvered spear-grass appears as a recollected, not a present, sight, and MS. D embeds it in something other than a poetics of vision. In MS. B, the Pedlar ends the speech in which he first laments Margaret by saying: "You will forgive me, Sir, / I feel I play the truant with my tale."[21] In MS. D, these lines become:

> You will forgive me, Sir,
> But often on this cottage do I muse
> As on a picture, till my wiser mind
> Sinks, yielding to the foolishness of grief.
>
> (116–19)

This is one of the revisions that newly emphasize the Pedlar's vulnerability to grief. At the same time, by implying that fixated seeing blocks the narration of the tale, it suggests that true meditative verse is to be associated with movement and utterance.

The Pedlar here brings out the central problematic of the poem, the tension between attachment and excursiveness. In the story, it is played out in Margaret's roaming, on the one hand, and her fixation on certain spots, like the road and the tollgate, which she imagines might be the site of news from elsewhere. In the Pedlar's narration, it is marked by what might seem contradictory principles—on the one hand, the importance of memorializing what each "in his peculiar nook of earth" loved and, on the other, the spiritual distance we must achieve from "the passing shows of being." The meditative mind does not transcend but absorbs this tension; its centrality in the Pedlar's final speech is what makes it great "sentimental" verse—as opposed to mere moralizing, which would claim to transcend earthly attachments, or the false naive, which would represent the transfigured spear-grass as a present sight. The final contrast in the speech, between "an idle dream" and "meditation" (523–24)—which is to say the achieved transformation of the Virgilian dreamer into the imaginative poet—is produced by a mind that, in its motions, acknowledges the claims of the human and natural. Broadly and literally, the arresting sight of the spear-

there is a disagreement on larger issues. In my view, the revision of MS. B into MS. D produced the best version of the poem; Liu would argue that MS. D simply continues the poetic mystifications which MS. B, crucially in Wordsworth's career, set in motion.

20. *Natural Supernaturalism* (New York: Norton, 1971), 376. Hartman's treatment of *Excursion* 1 emphasizes "the visual theme" (*Wordsworth's Poetry*, 304).

21. MS. B, 170–71. The manuscript (Cornell, p. 203) shows that when Wordsworth drafted the spear-grass passage as the Pedlar's self-correction to his lament, he meant to retain these lines as the transition to the story of Margaret.

grass occurred "as once I passed," and if we examine these lines in slow motion, we can see their intricate doubleness. The present sight ("those very plumes . . . the high spear-grass on that wall") is made symbolic as the observer allows his mind its excursiveness—"By mist and silent rain-drops silver'd o'er, / As once I passed"—and then returns to a moment of meditative stasis ("did to my heart convey / So still an image of tranquillity"). This doubleness of motion and stasis is then repeated within the moral sensibility—first in the evocation of "uneasy thoughts"; then in the faintly obsessive repetition of words that convey feelings aroused by physical change ("what we feel of sorrow and despair / From ruin and from change"); and finally in "all the grief / The passing shews of being leave behind," where we cannot tell whether the evanescence of being, properly understood, puts grief in the past, or whether human life deposits the grief we feel as an unavoidable residue of its passing. The meditative rhetoric of the speech is due not to iconicity but to the way the verse transforms the direct vocalizing of older pastorals. "There is a cumulative movement in the Pedlar's lines," Seamus Heaney rightly observes, "that does not so much move the narrative forward as intensify the lingering meditation. We know that the phrase 'the still, sad music of humanity' will apply to [these lines], but it is too abstract, not kinetic enough."[22] This "music of understanding," as Heaney calls it, appears not only in verse movement and vocalizing gestures (e.g. the repetition of "so calm and still"), but in the very image itself of the spear-grass. For the "mist and silent rain-drops" with which it is "silver'd o'er" transform the tears once attributed to nature, whose fictional laments in the older pastoral become the assonance and alliteration that bespeak the silent raindrops. The word for mental rehearsal with which the Pedlar crowns his speech is the one Virgil chose to represent the music of the shepherd in repose:

> *Tityre, tu patulae recubans sub tegmine fagi*
> *silvestrem tenui musam* meditaris *avena.*

But much as it owes to and is engaged with Eclogue 1, *The Ruined Cottage* is a profound rewriting of the representative situation of Virgil's poem—the contrast between the shepherd who is at home in a known world and his exiled companion. As the title suggests, the condition of literally being at home is a thing of the past; both Wordsworth's interlocutors are travellers on foot, and the scene of their meeting is not, as in Virgil, the native ground they once shared, but its opposite—a spot which neither has inhabited and which is no longer habitable, except metaphorically and metonymically. The fundamental question of being at home in the world—which *The Ruined Cottage* can be seen

---

22. Seamus Heaney, *Preoccupations: Selected Prose, 1968–1978* (New York: Farrar, Straus, and Giroux, 1980), 66. I have reversed the order of the two sentences I have quoted. It is not irrelevant that Heaney's account of Wordsworth's verse takes its departure from the poet's habit of composing while pacing steadily to and fro.

to share with earlier pastorals, like *The Shepheardes Calendar, As You Like It,* "Lycidas," and "Upon Appleton House"—is thus reconceived. The relation of complex and simple—whether seen in the poet's double self-representation in Eclogue 1 or the encounter of courtier and rustic in Renaissance pastoral—is not represented by a situation in the present but is projected over time, so that it answers most directly to Schiller's categories of naive and sentimental.

Wordsworth's poem does not court what Schiller might have called the idyllic fallacy—the attempt to satisfy the modern imagination by naive, i.e. putatively present, representations of simple life. Like any good pastoral elegy, it is aware of the conditions of redeeming the loss it mourns, and it shows this awareness by the way representing the ruin allows the imagination to reinhabit it. Let us return to the Pedlar's lament for Margaret, and continue beyond the last lines we quoted:

> She is dead,
> And nettles rot and adders sun themselves
> Where we have sate together while she nurs'd
> Her infant at her breast. The unshod Colt,
> The wandring heifer and the Potter's ass,
> Find shelter now within the chimney-wall
> Where I have seen her evening hearth-stone blaze
> And through the window spread upon the road
> Its chearful light.
>
> (108–16)

The first lines adhere to the practice of the older pastoral elegies, in that they represent fecundity reversed. But the description that follows is surprisingly benign: the beasts are mild and innocent, and they have simply made the cottage the site of their own domesticity.[23] The shift from the lurid contrast between adders and nursing babe replicates, at the level of representation, the change in utterance from the older poets' plangent laments to modern meditation. What seems to engage Wordsworth in this description is the breakdown of the boundaries between the cottage and its surroundings. The violated positive value, corresponding to the nursing babe in the preceding lines, is the human domesticity that has been displaced by the animals'. But this is not, as we might expect, represented by an interior scene around the hearth, but rather by perception of the fire as it "through the window spread upon the road / Its chearful light." This is a view from the outside, and the sense of everything in its place (another way of stating the value violated in this scene) comes from a personification that makes the cottage resemble the young Margaret as she greeted travellers and gave them refreshment. The naive version of being at

23. Compare the Gothic effect of the superficially similar scene in the "Incipient Madness" fragment, ll. 26–34 (Cornell, p. 471).

home is represented as innocent self-possession. It is the antitype of the cottage as we first saw it, "four naked walls / That stared upon each other."

The sentimental mode of self-possession is brought out by the lines which conclude the Pedlar's next description of the cottage and its desolation:

> Looking round, I saw the corner-stones,
> Till then unmark'd, on either side the door
> With dull red stains discoloured, and stuck o'er
> With tufts and hairs of wool, as if the sheep
> That feed upon the commons thither came
> Familiarly and found a couching-place
> Even at her threshold.
>
> (330–36)

The elements of the earlier passage are heightened here: animals who are not only domestic but are the archetype of innocence obliterate the boundary of the cottage by making it their "couching-place." There is a pastoral appeal in these lines that can be understood most clearly if we turn to a poem written a few years after *The Ruined Cottage*, a modest "Inscription: For the House (an Outhouse) on the Island at Grasmere" that appeared in *Lyrical Ballads* (1800). "Rude is this Edifice," the poem begins, and its first half justifies the homely effort of the "Vitruvius of our village" who built it. The second half, rewriting Virgil, derives direct imaginative benefit from the elements in which we saw the ruin of Margaret's cottage:

> It is a homely pile, yet to these walls
> The heifer comes in the snow-storm, and here
> The new-dropp'd lamb finds shelter from the wind.
> And hither does one Poet sometimes row
> His pinnace, a small vagrant barge, up-piled
> With plenteous store of heath and wither'd fern,
> A lading which he with his sickle cuts
> Among the mountains, and beneath this roof
> He makes his summer couch, and here at noon
> Spreads out his limbs, while, yet unshorn, the sheep
> Panting beneath the burthen of their wool
> Lie round him, even as if they were a part
> Of his own household: nor, while from his bed
> He through that door-place looks toward the lake
> And to the stirring breezes, does he want
> Creations lovely as the work of sleep,
> Fair sights, and visions of romantic joy.[24]

24. Lines 13–29, in *Lyrical Ballads*, ed. R. L. Brett and A. R. Jones (London: Methuen, 1963), 172.

This is clearly a version of the Virgilian shepherd, stretched out on his bed of green leaves.[25] In Eclogue 1, Meliboeus's goats both populate and bound (literally "define") his world. Known location and relations determine the form of the herdsman's utterance, a direct address to the objects of his care, even while its occasion, the temporal threshold of separation, explains its rhetorical character—the plangency of the repeated negatives and the poignancy of the closing description of the goats feeding. Wordsworth's poem revises the Virgilian shepherd along the lines we have seen at the beginning of *The Ruined Cottage*: he contemplates not a fixed sight but ambiguously located visions (are they entirely within his head? or aspects of the world he sees? or imaginative colorings of that world?) Moreover, it is not only the Virgilian green couch that makes this pastoral hut a site of imaginative power, but also the companionship of the sheep, who "lie round [the poet], even as if they were a part / Of his own household." The intrusion of the sheep, which is a sign of the ruin of Margaret's domestic integrity, can also manifest the way the latter-day poet makes his home in the world.

The sentimental, then, is founded on the ruins of the naive. One place we can locate this phenomenon in *The Ruined Cottage* is in the last word added to the description of the sheep on the cottage threshold. What the Pedlar imagines (for this little scene too is an example of the poetry prompted by trivial remains, in this case the red stains and bits of wool) is that the sheep "thither came / Familiarly and found a couching-place" (cf. Ms B: "As to a couching-place and rubbed their sides"). "Familiarly" registers Margaret's tragedy with doubly ironic reference—it suggests both the loss of her husband and the decay of her household—yet it partakes more of her own innocence than of narratorial complexity. Its appeal, however, is neither facile nor (in our current sense) sentimental. For it is this word that registers the hold of Margaret's story on both the narrator ("He had rehearsed / Her homely tale with such familiar power," 208–9) and the Pedlar:

> Sir, I feel
> The story linger in my heart. I fear
> 'Tis long and tedious, but my spirit clings
> To that poor woman: so *familiarly*
> Do I perceive her manner, and her look
> And presence . . .
>
> (362–67, my emphasis)

25. Prompted by this passage, as well as the beginning of *The Ruined Cottage*, my phrase conflates Meliboeus's description of himself *viridi proiectus in antro* and Tityrus's answering invitation to spend the night *fronde super viridi*.

To know Margaret's story "familiarly" is both to feel its poignancy, to experience it on its own terms, and at the same time to give it a sustaining representation, such as is suggested by the innocence of the intrusive beasts and by the various overgrowings that are as remarkable for descriptive felicity as for symbolic suggestiveness:

> The honeysuckle crowded round the door . . .
> . . . knots of worthless stone-crop started out
> Along the window's edge . . .
> . . . . . . The border-tufts—
> Daisy and thrift and lowly camomile
> And thyme—had straggled out into the paths
> Which they were used to deck.
>
> (308–20)

Wordsworth's poetry, like pastoral in general, has always been open to the charge of being unduly aesthetic or benign in its accounts of suffering—of making comfort, we might say, too comfortable. *The Ruined Cottage* escapes this charge because naive and sentimental in it are related in the way, in the older pastoral, the poet is related to the simple figures who represent him by virtue of his representing them. The tension between attachment and excursiveness, which marks the meditative imagination of narrator and Pedlar, is played out naively, in the story, not only by the psychological deterioration of Robert and Margaret, but also in the way it makes each of them a figure of the poet:

> Ill fared it now with Robert, he who dwelt
> In this poor cottage; at his door he stood
> And whistled many a snatch of merry tunes
> That had no mirth in them, or with his knife
> Carved uncouth figures on the heads of sticks.
>
> (161–65)

Robert stands at the threshold of the cottage, whereas before he was either at his loom or plying his spade "behind the garden-fence" (126). His disrupted domesticity manifests itself, in the absence of real work, in "casual task[s] / Of use or ornament" (167–8) that are clearly a parody of poetry—which is to say that they suggest the neoclassical poetry of the fancy whose "strange, / Amusing but uneasy novelty" (of Robert, 168–69) Wordsworth stigmatized in the preface to *Lyrical Ballads*. This suggestion of the mode of poetry Wordsworth meant to supersede is of course important, but far more significant is the way Margaret's sufferings ground the work of the Wordsworthian imagination. Her suffering puts her in the position of the Virgilian dreamer:

On this old Bench
For hours she sate, and evermore her eye
Was busy in the distance, shaping things
Which made her heart beat quick.

(454–57)

Even more important, she is a pastoral interlocutor, one of the important voices
in her own tale. We first hear her at the climactic moment of part 1, when the
Pedlar concludes his account of Robert's deterioration:

One while he would speak lightly of his babes
And with a cruel tongue: at other times
He played with them wild freaks of merriment:
And 'twas a piteous thing to see the looks
Of the poor innocent children. "Every smile,"
Said Margaret to me here beneath these trees,
"Made my heart bleed."

(179–85)

"At this the old Man paus'd, / And looking up to those enormous elms," seeks
the "natural wisdom" that their repose conveys to him. But we ourselves cannot
so easily turn away; along with the narrator we have felt the "familiar power" of
this story and must hear it to the end. "The heart-piercing immediacy" of Margaret's words, as F. R. Leavis rightly says, is thus essential to the imaginative
work of the passage and the poem.[26] Margaret's words suggest not only vulnerability to suffering but the observer's distress at the suffering of another—precisely what Robert could not tolerate, looking at his family, and what the poem
as a whole seeks to make familiar to us.

Were this first utterance all, we might consider it to be marked as purely
naive—an example of the transparent expression of emotion that Wordsworth
attributed to the speech of country people. (A sign of its naivety is the fact that
Leavis's interpretive phrase does little more than reiterate it.) But in part 2,
Margaret's speeches, both direct and indirect, are crucial to the narration of her
tale (253–73, 340–61, 396–99, 425–31, 436–43). She most becomes the
poet in the longest of her direct speeches, which occurs after the Pedlar has
observed signs of neglect in the cottage and garden. While Margaret is setting
supper on the table, she says:

26. F. R. Leavis, "Wordsworth: The Creative Conditions," in *Twentieth-Century Literature in Retrospect*,
ed. Reuben A. Brower (Cambridge: Harvard University Press, 1971), 334. The main point of Leavis's account is that the narrator, with his intense, disturbed feelings, is as important to the poem as
the Pedlar.

"I perceive
You look at me, and you have cause. Today
I have been travelling far, and many days
About the fields I wander, knowing this
Only, that what I seek I cannot find.
And so I waste my time: for I am changed;
And to myself," she said, "have done much wrong,
And to this helpless infant. I have slept
Weeping, and weeping I have waked; my tears
Have flow'd as if my body were not such
As others are, and I could never die.
But I am now in mind and in my heart
More easy, and I hope," said she, "that heaven
Will give me patience to endure the things
Which I behold at home."

(347–61)

The lines are remarkable not only for the affecting simplicity with which Margaret recounts her behavior but also because they rise, at two climactic moments ("what I seek I cannot find" and the final lines) to powerfully "sentimental" formulations. This is not just the speech of a character, but great Wordsworthian verse. Margaret's powers of utterance here represent those of the poet who represents her: they are powerfully enabled by and poignantly felt to enact the excursive wandering that is compelled, paradoxically, by her fixation. Similar paradoxes of expressive outflowing and persistent attachment appear in Margaret's account of her uncontrollable weeping, in which her body seems to act out the dissolution of boundaries that has already been evident in her other mortal house, the cottage. These two dwellings of the spirit, Margaret's body and the cottage that at times represents it, are at the end interchangeable and utterly permeable:

And so she lived
Through the long winter, reckless and alone,
Till this reft house by frost, and thaw, and rain
Was sapped; and when she slept the nightly damps
Did chill her breast, and in the stormy day
Her tattered clothes were ruffled by the wind
Even at the side of her own fire.

(480–86)

"Yet still," the poem goes on

> She loved this wretched spot, nor would for worlds
> Have parted hence; and still that length of road
> And this rude bench one torturing hope endeared,
> Fast rooted at her heart, and here, my friend,
> In sickness she remained, and here she died,
> Last human tenant of these ruined walls.
>
> (487–92)

The question that the poem has raised is what it means to be a "human tenant of these ruined walls." The tragic answer is represented by Margaret's final state, in which the potential power of a love "fast rooted at her heart" is thwarted by its objects—"this rude bench" and "that length of road," a locution which suggests how even a site of movement is fixated by grief. The sustaining answer, the achievement of Wordsworthian pastoral, is represented by the final lines, where the Virgilian bower becomes, by its permeability, the site of the humanized imagination. Sitting "beneath the trees," we feel the "mellow radiance" of the sun; "admonished" to leave by the "sweet hour" of evening, we are led thence by the song of birds—first warbling within, "from those lofty elms," and then from outside as "other melodies, / At distance heard, peopled the milder air." For all their descriptive appeal, these lines are a sentimental version of the end of Eclogue 1, where the distant sight of chimney smoke and mountain shadows mark the limits of the herdsmen's world. The "verbal music" for which Virgil's lines are famous becomes doubly self-conscious in the modern poet—by the foregrounding of melody itself as what the verse represents, and by the formulations (the openness of "other melodies," the metaphor of "peopled") which intimate that what leads away from the "silent walls" and to "a rustic inn, our evening resting place" is "the still, sad music of humanity."

II

Because of its importance in Wordsworth's writing career and its direct revision of the traditional eclogue, *The Ruined Cottage* can be seen as the work that made possible a modern pastoral in English. What is not clear is how to represent Wordsworthian and post-Wordsworthian pastoral, or, to put it another way, what form to give a literary history of modern pastoral poetry. We should certainly begin by recognizing the range and vitality of Wordsworth's own pastorals. *Lyrical Ballads* (subtitled "With Pastoral and Other Poems" in the editions of 1802 and 1805) include the large-scale narratives "Michael" and "The Brothers," the ballad-lyric "Hart-Leap Well," various lyrical transformations of eclogue, and several poems that employ the figure of the Virgilian shepherd *proiectus in antro*, of which "Nutting," a consciously revisionist pastoral, is the most important. *Poems, In Two Volumes* (1807) includes two new types of Wordsworthian pastoral—various encounters and reflections (including "The Solitary Reaper") in "Poems Written During a Tour of Scotland," and addresses to birds and flowers, which, summing up or inspiriting their locales, come to represent the poet. In addition, the major lyrics of the 1807 volumes have decided pastoral affinities and aspects. "Resolution and Independence," which begins with reminiscences of Spenser's "Prothalamion," modernizes two eclogue types, the meeting of courtier and rustic and the dialogue between a young and an old shepherd; "Elegiac Stanzas" ("Peele Castle") concerns the way representations of nature provide a fit home for the spirit; the balladic, quasi-primitive "Song, at the Feast of Brougham Castle" locates itself poetically with a pastoral coda; the volume's final poem, the "Ode" which was later called "Intimations of Immortality," here states its ambition with a pastoral epigraph, the initiating phrase (*paulo maiora canamus*) of Virgil's fourth Eclogue. And beyond Wordsworth's shorter poems, there are, in *The Prelude, The Excursion,* and the extant fragment of *The Recluse* ("Home at Grasmere") remarkable pastoral episodes and passages and, particularly in *The Prelude,* searching criticism of pastoral.

There is no doubt, then, that Wordsworth is one of the great pastoral poets (which is not the same as saying, as I hope is clear by now, that he is one of the great nature poets). But it is not easy to conceive the whole formed by these numerous parts. Just as it is difficult to say why Wordsworth identified certain poems (and only those) as pastorals, so it is difficult to argue that one's own list of his pastorals forms a group that is both coherent and distinct.[27] In revising traditional pastoral usages, Wordsworth undid the stabilities which underlie them and which convey to the reader the sense of a definable literary kind. Consider "The Two April Mornings," which is clearly a version of pastoral elegy:

> We walked along, while bright and red
> Uprose the morning sun,
> And Matthew stopped, he looked, and said,
> 'The will of God be done!'

> A village Schoolmaster was he,
> With hair of glittering grey;
> As blithe a man as you could see
> On a spring holiday.

27. In *Lyrical Ballads* (1800), each of the following poems is subtitled, "A Pastoral": "The Oak and the Broom," "The Idle Shepherd-Boys," "The Pet Lamb," and "Michael" ("A Pastoral Poem"). "The Brothers" is identified as pastoral in the table of contents and in a note to the poem. The 1802 and 1805 editions were titled *Lyrical Ballads, With Pastoral and Other Poems.* A later poem, "Repentance" (*Poetical Works,* ed. de Selincourt, 2.46) was subtitled "A Pastoral Ballad" when published in 1820.

And on that morning, through the grass,
10   And by the steaming rills,
We travelled merrily to pass
A day among the hills.

'Our work,' said I, 'was well begun;
Then, from thy breast what thought,
Beneath so beautiful a sun,
So sad a sigh has brought?'

A second time did Matthew stop,
And fixing still his eye
Upon the eastern mountain-top
20   To me he made reply.

'Yon cloud with that long purple cleft
Brings fresh into my mind
A day like this which I have left
Full thirty years behind.

And on that slope of springing corn
The self-same crimson hue
Fell from the sky that April morn,
The same which now I view!

With rod and line my silent sport
30   I plied by Derwent's wave,
And, coming to the church, stopped short
Beside my Daughter's grave.

Nine summers had she scarcely seen
The pride of all the vale;
And then she sang!—she would have been
A very nightingale.

Six feet in earth my Emma lay,
And yet I loved her more,
For so it seemed, than till that day
40   I e'er had loved before.

And, turning from her grave, I met
Beside the church-yard Yew
A blooming Girl, whose hair was wet
With points of morning dew.

A basket on her head she bare,
Her brow was smooth and white,
To see a Child so very fair,
It was a pure delight!

No fountain from its rocky cave
E'er tripped with foot so free,   50
She seemed as happy as a wave
That dances on the sea.

There came from me a sigh of pain
Which I could ill confine;
I looked at her and looked again;
—And did not wish her mine.'

Matthew is in his grave, yet now
Methinks I see him stand,
As at that moment, with his bough
Of wilding in his hand.[28]   60

This is a lyricized eclogue, a dialogue in a *locus amoenus* between an older and a younger "shepherd." In dwelling on the pathos of the death of a young country-woman, loved as a child by one of them, it recalls *The Ruined Cottage;* the connection with an anniversary, which prompts the memorial utterance, confirms the filiation with pastoral elegy. Nevertheless, analogies with older pastoral are somewhat forced. First, the April morning is not a genuine anniversary, a day established for commemoration, and the utterance prompted by memory is both spontaneous and unwilling. Traditional pastoral elegies are formal performances on set occasions,[29] and thus replicate internally the generic stability that characterizes older pastorals. Even in "Lycidas," which pushes generic understandings to their limits, the speaker can ask, "Who would not sing for Lycidas?" Both the allusion to Virgil and the rhetorical nature of the question bear witness to the idea underlying generic conventions—that certain forms of expression are appropriate to certain occasions. In "The Two April Mornings" it would be impossible to say, "Who would not sing for Emma?" Only Matthew can commemorate her. His loss is as individualized as the sight of the reddened cloud which causes him to recall it. This natural event, which is charged with meaning only for him, is the equivalent in lyric of the ruins and remains which, in Wordsworthian narrative, can only reveal their human meaning through a narrator with particular knowledge. "The Two April Mornings" is thus radically anecdotal. (In a letter objecting to Wordsworth's poetic egotism, Keats singled it out for aggrandizing a mere incident).[30]

28. This is the text of *Lyrical Ballads* (1800), as printed in Gill, 140–42.

29. These are not necessarily anniversaries, but the set occasions that produce funeral laments, shepherds' gatherings for song, are of a piece with the anniversary celebrations that are frequently envisaged.

30. To J. H. Reynolds (3 February 1818), in *The Letters of John Keats: 1814–1821*, ed. Hyder Edward Rollins, 2 vols. (Cambridge: Harvard University Press, 1958), 1:224.

But even Matthew cannot "sing" for his daughter. The public, performative character of song implies that the master-singers of older pastoral can turn the pain of loss into achieved, formal utterance. In "The Two April Mornings," as in *The Ruined Cottage*, the metaphor of song is not adequate to the expression of loss: the vocal memorializing of traditional pastoral gives way to individual thoughts and their more ambiguous potentiality for poetic generalization. The pain registered by the sighs that escape Matthew is not transformed, or even fully expressed, by the narration with which he explains them. His final words are a forcible conclusion, but not a resolution. If "And did not wish her mine" implies "because she could not replace *my* child," it has an elegiac inflection; but it may also mean, "I have accepted her loss and do not want to relive its pain." This latter sense, which cannot but be felt as continuing in the present, gives Matthew's words the abruptness and opacity of the "sigh of pain" which was the only external manifestation of his thought. There is a gap between feeling and utterance even at the end of his narration, just as, at the beginning, the reddened cloud which provoked his sigh has the aspect of an open wound.

The poem's commitment to the arbitrariness of individual experience reveals the poetics that undid a literary system of genres and conventions. Yet "The Two April Mornings" is clearly a pastoral, and foregrounds its poetics so as to bring out the necessity of giving pastoral a modern form. At the center of the poem is a potential impasse between Matthew's "silent sport," associated (29–32) with his daughter's grave, and the memory of her singing, whose natural spontaneity he briefly revives when his exclamation breaks through the syntax of the sentence (35). How can the poem go beyond the point, marked by almost redundant expressions in the next stanza (36–40), at which the memory of love is intensified by the finality and silence of death? This is a problem of very wide bearing in Wordsworth, but it is also the fundamental question of pastoral elegy: how does the world of survivors sustain itself after the loss of the person who defined for it the fullness of human life? The structure of this problem remains, even though the Romantic understanding of its terms is different from that of earlier epochs. (The child, a creature of nature, replaces the hero who controls it; spring and summer are a fulfillment, rather than the initial stages of life and experience; hence the nightingale [36] becomes newly problematic, because more uncertainly analogous, as a figure of the poet.)

In "The Two April Mornings," Wordsworth addresses the problem of sustaining memory in pastoral terms and by pastoral means. Matthew's meeting with the "blooming Girl" is a sign that nature renews humanity in the life of children; but at the same time, this general promise is crossed by particularities of attachment and loss, which assume an equal presence in what we understand to be the continuities of human life. The anecdotal mode beautifully conveys the pastoral qualification of the renewing image, not only by implying the particularities of Matthew's experience, but also by questioning the status of poetic expression. The stanza that most conveys the girl's symbolic import (beginning, "No fountain from its rocky cave," 49) is less direct than it may appear. Its omission would not be noticed, so far as the recounted episode is concerned; we can therefore ask whether it expresses Matthew's remembered response to the girl, as if continuing the vein of "It was a pure delight!" (48) or is rather a retrospective reflection and representation. To raise this question shows that Matthew is a figure of the Wordsworthian poet, whose presence is then doubled and intensified in the final stanza, when the speaker memorializes Matthew. This stanza (and hence the framing conception of the whole poem) is directly reminiscent of pastoral elegy. Though it replicates the older speaker's experience—the absoluteness of death ("Matthew is in his grave") prompting a vivid recollection—it does so in a way that stabilizes its double aspect. Where Matthew's memories, open-ended and even excessive, border on inexpressibility, the speaker's final memory is a vivid image, less directly symbolic than that of the blooming girl, but equally iconic. What is particularly impressive is the fidelity of Wordsworth's pastoralism both to what he understood as the modern conditions of poetry and to the conceived "strength relative to world" of the poem's speaker. The manner of the ending sharply qualifies the sense in which the two companions in this eclogue can be said to have undergone and found words for a common experience. The speaker's memory does not absorb or supersede Matthew's; there is thus no suggestion of the poet's privilege such as would replace the power of song in older pastoral. Rather the summary image is leavened by a sense of attachment to the anecdote and awe at the older man's experience, as the ending sustains—in "as at that moment" and the suggestiveness of "wilding"—the vividness and human difficulty of his last words.

Because of the way "The Two April Mornings" revises pastoral usages, its connections with other Romantic and post-Romantic poems have less to do with genre than with situations, motifs, imaginings, and purposes that belong to poetry in a broad sense. Within *Lyrical Ballads*, it has more important connections with the Lucy poems than with the indubitably pastoral "Poor Susan." Similarly, the way it resembles "Resolution and Independence"—beginning in the joyfulness of spring, the sudden irruption of melancholy, the consequent instructive utterance of an older shepherd—shows not that the two poems share pastoralism as such, but that they are (quite different) pastoral realizations of a fundamental "plot" in Wordsworth's poetry. A reader of Wordsworth should always be alert to the topoi and representations of pastoral and to its modal possibilities. But he or she has to emulate the poet and reinvent the uses of pastoral on each occasion. And what holds for reading Wordsworth holds for reading other modern poets and seeing their connections with him. We know that Hardy admired "The Two April Mornings," but it affected his poetry as a lyric of memory.[31] Hence its influence can be clear in poems one would never call pastoral—for example, "The Rejected Member's Wife," with its vivid concluding image of the woman as she will be remembered.

There is a significant body of modern pastoral—works of fiction, as we shall see in the last chapter, as well as poetry. But the context of each pastoral work is no longer the intertextual genre but the writer's works and endeavors as a whole (in which intertextual relations of various sorts may of course be important). This is true even of self-styled idylls and eclogues. There are more of these than one might expect, but in English, at least, they scarcely continue or reconstitute a genre or tradition. Though individually they may have revealing connections to older pastoral (whether to "make it new" or to play against it), their interest lies less in relation to each other than to their occasions and the individual poets' works.[32] Tennyson's consciously Theocritean "English idylls" have more significance as one of his attempts to bring together traditional forms and contemporary concerns than in any likeness to or difference from, say, Frost's rural dialogues or the eclogue ("Shepherd and Goatherd") in which, among other forms, Yeats commemorated Robert Gregory. The variety of modern pastoral is of a piece with the variety of modern poetry. I want to exemplify this—both the pastoralism and the variety—in lyrics by Wordsworth, Tennyson, and Hardy, and then, to conclude this necessarily brief treatment, in poems by Stevens and Frost.

III

Wordsworth's "To the Cuckoo" is one of his most esteemed, yet least discussed lyrics:

> O blithe New-comer! I have heard,
> I hear thee and rejoice:
> O Cuckoo! shall I call thee Bird,
> Or but a wandering Voice?
>
> While I am lying on the grass,
> I hear thy restless shout:
> From hill to hill it seems to pass,
> About, and all about!

---

31. In a letter to Frederick Locker (later Locker-Lampson), praising his poem "The Old Stonemason" and the "sudden power" of its last verse, Hardy says, "The only poem which has ever affected me in at all the same way is Wordsworth's 'Two April Mornings.'" *The Collected Letters of Thomas Hardy*, ed. Richard Little Purdy and Michael Millgate, vol. 1 (Oxford: Clarendon Press, 1978), 69.

32. This point is implicit is Stuart Curran's treatment of self-styled eclogues in his chapter on "The Pastoral" in *Poetic Form and British Romanticism* (New York: Oxford University Press, 1986), 85–127. The most important examples are Southey's *Botany-Bay Eclogues*, Byron's "The Blues: A Literary Eclogue," and Shelley's "Rosalind and Helen: A Modern Eclogue."

To me, no Babbler with a tale
Of sunshine and of flowers,   10
Thou tellest, Cuckoo! in the vale
Of visionary hours.

Thrice welcome, Darling of the Spring!
Even yet thou art to me
No Bird; but an invisible Thing,
A voice, a mystery.

The same whom in my School-boy days
I listened to; that Cry
Which made me look a thousand ways;
In bush, and tree, and sky.   20

To seek thee did I often rove
Through woods and on the green;
And thou wert still a hope, a love;
Still longed for, never seen!

And I can listen to thee yet;
Can lie upon the plain
And listen, till I do beget
That golden time again.

O blessed Bird! the earth we pace
Again appears to be   30
An unsubstantial, faery place;
That is fit home for Thee! [33]

The loose sense in which "To the Cuckoo" is pastoral is suggested by Bradley's remark that it is an "entirely happy" poem. [34] This is not the critical vocabulary we favor these days, but it indicates the way the poem accommodates polarities that are elsewhere more problematic—childhood and adult experience, imagination and reality, heaven and earth, the mystical and sacramental, [35] and, looking back to our account of *The Ruined Cottage*, excursion and fixity. The harmonizing process can be traced through the ways of naming the cuckoo—from the dichotomy of the opening question ("bird" or "wandering voice"?) to the

---

33. This is the first published text (*Poems, In Two Volumes*, 1807), as reprinted in Gill, 245. Wordsworth kept tinkering with the second and third stanzas, and the reader will encounter these later versions in other editions of his poetry. In my view, his revisions slightly weaken the poem, by enhancing the speaker's initial ability to define the bird.

34. A. C. Bradley, *Oxford Lectures on Poetry* (Bloomington: Indiana University Press, 1961), 131.

35. These are the terms of David Ferry's analysis, in *The Limits of Mortality* (Middletown: Wesleyan University Press, 1959), 33–36. Ferry calls "To the Cuckoo" "a marvelous case of a poem in which the two sorts of vision are brought into precarious but successful balance" (33).

firmly declared "O blessed Bird." This final epithet joins the two elements and maintains their poise by tying the ethereal adjective to the ordinary noun (a tactic repeated in "an unsubstantial, faery place"). The subtlety of the process can be seen in the way the epithets in the middle stanzas are revised. The two negatives ("no Babbler" and "no Bird") are countered not by single competing epithets but, in the first case, by a whole imaginative action (11–12) and, in the second, by a string of implicitly compatible namings (15–16). These alternatives, which suggest a freer, more open imaginative experience, are at the same time qualified by the phrase, "to me." This individuating of the speaker makes the poem very different from its eighteenth-century model, Michael Bruce's "Ode: To the Cuckoo" (1770).[36] The lines beginning "To me, no Babbler" almost explicitly reject the older kind of representation; but what replaces it, the apparently general claim that the bird tells of "visionary hours," is true, in the first instance, for a particular speaker. Hence the qualifying addition of individual time as well as perception ("Even yet though art to me"), and the opening up of these implications in the stanzas about the speaker's boyhood. The lyric rhetoric changes in these stanzas. Vocative formulas give way to namings ("that Cry," "a hope, a love") that integrate the meaning of earlier epithets ("voice," "babbler," "darling") into actions which are descriptively and psychologically realistic, and which, for that very reason, assimilate the speaker's inner experience to the unfocused motion that had at first been attributed solely to the bird ("wandering Voice," "restless shout").[37] The integration in memory of the speaker's past and present selves enables the imaginative confidence of the final stanza.

Granted that this is a plausible overview of "To the Cuckoo," how precisely should we think of it as a pastoral lyric? An interestingly mistaken comment by Matthew Arnold suggests why it matters to specify the mode of the poem. By way of arguing that Homer should not be translated into ballad stanzas, Arnold

36. For the likelihood that Wordsworth knew this poem, which he read in a volume by John Logan (below, n. 40), see *Poetical Works*, ed. de Selincourt, 2.502. Bruce's poem (pub. 1770) can be found in Roger Lonsdale's *New Oxford Book of Eighteenth Century Verse* (1984); it differs in only a few details from Logan's version, which was apparently plagiarized. See William Gillis, "A Scottish Source for Wordsworth," *Studies in Scottish Literature*, 3 (1965): 62–64.

37. Wordsworth's own comments on the poem, in the 1815 Preface, make clear the pertinence of descriptive accuracy to its effect:

> This concise interrogation ["Shall I call thee Bird,/Or but a wandering Voice?"] characterises the seeming ubiquity of the voice of the Cuckoo, and dispossesses the creature almost of a corporeal existence; the imagination being tempted to this exertion of her power by a consciousness in the memory that the Cuckoo is almost perpetually heard throughout the season of Spring, but seldom becomes an object of sight. (Gill, 632)

"To the Cuckoo" was one of the poems Coleridge singled out to illustrate "the perfect truth of nature in [Wordsworth's] images and descriptions as taken immediately from nature." *Biographia Literaria*, ed. Engell and Bate, 2.148–49.

says that this poetic form is not so inherently limiting in "purely emotional poetry." He cites the penultimate stanza of "To the Cuckoo" ("And I can listen to thee yet," etc.) to show that "the lyrical cry, though taking the simple ballad-form, is as grand as the lyrical cry coming in poetry of an ampler form."[38] But there is no lyrical cry in the stanza cited. Its performance cues do not call for such utterance, and its emphasis is on lying still and listening: we might, indeed, cite it to illustrate the idea of "emotion recollected in tranquillity" or the shift we have observed in Wordsworthian pastoral from utterance to meditation. Arnold's mistake sharpens our awareness of the way "To the Cuckoo," to recall our definition of mode, reflects the conceived strength relative to world of its speaker. It has a very different character from "To a Sky-Lark," another 1807 poem, in which the attempt at ecstatic identification with the bird's song obliterates the distinction between it and the human speaker:

> Up with me! up with me into the clouds!
>   For thy song, Lark, is strong;
> Up with me, up with me into the clouds!
>   Singing, singing,
> With all the heav'ns about thee ringing,
>   Lift me, guide me, till I find
> That spot which seems so to thy mind![39]
>
> (1–7)

The difference in mode, the expressive power conceived to be generated by verse form and rhetorical manner, is very instructive, the more so as the poem concludes, after twenty more lines of irregular gesticulations, with an attempt at pastoral stabilizing:

> Joy and jollity be with us both!
> Hearing thee, or else some other,
>   As merry a Brother,
> I on the earth will go plodding on,
> By myself, chearfully, till the day is done.
>
> (25–29)

This resembles the last stanza of "To the Cuckoo," which also represents the poet's earthly motion. But here we have the merely contrastive "plodding," instead of the beautifully gauged "the earth we pace," which foregrounds the simple, measured movement of the verse—the most one can do, the poem is aware, to capture the cuckoo's voice and movement, or what we infer of one

---

38. Matthew Arnold, "On Translating Homer," in *On the Classical Tradition*, ed. R. H. Super (Ann Arbor: University of Michigan Press, 1960), 209.

39. Gill, 238.

from the other. The modal comparison with "To a Sky-Lark" brings out the pastoral measuring of the apparently full affirmation that concludes "To the Cuckoo." The astonishingly plain line, "Again appears to be," reintroduces the qualifications of individual perception and lived time. This modulation of the strength suggested in "O blessed Bird" determines the force of the claim in the last line. It sounds as if hearing the cuckoo makes the earth a "fit home" for us, but the effect of the pure apostrophe (addressing only the unsubstantial pronoun) is to sustain the modality of this pastoral motif: the earth becomes the realm of the imagination only for the duration of the bird's song and of the poem that represents it.

The mode of "To the Cuckoo" can be further specified and explained by the character of the speaker. His pastoral genealogy is evident in his posture, a lyric distillation of Virgil's supine figure, who half-absorbs, half-creates an imaginative world which centers on his perceptions.[40] In the course of the poem, this figure gains the power to "beget / That golden time" and to invoke the "blessed Bird" by being a pastoral speaker in the sense we have defined— one who takes on the characteristics of the simple creature(s) he encounters. In "The Green Linnet," another 1807 poem, this is a fairly straightforward relationship between speaker and creature addressed. In "To the Cuckoo," the speaker's accommodation to the bird is made possible by another pastoral relation, to his boyhood self. The earlier contrast between his earthbound stillness and the ubiquitous voice in the skies is reduced to the difference between the boy's past movements ("did I often rove") and the present stillness which becomes fruitful by recalling them: their harmony is confirmed in "the earth we pace," which is the mean between the motion and the stillness represented in the two preceding stanzas. The enabling connection with boyhood is first established by the descriptive directness of the fifth stanza. The cuckoo's cry can be felt to be "the same" (17), because its effect on the boy is so like its present effect; at the same time, the boy's response integrates the restlessness attributed to the bird's voice and the aural effect on the adult listener. (The poem thus addresses an instability in the opening lines. They suggest that one rejoices because the bird is "blithe," but of course it is the unexplained feeling of joy that prompts the epithet: the work of the poem is to acknowledge and justify the connection.) The rapprochement of boy and adult is even fuller in the next stanza (21–24), because it modifies the sense that the child is in a privileged relation to nature with the idea that it was naive of the boy to think he could

---

40. The volume of John Logan's *Poems* (London, 1781), which contains his version of "Ode: To the Cuckoo" and which Dorothy Wordsworth's journal (June 3, 1802) says she and William were reading, two months after she first reports him working on the cuckoo poem (March 23, 1802), has, as its epigraph, the lines from Virgil's first Eclogue about Meliboeus *proiectus in antro*.

find the cuckoo. This opens up the pastoral relation with the adult, who lends the authority of his own recognition—that the bird can only be known in the feelings it arouses—to the crucial line, "And thou wert still a hope, a love." This characterization of the bird, merging memory of the past with present awareness, can be felt as a present truth, just as the potential pathos of "Still longed for" is counteracted by its accuracy as a representation of the boy's naiveté. If the bird's annual return in spring suggests that we can rely on the imaginative enhancement it represents, this is because the memory of boyhood is accessible—that is (to add the crucial reminder) *in this poem*, for all depends on this being an unproblematic account of the glad animal movements that elsewhere are a trouble to the poet's dreams.

If "To the Cuckoo" is characteristically Wordsworthian, "Come down, O maid," the last lyric in *The Princess,* is quintessentially Tennysonian:

> Come down, O maid, from yonder mountain height:
> What pleasure lives in height (the shepherd sang)
> In height and cold, the splendour of the hills?
> But cease to move so near the Heavens, and cease
> To glide a sunbeam by the blasted Pine,   5
> To sit a star upon the sparkling spire;
> And come, for Love is of the valley, come,
> For Love is of the valley, come thou down
> And find him; by the happy threshold, he,
> Or hand in hand with Plenty in the maize,   10
> Or red with spirted purple of the vats,
> Or foxlike in the vine; nor cares to walk
> With Death and Morning on the silver horns,
> Nor wilt thou snare him in the white ravine,
> Nor find him dropt upon the firths of ice,   15
> That huddling slant in furrow-cloven falls
> To roll the torrent out of dusky doors:
> But follow; let the torrent dance thee down
> To find him in the valley; let the wild
> Lean-headed Eagles yelp alone, and leave   20
> The monstrous ledges there to slope, and spill
> Their thousand wreaths of dangling water-smoke,
> That like a broken purpose waste in air:
> So waste not thou; but come; for all the vales
> Await thee; azure pillars of the hearth   25
> Arise to thee; the children call, and I
> Thy shepherd pipe, and sweet is every sound,

>   Sweeter thy voice, but every sound is sweet;
>   Myriads of rivulets hurrying through the lawn,
> 30   The moan of doves in immemorial elms,
>   And murmuring of innumerable bees.[41]

There is no question that this is a pastoral lyric. The speaker is a shepherd; it is called "a small sweet Idyl" (*Princess* 7.175–76); it speaks on behalf of the life of the valley, sociable and nurturing, as opposed to the mountain's lone austerities. It seems to be an invitation of a type familiar from earlier pastorals. Yet Tennyson himself observed that though the poem "is said to be taken from Theocritus, . . . there is no real likeness except perhaps in the Greek Idyllic feeling."[42] "Come down, O maid" reduces, almost to the vanishing point, the sense of dramatic situation and speaker's presence that are marked features of its putative models. It is precisely in Idyll 11, in which the monster Polyphemus appears as a lovelorn swain, that a Theocritean herdsman is most fully represented as a character, and Corydon, in Eclogue 2, stands out similarly among Virgil's shepherd-singers. Both are comic figures, explicitly observed by the poet and conscious themselves of how they appear to others. None of this is true of Tennyson's shepherd. He has no character at all, and his first words mark the difference in his presence as a speaker. "Come down, O maid, from yonder mountain height." What is the situation here? The mountain seems at a considerable distance. Do we imagine that the shepherd halloos to the maiden up there? (Polyphemus and Corydon know that their apostrophes fall on no ears; Virgil's phrase *studio iactabat inani* [Ecl. 2.5], makes the comic emptiness explicit.) And apart from the question of physical distance, "yonder" suggests a speaker who is looking up from the valley, not an auditor standing on the heights.

If such questions are inappropriate, it is because this speaker, unlike his dramatically presented prototypes, has the character of a Romantic lyricist, meditating on the spiritual appeal and claims of two landscapes, as we know Tennyson did in composing this poem.[43] Already by the second and third lines he speaks as much to himself as to the *ferne Geliebte*. And what can it mean to urge the maid to cease

>   To glide a sunbeam by the blasted Pine,
>   To sit a star upon the sparkling spire?

41. The text is from *The Poems of Tennyson*, ed. Christopher Ricks, "Second Edition Incorporating the Trinity College Manuscripts," 3 vols. (Berkeley & Los Angeles: University of California Press, 1987), 2.286–88.

42. Quoted in Ricks's notes.

43. See A. Dwight Culler, *The Poetry of Tennyson* (New Haven: Yale University Press, 1977), 147–48.

These lines, which presumably represent the mountain maiden's actions, have all their life in the beholder's vision, which sees some spirit of the heights, a sort of Alpine nymph or elf. The persuasions are thus not addressed to an independent moral agent, but rather to a poetic self, which is asked to dwell elsewhere and, in effect, seek another muse. Hence no one is bothered by what should seem exceedingly odd—that the speaker invites whomever he is addressing to seek out Love as a third-person personification, instead of saying, "Come *to me*," as his classical predecessors do. This shepherd dwells not in a locale that defines him, but wherever his imagination takes him. The initial descent to the valley (8–12), despite its somewhat programmatic force, leads us back to the "splendor of the hills" and a passage that Ruskin called "one of the most wonderful pieces of sight in all literature."[44] The fluidity of this movement and its very grammar dissipate the clear sense of "I" and "you" on which persuasion depends.[45] The subject of "nor cares to walk" (12), which returns us to the mountains, is Love—presumably a metonym of the speaker, but primarily a Keatsian personification who, as in "To Autumn," gives an earthly landscape its poetical character. The shift to the second person in the next two lines has the effect not of restoring a dramatic relation, but of sustaining the poem's fluidity of identification and address. It is utterly implausible that the maiden would have set out to "snare" Love. The imagined action is part of the poetical seeking that sustains the movement of the verse, and thus, overriding the grammatical shift, continues the sense of "nor cares to walk."

The poem's movement reflects not only an attenuation of the pastoral lover's ego, but a post-Romantic transformation of his imaginings. If the classical prototype of the valley of love is Polyphemus's cave and its setting,[46] the mountain scenes bear traces of Virgil's suffering lovers. The idea that Love was "dropt" on the heights may recall the hapless lover of Eclogue 8, who imagines the birth of the cruel god in remote mountains (8.43–44); snowy wastes are the terrain on which Gallus, the dying lover of Eclogue 10, repeatedly imagines

---

44. Quoted in Christopher Ricks, *Tennyson*, 2d ed. (London: Macmillan, 1989), 194.

45. Critics of Tennyson, including such acute readers as Ricks and Herbert F. Tucker (below, n. 48), treat "Come down, O maid" as a poem that is more dramatic and ethical, more involved in competing social values, than I take it to be. Their interpretations are largely determined by the poem's place in the narrative of *The Princess*, which, indeed, they could accuse me of ignoring. A similar objection might be made by Owen Schur, whose account of the poem takes its bearings from the situation and the play of gender in *The Princess: Victorian Pastoral* (Columbus: Ohio State University Press, 1989), 126–41.

For all that, "Come down, O maid" and several other lyrics have long since been separated from the whole "medley" of *The Princess*, as Tennyson called it. Most readers will know the poem (without loss, in my view) as an anthology piece.

46. Tennyson may have been especially responsive to the epitome of Theocritus's lines which appears as a quoted song in Virgil's ninth Eclogue (39–43).

himself and his faithless mistress. Virgil's shepherds project their desires onto various settings, where they stage themselves and other figures. Tennyson and his singer directly represent a landscape that is vaguely eroticized—e.g. in the obscurely gendered play between passive and appetitive experience, first registered when "red with spirted purple" is followed by "foxlike in the vine." Eroticized landscapes need hardly be traced to a pastoral source. But their deployment in "Come down, O maid" reflects the weak structure of the Virgilian shepherd's imaginings, which move readily, because haplessly, among various scenes of love. An early draft of lines 7–19 (in which, as it happens, the icy regions are explicitly a site of suffering) shows how Tennyson chose not to organize the poem:

> . . . and cease
> To glide . . .
> To sit . . .
> To hang a flower on furrowed stairs of ice
> That roll the torrent from their dusky doors
> Where there is death among the silver horns
> And madness in the stream and in the snow.
>   But leave the cold, the death, and let the wild
> Lean-headed Eagles, etc.[47]

Tennyson evidently considered representing the realms of ice in a single passage, which would have been left behind as a negative landscape. The final version, alternating valley and mountain scenes, distributes more evenly their values and their erotic suggestions. The effect is to mitigate both ethical rejection of "the splendour of the hills" and imaginative loss in leaving them. The brilliant visuality of "silver horns," "white ravine," and "firths of ice" (13–15) complements, rather than competes with, the Keatsian appeal to other senses in the preceding lines. The "azure pillars of the hearth" may, by their purposiveness, make an ethical contrast with the "wreaths of dangling watersmoke,"[48] but the unusual locution (it seems to refer to chimney smoke) accommodates domesticity to the scene that has been left—both in "azure," usually an epithet of the sky, and in the grandeur of "pillars." If there is purposiveness here, it is in the faint phallicism of "arise to thee," which makes very remote literal sense. Similarly, the feeling of submerged ego in the "furrow-cloven falls"

---

47. This draft is in the Trinity manuscripts, as reported in Ricks's edition. Note that the rejected "flower," with its traditional associations, more decisively represents an actual maiden than the "sunbeam" and "star" which Tennyson retained.

48. Herbert F. Tucker, *Tennyson and the Doom of Romanticism* (Cambridge: Harvard University Press, 1988), 374.

and the mountain torrent carries over when they become "myriads of rivulets hurrying through the lawn."

Yet for all its transformation of the traditional shepherd-singer, "Come down, O maid" retains a sense of his presence as speaker. In this way it differs from the two other great lyrics of *The Princess*, "Tears, idle tears" and "Now sleeps the crimson petal." Herbert F. Tucker calls all three of these lyrics "poems of the puzzled will, chants invoking some impersonal power that floods up from unfathomable psychic depths to engulf the conscious self."[49] The signs of "ego loss" in the other two poems, the "apparent independence of . . . language from any willing intelligence,"[50] can be discerned in the fluidity of ego and the shifting grammar of "Come down, O maid," which could be described as a spilling forth, as if to let the torrent dance us down, of phrase and image from its initiating sentence. But even though the shepherd is not a continuous first-person presence, the verse is carried along by hortatory verbs, which repeatedly give a lift suggestive of a willing agent. The most remarkable passage, in this respect, comes after eight lines (10–17, the valley and mountain scenes) in which there are no hortatory verbs. They return in such a way as to suggest a defined speaker and auditor ("But follow . . . let the torrent . . . let the wild . . . leave"), were it not that the most vivid actions are located in the surrounding scene (the torrent dancing, the eagle yelping), until, in a beautiful Tennysonian effect, "and leave" (21) is rhymed grammatically with the third-person effect of "and spill" (strictly speaking, the latter verb is an infinitive). Once again the speaker's identifications prove to be fluid, yet the suggestions of ego and will are not without their effect. Despite Ruskin's praise, "slope, and spill" are not strictly descriptive, though their personifying force does not emerge until "That like a broken purpose waste in air" (23). "Like a broken purpose" draws on the hint of personification in "dangling water-smoke," while its surprising human analogy moves the verse forward to the most intense of the hortatory addresses: "So waste not thou; but come." This has a strong feeling of address to another, but even so, the phrase has a different inflection from the petitions addressed to Marvell's coy mistress or Cervantes's mountain shepherdess Marcela. The maid is urged to reject not an attitude or a way of life, but lyrical self-identification with the water-smoke. Similarly, leaving the eagles to "yelp alone" is an alternative felt through (and indeed for) the lyric speaker.

What he offers instead of lone yelpings are the full voicings of the final passage (24–31). The flexibility of the phrases, both their length and their placement in and across the lines, suggests enough dramatic presence to produce the only "I" in the poem. Hence echoing repetition (the "rhyming," by

49. Tucker, 362.
50. Tucker, 363, 370.

phrase structure and line position, of "Await thee" and "Arise to thee") leads to the explicitly represented "call" and "pipe." But just as the landscape has been delicately eroticized by the waiting vale and the rising pillars, so the shepherd whose desire manifests itself as music and the maid whose sound is even sweeter disappear into the resonant setting with which the poem concludes. These lines are a tissue of Theocritean and Virgilian reminiscences, all of them of passages in which there is a sense of plenitude and well-being in settings replete with natural music.[51] But where the classical landscapes never lose sight of the human beings at their center, Tennyson's is a site of ego loss. It is impossible to hear the shepherd's voice, as represented utterance, after "Sweeter thy voice, but every sound is sweet." Nevertheless, this line's neat balance and sense of discrete elements, which emulate its Theocritean source,[52] carry over to modulate the auditory excessiveness that follows. The serial listing and the caesuras of the final lines give a sense of measure, so that the abundant alliteration and the hypermetrical effects suggest a benign version of the spilling previously rejected. Perhaps most remarkable is the way "immemorial," which might seem to open up "the depths of some divine despair," is attuned to present music by the murmuring of the last line. The elms are "immemorial" in that the form in which we see them exceeds what we can know or remember; there is also the suggestion (since the unusual word is unusually applied to a natural object) that the elms are incapable of memory and thus resist personification. The poem accepts these implications of human and poetic limitation by turning to the bees, who give this poet, as they did his classical masters, a promise of appropriate scale. There is a similar domestication of potential awe when the mountain torrent is multiplied into "myriads of rivulets." One might expect Tennyson, of all post-Romantic poets, to seek in pastoral what one critic calls "the uses of nostalgia." But his use of ancient bucolic, both in this lyric and in his English idylls, suggests that he saw it as a means of accommodating his melancholy to experience in the present world. Though his landscapes of love are usually elegiac, the pastoralism of "Come down, O maid" sustains its diffused eroticism in the present.

Wordsworth and Tennyson evidently thought of their poems as nourished by traditional pastoral poetry, even though the underlying poetics of their engagement is radically different from what it is in Spenser, Marvell, or Pope. Hardy's poems, in which the rhetoric and conventions of earlier pastoral have no apparent afterlife, show even more clearly that modern pastoral lyric is not a specifiable subgenre, but a modal variant of modern lyric in many of its forms. I want to begin with "Drummer Hodge," one of several poems Hardy wrote

51. Theocritus, Id. 1.1–7, 7.135–42; Virgil, Ecl. 1.53–58.
52. Idyll 1.1–3, 7–8, quoted above, chap. 1.

about the Boer War, because, though indubitably pastoral, it is strikingly different from "To the Cuckoo" and "Come down, O maid":

I

They throw in Drummer Hodge, to rest
    Uncoffined—just as found:
His landmark is a kopje-crest
    That breaks the veldt around;
And foreign constellations west
    Each night above his mound.

II

Young Hodge the Drummer never knew—
    Fresh from his Wessex home—
The meaning of the broad Karoo,
    The Bush, the dusty loam,
And why uprose to nightly view
    Strange stars amid the gloam.

III

Yet portion of that unknown plain
    Will Hodge for ever be;
His homely Northern breast and brain
    Grow to some Southern tree,
And strange-eyed constellations reign
    His stars eternally.[53]

One hears a note of protest in the first two lines, which register both the brutality of war itself and the indifference of those responsible for this particular war.[54] But the clash between "rest" and "just as found" is given a different inflection by the lines that follow, which place the dead drummer in a landscape whose elements and scale recall Wordsworth's Lucy poems. Unlike Wordsworth's, it is not an English landscape. But the poem brings it equally home by the relation it establishes between the rustic subject ("Hodge" is a stock name) and the poet and reader who contemplate him. Though the final lines of each

53. This and all other poems by Hardy are quoted from *The Complete Poems of Thomas Hardy*, ed. James Gibson (London: Macmillan, 1976). Miscellaneous information about the poems is taken from this edition.

54. These are both characteristics of the voluminous body of poetry opposing the Boer War. See M. van Wyk Smith, *Drummer Hodge: The Poetry of the Anglo-Boer War (1899–1902)* (Oxford: Clarendon Press, 1978).

stanza, with their recurring words and images, are almost like a refrain, their differences show the emergence of this pastoral relationship. The first phrase for the stars, "foreign constellations" implicitly places us elsewhere from where they are seen. (By the same token, "kopje," the most pointedly foreign of the South African terms, appears in the first stanza.)[55] In the next stanza, we take in these constellations more as the drummer himself did. Where "each night" of stanza one measures the even and indifferent pace of time post mortem, "why uprose to nightly view" revives the displaced soldier's experience, and makes "strange stars," partly because of the plain diction, represent his sense of the overarching sky. The last stanza completes the bringing together—across the separations of class, geographical distance, and death itself—of the observer and the soldier. As in "Transformations" ("Portion of this yew / Is a man my grandsire knew"), Hardy imagines the deceased's assimilation to nature with as much specificity as he attends to the realities of his life. "Portion of that un-known plain" is poised between lived experience ("I am stuck here") and physi-cal death. Hence "breast and brain" recall the sentient being, as well as name parts of the body. The grave grotesquery of these lines incorporates us in the "unknown plain" of death, and our participation in Hodge's fate is completed by the final version of the "refrain." Its grandeur and scope might seem to derive from the broad external view of stanza I. But to view constellations as "strange-eyed" is to have looked to them for a sense of place and relation, and "his stars" gives the accident of the drummer's life the dignity of fate. The closing lines thus confirm the way he has become a representative figure: his naive sense of not being at home meets and is the means of expressing the observer's sense of life's fundamental displacements.

"Drummer Hodge" is a pastoral version of an important kind of Hardyan lyric—the poem of cosmic questioning, in which God or nature or world forces are often directly represented or confronted. Because of the speaker's self-representation through (though not precisely as) the drummer, it avoids the failures of tone that can afflict these poems (often because the first-person speaker is ponderously or uncertainly conceived, as in "God-Forgotten" or "Na-ture's Questioning"). But this is not because "Drummer Hodge" is a wholly dif-ferent kind of poem. On the contrary, what seems to have made it a pastoral is precisely its incorporating the scale and concerns of these other poems. For we cannot imagine that Hardy set about to write a pastoral in the sense that Ten-nyson intended to write an idyll. The poem, one assumes, was prompted by the

---

55. The others are karoo, veldt, and bush. The last two are now standard English, but OED attests that all three were well established before Hardy wrote this poem (November 1899). "Kopje," on the other hand is first recorded in 1881, and the first two (of three) citations mark it as a foreign term. The third, from the *Atheneum* of September 30, 1899, brings out some of the pointedness of "Drummer Hodge": "The gallant deeds of the kopje and the karroo."

news Hardy recorded in a note accompanying its first publication: "One of the Drummers killed was a native of a village near Casterbridge." "Then Hodge is no abstraction," one commentator rightly says.[56] But if so we must ask why Hardy used the type name, to which he elsewhere objected. A lengthy passage in *Tess of the d'Urbervilles* develops the opposition between "the typical and unvarying Hodge" of vulgar imagination and the reality, as Angel Clare discovers it, of his rustic companions—"men every one of whom walked in his own individual way the road to dusty death."[57] Hardy had made this argument some years earlier in an essay on "The Dorsetshire Labourer" (1883). If you had lived among these folk, he says, the "supposed real but highly conventional Hodge" would "become disintegrated into a number of dissimilar fellow-creatures, men of many minds, infinite in difference."[58] Where the prose passages say, "Hodge is as individual as you," the pastoral poem says, "You and he are essentially in the same situation." As Hodge becomes representative of all human beings, his name becomes conventional in a pastoral sense. But, to say it again, this is not because it had the same force for Hardy as "Lycidas" or "Damon" had for Milton. Rather, certain elements of Hardy's cosmic poems—the sense of being out of place on earth, the impersonal presence of the heavenly bodies, the finality of the grave—came into play to make the poem (which may indeed have begun as a protest against stereotyping) a version of pastoral.

In poems so concerned as Hardy's with questions of strength relative to world, pastoral expression is one manifestation of more general lyric characteristics, such as ironic reserve, diffident first-person presence, and openness to feeling and to sense impression. The conception of "The Subalterns," one of his most telling cosmic fables, leads to a form of expression as genuinely pastoral as, but very different from, that of "Drummer Hodge." Hardy imagines that "the leaden sky," the North Wind, Sickness, and Death are not ultimate phenomena or powers, as they may be in other poems, but are themselves dependent on higher forces. In each of the first four stanzas, one of these "subalterns" addresses the human subject of the poem and regrets its inability to keep from afflicting him. This imagined solicitude, which oddly recuperates some of the faith it ironizes,[59] enables the wry acceptance with which the lyric speaker concludes the poem:

56. J. O. Bailey, *The Poetry of Thomas Hardy: A Handbook and Commentary* (Chapel Hill: University of North Carolina Press, 1970), 120.

57. *Tess of the d'Urbervilles*, ed. Scott Elledge (New York: W. W. Norton, 1979), 100 (chap. 18).

58. *Thomas Hardy's Personal Writings*, ed. Harold Orel (New York: St. Martin's Press, 1966), 166, 170–71.

59. Cf. John Crowe Ransom's comment that "each of the . . . Subalterns throws in an intimate phrase taken from the language of faith, to indicate how strange it is to have to victimize so good a creature." *Selected Poems of Thomas Hardy*, ed. John Crowe Ransom (New York: Collier Books, 1966), xv. It is Ransom who calls these cosmic poems "fables" (x).

> We smiled upon each other then,
> And life to me had less
> Of that fell look it wore ere when
> They owned their passiveness.

No comment on this poem could be better than Irving Howe's praise of "the Hardyan tone, a democracy of comradeship in a shared plight."[60] But Howe's elaboration of this remark shows why one should recognize the poem's pastoralism. In the final stanza, Howe says, "Hardy speaks in his own voice": "The resolving voice is the voice of the mature Hardy, a poet supremely honest before his dilemmas and failures, no matter what the cost."[61] "The Subalterns" is certainly a version of first-person lyric: the four figures are all metonyms of the human speaker (two representing the natural scene in which he lives, two the ills that flesh is heir to). But it is so good a poem precisely because Hardy does not "speak in his own voice" in Howe's sense. Rather, first-person utterance is shared among the gathered speakers, made equal by their vulnerability to a greater power. By the time the poet speaks, he has already "owned his passiveness" by representing his imagined companions as speaking for him.

Almost any type of Hardy poem can be a pastoral, but none need be. There is a group of poems that are putative utterances or reflections by simple creatures or natural objects.[62] Despite appearances, such poems may not count as pastoral when the trick too transparently invites us to read them as normal first-person lyrics. But in "While Drawing in a Churchyard," most of which is spoken by a yew tree, the human speaker's emergence in the final stanza places the yew as a representative simplification of the meditating human subject. Of all the types of Hardy's poems, those involving memory are the most interesting to examine for pastoral modalities, for these poems regularly invite us to consider the status as present representation of what is said to be a recollection. One such poem, "She Hears the Storm" has a rural speaker and is perhaps indebted to "The Two April Mornings":

> There was a time in former years—
> While my roof-tree was his—
> When I should have been distressed by fears
> At such a night as this!
>
> I should have murmured anxiously,
> 'The pricking rain strikes cold;

60. Irving Howe, *Thomas Hardy* (New York: Macmillan, 1967), 174–75.

61. Howe, 177.

62. Among these poems are "The Caged Thrush Free and Home Again," "The Puzzled Game Birds," "Wagtail and Baby," "Starlings on the Roof," "The Moon Looks In," "The Calf," "The Yellow-Hammer."

His road is bare of hedge or tree,
  And he is getting old.'
But now the fitful chimney-roar,
  The drone of Thorncombe trees,
The Froom in flood upon the moor,
  The mud of Mellstock Leaze,

The candle slanting sooty-wick'd,
  The thuds upon the thatch,
The eaves-drops on the window flicked,
  The clacking garden-hatch,

And what they mean to wayfarers,
  I scarcely heed or mind;
He has won that storm-tight roof of hers
  Which Earth grants all her kind.

As in Wordsworth's poem, the utterance of a countryperson is prompted by a natural occurrence which calls up memories of love and its cares; the finality of the grave, possessing the loved one, in some sense possesses the speaker. The power of Hardy's poem comes from the fact that though the woman claims not to heed the storm and its effects, the stanzas about them make them vividly, even relentlessly, present. We can regard these stanzas either as the unexpected influx of old feelings (a familiar phenomenon in Hardy's poems) or as a belated utterance, like that of pastoral elegies, in which strength and coherence of expression are enabled by the act of memory. Though it too shows a similar doubleness—for it makes evident the pressures of recurrent feeling—"The Two April Mornings" is more obviously committed to the poetics of pastoral memory. But the pastoral character of "She Hears the Storm" can be seen in the last stanza. The speaker's presence is felt not (as in other poems) in the particularities of past experience, but in a representative relation to the world of present awareness.[63] The epigrammatic finality of the last stanza is modulated by the vulnerabilities of love (for the woman has in fact imagined and traced her husband's final journey home) and of the mortal body, which finds its fit habitation only in the grave.

IV

Wordsworth's reinvention of pastoral took its character from, among other things, the weakened presence of the heroic modes against which older pastoral defined itself. Romantic poetry itself provides the heroic imaginings

63. Hardy changed the title from "The Widow's Thought," in manuscript, to the published version's "She Hears the Storm."

which generate and define some modern pastorals. Wallace Stevens's "The Plain
Sense of Things" epitomizes such poems:

> After the leaves have fallen, we return
> To a plain sense of things. It is as if
> We had come to an end of the imagination,
> Inanimate in an inert savoir.
>
> It is difficult even to choose the adjective
> For this blank cold, this sadness without cause.
> The great structure has become a minor house.
> No turban walks across the lessened floors.
>
> The greenhouse never so badly needed paint.
> The chimney is fifty years old and slants to one side.
> A fantastic effort has failed, a repetition
> In a repetitiousness of men and flies.
>
> Yet the absence of the imagination had
> Itself to be imagined. The great pond,
> The plain sense of it, without reflections, leaves,
> Mud, water like dirty glass, expressing silence
>
> Of a sort, silence of a rat come out to see,
> The great pond and its waste of the lilies, all this
> Had to be imagined as an inevitable knowledge,
> Required, as a necessity requires.[64]

This is one of many late Stevens poems that represent the imagination in a state
of wintry reduction. The pastoralism suggested by its title becomes clear when
we align it with a similar poem of equal length, the penultimate section of "An
Ordinary Evening in New Haven":

> The last leaf that is going to fall has fallen.
> The robins are là-bas, the squirrels, in tree-caves,
> Huddle together in the knowledge of squirrels.
>
> The wind has blown the silence of summer away.
> It buzzes beyond the horizon or in the ground:
> In mud under ponds, where the sky used to be reflected.
>
> The barrenness that appears is an exposing.
> It is not part of what is absent, a halt
> For farewells, a sad hanging on for remembrances.

---

64. This and other poems are quoted from *The Collected Poems of Wallace Stevens* (New York: Alfred A.
Knopf, 1954).

It is a coming on and a coming forth.
The pines that were fans and fragrances emerge,
Staked solidly in a gusty grappling with rocks.

The glass of the air becomes an element—
It was something imagined that has been washed away.
A clearness has returned. It stands restored.

It is not an empty clearness, a bottomless sight.
It is a visibility of thought,
In which hundreds of eyes, in one mind, see at once.

Here we have a similar array of images—fallen leaves, mud, ponds without reflections—and, beginning in the middle of the poem, a similar movement of recovery from their implications. But "An Ordinary Evening" is in Stevens's late heroic manner—the philosophizing mode whose scope and austere grandeur are evident in the final tercet quoted. The lines about absence in the two poems are similar in their formulable meanings, in that they both resist the elegiac desire to make the sense of absence restore, of itself, that which is gone. But the philosophical manner of "An Ordinary Evening"—impersonal, declarative, defining—makes its lines about absence different from their analogue in "The Plain Sense of Things," where it is quite ambiguous whether "the absence of the imagination / Had itself to be imagined" is a statement of resolve or an acknowledgement of vulnerability.

All this may only say that "The Plain Sense of Things" is lyric: the needs, susceptibilities, and bafflements of a first-person speaker (even one distributed into "we") are strongly felt, as they are not in the more philosophical poem. What makes it a pastoral lyric emerges most clearly in the last two stanzas. The imagination dwells in the single scene of its deprivation, and discovers its ability to reanimate the scene in the rat, the figure who transforms the silence suggesting lifelessness to a manifestation of concentrated attention. The rat, to say the least, ironizes traditional pastoral lowness, but it is a pastoral figure nonetheless—a grubby representation of what the poet himself requires, to be at home in this scene and to enact a direct interest in it.

The rat's pastoral character is due in part to the emergent voicing of the final lines. The "music of understanding" (to use Heaney's phrase about Wordsworth) is first felt in the return of the main theme ("the plain sense of it"), then in the undoing of silence by the breathing continuance of "Of a sort," and finally in the lift at the beginning of the last stanza:

> . . . water like dirty glass, expressing silence

> Of a sort, silence of a rat come out to see,
> The great pond and its waste of the lilies, all this
> Had to be imagined . . .

If we take "the great pond and its waste of the lilies" as the object of "see", the enjambment produces a strong vocal energy which is continued in "All this / Had to be imagined." But the comma after "see" can also isolate the phrase about the rat and make the next line not climactic but merely summarizing, even simply repetitious. Similarly, one can regard the "waste of the lilies" as grandly austere or as a recurrence of the realities of mud, dirty water, and flies. There is a poise between thwarted and renewed powers that is summed up by the play between the meaning of the final lines and the dignity of their formulation. This doubleness is captured in the rhetoric of the last line, where what we might call the meaningful tautology of "Required, as a necessity requires" counteracts the earlier despair of repetition. To see the qualification and ambiguity in this conclusion, consider the emergence of voice at the end of "Evening Without Angels":

> . . . Evening, when the measure skips a beat
> And then another, one by one, and all
> To a seething minor swiftly modulate.
> Bare night is best. Bare earth is best. Bare, bare,
> Except for our own houses, huddled low
> Beneath the arches and their spangled air,
> Beneath the rhapsodies of fire and fire,
> Where the voice that is in us makes a true response,
> Where the voice that is great within us rises up,
> As we stand gazing at the rounded moon.

Though an earlier poem, this has its likenesses to "The Plain Sense of Things"—the bareness of earth, the huddled houses—and it has clear filiations with the end of Virgil's first Eclogue. But if this passage begins by modulating to the minor, "seething" and "swiftly" bear witness to its capacity, in the final lines, to revive a sense of major man. By comparison with these lines, the voice of "The Plain Sense of Things," is, like Spenser's Colin Clout, that of the shepherd in winter.

I have compared "The Plain Sense of Things" with other poems in order to bring out its pastoral character. But no more than in the case of Wordsworth and Hardy should we seek to identify pastoral lyrics as a separate group within Stevens's work. Rather, these poems are a modal variant of the single, grand project that constitutes the *Collected Poems*. The later poems, in which the imagination's claims are modulated by a reduced sense of its powers, are perhaps most amenable to pastoral. My own list of Stevensian pastorals would include "The Final Soliloquy of the Interior Paramour," "The World as Meditation," "The Planet on the Table," "The Hermitage at the Center," "Of Mere Being," "An Old Man Asleep," and "Not Ideas about the Thing but the Thing Itself" (these last two revealing what we might call the pastoralism of the letter). But throughout his career, Stevens was capable of pastoral modulations, and some of his most distinctive poems have figures at their center who, in their representative reduction, are post-Romantic relatives of the literary shepherd—"The Snowman," "Peter Quince at the Clavier," "The Man on the Dump," "A Rabbit as King of the Ghosts." None of this is surprising. Stevens, of all our great modern poets, seems most committed to sustaining the heroic character of the Romantic imagination, as best he can. His relation to Shelley and Whitman is not at all dissimilar to Theocritus's relation to Homer and Hesiod. From the nature of the case, one could anticipate that pastoral would be one of the forms taken by his recuperative ironies.

Pastoral in Stevens is one register in a large, central poetic project. Frost, on the other hand, is a pastoralist of Theocritean and Wordsworthian range and variety. Readers will think first of the rural dialogues that define *North of Boston*, his second volume of poems, and that appear throughout his career. Both Frost and his reviewers referred to these poems as eclogues; even without the poet's testimony that he "first heard the speaking voice of poetry in Virgil's *Eclogues*," we would recognize the enabling influence of these and Theocritus's bucolics.[65] Nevertheless, not all these poems sustain, if we may put it this way, the mode of their genre. "Frost's dramas," Reuben A. Brower observes, "often have . . . a decisiveness and completeness not matched in ancient pastoral."[66] Some of the greatest ("Home Burial," "A Servant to Servants," "The Fear") are too troubled, even tragic, in their realism to count as pastorals. In "The Death of the Hired Man," indeed, we still experience the reconciling effect of voices in dialogue (though not the intensity of loss expressed in some pastoral elegies), and both of Frost's witches ("The Witch of Coös" and "The Pauper Witch of Grafton") know and provide the pleasures of performative utterance. But the poems that most resemble traditional or Wordsworthian eclogues are in the second rank of Frost's work ("The Mountain," "The Black Cottage," "West-running Brook"). "Build Soil—A Political Pastoral," in which Tityrus badgers Meliboeus, is one of the worst things he ever wrote. In any case, these poems belong to the history of pastoral narrative and dialogue; in an account

65. In a letter to John Bartlett (1913), Frost spoke of what eventually became *North of Boston* as having the provisional title *New England Eclogues;* another letter of the same year refers to his having given his blank-verse poems "a sort of eclogue form." Both letters are quoted in William H. Pritchard, *Frost: A Literary Life Reconsidered* (New York: Oxford University Press, 1984), 74–75, 103. Pritchard also cites a review in which Edward Thomas calls the poems of *North of Boston* "a unique type of eclogue" (89). Ezra Pound also called it a "book of New England eclogues" in a review: *The Literary Essays of Ezra Pound*, ed. T. S. Eliot (Norfolk: New Directions, 1954), 385. The remark about Virgil is quoted by Reuben A. Brower, *The Poetry of Robert Frost: Constellations of Intention* (New York: Oxford University Press, 1963), 156–7.

66. Brower, 163.

of modern pastoral, they would figure in a chapter that begins with "Michael" and "The Brothers."

Even without the rural narratives and dialogues, the variety of Frost's pastorals is remarkable. We begin with an unusual and relatively unfamiliar poem:

Two Look At Two

Love and forgetting might have carried them
A little further up the mountainside
With night so near, but not much further up.
They must have halted soon in any case
5   With thoughts of the path back, how rough it was
With rock and washout, and unsafe in darkness;
When they were halted by a tumbled wall
With barbed-wire binding. They stood facing this,
Spending what onward impulse they still had
10   In one last look the way they must not go,
On up the failing path, where, if a stone
Or earthslide moved at night, it moved itself;
No footstep moved it. 'This is all,' they sighed,
'Good-night to woods.' But not so; there was more.
15   A doe from round a spruce stood looking at them
Across the wall, as near the wall as they.
She saw them in their field, they her in hers.
The difficulty of seeing what stood still,
Like some up-ended boulder split in two,
20   Was in her clouded eyes: they saw no fear there.
She seemed to think that two thus they were safe.
Then, as if they were something that, though strange,
She could not trouble her mind with too long,
She sighed and passed unscared along the wall.
25   'This, then, is all. What more is there to ask?'
But no, not yet. A snort to bid them wait.
A buck from round the spruce stood looking at them
Across the wall as near the wall as they.
This was an antlered buck of lusty nostril,
30   Not the same doe come back into her place.
He viewed them quizzically with jerks of head,
As if to ask, 'Why don't you make some motion?
Or give some sign of life? Because you can't.
I doubt if you're as living as you look.'
35   Thus till he had them almost feeling dared
To stretch a proffering hand—and a spell-breaking.

Then he too passed unscared along the wall.
Two had seen two, whichever side you spoke from.
'This *must* be all.' It was all. Still they stood,
A great wave from it going over them,   40
As if the earth in one unlooked-for favor
Had made them certain earth returned their love.[67]

Brower's proposal that this poem is "a compression of the pastoral form as it appears in Theocritus and Virgil" is prompted by his recognition that, for the modern reader, it is difficult to define generically: it mingles narrative, dramatic, and lyric in a way that most distinctly recalls a Theocritean idyll, a "little picture" or casual scene made resonant.[68] It certainly has the hallmarks of pastoral as we have come to understand it. It is an exercise in suspension: the event's and the poet's unwillingness to declare the encounter complete produces, when it is over, a final sense of "unlooked-for favor" that is poised against the officially framing world of night and rough paths, rock and earthslide. If the poem's initial convening is not conventional, since it does not assume the likeness of its participants, it comes to suggest the way they belong together, as it fulfills the symmetry promised by the title. As we shall see, the poem is responsive to the questions we have been putting to pastorals. But it gives a Frostean twist to them, and thus reveals the way in which it emerges from and modulates concerns found in other, quite different poems.

   To begin, this encounter seems to invert the pastoral relation of complex and simple, in that the humans are represented in simpler terms than the animals. They think in unison and only repeat their initial brief thoughts, "This is all." The deer are differentiated by sex, and it is they who reach out, in the thoughts attributed to them, to the challenging stillness of the human couple. The humans' imputed likeness to a boulder, recalling the first appearance of Wordsworth's leech-gatherer, is one indication that this poem ironizes the relations we anticipate in such poems. It does so, in general, because of Frost's skeptical view of the way in which nature corresponds to human nature. But the poem is more particularly determined by the attitude that, as Richard Poirier argues, human love must precede a sense of connection with the natural world: "A man alone," he says (apropos of "The Most of It") "cannot see or hear anything in nature that confirms his existence as human. If he is alone, he cannot 'make' the world; he cannot reveal himself to it or in it; he becomes lost to it; it remains alien."[69] Poirier's own emphasis is on poems that express this view with a certain grandeur, whether tragic ("The Subverted Flower"), ironic ("The

67. This and all other poems are quoted from *Complete Poems of Robert Frost* (New York: Henry Holt, 1949).

68. Brower, 156.

69. Richard Poirier, *Robert Frost: The Work of Knowing* (New York: Oxford University Press, 1977), 71.

Most of It"), or strong in successful overcoming ("Putting in the Seed"). The only pastoral version he recognizes, of love discovering something responsive in nature, is "Never Again Would Birds' Song Be the Same." But that poem has a lyric protagonist who is unique in Frost: it is Adam himself, no longer Milton's "grand parent," but still retaining some of the authoritative naiveté and vulnerability of the traditional swain. "Two Look at Two" is a pastoral of ordinary humans, who receive from earth a kind of "counter-love" that is denied the lone protagonist of "The Most of It." It is precisely the simplicity with which they are represented, betokening their mutual love, which permits the playful humanizations of the deer. The encounter with the buck brings out the way human love finds a place for itself in the world:

> Thus till he had them almost feeling dared
> To stretch a profferring hand—and a spell-breaking.
> Then he too passed unscared along the wall.

They are tempted to reach out in order to affirm a likeness; their refusal is a sign that they need not. When the buck moves along the wall, he in one sense breaks the spell they had wanted to maintain; on the other hand, the symmetry with the doe's action, the calm of "unscared," and the spondaic "he too passed" sustain it. Some deep quality of trust has been maintained. The couple's security with each other, expressed by not needing to affirm a likeness, therefore finds it: "Two had seen two, whichever side you spoke from."[70]

If the encounter with the buck humorously reverses the plot of "The Most of It," its upshot affirms, with pastoral wit and gratitude, the moral of "All Revelation":

> Eyes seeking the response of eyes
> Bring out the stars, bring out the flowers,
> Thus concentrating earth and skies
> So none need be afraid of size.
> All revelation has been ours.

This is as strong as any affirmation in Frost. The question, as often in pastoral cases, is what to make of the diminished expression of it in "Two Look at Two." We can locate its comparative "weakness" in the opening passage:

> When they were halted by a tumbled wall
> With barbed-wire binding. They stood facing this,
> Spending what onward impulse they still had
> In one last look the way they must not go,
> On up the failing path . . .

---

70. The first poem of "The Hill Wife" represents the opposite situation: too much care for the presence of the birds outside the young couple's house is a sign that they care too little for each other.

In his essay, "The Constant Symbol," Frost says that a poem or any other human undertaking, "be it in art, politics, school, church, business, love, or marriage," is to be "judged for whether any original intention it had has been strongly spent or weakly lost. . . . Strongly spent is synonymous with kept."[71] "Two Look at Two" is certainly about something "kept," but "spending what onward impulse they still had" seems short of "strongly spent." "'This is all,' they sighed." Yet just as the barrier of the wall will enable a pastoral connection, so the recognition of limits intimates a strength in their acceptance. The writing is of a wonderful firmness and poise. The "onward impulse" is not simply checked by the couple's sense of reality—the "rough" path, "unsafe in darkness," by which they have come to this place of "love and forgetting"; it also realizes itself in the act of imagination, shared between couple and poet, which conceives the loneness of earth's movements on the path not taken.

It is difficult to keep the poet himself out of the scene and its small drama. (Indeed, his performative presence makes this a finer poem than the more ambitious "West-running Brook," which is cast in the form of an eclogue.) The narrator does not exactly merge with the couple, but is rather associated with them in a sort of pastoral equality; several lines can be heard, as if simultaneously, as his utterances and as the couple's observations or imputed thoughts. The pastoral performance is most remarkable when the poet represents himself not only in the human lovers but also in the other couple, the deer. The doe's puzzlement is a piece of virtuoso inference, in which the speculative image of the upended boulder is anchored by the realistic observation of the animal's "difficulty of seeing what stood still." But it is the actual impersonation of the doe which—since it easily shifts to the couple's view ("they saw no fear there")—allows the sense of equality and security on both sides of this confrontation. The comic bravura with which the buck is represented accommodates recognitions that, as Frost himself might say, could make trouble in other poems. The mock archaism of line 29 ("This was an antlered buck of lusty nostril") opens a window onto sexuality, while the thoughts attributed to him, too humanized to make them seem merely plausible of an animal, are a version of what the poet himself, in another mood, might think of these mild lovers. The intimated challenge—it is as if he himself "almost dares" them—lends his authority to their persistence in stillness, so that their not making the "spell-breaking" gesture sustains the spell he is weaving. If these lines carry to a certain limit pastoral tricks of (self)representation, the next line, "Then he too passed unscared along the wall," is a masterstroke of suspension. It both breaks and maintains the spell, as we have said; it connects the couple's observation

---

71. *Robert Frost on Writing*, ed. Elaine Barry (New Brunswick: Rutgers University Press, 1973), 129. Frost wrote "The Constant Symbol" as the preface to the Modern Library edition of his poems (1946). The passage quoted is one of the central emphases of Poirier's book.

with the poet's narration; and in repeating the earlier line (24) about the doe, it brings out the double aspect of the poem, both completing its formal balance ("two had seen two") and indicating the character of its movement ("passed unscared"). Similarly, the release of the final lines is both enabled and measured by the shared representation of "'This *must* be all.' It was all. Still they stood." The rightness of tone—the "great wave" poised against "still they stood," so that it has the effect of an "unlooked-for favor," not of a rhetorical flood— derives from the poet's finding his presence and his poem in representing the two pairs and their coming together.

Frost's first-person poems so often involve country knowledge and have the flavor of rural speech, that it seems obvious to interpret them as pastoral self-representations. But the principle extends beyond the circle of such poems as "Mowing," "Hyla Brook," and "The Pasture." "The Wood-Pile" sets a kind of limit of pastoral expression and, like "Two Look at Two," has connections with very different poems. On the one hand, its plot is similar to that of an indubitable pastoral, "The Tuft of Flowers": a man alone and feeling his isolation has his attention captured by a small creature, who leads him to see something that makes him recognize the humanity of human work, and so to alleviate his loneliness. But where "The Tuft of Flowers" is affirmative in its rhetoric and in the way it represents both nature and work, it is possible to associate "The Wood-Pile," as Poirier does, with "Desert Places" and "Acquainted With the Night," poems that seem the antithesis of pastoral. Hence "The Wood-Pile" strikes two of Frost's best critics quite differently. Poirier insists on its bleakness, while William H. Pritchard values its "teasing character," its refusal to provide "a meaning not evidently on the surface."[72] Though there does not seem much room here for pastoral colloquy, I think there is truth in both these views, and that the poem's pastoralism provides a mean between them.

Bleakness is certainly the word for the scene in which the lone speaker of "The Wood-Pile" finds (or fails to find) himself:

> The view was all in lines
> Straight up and down of tall slim trees
> Too much alike to mark or name a place by
> So as to say for certain I was here
> Or somewhere else: I was just far from home.
>
> (5–9)

But unlike the snowy landscapes of "Desert Places," "The Onset," and "Stopping By Woods on a Snowy Evening," this does not threaten or tempt the speaker with obliteration. Its challenge is of a piece with the manner of the begin-

72. Poirier, 138–44, 153–55; Pritchard, 101–3.

ning (which, as in "Two Look at Two," expresses hesitancy about going or returning):

> Out walking in the frozen swamp one gray day,
> I paused and said, 'I will turn back from here.
> No, I will go on farther—and we shall see.'
> (1–3)

The casual tone of Frost's blank verse, savvy and capable of whimsical choice, is quite different from the more plangent accents of the rhymed and stanzaic lyrics just mentioned. What this speaker wants to do in this landscape is to "mark" it, "so as to say for certain I was here." The wood-pile is that mark, but we cannot indulge in calling it, as does one study of Frost's pastoralism, a "symbol of man's creativity."[73] The question is whether the poem sustains the more modest pastoralism of which the model is "The Tuft of Flowers." Does the discovered trace of human activity make this speaker feel, as his predecessor does, "a spirit kindred to my own; / So that henceforth I worked no more alone"? Here are the reflections that conclude the poem:

> I thought that only
> Someone who lived in turning to fresh tasks
> Could so forget his handiwork on which
> He spent himself, the labor of his ax,
> And leave it there far from a useful fireplace
> To warm the frozen swamp as best it could
> With the slow smokeless burning of decay.
> (34–40)

Does this "handiwork" represent the poet's?—for this is what would make for a sense of connection, since the speaker is not (as he is in "The Tuft of Flowers") a fellow worker. The question may best be approached by another one: does the dictum "strongly spent is synonymous with kept" apply to the "handiwork on which / He spent himself, the labor of his ax"? The lines leave us suspended, in doubt. "Turning to fresh tasks" suggests "strong spending," but this is counterbalanced (since it calls "keeping" into question) by the uselessness of the wood-pile, its slow dissolution back into nature.

This ambiguity is a Frostean version of the traditional shepherd's strength in weakness, and it is played out in the speaker's representation of the scene in which he finds himself. The work of the wood-pile comes to represent that of the poem, because the poem's virtuosity—striking in the last line, but more quietly evident throughout, in felicities of observation and description—never

73. John F. Lynen, *The Pastoral Art of Robert Frost* (New Haven: Yale University Press, 1960), 145.

fails to sustain an ironic play between the narrator's sensible tone and the awareness that he is at the limits of the human. This doubleness is most evident in
the treatment of the bird, who leads the speaker to the wood-pile, as the butterfly leads the speaker to the tuft of flowers. Where the butterfly is directly
humanized, the bird is the occasion for questioning what it means to find ourselves in ("fellow," shall we call them?) creatures. There is first the witty ambiguity of

> He was careful
> To put a tree between us when he lighted,
> And say no word to tell me who he was
> Who was so foolish as to think what *he* thought.
>   (10–13)

"Who" may refer to either bird or speaker, so the bird's comic worry redounds
on the poet's procedures. What is impressive is that the humanizing impulse is
not, as elsewhere, firmly denied ("and that was all," "I meant not even if asked, /
And I hadn't been"), but rather floated out as something that can be dangerous
in human isolation. I think Poirier is wrong to emphasize the speaker's anxiety
and paranoia, but the joking gives these possibilities some play:

> He thought that I was after him for a feather—
> The white one in his tail; like one who takes
> Everything said as personal to himself.
> One flight out sideways would have undeceived him.
> And then there was a pile of wood for which
> I forgot him and let his little fear
> Carry him off the way I might have gone.
>   (14–20)

With this acknowledgment of another road not taken, the description of the
wood-pile, though its terms are prosaic, has the character of a "fresh task," of
properly focused attention. It also represents the poet's work in that the accidental binding and the shifting support of the neatly cut and stacked pile suggests the formalism of Frost's verse, always modifying metric regularity with
the natural movements of voice and impulse. The loneliness of "The Wood-
Pile" is not assuaged by a direct claim of fellowship, as in "The Tuft of Flowers"
("'Men work together,' I told him from the heart, / 'Whether they work together or apart,'"); but on the other hand, this is not "Desert Places," where "the
loneliness includes me unawares." The speaker's awareness that he himself is "far
from a useful fireplace" is balanced by his observation of the wood-pile and his
understanding that it represents an expense of spirit. Its handiwork and the

poet's come together precisely in their "uselessness," of which the stunning last line is both sign and vindication.

One sign that "The Wood-Pile" is at the limits of pastoral expression is that the bird is "careful . . . to say no word." Most of the birds in Frost's poems are there for their songs. Several of these poems have a somewhat programmatic force, and the message is apparently to deny the claims implicit in Romantic representations of birds. "The Oven Bird," a belated bird of midsummer, "knows in singing not to sing"; the speaker of "Come In" recognizes that the invitation sensed in the thrushes' song was never issued; "The Need of Being Versed in Country Things" is to understand that the birds' song does not lament human loss. But pastoral is founded on irony, and its use has been to answer the oven bird's question, "what to make of a diminished thing." So although Frost's poems seem to reject Romantic poetics and ideas of pastoral based on them, his bird poems characteristically establish a pastoral relation between the human speaker and the natural singer he represents. This relation is most direct in "The Oven Bird":

> There is a singer everyone has heard,
> Loud, a mid-summer and a mid-wood bird,
> Who makes the solid tree trunks sound again.
> He says that leaves are old and that for flowers
> Mid-summer is to spring as one to ten.
> He says the early petal-fall is past
> When pear and cherry bloom went down in showers
> On sunny days a moment overcast;
> And comes that other fall we name the fall.
> He says the highway dust is over all.
> The bird would cease and be as other birds
> But that he knows in singing not to sing.
> The question that he frames in all but words
> Is what to make of a diminished thing.

We can take our bearings from Brower's account of this, for him, definitive Frostean poem: "The poetry is not in [the] idea alone [of "things being less than they were"] but in the metaphor of loss-and-song expressed 'in all but words' through many sorts of indirection." This is certainly suggestive of pastoral, but Brower resists making the bird a representative singer: "Readers who see in the poem a symbol of Frost the poet or a veiled *ars poetica*, should note that the symbol is not the bird but the poetic art, the 'feat of words' as a whole."[74] Brower's anxiety to keep the bird in his place is probably due to his

74. Brower, 30, 31.

thinking that it can be "symbolic" only on Romantic terms.[75] But he then has to insist on distinctions that are somewhat forced. Of course it is the case that "the song in the poem is not just any oven bird's song, but the singing *made* by the poet's words." This would be true of any poem about any bird at any time. (Hardy's "Shelley's Skylark" is a poem about this fact.) What is more to the point is that the poet's utterance seems to be sustained by what is imputed to the oven bird—by the mimetic suggestions of the opening lines and by the thrice repeated "he says." The reserve with which this personification is used might seem to show that, despite its presence, it is disposable. "He says the early petal-fall is past" need mean no more than that the oven bird's singing, heard by "everyone," means that it is summer. And the personification fades from the next two lines, which avoid being attributed to the bird as lament and seem to be a human extrapolation of "petal-fall." But the poet is not through with the bird nor the bird with the poet. "And comes that other fall we name the fall" can evoke the pathos of "early petal-fall" if taken as directly uttered by the poet; but this tone is checked and qualified (turned, as it were, from song to speech) by the equal possibility that "comes" is in indirect statement, still dependent on "He says." The final use of "He says," in the next line, need not be taken as a personification at all. But its referential force ("Hearing this bird's song means that," etc.) sharply reminds us to get our bearings on past and future from our sense of present reality. Recollecting the character of the bird's song is crucial here, since the modulation of the poet's tone is due to this reminder from outside of the way things are.

The oven bird is a creature represented by the poet, rather than a metaphor (which can always threaten to become a "symbol") which is at his disposal. Traditional pastoral would take the double meaning of "represented by the poet" as given; Frost (not unanticipated by Wordsworth and Hardy) separates the two meanings and makes a realistic account of the bird serve as the foundation for discreet identification with it. This is nowhere more evident than in a line that seems the poet's alone: "The bird would cease and be as other birds." How can the speaker know this? It has an air of plausibility, because other birds do not sing so late in the year. But it can be said to be true only of the self-representation the bird has become. Hence the conduct of the poem leads us to accept, of the speaker's relation to the bird, Empson's formula for the "double attitude . . . of the complex man to the simple one": "I am in one way better, in another not so good" (*SVP*, 15). If the poet is superior to the bird because, as Brower suggests, he can formulate the paradox that "he knows in singing not to

---

75. He may also have been siding with Frost's own reaction to the eagerness with which his friend Sidney Cox sought to make something of this poem. Cox began a fan letter about *Mountain Interval* (the volume in which the poem appeared), "Dear Oven Bird"; Frost was not pleased. The incident is recounted by Pritchard (148–49), who comments, "Surely Cox had a point."

sing," the bird contributes to the poet its one advantage over him—its persistence in simply being itself. The song that seems to frame a question answers it by its very existence. The gnomic manner of the final lines, qualifying active questioning by the mode of utterance, emulates the self-sustaining character of (even this) bird's song.

Frost's bird poems can be understood as a post-Romantic alternative to the one laid out in Stevens's "Autumn Refrain." Conscious of his distance in both time and space from the nightingale of English Romantic poetry ("not a bird for me"), the speaker of that poem is reduced to intuiting, underneath "the stillness of everything gone," "some skreaking and skrittering residuum," something that "grates these evasions of the nightingale." When "Lycidas" mocks those who "grate on their scrannel pipes of wretched straw," it expresses a confidence in knowing the proper music of the oaten flute. "Autumn Refrain" is at a real impasse: its "skreak and skritter of evening" invert Romantic bird song, without being able to deny the impulses or ambitions it represents. It is, as John Hollander says, "the poem of a silent time," which is "forced back on its own meager musical resources."[76] Stevens's late pastoral lyrics recuperate both meager music (e.g. in the "scrawny cry from outside" which initiates "Not Ideas about the Thing but the Thing Itself") and silence itself, in "The Plain Sense of Things." Nevertheless, it remains the case that, as Hollander puts it, "there will be no easily audited poetic bird for Stevens."

Frost's American birds are more readily heard, because he is less invested in the fiction that their sounds authorize the poet's. His modern, ironizing relation is less to the loftier strains of nightingales and skylarks than to the kind of modulation already evident in another of Wordsworth's 1807 poems:

> O Nightingale! thou surely art
> A Creature of a fiery heart—
> These notes of thine they pierce, and pierce;
> Tumultuous harmony and fierce!
> Thou sing'st as if the God of wine
> Had helped thee to a Valentine;
> A song in mockery and despite
> Of shades, and dews, and silent Night,
> And steady bliss, and all the Loves
> Now sleeping in these peaceful groves!
>
> I heard a Stockdove sing or say
> His homely tale, this very day.
> His voice was buried among trees,

---

76. John Hollander, "The Sound of the Music of Music and Sound," in *Wallace Stevens: A Celebration*, ed. Frank Doggett and Robert Buttel (Princeton: Princeton University Press, 1980), 249.

Yet to be come at by the breeze:
He did not cease; but cooed—and cooed;
And somewhat pensively he wooed:
He sang of love with quiet blending,
Slow to begin, and never ending;
Of serious faith, and inward glee;
That was the Song, the Song for me![77]

The second stanza makes its pastoral alternative clear from the beginning—in allowing the equivalence of "sing or say," in heeding a bird's "homely tale," and in shifting to the anecdotal mode from the energies of apostrophe in the first stanza. But its pastoralism is as Romantic as the loftier mode it corrects, in that it does not question the notion that some bird's song represents and authorizes the poet's: it cooes its evasions of the nightingale.

Whether or not Frost knew this poem, it is a suggestive prototype of the "mid-wood" poems in which occur his most direct evocations of bird song— "The Oven Bird," "Come In," and "Acceptance." The latter indicates both his relation to and distance from Wordsworth:

When the spent sun throws up its rays on cloud
And goes down burning into the gulf below,
No voice in nature is heard to cry aloud
At what has happened. Birds, at least, must know
It is the change to darkness in the sky.
Murmuring something quiet in her breast,
One bird begins to close a faded eye;
Or overtaken too far from his nest,
Hurrying low above the grove, some waif
Swoops just in time to his remembered tree.
At most he thinks or twitters softly, 'Safe!
Now let the night be dark for all of me.
Let the night be too dark for me to see
Into the future. Let what will be, be.'

Though the poem indulges in some miming of bird sounds ("murmuring," "twittering"), it is not certain to what extent their familiarity and friendliness speak for the poet. The sounds are inferred, not conveyed to the speaker by an obliging breeze.[78] Frost himself encouraged a dark reading of "Acceptance." When

---

77. Gill, 331.

78. Or rather, Wordsworth has a firmer belief in the poet's powers of inference and the directness with which he can represent the natural world. His comment (in the preface to *Poems*, 1815) shows the intent of the personification in "His voice was buried among trees,/Yet to be come at by the breeze": "The breeze, gifted with that love of the sound which the Poet feels, penetrates the shade in which it [the bird's voice] is entombed, and conveys it to the ear of the listener" (Gill, 632).

first published, in *West-Running Brook,* its last two lines were printed as an epigraph to a group that was headed *Fiat Nox* and that included "Once by the Pacific," "Bereft," "Tree at My Window," and "Acquainted with the Night." "The speaker's perch" in these poems, as Pritchard observes, "is very much a threatened perch."[79] But whatever the force of its final lines in isolation, "Acceptance" is true to the pastoral suggestions of its title. The birds' plain sense of "the change to darkness in the sky" corrects and stabilizes the speaker's somewhat extravagant expectation that nature will cry out in response to the conflagration of the sunset. Hence the birds' murmuring and twittering are not treated ironically. But their very presence shows why this is a lesser poem. The sounds of the birds and of the human voice are further apart here than in poems, like "The Oven Bird," which enact the myth of origins advanced in "Never Again Would Birds' Song Be the Same"—that it is the human voice that gives bird song its "oversound," and enables it to convey a "tone of meaning but without the words."

Frost's belief in the priority of the speaking voice enables him to recover pastoral bird song. An easy-going idyll like "Our Singing Strength" can humanize while entertaining the Romantic version—

> In spring more mortal singers than belong
> To any one place cover us with song—

before it is shifted downwards to the modern form evoked by the poem's circumstances. These are that a freak spring snowstorm leaves the birds no perch or landing place except the open road, where they meet the poet (shades of Theocritus 7!) and join their "talking twitter" to his casual rhyming, thus constituting together "our singing strength." More revealing than this easy sharing is "The Need of Being Versed in Country Things," which modulates Romantic impulses and accents:

> The house had gone to bring again
> To the midnight sky a sunset glow.
> Now the chimney was all of the house that stood,
> Like a pistil after the petals go.
>
> The barn opposed across the way,
> That would have joined the house in flame
> Had it been the will of the wind, was left
> To bear forsaken the place's name.
>
> No more it opened with all one end
> For teams that came by the stony road
> To drum on the floor with scurrying hoofs

---

79. Pritchard, 189.

And brush the mow with the summer load.

The birds that came to it through the air
At broken windows flew out and in,
Their murmur more like the sigh we sigh
From too much dwelling on what has been.

Yet for them the lilac renewed its leaf,
And the aged elm, though touched with fire;
And the dry pump flung up an awkward arm;
And the fence post carried a strand of wire.

For them there was really nothing sad.
But though they rejoiced in the nest they kept,
One had to be versed in country things
Not to believe the phoebes wept.

This poem may seem anti-pastoral, because it recognizes that the wasted human scene has become a fit home for birds. But one needs to be versed in country things not simply to register this irony, but to understand and represent human loss and emptiness. All the poetry is in the speaker's comparisons and personifications and the various modalities of desire they convey. Hence the poem is willing, in its central mention of bird song, to court the pathetic fallacy it will later profess to deny: "Their murmur more like the sigh we sigh / From too much dwelling on what has been." The strength of "The Need of Being Versed in Country Things" is not that it denies that "the phoebes wept," but that it can afford to be ready to believe it. The birds can represent the poet because they are at home in a ruined habitation, which, like Wordsworth's, is a site of the latecomer's meditation.

Eight

PASTORAL NARRATION

I

"According to our Idea of Shepherds, Tales and Narrations become them very well," said Fontenelle.[1] Though we tend to think of pastoral as a mode of lyricism, narratives were once its most prominent single form. The *Arcadia's* of Sannazaro and Sidney, Montemayor's *Diana*, and d'Urfé's *L'Astrée* were among the most widely read and influential works of the later Renaissance. Their imitators were legion—among them Cervantes, who first tried his hand as a writer with a pastoral romance called *La Galatea*. The length and unfamiliarity of these works make them difficult to use effectively in a study like this one. Fortunately, they have a great (and much shorter!) ancient prototype. *Daphnis and Chloe*—presumably written by one Longus in the later second century A.D.—did not become a literary model, determining generic and modal characteristics, in the way Theocritus's Idylls and Virgil's Eclogues did. But it is the equal of these works in literary distinctiveness and brilliance; with its interest in both sexuality and the erotics of narration, this may be the time for renewal of interest in it; and, what is most to our purpose here, it enables us to see the character

---

1. Bernard le Bovier de Fontenelle, "Of Pastorals," in Le Bossu, *Treatise of the Epick Poem*, trans. Peter Motteux (London, 1695), 292.

of pastoral narration. The analysis that follows presents *Daphnis and Chloe* as an example of pastoral narration, with particular attention to the way "pastoral" and "narration" are related to each other. We will eventually see that there is a certain contradiction between pastoral representations and the more dramatic plots, situations, and types of characterization that we associate with prose fiction. But we shall also see that pastoral usages and modes of representation are affected by appearing in prose fiction and produce a distinctive form of it.

Daphnis and Chloe is one of several extant "Greek romances" that were written in the early Christian era, and is the only pastoral romance among them.[2] Its pastoralism is evident in several ways. Where the other romances put a central pair of lovers through a variety of extravagant adventures, *Daphnis and Chloe* keeps them down on the farm, or at least out in the meadows. The entire action takes place in and around a country estate on the isle of Lesbos; this locale is predominantly represented as a *locus amoenus*, whether a setting for love or the site of country festivals, rather than as a rural working world. The hair-raising actions of the other romances take the form here of incursions into the lovers' idealized meadows and groves—first by a rustic of coarser grain, enamored of Chloe, and then, more prominently, by two sets of marauders from outside— Phoenician pirates and a group of rich young urbanites on a hunting excursion. These episodes are thematically relevant to, but do not themselves convey, the main action of the romance—the growth into sexual knowledge of its eponymous hero and heroine. Like Spenser's Pastorella and Shakespeare's Perdita, each is a castaway child of wealthy parents and is discovered in the fields by a rustic foster-parent. They grow up together, tending their herds of goats (Daphnis) and sheep (Chloe), and as their companionship turns to love, they find themselves eager to find, but unable to figure out, how to allay the pangs of desire they feel. The implausibility of their persistent ignorance is matched only by the sophistication and charm with which Longus conducts his tale of delayed gratification. The main question about *Daphnis and Chloe* has always been whether it is a particularly accomplished piece of "soft porn," as a recent reviewer calls it, or has the dignity and claim on our attention of other ancient masterpieces. (Goethe thought it manifested "the highest art and culture," and said that "one would have to write an entire book to do justice to all its merits.")[3] For us this question will be subsumed by a consideration of two more

---

2. They are now conveniently gathered in B. P. Reardon, ed., *Collected Ancient Greek Novels* (Berkeley: University of California Press, 1989). It is now common to refer to these works as "novels," but I prefer to reserve that term for the realistic fiction of modern, bourgeois Europe.

3. In the conversations with Eckermann (March 21, 1831), as quoted in William E. McCulloh, *Longus* (New York: Twayne, 1970), 106. Brian Vickers refers to *Daphnis and Chloe* as "soft porn" in *Times Literary Supplement*, April 20, 1984, 427.

particular matters—the character of *Daphnis and Chloe* as a narrative and its character as a pastoral.

From the brief account just given, it will be seen that *Daphnis and Chloe* is susceptible of being described as a straightforward plot, with a beginning (the finding of the children, their original innocent companionship), a middle (discovering the ways of love and overcoming the impediments posed by those who invade their turf and seek to carry off one or the other of them), and an end (the revealing of their true identities and their marriage and sexual union). The sense of strong plotting emerges particularly in Book 4, in which the situations, conflicts, and resolutions are derived from stage comedy. The plot movement is supported by a seasonal pattern. Books 1 and 2 take us from spring to autumn; the seasonal deadpoint of winter, at the beginning of Book 3, gives way to a second spring-to-autumn sequence, which finally unites the lovers in Book 4. It is thus not surprising that the most useful critical introduction to *Daphnis and Chloe*, by William McCulloh, claims that "the linear progression of the seasons fixes the movement of the action"; that "the movement of the year supports and parallels the phases of the growing passion of Daphnis and Chloe"; and that "the love of Daphnis and Chloe is a natural growth, like the year and their own maturation."[4] Another critic moralizes the plot: "For human beings . . . nature takes its proper erotic course only through troubles that develop knowledge and culminate in marriage. In fact, this process of erotic maturation constitutes the action of *Daphnis*."[5]

All very well, but to anyone who has read *Daphnis and Chloe*, such accounts will seem unduly solemn. Rosenmeyer gives a much truer sense of the main characters and the whole book: "The simplicity of the characters ensures their day-for-day well-being and their ultimate survival. The naiveté of the writing protects the pastoral experience against the profundities and the syntheses which the plot, like any plot, is always on the verge of triggering."[6] Moreover, reading for plot, in this romance, leads one to ignore its main sources of appeal—to our sexual sophistication, continually engaged by the lovers and amused by their inability to get the point, and to our literary sophistication, which savors a variety of expert rhetorical performances. Though the book can be represented in terms of plot, it is more accurately described as a series of set pieces. These include not only the lovers' dealings with each other, but descriptions of landscape, set speeches in various contexts, accounts of musical performance, the serio-comic adventures, and three etiological myths (one in each of

4. McCulloh, 68–69.

5. Arthur Heiserman, *The Novel Before the Novel* (Chicago: University of Chicago Press, 1977), 136.

6. Thomas G. Rosenmeyer, *The Green Cabinet: Theocritus and the European Pastoral Lyric* (Berkeley & Los Angeles: University of California Press, 1969), 48.

the first three books). The writing ranges from pellucid simplicity in narrative passages to artful elaboration in the descriptions and speeches; the prose is shot through with literary allusions, and some of the episodes themselves are re-workings of prior texts—not only narratives but, in one instance, a lyric by Sappho, the preeminent poet of Lesbos. Indeed, one can think of the book as a continual narrativizing of lyric.

Our concern is with the way the divergent descriptions of *Daphnis and Chloe* conceive or imply its pastoralism. In readings which emphasize plot development, the benign landscapes, the symbolic gardens, and the supervising role of Pan and the Nymphs represent an organic relation between nature and human beings. The central metaphor of maturation is thought to make this a pastoral romance. The alternative view emphasizes rhetorical parts, not the narrative whole, and involves a different idea of the book's pastoralism. The best such account, by Thalia A. Pandiri, argues that "the work is quintessential pastoral, less because of its shepherd protagonists than because of the author's narrative strategy, with its mixing of genres and the cool distance it establishes between character and reader." This distance is achieved by "the author's emphasis on the pastoral scene as artifact, a crafted work to be viewed and admired by the connoisseur."[7] Pandiri takes this artifice to be represented by the garden of Philetas, an old shepherd who seeks out Daphnis and Chloe to instruct them in the ways of love. She calls his garden "a suitable emblem" for the work as a whole, because "carefully landscaped, protected on all sides from wild nature by a barrier, it creates the illusion of a free natural setting as it ought, ideally, to be."[8] This is the aspect under which she sees all the episodes of the book. The repeated incursions of violence have for her a double valency. On the one hand, they remind us of the rough realities to which the world of pastoral play is vulnerable. On the other hand, these reminders are precisely of an artistic road not taken. They "can be put out of mind so long as the pastoral landscape seems relatively encapsulated"; they serve to alert us to the writer's "self-conscious and ordered craft" and to make us realize "how art embellishes and reshapes"—"how little a pastoral paradise owes to nature and how much to the discerning aesthetic sense of an urban sophisticate."[9]

Pandiri's emphasis on artful set pieces takes its cue from the first sentences of the book, narrating its ostensible occasion: "When I was hunting in Lesbos,

---

7. "Daphnis and Chloe: The Art of Pastoral Play," *Ramus* 14 (1985): 116.

8. Pandiri, 118. There is no question that this passage can stand as representative of literary craft. Philetas was the name of a famous Alexandrian poet, cited as a model in Theocritus's seventh Idyll; Longus's Philetas encounters in his garden a mischievous boy who turns out to be Eros, the supervising deity of this romance; and his discourse is shot through with reminiscences of Theocritus and Virgil's Eclogues. So the question is not whether but what kind of model for writing Philetas and his garden provide.

9. Pandiri, 125. The other quotations in this sentence are from pp. 124, 119, 121.

I saw the most beautiful sight I have ever seen, in a grove that was sacred to the Nymphs: a painting that told a story of love."[10] This painting represents scenes from a tale which the author proceeds to narrate in the four books of the romance. This beginning certainly seems to justify representing *Daphnis and Chloe* as a series of well-wrought scenes. But the consequence of Pandiri's treatment is that she ignores the main action of the book. You can scarcely tell from her account that the author and reader are constantly attending to Daphnis and Chloe's desire for each other and to the sexual knowledge that they seek to acquire. Even her account of the harsher realities that the artist fends off emphasizes not "unruly passion and ugliness" (once mentioned, 119), but elements of "hard pastoral"—the rustic labors, the physical coarseness, and the narrow social and economic calculations of Daphnis and Chloe's foster-parents and their world. Where the interpreters who emphasize organic growth exaggerate the main action of the romance, this version of pastoral, with its emphasis on landscape and on art's opposition to nature, tends to lose sight of it.[11]

If emphasizing "the *hortus conclusus* of literary pastoral"[12] leads to representing *Daphnis and Chloe* as a series of "little pictures"—to recall what was once thought to be the meaning of "idyll"—we can see the book as a pastoral *narration* by attending not to scene and landscape, but to the herders who are its

10. I quote the translation by Christopher Gill, in Reardon's collection (above, n. 2); references are to book and paragraph, rather than page, so that the reader can locate the passage in the Loeb edition and other translations. The most widely available translations in recent years have been those of Moses Hadas, which McCulloh rightly criticizes as sluggish, and Paul Turner (Penguin, recently reprinted). Turner and Gill both seek to convey the lucidity and lightness of Longus's writing, but Gill pays more attention to his rhetorical artfulness. I occasionally substitute a sentence or phrase of Turner's in Gill's translation, when it seems to me more felicitous English or truer to the Greek. All such substitutions are noted.

11. Since I am more interested in the question of pastoral narration than in the interpretation of *Daphnis and Chloe*, I have omitted from this account the view advanced by H. H. O. Chalk that the romance draws on religious sources and is an allegory of cosmogonic Eros: "Eros and the Lesbian Pastorals of Longos," *Journal of Hellenic Studies* 80 (1960): 32–51. This lofty interpretation is motivated by a desire to rescue the book from the charge of triviality. Most subsequent interpreters back off from Chalk's largest claims, but his article remains influential. Though he emphasizes the larger themes and movement of the romance, his view of pastoral is close to Pandiri's: he very much wants to see it as the product of urban intellect and art, rather than as a commitment to rural innocence.

In a recent, impressive essay, Froma I. Zeitlin combines these two ways of construing *Daphnis and Chloe*: "The Poetics of Erōs: Nature, Art, and Imitation in Longus' *Daphnis and Chloe*," in *Before Sexuality: The Construction of Erotic Experience in the Ancient Greek World*, ed. David M. Halperin, John J. Winkler, and Froma I. Zeitlin (Princeton: Princeton University Press, 1990), 417–64. Her interpretation centers on the reader's erotic engagement with the text and, though not executed with solemnity, seems to me rather too grand—for reasons, I would argue, that go with taking the heart of pastoral to be "a nostalgia not only for rusticity and benign nature, but more primordially for the green fields of childhood or dreams of the Golden Age" (426).

12. Pandiri, 133.

principal characters. We can begin with Philetas, whose role as a gardener has a different dynamic, and hence a different place in the romance, from the static identification of him with "a sheltered haven," whose artful construction shuts out the unruliness of love. For one thing, Philetas has not always had a garden; he turned to gardening only after "I stopped being a herdsman because of my age" (2.3), and his life as a herdsman is associated with having been a lover. The very existence of his garden is thus of a piece with the encounter which, he tells Daphnis and Chloe, prompted him to seek them out. Charmed by the intruder he finds there, a mischievous boy with golden hair and glistening body, Philetas promises that he can pick the fruit at will, if he only will give him one kiss. But the boy, who is Eros, refuses to allow the old man to get caught up again in the pursuit of love: "Your age won't save you from chasing me after your one kiss (2.5)." The love-god was once, indeed, in attendance on Philetas, "when, as a lusty young man, you used to graze your large herd of cows . . . [and] while you played the pipes beside those oaks when you were in love with Amaryllis" (2.5). But now Eros is "shepherding" (*poimainō*) Daphnis and Chloe, and his gift to Philetas, now that he is old, is to make his garden flourish. Philetas's garden is thus conceived less in terms of his own cultivation of nature than as an accommodation of the love-god and as a displacement and stabilizing of erotic energies.

We can now see more clearly how the Philetas episode is a model for the aesthetics of *Daphnis and Chloe*. By recognizing where he is in relation to love, this avatar of the Alexandrian poet becomes the pastoral representative of the narrator. The author's Prologue promises the reader precisely what Philetas offers Daphnis and Chloe—instruction in love.[13] And the writer's enabling condition is the one Eros ensured Philetas by refusing him the kiss and its consequent turbulence: "As for me," says the narrator, "may the god Love let me write about others' passions but keep my own self-control." Aesthetic mastery of erotic energies occurs most importantly, then, not in the garden as a picture or a representation of nature, but in the transformation of desire into rhetorical performance, in Philetas's whole narration and discourse of love. When Daphnis and Chloe ask him about Love's power, he replies with a mini-hymn to the cosmogonic Eros, who rules the elements, the stars, and his fellow gods (2.7). This is the kind of discourse serious interpreters want to hear (Heiserman compares it to "the idea of Love grasped by Dante in paradise"); it turns desire into transmittable wisdom.[14] But Philetas also knows that the young lovers stand in need of practical counsel. He concludes, therefore, not in the empyrean, but

13. The narrator says he composed the work "as an offering to Love, the Nymphs, and Pan, and something for mankind to possess and enjoy. It will cure the sick, comfort the distressed, stir the memory of those who have loved, and educate those who haven't."

14. Heiserman, 137. The passage is of course at the center of Chalk's interpretation.

by telling them that "there is no medicine for Love, no potion, no drug, no spell to mutter, except a kiss and an embrace and lying down together with naked bodies" (2.7).

The rhetorical and aesthetic transformation of passion, familiar to us in other pastorals, is a fundamental motive of the first two books of the romance. In Book 1, the lustful shepherd Dorcon is doubly tamed and transformed. His attempted rape of Chloe in the guise of a wolf—to which he resorts after failing to win a kiss from her in a verbal contest with Daphnis—leads to his being mauled by the guard-dogs, from whom he is rescued by none other than Daphnis and Chloe, who innocently think his disguise is a mere "pastoral game" (1.21). Two seasons but only a few pages later, Daphnis is abducted by pirates, who also take some of Dorcon's cows. When Chloe hears Daphnis calling to her from the ship and runs to the shore, she finds Dorcon badly wounded by the pirates. All the Greek romances are in the business of handling such extremities, but the means here are pure pastoral. Dorcon tells Chloe that she can rescue Daphnis if she will take up his pipes—which, he points out, have won many contests—and "play on them that tune I taught Daphnis once, and Daphnis taught you" (1.29). This is a familiar topos of pastoral tradition (literally, a handing on), but nowhere else does normally transmitted song have such effects. Chloe gives the dying Dorcon the kiss that is all he asks as his reward and then plays the tune; Dorcon's cows, hearing it, leap from the ship and capsize it; Daphnis comes safely to shore, holding on to the horns of two cows. To "honor the memory of their benefactor," Daphnis and Chloe plant trees and offer first-fruits at his burial:

> They also poured out libations of milk, squeezed some grapes, and smashed a number of pipes. They heard the cows mooing sadly and saw them running wild while they mooed. And they supposed, cowherds and goatherds as they were, that this was the cows' way of mourning for the dead cowherd. (1.31)

This mini-version of a pastoral elegy is one of the two set pieces that bring Book 1 to an end. The rural rites and the pitiful moosic, within the fiction, and the merrily ironic narration both serve to dissipate grief for Dorcon and to make him a herdsman of note.

Similarly and on a grander scale, Book 2 sustains the promise of Philetas's narration by turning the aggressive invasion of a protected locale and painful emotions into aesthetic pleasure. It is the thought of their own love pains that leads Daphnis and Chloe to recognize what they are experiencing, when like dutiful students they compare notes after Philetas's lecture. Their attempts to follow his practical advice—to kiss and embrace and lie naked together— might have led them, says the narrator, to "discover the real thing" (2.11, trans. Turner), when their world is troubled by another incursion. Some rich young men from Methymna, out on a holiday, become involved in a brawl with Daphnis and other rustics. The mutual misunderstanding in this brilliantly staged encounter of city and country is submitted to the judgment of Philetas, whose decision leaves the Methymneans unsatisfied. They therefore return for a raid on the countryside, in the course of which they abduct Chloe, along with her and Daphnis's flocks. This time the rescue is the work not of an ordinary set of Pan-pipes, but of the god himself, who terrorizes the abductors by extraordinary occurrences on their ship and by the sound of his own pipes, which "did not give pleasure to those listening, as pipes usually do, but terrified them, like a war trumpet" (2.26).

After this climax, which is the strongest manifestation of the various powers who govern the tale, the final third of Book 2 restores the normal pleasures of piping. Pan's pipes, now sounding sweetly, lead Chloe and her flock home, and are explicitly domesticated in the ceremonies which thank the rural god. These culminate in a triple episode of pleasurable utterance and instruction. The old shepherd Lamon, Daphnis's foster-father, begins by telling the story of Pan and Syrinx, the origin of the pipes (Gr. *syrinx*); Dryas, Chloe's foster-father, concludes with a dance miming the work of the vintage. The centerpiece is Philetas's performance on the Pan-pipes, in which normal piping borders on the god's own powers. When asked to perform, Philetas refuses to use Daphnis's pipes, as being "too small for his great art, because they were made to be played in a boy's mouth" (2.33, my modification of Gill). He sends his son (conveniently named Tityrus) home for his own pipes, a large instrument which "you could have imagined . . . was the very instrument that Pan first put together." On these pipes, Philetas performs a summa of pastoral song:

> You would have thought you were hearing several flutes playing together, so strong was the sound of his piping. Gradually reducing his force, he modulated the tune to a sweeter sound [compare the modulation in the story to normal piping and its benignity] and displayed every kind of skill in musical herdsmanship: he played music that fitted a herd of cows, music that suited a herd of goats, music that flocks of sheep would love. For the sheep the tune was sweet; for the cows it was loud; for the goats it was sharp. In short, with that one pipe he imitated all the pipes in the world. (2.35; last sentence, trans. Turner)

The phallic implications of the old man blowing his big pipes instead of Daphnis's little-boy ones are played out after Dryas's dance of the vintage. Prompted by the old man's performance, Daphnis and Chloe spring to their feet and dance out the story of Pan and Syrinx. At the climax of their dance, "*Daphnis took Philetas's big pipes* and piped a plaintive tune, like one in love, then a romantic tune, like one who tries to win his love, and then a tune that sounded a rallying call, like one looking for his lost love" (2.37, my emphasis). Philetas thereupon gives his pipes to Daphnis, who "present[s] his little one[s] as an offering to Pan" (trans. Turner). This scene seems the perfect midpoint of *Daphnis and Chloe*). The transformation of Pan's savage force into the cultural harmonies of the herdsmen's world here becomes the rite of passage by which the young lovers dance their way into adult sexuality. The pastoral set piece thus becomes a crucial episode in the romance plot.

But the episode proves not to work this way. The assumption that underlies our amusement at Daphnis and Chloe's innocence—that there is a ready and easy way to lovemaking—is belied by the book's representation of adult sexuality. As John J. Winkler has argued, in a powerful "reading against the grain," violence is at the heart of the "erotic protocols" of Daphnis and Chloe's world.[15] This has already been apparent in Dorcon's attempted rape and it is strongly suggested by the features of the Methymnean episode—not only the abduction of Chloe and the fearsome intervention of Pan, but the fact that the raiders originally came to the countryside on a hunting expedition. Philetas's narration of Eros at play in his garden gives a benign cast and the promise of a harmonious outcome to the type of episode in which a protected locale is invaded. But Winkler would say of Philetas's mythologizing what he says when Daphnis takes up the old herdsman's pipes and completes the circle of instruction—that in such episodes, "Longus . . . notices the continuity from generation to generation of the cultural forms which enshrine erotic violence and at the same time conceal it."[16]

Longus's consciousness of these tensions is apparent in his description (4.2–3) of another symbolic garden, that of Dionysophantes, the Mytilenean aristocrat who owns the country estate of which Lamon is caretaker and who proves to be Daphnis's father. This garden, a marvel of cultivation, provides fruits and flowers of all seasons and unites the works of art and nature. In its midst is a temple to Dionysus, decorated with paintings of subjects related to the god. Each of these paintings "recalls death, mutilation, or loss of self," so that, as Winkler puts it, "the garden is a microcosm of the pastoral world— protected, fertile, flowering, with a structure of recollected and institutionalized violence in the center."[17] This garden, unlike Philetas's, is victimized by an intruder who cannot, like the Eros he exemplifies, be sublimated into cultural use. A cowherd named Lampis, who seeks Chloe's hand in marriage, is aware that when Dionysophantes comes to visit his garden (the event that has prompted the description of it), Lamon the gardener will obtain his consent to

15. "The Education of Chloe: Hidden Injuries of Sex," in *The Constraints of Desire: The Anthropology of Sex and Gender in Ancient Greece* (New York & London: Routledge, 1990), 101–26.

16. Winkler, 120.

17. Winkler, 123. Pandiri, making a different emphasis, says that the point is precisely that we are to be aware how much violence is kept at bay by the accomplishments of art (139, n. 25).

the marriage of Daphnis and Chloe. In order to arouse Dionysophantes's displeasure at those in charge of the garden, Lampis breaks in at night and spoils the flowers: "he dug some up, broke others off, and trampled the rest down like a pig" (4.7).

If such invasions and violations are the ways of adult sexuality, how can a pastoral process lead Daphnis and Chloe to learn, as the last words of the book put it, that "what they had done in the woods had been nothing but shepherds' games" (4.40)? The answer, briefly, is that it cannot. The image of Lampis's fouling the garden can appear in the mouth of Virgil's Corydon, because it expresses the rustic's hapless dismay at the power that has victimized him:

> *heu heu, quid volui misero mihi? floribus Austrum*
> *perditus et liquidis immisi fontibus apros.*
>
> (Ecl. 2.58–59)
>
> How could I, desperate wretch, want to unleash
> Tempests on flowers and boars on crystal springs?

Longus's image, which perhaps recalls these lines, is coolly impersonal, as if to acknowledge the way things are. Hence it is not surprising that the urbane artist draws on other than pastoral elements in his repertoire, in order to complete the lovers' education. The crucial instructor proves to be not Philetas, but a young townswoman named Lycaenion, on the scene not as a native, but because she is married to an old farmer, who is physically past his prime. She seeks Daphnis as a lover and, having overheard one of his scenes of sexual frustration with Chloe, schemes to satisfy herself by offering the lesson he needs. Though her name means "little wolf" and she is thus the female counterpart of Dorcon, Lycaenion does not principally derive from the fictions of pastoral. She is an adaptation of a figure in New Comedy—"the party girl or hetaira, who—especially in Menander—is often a kind of heroine. . . . Wolf was slang for prostitute; the diminutive suffix [in her name] is frequent in the names of professional sweethearts. As often in comedy, she helps a boy-girl pair out of difficulties."[18]

All the commentators agree that Lycaenion is sympathetically presented; the tone of the scene in which she guides Daphnis "on the road he had been searching for" (3.18) is thus continuous with the witty pastoralism of Books 1 and 2. But as an instructor in love, she quite undoes the pastoral presence of Philetas, whose cultural centrality—given the allusiveness of his name (above, n. 8), the character of his discourse, and his powers of song—has as much claim on the sophisticated reader as on his young auditors in the story. This is most evident in the last of the lies with which she carries out her scheme. The first

18. McCulloh, 58.

two are (to her husband) that she must help a neighbor in childbirth and (to Daphnis) that she needs help in finding a goose that has been snatched away by an eagle. When she gets Daphnis in the woods, she persuades him to accept her lesson in love by saying that the Nymphs had appeared to her in a dream and told her to assist him in his plight. None of these falsehoods reflects badly on Lycaenion as a person, but the last registers a decisive shift in the romance. The readers who suspend their disbelief, as well as the rustics in the story, have a stake in crediting the various appearances and actions of the minor deities who look out for Daphnis and Chloe, for they express our solicitude for their innocence and well-being. When Lycaenion achieves her—and the author's— ends by making a frank lie out of what had earlier been an enabling fiction (e.g. 1.7, where the Nymphs appear in dreams to Lamon and Dryas, and 2.23, where they appear to Daphnis), the terms of our relation to Daphnis and Chloe have to change.

It is no surprise, then, that *Daphnis and Chloe*'s character as a narration changes after the Lycaenion episode. A rapid conclusion seems in the offing: "When the lesson in lovemaking was over, Daphnis still had a shepherd's un- derstanding and was eager to run to Chloe and do what he'd been taught right away, as if frightened that he would forget it if he waited" (3.19). But Lycaenion checks him by warning him that "if Chloe has this sort of wrestling match with you, she will cry out and weep and will lie there, bleeding heavily." This mo- ment is, for Winkler, the heart of the cultural dilemma of *Daphnis and Chloe*— that female pain is thought to be inseparable from the fulfillment of male desire. The formal manifestation of this dilemma is that this moment of revelation pretty much brings to a halt the love plot as it has so far developed.[19] The narrative path to the final bedding of the pair is a double one, and neither much involves pastoral representations. On one side, that of sexuality, the denoument comes from a quite new complication. The aristocratic party that comes to the country in Book 4 includes a homosexual parasite named Gnathon (= "jaws" or "full mouth"), whom Longus describes as "nothing but a mouth and a stomach and what lies underneath the stomach" (4.11) and who is another figure from New Comedy. Repulsive as he might seem to be, it is Gnathon who assumes the role of instructor in love in Book 4. He does not succeed in persuading Daphnis to play the role of a she-goat (4.12), but Longus does give him a pretty little speech to his master about the gods humbling themselves for love (4.17)—a topos that the disguised Florizel will rehearse to Perdita (*Winter's Tale*

---

19. Cf. 3.24: "One day, they lay down together naked, covering themselves with a single goatskin; and Chloe would easily have become a woman if the thought of the blood had not disturbed Daphnis. He was understandably frightened that one day he might not be able to control himself, and so he did not allow Chloe to undress often. Chloe was amazed at this, but she was ashamed to ask the reason."

4.4.25–30). Along with this new plot strand, social impediments to the lovers' union become evident, now that they are no longer children. Neither Lamon nor Dryas wants his foster-child to go cheap in a marriage arrangement (each, unknown to the other, holds the same trump card, the knowledge of the child's wealthy parentage). Daphnis wins Dryas's consent to the marriage only when he discovers a large sum of money—a bonus, in the increasingly complicated plot, from the Methymnean episode. But final permission for the marriage must await the master's visit in Book 4, which is much occupied with entanglements and coincidences (some occurring in the city of Mytilene) that reveal Daphnis and Chloe's true parentage.

Pastoralism does not disappear from the last two books, but such episodes as occur do not constitute or sustain narrative motives. The most interesting episode immediately follows Lycaenion's instruction and warning. Daphnis and Chloe are in the fields eating and kissing (the limit of what the frightened Daphnis has decided to seek from Chloe). A fishing boat passes in their sight, and they hear both the chanty sung by the oarsmen and its echo, which the contours of the land make sound with perfect clarity. "Daphnis knew what was going on and gave his attention only to the sea. . . . But for Chloe this was her first experience of what is called an echo" (3.22). This formulation would have been appropriate—and is manifestly displaced from—the expected scene of love-making. Inhibited from teaching Chloe what he has learned, Daphnis becomes another narrator and purveyor of cultural knowledge. This is not the first time he has assumed this role. In Book 1, he tells the story which explains to Chloe the song of the wood dove (*phatta*). She was a young cowherd, with a beautiful voice, who asked the gods to turn her to a bird when a neighboring cowherd, whose voice was "stronger like a man's but still sweet like a boy's," lured away her best cows with his singing (1.27). This story directly suggests Daphnis and Chloe's situation as lovely fellow herders, and in its delicacy and pathos, particularly in the way it balances youthful likeness and sexual difference and addresses the boy's dominance of the girl, seems to move their incipient love along. The story of Echo has a quite different relation to the narrative. Its occasion does not express, but rather strongly displaces, the lovers' sexual situation. Hence the paragraph devoted to the fishermen and their echoing song, though a fine set piece in itself, feels like an arbitrary intervention in the narrative.

What the fishermen's song represses returns in the inset story of Echo. She is said to have been the daughter of a Nymph and a mortal father, who was raised by the Nymphs and educated by the Muses. This double upbringing makes her wonderfully skilled in music and leads her to shun all men. Her artistry and resolute virginity enrage Pan, who avenges himself by maddening the local herdsmen until, "like dogs or wolves, they tore her apart and scattered her limbs [*melē*]—which were still singing—over the whole earth" (3.23). This Dionysiac account of the origins of echo occurs uniquely in *Daphnis and Chloe*. The sharp disparity between its violence and the benign occasion of its telling is replicated in its bearing on the narrative. First, unlike the somewhat similar story of Syrinx, it does not suggest any pleasurable transformation of brute passion. Sexuality here remains unalterably savage; its needs and urgings are neither modified nor manifested in Echo's sounds, which are wholly identified, by the telling pun *melē* (= both "limbs" and "songs"), with her scattered limbs. Similarly, the conclusion of Daphnis's tale suggests his own impasse. He says that the earth now echoes Pan himself, when he plays on his pipes, and that the god chases the sound all over the mountain. It may be true, as Chalk says, that "throughout the book [Daphnis] acts the part of Pan the musical shepherd,"[20] but neither way in which Daphnis could identify himself with Pan here will lead his love to its completion. He cannot and will not emulate the god in his animal sexuality, and Pan's chastened pursuit of echoes, the reiteration of which delights Chloe, leads only to the dead end of the kisses with which she rewards his tale.

We seem to have uncovered a central contradiction in pastoral narration. Desire can either be represented in pastoral modes—in which what is unruly and unsatisfied is stabilized by the pleasures of utterance and performance—or it (as well as other forms of self-seeking) can give rise to statements and acts that effect change and that thus generate a normal plot, with its entanglements, rhythms, and resolutions. But not, apparently, both. The most recent translator of *Daphnis and Chloe* speaks of the "rather paradoxical implications" of "Longus's decision to make his novel a pastoral one": "What is characteristic of the Greek novel in general is the forward thrust of its narrative movement. . . . What is typical of pastoral poetry, on the other hand, is its intensely static quality."[21] In a quite different critical mode, the pastoral thematics of Renato Poggioli, we are told that "the pastoral insists on the preliminaries of love rather than on its final consummation" and that "the pastoral does not like happy endings as such precisely because it does not like happiness to end."[22] If all this is so, what account do we give of the pastoralism of *Daphnis and Chloe?* On the one hand, it seems to display the contradiction of pastoral narration by coming apart in the middle of Book 3, after Lycaenion's instruction. At the same time, its pastoralism is at the heart of its literary distinction and appeal. As one of its more unflappable interpreters says, "It may be true [in the words of the Prologue]

---

20. Chalk, 45.

21. Gill, in Reardon, 286.

22. *The Oaten Flute: Essays on Pastoral Poetry and the Pastoral Ideal* (Cambridge: Harvard University Press), 54, 56.

that 'no one has ever escaped Love altogether, and no one ever will,' but on the evidence of this novel no one would wish to."[23] This seems a natural response to *Daphnis and Chloe,* and yet it is really quite astonishing. The "evidence" of the book includes Pan's rutting rages, Gnathon's repulsive attempts to have his way with Daphnis, and the animal antics of the mature young herdsmen, Dorcon and Lampis. The males who are at peace with love are old men past their prime. As for women, might they not reasonably avoid the victimization that the men take for granted and that is mythologized in the stories about Pan? It is Daphnis and Chloe in their unshakeable innocence who save love for the normal—i.e., as Winkler reminds us, the culturally accepted—adult world. There is, it seems to me, no particular value attributed to their growing up—quite the reverse— nor is value reposed in the sophisticated sensibility as it is represented by Dionysophantes and the other Mytilenean visitors who make the plot work out. Even though the romance as a whole cannot sustain the pastoralism of the first two and a half books, it is this that makes it survive as a classic.

II

In exploring the relation between pastoral and narrative, we have treated *Daphnis and Chloe* as, in effect, a sequence of prose eclogues, in which literary performance absorbs and stabilizes the characters' erotic energies and, with them, the dynamics of plot. But the book's pastoralism involves not only the performance of its set pieces, but also the relationship it establishes between the urbane reader and the naive hero and heroine. We now turn our attention to the way Daphnis and Chloe and their various actions are represented. Here is the paragraph that introduces us to them as goatherd and shepherdess:

> It was the beginning of spring, and all the flowers were in bloom, in the woods, in the meadows, and on the hills. Now there was the hum of bees, the sound of sweet-singing birds, the skipping of newborn lambs. The lambs skipped on the hills; the bees hummed in the meadows; the birds filled the copses with the enchantment of their song. Everything was possessed by the beauty of spring; and Daphnis and Chloe, impressionable young creatures that they were, imitated what they heard and saw. They heard the birds singing, and they sang; they saw the lambs skipping, and they leapt about nimbly; they copied the bees and gathered flowers. They scattered some of the flowers in the folds of their clothes; and they used the rest to weave little garlands, as offerings to the Nymphs. (1.9)

23. R. L. Hunter, *A Study of "Daphnis and Chloe"* (Cambridge: Cambridge University Press, 1983), 42.

It is easy to feel the charm of this, but in what does it consist? Daphnis and Chloe's naive imitation of the sights and sounds about them is the most obvious element, but what secures our attention to them is the art of the opening sentences. Gill's translation accurately conveys the disposition of the various elements (woods, meadows, hills; bees, lambs, birds; humming, skipping, singing) but cannot emulate the economy of the Greek and sacrifices some of its rhythmical vibrancy. Still, we are sufficiently acculturated to such representations that we can feel the force of the climactic detail, the "enchantment," of the birds' singing. (The verb here, *katēdon*, "charmed, sang a spell," is a compound of *aeidō*, "sing.") This word makes explicit the way the prose has engaged us, and a repetition of the note it sounds, in the statement that the season "possesses" all things, ushers in Daphnis and Chloe. We therefore apprehend their actions less in what the Romantics conceived to be the situation of adults contemplating children—between whom a shadow has fallen or a gulf is fixed—than as prior participants in mimetic pleasures, of which these innocents permit us to see and acknowledge the foundations. The account of Daphnis and Chloe makes this explicit. It does not remain where it begins, at a kind of still point of mimetic simplicity ("hearing the birds singing, they sang"), but builds more complex clausulae and actions until the youths go beyond the pattern of imitation and weave their garlands as the narrator weaves his prose.

Longus's writing, though sophisticated, is not separate from or at odds with, but rather a means of access to, Daphnis and Chloe's innocence—which therefore appears to us not as a lack (what they don't know) but as a valuable freshness of experience and apprehension. Chloe's first love deed is a famous bit of naiveté. Daphnis has fallen into a pit dug for a marauding wolf, and since no rope can be found to haul him out, she unwinds her breast band and uses that. This carries no erotic charge—neither Daphnis nor the narrator nor even Dorcon, who is present, pauses over it. But eros begins as a consequence of this event. The muddied Daphnis goes to wash in the Nymphs' spring, and Chloe, gazing at him, thinks he is beautiful: "as he had never seemed beautiful to her before, she thought that this beauty must be the result of washing" (1.13, Turner). Thus begins a series of metonymies on which are founded much of the humor of *Daphnis and Chloe* and also much of its mythopoetic force. Metonymic connections derive from contiguity—unlike metaphor, which connects objects or phenomena by perceived likenesses, or synecdoche, which claims an inherent relation of part to whole. Hence the joke in Chloe's thinking that bathing or music (when she sees him playing his pipes the next day) makes Daphnis beautiful: the novice lover takes the cause for the effect and mystifies what is contingent. Similarly Daphnis, when his turn comes, puzzles over the wretchedness he feels (1.18) by objectifying the apparent properties of the kiss with which Chloe rewarded his getting the better of Dorcon in their boasting contest. Metonymy is a trope we associate with prose narrative and particularly with the realistic novel. But it is also appropriate to pastoral, in which, as Rosenmeyer has argued, the ethos of cultivated simplicity produces a rhetoric of discretely apprehended pleasures. The force of metonymy in Longus's narrative can be felt in the pithy formulation with which he sums up the lovers' innocence and their suffering: "They felt pleasure at seeing each other and pain at leaving each other. They wanted something, but they didn't know what they wanted. The one thing they knew was that he had been destroyed by a kiss and she by a bath" (1.22).

More than once we are told that a character does or does not know "what love means" (literally, the deeds or actions of love, *ta erōtos erga*). The question of *Daphnis and Chloe*—put one way it is the problem of its prurience, in another way the problem of its pastoralism—is what the knowing reader makes of the acts and experiences of its hero and heroine. Although we know what Daphnis and Chloe "really" want, Longus's writing ensures that we do not disallow what they themselves know—the power they attribute to objects and contingent events. One could hardly read a work of fiction without crediting such details, and the power of the contingent is here an explicit issue. When Daphnis takes his fatal bath, Chloe washes his back: "As she did so, his flesh yielded so gently to her touch that she surreptitiously felt her own several times to see if his was more delicate than hers" (1.13). McCulloh worries that this is lubricious, perhaps because he imagines that "Chloe's fingers sink luxuriously into Daphne's flesh."[24] On the contrary, what seems remarkable here is the sense of fresh discovery of another—hence the inception of desire—and consequently of one's self. The naive immediacy, both of touching and self-regard ("Is it him? Is it me?"), captures an erotic moment that prevents any riper imaginings. The importance of respecting Chloe's naiveté emerges when she seeks to understand her experience in terms of the contingent and the contiguous—what she touches and what she perceives around her:

> How many times I've been scratched by brambles, and I've not wept! How many times I've been stung by bees, and I've not cried out! But the thing that's stinging my heart now is sharper than all those things. Daphnis is beautiful—but then so are the flowers. His pipes make a beautiful sound—but then so do the nightingales. And yet I care nothing for those things. I wish I were his pipes, so he could breathe into me. I wish I were his goat, so I could be led to graze by him. (1.14)

The commentators remind us that these are the topoi of love poetry, but the point, it seems to me, is not a narrowly literary awareness. On the contrary, our engagement with incipient self-consciousness undoes its fixed and devel-

24. McCulloh, 69.

oped forms. Chloe's sweet questionings, to use Stevens's phrase, lead us back to a foundational point of experience, in which sensory pleasures and pains and sensual desire seem exchangeable with or versions of each other. Hence rather than prompting a literary awareness that protects or distances us, Chloe's soliloquy seems to return us to the springs of love poetry—what it is that has made us so represent desire to ourselves.

As this passage suggests, Longus's mode of pastoral narration merges with and affects his "prosing" certain conventions of pastoral poems. Here is Dorcon wooing Chloe:

> First of all, he brought presents for them both: for Daphnis, a cowherd's Pan-pipe, the nine reeds fastened together with bronze instead of wax; for Chloe, a bacchant's fawnskin, whose colors looked as if they'd been painted on. From then on they regarded him as their friend, but gradually he stopped paying attention to Daphnis, while every day he brought Chloe a soft cheese, a garland of flowers, or a ripe apple. One day, he brought her a newly born calf, a wooden cup with ivy tendrils carved on it and inlaid with gold, and some chicks of mountain birds. Having had no experience of the methods employed by lovers, she took the presents with pleasure; indeed, her pleasure was greater because she now had something that she could give to Daphnis. (1.15, Gill, with details from Turner)

These gifts resemble, and some are identical with, what Theocritus's Polyphemus offered Galatea (Idyll 11) and Virgil's Corydon offered Alexis (Eclogue 2). This paragraph of narration is thus another authorial set piece, directly appealing to the literary awareness that partly constitutes the reader's sophistication. But as much could be said were such an inventory to appear in an eclogue or lyric—as it does, for example, in Marvell's "Damon the Mower." The particular question that concerns us is what difference it makes to have it appear as an incident in prose fiction. One obvious difference is that these items and their social uses become part of a consistently represented world. Garlands and nestlings have a connection with Daphnis and Chloe's springtime pleasures; pipes bound in bronze come from the adult world, conscious of what things are worth, as opposed to the pipes bound with wax, making which was one of Daphnis's "pastoral and childish toys" (1.10). None of this represents a sharp break with Theocritean or Virgilian bucolic. Ancient pastoral is a reduction of epic, not a branch of lyric: the gifts of rustic lovers, like other objects represented in bucolic poems, suggest a known and inhabited world.

But *Daphnis and Chloe* makes evident a further consequence of adapting a poetic convention to prose fiction. The world of which it becomes part is a social world, populated by various characters who variously engage us. Hence our relation to the rustic lover and his gifts has a different character from either our sophisticated amusement at Polyphemus or our lyric engagement with Corydon.[25] The most revealing detail is the cup inlaid with gold. The Greek phrase is *kissubion diachruson,* and the translations show the complexities of interpretation. Hadas's "gilt ivy cup" is unpacked by Turner in the direction of plainness, "a wooden bowl decorated with gold," and by Gill in the direction of elaboration, "a wooden cup with ivy tendrils carved on it and inlaid with gold." Turner represents it simply as one among several objects available to Dorcon; Gill's version (which might on the face of it seem unwarranted) has in mind the cup's literary provenance. The word *kissubion* is used of and recalls the decorated cup which appears, in Theocritus's Idyll 1, as the bucolic reduction of the shields of Achilles and Hercules. As Halperin has shown, in a splendid piece of philologico-literary interpretation,[26] Theocritus was dignifying, in his new mode of poetry, an object that in Homer is coarse and marginal, belonging only to Polyphemus (*Od.* 9.346) and Eumaeus the swineherd (*Od.* 14.78, 16.52). One way he did so was to change the literary rationale of the word (which seems related to *kissos,* ivy) from "an object [of coarse associations] made of ivy wood" to what it explicitly is in Idyll 1—an object decorated with an ivy pattern (hence Gill's translation). The question is: what is a *kissubion* doing here? With respect to Dorcon alone, the literary associations, like the gold inlay, bring out the pretentiousness of his gifts; if he were a Theocritean speaker, he might be the anonymous goatherd of Idyll 3, who bathetically complains to his love in a song laced with Homeric locutions. On the other hand, taking the cup purely as an object in a world leads Halperin to say that Longus here "prettifies the life of the countryside by adorning its humble artifacts with sophisticated embellishments—belts of straw and ivy buds with coral clasps and amber studs."[27] Halperin shrewdly appeals to the courtly refinement of the lyric speaker whom Marlowe distilled from Polyphemus and Corydon. But in the context of Longus's narration, our sophisticated enjoyment finds another possible representative than the precious lyricist or the amused viewer (as one might imagine Dionysophantes to be) of the rustic putting on airs. As the paragraph concludes, our interest in the inventory of gifts becomes associated with Chloe's artless pleasure in them. The impulse to evaluate or distance ourselves dissolves in the feeling that all these good things can be readily and innocently apprehended and exchanged: perhaps the original and perhaps the best form of our sensory and literary pleasures, but in any case a liberating way in which to experience them. I do not mean to pin down the literary force of Dorcon's gifts to Chloe's take on them. Marvell sufficiently reminds readers of English

25. Cf. Rosenmeyer, 60–62, for a fine discussion of the differences between the two poems.

26. David M. Halperin, *Before Pastoral: Theocritus and the Ancient Tradition of Bucolic Poetry* (New Haven: Yale University Press, 1983), 167–74.

27. Halperin, 174.

how teasingly elusive pastoral simplicities can be, and the suggestions of Longus's *kissubion* seem to me a fine instance of what McCulloh calls his "Mozartian ambivalence."[28] What is certain, I think, is that prose fiction by its nature—its entailing fuller situations and the presence of different characters—provides the writer with new possibilities of pastoral realization.

To say it again, what is different here is not wholly new to pastoral. Most idylls and eclogues have more than one bucolic speaker (though Idyll 11 and Eclogue 2 are essentially monodies), and the wooing situation is a staple of Theocritus's and Virgil's implied worlds. But in *Daphnis and Chloe* we see what happens when the narrative potentialities of bucolic are fulfilled. These narrative realizations remain distinctly pastoral. The wooing triangle, which in another mode could produce conflict or tangled feelings, is reduced to the giving of gifts, and the main expression of feeling, Chloe's, captivates precisely because it is invested in these objects. Furthermore, this scene exemplifies (though it has a comfortable relation to) the contradiction between pastoral representations and "normal" narrative motives and energies. The paragraph we have discussed is introduced by the statement that Dorcon, who had fallen in love with Chloe when he helped her pull Daphnis out of the wolf-pit (maybe he did notice her loosening her breastband), was "determined to have his way either by giving presents or by using force" (1.15). This makes the gifts merely instrumental; since Dorcon looks only to what they will do for him, one does not attribute to him either Polyphemus's naive satisfaction in what his gifts show him to be or Corydon's extraordinary "sentimental" investment in his offerings, which become the terrain on which the rustic's and the poet's sensibilities meet.[29] Here the valuing of the gifts for themselves resides entirely in Chloe, who can take pleasure in them because she "had no experience of the methods employed by lovers." This formulation brings us close to the center of the plot. "Inexperienced" (*apeiros*) speaks for itself, and the word Turner well translates as "methods" (vs. Gill's "wiles") is *technē*, the key term in the book for the action that Daphnis and Chloe are trying to learn ("techniques of love," as we now say).[30]

Knowledge of *technē* is precisely what writer and reader have: it is the term the narrator uses when he says the painting he seeks to emulate combines great artistic skill with a romantic subject. It is such artistic knowledge that produces,

---

28. McCulloh, 41.

29. See especially Ecl. 2.45–55, a passage much imitated by Renaissance poets, and not only in erotic poems. One line (*et vos, o lauri, carpam et te, proxima myrte*) provided the opening of *Lycidas*.

30. Daphnis begs Lycaenion to teach him "the skill [*technēn*] that would make him able to do what he wanted to Chloe" (3.18). Cf. the description of the "simple, unsophisticated kiss" (*adidakton kai atechnon*) with which Chloe rewards Daphnis's victory over Dorcon in the self-praising contest (1.17).

insofar as the book's pastoralism is concerned, the transformations of desire that culminate in and center on the figure of Philetas (who had refused to use Daphnis's pipe as too small for his great art [*megalēn technēn*]). But Longus's mode of narration also leads us to associate ourselves with Chloe's artless inexperience, and it is this side of *Daphnis and Chloe* which makes it a pastoral narrative, a mode of pastoral distinct from the idylls and eclogues in which Philetas would feel at home. The larger purposes of the tale are announced at the climax of Daphnis and Chloe's adventures, when the voice of Pan terrorizes the Methymnaean abductors: "Most unholy and impious of men, what madness has driven you to act so recklessly? You've filled the countryside I love with war; you've driven off herds of cows, goats, and sheep that are under my care; you've dragged from the altars a girl whom Love has chosen to make a story [*muthos*] about" (2.27). *Muthos* here lies somewhere between English "story" and "myth"—more significant than the former, less grand and "world-historical" than the latter.[31] *Muthos* and *muthologeō* (tell a *muthos*) are used of the three etiological tales in *Daphnis and Chloe*. There is an implicit differentiation, not only from *logos* (historic truth, a Platonic distinction which is evoked, with unclear force, at 2.7),[32] but also, it would seem, from *historia*, which is the word used of the painting that the narrator first sees and that suggests an account that is written (or, as here, otherwise inscribed) and based on learned inquiry. A *muthos*, by contrast, suggests a significant tale that would be handed down orally among a community (the first meanings of the word, as in Homer, are "word" and "speech").[33]

How does the author who had been "seized by a yearning to depict the picture in words" come to narrate a *muthos*, rather than a *historia?* The writer's fictive self-representation as an unlettered singer, which is at the heart of the bucolic tradition, makes an appearance in *Daphnis and Chloe*, when Philetas becomes the instructor in love, but is not otherwise involved in the production of the tale. But the conscious simplicities of Longus's style are suggestively like the mode of narration indirectly attributed to Chloe, when she tells Daphnis how she escaped the Methymnaeans: "She recounted everything: the ivy on the goats, the howling of the sheep, the pine that grew on her head, the fire on

31. Turner's translation (which I have substituted in Gill's) catches the emphasis better than Gill's own ("a girl whom Love wants to make the subject of a story"). There is something to be said, at this moment, for Hadas's more old-fashioned ways: "a maiden of whom Eros wishes to fashion a tale of love."

32. Hunter, 47, 114, on the Platonic distinction; McCulloh on 2.7: "it is hard to catch the precise point of the contrast here" (98).

33. Cf. McCulloh, 26, on the "subsurface tradition of the oral tale" in *D&C*, and Hunter, 17, on the way the names of the foster-parents "deepen the sense that we are reading a local *muthos* or aetiological tale." The story of the wood dove is called *ta thruloumena*, from the word for "chatter" or "babble." Gill translates, "a story that had often been told" (Turner: "that was on everyone's lips").

land, the noise at sea, the two kinds of piping—the warlike and the peaceful—the night of terror, and how although she did not know her way home, music pointed the way."[34] The hallmark of this style is enumeration—events identified by noun-phrases and connected paratactically. This degree-zero of pastoral narration—which bears out, in narrative contexts, Rosenmeyer's emphasis on the inventory in pastoral lyric—is neatly summed up in "L'Allegro":

> And every shepherd tells his tale
> Under the hawthorn in the dale.
> (67–68)

Narration merges with enumeration here, not only because of the double meaning of "tells" and "tale" ("tally" and "story"), but also because the chiming of the noun with the verb makes us apprehend the double sense with a simplicity that is prior to the pointedness of a pun.

Longus does not emulate a mode of sheer enumeration (that experiment in recounting has been left for the modernism of our own times), but the sense of attending to individual items and their ready exchangeability, which we have already noted in Chloe's pleasure at Dorcon's gifts, is at the heart of his mythologizing the two innocent lovers. Pastoral metonymies continue to characterize their experience when summer arrives and expresses the greater warmth they begin to feel. Daphnis, confused by the heat, "kept plunging into rivers," while Chloe turns to cheese-making, a rather troublesome task. "But then she washed her face, put on a garland of pine twigs, wrapped her fawnskin around herself, and, filling a bucket with wine and milk, she shared a drink with Daphnis" (1.23). This description produces a rather weird wooing scene, a sort of metonymic farce. It begins unsurprisingly:

> When midday came, their eyes were captivated. Chloe, seeing Daphnis naked, was lost in gazing at his beauty and felt weak, unable to find fault with any part of him. Daphnis, seeing her in a fawnskin and garland of pine holding out the bucket, thought he was seeing one of the Nymphs from the cave. (1.24)

Such erotic wondering can be the basis of a familiar sort of mythologizing: it may suggest Petrarch and would not be foreign to Virgil's Corydon. But here is what it leads to in our hero and heroine:

> He snatched the pine garland from her head and put it on his own, after kissing it first. She put on his clothes when he was bathing and naked, and she too kissed them first. Sometimes they threw apples at each other, and tidied themselves up by combing each other's hair. She said his hair

---

34. 2.30, trans. Gill, except that I have substituted Hadas's more accurate "recounted" for *katelexe*, which Gill and Turner render "told."

was like myrtle berries, because it was dark; he said her face was like an apple, because it was pink and white. He taught her how to play the pipes too; and when she started to blow, he snatched the pipes and ran his lips along the reeds. He gave the impression of correcting Chloe's mistakes, but really it gave him an excuse for kissing her by means of the pipes.

The difference between these kisses and the kiss which has already set Daphnis aflame (the kind of kiss against which Eros warns Philetas) repeats the difference between Dorcon's and Chloe's sense of his love gifts and anticipates the large division in *Daphnis and Chloe* between innocent love and adult sexuality. Compare the different irony, tinged with pathos, of Ovid's account of Phoebus embracing the transformed Daphne:

> *Hanc quoque Phoebus amat positaque in stipite dextra*
> *sentit adhuc trepidare novo sub cortice pectus*
> *conplexusque suis ramos ut membra lacertis*
> *oscula dat ligno; refugit tamen oscula lignum.*

> But even now in this new form Apollo loved her; and placing his hand upon the trunk, he felt the heart still fluttering beneath the bark. He embraced the branches as if human limbs, and pressed his lips upon the wood. But even the wood shrank from his kisses.[35]

These kisses are in one way as comic as Daphnis and Chloe's, but they are shot through with the frustration neatly represented by the rhythm and word order of *oscula dat ligno*. The de-eroticized kisses of Daphnis and Chloe, absurd as they are, are charming because they are pure gestures of valued contact. They express one ideal way of noticing and being pleased by the properties of what we love.

The larger uses of these metonymies begins to emerge a few paragraphs later, when Daphnis tells Chloe the story of the wood-dove:

> There was a young girl, young girl, as beautiful as you are; and she had a herd, like you, keeping many cows in a wood. She was a beautiful singer too, and her cows enjoyed her singing. She managed her herd without hitting them with a stick or prodding them with a goad; sitting under a pine and garlanded with pine, she sang the story of Pan and Pitys. (1.27)

Pitys was a nymph who was changed to a pine tree (Gr. *pitys*) because of Pan's aggressive love; her story resembles those of Syrinx and Echo. The pine was sacred to Pan, but this myth is very sparsely documented before Longus, who

---

35. *Metamorphoses*, ed. and trans. Frank Justus Miller, 3d ed. (revised by G. P. Goold), 2 vols. (Cambridge: Harvard University Press, Loeb Classical Library), 1.553–56.

makes more of it than any previous writer.[36] When the cowherdess of Daphnis's tale sings of Pan and Pitys, she not only anticipates her own unhappy transformation but already suggests, even in this rather sweet tale, that sexual difference has fearsome consequences. But beyond these suggestions, the mention of Pitys marks the way Chloe and her pine garland are being differently mythologized. If the pine garland, though dear to Daphnis, does not seem to be unusually important, that is part of the point: the pastoral alternative to erotic mythologizing, with its magnification of sexual fulfillment and its displacement onto surrogate objects, is the even enumeration and exchange of each and every item that pleases. (This might indicate the difference between a pastoral narration and "soft porn.") As the use of the two pine-nymphs in Book 2 shows, Chloe becomes an alternative to Pitys.

Early in Book 2, when Philetas speaks of his own youthful love woes, Pitys is associated with the pains of love and with better known myths of Pan: "I called on Pan to help me, since he himself had been in love with Pitys. I praised Echo for calling after me the name of Amaryllis" (2.7). Before Pitys reappears, at the end of Book 2 (where, we recall, the tale of Syrinx is prominent) the pine figures importantly in the story of the Methymnean raid. The obvious moment to single out is Chloe's appearing "with a garland of pine on her head" when Pan terrorizes her abductors (2.26). But this wondrous sight emerges from and returns to references to the pine as it figures in Daphnis and Chloe's ordinary world. Instructed by the Nymphs in a dream, Daphnis goes to the pine tree to honor Pan and seek his help after Chloe's abduction (2.23–4); when she returns, their thank-offering is the sacrifice of a he-goat, crowned with a pine garland, at the pine tree— "a pastoral (*poimenikon*) offering," as Longus says, "to a pastoral god" (2.31). These references to the pine, which single out Chloe by associating her with a valued object, are significant but not erotically charged. However much erotic transformation seems to lie in store for her, it is not the means in Book 2 by which Pan or the narrator make her the object of our attention.

The power of naive pastoral metonymies produces the final episode of Book 2, which answers, on Chloe's behalf, the old men's mythologizing of Pan and his pipes. After Daphnis's Pan-dance, when he takes up the bigger pipes (at which point Chloe, enacting the myth, "disappeared into the wood, as though into the marsh"), he and Chloe return to the status quo before the Methymnean raid. They take their flocks out in the morning and act according to Philetas's instructions: "They saluted first the Nymphs and then Pan, and then sat under

---

36. The story is not in Ovid. The myth is mentioned before Longus only by Theocritus (*Fistula*.4– 5) and Propertius (1.18.20)—brief circumlocutions, neither of which names the nymph—and Lucian, *Dialogues of the Gods*, "Pan and Hermes." See Philippe Borgeaud, *The Cult of Pan in Ancient Greece*, trans. Kathleen Atlass and James Redfield (Chicago: University of Chicago Press, 1988), 78.

the oak, playing the pipes. Then they kissed each other, embraced, lay down together, and—after doing nothing more—got up again" (2.38). Nevertheless, all this makes them warmer, and they start competing about who loves the other more. "Daphnis went to the pine and swore by Pan that he would never live alone, without Chloe" (2.39). Chloe swears the same by the Nymphs, but then she is troubled and asks for a second oath:

> "Daphnis," she said, "Pan is a romantic [*erōtikos*] god and an unreliable one. He fell in love with Pitys; he fell in love with Syrinx; he never stops pestering the Dryads and bothering the Nymphs that guard the flocks. If you fail to keep the oaths you swear by him, he'll fail to punish you, even if you go after more women than there are reeds in the pipes." (2.39)

What then should Daphnis swear by? The logic of our argument might suggest the pine itself, but as an object its value depends on the god with whom it is associated. What Chloe proposes, as the appropriate gods of shepherds and goatherds (*poimenōn kai aipolōn idious theous*, the final words of Book 2) are the sheep and goats themselves. Of all there is in Daphnis and Chloe's world, it is their animals—viewed not as symbols or sources of instruction (they come to grief in Book 3 trying to imitate the goats) but as companions—who are most continually associated with their love. Daphnis swears by them in a manner proper to a metonymic oath—by holding a she-goat with one hand and a he-goat with the other. Their actions in their world bring them to a point where they match and answer the usual pastoral mode, represented by Philetas and his old companions, of stabilizing eros by vocal sublimations.[37]

So far as *Daphnis and Chloe* goes, there is probably more to be said, or at least to be justified in argument. I would say that Book 4 shows that Longus is

---

37. I should make it clear that the naive metonymic mode of representation, though more directly associated with narration than the stabilizing utterances represented by Philetas, equally encounters the impasse, in the narrative, of the lovers' acquiring sexual knowledge. We earlier cited Longus's remark that Daphnis and Chloe "might really have done something" on the basis of Philetas's instructions (2.11), had the Methymnean raid not occurred. In fact, it seems clear that nothing of the sort would have happened. After Book 2, there is a further blocking episode at the beginning of Book 3, when winter keeps Daphnis and Chloe apart. This produces some wonderful moments of contact between the lovers, including a reprise of the metonymic kissing routine (3.8), but when spring returns, the lovers are back to the familiar difficulty (3.14, where they try to imitate the goats). It takes Lycaenion to show Daphnis what Philetas was getting at, and then the jig is up.

We can thus see that the Methymnean raid is not an interruption but a displacement of the sexual plot. The episodes it produces—Pan's rescue of Chloe, the celebrations of Pan, the myth of Pan and Syrinx, Philetas's pan-pastoral song, and Daphnis and Chloe's oaths—are the culmination of the pastoral poetizing of *Daphnis and Chloe*. The point of this poetizing, to say it again, is to transform erotic energies into stable ceremony and utterance. Our point here has been that the comic depiction of Daphnis and Chloe is pastoral in this sense and gives the lovers' innocence a mythic presence.

conscious of his pastoral mythologizing: on several occasions, Daphnis strikes the city visitors as wondrous, even god-like, and the story ends with Daphnis and Chloe deciding to have a country wedding and to spend their lives in the country, and with their establishing "an altar to Love the Shepherd" (4.39). At the same time, the way they have become spectacles for the city folk indicates that their full pastoral presence—what makes this the *muthos* that Longus-Eros intended—is the work of the first half of the book. I am also struck by the degree to which the account I have given of Books 1 and 2 emphasizes Chloe, whereas Daphnis is the central figure in Books 3 and 4; my very different kind of analysis thus suggests the pertinence of Winkler's critique, however one finally evaluates it. (He would, I imagine, have found my account too complicitous with Longus's pastoralism; for my part, I would say that his use of *Daphnis and Chloe* for what he calls an anthropological analysis makes him undervalue the way literary realizations help us live with cultural antinomies, not by mystification but by way of ironic acceptance and self-awareness.) What I want to bring out now are not specific interpretive issues, but what *Daphnis and Chloe* shows us about pastoral narration. A brilliant critic of the novel remarked, when I told him I was writing about the pastoral novel, that it seemed to him a contradiction in terms. Our analysis of *Daphnis and Chloe* has produced a similar thought about, in Arthur Heiserman's phrase, "the novel before the novel." Nevertheless, we have also seen that prose narrative realizes certain interests and potentialities of pastoral fictions and conventions, and that encountering them in such a narrative brings out distinctive aspects of the stake we have in them. Were we not aware of the motives of "normal" narrative and their relation to an idea of adult sexuality, neither the unshakeable innocence of Daphnis and Chloe nor its pastoral representation would have the mythopoetic presence that distinguishes their tale.

The point is to recognize the double aspect of pastoral narration. From its beginnings, pastoral was motivated by an attitude towards heroic poetry and established its literary presence with reference to it; similarly, pastoral narrations need not exclude and are often made more vital by the pressures of worldly realities and the full array of narrative motives and conventions. Lodge's *Rosalynde* is a "purer" pastoral than *Daphnis and Chloe*, because it keeps sex and self-seeking out of its pastoral locale; they are part of the world of wars and family conflicts from which Rosalynde and her companions flee, but they are not found in the Forest of Arden, or even allowed to enter it as foreign invasions. For this reason, *Rosalynde* is not only a less interesting book than *Daphnis and Chloe*, but a less interesting pastoral. The question to ask of a pastoral narration is whether its use of and engagement with narrative realities and motives enables pastoral realizations or whether—as can be argued of Cervantes' *Galatea* and is certainly the case with Sidney's *Arcadia*—they do them in. Given the inherent contradiction, we may be surprised to find that pastoral narrations (and, as we shall see in the next chapter, pastoral novels) succeed on their own terms. And when we consider the example of Cervantes, at the end of this chapter, we will see that the literary importance of pastoral narrations is not confined to instances of generic purity or modal uniformity.

III

The number and variety of pastoral narratives in European literature of the sixteenth century defy treatment in a book like this. Moreover, they emphatically show that Renaissance pastoral, far from being simply transnational, everywhere reflects cultural histories and interests that belong to specific languages and political-social entities. Sidney's *Arcadia*, which students of English literature naturally take to represent the pastoral romance, is utterly untypical of the genre.[38] It resists and ironizes the fundamental convention that true lovers are fittingly represented as shepherds, and it manifests its discomfort by assigning its pastoral narrations to eclogues which are formally segregated from the prose narrative and are fictionally explained as performances, for a court in exile, by local shepherds who have no part in the events of the romance proper. But if the variety and cultural specificity of Renaissance pastoral narratives prohibit a comprehensive treatment, an analysis of Jorge de Montemayor's *Diana* (1559), the first and best of them, will enable us to address certain general questions. How do pastoral representations—and specifically their original form in eclogues—give rise to narrations? What is the character of these pastoral narrations? How could pastoral usages be a narrative resource for writers in the Renaissance?

In speaking of *Daphnis and Chloe* as "pastoral narration," we mainly had in mind Longus's handling of the tale—on the one hand, matters of style (the rhetorical simplicity he cultivates throughout) or, on the other, the way individual parts are organized and connected (e.g., the emphasis on set pieces and the consequent dissipation of dramatic conflict and the energies of plot). But "pastoral narration" can also refer to tales told by pastoral characters. In *Daphnis and Chloe* such *mythoi* are modes of instruction and thus sustain the separation, which it is their cultural function to overcome, between innocence and experience. In sixteenth-century works, pastoral figures characteristically tell their own stories. Such narrators speak with authority in one sense (knowing what they tell, which is usually their own experience), but they do not have a privileged relation to their auditors. Just as in formal eclogues, auditors are peers

---

38. See Peter Lindenbaum, *Changing Landscapes: Anti-Pastoral Sentiment in the English Renaissance* (Athens: University of Georgia Press, 1986), 30–34, and especially the acute account of Sidney's "disabling the solutions of earlier pastoralists" in Judith Haber, *Pastoral and the Poetics of Self-Contradiction: Theocritus to Marvell* (Cambridge: Cambridge University Press, 1994), 62.

and speak responsively, so Renaissance pastoral narrations assume or establish a parity between speakers and listeners: "my story," in pastoral conditions, tends to become "our story."

Such pastoral narrations appear before the *Diana*, notably in Iacopo Sannazaro's *Arcadia* (1504), the work that more than any other brought classical pastoral into the vernacular literatures of Europe. The *Arcadia* has entered literary history as a "pastoral romance," because its poems—vernacular eclogues and Petrarchan lyrics (canzones and sestinas)—alternate with prose pieces. But it was first conceived as a development of the Virgilian eclogue book. Its ten poems (later expanded to twelve) were on occasion collected by themselves, and the prose pieces are themselves heavily imitative of ancient verse pastorals.[39] The *Arcadia* is thus a sort of double eclogue book, particularly in the first five sections, where the prose pieces and poems are about equal in length, and the prose describes settings, static situations, and bucolic rituals. (When fictional difference and change emerge, in its later sections, the *Arcadia* displays some of the contradictions of pastoral narration that we observed in *Daphnis and Chloe*.) Beyond its formal innovation, the *Arcadia* is a prologue to the *Diana* in its revaluation of the passionate shepherd. The serious lover, as we already have had occasion to observe, is not the norm in classical pastoral. Theocritus's Daphnis, obscurely defining himself by his love, bids farewell to the pastoral world before he dies. Virgil's Gallus, modelled on Daphnis and dying of love metaphorically, imagines himself out of Arcadia—and in some sense takes the poet with him, for his monologue leads to the conclusion of Virgil's Eclogue book. The figure of the lover can remain ambiguously pastoral in Renaissance writings, despite the cultural centrality of love as emotional experience and motive to poetry. In Sidney's *Arcadia*, the most striking Gallus figure— Philisides, the author's self-representation—appears mainly in the verse eclogues, i.e. apart from the prose narrative, and even there is problematically separated from his peers. But Sannazaro's *Arcadia* had already gone a long way towards assimilating the Petrarchan lover to the literary shepherd, and in the *Diana* the Gallus figure becomes the norm of pastoral experience and the foundation of pastoral romance.

In pastoral elegy, a dead and exceptional herdsman is commemorated by his fellows, so as to ensure the continuity of the diminished social group. The laments, recollections, and mimings which represent the dead herdsman are definitive, we have argued, of pastoral poetry, because they define what becomes of poetry and its power in the absence of a hero. Even more than Thyr-

---

39. Of the sixteen manuscripts listed in Iacobo Sannazaro, *Opere Volgari*, ed. Alfredo Mauro (Bari: Laterza, 1961), two present the ten eclogues (of the first version of *Arcadia*), without the connecting prose passages. Quotations from the *Arcadia* are from Iacopo Sannazaro, *Opere*, ed. Enrico Carrara (Turin: UTET, 1952).

sis's song of Daphnis—which is clearly a performed song—the monologue of Virgil's Gallus tests the limits of pastoral utterance. It takes the imagination beyond the boundaries of the pastoral world, but it is produced in a situation of pastoral convening, and the poem exploits the ambiguity of performance in its Theocritean model by making ambiguous whether we are to conceive the speaker of the love complaint as the lover himself or the Arcadian poet who represents him. The *Diana* translates these poetics to a post-Petrarchan situation. The pastoral world of the romance consists of lovers bereft of those they loved—i.e. in the situation of pastoral elegists—but who are modelled on Gallus, i.e. on the heroic figure originally lamented.[40] This paradox in the new imagining of pastoral community is reflected in the way Book 1 of the *Diana* constitutes it. The first sentence introduces one of the main figures in terms that both suggest his literary genealogy and promise a narrative account:

> Downe from the hils of *Leon* came forgotten *Syrenus*, whom love, fortune, and time did so entreate, that by the least greefe, that he suffered in his sorrowfull life, he looked for no lesse then to loose the same.[41]

Where Sannazaro, more closely imitating Virgil, stages such a figure amidst his less troubled fellows (*Arcadia*, Poesie 3 and 5), Montemayor gives him an opening scene a la Petrarch. Sireno returns to the fountain where he fell in love with Diana and proceeds to renew his woe first by a song sung to a lock of her hair and then by rereading a letter in which she pledged her love to him. At this point, he sees another shepherd, Silvano, approaching the same spot and overhears him sing a complaint against Love. The two then make themselves known to each other: they prove not only to have been old acquaintances but fellow sufferers in the same love, for the romance's eponymous heroine, Diana. By staging solo utterances as such—overheard, but not consciously in the presence of auditors—Montemayor paradoxically reduces their isolation and increases the sense of shared plight which is one of the fundamental implications of pastoral representation. Where Theocritus's and Virgil's Arcadian auditors, with their mixture of sympathy, mockery, and incomprehension, frame the hero's or lover's self-centered utterance and bring out its extravagance, Montemayor's overhearers take love complaints at their own valuation and recognize their own experience in them. Humanity, in the *Diana*, is divided between those who are at liberty and those who have suffered for love. So too is the

---

40. They are not modelled on lovers in the Polyphemus-Corydon line, which ends in Marvell's Mower, because the love represented is characteristically between equals.

41. *A Critical Edition of Yong's Translation of George of Montemayor's "Diana" and Gil Polo's "Enamoured Diana,"* ed. Judith M. Kennedy (Oxford: Clarendon Press, 1968), 10. All quotations will be from this edition, with page numbers noted parenthetically in the text. Citations of the Spanish text are from Jorge de Montemayor, *Los siete libros de la Diana,* ed. Enrique Moreno Báez (Madrid: Real Academia Española, 1955).

potential audience of the book, *its* overhearers: early on and frequently there-after, it is made clear that the reader is assumed to be one who understands love by having experienced its sufferings. The Arcadian community—which in Virgil and Sannazaro could scarcely contain the passionate lover—has now become a community *of* such lovers.[42]

However, it is not evident why there should be any narrative interest in Montemayor's reconception and restaging of the pastoral world. The opening episode of the *Diana*, in which the two shepherds exchange love laments, would be quite unsurprising as an eclogue. One of the founding poems of Spanish Golden Age literature, Garcilaso de la Vega's Egloga 1, is just such a poem, and the reunion of Sireno and Silvano ends by their singing a duet that could have served as a poem in the *Arcadia*. But the place of narrative becomes clear when a third woebegone lover joins the first two. Sireno and Silvano see a shepherd-ess approaching, and hearing her sing a plaintive sonnet, recognize, as one would expect, the experience they share. At the same time, such lyric outbursts are not the whole of the way even pastoral lovers make themselves known to each other. Selvagia, the newly arrived shepherdess, greets Sireno and Silvano with a question that is almost a motto for this romance: "What doe you in this greene and pleasant medow, despised Shepherds [*desamados pastores*]?" (29). They ask the same of her. The upshot of their conversation, which begins by discussing men and women as lovers, is that Sireno asks Selvagia to tell them her story: "Vouchsafe to tell us the substance of thy love, and all the occurrents which have hitherto befallen thee therein" (32). This story, which concludes Book 1, can be looked at in two ways. On the one hand, its tale of four crossed lovers (not unlike the mixups and betrayals of *A Midsummer Night's Dream*), con-cludes in the manner of an eclogue, as the lovers, finding themselves and their flocks together in a forest, sing their loves and discontents to each other in a series of solo lyrics. Strictly speaking, these lyrics are resung by the narrator Selvagia, who then joins her auditors, Sireno and Silvano, in three more lyrics that conclude Book 1. The project of the *Diana* might thus seem scarcely dif-ferent from that of the *Arcadia*—to strengthen the way in which a series of eclogues forms an eclogue-book. But at the same time, Selvagia's story is more like a story in our sense—i.e., in Renaissance terms, more like a novella—than anything in Sannazaro. Thus, though "the substance of her love," to recall Sir-eno's initial request, may be similar to that of the two shepherds, loving but unloved, whom she addresses, "the occurrents which have hitherto befallen [her] therein" are quite different. Seen in this light, the *Diana* is not an eclogue book, but a collection of tales.

At the beginning of Book 2, when the three new friends have reconvened

---

42. See Haber (63ff.) for an account of the way, in his *Arcadia*, Sidney undoes the pastoral conven-tion by which overhearing a love complaint leads to "a fellowship based on mutual isolation."

at the fountain and treated us to yet two more love complaints—i.e. when we may well think that this really is another eclogue book—Silvano greets Selvagia by speaking of "the diversitie of so many unaccustomed mishaps, that daily harme us woefull and true lovers" (56). This sounds rather like one of the headings that set the day's storytelling agenda in the *Decameron* and its Renaissance imitations, like Marguerite de Navarre's *Heptameron*. (In both these collections, we should note, the fictional occasion is a retreat from a present danger to a pastoral locale, which provides the space for storytelling on set themes.) In Book 2, a new shepherdess enters the scene, with a story adapted from Matteo Bandello's *Novelle*, and in the next book the ever-expanding group of pastoral lovers meets yet one more likeness of itself, a shepherdess whose tale adapts to rural circumstances the kind of town-centered love entanglement that one finds in Boccaccio. (We might entitle it, "How a father asked his son to help him woo the maiden he loved and the consequences for them both.") In one of its aspects, Montemayor's project is to give a collection of love tales greater aesthetic, thematic, and philosophical unity than one finds in the larger collections of *novelle*.

The pastoralism of the *Diana* is the main means of achieving this unity— and not only because the eclogue-like narrative conventions continually remind the characters and the reader that, in Robert Graves's words, "there is one story, and one story only." The *Diana's* pastoralism also involves the fact that the lovers, unlike narrators in the Boccaccian tradition, tell their own stories, and do so in a manner that is specific to pastoral. At the beginning of Book 6, Felismena—the Bandello heroine whose unhappy love has caused her to withdraw from town and court and assume pastoral guise—finds herself with a "real" shepherdess, Amarillidi, and they mutually request an account of each other's lives (*cuenta de sus vidas*). The narrator remarks that this is a perfectly natural thing (*cosa muy natural*) for those who find themselves in the same situation, and one of course finds characters giving such accounts in many kinds of fiction. In one of Cervantes' "exemplary" novellas, "The Little Gypsy Girl," two young noblemen find themselves disguised in a gypsy camp; they naturally ask each other, "What are you doing here?" Their stories answer that question in a manner consistent with what we think of as narrative situations—i.e. representing their lives as part of ongoing and as yet uncompleted actions (they not only say how that got to the gypsy camp but where they think they are going). Their stories thus do not count as pastoral narrations, even though "The Little Gypsy Girl" itself has a number of pastoral aspects. When "real" shepherds, like Virgil's Tityrus or Spenser's Melibee, recount their histories, they not only mean to explain their present situations, they also regard those situations as unchanging: in telling what has happened to them, they define what they are. This is the case with each of Montemayor's lovers. The stories they tell have no envisaged future, but simply lead up to and define the various states of love-woe which they discover to each other.

It is pastoral narration so conceived that enables Montemayor to engage the problematics of representing Gallus, and thus make pastoral discourse "adequate to the task of evoking the intricacies of sentimental life."[43] The crucial ambiguity in the tenth Eclogue concerns the putative speaker of Gallus's complaint. Its Theocritean prototype is unambiguously a performed song, as are the two love complaints in Virgil's Eclogue 8. But in Eclogue 10, the multiple meanings of the opening phrases—*Gallo carmina sunt dicenda* and *carmina Gallo*—alert us to the doubleness of the poem as a whole. If the framework of Arcadian figures and the idea of singing for Gallus suggest that his complaint is the Arcadian narrator's representation of him, the length and urgency of his utterance suggest, by the usual understanding of fiction and drama, that he speaks "for himself," in the here and now. The ambiguous ending of the poem, which concludes the Eclogue book and in which threatening darkness comes to the landscape, brings out the uncertainty of what it means to say that the poet's voice has become his.

Montemayor transfers these poetics to the treatment of his great theme of memory. The epithet *olvidado* (forgotten), applied to Sireno in the opening sentence, echoes throughout the *Diana*. The great sin against love is to forget the person who loves you; the great anguish is to be forgotten (*olvidado/a*) by her/him whom you love; the great heroism is to remain true to your own experience of love, which means to hold it in memory. When Montemayor's lovers tell their stories, they can be thought to be narrating past events so that their auditors will understand their present condition: the past events are narrated in prose, the present condition is manifested by the verse complaints that were overheard by others and prompted their requests for the explanatory story. But this division between past and present, prose and verse, story and lyric is far from simple. It is obvious that retelling a story to others can also revive it for oneself, and Montemayor brings out this doubleness by having his narrators resing the songs that variously prompted and confirmed their loves or witnessed their failure. Montemayor is attentive to moments in which the narration of past events revives memory and is felt to be a present reality, but it is rehearsing the songs which particularly brings out the presence of the past.

This use of repeated songs is a striking indication of the way pastoral devices can become usages of narrative—by which I mean, of course, not simply that they appear in narratives but that they bring out their values, the human realities which narrative fictions bring to life and the human uses to which they

---

43. I adapt this phrase from Mary Gaylord Randel, "The Language of Limits and the Limits of Language: The Crisis of Poetry in *La Galatea*," *Modern Language Notes* 97 (1982): 257.

are put. The representation of repeated songs as acts of memory not only extends the possibilities of individual pastoral narrations but also lays the groundwork for the largest narrative structures of the book. Carroll B. Johnson, analyzing the tension in the *Diana* between lyric and narrative motives, raises the question of how the book as a whole will get beyond the condition of Book 1, in which all the figures are in permanent states of love-woe and the book formally is one gigantic eclogue.[44] How, in other words, will the *Diana* become a pastoral *romance?* To put it in terms of the thematic triad introduced in the opening sentence, how will Fortune and Time enter into a pastoral representation of Love? The foregrounding of lovers' memories suggests the answer so far as time is concerned. Insofar as their present situations—however similar (and therefore susceptible of "pure" pastoral representation)—have been determined by events which took place in the past (and which, summarized, sound like the stuff of novellas), then it is implicitly possible that these situations can change and that the forgotten lover can look forward in hope: throughout the romance, the characters take up both these questions for discussion and debate. The fundamental principle of the *Diana* is that those who love deserve to be loved; its great promise is that fidelity to one's experience in love will be rewarded. But what machinery can a pastoral narrative use to fulfill such a promise? This is the province of Fortune, which works in various ways in the *Diana*. The most notorious, because it is stigmatized by Cervantes' Priest during the purging of Don Quixote's library (*Don Quixote,* 1.6), is the magical waters of the good Felicia, whose palace, the subject of Book 4, sits in the center of the romance. But the *Diana's* basic means of bringing about change is a less ostentatious piece of romance machinery and more directly arises from its pastoral narrations.

The first half of Book 2 brings Sireno, Silvano, and Selvagia together with three nymphs, under circumstances to be spelled out below. As they chat amiably, three savages rush out of the woods and attack the nymphs; the shepherds fight bravely, but there is no rescue until a beautiful huntress emerges from the woods and slays the savages. Though this episode has puzzled some commentators, its point seems clearly to represent the poles of lust and chastity, represented by bestial and semidivine creatures, between whom are situated the human lovers, motivated by both desire and pure affection. This emblematic representation is confirmed as the narrative returns to its usual mode of pastoral narration. The heroic huntress turns out to be not the goddess Diana, as we might well have thought, or even an avatar like Spenser's Belphoebe. Rather, she is the heroine from Bandello, named Felismena, whom unhappy love has driven from town and court to take up a pastoral guise. She tells her story precisely to convey to the nymphs—who identify themselves as in the entourage of the wise Felicia, "whose course of life . . . is to cure and remedie the

---

44. "Montemayor's *Diana:* A Novel Pastoral," *Bulletin of Hispanic Studies* 48 (1971): 20–35.

passions of love" (79)—just how wretched and unreasonable human love can be. Her long story, one of the sources of *Two Gentlemen of Verona* and containing an episode reminiscent of Viola and Olivia in *Twelfth Night*, leads the nymphs to understand what their nature almost forbids them to (a lesson Belphoebe, for example, never learns):

> When the Nymphes had heard faire *Felismenas* tale, and understoode what a great Lady she was, and how love had made her forsake her naturall habite, and taken upon her the weedes and life of a shepherdesse, they were no lesse amazed at her constancie and zeale, then at the great power of that cruell tyrant, who absolutely commands so many liberties to his service. And they were mooved besides to no small pittie, to see the teares and burning sighes wherewith the Ladie did solemnize the history of her love. (103)

It is their newly aroused feeling for the plight of human lovers that prompts the nymphs to propose taking Felismena and the three "real" shepherds to Felicia's palace. This is the machinery that initiates change in the *Diana*, and it clearly has less to do with romance coincidence or magic, which would require a considerable suspension of disbelief, than with the reader's response to the tales of love he or she has heard. The nymphs complete the way in which readers come to fill the available roles in Montemayor's pastoral world. If before we have been identified as fellows in the experience of love and as sympathetic auditors to love's tales, the nymphs bring out two further elements of any reader's role— the immunity from the literal experience of what is reported on the page and at the same time the possibility of combining sympathy with a wider perspective—in this case a feeling and, in a modest way, an ideology of the way the world takes care of lovers. This is yet another way in which we can think of the *Diana* as expanding the scenario of Eclogue 10—in this case the Arcadian herdsmen, demigods, and human sympathizers who surround Gallus—and it is the main means by which this pastoral brings about its changes.

The book devoted to Felicia's palace has less to do with the main concerns of the *Diana* than one expects. If our attention picks up when Orpheus appears, it quickly flags when his song settles into praise of some two dozen ladies of the Spanish court. (There is also a long Moorish tale, which appeared in many editions and which Yong translates, but which all modern editors reject as a nonauthorial interpolation.) The lovers' sojourn with Felicia ends in a threefold way. Belisa, the grieving shepherdess whom the travelling group encountered in Book 3, remains in the palace, where she will eventually be united with her lover, Arsileo. Felismena herself is sent back to the world in her pastoral guise. In Books 5, 6, and 7, she takes on the role of main pastoral auditor; in Book 7 she is finally united to her lover, Don Felis, in sufficiently implausible circumstances. Though Felicia provides an elixir to heal Don Felis's physical wounds, the potions that affect the lover's inner condition are administered only to the three shepherds of Book 1. There is no agreement about what these potions mean; one cannot even tell whether they are allopathic or homeopathic. The potion given to Selvagia and Silvano makes them fall in love with each other and thus fulfills the promise that those who love deserve to be loved. But the potion given to Sireno makes him forget his love of Diana, and this leads up to the final way in which pastoral usages serve narrative purposes in the *Diana*.

The story of Sireno and Diana, which the title suggests is the central one of the romance, involves the most remarkable adaptation of pastoral devices to narrative purposes. Unlike any of the other lovers, Sireno does not tell his own story. Rather, it is already known to his world (including the reader, who is informed of his enforced absence and Diana's marrying another in the "Argument" to the book), and it is twice told to him, primarily by means of repeated songs. Early in Book 1, Silvano repeats to Sireno a song he overheard him singing to Diana. (Shortly thereafter, Silvano repeats for Sireno the song he overheard Diana singing, lamenting Sireno's absence.) In Book 2, when Sireno, Silvano, and Selvagia have come together after overhearing each other's renewed laments, they overhear yet another song. This draws them to a flowery meadow, where they see three nymphs sitting by a stream. When they have finished their song, one nymph asks, "Are these (*Cynthia*) the river bankes, where the Shepherd *Syrenus* went up and downe, tormented and lost for the love of the faire Shepherdesse *Diana*?" (59) Indeed they are, and Cynthia proceeds to sing a song of some 400 lines, recounting the occasion (including the lovers' sad songs) when Sireno and Diana parted before he went off on an obscure but unavoidable mission.

This odd way of recounting the story of Sireno and Diana brings out the doubleness of pastoral narration, as it derives from the Gallus eclogue. On the one hand, what Sireno hears has the effect on him that the rehearsals of events and songs have on the lovers who tell their own stories. He responds to Cynthia's song in the following way:

> Unfortunate *Syrenus* all the while the Nymph with her sweete song did manifest his old cares and sighes, forgot not to breath them out so thicke, that *Sylvanus*, and *Selvagia* could not by any meanes comfort him: for he was now no lesse pensive then [than] at the very time, when he passed [experienced] them, marvelling much how she knew of these particulars which passed betweene him and *Diana*. (74–75)

On the other hand, just as these stories, unlike the ostensibly direct representations of high romance, are explicitly told to others, so the songs within them have not only the putative immediacy of lyric but also "reach for a wider audience," as Mary Gaylord Randel says of the verse in Cervantes' *Galatea:* "While claiming to be in some sense more intimate [than prose], poems become at the same time more impersonal."[45] Thus Sireno's distress, while he hears Cynthia narrate his parting from Diana, is played off against the responses of the other auditors. "Faire *Cynthia* having made an end of her sweete song, *Doria* and *Polydora* [the nymphs] wondred that a Shepherdesse could be the cause, that love kindled such burning flames, and marveiled no lesse how time had cured her greefe, which seemed at their farewell to be remedilesse" (74). Even Silvano and Selvagia, while trying to comfort Sireno, "were no less astonished at the passing sweete grace, wherewith *Cynthia* both song and plaied the same" (75).

This doubleness—clearly of a piece with pastoral memorializing, in which feelings of loss are mitigated by the rites of commemoration—underlies the way in which the lovers of the *Diana* become representative. Sireno has scarcely had time to be "almost out of his wits" that the nymphs know his story, when Cynthia goes on to say, "And among these river banks are many other faire Shepherdesses, and enamoured Shepherds, where love hath shewed his mightie power and effects, and some cleane contrary to that they hoped for" (59). This generalizing observation would seem to suggest that the representative is at the expense of fictional particularity.[46] It is a partial corrective to recognize, as is explicit when Felismena's story reads a lesson in love to the nymphs, that love, for Montemayor, is represented only by those who have individually felt its effects. But the question remains: how much does representing the experience of love entail, for the writer, the fictional particularities that one finds in novellas? Felismena's story, which brings a tale of Bandello's to a pastoral locale, shows one way in which the *Diana* suspends the potential tension between particular and general. But the story of Sireno and Diana is the most remarkable example of the way pastoral representation can admit the proto-novelistic realities that Montemayor's conception of love entails. The odd way in which Sireno's story has been taken from him in Books 1–3 pays off in the last three books, when Diana herself appears on the scene, and we are in a position to see their story precisely as a tale of *two* persons, rather than, as in all the other cases, as the story of one faithful, suffering lover. Much of what Sireno heard in the first three books represented not his own but Diana's love and grief (however unaccountable, given her ultimate infidelity). The later books change their situation entirely by means of two plot devices. First, Felicia explains to Sireno that she cannot make him happy in love without violating Diana's marriage bond, so she gives him a potion to make him forget his love. Shortly thereafter the three original shepherds return home and learn, from Diana herself, that

---

45. Randel, 262.

46. Thus Bruce W. Wardropper's important and influential article on the *Diana* privileged its idealizing aspects and criticized the older realistic and novelistic assumptions that had made it appear "decadent" and suchlike. "The *Diana* of Montemayor: Revaluation and Interpretation," *Studies in Philology* 48 (1951): 126–44.

she was forced into her marriage by her parents. This explanation, superficially more realistic than Felicia's magical waters, is really just as implausible, once we start asking why no one in the neighborhood knew this earlier, why Diana did not write or tell Sireno, and suchlike. But the point is not the plausibilities of plot, but the representation of love realities that the new situation permits.

It is never clear whether Diana married on compulsion and is therefore exculpated. That is not the point. It is rather that she has an account of this story that she believes as strongly as Sireno does and that leads to the most genuinely novelistic entanglements of the *Diana*. The possibility for this has been established by the earlier accounts of her love and its sorrows—which make her as representative a lover as Sireno—and it is realized by a new mode of pastoral representation that becomes prominent in the last three books. One of the main and most influential features of the *Diana* is its taking up *cuestiones de amor* (so that one of its achievements is to be not only a collection of tales but also a courtly conversation, like *Il Cortegiano*). This is evident from the start—e.g. when Sireno and Silvano in Book 1 discuss whether he is worse to have loved and been betrayed or to have been rejected from the beginning. But it becomes formalized at the end of Book 4, when the sojourn in Felicia's palace ends with groups of lovers and nymphs taking up three questions: how can it be said that true love is born of reason? why do true lovers cling to their grief? and why does love cool because of absence? When Felismena, still as a shepherdess, returns to the world, these love debates take the form of eclogue-like convenings. Her first encounter is overhearing the lament Arsileo sings at the request of Amarillidi, his companion in love-woe. This is a double sestina, a form that in Petrarchan lyric is directly expressive of grief, but that in this pastoral context is also sung for another. It is sung directly for another (Amarillidi), unwittingly for yet another (Felismena), and thus, so are the lovely workings of love, time, and fortune, ultimately for the other who most counts, Arsileo's lover, Belisa. On hearing the lament, Felismena steps forward to reveal that Belisa is alive, longing for her lover and safe at Felicia's palace, whither Arsileo immediately departs. When Felismena and Amarillidi are left alone, they ask, as we have already noticed, about each other's lives. This leads not, as we might expect, to a narration by Amarallidi, but to a debate between her and Filemon, her jealous lover. The question is whether he is entitled to be jealous of Arsileo. It is staged in a pastoral way, with Felismena the shepherdess invited to be judge, and resolved by the fact that Filemon's final argument—that his jealousy is unreasonable, but that unreasonableness is precisely what is normal in love—carries the day without any need for Felismena's separate judgment. In other words, the account fictionally enacts the convention of singing contests, that both contestants "win" or are worthy of prizes.

These disputes about love run throughout the final three books and are staged eclogues, both in setting and occasion. The final meeting of Diana,

Sireno, Silvano, and Selvagia is the most novelistic passage in the *Diana* not because it is a new departure from the other pastoral representations, but because
of the way it registers differences within what seems to be the usual gathering
of shepherds. The episode occurs in Book 6, after the scene between Amarillidi
and Filemon. Diana, in search of a lost lamb,[47] meets Silvano (her former lover)
and Selvagia, who are now, thanks to Felicia, lovers themselves. They discuss
their situation and the *cuestiones de amor* implicit in it, just as Amarillidi and Filemon have in the scene that begins Book 6. But the difference here is that the
situation Diana and her friends discuss is in the past and is different from the
situation in which they now find themselves. Hence there are troubling under-
currents of feeling—wonderfully observed by Montemayor, who, as several
commentators point out, was an experienced courtier writing for a court audience—and these affect the most familiar pastoral conventions. Diana, admit-
ting some fault and aware that she should accept the present love of Silvano
and Selvagia, asks them to "sing some song, to entertaine the time, and to passe
the heate of the day away" (218). This they do, but the song reflects Selvagia's
displeasure at Diana's conversation with Silvano and is represented as a way of
getting back at her. The three are then joined by Sireno, via the usual machinery: coming to meet Selvagia and Silvano, he encounters Diana's sheep, who
recognize him as they did in the old days. "With the thoughts, that the memorie of such a thing did put before his eies" even though Felicia's waters had
"made him forget his olde love" (220), Sireno sings a song ("Passed contents, /
O what mean ye?"). Diana, who is with Silvano and Selvagia, overhears this
song, and she and Sireno fall into a discussion of what they owe each other. It
is very similar to what we heard from Amarillidi and Filemon and what Felismena, in her last pastoral encounter, will hear from the Portuguese shepherds,
Duarda and Armia, in the seventh and final book. But Sireno and Diana are in
a situation that will not admit of resolution: Fortune and Time have, in their
case, worked at cross-purposes with Love. Hence their debate becomes a quarrel, until it reaches an impasse that is a standoff between them and between two
key terms of the romance and its ideology of love: Diana says that Sireno's
(new) liberty is a strange thing and he retorts that her (past) oblivion was
stranger still. Sireno seeks to relieve the tension by proposing a song, but the
usual pastoral means of resolution now occur with a difference. Silvano takes
up his invitation, but so that they can sing in harmony, he says, "Let us imagine
that we are both in the same case, as this Shepherdesse made us live, when we
filled these hils and dales with our amorous complaints" (223–24). To recall the
past in song this way is precisely to have gone beyond pastoral narration. For

---

47. This is a vestige of eclogue, perhaps derived from the story of Carino in Sannazaro's *Arcadia*
(prosa 6), and ultimately going back to the third Eclogue of Calpurnius Siculus (fl. 50–60 A.D.), an
imitator of Virgil who was much imitated by Renaissance pastoralists.

Silvano and Sireno are now play-acting what was, rather than recalling it in order to make manifest their present condition.

IV

The *Diana* ends on the brink of something like novelistic narration. Since our interest is in its mode of narration, the next stage of our story is not its famous sequel, Gaspar Gil Polo's *Diana Enamorada* (whose interests are in the morality and ideology of love), but the pastoral narrations of Cervantes. His first published work, the pastoral romance *La Galatea*, has many proto-novelistic aspects. There are characters who are not in pastoral costume and a good deal of violence (including a startling murder at the very beginning); compared with its predecessors, it contains less recollection and more events that occur in the narrative present.[48] Though Cervantes never renounced *La Galatea*,[49] it conveys a sense of confinement by its own conventions that is not at all surprising in the future author of *Don Quixote*. What is surprising is that pastoral episodes prove to have an important and enabling role in the fictional endeavor of *Don Quixote*. In the course of ironizing chivalric heroism, Cervantes recovered values of pastoral convenings and narration that had threatened to break under the burdens imposed in his pastoral romance.

Towards the end of his adventures, Don Quixote comes upon a group of aristocrats masquerading as shepherds and gets it into his head to turn Arcadian shepherd himself (2.58). This episode is often thought to epitomize the Cervantean attitude towards pastoral—not only because it suggests that pastoral replaces chivalric romance as the stuff of Quixotic fantasy, but also because its mockery seems consonant with a famous passage in "The Dogs' Colloquy," in which one of the canine interlocutors reports that what he saw, when he lived with real shepherds, completely gave the lie to the pastoral books read by his former master's lady. But the pastoral episodes of Part 1 (1605) are a major resource in what became a central endeavor of Cervantes' masterpiece, the making of fictions while interrogating them. They are different from and more important than the pastoral episodes of Part 2 (1615). It is no mistake that Don Quixote's Arcadian scheme is prompted by an aristocratic masquerade. Both in adventures on the road and in events staged by others to see the two protagonists perform, disguise and theatricality are the central means by which Part 2 addresses questions of fiction and reality. The definitive Quixotic episode in

---

48. This point is made in an extremely useful article by Elizabeth Rhodes, "Sixteenth-century Pastoral Books, Narrative Structure, and *La Galatea* of Cervantes," *Bulletin of Hispanic Studies*, 66 (1989): 353.

49. He left it unfinished, but in his final work, the idealizing *Persiles y Sigismunda*, he promised to complete it.

this part of the novel is Master Pedro's puppet show, in which the knight leaps on stage and lays low the pasteboard Saracens he sees there (2.26). In Part 1 the life of fiction is predominantly represented by storytelling. Interpolated tales occupy most of the middle chapters, and at least one encounter on the road, the freeing of the galley slaves (1.22), itself involves storytelling. As if to mark the difference between the two parts of the novel, Gines de Pasamonte, who in that episode boasts of writing his autobiography, reappears in Part 2 as Master Pedro, the puppeteer.

The first interpolated story in *Don Quixote* is the product of a pastoral episode, which seems to have been placed so as to foreground certain conventions of producing and exchanging tales.[50] After the attack on the windmills and the battle with the Basque (1.8–9), Don Quixote and Sancho Panza come upon some goatherds, who welcome them to their evening meal (1.11). The best-known piece of pastoralism in this chapter is Don Quixote's speech on the Golden Age, but more important to the book's procedures are the way it arises and the way it is received. The knight's speech is prompted by some acorns he is served, and in that respect "this harangue, which might well have been spared" (87) is another instance of his inappropriate responses to quotidian realities. But for the first time in the novel, no conflict results. For one thing, the knight does not wholly misread the world as a text here, for acorns are a familiar authenticating detail in representations of primitive simplicity. As for the goatherds, their bemused response to the knight's high-flown rhetoric prompts them to offer some entertainment in return—a love song by one of

---

50. This is my strong interpretive claim about what seems an indubitable fact—that Cervantes originally planned to put the story of Grisóstomo and Marcela in the Sierra Morena chapters, along with the stories of Cardenio and Dorotea, and then shifted it to an earlier position. The evidence is internal—fictional inconsistencies (chiefly concerning the stealing of Sancho's ass), errors in book production (e.g. mistakenly placed chapter headings), and the fact that chapters 11–14 are, anomalously for this part of the novel, set in the mountains. The argument was first spelled out by Geoffrey Stagg, "Revision in *Don Quixote,* Part I," in *Hispanic Studies in Honour of I. González Llubera,* ed. Frank Pierce (Oxford: Dolphin Book Co., 1959): 347–66. For an even more detailed account, which attempts to identify every stage in the composition of part I, see R. M. Flores, "Cervantes at Work: The Writing of *Don Quixote,* Part I," *Journal of Hispanic Philology,* 3 (1979): 135–60. A brief account of these matters will be found in E. C. Riley, *Don Quixote* (London: Allen & Unwin, 1986): 73–74.

Neither Stagg nor Flores offers much explanation of why Cervantes moved this first pastoral episode. Their very brief remarks (Stagg, 356; Flores, 146) are repeated in Riley's statement that "Cervantes could very well have decided to thin out the cluster of extraneous stories crowding the central section of part I" (74). Reading an author's intentions is a tricky business, but I hope to make evident a stronger literary motivation than has hitherto been recognized for shifting chapters 11–14 to their prominent early position in the novel.

All citations to *Don Quixote* are by part and chapter (e.g. 1.11), followed by page number in the translation by J. M. Cohen (Harmondsworth: Penguin, 1950). Citations in Spanish are from Luis Andrés Murillo, ed. *El Ingenioso hidalgo Don Quijote de la Mancha I* (Madrid: Castalia, 1978).

their number, who can "show this gentleman, our guest, that even in the mountains and woods there are people who know something about music" (87). The chapter as a whole thus takes the form of an eclogue: a rural gathering, with its atmosphere of hospitality, equality, and simple pleasures, has been the occasion for the exchange of pleasurable utterances. The eclogue model returns three chapters later, at Grisóstomo's funeral (1.14). The chapter begins when the gentleman Vivaldo reads aloud one of the dead lover's poems. His recitation closely replicates a founding convention of pastoral elegy, the repetition, by one of the gathered company, of the dead shepherd's dying complaint. As Vivaldo is about to recite another poem, the shepherdess Marcela suddenly appears and delivers the eloquent self-defense for which this scene is famous. Though her speech displaces the poem we were about to hear, it sustains the pattern of an eclogue, for in its length and formality it answers to and balances the dead shepherd's complaint.

The author of *La Galatea* would certainly have been conscious of these eclogue patterns. The question is how he turns pastoral usages to account in the fictional form he was inventing in *Don Quixote*. If we come to these chapters from the Spanish pastoral romance, we can see that some degree of irony distances author and reader from its fictional conventions. In a pastoral romance, as here, eclogue machinery generates love stories; but in accordance with the central fiction that all shepherds are lovers (and vice versa), the narrators and auditors of the various love stories are the interested parties themselves. In these chapters of *Don Quixote*, the story of Grisóstomo and Marcela is told by neither party, but by one of the goatherds. By the same token, Grisóstomo's complaint, which in a pastoral romance would be directly uttered and would be overheard by other shepherds (i.e. lovers in similar plights), is a written poem recited by a gentleman spectator. Similarly, in the first "eclogue chapter," Cervantes represents Antonio's love song, for no reason internal to his story or situation, as written by his uncle the priest. These bracketing and distancing devices would seem to undermine the putative reality of the fictions of pastoral romance. But the effect is not satiric. Pastoral writing, after all, is amenable to the play of irony. Even in straightforward pastoral, irony is inherent in the reduction of heroic modes, the claims of strength in humility, and the doubleness of representation and self-representation (these are and are not shepherds). Self-consciously acknowledging its fictions, while maintaining the pretense of their reality, has been a pastoral capacity since its Alexandrian beginnings. We can therefore understand why these chapters of the *Quixote* reveal a more delicate and interesting relation between Cervantean realism and pastoral fiction than the paradigm of Quixotic lunacy might lead us to expect.

The simplest illustration of this relation occurs in a later episode. When Sancho Panza is dispatched to tell Dulcinea of his master's carryings-on in the

Sierra Morena, he meets the priest and barber of his village (1.26), who return with Sancho to the mountains in order to bring Don Quixote home. While reposing in a *locus amoenus*, they are surprised to hear a voice singing sweetly: "for although report has it that shepherds with excellent voices are to be found in woods and fields, that is rather poetic exaggeration than sober truth" (1.27, 224). Despite its suggestion of "The Dogs' Colloquy," this proves not to be a dismissal of pastoral convention. On the contrary, the device of an overheard love lament leading to the story that explains it is straight out of pastoral romance. Furthermore, the reality of this episode tends to confirm the so-called exaggerations of the poets. For the voice is that of Cardenio, whose love despair has driven him to the wilds, where he lives, wretchedly clothed, among the goatherds. He is thus a ragged version of the conventional lovelorn shepherd, earlier represented by Grisóstomo. If the tale he proceeds to tell the priest and the barber is "true," is not its upshot, the figure he now cuts and the life he leads, equally "true"?[51]

Like so much else in the *Quixote*, Cervantes' local ironies about pastoral readily change their aspect, and here serve to enhance its fictive reality.[52] The story of Grisóstomo and Marcela is made more credible by having the goatherd Pedro awkwardly narrate it and frankly register its strangeness, though in respect to pastoral romance this is a mildly ironizing device. This move towards a kind of realism also makes more plausible, because it motivates, the two lovers' pastoral roles. In a pastoral romance, they would simply "be" shepherds. But in this story, which does not presume upon the convention, they are well-to-do villagers, each of whom becomes a shepherd at a decisive moment. Grisóstomo has returned home from the university (where, presumably, he learned to turn out more sophisticated love poems than those written by Antonio's uncle), and has become an important local figure, using his knowledge to build up the family fortune and writing plays to be acted at church festivals. He dons a shepherd's outfit when he falls in love with Marcela and wishes to be with her

51. One result of the fictions that immediately follow Cardenio's tale—Dorotea's tale (1.28) and her being disguised as the Princess Micomicona (1.29) to deceive Don Quixote—is that Cardenio dons the herdsman's outfit she had been wearing and appears to the company at the inn as a "real" shepherd: "Everyone in the place was struck by Dorothea's beauty, and by the handsomeness of the shepherd [*zagal*] Cardenio" (277). This, for the moment, straightforward identification of Cardenio is a nice example of what Leo Spitzer calls Cervantes' "linguistic perspectivism." Leo Spitzer, "Linguistic Perspectivism in the *Don Quijote*," in *Linguistics and Literary History* (Princeton: Princeton University Press, 1948): 41–85.

52. For a similar point about the episode with the goatherds, although it frames its account of pastoral rather differently, see Alban Forcione, "Sancho Panza and Cervantes' Embodiment of Pastoral," in *Literature, Culture, and Society in the Modern Age: In Honor of Joseph Frank, Stanford Slavic Studies* 4:1 (1991): 57–75, esp. 57–60.

in the hills. So far is this from being conventional behavior, it surprises everyone in the story; so too, for the reader, it registers the lover's emotional extravagance and represents the course from which he will not turn back.

Nor is this a story of the rich boy falling for a simple shepherdess.[53] Marcela is the local heiress, who finds herself besieged by suitors. Frank to them all about her unwillingness to marry, she, like Grisóstomo, suddenly appears in herding attire and goes into the fields to tend a flock. In justifying herself, Marcela conveys the moral significance and psychological weightiness of this change of costume: her defense of her freedom and her right to determine her life makes one take it seriously as a characterological choice. Grisóstomo and Cardenio similarly make pastoral conventions real—the one by his death, the other by his madness. In all these cases, there is a remarkable balance—part of what makes Cervantes the founding genius of the novel—between the mildly ironic realism that brackets these characters as literary and the realistic reinvestment in them that makes us give credence to their fictional acts and fates. And marking Grisóstomo and Marcela as literary has a further effect on the *Quixote's* extraordinary play between perspectivist irony and its air of reality or plausibility. The pastoral lovers' unshakeable and single-minded spiritual commitments produce a suggestive likeness, the first of many such rapprochements, to the hero and his mad enactment of a literary role. When Marcela departs from the scene of the funeral, leaving "everyone as amazed at her good sense as at her beauty" (110), Don Quixote leaps up to forbid anyone from pursuing her. As his speech on the Golden Age had imagined a life like the one Marcela leads, so the extravagance of the comic knight and the heroic shepherdess bring them together here, in a Quixotic version of the companionship of pastoral romance.

More ordinary kinds of pastoral companionship are also evident in these chapters, particularly in the relations between speakers and auditors. The idea that utterance leads to shared pleasure, rather than conflict (as in drama) or singular expression (as in lyric) is a founding idea of pastoral, represented in various conventions of exchanged song. These early chapters of *Don Quixote* enlarge the pastoral circle to include whoever comes into the goatherds' world. Their generous, accepting response to Don Quixote's speechifying is matched, in the next chapter, by the knight's acceptance of Pedro's malapropisms, his commending the *muy buena gracia* with which he tells Grisóstomo's story, and his concluding thanks for "such a delightful story" (95). The pastoral circle extends further when Don Quixote encounters Vivaldo and his companions on the way to Grisóstomo's funeral (1.13). This meeting begins like one of the

---

53. Grisóstomo is the son of a *hidalgo*, whereas Marcela's father is a farmer (*labrador*). On the other hand, we are told that he is even richer than Grisóstomo's father (1.12, 92).

usual adventures: "They had gone less than a mile when they came to a cross-road, where they saw approaching them along another track some six shepherds dressed in black skins, with their heads crowned with garlands of cypress and bitter bay" (96). But on this terrain, the knight sees others for what they are; the two parties exchange courteous greetings and discover they are heading for the same place. Just as no misapprehension on Don Quixote's part initiates physical conflict, so Vivaldo, who immediately discerns his companion's madness, courteously draws him out, allowing him to display his earnest foolishness in a manner different from that of the roguish innkeeper who stages the mock ceremony in which the old gentleman is knighted (1.3).

Renaissance pastoral need not extend itself unduly to include a bookish knight who praises the golden world and a gentleman who, with all his wits about him, pauses in his journey for a literary spectacle. Granted that Cervantes sustains pastoral values while exposing the usual pretense that all inhabitants of a pastoral world are shepherds, we may still feel that these chapters are set apart from the rest of *Don Quixote*. But pastoral figures and conventions recur at crucial moments, as the novel elaborates the interests that derive from pastoral usages. This is seen most clearly in the way Cardenio's tale is interpolated into the main narrative. When Don Quixote and Sancho withdraw to the Sierra Morena, they come upon abandoned saddlebags, in which Don Quixote finds, to his intense interest, a notebook containing a love poem and a love letter. He sets out to find his fellow in amatory affliction, and almost immediately sees him leaping among the rocks. But before they actually meet, he and Sancho come upon a goatherd, and it is he who tells them about Cardenio's appearance in the mountains and his condition (1.23). Suddenly Cardenio appears and agrees to tell his "sad tale," on condition that he not be interrupted. When the knight is unable to restrain himself, upon hearing *Amadís de Gaul* mentioned, the interruption leads to an exchange of blows and Cardenio dashes away (1.24). His tale is therefore completed three chapters later, when the priest and barber overhear his courtly love songs and decide to seek out their singer.

The double pastoral staging of Cardenio's tale and the division between its two hearings bring out a doubleness in the way pastoral represents literary community.[54] On the one hand, pastoral encourages an attitude, already exemplified by the goatherds' and Vivaldo's response to Don Quixote, of hearing people out and taking them on their own terms—a golden rule which, out on

---

54. It is worth noting that the pastoral staging is quite unnecessary for fictional purposes. Don Quixote and Cardenio could have met directly, with no loss of intelligibility or (as these things go) plausibility; the priest and barber too could have directly come upon Cardenio, whose story Sancho had already told them. The very disposability of the pastoral framework prompts us to ask what it contributes.

the road, neither the knight nor those he encounters is able to observe. The priest's and barber's disinterested concern for Cardenio and Dorotea (whose tale is introduced by yet another piece of pastoral overhearing) exemplifies this attitude; in broad literary terms, it leads to accepting stories as stories, self-contained, interesting, and entertaining. Yet at the same time, the pastoral assumption that all persons are alike leads to the idea, well exemplified by pastoral romance, that all stories come together and that listeners will have an interested, as well as a disinterested, concern in any story they hear. This notion is foregrounded when Cardenio hears Dorotea's tale and realizes that each is the missing link in the other's story. But the implausibility of these interlocking plots, which are also a marked feature of *La Galatea*, tends to obscure what is most interesting in the ambiguities of pastoral listening. These emerge, indeed burst out, when Don Quixote is an auditor. Don Quixote's interest in what he hears makes the pleasure he expresses lead to disrupting the pastoral acceptance of a tale on its own terms.[55] It would be one thing if the knight were simply an outsider to pastoral occasions (i.e. if *Don Quixote* exhibited the simplifications one finds in imitations of it). But as the interlude with the goatherds shows, he is a potentially pastoral figure himself. (His attempt to outdo the mad behavior of other lovers comes to no more than inscribing poems on trees and calling on nymphs and fauns—precisely the pastoral behavior multiplied all over the mountains of *Don Quixote*.)[56] In all the pastoral episodes of Part 1, the knight and the speaker emerge as likenesses of each other—most strikingly when he meets Cardenio, when mad knight and mad lover gaze at each other, as if conscious of their mutual mirroring (1.23), but also when he champions Marcela and, as we shall see, in the concluding tale of the goatherd Eugenio. By raising the possibility of likenesses among all listeners, the pastoral framing of the interpolated tales makes us ask how other characters and we as readers define ourselves in relation to Don Quixote—and particularly in respect to the central question he embodies, the way we discover ourselves in the stories that give us pleasure.

This question is directly addressed when the company leave the Sierra Morena and return to the inn where Sancho had been tossed in a blanket and where he later met the priest and the barber. The first episode at the inn—

---

55. The most memorable instance is his inability to pay attention to Sancho Panza's tale of Torralba and the goatherd (1.20), which breaks up when Don Quixote fails to keep track of the goats as they cross the river, one by one. This is a reductio ad absurdum of both pastoral narration and pastoral listening.

56. See 1.26, where Don Quixote acts like Marcela's troop of pastoral lovers (1.12) and the lovers of Leandra who accompany the goatherd Eugenio to his pastoral retreat (1.51). Though he inflects these matters differently, I am much indebted to Timothy Hampton's discussion of Don Quixote and Cardenio as doubles, in *Writing from History: The Rhetoric of Exemplarity in Renaissance Literature*, (Ithaca: Cornell University Press, 1990): 257–63.

which will become a site of further storytelling[57]—is a discussion of the truth and value of chivalric romances. The two main antagonists, the priest and the innkeeper, represent "the usual division Golden-Age writers made between the two classes of the public, the *discretos* and the *vulgo*."[58] Among other fictional representations of literary discussions, the scene's literary ancestry includes the pastoral romance, where auditors often praise and comment on what they hear. As E. C. Riley, who points out this connection, says, Renaissance pastoral "had a good deal to contribute to the growth of literary self-consciousness."[59] But in its usual forms, pastoral envisages a homogeneous group. Riley cites the various responses to a song in Sannazaro's *Arcadia*:

> Alcuni lodarono la giovenil voce piena di armonia inestimabile; altri il modo suavissimo e dolce, atto ad irretire qualunque animo stato fusse più ad amore ribello; molti comendarono le rime leggiadre, e tra rustici pastori non usitate; e di quelli ancora vi furono, che con più ammirazione estolsero la acutissima sagacità del suo avvedimento.[60]

These praises may testify, as he says, "to a certain artistic discretion," but they are not at odds with each other; indeed, the sentence, with its rhythmic parallels, strongly suggests that all these points would be appreciated by any single reader or auditor. In Cervantes' inn, on the other hand, there is a marked self-centeredness in the innkeeper's enthusiasm for knightly combat, his daughter's for love complaints, and the maid's for the waiting women who keep watch. The scene might even be called, for this reason, an antipastoral, were it not that, as a whole, it recovers the cohesiveness of the assembled company by means of the novelistic pastoral, as we may call it, that Cervantes has been developing.

---

57. As such, it can be regarded as a version either of the gathering places of Renaissance story collections, like the *Decameron* and the *Heptameron*, or of the locales in which shepherds gather in pastoral romances. Anthony Close, one of the few critics to see the enabling presence of pastoral romance in *Don Quixote*, suggests that the inn can be thought of as a "low-grade equivalent" of Felicia's palace in the *Diana*. Anthony Close, "Cervantes' *Arte Nuevo de Hazer Fábulas Cómicas en este Tiempo*," *Cervantes* 2 (1982): 16. The basis of the analogy is that this is the locale to which the various lovers journey and where they are set on the way to reunion. But the mundane reality, both of the inn itself and of some of those who arrive there (like the barber, reclaiming "Mambrino's helmet"), suggests that this may be less an ironic parody of the magical palace than an "ordinary" pastoral locale, transformed by Cervantean realism.

58. E. C. Riley, *Cervantes's Theory of the Novel* (Oxford: Clarendon Press, 1962), 108. See also Alban K. Forcione, *Cervantes, Aristotle, and the "Persiles"* (Princeton: Princeton University Press, 1970), 103–15.

59. Riley, *Theory*, 33.

60. *Arcadia*, Prosa 4. "Some praised the youthful voice, full of priceless harmony; others the unusually sweet and gentle mode of song, such as could beguile the heart of anyone, however resistant to love; several complimented the graceful rhymes, not commonly used by rustics; and there were some who, with more admiration, extolled the exceptional acuteness of his wit."

The heart of the scene's pastoral feeling is the innkeeper's speech on behalf of the romances:

> I really think there's no better reading in the world. I have two or three of them here and some other writings. They've truly put life into me [*me han dado la vida*], and not only into me but into plenty of others. For at harvest time a lot of the reapers come in here in the mid-day heat. There's always one of them who can read, and he takes up one of those books. Then as many as thirty of us sit round him, and we enjoy listening so much that it saves us countless grey hairs. At least I can say for myself that when I hear about those furious, terrible blows the knights deal one another, I get the fancy to strike a few myself. And I could go on listening night and day. (1.32, 277)

Empson calls this speech "beautiful and unexpected" (*SVP*, 189). The harvest setting, the sense of shared work and leisure, cast an idyllic glow on the unifying effect attributed to the pleasures of reading. This background pastoral shapes our sense of the present occasion, transferring the homogeneity of the reapers to the heterogeneous company at the inn. In the light of this speech, the individuated enthusiasms of the innkeeper, his daughter, and Maritornes the maid are seen to share a pleasure that is naive, but also capable of *dando la vida . . . a otros muchos*.

Beyond the "horizontal" cohesion of the innkeeper's household, the pleasures of reading are felt "vertically," bringing together the *cultos* and the *vulgares*, the literate and the semi- or non-literate members of the group. The priest, as has often been observed, is a connoisseur of romances. His formula for their legitimacy—they are allowed "to divert our idle moments" (*para entretener nuestros ociosos pensamientos*)—is a *discreto* view that could well be consonant with the innkeeper's sentiments. But he keeps himself at arm's length from his antagonist and tends to represent these books as fit only for the entertainment of a leisured class. In this chapter, it is a brief intervention by Dorotea that suggests the way *Don Quixote* brings readers together. When the innkeeper's daughter says she sometimes cries for pity at the knights' complaints about their ladies, Dorotea asks, "Then you would give them some relief, young lady, if they were weeping for you?" Simply to ask this question suggests that extravagant fictions can have the claims of reality, in that they represent situations in which one might imagine oneself. The Cervantean twist is that this particular situation is the one in which Dorotea actually *has* found herself: it and its consequences are the very reason for her being at the inn. Nor is this the only mirroring of life and books that sustains her sense of literary participation here. For she speaks to the innkeeper's daughter as the Princess Micomicona, the part she is playing in the plot to bring Don Quixote home, and she brings off this role so well because she is herself an adept in the books of chivalry (1.29). The zest with which she plays the Princess and her resourcefulness in fictive tight spots (1.30) have already shown the degree to which the pleasures of books animate her.

These pleasures are ours too, and it is the way they are conveyed in the storytelling interlude at the inn that shows why *Don Quixote* is more than a Borgesian hall of mirrors. The pastoralism of the innkeeper's speech includes the representation of reading as an oral phenomenon and thus, for its audience, a directly shared experience. This is another instance of Cervantes' recuperating pastoral values by exposing (via the specifications about literacy) a conventional pretense, in this case that the shared tales of pastoral romance are oral. *Don Quixote* itself is deeply concerned with the consequences of literacy—both the isolation of reading, which has led the knight himself to build castles in the air, and its social diffusion, which aroused anxieties about the vulgar such as the priest displays.[61] Telling tales counteracts the recipient's isolation, and Cervantes' interpolated tales programmatically, it would seem, maintain the fiction that readers are auditors. So much, of course, could have come from the tradition of novella collections, like the *Decameron* (though it is not a convention Cervantes observed in his own *Novelas ejemplares*). Pastoral makes explicit the idea of audience cohesion, and the novelistic pastoral of *Don Quixote* brings together a heterogeneous group, capable of including unforeseen auditors and tale-tellers.[62] This expansion of the "story group" is the whole plot of the chapters at the inn (1.32–46). New characters appear at intervals, to complete the tales we have heard and introduce us to new ones. All these stories are interpolated into the main narrative line, but they are progressively less literary and more oral-dramatic, and increasingly enter into present novelistic reality. "The Tale of Foolish Curiosity" (1.33–34) is a written story which the priest reads to the company. "The Captive's Tale" (1.39–41) is the story of its narrator, who arrives at the inn with his Moorish bride, the tale's living happy ending. The final tale, that of Doña Clara and Don Luis (1.43), is not a simple narration, because it begins as a present occurrence outside the inn (a love song by Don Luis, disguised as a muleteer), it is told in explanatory fragments, and because, when we hear it, it is not yet finished. The next and final "adventure" at the inn is neither new nor interpolated, but rather completes an episode begun earlier in the main narrative.

The last character to arrive at the inn is the barber from whom Don Quixote took the basin which he imagines to be Mambrino's helmet (1.21). When the barber starts a fight with Sancho, over the packsaddle which had also been taken from him, Don Quixote proposes to settle the matter by producing what he claims is indisputably Mambrino's helmet. At this point the barber of Don

---

61. Riley, *Theory*, 43.

62. Unforeseen auditors and tale-tellers are a notable feature of *La Galatea*, which has an immense cast of characters for a pastoral romance. But they are all, of course, "shepherds."

Quixote's village ("our barber," as Cervantes calls him) decides to "give them all a laugh by carrying the joke [*burla*] further" (1.45, 404). This is a perfect instance of the way literary responsiveness contributes to the comic texture of *Don Quixote*, what Spitzer called its "linguistic perspectivism." The situation is not really a *burla*, which properly refers to a trick played on a character (like the trick which Maritornes and the innkeeper's daughter, drawing on their own knowledge of the romances, have just played on Don Quixote, 1.43). At the moment, the dispute about the helmet is simply a crazy conflict due, as usual, to the knight's mad self-confidence. "Our barber" turns it into a *burla* by appreciating what makes it amusing and stepping into it in such a way as to sustain its craziness. He protests, backing Don Quixote, that the basin *is* a helmet, and the rest of the company spontaneously enters in to consider, in addition, whether the mule's packsaddle might not indeed be a horse's harness. Like the roles in the priest's masquerade to bring Don Quixote home, these improvised parts bear witness to aesthetic pleasures. But here the text is neither the romances nor the novellas we have been hearing. It is what the book represents as life itself, made "poetic" for us by Don Quixote's inexhaustibly surprising lunacy.

This return to Don Quixote and the real world brings out a neglected element in the work's comic energies. Running in tandem with the putative written source of the knight's history, the manuscript of Cide Hamete Benengeli, is an ongoing oral narration, as various characters meet and tell each other about the mad knight's adventures.[63] Of the novel's self-reflexive representations in Part 1, it is less the jokes involving Cide Hamete's manuscript than these moments of retelling and their amplification into ad hoc role-playing that capture the spacious humor and pervasive gaiety of which Mann and Auerbach speak.[64] The barber's improvisation on Mambrino's helmet—providing his companions with sport, the reader with a new chapter, and the story of the helmet with a conclusion—is a rich example of the way oral performance sustains "The History of Don Quixote." It was a retelling of Don Quixote's story that prompted the innkeeper's speech in defense of romances, and the final flurry about the helmet brings out the force of Empson's comment on that speech: "Clearly it is important for a nation with a strong class-system to have

63. E.g., Sancho telling the priest and the barber about Don Quixote's adventures (1.26): "The pair of them were amazed at Sancho's tale. For, although they already knew the nature of Don Quixote's madness, they were astonished afresh every time they had news of him" (218). The next chapter (1.27) begins with the innkeeper and his wife giving the priest and the barber their own account of Don Quixote's behavior and of Sancho's blanket tossing.

64. Thomas Mann, "Voyage with Don Quixote," in Lowry Nelson, Jr., ed., *Cervantes: A Collection of Critical Essays* (Englewood Cliffs: Prentice-Hall, 1969), 49–72. Erich Auerbach, "The Enchanted Dulcinea," in *Mimesis: The Representation of Reality in Western Literature*, trans. Willard R. Trask (Princeton: Princeton University Press, 1953), 334–58.

an art-form that not merely evades but breaks through it, that makes the classes feel part of a larger unity or simply at home with each other." For the reapers at the inn, the chivalric romances are the art-form that brings readers, figured as listeners, together. But, Empson continues, "this may be done in odd ways, and as well by mockery as admiration." When the scene at the inn is shifted to its present company, we see that it is not the romances but *Don Quixote* itself that makes readers feel at home with each other. The pastoralism of Part 1, creating auditors of and participants in the knight's story, adumbrates what is narrated in Part 2, "the creation of a new 'community,' the community of readers of part 1—all infected with *quijotismo*."[65]

These various issues we have touched on—fiction and reality, the value of entertainment, the uses of reading—can be pursued in the *Quixote* without reference to pastoral. But it is Cervantes himself who turns to pastoral for versions or representations of his novelistic endeavor, and nowhere more prominently than at the end of Part 1. The famous discussion of books of chivalry undertaken by the Canon of Toledo (1.47–48)—a longer, intellectually elaborated version of the earlier scene at the inn—is frequently examined and mined for its views. But very little attention has been paid to the fact that it concludes with one of the most fully developed pastoral passages in the novel. After Don Quixote speaks out against the canon (1.49), he puts his own argument into action with an improvised narration of a hypothetical romance episode, a knight's descent, through a lake of boiling pitch, to a wondrous underworld (1.50). This spellbinding performance is followed by the arrival of a new character, a herdsman in pursuit of a wayward goat. He produces his own bit of rhetoric—a piece of flirtatious mockery, with which he settles down the she-goat—and then apologizes for it, saying that though a peasant, he knows "how to converse with men and beasts." This prompts the priest to say: "I can very well believe that, for I already know by experience that the mountains breed scholars, and sheepcotes contain philosophers" (444). This impeccable pastoral sentiment is justified in the next and penultimate chapter (1.51), when the goatherd, Eugenio, proceeds to tell his story, the last of the interpolated tales in Part 1.

However puzzling this tale is, it seems clear that Cervantes consciously made space for it as his novel approached its end. One effect of the interlude at the inn is that a new plot must be devised to bring Don Quixote home. Dorotea has been united with the lover who betrayed her, and therefore can no longer play the Princess Micomicona. The priest and the barber therefore tie up and cage Don Quixote, persuade him that he has been enchanted, and bring him home on an oxcart. Having bound and confined the hero who makes everything happen, the author might well have settled for a swift conclusion.

65. Hampton, 273.

Instead, he uses the first pause in the journey to stage the reflections on fictions and the two examples of their production that we have just summarized and that give a stronger sense of closure to Part 1 than the brief incidents and gestures that follow in the final chapter (1.52). The first part of this metafictional sequence, the canon's discourse and the priest's answering disquisition on stage plays (1.47–48), takes place on the road—prompted by the canon's overhearing some nonsensical passages from the masquerade staged by the priest and his being told, in one of the recursive narrations referred to so frequently, "Don Quixote's strange history" (*la peregrina historia de don Quijote,* 424). This interlude is extended, under specifically pastoral auspices, when the group stops in "a green and pleasant place" (434), where the oxen can graze and where the canon provides an al fresco meal, "so as to enjoy the scene and the conversation of the priest . . . and to hear Don Quixote's adventures in greater detail" (431). This *locus amoenus* provides fictional space for the canon's sympathetic attempt to disabuse Don Quixote, the knight's defense of the romances, and the arrival of Eugenio, who confirms the pastoral underpinnings of the occasion.

It is perhaps easier to show that the goatherd's tale is given a significant place at the end of Part 1 than to say just what its place or function is. It certainly recapitulates the earlier interpolated tales. In its main outline it is most like the other goatherd's tale of Grisóstomo and Marcela. The heroine Leandra is, like Marcela, the richest girl in the village and besieged by suitors, and the upshot of the story is to leave all her lovers frustrated and carrying on as woebegone shepherds. The reason, however, is the reverse of Marcela's exceptional purity and integrity. Leandra's head is turned by an attractive braggart, with whom she runs away; having discovered her stripped of clothes, jewels, and money (though not, it is averred, of her virginity), her father puts her in a nunnery. This part of the story has affinities with the tales of Dorotea, Cardenio, and the Captive.[66] But Eugenio's tale does not maintain the idealizing and romantic mode of its predecessors. Leandra is shallow and fickle, and her seducer, Vicente de la Roca, is a low-life version of Grisóstomo. He is the son of a poor local farmer; he has been away not at university but to the wars; his literary skills are not *cultos* but demotic. In an evident parody of the costume changes undertaken by the characters in the other tales, he is a cheap fancy dresser, able to recombine the elements of his few outfits into a multitude of costumes. The ultimate mirroring detail, adding a self-reflexive twist, is that Vicente is a master storyteller, the fabricator of adventures that leave the villagers spellbound. As so often in *Don Quixote,* the parody and realism here are not merely negative, but reopen fundamental issues about fiction. For Vicente's

---

66. Edwin Williamson, "Romance and Realism in the Interpolated Stories of the *Quixote,*" *Cervantes* 2 (1982): 57.

mendacious tale-spinning implicitly questions the convention of the preceding tales—that however improbable, they are told to us by honest narrators.

Among the interpolated tales, Eugenio's is the one in which the romance and high realism that define one main type of novella are most infiltrated by the low realism that defines another.[67] Its ending is a downgraded version of Grisóstomo's. Eugenio and his companion Anselmo withdraw to the country-side and, though occupying themselves in love complaints, actually acquire and tend herds. They are followed by Leandra's other lovers, who disport them-selves so that, Eugenio says, "this place seems to have become the pastoral Arcadia" (449). In the mouth of the disgruntled Eugenio, this account has the air of parody. And yet in two important ways, the end of his tale is straight pastoral. The roles to which Anselmo and he devote themselves—the one com-posing verses to complain of his beloved's absence and the other scorning the fickleness of women—are staples of Renaissance pastoral, in which debates between mockers and devotees of love are a familiar kind of eclogue or scene. Furthermore, in both its mode of resolution and its function for its narrator, Eugenio's tale closely resembles the narrations in pastoral romances. When pas-toral speakers tell their stories of love denied, they treat their present situations not as stages in unfinished actions, but as conditions that define who they are. Cardenio and Dorotea conceive themselves in this way when we first hear their stories, but their very encounters with other characters, including each other, lead to changes of costume and the successful completion of their romances. Eugenio neither imagines nor seeks a change in his condition. He has a reliable and pleasant way of life, and he clearly takes pleasure in the kind of perfor-mance his story represents, as if he were a rural version of Vicente de la Roca (indeed one may ask, without expecting an answer, whether his own story is more to be believed than Vicente's). What makes him a pastoral figure, unlike the other demotic tale-spinners, is that he is not self-seeking and that, insofar as his tale is true, it is the only one he has to tell. Hence he concludes in full pastoral character, by inviting the company to his nearby cottage for a country repast.

We can best understand the purposes of Eugenio's ambiguously pastoral tale by considering its effect on its audience. Each tale in a conventional pas-toral romance finds listeners who are appreciative in the double sense (inter-ested and disinterested) of which we have already spoken: they are pleased by what they hear, and they find their own plights reflected in it. Eugenio's audi-ence divides these two aspects of appreciative listening. His tale "much de-lighted all who heard it" (1.52, 450), and it receives from the canon the pre-

67. These are the two main types of story in Cervantes' own *Novelas ejemplares*. See William J. Entwistle, *Cervantes* (Oxford: Clarendon Press, 1940), 87–99.

dictable compliment of a courtly or urban outsider who enters the world of Renaissance pastoral: "the manner of its telling," he says, "made the narrator appear more like a polished courtier than a rustic goatherd." But there is one auditor whose appreciation resembles that of true pastoral listeners, for he too is living his life according to a literary model and finds himself in an apparently unchanging condition of unfulfilled desires. We are already aware, from his "Knight of the Lake" narrative, that Don Quixote forms a heroic-pastoral pair with Eugenio, and it is he who is "most liberal" in complimenting the goatherd's tale. But the form of his praise, a crazy repetition of his championing Marcela, is a proposal to rescue Leandra from her nunnery. This split response among Eugenio's auditors—taking the story as entertainment, on the one hand, and a call to action, on the other—plays out one of the main issues discussed by the canon and the priest, the relation between pleasure and profit in our experience of books and plays. It upshot here is farce and, to remind us, for one last time, that the issue is audiences' or readers' responsiveness, the precipitating cause is again the barber's stepping in to participate in Don Quixote's looniness. Eugenio asks who is the man who looks and talks this way, and the barber replies, "Why who should it be but the famous Don Quixote de la Mancha, the redresser of injuries, the righter of wrongs?" etc. "Either your worship is joking," the goatherd rightly says, "or the gentleman must have some of the rooms in his brain vacant" (451). Don Quixote explodes in anger, hurls a loaf of bread at Eugenio, and the two start brawling.

Is this the promised end of this great comic fiction? The *discretos*, the priest and the canon, as well as their companions, seem perfectly happy to have it be so, for they prevent Sancho Panza and everyone else from intervening. With "everyone enjoying the sport" (*estando todos en regocijo y fiesta*, 452), the fight might continue indefinitely, were it not interrupted by the sound of a trumpet, which calls Don Quixote to his very last adventure, brief and equally farcical. The problems of closure are evident in this final chapter, and they include this final handling of the relation between the pleasure and the reality of fictions. If the brawl represents the sheer comedy of "The History of Don Quixote"—for its sudden outburst is hilarious, and why should we not enjoy it, like everyone else, *discretos* and *vulgares* alike?—Eugenio and his ambivalently parodic tale seem to be an attempt to give a final turn, drier in its comedy and ironically self-conscious, to the issues that the *discretos* had just been discussing. Pastoral writing, with its capacity to suspend dilemmas and conflicts short of resolving them, may have seemed to Cervantes a way of stabilizing matters, while leaving ironic perspectives open. Whether or not it achieves this ambiguous closure, the episode shows once again that pastoral was an essential element in—and even, perhaps, the main single model for—his exploring the uses of fiction and the life of books, which is the beginning and the end of *Don Quixote*.

Nine

PASTORAL NOVELS

Though "the pastoral novel" might surprise no one as a topic, it suggests different general definitions and different sets of examples to different readers. Unlike other forms of pastoral, pastoral novels are conceived and motivated as novels and not in terms that derive from the bucolics of Theocritus and Virgil. There are certainly novels of country life, just as there are novels that express longing for a simple world and novels in which nature can be seen as a protagonist. But it is far too open a question whether any or all of them are to be called pastoral. Balzac's *The Peasants? Wuthering Heights? Tess of the d'Urbervilles? Lady Chatterly's Lover? Nostromo?*[1] To call Hardy's *The Woodlanders* a pastoral elegy may be useful heuristically in an introduction for students.[2] But it is scarcely

---

1. These examples are taken, respectively, from the following: Rudolf Zellweger, *Les débuts du roman rustique: Suisse, Allemagne, France, 1836–1856* (Paris: E. Droz, 1941), 112–19; Julian Moynahan, "Pastoralism as Culture and Counter-Culture in English Fiction, 1800–1920," *Novel* 6 (1972): 20–35; Harold E. Toliver, *Pastoral Forms and Attitudes* (Berkeley & Los Angeles: University of California Press, 1971), 278–91; Michael Squires, *The Pastoral Novel* (Charlottesville: University Press of Virginia, 1974); John Bayley, *Tolstoy and the Novel* (London, 1966), 148. See the rather discouraged survey of the field by David Raphael Thuente, "Pastoral Narrative: A Review of Criticism," *Genre* 14 (1981): 247–67.

2. Thomas Hardy, *The Woodlanders*, ed. David Lodge (London: Macmillan, 1974), 9: "*The Woodlanders* belongs to the genre of pastoral elegy."

intelligible to ask, "Is *The Woodlanders* a pastoral elegy?" (Whereas it is certainly intelligible to ask whether Shelley's "Adonais" and Arnold's "Thyrsis" are pastoral elegies.)

Since the novel is the characteristic form of the epoch in which the literary system ceased to be expressed by clearly defined and related genres, it seems neither useful nor plausible to claim for the pastoral novel the literary motivation or generic coherence of older forms. Rather, a piece of fiction can be called pastoral when its author—for whatever reason, with whatever awareness, and concerned with whatever subject or theme—has recourse to usages which are characteristic of older pastorals and which in turn make a tale or novel pastoral in mode. The art critic and writer John Berger may or may not think of his *Pig Earth* as a pastoral: the word might suggest to him an idyllic unreality that is the opposite of what he means the book to convey, the actualities of life in the French village where he has lived for many years. But Berger's project has a genuinely pastoral character. As he describes it, it derives from his being both an inhabitant of and a permanent outsider in his village and, more specifically, from his being a writer. This occupation, while it belongs to another world from the one he inhabits, also makes him eligible to be part of the village's ongoing cultural life, which he describes as "a living portrait of itself . . . constructed . . . out of words, spoken and remembered: out of opinions, stories, eye-witness reports, legends, comments and hearsay."[3] *Pig Earth* is thus a sophisticated writer's representation of countrymen and of himself as one of them, and its narrations blur the boundaries between oral and written. It is therefore not so surprising that it resembles an eclogue book, with short prose narrations, several of which concern the care of cattle and goats, alternating with poems that represent fundamental realities of the villagers' lives.

It is not the mere alternation of poems and prose that makes *Pig Earth* resemble an eclogue book, but the character of the individual prose pieces. The representational intent of the first half dozen (of eight) makes them self-contained and modest in length. Even when they are the occasion for the protagonists' individual memories, these pieces concern episodes which typify the lives of all the villagers; the sense of experience common to all is further sustained by the presence, throughout the narrations and the poems, of gestation, sustenance, winter and death, as realities in the lives of humans and domestic animals. The pastoralism of these prose pieces is also evident in their mode of narration. Perhaps surprisingly—since Berger emphasizes the role of gossip and storytelling in the communal self-portrait—only one of them is attributed to a peasant narrator. All the others are told in the third person, presumably by the author; but the point of view is persistently that of the protagonists, and

3. *Pig Earth* (New York: Pantheon, 1979), 9.

there is everywhere a feeling that details and past events are authenticated by what the author has been told. (It is impossible to determine how much of these narrations is fictional, and how much is based on real persons or experiences, or on reported or accepted truth.) In this unusual "way of telling," in which the narrator's apparent authority depends on experience he has shared with his subjects and what they have allowed him to know, Berger has worked out his own version of "putting the complex in the simple," just as, for the book as a whole, he has devised a form that resembles an eclogue sequence.[4]

As one might expect, nineteenth-century fiction provides more straight-forward, less idiosyncratic examples of the pastoral novel than *Pig Earth*. We must again remind ourselves that novels about rural life are not necessarily, perhaps not even usually, pastoral in form or mode. But even in the case of the two great and definitive examples on which this chapter will concentrate, *Silas Marner* and *The Country of the Pointed Firs*, there is considerable uncertainty of critical treatment. *Silas Marner*, to which we turn first, is often treated as just another one of Eliot's novels, despite its drastically unheroic protagonist and its unusual brevity. Even in a well-known account of the novel as celebrating the traditional ways of village life, the word "pastoral" does not appear, and perhaps is consciously avoided.[5] Insofar as there is an accepted account of what makes *Silas Marner* unusual, it is that it is a "fable" or a "parable." So even if our ambitions in literary definition go no further than defining by example, we are still a considerable ways from understanding why *Silas Marner* should be called a pastoral novel or why seeing it as one makes a difference to understanding its distinctive greatness.

---

4. I take the phrase "way of telling" from the title of Berger's and Jean Mohr's *Another Way of Telling*, an experiment in narrating by means of photographs. The last two prose pieces in *Pig Earth* are third-person narrations of the usual sort and are correspondingly longer than the first six pieces. This difference, Berger tells us, reflects the order in which the stories were written, but more important, it seems to me, is the fact that the last two stories are the first in which the protagonists' lives are significantly affected by the outside world. They thus lead to the second and third volumes of the trilogy (of which *Pig Earth* is the first), in which the stories are "set against the disappearance or 'modernisation' of village life" (prefatory "Note" to *Once in Europa* [New York: Pantheon, 1987], xiii). In "An Explanation" prefixed to *Pig Earth*, Berger says that the opening sketches "have a sharp-ness of foreground focus, a sense of the present, such as I could not now achieve" (13). Seen in the context of the whole trilogy, this characteristic (reminiscent of Rosenmeyer's account of pastoral), confirms the pastoral project of *Pig Earth*. If, as Berger says in the "Historical Afterword" that con-cludes the book, "peasant life is a life committed completely to survival" (196) but cannot be ex-pected itself to survive the conditions of modern life, then this book by an urban writer, who is also their neighbor and fellow worker, may be the only way this "class of survivors" will endure.

5. Q. D. Leavis, introduction to *Silas Marner* (Harmondsworth: Penguin Books, 1967). Cf. "George Eliot is not sentimental," 17; "the cottagers are not idealized," 39. All references to *Silas Marner* will be to this edition.

I

Definition involves differentiating as well as specifying, and *Silas Marner* is most usefully distinguished from *Adam Bede*. The two works have always been felt to have a great deal in common. Set around 1800, further back in time than any other of George Eliot's English novels, they consciously represent rural life before the changes wrought by commerce and industry in the nineteenth century. Each concerns and in some way celebrates the unchanging life of a village and the way the central figure confirms his life within its boundaries. As a writer of fiction, George Eliot means to be a realist; much of *Adam Bede* is in the spirit of the German writer Riehl, whom she praised in an essay entitled "The Natural History of German Life." But the realism of both these novels is infused with a tender attentiveness which contemporaries understandably called "charm." The very likenesses between the two books, precisely because they make both seem pastoral in a broad sense, have probably obscured the way *Silas Marner* is formally and modally a pastoral novel, as *Adam Bede* is not. There are many symptoms of this difference—for example, the broader social scope of *Adam Bede*, its heroic protagonist, and the centrality of Hetty Sorrel's tragedy. But the most revealing comparison, for our purposes, concerns its most explicitly pastoral episode.

Near the end of *Adam Bede* is a long chapter called "The Harvest Supper." This is very much a set piece by an author for whom Theocritus was a favorite poet and who quotes Virgil's Eclogues in her preparatory notes for describing trees.[6] The most explicit trace of generic self-awareness is the remark, concerning the antagonism between two laborers at the festive meal, that "when Tityrus and Meliboeus happen to be on the same farm, they are not sentimentally polite to each other" (562). The learned narrator also displays some bucolic wit, in the Theocritean sense of ironizing the heroic, when she asks of the traditional harvest song the question that was then being put to the Homeric poems, "whether it came in its actual state from the brain of a single rhapsodist, or was gradually perfected by a school or succession of rhapsodists" (563).[7] In

6. For Theocritus, see below, n. 11. Joseph Wiesenfarth, "George Eliot's Notes for *Adam Bede*," *Nineteenth Century Fiction* 32 (1977): 147. References to *Adam Bede* will be to the Penguin edition, ed. Stephen Gill (Harmondsworth, 1980).

7. Cf. Frank M. Turner, *The Greek Heritage in Victorian Britain* (New Haven: Yale University Press, 1981), 138–40. Eliot's jesting is more interestingly motivated than it might at first appear. The chapter before "The Harvest Supper" ends by evoking, in the novel's frankest nostalgia for the preindustrial past, the figure of Leisure, who "never went to Exeter Hall [identified with Evangelism], or heard a popular preacher, or read *Tracts for the Times* [by Newman et al.] or *Sartor Resartus*" (558). As Turner points out (140–54), the question of the nature and authority of the Homeric writings was intimately connected, for the Victorians, with analogous questions about the Bible. So the joking about the rhapsode of the harvest song is a gesture of relaxing the grip of contemporary intellectual dilemmas.

an often-quoted vignette, the narrator expresses her sense of solidarity with Old Kester, noted for his skill at thatching hayricks and his pride in his work, which is likened to "some pagan act of adoration" (562). And beyond these highly literary moments, the whole chapter has motives and dynamics like those of an eclogue. Not only is the supper a rural convening with its prescribed stages and moments of celebration; when an episode of mutual mockery seems to be getting out of hand, the occasion is saved by breaking out the songs that the company had been anticipating.

But what motivates the harvest supper as an event in a novel? Its function is not nearly so clear as that of the birthday feast to celebrate Arthur Donnithorne's coming of age (chapters 22–26). There the festive celebration reflects a major dramatic motive, Arthur's good intentions as the future lord of the estate, and occasions events (Adam's appointment to manage the woods, the accidental revelation of Arthur's gift to Hetty) that are steps to undoing his promise. By contrast, the harvest supper is unanticipated as a communal event and has no dramatic significance for its hosts, the Poysers. Its sole novelistic motivation is to give Adam a final opportunity to see Dinah, in the hopes of persuading her to marry him, before she returns to her solitary life of preaching and social service. Though Dinah seems to have promised to stay for the supper, it emerges that she has left the day before. But neither her departure, nor the revelation of it, nor Adam's reaction to it are represented in a novelistic manner. Just as Dinah's reasons for leaving (presumably she was unwilling to see Adam again, for fear of giving way) go unstated, so the news of her departure emerges at the supper in a context of conventional male joking. Most tellingly, we see nothing of Adam's disappointment beyond the mere fact of his leaving early with Bartle Massey, the misogynist schoolmaster. But if, for the moment, we regard the chapter as an eclogue, it handles the disappointed lover's case as we would expect, by displacing it into song—young David's rendition of "My love's a rose without a thorn," which diverts the company from the contentious jesting which was itself the occasion for telling Adam Dinah had left. What we have, then, is a rural ritual that is otherwise unmotivated by anything that concerns the Poysers or the village community, while the novelistic situation, Adam's anticipated meeting with Dinah, is handled in purely pastoral terms. "The Harvest Supper" is thus an instance of the conflict many critics have noted in *Adam Bede* "between framing, perfecting and completing (the pastoral impulse), and narrative movement with its dangers and freedom, its possibilities for radical change."[8] With its conscious pastoralism, "The Harvest Supper" contributes to the main novelistic inadequacies of *Adam Bede*—its

8. Gillian Beer, *George Eliot* (Bloomington: Indiana University Press, 1986), 64. Cf. Ian Gregor, "The Two Worlds of Adam Bede," in Ian Gregor and Brian Nicholas, *The Moral and the Story* (London: Faber and Faber, 1962), 13–32.

failure to give any inward, psychological account of Dinah's decision to marry Adam and its inability to make good on the claim that Adam's suffering for Hetty has shaped and tinged his new love.

Our concern is less to confirm a critique of *Adam Bede* than to recognize the potential contradiction between pastoral and novelistic representations. "The Harvest Supper" has the further advantage of providing a direct comparison, as a rustic social gathering, with chapter 6 of *Silas Marner*, which recounts an evening's conversation at the Rainbow Inn. From the time the novel was published, this scene was singled out by reviewers and critics. In various formulations all sound the note struck by Henry James, when he says, "Never was a group of honest, garrulous village simpletons more kindly and humanely handled."[9] The most searching version of this praise is Leslie Stephen's:

> She is awake to those quaint aspects of the little world before her which only show their quaintness to the cultivated intellect. We feel that there must be a silent guest in the chimney-corner of the "Rainbow," so thoroughly at home with the natives as to put no stress upon their behaviour, and yet one who has travelled out of sight of the village spire, and known the thoughts and feelings which are stirring in the great world outside. The guest can at once sympathise and silently criticise; or rather, in the process of observation, carries on the two processes simultaneously by recognising at once the little oddities of the microcosm, and yet seeing them as merely one embodiment of the same thoughts and passions which present themselves on a larger scale elsewhere.[10]

The last sentence calls to mind "the pastoral process of putting the complex in the simple." But the scene at the Rainbow is a pastoral in a narrower sense than Empson's. Though it has no specific traces of literary self-consciousness, such as we find in "The Harvest Supper," it is equally a novelistic version of an eclogue. Its rough wit, in which the contentious and the sociable oscillate back and forth, as if versions of each other, is reminiscent of the author's "beloved Theocritus."[11] The development of the conversation—both the allowance for mockery and contention and the conscious direction of the talk into specific performances—is formal and programmatic. Old Mr. Macey's stories of the

---

9. Henry James, *Literary Criticism: Essays on Literature, American Writers, English Writers*, ed. Leon Edel (New York: The Library of America, 1984), 917. This is from an article, "The Novels of George Eliot," published in 1866, just after the publication of *Felix Holt*.

10. David Carroll, ed., *George Eliot: The Critical Heritage* (London: Routledge & Kegan Paul, 1971), 471–72. Hereafter cited as *Critical Heritage*.

11. Gordon S. Haight, ed., *The George Eliot Letters*, 9 vols. (New Haven: Yale University Press, 1954–78), 8: 481. It must be said that the several citations of Theocritus in Eliot's works are from different Idylls and are of a different character from Idylls 4 and 5, the poems that are closest to the pastoralism of the "Rainbow" chapter.

Lammeter wedding and of Cliff's stables are as well known and as eagerly anticipated as the songs of the master singers of traditional pastoral. This is not an idle comparison, for Mr. Macey has been in his time the leading singer in the village, and around him revolves a conversational skirmish about musical abilities. What the company expects to hear, however, is not a song but a tale, because, as befits a novel, Mr. Macey is also the village storyteller. The transition from one to another of his stories epitomizes the literary character of the scene:

> Every one of Mr. Macey's audience had heard this story many times, but it was listened to as if it had been a favourite tune, and at certain points the puffing of the pipes was momentarily suspended, that the listeners might give their whole minds to the expected words. But there was more to come; and Mr Snell, the landlord, duly put the leading question. (102)

This answers precisely to Leslie Stephen's account. One takes the first sentence to be an outsider's observation, yet it is so close to the scene that the beginning of the second—"but there was more to come"—registers the anticipation of all the listeners, ourselves now included. Similarly, the comparison of the story to "a favourite tune," though it may remind us of the eclogues of which this company has never heard, is drawn from their own world and indeed their own estimation of Mr. Macey. As with the details, so with the chapter as a whole. We cannot attribute its programmatic character and formal disposition simply to the author, because these very aspects are (represented as) produced by the characters themselves—not only the landlord, whose conscious social role brings to mind the shepherds who invite and judge traditional singing contests, but the whole group of men, who know what to expect of each other and their evenings together.

When we ask of this chapter what we asked of "The Harvest Supper"— how does it function in the novel?—we can see the difference between *Silas Marner* and *Adam Bede*. To begin with, it is strongly motivated as an element of the plot. When Silas discovers that his gold has been stolen, his anguish prompts him to do what he has not done in the fifteen years he has lived in Raveloe—reach out to the villagers whom he has known only as customers and who only know him as a suspiciously odd and solitary person. He rushes to the Rainbow expecting to find there "the powers and dignities of Raveloe" (94), and though on this night, exceptionally, they are not there, his action in fact leads to public knowledge of his loss and thus to the first stages of his neighbors' concern for him and of his "consciousness of dependence" on them (135). But this plot articulation, which seems strong and direct when summarized, is achieved in the mode of pastoral narration. The tension which ends chapter 5, where Silas runs to the village and turns into the Rainbow, is diverted and relaxed by the opening sentence of chapter 6: "The conversation, which was at a high pitch of animation when Silas approached the door of the Rainbow, had, as usual, been slow and intermittent when the company first assembled" (95). As it unfolds, this sentence creates a narrative articulation that is specifically pastoral. For after the long relative clause at the beginning, the main verb phrase could well have been "stopped when Silas entered." Instead, the sentence turns us back to the beginning of the evening, thus dissipating dramatic expectation and enabling the set piece, the prose eclogue, that follows.

Pastoral narrations have no difficulty suspending action; the trick is to resume it. *Silas Marner* is masterful in this respect. If the scene at the Rainbow suspends the drama of Silas's arrival, it motivates its resumption by the final episode in the evening's social ritual—a familiar quarrel about the reality of ghosts which is generated, as the company expects it to be, by Mr. Macey's story of Cliff's stables. When chapter 7 begins with the men catching sight of Silas, their surprise at seeing the weaver in their midst, "looking round at the company with his strange unearthly eyes" (106), is augmented by their anxiety that he may be an unwelcome proof in the argument they have been conducting. Simply as a return to the action, the moment is not unlike Silas's snapping out of one of his cataleptic trances, but the broader effect of the evening's conversation is a function of its pastoralism. Both its themes (as we shall see later) and its dynamics determine the subsequent representation of Silas's loss and his plight. For as the villagers and the constituted authorities take cognizance of the theft, they develop a communal story to explain it that becomes one of the local tales, like those told by Mr. Macey.

In combining irony at the expense of the village fabulations with a sympathetic sense of what gives rise to them, the account of this new story exemplifies the "humor" which contemporary reviewers and critics took to be the hallmark of George Eliot's country scenes.[12] But is it genuinely pastoral in mode? If the conversation at the Rainbow reveals the way in which Raveloe will represent what has happened to Silas, does it also shape the novelist's representation of his loss and plight? Or to put it in terms of traditional pastoral, if the scene at the Rainbow is a prose eclogue, is the narrator herself represented by the local speakers?[13] At first glance the narrator of *Silas Marner* seems like those of George Eliot's other novels: she is "omniscient" in respect to the characters and their lives and given to general reflections that arise from the story she tells. One contemporary reviewer said that "as there is less of dialogue and more

12. See *Critical Heritage*, 172–73, 176, 184, 188. On humor, see Harry Levin, *Playboys and Killjoys: An Essay on the Theory and Practice of Comedy* (New York: Oxford University Press, 1987), 175–91.

13. Eliot does not follow the precedent of George Sand's *romans champêtres*, which she much admired, in attributing Silas Marner's story to a local narrator. Indeed, in this respect, she is closer to George Sand in *Adam Bede*, where she occasionally presents herself as someone actually acquainted with the scene and characters of the novel. Cf. especially p. 225 (chap. 17).

of narrative . . . than is usual in the novels of this author, she appears to have felt the necessity of elaborating her own remarks to the uttermost."[14] The initial observation is correct, but the implication drawn is misleading. From the beginning, as in the Rainbow scene, the narrator's discourse is close to the characters and their points of view. We might expect the narrator to establish a sense of identification with Silas, the unlikely protagonist and object of our concern. But her closeness to her characters is equally striking in the passages concerning the inhabitants of Raveloe, where the predominant narrative technique is "free indirect style" (*style indirect libre*), or "represented thought and speech."[15] It appears in the novel's first paragraph, to convey the rustic suspicion of weavers, and comes fully into play when Silas, using his knowledge of medicinal herbs, gives the cobbler's wife a preparation of foxglove, to relieve the symptoms of heart disease.

> Sally Oates's disease had raised her into a personage of much interest and importance among the neighbours, and the fact of her having found relief from drinking Silas Marner's 'stuff' became a matter of general discourse. When Doctor Kimble gave physic, it was natural that it should have an effect; but when a weaver, who came from nobody knew where, worked wonders with a bottle of brown waters, the occult character of the process was evident. Such a sort of thing had not been known since the Wise Woman at Tarley died; and she had charms as well as 'stuff': everybody went to her when their children had fits. Silas Marner must be a person of the same sort, for how did he know what would bring back Sally Oates's breath, if he didn't know a fine sight more than that? (66)

This rural ventriloquism pervades the narrative in the early chapters. We first learn of the cure of Sally Oates at the beginning of Silas's story, when it is mentioned, in a long paragraph in indirect style, as something we already know about. It is in this same paragraph that we first hear of Silas's catalepsy, which is not so named, but is noted through the eyes of Jem Rodney, the mole catcher, who has come upon Silas in the middle of a fit.

Free indirect style, when it represents rural characters, is an obvious means of "putting the complex into the simple." But what motivates this novelistic pastoral? There is a clear sense in which Silas Marner himself is a pastoral figure. Socially humble, innocent, his life determined by loss and reduced to a simple round of activity, he is nevertheless made to seem representative in his suffering and his needs. A sentence that seems to dehumanize him—"he seemed to weave, like the spider, from pure impulse, without reflection"—is followed by one suggesting, as in traditional pastoral, that sophisticated persons are to see

14. E. S. Dallas, in *Critical Heritage*, 184.
15. See Ann Banfield, *Unspeakable Sentences* (Boston: Routledge and Kegan Paul, 1982).

themselves in this figure: "Every man's work, pursued steadily, tends in this way to become an end in itself, and so to bridge over the loveless chasms of his life" (64). Our connection with Silas emerges with more particularity, when we think of him—again in a way prompted by traditional pastoral—as an authorial self-representation. Apart from autobiographical connections (to be mentioned later), the comparison of Silas's hoarding to a prisoner's absorption in the marks he makes on his wall (67) brings out a likeness to the work of writing;[16] similarly, the novelist's imagination is not unlike Silas's devotion to his coins, whose "bright faces . . . were all his own" (65), and which become his "familiars" and companions (68), even his children (70).

At one point, the narrator makes explicit the likeness between Silas's work and that done in her world: "The same sort of process has perhaps been undergone by wiser men, when they have been cut off from faith and love— only, instead of a loom and a heap of guineas, they have had some erudite research, some ingenious project, or some well-knit theory" (68–69). But more important than this quotable, familiarly Eliotic general appeal—in which condescension perhaps leaks in through the single word "perhaps"—is the pastoral form the analogy then assumes. In the next sentence, Marner's physical appearance, bent "into a constant mechanical relation to the objects of his life," is said to convey "the same sort of impression as a handle or a crooked tube, which has no meaning standing apart." Though one can recast this as a withering remark (think of it in the mouth of Mrs. Poyser), it does not have that effect. Rather the metaphor immediately recurs as a link between character and narrator, in the beautiful Wordsworthian anecdote of Silas's water jug:

> It had been his companion for twelve years, always standing on the same spot, always lending its handle to him in the early morning, so that its form had an expression for him of willing helpfulness, and the impress of its handle on his palm gave a satisfaction mingled with that of having the fresh clear water. (69)

The physical "impress," transforming the earlier visual "impression," aligns the writer's work of felicitous representation with the character's satisfaction of a simple, daily need. The end of the anecdote completes the analogy, as it tells of fragmentation and reconstruction. Silas accidentally breaks his jug and though it "could never be of use to him any more, . . . he stuck the bits together and propped the ruin in its old place for a memorial."

But the account of Silas is only half the story of authorial self-representation and of the relation of complex persons to simple. Silas's lonely,

---

16. I am indebted for this point to an unpublished essay by Neil Hertz. Silas Marner's occupation as a weaver is sufficiently determined by novelistic considerations; nevertheless, it may be worth noting the traditional association of weaving and writing.

self-absorbed activity could not represent two elements that Eliot considered crucial in the imagination of both novelist and reader—understanding and sympathy. Their problematic character for Eliot, at this stage of her career, is seen in the bizarre story, "The Lifted Veil," written while she was working on *The Mill on the Floss.* Latimer, the first-person narrator of this story is cursed with an ability to know the thoughts of others, as if no veil existed between his mind and theirs. This is, one might think, the novelist's power, but for Latimer—a poet in temperament, but incapable of achieved utterance—understanding and identifying with the "normal" world produces only a sense of persecution. Much of this story is refigured in that of Silas Marner, whose "inward life had been a history and a metamorphosis, as that of every fervid nature must be when it has fled, or been condemned to solitude" (56). In *Silas Marner,* the plight of this protagonist is not relieved merely by the generosity of narrator and reader, nor is the question of "The Lifted Veil"—in what mode can we know the inner life of others?—confined to our omniscience. Instead the narrator reposes part of (her representation of) the problem of knowing Silas in the people among whom he lives. Hence Raveloe's view is central to the opening chapters, giving us our very first sight of Silas (mischievous boys peeping at him, in his mysterious loom) and alternating with the narrator's accounts of his past history and present life. The double relation to Silas brings out why Eliot cast this tale, of which she imagined Wordsworth to be the ideal reader, in the form of a novel.[17] It also shows how *Silas Marner* is allied to earlier pastorals, in which sophisticated self-representation is a function of multiple pastoral figures.

After the chapter at the Rainbow, in which we first hear the villagers in their own voices, the narration is accommodated to the direct speech of Raveloe. We can see this at precisely the point at which Raveloe's story about the theft of Silas's gold seems to give way to the narrator's resuming her own account of his loss. When the excitement about the robbery dies down, the event settles into being the subject of such ongoing arguments as we have overheard at the Rainbow. "But while poor Silas's loss served thus to brush the slow current of Raveloe conversation, Silas himself was feeling the withering desolation of that bereavement about which his neighbours were arguing at their ease" (129). This sentence introduces two paragraphs expressing the narrator's sense of Silas's suffering, which is represented by his moaning to himself at night, "very low—not as one who seeks to be heard" (130). The next paragraph begins:

17. In a letter to her publisher, Eliot said: "I have felt all through as if the story would have lent itself best to metrical rather than prose fiction, especially in all that relates to the psychology of Silas; except that, under that treatment, there could not be an equal play of humour." The allusion to Wordsworth is in the same letter: "I should not have believed that any one would have been interested in [the story] but myself (since William Wordsworth is dead)." *Letters,* 3:382.

"And yet he was not utterly forsaken in his trouble." This engages the sympathy we have just been made to feel and, with its biblical ring, intimates a providential care that would seem allied to authorial omniscience. But what authenticates the sentence at this moment is a return to the inhabitants of Raveloe and their genuine, if narrow, sympathy for Silas. Several instances are given, but the main ones are two visits by well-wishers—old Mr. Macey, who treats the uncomprehending Silas to a complacently knowing discourse about his plight, and a new character, the first onstage female in the novel, the good-hearted Dolly Winthrop. She has come to bring Silas some cakes and to urge him to attend church on Christmas, which she vaguely but powerfully imagines will make him feel better and join him to his fellows. (Mr. Macey gave him the same advice, but being a tailor identified it most closely with purchasing a Sunday suit.) Silas senses her good intentions, but the two can scarcely understand each other. He says he has never been to church, because he called it "chapel," a word Dolly has never heard (137). Thus, "poor Dolly's exposition of her simple Raveloe theology fell rather unmeaningly on Silas's ears, for there was no word in it that could rouse a memory of what he had known as religion [in the dissenting sect at Lantern Yard]" (138).

Nevertheless, Dolly's and Silas's difficulty in understanding each other comes to represent our own sympathetic understanding. When Dolly presents the lard cakes she has baked, she remarks that they have letters pricked in them that she cannot read, but whose meaning she knows is good, because she has seen them on the altar cloth at church. Silas, to her surprise, can read them— IHS—and this small feat prompts her to further remarks on the goodness of the cakes and the letters. "Silas was as unable to interpret the letters as Dolly, but there was no possibility of misunderstanding the desire to give comfort that made itself heard in her quiet tones" (136). Two elements in the scene explain how Dolly's artless talk, Silas's attentive but thwarted responsiveness, and their very imperfect understanding of each other can sustain the narration at this point. The first is Dolly's confidence that one can sense a good meaning without knowing what words or letters mean. This question has already been at the center of Mr. Macey's story of the Lammeter marriage, the one his audience heard "like a favorite tune." It seems that the parson had mistakenly switched genders in the ceremony, asking the man to take the woman as his wedded husband and vice versa, and no one, including the couple, noticed. Mr. Macey, ever alert as the parish clerk, worries that the marriage will not be valid. He asks himself, "Is't the meanin' or the words as makes folks fast i' wedlock?" (101) and turns the question now one way, now the other. What makes this pastoral wit, on the author's part, is that we do not have a ready answer to Mr. Macey's question. We can feel, as R. H. Hutton said in a contemporary review, that at this moment, "a faint shadow of the intellectual phases of 'modern thought,'—just sufficient to remind the reader of the form which they take in the present day, without in any way marring the truth of the picture,—begins to fall on the discussion."[18] The fact that our first encounter with Raveloe talk produces this piece of comic-intellectual pastoral—it is not unlike passages in *Love's Labour's Lost*—makes it more plausible that Dolly Winthrop, who speaks from her heart not her head, knows what she is talking about when she says one can be sure of meanings while puzzling over the words. And this effect is secured by the fact that when it comes to interpreting IHS, we are not so superior to Dolly and Silas as we might think. We can read the letters, like Silas, and we know, like Dolly, that they have connections with the church. But what do they mean? If you think (as I did) that they stand for *in hoc signo* [*vinces*], someone will say, with equal authority, that they mean *Iesus hominum salvator*, or yet again, *Iesum habemus socium*. And in any case, all these interpretations derive historically from a failure to recognize that IHS are the first three letters of Jesus's name when written in Greek capitals. If you think you know unequivocally what the letters mean, you are less different from Silas and Dolly than you imagine; if you are aware of the various interpretations and the history of the letters, you recognize that your knowledge is an intellectual version of Dolly's puzzlement.[19]

After Silas's gold is stolen, a scene with Dolly marks each stage of his story. Her second visit occurs when she comes to advise him about caring for the baby Eppie (chapter 14); like their first scene, it plays their sense of trust in each other against their difficulty in comprehending differences of religion, gender, and the customs they grew up to believe are natural. At the beginning of Part II (chapter 16), before the stolen gold is found, it is Dolly to whom Silas tells the story of the injustice done to him in Lantern Yard and with whom he puzzles out the bad and the good in his life; when he returns from his trip to the site of Lantern Yard, it is she whom he tells, in what can be considered the last scene of the novel, that Raveloe is now his only home.[20] This reliance on the scenes with Dolly to carry Silas's story brings out what is distinctive in the narration of *Silas Marner*. George Eliot spoke of having sought to give *The Mill*

---

18. *Critical Heritage*, 176–77.

19. I do not want to claim to have been in any better position than my own or George Eliot's readers. The one thing I did know that Dolly and Silas did not is that I could look up "IHS" in the *Oxford Dictionary of the Christian Church*. To the information given there, OED adds yet another interpretation, *in hac salus* (in this [cross] is salvation), and a revealing citation, the only nineteenth-century example, from the *Daily News*, 1897: "The monograms IHS and XPC, which are so often to be seen in our churches, sorely puzzle a portion of the congregation."

20. My phrasing may seem oddly evasive, since any novel presumably has only one last scene. But George Eliot ends all her novels, except *Daniel Deronda*, with unnumbered chapters titled "Epilogue" (*Adam Bede, Romola, Felix Holt*), "Conclusion" (*The Mill on the Floss, Silas Marner*), or "Finale" (*Middlemarch*). This device creates the effect of a double ending. It is, indeed, less marked in *Silas Marner* than in its two predecessors, but it is still felt, since the "Conclusion" is a set piece devoted to Eppie's wedding. The final conversation between Silas and Dolly concludes the last of the numbered chapters.

on the Floss a certain epic breadth.[21] In her pastoral novel, by contrast, she casts her narration in a way that suggests "the slow current of Raveloe conversation." This effect arises not only from the scenes of conversation themselves, in which Dolly, for example, is allowed a certain repetitiousness and loquacity, but also in the way they arise. We have described the first of these scenes as a direct consequence of Raveloe's reaction to the theft of Silas's gold. But as with Silas's appearance at the Rainbow, the lines of action that lead to this scene are suspended, as the narrator interrupts her account of the investigation of the theft to return, for a chapter and a half (pp. 115–27), to the Godfrey Cass plot. The narrator's statement about the slow spiritual growth that will follow Silas's first "opening his trouble to his Raveloe neighbours" (108), is largely made good, in the chapters that follow, by the mode of narration.

II

But even if we recognize the pastoral mode of Silas's story, are we to say that the whole of *Silas Marner*, with its double plot, is a pastoral novel? One way to answer this question follows the traditional view that among Eliot's novels, *Silas Marner*, as James put it, "has more of that simple, rounded, consummate aspect, that absence of loose ends and gaping issues, which marks a classical work."[22] This view is responsive to the balancing and interweaving of the two plots and the way their well-articulated connections convey moral consequences. A recent critic explains the general view that *Silas Marner* is a "fable" by saying that it "is governed by two patterned stories that might be diagrammed."[23] The satisfying wholeness of *Silas Marner* does not entail, but is certainly compatible with, interpreting it as a pastoral. Though the two protagonists and their stories stand in a "high-low" relation to each other, the whole world of Raveloe, including the Cass family and their friends, is represented as provincial and simple. Nancy Lammeter is very much a fair shepherdess of the pastoral novel: her hands roughened by butter-making (147) do not disallow the imagery of birds and flowers that attends her, and primness and narrow probity, which are her strengths, determine the bounds of her life. Even on the painful side of the story, the treatment of Godfrey Cass is considerably milder than that of Arthur Donnithorne and Tito Melema, his amiably self-serving *semblables* in *Adam Bede* and *Romola*. In addition, the traditional division of George Eliot's career into "early" and "late" phases adds weight to the view that *Silas Marner* as a whole is

21. *Letters*, 3:317–18.

22. *Literary Criticism*, 916.

23. George Levine, "*Romola* as Fable," in Barbara Hardy, ed., *Critical Essays on George Eliot* (London: Routledge & Kegan Paul, 1970), 79.

a pastoral. If "George Eliot's early books owe their charm to the exquisite painting of the old country-life," as Leslie Stephen said, then *Silas Marner* clearly
belongs with the "early" novels, while *Romola*, which was published two years
later (1863), is the first of the "late."[24]

Though this division between early and late novels seems obvious, some
recent studies have drawn attention to what is new in *Silas Marner*, which is
therefore seen to have a different relation to George Eliot's career. Its writing
interrupted the work she had begun on *Romola*, and the two novels have more
in common than one would expect from their strikingly different modes.[25]
What primarily concerns us, however, is what it means to think of *Silas Marner*
not simply as harking back to the historical time and the artistic manner of its
predecessors, particularly *Adam Bede*, but as showing signs of difference from
them. It is George Eliot's first novel to focus on an outsider, the first in which
the protagonist's past is divided from his present, and the first to treat motifs
that remain important in her novels, such as blackmail and foster parenting.[26]
Some critics have drawn attention to the "autobiographical matrix" of *Silas
Marner*. It and "Brother Jacob" (which rather crudely concerns exposing the protagonist's past) were the first works wholly written after the main secret of
Eliot's own past, the authorship of *Scenes from Clerical Life* and *Adam Bede*, became
known to the public; one can also see connections with her intense concern
about the one earned by her novels and the fact that this period of her life was

24. *Critical Heritage*, 474–75. According to David Carroll, the editor of this volume, it was Stephen
who first made this distinction. However, it was implicit in contemporary reviews and accounts of
Eliot's novels. Cf. James's review of *Middlemarch*, in which, after praising its intellectual power and
genuine philosophic weight, he says: "These great qualities imply corresponding perils. The first is
the loss of simplicity. George Eliot lost hers some time since; it lies buried (in a splendid mauso-
leum) in 'Romola'" (*Literary Criticism*, 965). The sharp division between early and late novels is
maintained, though with a newly emphatic preference of the latter, in F. R. Leavis's influential
chapter in *The Great Tradition*.

25. We have already noted Tito Melema's resemblance to Godfrey Cass as a character type, but
not the fact that he too has a clandestine marriage (the children of which, in yet another parallel,
are ultimately taken care of by the titular figure). But Tito also resembles Silas Marner, in that both
are outsiders in communities where all the inhabitants are well known to each other. Another
outsider in *Romola*, Baldessare, is a tragic version of Silas. He too has a "fervent nature" (chap. 30);
a past betrayal of his love has made his mind too a blank and left him an outcast, with only an
obsession (in his case with revenge) to sustain his desire to live. Still other likenesses could be
detailed—e.g. the internalization, in the Florence of *Romola*, of the religious communities represented by Lantern Yard and the Raveloe church.

26. On blackmail, see Alexander Welsh, *George Eliot and Blackmail* (Cambridge: Harvard University
Press, 1985). On foster parenting, see Beer (above, n. 8). Both Welsh and Beer group *Silas Marner*
and *Romola* as transitional works. Welsh's analysis of the theme of blackmail is connected with the
larger point that *Silas Marner* is a "fiction of discontinuity, the story of a person cut off from his
past" (160)

critical in establishing her relation to her own foster children, G. H. Lewes's sons.[27] So far as the novel's form is concerned, it is the first, as Philip Fisher says, "that critics speak of by parts, a Marner half connected only at flash points with a Cass half. Each novel that follows can be divided similarly."[28] On this view, the novel's integrity, as John Preston puts it, is that "it brings [the two plots] together in the only way possible, by an imaginative understanding" of "what neither story separately can have, the knowledge of its connections with the other story."[29]

Critics who emphasize the separateness of the two plots of *Silas Marner* tend to treat it as a novel like any other, and thus have difficulty accommodating its pastoralism.[30] But they raise the question we need to ask, which is how the particular ways of this novel establish the privileged position of its reader. He or she is of course construed, as Leslie Stephen said, as "one who has travelled out of sight of the village spire, and known the thoughts and feelings which are stirring in the great world outside." But this knowledge, which puts us in a pastoral relation to Raveloe and its inhabitants, is itself given a pastoral representation. The distinctive tactics of the first chapter—drawing us first into the Raveloe world and then, via our identification with Silas, taking us back to Lantern Yard—has the effect of making us possess not knowledge of the great world as such, but knowledge of the two simple worlds in which the protagonist has lived. The treatment recalls dialogic eclogues, in which differing experiences and views are equally represented as those of shepherds. Eliot's pastoral construing of the reader is made explicit in the sentence that begins chapter 2:

27. Lawrence Jay Dessner, "The Autobiographical Matrix of *Silas Marner,*" *Studies in the Novel* 11 (1979): 251–82. Welsh, 161–68. Gordon S. Haight, *George Eliot: A Biography* (New York: Oxford University Press, 1968) (339–40), points out the importance of money as a theme in "Brother Jacob" and *Silas Marner,* but he scarcely hints at Eliot's eagerness (Dessner, 259, calls it greed) in her business dealings at this time.

28. Philip Fisher, *Making Up Society: The Novels of George Eliot* (Pittsburgh: University of Pittsburgh Press, 1981), 105.

29. "The Community of the Novel: *Silas Marner,*" in *Comparative Criticism: A Yearbook,* vol. 2, ed. Elinor Shaffer (Cambridge: Cambridge University Press, 1980): 125.

30. For Fisher the overall sense of "idyllic, hazy recovery" (115) makes it impossible to accept with conviction what Preston calls the Cass plot's *"other* story, in which there is no redemption, no rescue, no gift" (120). Preston accepts the invitation of the two plots, but at the expense of the pastoralism. For him, Raveloe is "as blind and mechanical" as Silas's own life there (117), and is no better, in its provincialism, than Lantern Yard. It is crucial to his account that the only true community in *Silas Marner* is that constituted by the novel itself. Everything depends on the reader's grasp of the double plot: "Marner's story . . . is going to get into the repertoire of tales told at the Rainbow. . . . But, like all their tales, it falls short of the true meaning of the events. . . . What seems strange in it, a blessing, a gift of grace, is in reality explicable, the visible consequence of another and invisible history" (125).

> Even people whose lives have been made various by learning, sometimes find it hard to keep a fast hold on their habitual views of life, on their faith in the Invisible, nay, on the sense that their past joys and sorrows are a real experience, when they are suddenly transported to a new land, where the beings around them know nothing of their history, and share none of their ideas—where their mother earth shows another lap, and human life has other forms than those on which their souls have been nourished. (62)

The final, naturalizing metaphors do not transcend social particularities and differences, for they confirm the assumption that selfhood consists in maintaining a fast hold on our own knowledge and experience; our ability to understand the two provincial worlds of chapter 1 shows our awareness of this condition, but not our freedom from it. After thus beginning chapter 2, the narrator enacts our self-understanding by returning to the "new land" of Raveloe by means of Silas and his sense of change. "There was nothing here, when he rose in the deep morning quiet and looked out on the dewy brambles and rank tufted grass, that seemed to have any relation with that life centring in Lantern Yard" (63). The understanding to which this sentence appeals—balancing the richly descriptive subordinate clause against the general moral force of the last quoted phrase—is construed as the ability to imagine more than one such world. It therefore introduces a full description, warm and sustaining, of the chapel services and the singing that Silas knew in Lantern Yard. Only then do we turn to his new home with a question which looks rhetorical in the usual sense, but which gains its force from its truth to his narrow experience: "And what could be more unlike that Lantern Yard world than the world in Raveloe?"

Silas Marner continuously appeals to and constitutes the reader's capacities in terms of paired phenomena that, taken individually, are of a pastoral simplicity and completeness. Our ongoing understanding of Silas and our overview of his conversations with Dolly are constituted by the initial pairing of Lantern Yard and Raveloe. But other aspects of the novel engage paired divisions within Raveloe's world—of class, as represented by the Red House (the Cass home) and the Rainbow, and also by the two rooms of the Rainbow; of gender (there is a shift, after Eppie arrives, from the world of men to the domestic world of women), and of generation. There are also thematic pairs, of which one of the most striking emerges in a formal pairing—when a conversation at the Red House brings out the significance of one of Mr. Macey's tales at the Rainbow. This concerns the first Mr. Lammeter, who both did and did not belong in Raveloe: he was a stranger, "from a bit north'ard," and yet (unlike his fellow northerner, Silas) he "know'd the rights and customs o' things" (100). At the New Year's party, a slightly tense discussion (itself informed by the division between old and young) is the occasion for characterizing his son, the present Mr. Lammeter:

His spare but healthy person, and high-featured firm face, that looked as if it had never been flushed by excess, was in strong contrast, not only with the Squire's, but with the appearance of the Raveloe farmers generally—in accordance with a favourite saying of his own, that "breed was stronger than pasture." (153)

We usually encode this duality as nature and nurture, but Mr. Lammeter's version, both by its metaphor and its aphoristic pith, brings out the novel's consistently pastoral mode of representation (also evident when we are informed that his favorite song is "Over the hills and far away"). The relative strengths of breed and pasture structure our sense of Silas's experience and underlie the climactic dramatic moment when Eppie chooses to remain with Silas, her foster father, and not to live with Godfrey, her newly confessed natural father. This crisis also brings into play the dualities of class and generation: "I wasn't brought up to be a lady," Eppie says, "and I can't turn my mind to it. I like the working-folks, and their victuals, and their ways. And . . . I'm promised to marry a working-man, as 'll live with father, and help me to take care of him" (234). The progress of this scene shows that the various dualities are neither simple nor neatly divided. When Silas, for example, defies Godfrey and says, "Your coming now and saying 'I'm her father' doesn't alter the feelings inside us" (231), "pasture" has acquired the force of "breed." But the fact that speeches and situations are open to being construed in these terms shows what is mistaken in Fisher's objection that "the harsh substance of the book provides the motive for the compensating surface of sentimentality" (109). Both the represented substance and the mode of representation of *Silas Marner* are determined by the pastoral doubling that pervades the narration and provides both novelistic texture and formal organization.

Pastoral pairings structure the plot of *Silas Marner*, most obviously in the exchange of Silas's gold for the child. Furthermore, time, the medium of plot, comes in clear and simple blocks—the present of Part I, in "timeless" Raveloe, set against Silas's past, fifteen years earlier, in Lantern Yard, and a symmetrical jump of sixteen years to Part II, in which we find Eppie grown up, Silas ready to give up his work, and Godfrey and Nancy married, childless, and middle-aged. But within this framework Silas experiences the drama of human time— the general problematics of purpose and hope, which is what gives interest and dignity to his narrow life, and the specific need to overcome his past experiences as he learns to trust the people he now lives among. Because he is thus defined by a continuous sense of self, he can be a serious novelistic protagonist, even though he is a "poor mushed creatur'" (130). Similarly, the two plots are not simply juxtaposed, but are connected by critical turning points. These, indeed, are something of a problem, for they more than once depend on chance occurrences. The traditional solution to this difficulty is simply to accept the novel as it is, to say, with F. R. Leavis, that its "atmosphere precludes too direct a reference . . . to our everyday sense of how things happen."[31] Recent critics have not accepted this argument. When they do not feel Fisher's impatience, they register ambivalence like Alexander Welsh's: "The chapter that brings Dunstan to the edge of the stone pit (ch. 4) is a model of George Eliot's ability to narrate circumstances, character, and the character's rationalizations in brief compass, but this effective realism scarcely conceals the commitment of the double plot to chance."[32] But if the realism is effective, it is likely to have done a better job of "concealing" than Welsh allows.

The artistic challenge, of course, is not to conceal strange occurrences, but to make them plausible. Eliot acknowledges the difficulty in one of the thematic dualities that arise from the conversation at the Rainbow. The concluding argument, about whether a "reasonable" person believes in ghosts, carries over into the investigation of the theft. Most of Raveloe attributes the theft to a pedlar, to whom are attached both the one apparent clue (a tinderbox found near Silas's cottage) and invented appurtenances like large earrings and a suspicious look. But a minority, led by Mr. Macey, hints that other than human hands may have been responsible. As the narrator sums it up: "When the robbery was talked of at the Rainbow and elsewhere, in good company, the balance continued to waver between the rational explanation founded on the tinder-box, and the theory of an impenetrable mystery that mocked investigation" (128). This controversy reflects the dilemmas of religious belief experienced by many Victorians, including George Eliot,[33] but it also bears on the conduct of the novel. Just as the invention of the guilty pedlar is a parody of novel-writing itself—taking a known object to have a metonymic relation to an event, and imagining other plausible facts that will build up a whole account of motives and actions—so the division of opinion brings to mind the double plot and its different perspectives. But its pertinence is not the neat division between superstition and rationality, but rather their joint presence in our minds, as in Raveloe's. If the villagers' "rational explanation" is generated by superstition, the reader discovers that plot workings which seem clear as day yield their own sense of mystery.

The most remarkable such moment is also the most important, the cataleptic fit that Silas undergoes when the infant Eppie crawls into his house. She is already there, when the narrator turns back, asking, "But where was Silas Marner while this strange visitor had come to his hearth?" (166) She answers

31. *The Great Tradition* (New York: Anchor Books, 1954), 63.

32. Welsh, 166. Beer (127–31) emphasizes the role of coincidence in *Silas Marner,* but mistakenly says that the theft of Silas's gold was made possible by one of his cataleptic fits (130).

33. See, e.g., U. C. Knoepflmacher, *George Eliot's Early Novels: The Limits of Realism* (Berkeley & Los Angeles: University of California Press, 1968).

this question by recounting the habit into which Silas had fallen, of looking out his door, "as if he thought that his money might be somehow coming back to him." Evening after evening he would stand "listening and gazing, not with hope, but with mere yearning and unrest" (in this he strongly resembles Godfrey). On New Year's Eve, some friendly but slightly heartless Raveloe jesting had increased his anticipation:

> Since the oncoming of twilight he had opened his door again and again, though only to shut it immediately at seeing all distance veiled by the falling snow. But the last time he opened it the snow had ceased, and the clouds were parting here and there. He stood and listened, and gazed for a long while—there was really something on the road coming towards him then, but he caught no sign of it: and the stillness and the wide trackless snow seemed to narrow his solitude, and touched his yearning with the chill of despair. [Here he is less like Godfrey than like Molly, to whom the last phrase applies with painful literalness.] He went in again, and put his right hand on the latch of the door to close it—but he did not close it: he was arrested, as he had been already since his loss, by the invisible wand of catalepsy, and stood like a graven image, with wide but sightless eyes, holding open his door, powerless to resist either the good or evil that might enter there. (166–67)

There are several things to notice about this passage. First, the fact that Silas's door is open—so that the infant is able to see the light towards which she crawls—is due to the realistically motivated looking outside. Second, the powerful atmosphere here is not that of fairy tale or English idyll, but of a Wordsworthian landscape as the site of spiritual extremity. But most important is the way the catalepsy is produced. In a beautiful bit of imitative writing, its onset interrupts our following Silas's action in closing the door; its naming, as the agent of the passive verb "arrested," is itself arrested by the information that Silas's loss of his gold had occasioned recurrences of his losses of consciousness. When it is finally named, "the invisible wand of catalepsy" fuses the rational and the mysterious and perfectly suspends their competing explanatory claims. On the side of rational explanation are the plausible fact just reported, about fits prompted by Silas's loss, and the term "catalepsy," which accurately names what both Raveloe and Lantern Yard consider otherworldly visitations.[34] On

---

34. The effect is enhanced by the fact that this is the first time in the novel the noun "catalepsy" is used. It was first mentioned in Jem Rodney's indirectly represented narration and then more fully described, but still not named, in the account of Silas's life in Lantern Yard (56). Two pages later it is mentioned as if we have already understood what it is: "It was at this point in their history that Silas's cataleptic fit occurred during the prayer-meeting" (58). The use of an adjectival phrase (suggesting a single occurrence, rather than a permanent condition) and its oblique placement in this sentence bring out, by contrast, the fullness and resonance of "the invisible wand of catalepsy."

the other hand, the metaphor of the invisible wand epitomizes the rhetorical skills, to which we have already submitted, of the sentence and the whole passage. But the metaphor confirms novelistic powers beyond the local context. Both its elements, invisibility and a magician's powers, connect our sense of the strangeness of this event to the represented feelings and beliefs, in the world of Silas and his neighbors, that have helped lead us to this climactic moment.

At the end of the long paragraph in which Silas, "in utter amazement," discovers the sleeping child, the narrator speaks of his "presentiment of some Power presiding over his life": "for his imagination had not yet extricated itself from the sense of mystery in the child's sudden presence, and had formed no conjectures of ordinary natural means by which the event could have been brought about" (168). Not only are those "ordinary natural means" the events of the Cass plot, but Silas, in any frame of mind, could have had no knowledge of them. It therefore seems, as Fisher and Preston suggest, that the power presiding over Silas's life is the novelist herself. But the sense of providential workings comes from pastoral representations. Though due to connections in the plot, it is always tied, as a matter of felt, represented reality, to Silas's sense of himself and his experience. (His first thought when he sees the child is that it is "his little sister come back to him in a dream—his little sister whom he had carried about in his arms for a year before she died, when he was a small boy without shoes or stockings" [167–68].) His presentiment when he discovers the child is not, so to speak, absolute, but is due to the stirring of "fibres that had never been moved in Raveloe—old quiverings of tenderness—old impressions of awe at the presentiment," etc. The question of whether benign powers supervise human life, which Dolly and Silas puzzle out together, is always represented as a matter not simply of general belief, such as Dolly expresses, but of Silas's need to believe that his life as a whole makes sense and to regain a sense of connection to the person he was in Lantern Yard. This is both pastoral, because centered on the simple person, and novelistic, because engaged with the felt character of an individual life.

The very integrity of *Silas Marner*, as of any good pastoral, makes evident its limitations and its own sense of them. It does not, for example, attempt to represent the rural world in the manner of Riehl's "natural history." We see nothing of what we do in *Adam Bede*: the village at work, agricultural production, the church and the clergy. What we do see is what might have been predicted from Renaissance pastoral romances: festive social gatherings (both quotidian and seasonal), a wide range of conversation and music-making, and, on the side of practical life, much attention to food. There is a similar awareness of limitations—a sense of how much novelistic reality a pastoral can absorb—in the treatment of Silas himself. When she replaces his hoarded gold, the child Eppie not only connects him to a living world, but seems to introduce the principle that underlies most novels:

The gold had kept his thoughts in an ever-repeated circle, leading to nothing beyond itself; but Eppie was an object compacted of changes and hopes that forced his thoughts onward, and carried them far away from their old eager pacing towards the same blank limit—carried them away to the new things that would come with the coming years. (184)

But the apparent launching of Silas and Eppie on the tides of change does not survive even this sentence, which concludes by emphasizing retrospection and the timeless life of the village.[35] Just as the novel skips over the years in which Eppie grows up (and in which Godfrey and Nancy come to marry), so her life with Silas is represented by set pieces, like the failed discipline of the coal hole, and static images of the organic, like their romps in nature.

If some of this writing is too charming by half, as if unwittingly to exemplify the limitations of a pastoral, the author's clear understanding of those limitations emerges in the episode with which Silas's story concludes. One sign of his new life in Raveloe has been his desire to understand what happened to him in Lantern Yard, particularly the fact that the case against him was decided by casting lots (the novel's most explicit encoding of the question of whether there are guiding reasons behind chance occurrences). With everything in his life apparently settled—his gold recovered, Eppie grown up, his household about to be completed with her marriage—he decides to return to Lantern Yard, both to see if his innocence had been established after he left, and to question the minister about the biblical practice that had condemned him. When he and Eppie reach the unnamed city and Silas at last locates the lanes and alleys he knew, they find not Lantern Yard, which has completely disappeared, but "a large factory, from which men and women were streaming for their mid-day meal" (240). It is a stunning glimpse of the urban, industrial England that Silas and Raveloe do not know, and it is equally stunning for the clean break it makes with Silas's past. "The old place is all swep' away," Silas tells Dolly Winthrop. What is amazing is the feeling that it is truly gone—that there is no residue of the past that had for so long possessed his spirit. "The old home's gone; I've no home but this now" (240). As a novelistic character, he had been defined by Lantern Yard and by his need to connect his present and future to his past; as a pastoral figure, he can now wholly accept his new home.

This new identity of self and habitation, achieved as if by transformation, might appeal to anyone, and to no one more than Marian Evans, who insisted on calling herself Mrs. Lewes but was known to the world as George Eliot. But against the attractive simplification of Silas free of his past, the author places Godfrey, who will always live with the consequences of his misdeeds and eva-

---

35. " . . . the new things that would come with the coming years, when Eppie would have learned to understand how her father Silas cared for her; and made him look for images of that time in the ties and charities that bound together the families of his neighbours."

sions. The final scenes of Godfrey and Nancy in the childless Red House are wonderfully done, and in one sense are fully novelistic, with their awareness of what character determines and the ineluctability of the past. But they are done on a small scale and are balanced against the final episodes concerning Silas and Eppie. In the way they accept their life together, as well as in the way the author uses them as fictional elements, Godfrey and Nancy express characteristically pastoral attitudes—that losses and absences underlie the need for community, and that we come to terms with life by accepting limitations. The more fully novelistic representation of the two of them does not dominate or engulf the simplicities of Silas's story, as Dorothea's, Lydgate's, and Bulstrode's stories outweigh that of the Garths in *Middlemarch*.

The high realism of *Middlemarch* perhaps obscures the fact, evident in *Romola*, *Felix Holt*, and *Daniel Deronda*, that George Eliot constantly experimented in fictional form. *Silas Marner*, the last and most successful of her early experiments in shorter forms, shows that the potential contradiction of a pastoral novel could be overcome—that the apparently disparate modes of representation could be accommodated to each other. But this generic achievement does not adequately represent the artistic motivation of *Silas Marner*. If we think of Eliot's works as a linear progression, *Silas Marner* interrupts and suspends the project of *Romola*, with its enormous thematic, aesthetic, and reconstructive ambitions. We can also view it as her stepping back from the moral and psychological pressures of *The Mill on the Floss*, particularly her identification with a protagonist at odds with the world of her youth. Seen from this perspective, the story of Silas—the innocent, misunderstood outsider and the figure, untroubled by sex, for whom childhood heals the rift between youth and age— refigures Maggie Tulliver's dilemmas. But though *Silas Marner* imagines the situations and moral pressures of the novels that surround it in terms of the world of *Adam Bede*, it does not try to replicate the earlier novel. Its pastoral modesty and finish show that Eliot well understood the extent to which this tale could express what now seemed urgent to her as a novelist. *Silas Marner* scales down the scope and claims of its predecessors so as to inaugurate a new project, that of reconceiving the world of her novels and the relationship between social and moral ties. It can thus be thought to replicate, within her career, the traditional place and use of pastoral—as a reduction, which is both homage and critique, of heroic modes which it seeks to "make new."

III

Sarah Orne Jewett's *The Country of the Pointed Firs* is more idiosyncratic than *Silas Marner*; indeed, critics have been rather baffled to know what to call it. It is widely agreed that it is not a novel. Its action—the narrator's summer visit to a coastal village in Maine—is simply a framing device: it does not produce the entanglements and consequences of a plot or even of a novelistic situation. Most recent critics have argued that the book's parts are more than "loosely connected sketches," as F. O. Matthiessen called them,[36] and have emphasized various ways in which it is thematically and emotionally unified. But they have been hard pressed to identify what gives the book its formal coherence. My own resolution of this problem (the reader will not be surprised to hear) is that *The Country of the Pointed Firs* is a pastoral. Not only its rural subject matter but its central interests—sustaining life in a time of decline and the way community and isolation are mutually implicated—led Jewett to pastoral usages and representations. In the work which most deeply realized her project as a writer, she rediscovered, for realistic fiction, the form of the eclogue book.

One could argue that Jewett was a pastoral writer throughout her career. The framing action of her first book, *Deephaven* (1877), is the same as that of *The Country of the Pointed Firs* (1896), and is familiar to us from Renaissance pastorals: outsiders from the city visit the country and discover the human fullness of a rural world, in this case the declining port of Deephaven and its adjacent farms. Jewett's literary self-consciousness is shown by references, at key points late in the book, to *As You Like It* and to the Ladies of Llangollen—a famous eighteenth-century pair, whom the narrator and her friend Kate imagine they might emulate and "remove ourselves from society and its distractions."[37] Fifteen years later, she wrote to an admirer, "You know there is a saying of Plato's that the best thing one can do for the people of a State is to make them acquainted with each other, and it was some instinctive feeling of this sort which led me to wish that the town and country people were less suspicious of one another."[38] These proto-Empsonian sentiments were repeated in the preface to a new edition of *Deephaven* (1893) where she associated her endeavor as a writer with George Sand's rural novels.

Most of Jewett's contemporaries praised her for her faithful rendering of the people and countryside of New England—thus preparing for her entry into literary history as a regional writer. But one critic raised, without naming it, the question of her pastoralism. Charles Miner Thompson, summing up Jewett's career in 1904, turned his attention from the people she writes *about* to the people she writes *for*:

> The audience which she seeks, quite naturally and unconsciously, is made up of the people of her own social and intellectual class. . . . The attitude is always felt to be that of an observer *de haut en bas*. No attentive reader,

36. Francis Otto Matthiessen, *Sarah Orne Jewett* (Boston: Houghton Mifflin, 1929), 101.

37. In Sarah Orne Jewett, *Novels and Stories*, ed. Michael Davitt Bell (New York: Library of America), 135. The reference to *As You Like It* is on pp. 120–21.

38. Sarah Orne Jewett, *Letters*, ed. Richard Cary (Waterville, Maine: Colby College Press, 1967), 83–84.

I think, can escape the conclusion that she has always written as a "summer visitor" for "summer people."[39]

This criticism, a familiar observation about or charge against pastoral writing, is potentially more severe than Thompson meant it to be. Jewett, sensing this, said in a letter to him: "It was hard for this person (made of Berwick dust) to think of herself as a 'summer visitor,' but I quite understand your point of view; one may be away from one's neighborhood long enough to see it quite or almost from the outside, though as I make this concession I remember that it was hardly true at the time of 'Deephaven.'"[40] It was indeed hardly true of Jewett when the book was published, but the fact remains that the narrator represents herself and her companion precisely as summer visitors. Moreover, the general question of the (rural) writer's relation to her materials was one of which Jewett was keenly aware. In a well-known letter to Willa Cather, she said:

> I want you to be surer of your backgrounds. . . . You don't see them [e.g. "your Nebraska life"] yet quite enough from the outside, —you stand right in the middle of each of them when you write, without having the standpoint of the looker-on who takes them each in their relations to letters, to the world.[41]

Whether or not Jewett observes, as Thompson says, *de haut en bas*, she always writes as an observer. It is well known that the powers she brought to her fiction were cultivated by accompanying her physician father as he visited his patients in Berwick and the surrounding countryside. One can feel in her stories both the child's patient observation and the assessment of human pain and difficulties that her father shared with her. And there is at least prima facie reason for Thompson's limiting phrase. Jewett belonged to the economic and social elite of her region. One grandfather was a shipbuilder and merchant, whose wealth ensured her economic independence, and her family network included many professional people, of whom her father, a professor at Bowdoin, was not the least distinguished. From the age of twenty, when the *Atlantic Monthly* accepted a story, she moved in the literary and intellectual circles of Boston, where she frequently visited, and her circle of international acquaintances included Arnold, Tennyson, and Henry James. From 1881, she lived in Boston with Annie Fields, the widow of an eminent publisher. The sense of the larger

39. In Richard Cary, ed., *Appreciation of Sarah Orne Jewett: 29 Interpretive Essays* (Waterville, Maine: Colby College Press, 1973), 43–44. Among Jewett's later critics, Paul John Eakin has most usefully drawn out the implications of Thompson's remarks, though along somewhat different lines from mine. Paul John Eakin, "Sarah Orne Jewett and the Meaning of Country Life," *American Literature*, 38 (1967): 508–31; in Cary, 203–22.

40. Sarah Orne Jewett, *Letters*, ed. Annie Fields (Boston: Houghton Mifflin, 1911), 196–97.

41. *Letters*, ed. Cary, 248.

social and intellectual world as her audience therefore came readily to her. But the question Thompson raises is literary, and what interests us, therefore, is not Jewett's life as such but her authorial self-representation. *Deephaven* is limited in the way Thompson suggests not simply because the narrator is a summer visitor but also because she is accompanied by her bosom friend Kate, who is her constant and best companion. The society these budding Ladies of Llangollen provide for each other gives them too secure and external a relation to the country folk among whom they find themselves. Hence many passages, including some that are well written and affecting, bring to mind the outlook of tourists or charitable visitors.

The life of the rural and coastal regions of New England was Jewett's subject matter throughout her career, but *The Country of the Pointed Firs* uniquely opened up her relation to it as a writer. The narrator is a central figure in *The Country of the Pointed Firs*, and both in its parts and as a whole, it is distinct from her other fiction. Its chapters are very short, and even when grouped into larger units are different from her independent sketches and stories. These latter, deficient though they are in plot, characteristically revolve around a turning point in someone's life or a situation that is in some ways critical. In *The Country of the Pointed Firs* the turning points and critical situations are all in the past; the present time of the book consists of "uncritical" conversations and visits, which are occasions on which the narrator is told stories of the past, and which provide her opportunities for reflection. The immediate afterlife of the book shows that Jewett recognized its difference from the bulk of her work. She continued to think of Dunnet Landing as a fictional world and wrote four additional stories which are told by the same narrator, involve Mrs. Todd and her brother William, and assume a knowledge of their world. But they are much more in the manner of her independent stories and sketches, and (for this reason, I am suggesting) she never incorporated them into an edition of *The Country of the Pointed Firs*.[42]

The narrator of *The Country of the Pointed Firs* is herself a writer, who experiences a (very mild) crisis of writing soon after she has taken up her sum-

---

42. They were, however, incorporated into the posthumous edition for which Willa Cather wrote a preface: *The Best Short Stories of Sarah Orne Jewett* (Boston: Houghton Mifflin, 1925). This expansion of the book was the publisher's doing, though Cather accepted it (see June Howard, ed., *New Essays on "The Country of the Pointed Firs"* [Cambridge: Cambridge University Press, 1994], 20); commentators agree that the effect was to weaken it. The recent Library of America edition (above, n. 37) presents the book as originally published, with the four later stories ("A Dunnett Shepherdess," "The Foreigner," "The Queen's Twin," "William's Wedding") appended; the same arrangement is in the most available paperback edition, *The Country of the Pointed Firs*, ed. Mary Ellen Chase (New York: W. W. Norton, 1982). All quotations will be from this latter edition and will be cited parenthetically in the text (chapter number, in small roman numerals, followed by page reference).

mer's residence with Mrs. Todd, the herbalist of Dunnet Landing. She is so immediately accepted into Mrs. Todd's life and world—being left to dispense medicines from the house, while her landlady goes off to gather herbs—that she becomes anxious about the writing she intended to do and therefore, "selfish as it may appear," seeks out a "retired situation" in which to work during the day (iii, 9). She rents the local schoolhouse, isolated high on a hill with a splendid view. The first full account of her there opens up the concerns of the book:

> One day I reached the schoolhouse very late [chapter iv begins], owing to attendance upon the funeral of an acquaintance and neighbor, with whose sad decline in health I had been familiar, and whose last days both the doctor and Mrs. Todd had tried in vain to ease. The services had taken place at one o'clock, and now, at quarter past two, I stood at the schoolhouse window, looking down at the procession as it went along the lower road close to the store. It was a walking funeral, and even at that distance I could recognize most of the mourners as they went their solemn way. Mrs. Begg had been very much respected, and there was a large company of friends following to her grave. She had been brought up on one of the neighboring farms, and each of the few times that I had seen her she professed great dissatisfaction with town life. The people lived too close together for her liking, at the Landing, and she could not get used to the constant sound of the sea. She had lived to lament three seafaring husbands, and her house was decorated with West Indian curiosities, specimens of conch shells and fine coral which they had brought home from their voyages in lumber-laden ships. (iv, 12–13)

This paragraph bears witness both to Jewett's general fictional powers and to some that are specifically pastoral. There is, first, the economy with which the narrator registers different elements of sympathy—the painfulness of the deceased's last days; the information (which assumes we know and understand the regional phrase) that it was "a walking funeral"; the sense of sharing the reported view that "Mrs. Begg had been very much respected," so that the narrator, from her observer's distance, can be felt to be among the "company of friends." The final details bring out aspects of the pastoralism that is introduced by the outsider's perspective—the witty revelation of town-country distinctions within the world of Dunnet (which for us is all "country"), and the shells and coral which are the reductions and remnants, but still the lovely souvenirs, of a past age of commerce. A page later, the narrator sees the funeral winding its way and disappearing against the backdrop of the summer sky and "the bay-sheltered islands and the great sea beyond," while "the song sparrow sang and sang, as if with joyous knowledge of immortality" (iv, 14). The passage seems a perfect example of what Robin Magowan, seeking to define the book's pastoralism, calls Jewett's "art of landscape."[43]

Yet when the narrator turns to her writing, it is with dissatisfaction and distraction. "For the first time I began to wish for a companion and for news from the outer world"; she worries about having left the funeral after the church services and so made it evident "that I did not really belong to Dunnet Landing" (iv, 15). This expression of social uneasiness reveals what the distant, seemingly perfected view of the funeral could not represent adequately—the mourners themselves. As the passage continues (immediately after the lines quoted above) the narrator singles out two mourners, who suggest different ways in which she must get closer to the scene she means to represent. One is Mrs. Todd, grieving for the friend of whom (the narrator recalls) she had said they had "both seen trouble until they knew the best and worst on 't"; the other is Captain Littlepage, "the one strange and unrelated person in all the company." What the narrator's subsequent dissatisfaction suggests is the inadequacy of viewing Dunnet Landing from a distance and of seeing its inhabitants primarily as belonging to a landscape. To know this world means sounding more fully the "trouble" in the lives of its inhabitants and knowing, as opposed to knowing about, those who seem "strange and unrelated."

Jewett's self-consciousness as a writer and her consciousness of pastoral usages appear in the sentences that precede the narrator's expression of social displacement. Bees keep hovering over her ink bottle,

> which I had bought at the Landing store, and discovered too late to be scented with bergamot, as if to refresh the labors of anxious scribes. One anxious scribe felt very dull that day; a sheep-bell tinkled near by, and called her wandering wits after it. The sentences failed to catch these lovely summer cadences. (iv, 14–15)

This wittily disallows writing as the means of pastoral representation—first, in the way country ink "flowers" and undoes its apparent purpose, and then because what the narrator says of the sentences she has been writing is not true of the ones we have been reading. This is the last we hear of the narrator writing or as a writer. From this point on, the representation of Dunnet Landing and its inhabitants centers on social encounters and occasions. The narrator, who had felt on the margins of Mrs. Begg's funeral, increasingly becomes part of the Dunnet community. This development, one of the genuinely unifying elements of the book, can be seen in the three central episodes—the visit to Mrs. Todd's mother on Green Island (chaps. viii–xi), the visit of Mrs. Fosdick when the narrator is allowed to hear the story of "poor Joanna" (chaps. xii–xv),

---

43. Robin Magowan, "Pastoral and the Art of Landscape in *The Country of the Pointed Firs*," *New England Quarterly* 36 (1963): 229–40, in Cary, *Appreciation*, 187–95.

and the Bowden reunion (chaps. xvi–xix), where the narrator is practically one of the family. In becoming part of Dunnet, the narrator reenacts the older convention of the poet representing himself as a shepherd. When she comes down from the schoolhouse and leaves her pen and ink behind, she no longer represents Dunnet *de haut en bas*. In this respect, the pastoralism of *The Country of the Pointed Firs* differs from that of *Silas Marner*, in which the pastoral sympathies and accommodations remain those of an omniscient narrator.

Each of the episodes in the book is a version of pastoral, but the central one (the story of Joanna Todd, chap. xii–xv) most fully displays Jewett's revivification of pastoral usages. It begins with a meeting of two rural figures, Mrs. Todd and her old friend Mrs. Fosdick, who lives at a distance and has come for the only extended visit we see in the book. Their first evening together (chap. xii) is less obviously like an eclogue than the Rainbow scene of *Silas Marner*, because the social ritual of the visit less clearly dictates specific speeches, and because the interlocutors are not seen as simpler folk than the narrator who observes them. But though the conversation at first seems to the narrator "a borderless sea of reminiscences and personal news" (60), it shapes itself so as to end with a familiar set piece, and thus serves, in the manner of pastoral exchanges, to meet expectations while enlivening the moment. "There," says Mrs. Fosdick as the evening concludes, "it does seem so pleasant to talk with an old acquaintance that knows what you know. I see so many of these new folks nowadays, that seem to have neither past nor future. Conversation's got to have some root in the past, or else you've got to explain every remark you make, an' it wears a person out" (61). What is remarkable about this oft-quoted sentiment is that it rings true for the narrator. In the course of the chapter, she has become one of the rural company; she has become, as she enables the reader to be, a willing and sympathetic listener. If George Eliot's narrator resembles (in Leslie Stephen's words) "a silent guest in the chimney-corner of the 'Rainbow,'" Jewett's narrator represents herself as a further reduction of a pastoral listener:

> Mrs. Fosdick had been the mother of a large family of sons and daughters. . . . I soon grew more or less acquainted with the histories of all their fortunes and misfortunes, and subjects of an intimate nature were no more withheld from my ears than if I had been a shell on a mantelpiece. (59)

This is not an idle metaphor. That shell would not have been picked up on a local beach (in our current manner, as summer visitors), but would have been an exotic specimen, like Mrs. Begg's conches and coral, brought home from a voyage. It thus represents Dunnet's domestication of the larger world and can stand for the narrator's new position, as the outsider now at home. More than that, it recapitulates what has put her and Mrs. Fosdick at ease with each other—her discovery, which is at once an implicit self-representation and a newly revealed aspect of the world of Dunnet, that Mrs. Fosdick, "like many of the elder women of that coast, had spent a part of her life at sea, and was full of a good traveler's curiosity and enlightenment" (59).

The chapter that brings Mrs. Fosdick on the scene lays the groundwork for the book's fullest narration of a story from Dunnet's past. It concerns Joanna Todd, who was abandoned by her betrothed and immediately decided to withdraw to Shell-heap Island, which her father had owned and had used for fishing and harvesting clams. "Poor Joanna" she is called by the two old friends who share the telling of her story, but they also convey the stature she acquires in determining to live forever apart from others. Her calm poise in turning away her former neighbors attains a spiritual dignity, "so above everything common," when Mrs. Todd, who had become her cousin by marriage, beseeches her to return:

> "I haven't got no right to live with folks no more," she said. "You must never ask me again, Almiry: I've done the only thing I could do, and I've made my choice. I feel a great comfort in your kindness, but I don't deserve it. I have committed the unpardonable sin. . . . I have come to know what it is to have patience, but I have lost my hope. You must tell those that ask how 'tis with me," she said, "an' tell them I want to be alone."
> (xiv, 76)

Many readers have noted the Hawthornian cast of this speech, and it is not only the literary echo that brings to mind a sterner and less commonplace past. Both Mrs. Todd and Mrs. Fosdick think of Joanna as belonging to a time when there were "a lot o' queer folks" about: "there was more energy then, and in some the energy took a singular turn" (xiii, 64). Mrs. Fosdick's generous good sense gives the thought an almost comic turn, when she says, "We don't seem to hear nothing about the unpardonable sin now, but you may say 'twas not uncommon then" (xiv, 77). Shell-heap Island itself embodies a more remote and awe-inspiring past. It was an Indian ceremonial ground, of which only the shell-heap and some stone relics remain. But Mrs. Fosdick recalls that "queer stories" were once told of it and "some o' the old folks was kind o' fearful about it" (xiii, 63).

In telling this story, Jewett reinvents pastoral usages for and by means of her particular vein of realistic fiction. Assigning the story to two narrators itself recalls pastoral dialogue, especially since Mrs. Fosdick and Mrs. Todd divide between them two fundamental powers of a novelistic narrator—worldliness and observational sharpness, on the one hand, and on the other, sympathy and a sense of considering one's words. Even more telling is the place provided for the reader. The skill of the episode, viewed as a piece of realistic fiction, is the way it mingles information and explanations, such as any new listener needs, with a conversation between old friends, who recall events to each other and mull over a fate that troubles them both. It is common in Jewett's fiction to have a story emerge from a conversation between friends. But she here opens up this convention and, so to speak, interprets it for herself by the way her interlocutors include the narrator—who, like the reader, is new to the story—in a circle of understanding whose conditions are set by these rural speakers.

In addition to the pastoral character it acquires from its manner of telling, the story of Joanna particularly resembles a pastoral elegy. It memorializes a lone and heroic "shepherdess," whose fate embodies the character of a past time and whose memory serves as a bond in the diminished community of the present. One of the affecting elements of Mrs. Fosdick's and Mrs. Todd's stories is the way Dunnet continued to look out for Joanna during her self-imposed exile—watching for signs of trouble, leaving food and supplies for her, and finally showing up in full force for her funeral, "same's if she'd always stayed ashore and held her friends" (xiv, 78).[44] Joanna's story is central (both literally and figuratively) in *The Country of the Pointed Firs*, because it reveals the conditions of community in Jewett's world. One would think that the forbidding isolation of her island would be contrasted with the social world of Dunnet. But one of the surprising things about the book is that we see very little of the town itself and none of its normal social gatherings, like the church services and meetings that are occasionally mentioned.[45] The human landscape of Jewett's country resembles that of Sidney's Arcadia, where the houses "were all scattered, no two being one by th'other, and yet not so far off as that it barred mutual succour— a show as it were of an accompanable solitariness, and of a civil wildness."[46] The inhabitants of Dunnet live lives of "accompanable solitariness." Mrs. Todd's house seems to be at the end of town, and the representative good place is Green Island, where, her mother, Mrs. Blackett, and her brother William live. As a symbolic locale, it is the opposite of Shell-heap Island, one name suggesting fertility and the other accumulated dead matter. But it is still an island, and

44. The details of Dunnet's attention to Joanna might seem to be due solely to the realism of regional fiction, but its first manifestation recalls the repertory of traditional pastoral. Joanna (in the manner, we may think, of Cervantes' Marcela), tells the curious fishermen of the region to leave her alone, but this does not deter a *pastor fido*, bearing rural gifts: "There was one man who had always set everything by her from a boy. He'd have married her if the other hadn't come about an' spoilt his chance, and he used to get close to the island, before light, on his way out fishin', and throw a little bundle 'way up the green slope front o' the house," etc. (xiii, 67)

45. Dunnet, to be sure, is not much of a town; the narrator mentions occasionally having "sailed up the coast to a larger town . . . to do some shopping" (viii, 32). But it does have a church, a doctor (who is on good terms with Mrs. Todd, the herbalist, but who has only a walk-on part), and selectmen, from two of whom, the narrator mentions, she rented the schoolhouse (iii, 9). See below, n. 56.

46. Sir Philip Sidney, *The Countess of Pembroke's Arcadia (The New Arcadia)*, ed. Victor Skretkowicz (Oxford: Clarendon Press, 1987), 11.

Mrs. Blackett's visits, even with her daughter, are subject to conditions of weather and of physical hardiness. One of the affecting moments at the Bowden Reunion, the book's climactic representation of community, is the leavetaking of the old people, who know that with "the steady, hard work on the farms" and "the difficulty of getting from place to place," they cannot expect to see one another again very soon. "It gave one," the narrator reflects, "a new idea of the isolation in which it was possible to live in that after all thinly settled region" (xix, 109). Mrs. Blackett is much beloved in her world, but as with Joanna, the main expressions of affection are keeping an eye on her island and the fact that, to adapt what Mrs. Fosdick says of the supplies left for Joanna, "a good many old friends [have her] on their minds" (xiii, 67).

The narrator's enabling power is what she shares with all the good folks of Dunnet and particularly, on its profounder and more troubled side, with Mrs. Todd—the power of thinking about others and what Wordsworth calls the "peculiar" attachments of their lives. She becomes one of this rural community as she values and emulates their steadfast affection for each other. When she asks Captain Bowden to take her to Shell-heap Island, his willingness to make the difficult landing changes markedly when he learns that she knows about Joanna (he at first thought she wanted to look for Indian relics) (xv, 79–80). Thinking of one another is the common mode of social connection in Dunnet. At the end of the visit to Green Island, Mrs. Blackett confirms her immediate sense of friendship with the narrator by promising that "William an' me'll be talkin' about you an' thinkin' o' this nice day" (xi, 51) and by inviting her to sit in her rocking chair, so that she can "think o' your settin' here to-day" (54). When the narrator leaves the Bowden reunion, she says she "parted from certain new friends as if they were old friends; we were rich with the treasure of a new remembrance" (xix, 110). Quoted by itself, this might suggest too grand or sentimental an account of community in Dunnet. But it is leavened in true pastoral manner—that is, by registering alternative perspectives without prompting conflict of judgment or ironic focus. Just before this, the narrator ends the paragraph about the old folks parting by saying, "I heard the words 'next summer' repeated many times, though summer was still ours and all the leaves were green" (110). This sentence qualifies the sense of possessing the moment and beautifully measures its pathos. The idyllic stasis that has been "ours" at the Bowden reunion is about to become the scene of a memory and therefore (here is the resistance to pathos) something that enhances expectation. In a life of severity, one does not need winter's icy fang to cherish the time of greenness. Despite their literary refinement, the narrator's thoughts here are of a piece with the world she represents. Riding home with her, Mrs. Todd observes, "Those that enjoyed it best 'll want to get right home so's to think it over" (111). It is from her new/old friends that the narrator knows how to value such episodes of meeting and parting.

It is in the treatment of visits that we can see how *The Country of the Pointed Firs* differs from a novel to which it is often likened, Elizabeth Gaskell's *Cranford*.[47] Both books are short fictions about backwater societies dominated by women. (Or at least that is the accepted view of *Cranford*. It is, in important ways, dominated by men, both as objects of admiration and as agents in the novel's action. Dunnet Landing, on the other hand, is indeed a world of women, and its men are marginalized. That is part of the story Jewett has to tell, the way a community compensates for its loss of economic and social power, and it is a main reason her fiction takes the form of a pastoral.) *Cranford* visits are prompted and energized by events of the moment, and are carefully prepared for; within their world, they are always eventful or consequential; they are recollected not in tranquillity but in a spirit of assessment, sometimes of agitation or resentment; they are the heart of what we see of human relations. *Cranford*, in other words, is a novel of manners in the main nineteenth-century tradition. It deserves its reputation as a minor masterpiece of affectionate wit, but from our standpoint what counts is that it depends on sustaining the narrator's youthful, witty, worldly view of the Cranford ladies' provincialism (unlike Jewett's narrator, she remains an outsider, despite frequent visits). A single phrase, as the ladies arrive to meet the aristocratic Lady Glenmire, reveals the mode of the novel:

> And with three new caps, and a greater array of brooches than had ever been seen together at one time, since Cranford was a town, did Mrs. Forrester, and Miss Matty, and Miss Pole appear *on that memorable Tuesday evening.*[48]

The narrator's justness of tone, clearly ironic but not dismissive, comes from being able to take the evening at the ladies' valuation—which in turn makes it equally memorable, as a novelistic scene, for the reader. But the difference remains between what "memorable" means to the ladies, with their social pretensions and capacity for hurt feelings, and to the witty narrator/author and the reader she entertains.

In *The Country of the Pointed Firs* the distance between the two senses of "memorable" is closed. The most powerful stories in the book, the heart of several visits, are the characters' recollections, made memorable to us because, so the fiction has it, they are memorable to them. At times the narrator's inde-

---

47. See Joseph Allen Boone, *Tradition Counter Tradition: Love and the Form of Fiction* (Chicago: University of Chicago Press, 1987), 295–311. Boone would disagree with my subsequent statement that the society of *Cranford* is dominated by men, but I think it is sufficiently true and useful as a point of comparison with *The Country of the Pointed Firs*.

48. Elizabeth Gaskell, *Cranford/Cousin Phyllis*, ed. Peter Keating (Harmondsworth: Penguin, 1976), 120 (chap. 8). My emphasis.

pendent way of making a scene memorable is balanced against (indeed, almost seems to give way to) the characters' more concrete and literal recollections. The journey to the Bowden reunion leads out of the woods to "a wonderful great view of well-cleared fields that swept down to the wide water of a bay"— and beyond this "distant shores like another country" and "far-away pale blue mountains" (xvii, 93). The narrator calls it "a noble landscape" (94). But when Mrs. Todd and Mrs. Blackett look out, they see a known, which means an inhabited, scene. They identify a far-off town and its surrounding farms and speak of Mrs. Blackett's sister, who lived there and from whom she was "'most always separated" after they were married. "'I do love to look over there where she used to live,' Mrs. Blackett went on as we began to go down the hill. 'It seems as if she must still be there, though she's long been gone'" (94). To stop the quotation here would wrongly emphasize the pathos of loss. These country minds dwell on the way one makes a life. "She loved their farm," Mrs. Blackett continues—"she didn't see how I got so used to our island; but somehow I was always happy from the first." And Mrs. Todd chips in, "Yes, it's very dull to me up among those slow farms." The vigor and unexpected discrimination of this last phrase shows how little we need the distance of wit to understand how these speakers dwell within their world.

Given the assimilation of Jewett's narrator to the world of Dunnet, we might be tempted to modify Empson's formula and say, "You can say everything about complex people by a complete representation [vs. Empson's 'consideration'] of simple people" (*SVP*, 131). Yet the narrator never sounds like her Dunnet companions, and she does not merely record their stories and their present concerns and conversations. Her role in making Joanna's story memorable brings out the nature of her own pastoral presence. On the traditional model, we might expect her to become a third speaker in this prose eclogue. But during the conversation about Joanna, she is simply an absorbed listener; the story itself is entrusted to the local narrators, and the last words are Mrs. Todd's: "Some is meant to be the Joannas in this world, an' 'twas her poor lot" (xiv, 78–79). But in the next chapter, the narrator visits Shell-heap Island by herself, and her reflections there are her contribution to memorializing Joanna. They thus exemplify the shift we have already seen in "The Ruined Cottage," from the elegiac utterances of older pastoral to the modern mode of commemorative meditation:

> I found the path; it was touching to discover that this lonely spot was not without its pilgrims. Later generations will know less and less of Joanna herself, but there are paths trodden to the shrines of solitude the world over,—the world cannot forget them, try as it may; the feet of the young find them out because of curiosity and dim foreboding; while the old bring hearts full of remembrance. (xv, 81–2)

And when she contemplates Joanna's ruined cottage and drinks from the spring there, she thinks that

> now and then some one would follow me from the busy, hard-worked, and simple-thoughted countryside of the mainland, which lay dim and dreamlike in the August haze, as Joanna must have watched it many a day. There was the world, and here was she with eternity well begun. In the life of each of us, I said to myself, there is a place remote and islanded, and given to endless regret or secret happiness; we are each the uncompanioned hermit and recluse of an hour or a day; we understand our fellows of the cell to whatever age of history they may belong. (xv, 82)

These passages are important not simply for their thematic weight—they are clearly conscious of the paradox of "accompanable solitariness"—but also for the kind of authorial presence they establish. The great sentence about "a place remote and islanded" has been compared to a famous passage in *Moby Dick*:

> Consider all this [the treacherous destructiveness of the sea]; and then turn to this green, gentle, and most docile earth; consider them both, the sea and the land; and do you not find a strange analogy to something in yourself? For as this appalling ocean surrounds the verdant land, so in the soul of man there lies one insular Tahiti, full of peace and joy, but encompassed by all the horrors of the half known life. God keep thee! Push not off from that isle, thou canst never return![49]

The heroic tones of this paragraph bring out the pastoralism of Jewett's sentence. It engages but does not exhort the reader, and it mitigates heroic and tragic isolation by intimations of companionship, such as have already been exemplified by the story of Joanna's island. Even the one marking of utterance, "I said to myself," suggests an internal companion and modulates the declarative energies of the statement.

This sentence is too much in the narrator's character to be taken as authorial in the usual sense. But the sentence also brings out the lack of specificity about the narrator's life and character that sets her apart from the inhabitants of the world she represents. We do not know her age or home or even her name (she differs in all these respects from the narrator of *Cranford*); she seems to put aside the one thing, her writing project, which gives her a normal fictional

---

49. This paragraph concludes chapter 58 of *Moby Dick*. The comparison is made in Warner Berthoff's fine essay, "The Art of Jewett's *Pointed Firs*," *New England Quarterly*, 32 (1959): 31–53; in Cary, *Appreciation*, 144–61. Note that Jewett, who writes of bays, not of the open sea, inverts the analogy: the island is not the site of innocence, but the furthest representation of isolating trouble or loss (or, alternatively, secret happiness).

characterization and purpose. Though her reflections about Joanna reveal the depths of her thought and feeling, we do not know what, for her, is the place remote and islanded. We do know this of Mrs. Todd. It is (represented by) the patch of pennyroyal on Green Island, to which she takes the narrator as a gesture of unusual friendship. She confides that this, the place where she and her dear husband Nathan courted, is for her a site of double loss—reminding her both of her first and truest love (whose social standing prohibited their marriage) and of Nathan's death, when his ship sunk within sight of that headland. But even though the narrator is emptied of her own fictional character and thus marked as a figure of the author, she seems fully present in the Dunnet world, an equal participant in its "simple, nameless, unremembered acts of kindness and of love." Her odd selflessness makes her the truest companion of Mrs. Todd: she displays, in the mode of meditation and representation, the sympathetic energies and vigorous understanding that Mrs. Todd reveals in living speech and moral commentary. This is the deepest sense in which the author of *The Country of the Pointed Firs* "represents herself as a shepherd." Using Schiller's terms, we might say that the narrator is the "sentimental" version of Mrs. Todd's "naive." In terms of our analogy with traditional pastoral, we can say that throughout the book, they mutually represent each other.

Nowhere is such mutual representation more powerful than in the narrator's reflections in the pennyroyal patch, where she both characterizes Mrs. Todd and derives from her the character of her own deepest thoughts:

> She looked away from me, and presently rose and went on by herself. There was something lonely and solitary about her great determined shape. She might have been Antigone alone on the Theban plain. It is not often given in a noisy world to come to the places of great grief and silence. An absolute, archaic grief possessed this countrywoman; she seemed like a renewal of some historic soul, with her sorrows and the remoteness of a daily life busied with rustic simplicities and the scents of primeval herbs. (x, 49)

This passage is produced by pastoral machinery—its strength depends on Mrs. Todd's preceding speech, of equal length and an equally remarkable piece of writing—and brings out the need for the narrator's pastoral presence. For though it represents Mrs. Todd's spiritual stature, she can only be like Antigone in the narrator's reflections. Independent and authoritative though she is, she has no more powers of action than anyone else in Jewett's Dunnet, where nothing at all comparable to tragic action happens or is made to happen. All such events are in the past—the decline of voyaging and commerce, the deaths at sea of its men, the lost loves of its women. (Compare *Cranford*, which readers may remember as a town where nothing much happens, but which is propelled as a novel by a series of "dramatic" events—the deaths of Captain Brown and Mr. Holbrook, the visit of Lady Glenmire, the arrival of the Italian conjuror, the failure of the Town and Country Bank, the return home of long-lost brother Peter.) Like the narrator's, Mrs. Todd's powers are those of sympathy and understanding. This is true even of what she "does," which is to know the medicinal powers of herbs and where to find them.

The completeness of the book's pastoralism is shown in its form. In the absence of significant action and events, Dunnet is represented as the sum of its parts. The visit to Green Island is a formal epitome of the whole book. Like a short eclogue sequence, it is broken into duologues that renew or deepen or establish acquaintance in its widest sense: Mrs. Todd and Mrs. Blackett (chap. viii), the narrator and William (chap. ix), the narrator and Mrs. Todd (chap. x) and the narrator and Mrs. Blackett (chap. xi). The last three of these chapters have decided filiations with older pastoral. Chapter ix concludes with William's showing the narrator the splendid view from the island's highest point. "'There ain't no such view in the world, I expect,' said William proudly," and indeed it contains everything he knows of the world—the "pointed firs," the ocean with "a hundred other bits of island ground," and "the mainland shore and all the far horizons" (ix, 45). The final words of the chapter are the narrator's consciously pastoral reflections: "It was impossible not to feel as if an untraveled boy had spoken, and yet one loved to have him value his native heath." The next chapter begins with Mrs. Todd showing the narrator her family's portraits—portable epitomes of history—and ends with her memorializing her losses in the sacred grove ("'tis kind of sainted to me") of the pennyroyal patch (x, 48). In the final chapter, in which Mrs. Blackett also shows the narrator her inner sanctum with its Bible and rocking chair, she and William, like two shepherds in an eclogue, raise their thin, sweet voices to sing for their guests. The performance of "Home, Sweet Home" gives the sentimental song a finely tuned pastoral presence. The listeners are deeply touched, but the two old singers, utterly innocent of roaming 'mid pleasures and palaces, have no sense of their pathos and cannot sentimentalize their devotion to the island home they have never left. The performance of the other song is not represented, but its mere mention confirms the relation between literary belatedness and the scene's local piety. "Cupid and the Bee" is a latter-day version of a witty erotic lyric from late antiquity—the kind of poem on which Renaissance poets based poems about the pains of love,[50] but which is here sung by an old lady whose love is all friendship and domestic affection, her eros (unlike her daughter's) having vanished even out of memory.

There is some reason to think that Jewett might have thought of Theocri-

50. See chapter 6, n. 23.

tus's idylls as a model for the chapters of *The Country of the Pointed Firs*.[51] Whether or not this is so, her assumptions about the world she depicts led her to a form that resembles an eclogue book. It is a sequence of encounters, vignettes, and set pieces, whose cumulative force lies in thematic continuities and its clear, balanced organization, rather than in an event or a represented change or the experience of its main figures. Mrs. Todd is something of a unifying element, but becoming acquainted with Dunnet Landing means more than becoming acquainted with her. Of the five episodes that constitute the narrator's knowledge of Dunnet, the first and last are her own separate encounters with old men. Mrs. Todd is somewhat dismissive of both of them, but each, in his own way, is representative of this world. The formal arrangement of the whole book has the kind of balance characteristic of eclogue books, in which whole poems metaphorically "answer to" each other, on the model of the responsive songs within eclogues. In *The Country of the Pointed Firs*, the central story of Joanna is enclosed by episodes (the visit to Green Island and the Bowden reunion) in which we see the countervailing strengths of human connection. This central group is framed by the narrator's visits with the two old men, each of whom embodies the diminutions of Dunnet's world. Again in a way characteristic of eclogue books, this static formal balance is held in suspension with effects that are dynamic, in the sense that they use the temporal ordering of a sequence to register difference and direction. The most obvious dynamic in *The Country of the Pointed Firs* is registered by the first and the last chapters, which record the narrator's arrival in Dunnet at the beginning of the summer and her departure at the end (this symmetry means, of course, that the chapters also have the static effect of balancing each other and framing the whole book). The most strongly registered dynamic effect, as we might expect of an eclogue book, is thematic—the sense of climax at the Bowden reunion, which is the fullest representation of community and also the occasion for substantial reflections by the narrator. But another dynamic effect (in that it registers a difference) counteracts this sense of climax with a diminishing effect. The second of the visits with old men, which immediately follows the Bowden reunion, concerns a milder character and is narrower in scope than its counterpart earlier in the book.

The narrator's first visit is with Captain Littlepage, who seeks her out at the schoolhouse, after Mrs. Begg's funeral, and in effect shows her that the way out of her impasse as a writer is to become a friend and a listener. What she hears sums up the book's project, for Captain Littlepage embodies the belatedness of both Dunnet Landing as a world and of *The Country of the Pointed Firs* as

---

51. Cf. xii, 59, where the narrator says that Mrs. Todd "might belong to any age, like an idyl of Theocritus." Two eminent contemporaries associated Jewett's art with Theocritus—James Russell Lowell, commending her to his publisher in England (in Matthiessen [above, n. 36], 89), and Willa Cather, in her preface (above, n. 42).

a piece of writing. Once the captain of a merchant ship, he bears the marks both of a shipwreck in the Arctic that turned his wits and of the fact that his occupation is gone. Like some old shepherds in traditional pastoral, he is *laudator temporis acti*, and is not merely cranky in complaining that the opportunities of voyaging, now lost, promoted a "large-minded way of thinking" (v, 21). On the literary side, his very first words—"A happy, rural seat of various views" (v, 16)—call on the narrator to think of her schoolhouse as a version of Milton's Eden,[52] as if this were the only way properly to represent so choice a site; if he intends any irony, it reflects not on the scene itself, but on what he sees as the failure of present-day Dunnet to answer to heroic imaginings. What makes him a pastoral figure, an ironized and reduced version of the heroic rather than a crazed negation of it, is the hold he still has on the poetry that sustained him in his voyages; on his knowledge as a ship's captain and of voyaging as a way of life; and on his own personal dignity. His hold on us is the story he tells of a phantom city in the utmost northern regions. Along with the story of Joanna, this tale is what is left to *The Country of the Pointed Firs* of heroic American narration.[53] Reminiscent in general of Melville's nautical world and specifically recalling Poe's "Narrative of A. Gordon Pym," the tale is marked as a shadow of its predecessors both by Captain Littlepage's flashes of mental instability and by the fact that he does not claim to have been a witness of what he so passionately believes is true. The story was told to him by "old Gaffett," his sole companion on the remote Arctic island where he was sustained spiritually by recalling passages of Shakespeare and Milton. He is thus in the position of a pastoral performer—repeating a "song" that has been handed down, so as to maintain it in and for the present world. A more particular likeness to a pastoral reciter appears at the climax of his narration, when the words he repeats are not those of his informant but of the poet who alone might have represented such things unattempted:

> "Then there came a day," said Captain Littlepage, leaning toward me with a strange look in his eyes, and whispering quickly. "The men all swore they wouldn't stay any longer; the man on watch early in the morning gave the alarm, and they all put off in the boat and got a little way out to sea. Those folks, or whatever they were, come about 'em like bats; all at once they raised incessant armies, and come as if to drive 'em back to sea. They stood thick at the edge o' the water like the ridges o' grim war; no thought o' flight, none of retreat. Sometimes a standing fight, then soaring on main wing tormented all the air." (vi, 26)

52. *Paradise Lost* 4.247. The Captain (or Jewett) slightly de-Miltonizes the line by making "view" plural.

53. Larzer Ziff remarks Jewett's "implicit sense of her mind's having been opened in the great days of New England letters." Larzer Ziff, *The American 1890s* (New York: Viking, 1966), 286.

Captain Littlepage says of Gaffett that "it used to ease his mind to talk to an understanding person" (vi, 23), and he himself welcomes the narrator for just this reason. But what can Dunnet Landing, or we in our time, do with what he knows? "Some o' them tales hangs together toler'ble well," Mrs. Todd says, when the narrator reports this visit on the heights (vii, 29), and later, "You always catch yourself a-thinkin' what if [his 'great stories'] was all true, and he had the right of it" (xviii, 103). The chapter after the tale begins:

> Gaffett with his good bunk and the bird-skins, the story of the wreck of the Minerva, the human-shaped creatures of fog and cobweb, the great words of Milton with which he described their onslaught upon the crew, all this moving tale had such an air of truth that I could not argue with Captain Littlepage. (vii, 28)

These words give the Captain, as is implicit in his likeness to a pastoral reciter, some of the writer's authority. Though as a character, fitful and troubled, he represents the kind of poetic imagination this author knows she must leave in the past, the story he tells becomes authoritative for the book. Its conclusion looks back on the repetition of Milton's war in heaven:

> And when they'd got the boat out o' reach o' danger, Gaffett said they looked back, and there was the town again, standing up just as they'd seen it first, comin' on the coast. Say what you might, they all believed 'twas a kind of waiting-place between this world an' the next. (vi, 26)

"The Waiting Place" is the title of this chapter, and it becomes the title, in Kenneth Burke's larger sense, for other places that come to represent Dunnet Landing. Joanna's island, which the narrator calls a "hermitage"[54] and where she found herself "with eternity well begun," is obviously a "waiting place." But so too is Green Island, the first sight of which brings to mind the story the narrator has just heard. As she and Mrs. Todd stand talking about Captain Littlepage,

> a gleam of golden sunshine struck the outer islands, and one of them shone out clear in the light, and revealed itself in a compelling way to our eyes. Mrs. Todd was looking off across the bay with a face full of affection and interest. The sunburst upon that outermost island made it seem like a sudden revelation of the world beyond this which some believe to be so near. (vii, 29–30)

"That's where mother lives," Mrs. Todd exclaims, almost as if correcting the narrator's fantasy and alerting us to the fact that Green Island looks to and is

---

54. This is not simply the narrator's interpretive metaphor, but is in accord with Mrs. Fosdick's calling Joanna "a sort of nun or hermit person" (xiii, 65).

looked on by the world of the living. But there is truth in the narrator's sense that the outermost island on this piece of coast replicates, as a "waiting place," the outermost island of the known world in Captain Littlepage's tale.[55] Its human fertility is all in the past, and even as a dwelling place it is shadowed by the recognition, as Mrs. Blackett says, that "the time o' sickness an' failin' has got to come to all" (xi, 52).

The last "waiting place" in *The Country of the Pointed Firs* is the center of the final episode, the narrator's visit with Elijah Tilley. He is one of four old fishermen who have worked together since boyhood and seem as much given to conversation as "a company of elephants" (xx, 114) or "a landmark pine" (115). Mrs. Todd considers Elijah "a ploddin' man" (xx, 128), and there might be little else to say of him as a fictional character. But as a pastoral figure, he provides an alternative representation of the reduced possibilities of life in Dunnet Landing. The other old men in the book embody the ruin of large, indeed conventionally heroic, possibilities on sea and land.[56] Captain Littlepage has suffered in himself the historical decline of shipping, while the equally skittish and estimable "Sant" Bowden, filled with dreams of military command, is able to express them only by organizing the family procession at the Bowden reunion. Elijah Tilley, on the other hand, seems, like the women and the *senex puerilis* William, only to have become older while living the life he always knew. This in itself might make him a pastoral figure in a simple sense, but it is what we learn of him after the narrator breaks the ice and is invited for a visit that makes clear why he concludes Jewett's account of Dunnet Landing. He sums up his world by merging the opposites that once gave it meaning and reducing them within domestic confines. His ploughed field brings the sea to land by the way he has marked subsurface boulders by what he consciously calls "buoys." At home he is rather feminized: his main domestic occupation is knitting, and he is an impeccable housekeeper. His house itself, which surprises the narrator by its brightly painted exterior, seems to represent Dunnet living as Mrs. Blackett's does: in each the bright, cheerful kitchen is the center of life, though each maintains a carefully furnished parlor, expressing a "high respect for society in

55. The preceding paragraph, describing the book's definitive landscape, also picks up its metaphors from the Captain's tale:

> We were standing where there was a fine view of the harbor and its long stretches of shore all covered by the great army of the pointed firs, darkly cloaked and standing as if they waited to embark. As we looked far seaward among the outer islands, the trees seemed to march seaward still, going steadily over the heights and down to the water's edge. (29)

56. There are no young adult or middle-aged men. When the narrator sees Elijah's "carefully painted" and "neat sharp-edged" little house, she thinks it looks more like what you would expect to be the dwelling of "the smart young wholesale egg merchant of the Landing" (xx, 119). We have not heard of this character before, nor do we meet him or others like him.

the abstract" (xx, 124). (Interestingly, we get no detailed descriptions of the interior of Mrs. Todd's house; its domestic spaces are marked by the activities within them and by the living relation between the house and her herb garden).

The explanation of Elijah Tilley's domesticity makes it more deeply representative of Dunnet housekeeping. He maintains the house, keeping up its appearance and standards, as a tribute to "poor dear," his dead wife, whose memory is ever present to him. The last of the dwellings we see in Dunnet, the house brings together two ideas of pastoral place. Mrs. Todd had called Shell-heap Island "a dreadful small place to make a world of" (xiii, 66), but the same could be said of Green Island and indeed of all of Dunnet Landing. The human splendor of this country is precisely that its inhabitants have made a world out of small places. This is true of Joanna herself, who made her little hut a neat home, decked with lovely rush mats, and made companions of the island's birds and of the hens her faithful lover left for her. Elijah's house too makes a world of a small place, not simply because it embodies all "his" world, but because it includes some of the great world (the china set from Bordeaux that was his and his wife's pride and joy), and because it prompts in the narrator the ability to imagine, very much in the manner of Jewett in her stories and sketches, the life that was lived here. But Elijah's house is also "a shrine of solitude," "a place remote and islanded," and "a waiting place." Like a pedestrian Captain Little-page, his head filled with ghosts of the past, he sometimes looks out of his door and imagines that "poor dear might step right back into this kitchen" (xx, 121). Unlike Silas Marner, the sign of whose humanity is that he cannot give up hope and expectation, Elijah knows that his looking is all retrospective: "No, I sha'n't trouble the fish a great sight more" (xx, 122). And yet it is this that makes him welcome a visitor and endows him, like his love-lorn literary predecessors, with the power of utterance. When Mrs. Todd is told that the silent old man had been talking, she says immediately and correctly, "Then 'twas all about his wife" (xx, 127).

There is one more chapter after the narrator's visit with Elijah Tilley. Like the closing passages of eclogues and eclogue books, it represents the ending of a natural unit of time and a farewell to the scene it celebrates. Its title, "The Backward View," bears witness to the degree to which human presence, in the country of the pointed firs, is involved with retrospection. But the book is no more nostalgic than the people it represents. Rather it is one more instance of the pastoral resistance to nostalgia: the sense of loss produces less a yearning for the irrecoverable than a valuing of what remains. The narrator's backward view is most explicit in the final paragraph, with its last sight of the bay and its islands. But her farewell is most powerful, both in its human feeling and its analogy with the book's closure, in her last moments in the house, after Mrs. Todd abruptly departs, so as to avoid a parting scene:

The little house had suddenly grown lonely, and my room looked empty as it had the day I came. I and all my belongings had died out of it, and I knew how it would seem when Mrs. Todd came back and found her lodger gone. So we die before our own eyes; so we see some chapters of our lives come to their natural end. (xxi, 130–31)

One might think the last sentence too obvious, but it is precisely true to the effect of an emptied room, and its quiet strength comes not from literary self-reflexiveness but from the persistent acceptance throughout the book of the calm pain of endings. We see a final instance in the last sentence of the book when the boat heads out to sea "and when I looked back again, the islands and the headland had run together and Dunnet Landing and all its coasts were lost to sight"—just as, at the beginning of the summer, Mrs. Begg's funeral procession disappeared around the slope of the hill "as if it had gone into a cave" (iv, 14).

These absolute disappearances are modeled on death, the solitariness that is not accompanable. But as the narrator observes, at the time of leave-taking at the Bowden reunion, "even funerals in this country of the pointed firs were not without their social advantages and satisfactions" (xix, 110). These latter are the foundation of what remains after natural endings. The narrator leaves her emptied room and goes down to the kitchen, where Mrs. Todd has left some small packages—"a quaint West Indian basket which I knew its owner had valued," a lunch prepared for her voyage down the coast, "and a little old leather box which held the coral pin that Nathan Todd brought home to give to poor Joanna" (xxi, 131). This pin replicates another convention of pastoral closure—the gift which, by being well crafted, tangible, and valued by its giver, both represents feelings of obligation and gratitude and compensates for what in them is inexpressible. ("What can I give in return for such a song" says Virgil's Mopsus, before he and Menalcas exchange gifts at the end of their funeral celebration of the hero-shepherd Daphnis.) Because of the specifications and continuities possible in realistic fiction this gift has a poignancy un-exampled in earlier pastorals. One more of the objects from abroad with which Dunnet makes a world of a small place, this coral pin is densely associated with affection sustained against separation and loss—not only Nathan Todd's thoughts of Joanna, but also Mrs. Todd's of Nathan (for she values in him, the husband she did not deeply love, exactly that loyal affection he expressed in the original gift), and Joanna's of Mrs. Todd, to whom she returned the pin, asking her to wear it for her sake, when she came to Shell-heap Island and hoped that this token of love and regard would help bring Joanna back to the mainland. As a gift, it implicitly includes the narrator in these intimacies of affection and separation. Its value as a memento is not simply that it belonged to Mrs. Todd, but that it carries with it the fullness of living memories. Its power within the fiction thus recapitulates the power of this fiction. It conveys, on its small scale and on terms suggested by what it celebrates, the satisfactions and poignancy of a society whose passion and significant action are all in the nevertheless living past.

IV

As a literary category, the pastoral novel includes those works of realistic and post-realistic fiction (e.g., André Gide's *Paludes*, a meditation on Virgil's first Eclogue) in which theme or subject matter, usually but not necessarily rural, is given literary form that derives from or is made intelligible by the usages of traditional pastoral. Willa Cather's *My Ántonia*, conscious of both its indebtedness to Jewett and its belated relation to Virgil, is such a work, and so, in my view, is Michael Ondaatje's recent *The English Patient*. In a larger consideration of the pastoral novel than has been possible here, we would certainly want to include George Sand's rural novels—*La mare au diable, François le champi*, and *La petite Fadette*—because they give novelistic form to the pastoral erotics that are conspicuously absent from *Silas Marner* and *The Country of the Pointed Firs*. These erotics are very different from what we find in earlier pastoral, on the side of either physical appeal and desire, as in *Daphnis and Chloe*, or of idealizing devotion. George Sand's countryside, like that of nineteenth-century fiction in general, is not the open space of classical and Renaissance pastoral, in which shepherd meets shepherdess. (The most interesting analogue of *Daphnis and Chloe* in the age of realism, *Paul et Virginie*, is a Rousseauian tale set on the island of Mauritius.) The realities of rural life as Sand depicts them—work, economics, and familial situations—make romance unlikely. But in each of her rural novels, love emerges from a situation that seems not made for it, and it is this very improbability that makes the erotics pastoral, by sustaining a feeling of innocence. Certainly the interest of these novels is not confined to the local piety and representation of the life of the land that made them classics of French literature and staples of the school curriculum. Readers of Proust, for example, will be interested to know that *François le champi*, which figures importantly in the opening pages of *À la recherche du temps perdu*, is about a boy who marries his (foster) mother.

But just as pastoralism is more interesting in itself and more valuable as a literary resource in *Don Quixote* than in Cervantes' own pastoral romance, so some of the most interesting fictional pastoral is in books that do not, as wholes, count as pastoral novels. The best English example is Hardy's *The Woodlanders*—a particularly good example in this context, because it is so much better a book than his indubitably pastoral *Under the Greenwood Tree*. The place of pastoral in *The Woodlanders* is indicated by the title itself. On the one hand it includes the central figures and their world—the Wessex woods which provide the whole way of life of the hamlet in its midst. On the other hand, the title has a certain irony, in that the central action of the book concerns the efforts of Melbury, the local wood merchant, to enable his daughter to cease to be a woodlander. In an attempt to elevate her socially, he sends her away to boarding school and thus makes her unable, in spite of some abiding feelings, to return to her home fully enough to return the affections of the central male figure, Giles Winterborne, the representative woodlander of the book. Winterborne's intimate knowledge of the woods makes him appear, at one point, as a local deity,[57] but it is precisely the fullness and completeness of his woodland life that brings him to the tragic end which older pastoral averts for its passionate lovers. He cannot lay claim to Grace Melbury, now that she has been taken from his world, and he can neither love nor recognize the love of Marty South, the rather sexless co-worker who is devoted to him. This kind of love situation is typical of pastoral romances, but the world of the novel cannot generate a way to reward devotion and align the lovers properly. What has replaced Montemayor's sage Felicia and her potions is the force of historical change, both social and economic. It is Hardy's awareness of change that makes *The Woodlanders* both an excellent and a nonpastoral novel. But it is the pastoral center—the woodlands and the two main figures who wholly belong to them, Giles and Marty—who measure what is happening in the contemporary world and the figures who belong to and, more important, are moving into it.

It makes little sense, as we observed at the beginning of this chapter, to say that *The Woodlanders* "is" a pastoral elegy. But there is no doubt that this is the way to represent its ending. Giles Winterborne dies because of exposure to cold, incurred because of his devotion to Grace. (She had sought shelter in his hut from her scapegrace husband, and he would not risk her reputation by staying under its roof with her.) Grace recognizes that Giles died for her, and for eight months after his death, she accompanies Marty South to lay flowers once a week on his grave. In the final episode of the novel, Grace fails to meet Marty at their usual time. Marty's "sense of comradeship would not allow her to go on to the grave alone," but as she is waiting at the churchyard, she over-

---

57. This occurs when Grace Melbury, now Mrs. Fitzpiers, is met by Giles, coming from the woods:

> He looked and smelt like Autumn's very brother, his face being sunburnt to wheat-colour, his eyes blue as cornflowers, his sleeves and leggings dyed with fruit-stains, his hands clammy with the sweet juice of apples, his hat sprinkled with pips, and everywhere about him that atmosphere of cider which at its first return each season has such an indescribable fascination for those who have been born and bred among the orchards. Her heart rose from its late sadness like a released bough; her senses revelled in the sudden lapse back to Nature unadorned.

The Woodlanders, ed. James Gibson and Ian Gregor (Harmondsworth: Penguin, 1981), chap. 28, p. 261.

hears talk that tells her that Grace has returned to her husband. She therefore goes to the grave alone, puts fresh flowers in place of the ones she and Grace had laid the previous week, and utters the final words of the novel:

> "Now, my own, own love," she whispered, "you are mine, and only mine; for she has forgot 'ee at last, although for her you died! But I—whenever I get up I'll think of 'ee, and whenever I lie down I'll think of 'ee again. Whenever I plant the young larches I'll think that none can plant as you planted; and whenever I split a gad, and whenever I turn the cider wring, I'll say none could do it like you. If ever I forget your name let me forget home and heaven! . . . But no, no, my love, I never can forget 'ee; for you was a good man, and did good things!" [58]

This is, in the full sense, a novelistic version of pastoral elegy. It does not simply restage a pastoral elegy as an event in realistic fiction. Rather, the isolation which gives Marty her pastoral dignity here—the claim in her single-minded devotion to have understood Giles's story better than anyone else—comes about because the convening on which traditional pastoral elegies were founded has been disrupted by conflicts of feeling and social motive, on Grace's part, that make novels what they are.

58. Chap. 48, p. 439. The preceding quotation is on p. 438.

Index

Note: Page numbers in **boldface** indicate the most important discussions of works and topics.